KARA KUSH

Idries Shah's family have lived in Afghanistan
for a thousand years: since the time of Haroun
al-Rashid, the caliph of the Thousand and One
Nights. As warlords, mystics, men and women
of letters, they have been among the most
prominent of the country's patriots and
achievers.

Shah himself is the best-known contemporary Afghan writer, with a vast and growing
readership in both the East and West. He has
published thirty books in all the major
European languages: on travel, philosophy,
belles-lettres and comparative human
thought.

He has taught extensively in Europe and
America on a professorial basis and has been
widely acclaimed for the quality of his writing
as well as for his collections of Eastern teaching-
stories: a genre which owes its current name to
him.

He divides his time between Britain and the
Middle East, is married to Kashfi Kabraji, and
has three children.

by the same author

The Sufis
The Exploits of the Incomparable Mulla Nasrudin
Tales of the Dervishes
Caravan of Dreams
Nail Soup
Melon City
The Pleasantries of the Incredible Mulla Nasrudin
Reflections
The Dermis Probe
Thinkers of the East
A Perfumed Scorpion
Seeker After Truth
Learning how to Learn
The Hundred Tales of Wisdom
Neglected Aspects of Sufi Study
Special Illumination
A Veiled Gazelle
The Elephant in the Dark
Wisdom of the Idiots
The Magic Monastery
The Book of the Book
The Way of the Sufi
The Subtleties of the Inimitable Mulla Nasrudin
World Tales

IDRIES SHAH

Kara Kush

The Gold of Ahmad Shah

FONTANA/Collins

TO THE PEOPLE
OF AFGHANISTAN
and in homage to
The Leader of our Caravan:

All perfect he, and therefore won
His lofty place; and, like a sun
His beauty lighted up the night.
Fair are his virtues all, and bright.
Let peace and benediction be
On him and his posterity!

Saadi of Shiraz
From *The Rose Garden*

First published by William Collins Sons & Co. Ltd 1986
A continental edition first issued in Fontana 1986
This edition first published 1987

Made and printed in Great Britain by
William Collins Sons & Co. Ltd, Glasgow

CONTENTS

Book One: Nikolai is Here   15
    Tiger's Fort, South of the Soviet Border, in
    Afghan Turkestan
    SUMMER

Book Two: The Gold of Ahmad Shah   31
1 *Ura Pobeyda* – Hail Victory!   33
    Kalantut Village, North-West of Kabul,
    Afghanistan
    APRIL 23

2 'I thank the court for its clemency . . .'   58
    Guerrilla Headquarters, The Eagle's Nest,
    Paghman Mountains, North of Kabul
    APRIL 29

3 Karima: 'If you push me too far . . .'   77
    Kabul City and Jalalabad, South Afghanistan
    JUNE 7–8

4 Business on the Frontier   93
    Manchester, England and Istanbul, Turkey
    MAY 25–26

5 A Caravan for David Callil   99
    Inside Afghanistan, on the road west of Chitral,
    Pakistan
    MAY 31–JUNE 8

6 Bright Wolf   105
   The Eagle's Nest, Paghman Mountains, North of
   Kabul
   JUNE 8

7 Noor Sharifi, Hostage   110
   Pul-i-Charkhi Prison, Kabul
   MAY 2

8 A Formal Case has been Initiated   115
   The Great Castle at the mouth of the Paghman
   valley
   MAY 4

9 Captain Azambai, Soviet Red Army   123
   South of Khaja Rawash Airbase, Kabul Road
   MAY 2

10 The Treasure   134
   Kajakai, Kandahar Province, South-West
   Afghanistan
   APRIL 30–MAY 10

Book Three: Halzun, the Snail   161
1 Nurhan Aliyev, Uzbek Librarian   163
   Tashkent, Uzbek SSR, Soviet Central Asia
   MAY 24

2 The Artefacts Department   170
   Moscow, Union Capital, USSR
   MAY 26–30

3 A Passport for Tezbin, Carpenter   180
   Moscow/Kabul
   JUNE 2–11

Book Four: Hail Jamal, Son of Zaid!   189
  1 'This is your mission, Jamal . . .'   191
    The Airport, Hadiqa City, Narabia, Arabian Gulf
    JUNE 12

  2 Highness, I am Samir, servant of Akbar   197
    Peshawar City, North-West Frontier, Pakistan
    JUNE 13–17

  3 Send for Yunanian, the Chemist   207
    The Palace/The British Embassy, Hadiqa City,
    Narabia
    JUNE 18

  4 Thank you, Dr Anddrews   223
    Oxford, England
    JUNE 20

Book Five: A Mirza in a Mulberry Tree   227
  1 Hang the Bandit Scum!   229
    Kabul and Panjsher Valley, Afghanistan
    JUNE 9

  2 Compassionate leave for Mr Khan   243
    New Delhi, India
    JUNE 8–14

  3 Account Paid   247
    Kabul, Afghanistan
    JULY 14–16

Book Six: Daughter of Daniyel   281
  1 Prem Lal, KGB Rezident   283
    Kabul, Afghanistan
    JUNE 8

2   Fazli Rabbi, Innkeeper   295
    Jalalabad, Afghanistan
    JUNE 8

3   To the Castle of the Yusuf-Born   301
    The Path of Flight, Smugglers' Route, Jalalabad
    to Pakistan
    JUNE 9–19

Book Seven: Ataka! Ataka! Ataka!   319
1   Nanpaz the Baker   321
    The Castle, Paghman Valley
    JUNE 5

2   The Whirlwind to see Colonel Slavsky   327
    Below the Castle, Paghman
    JUNE 19

Book Eight: Nest of the Eagle   337
1   One hundred and fifty-eight – and
    volunteering   339
    Eagle's Nest, The Buddhist Monastery, Paghman
    Mountains
    JUNE 19

2   Silahdar Haidar, Weapon-Bearer, reporting,
    Komondon   350
    Eagle's Nest
    JUNE 20

3   Time to move on, Big One . . .   362
    Eagle's Nest/Kalan's Farm, Near Kabul
    JUNE 20

4   The Fourth Battle   368
    Valley Entrance, Paghman
    JUNE 24

Book Nine: Across the Hindu Kush   387

1   An Izba in Nuristan   389
    The Koh-i-Daman Foothills
    JULY 3

2   The Wild Ones of Murad Shah   400
    The Lower Paghman Range
    JULY 5

3   Land of the Living Prince   408
    Beyond High Serai
    JULY 11

4   We must cross Black Mountain . . .   419
    Qala Kavi, Central Mountains
    JULY 12

5   Kara Dagh is Icebound . . .   426
    The Great Pass
    JULY 14

Book Ten: The Wolves of Turkestan   433

1   Like lice on a dinner plate . . .   435
    The North Slope of Kara Dagh Mountain, Afghan
    Turkestan
    JULY 16

2   Guerrilla City   441
    Kurt Burj, 'Wolf Redoubt', Reed Forest, Afghan
    Turkestan
    JULY 17

3   The Gunboat *Jihun*   449
    Qizil Qala, Oxus River Port, Afghan–Soviet
    Border
    JULY 21

4 Leninised   464
On the Oxus River
JULY 21

5 March South . . .   470
Wolf Redoubt
JULY 21

Book Eleven: Southwards to Kandahar   475
1 Ride and Die!   477
High Hazara Land, Central Afghanistan
LATE AUGUST

2 The Mulla and the Water of Life   482
Baghran Town, Descending towards Kandahar,
South-Central Afghanistan
LATE AUGUST

Book Twelve: Ekranoplan, The Sea Monsters   487
1 Wild Horses   489
Southern Hazarajat
AUGUST–SEPTEMBER

2 Kandahar in Disguise   494
The Oasis of Panjtan, Kandahar Province
MID-SEPTEMBER

3 Council of War   499
The Oasis
MID-SEPTEMBER

Book Thirteen: Into the Abode of War   505
1 Target: Kandahar Airport   507
Pendergood's Army, In the Free Land,
Pakistan–Afghan Border; and Moscow
SEPTEMBER 15, Late Afternoon

2 **The Russians are Coming** 520
The Eagle's force, North of Kandahar City
2100 hours

3 **Pendergood's Army, approaching the Airport,** 522
18 kms from Kandahar
2140 hours

4 **The Eagle's force, north of Kandahar City** 527
2151 hours

5 **Pendergood's Army, Kandahar Airport** 532
SEPTEMBER 16, 0100 hours

6 **The Eagle's force, Herat Road boundary,**
Kandahar City 537
0230 hours

7 **Pendergood's Army, Kandahar Airport** 544
0800 hours

Book Fourteen: The Secret Weapon 549
1 Stand to Arms! 551
North of Kandahar Airport
SEPTEMBER 16, 1000 hours

2 **Kandahar Airport** 558
1200–1300 hours

3 **The Tanks must not get through** 567
1436 hours

Book Fifteen: Zoo-Bear 571
The Super-Redeyes
Almas Fort, the heights near Kandahar Airport
1600 hours

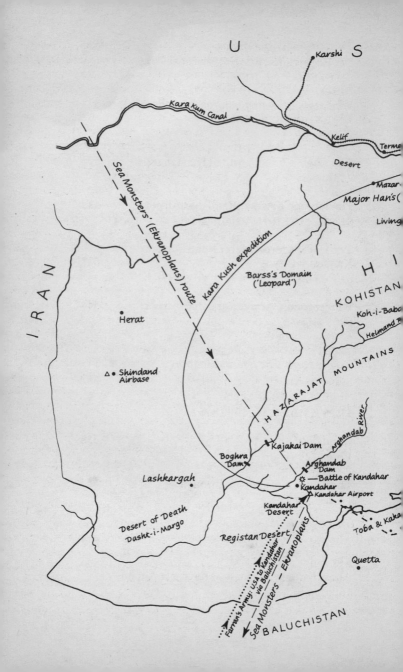

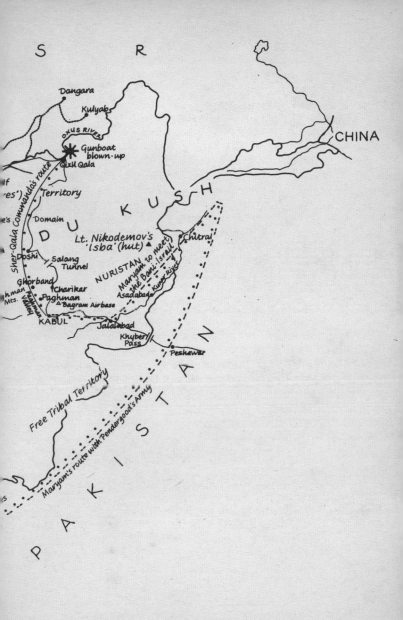

BOOK 1

Nikolai is Here

Tiger's Fort
South of the Soviet Border
Afghan Turkestan

SUMMER

Juma lay, waiting for death, by the parapet on the roof of his ancestral home.

Until five weeks ago, he had been a captain of the Seventh Infantry Division of the Afghan Army, stationed at Kabul. Then had followed a week under arrest, for slandering the Soviet people.

As the Russian grip on his country had tightened and the National Army crumbled, broken by purges and desertions, Juma had answered a more ancient, more pressing, call to duty. He was the twenty-fifth hereditary Battle-Lord of Sher-Qala, Tiger's Fort, a mile south of the Soviet–Afghan border, the Oxus River, and he had come home to lead his people, and to fight for freedom.

It seemed an age since the Russians had invaded Afghanistan, one of the few free countries left on their borders. It was three and a half years ago. The war was still on. Ten miles up the road from there, the Afghan port of Qizil Qala was crammed with tanks, landing-craft, Soviet equipment of all kinds. The only halfway decent ship on the mile-wide river was the ancient Afghan gunboat *Jihun*, busily ferrying the country's gold reserves, precious stones which were mined there – lapis lazuli, emeralds and rubies – and priceless ancient Greek, Buddhist and Islamic artefacts from the collection in the Kabul Museum, to help pay for the 'fraternal assistance' of the Soviet Limited Military Contingent, the new masters.

The Russians had, at last, broken through the barrier which had denied them warm-water ports of their own. To the south, Pakistan was wide open, all the way to the Arabian Sea. After that, the Gulf, the riches of Arabian oil, and the outflanking of Iran, were the next targets. Unless the Afghans, still fighting, could stop them. Twelve to sixteen million mountaineers, with only the world's vague sympathy, and their own determination, on their side.

But there was something that might enable the Afghans to evict the invader, reclaim their homeland, win their war. This lay in the secret which Captain Juma had entrusted to the village mayor.

What chance was there that the message would get back to a man who might do something, might just turn the tide in time, the man they called The Eagle? Not much.

The Russian helicopter gunships had been flying low these last few days. God willing, the summer clouds of north Afghanistan would keep them low, so that someone could, now and then, manage to shoot off a tiny rear rotor: the only way to get them down, if all you had was a World War I British Lee-Enfield .303, with second-hand cartridges filled with homemade black powder.

Captain Juma, of the former Royal Afghan, now People's Democratic, Army, screwed up his eyes to make out the distant profile of the light, scouting whirler, and guessed that it must be the forerunner of two or three more: the big ones they called the village-killers. They would have been called up by radio, because this community had harboured *badmashes*, 'villains', the communist word for the Muhjahidin, 'the strugglers' – the Resistance. And Juma had his own, special reason, for wanting them to come.

Last night near Sher-Qala, the village folk, the yokels, with utter foolishness, had lit a huge bonfire to celebrate the ambush of three Soviet tanks, just four kilometres down the road towards the provincial capital of Turkestan. They had knocked them out in broad daylight, too. Using only soft-drink bottles filled with petrol, plus a little shredded rubber – Molotov cocktails – they had burned out all three tanks, though with the loss of eight men and five women of the farming folk.

Usually the assault helicopters flew high past here, on their way to deal with the people of the more turbulent far west, along the plains of the boundary with the Soviet Union. Their targets were the ordinary people of the country: starvelings who tended the fields as best they could during the day, and crept out to attack at night. Just after dawn, the raiding parties, each of ten to thirty fighters, would return, carrying their wounded, from the raid. They would show Russian army pay-books, an officer's gaudy epaulette, boxes of almost unstrikable Estonian matches, buttons, cap-badges. Yesterday's day-raid had been too successful, and far too venturesome, for the Russians to ignore.

The best times were when the fighters brought back arms, grenades and ammunition. Often, too, there were things like canned food and candies: boiled sweets from Hungary which the Nikolais really loved. And metal mirrors. These were, oddly, engraved with the words, in Russian, 'to be used only for shaving'. Sometimes the village women, although most of them had been in action against the Nikolais, would weep when they saw these. Each could see, in her imagination, another mother, somewhere far to the north, saving up to buy one, and giving it to her conscript son. 'Nikolai, carry it in your left breast pocket. Do it for my sake: you never know . . .' There were letters, too, unposted, to Moldavia, Georgia, the Ukraine or Byelorussia. Trophies, certainly: but this detritus of death, this rubbish from soldiers' pockets, was the same the world over: sad and irrelevant.

Not irrelevant were the loading and defence instructions for the huge secret cargo of the treasure-ship; foolishly carried by an over-confident Russian officer, on an observation mission in one of yesterday's tanks. That was the sort of information that would change the course of the war. Taken from the Russian's body and carried to Juma, sick and useless, by his men.

The local Muhjahidin were still a travesty of a resistance force. Ragged, ill-equipped, careless and lacking cunning. They needed to be trained. Descendants of warriors, perhaps; but at this rate, how far were they from complete extermination? They were not afraid: Juma accepted that, but they were far from being the kind of soldiers that Afghanistan needed now. Giving themselves away with public displays of exultation at any success, firing shots wastefully and idiotically into the air, they regularly forgot that the cover of darkness was their great asset. Instead of letting the night cloak them, all too often they allowed themselves to be caught in the open in the mornings, and hunted by those satanic flying machines. Mind you, there were other fighters, like the seasoned warriors of the southland, who had had the Soviets on the run more than once; but Juma belonged to Turkestan.

A spasm of pain brought his thoughts back to the present. The villagers would not come back, he hoped: not for some time, anyway. He lay back on the straw which the blind cobbler, Haji Alim, had brought for him, near the upper turret of the baked clay building. By moving slightly, he tried to ease the pain, but it only increased: he felt the throbbing move higher, up now to his thigh. The wound was massively infected, the leg swollen and going blue. He hadn't been able to get it treated since the guard had slashed him with a bayonet as he jumped the barbed wire that night at Islahgah, the ideological-correction camp for politically unreliable soldiers, more than a fortnight ago. He had covered over a hundred and fifty kilometres in five days, most of it on foot, but sometimes helped by a friendly peasant with a donkey. Twice it was a man with a truck.

He had been planning his escape since he had discovered that his wife, held hostage for his good behaviour, had died of ill-treatment in the Pul-i-Charkhi prison. They had no children; now that Peri was gone, his duty was clear.

Juma had got home, had come back here to Tiger's Fort, still in his own uniform, to help train these people, to give them the knowledge he had gained at battle school. Without that they would be wiped out by those skills that he had learnt, but of which they had only dimly heard. His father had been their *Bashkan*, their chief. His family, alone in the village, had maintained the ancient fighting tradition, for seven hundred years. They were hereditary *noyons*, battle-lords, descended from the commanders of the Horde of Genghiz Khan. And the peasants, surely, could be trained. They would listen to him. It was really a matter of time, as Major Zaman had said. The Major had been trying to prepare him for this day.

Instructor-Major Zaman was an ancient veteran of the war with Britain in 1919, the year the Afghans had last regained their independence. He had lectured, speaking truly, that day ten years ago in the stifling classroom, a hero with the Star of Afghanistan on his tunic. '*Now hear and understand!*' Cadet Juma had jumped to full alertness, awakened by the raised voice from his daydream of the fair maidens, *peghlas* they called them thereabouts in the soft southern Pashtu, tripping to the brook which he could see through the window from his desk, the meadow bright with buttercups and daisies; and filling their clay jars with the family's daily drinking-water.

'*Hear and understand!* The Russians will come, make no mistake about it. The "Nikolais" may pretend to be our allies, but they will really come to rule. They took Kazakhistan in 1855: *and* that was after signing a treaty of alliance with the Kazakhs. Then they seized Kirghizia; and they had Northern Turkestan by 1876, a hundred years ago. By 1900 they had taken both the countries of the Turkomans and of the Tajiks, just beyond our present border: see, here, on this map. They have been trying to get into Afghanistan ever since. Next they will cross the Oxus. Any questions on that?'

'Sir!' It was Hatim; the tall, fair, keen youngster from Kamdesh, who always asked questions when he had a chance. The ageing Zaman had turned a bleary eye on him. That cadet's head looked as if it could do with a shave, but he was sitting at attention. 'Yes?'

'What's a "Nikolai", and why are they called that? Does it mean a Russian, and are they so called because of their Czar Nikolai?'

'They *are* the Russians, and most people here know that already. You come from Nuristan, and so you don't know very much, of course. I am not talking about old-time Russian emperors. Cadet Hatim: we are talking about here and now. Nikolai is a proper name with them, just as we call someone, say, Anwar. But, to us, Nikolai is like a made-up name. Just analyse it and you'll soon see what I mean.' The Major was addicted to illustrating his points with jocular mock-etymology.

'"Niko", in Dari means "good". "La" means "no"; so Nikolai means "I'm no good". In our interpretation, of course. It's a well-known joke. Now to some practicalities, please.'

When he was commissioned and posted to Kabul, Juma sat nightly in the capital's cafés, meeting many of the modern youth, the students, some of whom had been to Russia. They would always speak of the friendliness of Russian people, how they took you into their homes, made you welcome, yearned for world peace and universal brotherhood. When he had spoken to the Kabul students of the threat of the Nikolais, how they had laughed. Better read than he, they had explained that the name Nicholas was from the Greek; translated, it stood for no less than the stirring and idealistic phrase, *Victory of the People*. Was Major Zaman wrong? Juma had wondered. Were the invaders civilizers in disguise?

Forgive me for doubting, Major, I know now that you were right. And the students, too, perhaps, in their own way. But the sons of those happy, dancing, hugging Nikolais were here, in our country, today, killing women, maiming children. Victory: but for whom? And, no doubt, in their barracks and their messhalls, the Nikolais sang and danced as well. All empires spoke of peace and practised war.

What was it that Major Zaman had told them then?

'You notice that I do not talk of communism. The Army is not concerned with politics and never has been. Under whatever banner, Russia is, and always has been, expansionist. It so happens that Karl Marx, whom the Russians follow, had this to say about them, which I quote from the British scholar Walter Laqueur, who wrote in 1957, in *Communism and Nationalism in the Middle East*:

'"The policy of Russia is changeless. Its methods, its tactics, its manoeuvres may change, but the polar star of its policy – world domination – is a fixed star."' The Major lifted his finger in emphasis. 'In these circumstances, until the Russians do, perhaps, change, what can we, in Afghanistan, do?'

The Major had looked, sternly, at the attentive faces. 'There are, today, two hundred million people in the Soviet Union. There are twelve million of us. Their army is one of the best-equipped in the world, and we could not stand up to it in a conventional war. We cannot hope for outside help: we are a neutral country and always have been such. And nobody has ever helped us in any of our wars. But there is no record in history of a total-resistance army, helped by the people, ever having been beaten, however great the odds. Everyone must fight.

'Some might say that we are outnumbered sixteen to one. Look at it again, like this: there are *only* sixteen of them to one of us. But I say, "Die with honour, but take at least sixteen of the enemy with you." Long before they run short of men, they'll lose their stomach for the fight. That's the only language, gentlemen, that the Nikolais really understand. Above all, teach the people. As always, it is they who are our hope.'

The latest count showed 270 million Soviet people: more than twenty-two to one. But the principle was the same.

Juma's thoughts came back to the helicopters. He could hear the rhythm of more motors now; they were not far off. *I'm going to die all right: even if they don't see me or pick me up, I'm going to die quite soon. God grant they pick me up.* If they did not, the vultures would not be long. Vultures went for the eyes first . . .

He had refused to accept the precious rifle and the three pathetic rounds, used cartridges refilled with homemade gunpowder, that gave the bullets no real range, which the villagers had offered him when he was sending them away to shelter. In any case, he had been shaking with fever, sweat streaming down his face. What could he shoot in that condition?

'Sir, Battle-Lord: come with us. We'll find you a *hakim*, a leech. They know the power of herbs, they know how to heal.' The mayor spoke urgently.

'No, Haidar. I'm staying here. And you have work to do.'

'They'll blow you to pieces when they destroy the fort. You know what the rockets can do.'

'Do as I say, I am your chieftain, your *Bashkun!*'

'What can we do for you, then, *Bashkan?*'

'Carry me outside, up to the long flat rooftop *now*. The Nikolais, in *halikuptars*, are coming, coming soon.' How can one argue when one is so weak? But he must insist, must get it done.

The mayor, the Shahrdar Haidar, looked at him sideways. Ah, that was it. Captain Juma was very ill. The Russians had all kinds of Frankish medicines, and especially that powerful one, called *ontiboiotik*, which could cure even the most terrible wounds. They would, perhaps, take him to a military hospital, heal him there – or amputate the bad leg – and keep him prisoner, but alive. After all, he was of noble blood, and an officer. He might even join the Nikolais. People sometimes did such things, from gratitude . . . Or would the Russians make him talk – about the message to The Eagle? Things were so confusing. Obey orders, the Captain had said. Orders first, and we'll teach you how to think as well. But orders without thinking? Yes, in emergencies.

'Do it, take me up, Haidar? And keep watch from the foothills. Learn all you can from watching Nikolai. Always watch; see all you can, ask yourself what you have learned. It will help the homeland, I truly promise you. Get the message to Kara Kush, the leader called The Eagle: that is the most important thing of all. Now repeat the main points of the message.'

His fever-bright eyes searched Haidar's face.

'By my head and eyes, my Khan! "From Juma Sherzada in Turkestan to Komondon Kara Kush. The Russians plan to move the gold treasure of King Ahmad Shah, worth four hundred billion dollars, on the gunboat *Jihun* from Qizil Qala on the Oxus River to the USSR. For God's sake stop them. The most valuable consignment in history, while we bleed to death for lack of arms."'

'That's right, Haidar, and don't write it down.'

'I can't write anyway, master.'

'Take me up now, Haidar, you must!'

'Hearing is obedience, my Khan!' The mayor turned to the group of men. 'Let's take him up now.'

They carried Juma, gently enough, onto the roof, though now they avoided his eyes. Only the blind cobbler, feeling his way unhelped up the rickety ladder, brought an armful of straw and carefully pushed the bent dry stalks under Juma's leg on the dusty parapet. 'God sees all, my Khan,' he whispered.

I suppose he's sorry for me because he's blind; we're both wrecks, Juma thought. Just wrecks.

The throb of engines. Here they came. They were really near now. A scout, like a dragonfly, and two big gunships, Mi-24 attackers, over fifty feet long; the climbing sun glittered on their bulletproof gun-blisters. Juma could make out goggled faces now, peering through the front windows of armoured glass. He could sense the bomb-aimers ready, the fingers on the firing buttons and the Russian 'candies', explosive toys for the children to pick up, ready for release. Even after they had destroyed a village, the helicopters made a final pass and dropped, as if in derision, these brightly coloured packages, sometimes imitation playthings, dolls, or watches, women's combs, all sorts of nicknacks, among the ruins.

People came back to rebuild their homes and would find

these presents which blew off a hand or foot, or blinded those who picked them up. The adults soon came to know the toys: but they could never teach all the children not to touch them. The maimed children outnumbered the grown-up victims by ten to one.

Captain Juma pulled the fine muslin cloth, the customary 'three metres of white' which the villagers had left to be his shroud, foot by foot from the breast of his uniform jacket. Slowly, gasping with the pain, he rolled himself along the flat roof, laying it out as he went. It would do well enough as a signal, showing up better than his grey uniform against the red-brown clay. What a strange sensation. Was it possible to have so much pain that it could no longer hurt?

His head swam again; was he going to black out? Now he saw the picture of a tall young officer standing, smiling, in a brand new uniform, beside a graceful girl who was filling her water-jar from a cool stream. That would be the stream which brought the snow-water from the mountains beyond Paghman. It flowed, here, through a meadow, and they were standing in the shade of an immense mulberry tree.

'What is your name, *peghla*?' he asked.

Beautiful as a houri of Paradise, she turned her head modestly away.

'All right then, don't tell me. I'll run through some pretty girls' names, and I'll have guessed it when you blush! But don't misunderstand: I intend no disrespect. I am Captain Juma Sherzada, son of a chief, Battle-Lord of Sher-Qala, in the north. We are fighting to liberate Afghanistan. The great Major Zaman was my teacher, you know, when I was a cadet in these parts . . .'

A swirling, a stinging of his eyes, and he was back to consciousness. Two bulky ships were lurching down with their usual thumping clatter, sweeping in decreasing circles. The third one, a longer Mi-8, hovered warily, higher, almost like a hawk.

He was sure now. One of the big ones was going to land, here on the roof, while the other veered away. They had not come to bomb the fort this time. A helmeted figure, the navigator-gunner, was looking straight at Juma, through huge field glasses. Juma could now see the four munition pods, each armed with thirty-two 57-millimetre rockets fixed on the stubby wings, left and right of the hull. Two large, finned bombs were ready in their racks.

Now it was down: a beautiful landing, with no bump at all. The huge rotors, fifty feet in diameter and fourteen feet off the ground, were still stirring up the yellow sand and dust. The force of their wind, the downwash, almost blew Juma over the parapet. The stench from the burnt fuel of the twin turbos was overpowering. Although the big exhaust vented upwards, the rotors pushed a blanket of the abundant fumes back to ground-level.

The baked clay, hard as rock from centuries of sun, was as firm as any landing pad.

Juma struggled with his jacket buttons. There, that was all right now. The last task but one.

A door opened forward, and the automatic steps came down. Juma could just see the open door and bright lights in the cabin. There were four large, rectangular porthole-windows near him, and beyond them, on the fuselage, a big red star. The insignia of the Soviets, not of the Afghan Army.

A Russian officer, burly, self-assured, with bright gold lace and red parade shoulder-boards, surprisingly formal dress, jumped down and strode straight up to Juma, an automatic, a PM-Makarov, in his hand. He waved the weapon, speaking in good though accented Dari-Persian: 'Stand up and hold still!' He looked at Juma's rank, the bars still on his jacket.

'I am an Afghan officer, Comrade *Kapitan*, wounded and in need of medical attention, captured by the badmashes. I can't stand. Probably blood-poisoning in my leg, it's moving up . . .'

'You are former Captain Juma Sherzada, a deserter and a criminal. We know all about you, eater of filth! This is your own home pigsty, isn't it? Thought you'd get away from Islah-gah, eh?'

The Russian kicked Juma on his bad leg. The Makarov was inches from his face now; safety catch off. One shot was all it needed: execution.

'Organising resistance to the lawful forces of the State and you want treatment for a sore leg? The *Nizami*-KHAD, Afghan State Security, can show you, swine, what pain really means!'

He was going back to prison, Juma thought. The Russian

beckoned towards the brown and yellow camouflaged helicopter, squatting just six yards away. Two soldiers, immaculate in pressed grey Afghan Army field tunics, ran up to carry Juma to the aircraft. The Russian was a captain, these were Afghan majors and of course outranked him: but they ran, like eager dogs, to do their master's bidding. Juma was feeling very light-headed again. All those officers. Had the communists run out of ordinary aircrew? All this, for a miserable Turkestani village? Or to capture the great hero, Captain Juma, a miserable, dying traitor to the socialist cause, who had never fired a shot in anger?

The other helicopters set their courses homewards as the two men lugged him, a ragged bundle, distastefully along.

Juma was aware of being hauled up, into the very roomy cabin. It was, however, crammed with men. Three Soviet generals, map cases in their hands, binoculars slung round their necks, polished jackboots, gold wreathed hammer-and-sickle badges on red stars in their peaked caps, nodded with satisfaction to the men who held him.

As Juma was dumped on the floor, the nearest general, a podgy man with the wide face of an Uzbek, looked at him and wrinkled his nose: the suppurating wound stank. Then the Soviet officer assumed a twisted smile, and started to speak, his clipped pronunciation telling of his Turki origins.

'Comrade former Captain Juma, isn't it? What an interesting morning, and the day has hardly started! Here we are, studying counter-insurgency in the field and, *chuff!* – on our first time out we find a *renegat*, a traitor, sending his dupes to destroy our tanks in a particularly cowardly way. Yes, you filthy ape! We'll get something really worthwhile out of you. Before you're hanged!' The general's voice was now hoarse with fury, though he had, at first, tried to be smoothly sarcastic.

He looks just like the Devil, Juma thought. *Yes, that's it, the Devil, come to carry me away. In a dark, vicious, clattering bird, with foetid breath, out of this fair world, heading for Hell, Iblis from Jahannum, the Devil from Hell.*

Juma's throat ached, and a spasm from his leg made his vision swim. No, not devils, generals. Three *generals*? 'Die for a general?' He tried to clear his throat, shifted his arm to ease his leg. It only made the pain worse . . . *No, I mustn't say anything, do anything . . . No, I am NOT by that stream of sweet water, talking to a village maiden . . . I'm with the Nikolais* . . . He was shivering with fever, as if someone was shaking him, and now felt icy cold.

His head cleared a little as he counted three generals of the Soviet Army, several other officers – one at least was a major, that one over there. There was sure to be a colonel among them, too. Generals always liked to have their sycophants around when they were performing. The Mi-24s, he knew, could carry a crew of four as well as eight fully equipped troops.

The Russian captain slammed the armoured door and clipped it shut.

'All right, take off now. To Khanabad Headquarters.' The senior general must be speaking to the pilot through that throat-microphone, wobbling on his double chin.

The rotorcraft rose and wheeled in a wide arc, gaining height.

When it had reached what he guessed must be at least two hundred metres high, Captain Juma jerked, with all his remaining strength, at the string knotted to the ring-pulls of the firing pins in the two tiny, two and a quarter inch diameter grenades, strapped to his stomach with his belt. In three seconds they would explode.

'Juma Sherzada, twenty-fifth hereditary Noyon of Sher-Qala, reporting for duty,' he breathed. 'Come to battle, brave Nikolais . . .'

In the foothills near the fort, the small group of farmers, men, women and children from Sher-Qala, crouched sheltering among the rocks, almost invisible in their threadbare, grey-brown blankets. Two helicopters had been and gone away. One had landed, and it would be taking Captain Juma to hospital soon. Ah, there it was now, high up in the sky . . .

First it was there, rising steadily, slightly distorted in the shimmering heat, the very symbol of the invader's power. Then they saw the orange-red ball of fire, bright even in the sunshine, as the thing exploded, blown into a million shards.

'*Halak Shudand*! They're destroyed!'

'The *tiyara* is smashed, blown to pieces. They have gone to Hell!' Shouting with delight, the mayor tried to describe what he had seen to the sightless cobbler sitting silently beside him.

'To Hell, to Hell, they've all gone down to Hell, Haji!' He was dancing up and down now. Then he sat mute, speechless with ecstasy, gazing into the sky.

'It wasn't an amulet I felt, after all,' said the cobbler, 'strapped to our captain's stomach. And he was right: look and you will learn.'

Remembering Juma, the women began to wail in mourning.

'And the Battle-Lord is dead,' said Haidar; 'I must do as he commanded. He said "the task I give you could save our country, and perhaps the world".'

Shahrdar Haidar, hereditary weapon-bearer to the lords of Tiger's Fort, shook hands with the remnants of his people. Hands on hearts, they watched him go.

He took the dusty road which led southwards, through three hundred miles of occupied Afghanistan, across rivers and over mountains, to seek Kara Kush, The Eagle of Paghman, the man who had dared to raise the flag of rebellion against the most awesome political and military machine in the world. Kara Kush, who had taken up arms in the name of the people of a remote land in Central Asia, best known elsewhere for its dogs and carpets. But, as he reminded himself often enough on that long trek, a people who, alone in history, had resisted the all-conquering Arabs for a hundred years. Not to mention Alexander the Great – and the British Empire.

'Walk, ride, live off the land. Trust no stranger! Get to The Eagle! Give him the message!' Juma had said. Well, he could and would. He would obey orders. 'Obedience is the path to command.'

What had he learnt, from the last act of Captain Juma? First, remember the value of a ruse. Second, make any sacrifice. Third, he, Shahrdar Haidar, had thought that his master, the Noyon, could have sought healing from the enemy, or might even join them, out of gratitude. Don't be mistrustful. Trust Kara Kush, The Eagle.

'*Silah-Dar Mojud!*' How long had it been since the ancient war cry had echoed here! '*Here am I, the Weapon-Bearer* going into battle to help save the people whom my forebears, the Mongols, once came to conquer . . .'

*

There were five villages, in each of them no more than two hundred souls, whose people looked to Tiger's Fort as the centre of their community. With the Battle-Lord dead and the mayor trudging southwards to find the shadowy leader Kara Kush, the villagers returned to their fields and flocks. Kara Kush, after all, might not even exist. If he did, what could he do for Turkestan? *Shikast-i-kufar* – Defeat to the Infidel! was still the cry of the suicidal young, reared on tales of long ago, as they went out to die, riddled by Russian bullets, trying to destroy at least one truck from a convoy of perhaps dozens, as the invaders tightened their hold on northern Afghanistan.

And Soviet Northern Afghan Command did not forget the loss of their helicopter, even though they never discovered the real cause.

Two weeks after Captain Juma's death, four low-flying aircraft made three passes each, over the five villages. Instead of bombs, large metal canisters landed in the midst of the people, and a yellowish mist filled the village streets. According to the few survivors, those people or animals who were in the open and who breathed the vapour died almost at once. Anyone who touched the powdery deposit which settled on the ground, on walls and plants, also died.

Persistent rumours – and the direct accusation of the United States government – had claimed, for over two years, that the Russians were experimenting with 'yellow rain' in Laos, Vietnam and Afghanistan. According to the reports, this chemical warfare was based on a fungus, the deadly *Fusarium*. Although the Russians hotly denied the charge, it was noted that their scientists had recorded and described cases of accidental Fusarium poisoning in the USSR. Many people wondered if it was a coincidence that, after a mysterious substance was dropped by Soviet aircraft, illiterate Asian villagers could accurately report the symptoms of death through the ingestion of mycotoxins of the trichothecene group. They were hardly likely to have read the scientific literature.

The agent was extremely effective: almost everyone who was in contact with the mist died in great agony. It was worse than the plagues of typhus which had claimed so many lives before the Afghan Ministry of Health had stamped out the disease.

The Russian convoys were safe, at least for the time being.

BOOK 2

The Gold of Ahmad Shah

Soviet military units appear to have failed to develop strong primary-group attachments among the soldiers and between leadership elements and their men. This represents a potential for instability and fragmentation under combat stress. Therefore the effectiveness of Soviet military units in prolonged battle, when quick victories are not forthcoming . . . is open to question. Soviet military units could well begin to unravel if pressed hard enough in a conventional battle environment. From this perspective, Soviet units contain a great systemic weakness.

Professor R A Gabriel:
The New Red Legions

1 *Ura Pobeyda* – Hail Victory!

Kalantut Village
North-West of Kabul
Afghanistan

APRIL 23

In Afghanistan, someone who was six foot tall, with grey-green eyes and dark hair – if he spoke a local language perfectly – was almost certainly an Afghan. Adam Durany fitted that bill, having been born in the American-built town of Lashkargah, a hundred miles from the Pakistan border, where his father had been an engineer working on the great Kajakai Dam.

Following his father's bent, Adam had studied engineering in America; but, drawn to the land of his birth and its passion for modernization, he had returned to Afghanistan. Armed with a doctorate and understanding the people so completely, he soon acquired the Chair of Technology at the University of Kabul.

But the great transformation of the country, dreamed of since the war, had not come. Communist infiltration, intrigue and ultimately the Soviet invasion from the north to 'restore order and support the socialist government' had seen to that.

That was why Adam Durany was a rebel, a wanted man, an Afghan guerrilla operating from the stark fastnesses of the Paghman range of mountains to the north of Kabul. Dressed in the roughest of clothes, shirt and baggy trousers, he carried a Kalashnikov slung across his back.

When, on that December day, the huge Russian Antonov transports had landed at Kabul, and the tanks had rolled south along the Great Circle of all-weather roads the Russians had built for that very purpose, Adam stayed at his post – but not for long. Peasants tried to attack the tanks with sticks and stones; soldiers with only five rounds of ammunition tried to resist, air force men crashed their planes onto the teeming invaders: many others simply fled or resigned themselves to oppression.

But a plan was forming in Adam's mind. One day there would be a resistance movement: that was inevitable in a fiercely independent mountain land with a powerful military tradition. At first it would spring up locally, people rallying to their accepted chiefs. Thousands, however, would die, lacking the skills and the weapons needed to fight this new kind of war. There would have to be impregnable bases within Afghanistan, and friends outside. There would have to be exploits, too, to fire the people's imagination; and there would have to be scientific and technical knowledge.

When he reached this point in his reasoning, Adam remembered – Paghman.

His family were friends of the princely Sirdar Akbar of Paghman, and as a lad Adam had spent his summer vacations in the cool sun of the Paghman uplands. He had fished and skied, gone horse-riding and rambled all over the sprawling mountain ranges, so near to Kabul and yet so cool – bliss indeed after the summer heat of the 'Desert of Death' near his native Kandahar.

It was at the Paghman castle that he had met little Noor Sharifi, the daughter of the house. He had taught her to ride, to shoot, and to catch trout. One summer, though, Noor had suddenly seemed to be a child no longer. He remembered how he had thought that it was absurd to send a beautiful woman, his Noor, away to school. But that was the Sirdar's wish: a school in London, England. And so they had lost touch.

One day, in that last summer before she left, Adam had been on a particularly long hike deep in the mountains when he noticed a long, rather regular, shadow in the rocks just above him. The shadow turned out to be a slit which continued horizontally into the mass of the mountain. Scrambling along it, Adam found that the slit widened. He was in a man-made tunnel.

After making two or three turns, Adam entered an enormous cavern, with caves running in all directions from it. Astonishingly, the mountain hall was lit by daylight. Fissures, protected from view by the high spurs, ran into the cave's roof, each in turn catching the sun in its passage across the sky. A dim but adequate light suffused this extraordinary natural cathedral.

He understood at once that he had found one of the lost Buddhist cave-monasteries, abandoned a thousand and more years ago when the monks had emigrated, after the Islamic conquest.

He told nobody. The secrecy which had protected the place for so long seemed to capture him, too. Adam was no occultist, but something said to him that the monastery was sleeping: and that its time would come again.

Twenty years later, the realization came. The cave-monastery could be a virtually impregnable fortress from which a rebel army, thousands strong, could challenge the Red occupation. When the Russians moved into Afghanistan, the Paghman heights were snowbound. Adam waited four months, making preparations. In April he returned to the monastery to make quite sure. This time he found that there was another way in, which could be used by trucks and horses: skilfully concealed and easy to defend.

As he stood at one of the creeper-covered entrances to the smaller caves, Adam saw, high in the sky, a tiny flying figure. It swooped, then flew up again and hovered: *Kara Kush*, The Eagle. His old nurse had called him that when he was small, and it had become a pet name in the family. 'My little eagle, Kara Kush', she used to say. She was a Turkestani, and Kara Kush was a Turki word.

Adam remembered how the Persian-speaking boys at school had laughed when, foolishly, he had confided his pet name. 'Kara Kush, the eagle, ha, ha, ha!' A bully had come up to him, a boy three years older and very tough. 'Who's a stupid little Turkestani, then? Kara Kush, Kara Kush! Want a fight?'

The answer had come to him in a flash. 'In Turki it may mean "eagle", but in Dari-Persian, it can be said as "instant kill". Get away or I'll knock you down!' The other boys had cheered and then turned on the bully, who never troubled Adam again.

Kara Kush. He'd take that name, to beat the Red bully. It symbolized the Afghan people.

Back in Kabul, Adam had drawn his money, gradually,

from the bank, and sold everything of value. Food, scientific equipment, all kinds of tools and materials, were bought and carried, by him and his close friend, Qasim, to the Caves.

Then, subletting his apartment and giving out that he was going to attend a conference for a few weeks, he bought a return air ticket to nearby Pakistan.

Adam stayed only three days in Pakistan, before returning on horseback along the smugglers' route. It was also called the *Rahi Gurez*, the Road of Flight, and ran through the mountains south of Chitral. The people of Nuristan, a wild, untamed country, helped him reach Paghman and safety. Qasim was waiting: 'Victory – Kara Kush!'

Since then, *Girdbad*, the Whirlwind Battle-Group led by The Eagle, had grown from its original two men to a strength of some sixty-five would-be warriors. Each one had been double and triple-checked and tested for reliability even before he was allowed to visit the Caves. In rural Afghanistan, security was not difficult to operate: everyone seemed to know everyone else. And the information channels to Kabul, even to the highest quarters, were excellent. Nobody liked the puppet government.

Training and arms were the first priority. The ancient rifles, Lee-Enfield .303s from British Indian days, were next to useless, almost as bad as muzzle-loaders when faced by really modern weapons.

Yet around the country, in dozens of places, were dumps of the latest guns, mines, rocket-launchers which had been stockpiled by the Russians.

Over sixty men and only five guns. And the men, tired of training with dummy weapons, needed both guns and a successful exploit, something to raise their spirits. The Eagle cast an envious eye on the Russian supply centre near the village of Kalantut, some ten miles from his Paghman eyrie.

He planned to raid it now, reconnoitring with a patrol of five men.

Qasim called it an Attack Group. Whatever it was called, it consisted only of Adam, Qasim, old Khizrhayat who was seventy but an uncannily skilful tracker, Tirandaz, a level-headed local peasant and crack shot – and young Aslam Jan, fifteen years old but from a warrior family.

First, Adam decided, they would go into Kalantut village itself, to collect information and if possible, operate from there when evening came.

As they came near the first house they realized that something was disastrously wrong. There was no sound of village life: the smell of death hung in the air.

On the wall of a burnt-out stone barn they saw the words, whitewashed in Cyrillic, the Soviet war cry *Ura pobeyda!* Hail Victory!

All the cottage roofs were down, and blackened windows showed where the firebombs had done their work. The little mosque had been blasted by high-explosive shells, and the schoolhouse was still smouldering. Row upon row of machine-gun bullets had patterned the flimsy walls of a vine-covered teahouse under the solitary tree – the only one left from a row of eight graceful poplars.

More than fifty corpses, of old men, women and children, lay inside what was left of the houses. The bellies of the corpses were already swelling in the heat. Some of the faces looked strangely peaceful: some people had died contorted, burnt with flame-throwers or riddled with bullets from automatic rifles. For good measure, the village well had been wrecked by high-explosive grenades and the minute grocery shop looted. As was another, pitifully small, general store.

There was one survivor of the massacre: an old man, bleary-eyed with advancing cataract, who had been lying ill behind a stone-built cowshed when the attack began. He had crawled, painfully, to shelter, hardly knowing what he was doing: obeying even in his last hours, the imperative to survive. He had reached a depression in the ground, a culvert which had once fed a pond, now long since dry and partly filled with rubbish. This had shielded him from the bullets.

His name was Haji – 'pilgrim' – Abdurrashid. He said he was seventy-eight years old, but he looked much older than that. When Qasim found him, he had just dragged himself from his hiding place in search of water. It was obvious that he did not have long to live: and The Eagle wanted desperately to know any fact about the massacre, anything that might help to understand how it could have come about.

He got no explanation. The Haji lived for only an hour more.

All he could say was that the men of the village, whose ages ranged from fourteen to sixty-five, had fled six days ago, to escape conscription, and had thought that their families would be safe enough. None of them had been guerrillas.

Then, that morning, only a few hours before, Russian soldiers from the camp four kilometres away, heavily armed and riding armoured troop carriers, had surrounded the place and done all this, without provocation. '*Baz faisala shud*,' he said, 'Then it was over.' After the killings, the old man had heard the Russians rushing round the village streets, throwing explosives and fragmentation grenades, shooting and laughing. Women were screaming; some so badly hurt that they pleaded with the Russians to kill them quickly. This, he said, made the soldiers laugh all the louder.

'They were like madmen. They *were* madmen. This is not soldiers' work. I know, I have been in the Army, I have served my King.' He had no more to say and died soon after.

Aslam Jan found some spades but Adam knew that five men could not dig fifty graves in the time he had. They cleared the rubbish from the culvert in which the old man had taken refuge and carried the bodies there. They laid them side by side in a long, grotesque row and covered them with earth scooped out from the sides of the culvert.

Now the five men moved to the cover of a clump of bushes half a mile away, on an incline from which they could watch the Russian camp.

Three days before, Adam and his partisans had descended upon a Russian truck which had broken down and thus been separated from its convoy. There was no resistance from the soldiers guarding it, and the Afghans fell upon the tarpaulins with sharp knives, eager for loot, for guns. They found – a load of military bugles.

They belonged to a Russian parade-formation of musicians who doubled, as in other armies, as *pomashes*, medical order-lies, in active service conditions. Adam had distributed the instruments among the unarmed men of the Caves, and told them to get on with bugle practice.

Although he had not been able to arm the majority of the men, Adam was still determined to get into the camp – and get away with what loot he could obtain. The sixty would be itching to join the fight: but, armed or otherwise, such a large party would be seen quite easily if spotter planes were about.

Adam went over the plan once again making sure that his men understood. Qasim, speaking for the others said: 'We joined you in order to learn to obey, Eagle. What we have seen today may help to teach us. But for myself, I seek your permission to use, as my war cry when we attack the *Rouss*, the words *Ura Pobeyda!* Hurrah for Victory!'

'You have permission,' The Eagle said, 'and note this: for the purpose of this foray, we have a new name, the name of the dead village. We are now Mujahid Battle-Group Kalantut.'

From where they lay in the bushes they could see the Afghan flag, the black-red-green tricolour, hanging in the still air over the central administration building, a large square hut in the centre of the compound. Close to the barbed-wire perimeter fence, they identified a guardhouse and several low prefabricated huts. The camp itself was built on a hillside, with a brick building, probably an ablutions block, to one side. There was a great deal of scrub around, useful cover for an observer, and it was obvious that nobody had bothered to clear the ground for years. Even The Eagle, still a novice in guerrilla war, realized that the place was suffering from the slackness which poor organization and fifty years of peace had allowed to creep into the once efficient Afghan Army.

His information seemed accurate enough. This was undoubtedly the field armoury of the Afghan Eighth Infantry, now taken over by the Soviets. Too many modern weapons had been finding their way, through desertions and sympathy, into guerrilla hands and for some time now the Soviet Army had been steadily disarming the crumbling Afghan forces. Inside this camp, he felt sure, there would be no more than two or three Afghans acting as liaison officers and interpreters – in spite of that Afghan national flag.

The armoury, if The Eagle's Intelligence was right, contained mortars, machine-guns and rocket-launchers – in quantities enough to equip a division for war. And that was not to mention rifles and grenades, flame-throwers even. Adam and his friends, gazing at this prize, were the only members of his band who had any weapons at all: five Kalashnikov automatic assault rifles, some pistols and grenades, a flare or two for the signalling pistol, and a stick of dynamite. And in the Caves, now, three hundred and fifty of The Eagle's men and women, aching for action, were waiting for him to bring them arms.

Beyond the barbed wire, clear in his binoculars, Adam could see vast riches. As tempting as sweets to a child they lay there, piled in the open. Half concealed by tarpaulins, the guns and ammunition were neatly stacked, perhaps only recently seized from Afghan troops of doubtful loyalty to the rickety communist regime and now awaiting either storage or re-issue.

As night fell, the searchlights on the perimeter's observation towers were switched on and the thump of generators mingled with the clatter of jackboots as some two hundred men, obviously Russians, emerged from their quarters to line up on parade.

So the camp had an independent electricity and water supply. A huge water tank dominated the far side of the compound sitting on top of a watchtower. It was one of six such towers, each equipped with a searchlight. In each sat a sentry, and Adam noted that some of them were reading quietly. Like many other Russians, the watchtower sentries wore Afghan Army uniforms, a stratagem adopted by the Soviets in the odd belief that this would reassure the Afghan population. No dogs patrolled the wire, which was the usual fifteen feet high, but guards on foot, rifles slung across their backs, moved regularly around inside.

There was only a single radio mast with several stubby microwave antennae sprouting at intervals down its length, interspersed with round VHF receiving dishes. It looked almost like some weird metal creation offered as a profound piece of avant-garde art at a fashionable gallery.

Five against two hundred, maybe two hundred and fifty. What chance did they really have? 'As for numbers,' grinned the ancient Khizrhayat, catching Adam's thought and exposing naked gums, 'I would suggest that fifty to one is just about right for us.'

'Very well then.' The Eagle let him joke but did not smile. 'Now, as you know, if we are not back at the Caves, or haven't sent a signal' – he glanced at his watch – 'by two hours from now, the support group will set out and the attack will be on. We can only hope that if they come round by way of Kalantut village and see the destruction, their discipline will hold. If it doesn't the raid will be a disaster from the start. You now have three hours to rest. Be back here then, ready to take up positions and for any last-minute orders. Stay under cover, doubly careful, if there is any air activity. Make sure that you do not eat or drink for one hour before the time of action. We don't want people being sick over each other. Besides, vomit is bad for the rifles.'

Three of the band – young Aslam, the old man Khizrhayat and Tirandaz the sharpshooter, went off somewhere to sleep. The Eagle lay back, his head on his knapsack, rifle beside him. Qasim, similarly stretched, lay in the opposite direction so that they could scan the road that ran beside the camp in both directions.

Fifteen minutes before zero hour the five guerrillas re-assembled. They settled in the darkness behind the scrub about thirty yards from the armoury's outer fence. There seemed to be little activity among the Russians inside, nothing to suggest that they anticipated anything more than another quiet night.

Then, a little to his right, The Eagle thought he heard something move – perhaps only a rabbit. He froze, and opened his mouth slightly, in the way his father's hunter had taught him – a trick that increased the sharpness of one's hearing.

At first there was nothing. Then, suddenly, he felt a movement right beside him, and knew a real spasm of fear.

Out of the darkness, brilliant white and seemingly as large as a dinner plate, the huge flat face of an army flashlight glared straight at him, held at arm's length by the looming figure of a man.

Was it a Russian, creeping out illicitly from the camp? Or one of a patrol, checking the perimeter wire was intact? The Eagle was just registering that he could expect the hammer-blow of a bullet at any moment when the Russian, his long-service chevron and star suddenly visible as he jerked his flashlamp in fright, called out like a man who has seen a ghost. In a reflex action Adam brought up his Kalashnikov hoping to kill with the first stab of his short bayonet, and with luck to do it silently.

As he hurled himself at the man, the Russian spun sideways

then hared off towards the main gate, shouting wildly to the guardhouse to raise the alarm. Obviously he had been unarmed. The chevron and star insignia were worn only by men with five to nine years' service. If armed, he would not have run off like that.

The klaxons blared over and over again. Then the loud-speakers: '*Ataka! Ataka! Ataka!*' The Eagle could hear men running, oaths carried clearly on the still night air. The search-lights on the towers started to scan the area, seeming to pause at every rock and bush.

Adam cursed. Now the element of surprise was lost: and the support group had not yet arrived. He'd only given them two hours to march ten miles over rough country. Although lightly laden, they would have to jog-trot in the dim quarter-moon most of the way. Now he would have to call off the operation, and give the signal for retreat. This was beginning to look as bad as the fiasco of the bugles. What a commander he was turning out to be . . .

And then, even above the roar from the compound, from all around, like the sound of a mighty army on the march, and punctual to the second, came an incredible cacophony of sixty bugles. The support group, not a single weapon among them, had arrived.

A giant field-lighter flare exploded, brilliant white, high in the sky, and like some celebration firework, came floating gently down on its parachute, bathing the valley with its weird light. The Russians were trying to see exactly what they were facing.

The Eagle crept behind a less than adequate rock as machine-gun bullets at six hundred rounds a minute, whipped past him. He could see, and feel from their buzzing whisper, why the people called them 'messengers of death'. The glowing white tracers, fire-bullets interspersed with the lead ones, showed the gunners where their shots were going. Both these and the flare gave Adam a new piece of information. If the Russians needed such indicators they had no infra-red equipment to see in the dark. That might help to even out the odds just a little.

Adam's patrol group had moved as near as they dared to the camp before opening fire. Then, in a manoeuvre they had rehearsed for days, each man fired a short burst, moved sideways and fired again, ran on and fired once more, giving the impression that the place was surrounded by attackers shooting in relay time. All six of the perimeter searchlights were shot out before the second burst of firing was over.

Ten machine-guns were already chattering with the sound of the standard Russian light weapon – large magazines with a very rapid rate of fire. The type, an RPK, could cover eight hundred metres ahead, but needed reloading after only seventy-five rounds: just over a minute's firing. Not very efficient, compared to many a belt-feed gun. In fact the armoury should have been defended by the heavy Goryunovs, fed by 250-round chain-belts. It so happened that these were being checked, and the lighter weapon intended for squad support duty had been substituted.

As the flare died, its parachute and burnt-out corpse plopping into a giant oak tree not far from where The Eagle was huddled, a body fell heavily beside him in the hollow and young Aslam's voice spoke in his ear. 'Eagle, I have brought you a prisoner!'

Above the din of battle, The Eagle turned a furious face towards the boy and shouted, '*Zhawlan*, idiot. We can't take prisoners now!'

But the Russian, bent almost double behind Aslam, was gabbling. '*Gospodin*, sir, *zhalosty*, mercy . . .' He grabbed The Eagle's hand and started to kiss it as the sound of battle, trumpets, klaxons, grew ever louder.

'Aslam. Get back to your post!'

The boy plucked at Adam's sleeve. 'Eagle, listen. This man says we can get in there through a new sewage pipe. He wants to desert to us. Call off the others and we can try it.'

Call them off? And risk a trap? Anyway he had only two signal flares.

The Russian was jabbering again: '*Tovarish*, comrade, I am a *soratneek*, a comrade in arms . . .' This was like a low budget film, The Eagle thought. A veritable hail of bullets was coming straight at the rock before them, spraying ever more thickly as more and more guns opened up – and one of the enemy wanted to join them! He and Aslam, two-fifths of their fighting force, were crouching here talking to a Russian, while the other three guerrillas were keeping up the attack and might be killed at any moment.

On impulse The Eagle reached for his waistband and handed the Russian a Makarov pistol. The man took it eagerly and thanked Adam, bowing several times. Then, beckoning the two partisans to follow him, he moved off, holding the pistol at the ready. The firing had stopped for a moment: the Russians could obviously not see anything moving. Perhaps there was nobody left to move.

The Russian signalled to them, urgently, that they should move forward and to the left. Aslam Jan gripped The Eagle's shoulder in caution, nervous that their new ally should be so immediately trusted with a gun. In the dim moonlight The Eagle nudged Aslam and pulled the Russian back, gesturing for his weapon. The man handed back his gun without protest. The Eagle smiled, pushed an eight-round magazine into the empty butt and gave it back to the Russian. Aslam gaped. The Eagle was a real leader, a leader you could trust. Who else could have thought, on the spur of the moment, of such a perfect test?

The Eagle had arranged that if he fired a blue flare his group were to withdraw and regroup in a shallow gully some thirty metres to the west. Moments later, as the eerie blue of the flare died away, they assembled. The other three looked despondent, believing that the attack had been aborted. Covered in dust and leaves from crawling through the brushwood, oil from their still-hot weapons streaking their faces and arms, they cursed in whispers. As more flares burst, they saw the Russian and covered him with their guns.

To Aslam The Eagle said: 'Now, where did you find this man, and how did you know what he was saying?' The Eagle tried to see what the Russian looked like, and failed. All he could tell was that he was small and wiry and seemed to be continually bobbing about. There just wasn't enough light to inspect his face.

'He speaks Dari well enough. He just bounded up to me. He had wanted to desert for some time and all this confusion gave him the chance. Lots of others feel the same way, he says. Anyway, he's determined to desert. They still call people *preents*, he says, Russian for prince, as a sign of respect – and they're supposed to be communists!' Aslam Jan sounded delighted both with his first prisoner and with his assessment of Russian psychology. The Russian insisted on shaking hands all round, then on embracing his captors, or allies, or whatever they were.

'What's your name?' was all The Eagle could think of saying, at first.

Still crouched, the Russian gave him a snappy salute, and said, in passable Dari, '*Zelikov*, Roman, humbly reporting *komondon*!' He started to say something else.

'Silence and obey, *Zelikov*!'

'Thank you, *preents*.'

'*Chup sho* – silence!'

'*Da, da, preents*.'

Surely, thought Adam, the Russians would send patrols soon, to investigate the attackers' strength. Out here would become more unhealthy. So why not try to get into the camp through the drain as this impossible Russian was suggesting?

'Zelikov!'

'*Preents*?'

'Take me through the pipe into the camp.'

There was no point in risking the others. He told them, 'Back to your original firing stations. Red flare means all is well, enter the camp. No flare or message in one hour means disperse, reach home before dawn. In the event of my not returning, the butcher, Hoshnak Qassab, is my successor. Obey him implicitly.'

'I entrust you to God,' said Qasim.

'With faith in God. Let's go.' As they crept forward they could hear the sounds from the camp louder than ever. Extra searchlights were in action and were panning from side to side, though not to much effect. The engines of armoured personnel-carriers were being revved. A distorted voice came so incessantly from the loudspeakers that it could only be a recording of an endless-loop tape: '*Dushman! Dushman! Dushman! Ataka! Ataka!*' Bandit attack.

What exactly could the Russian tactics be, on a near-dark night, milling around inside a lighted camp surrounded by rocks, scrub and grass in which their opponents could hide and through which they could melt away if the Russians emerged? Presumably it was a standard military reaction. There had to be a formal answer to every problem. The Russians believed in the formula response to everything. They would, Adam thought, be better off sitting tight in their cosy defended positions, holding fire until they saw their attackers' next move. Another thought struck him. Perhaps the Russians were scared stiff.

The trumpeters, following their orders, had fallen silent. In a way it was a relief. The noise those sixty men made, none of them ever having blown a trumpet in his life, had a disturbing effect. Though you knew they were on your side you still felt disorientated.

They would start up their hellish clamour again after ten minutes, keep it going for two minutes, and then rest; then continue in that way until the order was countermanded. If that kept the Russians bewildered and their guns and attention directed outwards, and if the sewage pipe entrance to the camp was possible, miracles might yet be achieved.

Adam and Zelikov crawled on their bellies through the scrub towards the brick wall of the ablutions block. Evidently the pipe discharged from there. Flares of every size, colour and power, were shooting up into the sky, some bursting randomly like a fireworks display that had got out of hand; others dropping sedately on parachutes. The Russians were either afraid of the dark, or in a panic. Flares like that, especially the star shells, were almost always used singly, tactically, for giving orders, as The Eagle planned to use his. The way the Russians were using theirs was a mixed blessing, as The Eagle realized when he saw that Tirandaz had taken advantage of the illumination so prodigally provided by the Red Army to cripple their aerial. The bracket supporting it now hung at a crazy angle and one of the VHF dishes was hanging by its edge and reflecting the green, red and purple lights in the sky, like the fascia of some one-armed bandit from an amusement arcade.

Good. The Russians in there must be without radio now.

Only a few yards to go. Zelikov and the guerrilla chief climbed into a concrete pipe, two yards in diameter, jutting out from the brick wall. Inside it was almost dry but it stank, and they retched at first as they made their way some ten yards through the darkness, until the Russian pointed to a metal manhole cover just above them with light showing around its edges and accessible by a line of handgrips.

'No guard, inspection place. Here workshop, *gospodin preents*!'

Just like that. The way in. All that elaborate defence system of barbed wire and machine-gun posts and here was an unguarded door inviting visitors. Unbelievable! But was it unguarded? The Eagle decided to gamble.

They climbed up the handholds and Adam slowly pushed the manhole cover up. They clambered out and found themselves in a lofty workshop-cum-generator room with humming dynamos all around. The place was brightly lit, and smelt of diesel oil. And there wasn't a guard to be seen.

Zelikov was tugging at his sleeve. 'Kill *dinamos, preents*?'

The Eagle took in the crouching figure now, his obsequious manner, frightened face and pug nose, a comic-looking little man with a dirt-streaked face and close-cropped head. If they crippled the dynamos and put the lights out of action, how would they see their way round the camp? No, better to risk the light.

'No, Zelikov. We'll go to find the Commandant. Where is he?'

Zelikov stabbed the air with his gun. 'Commandant very bad, shoot us, *za-za-za*!'

Adam dug into him with the Kalashnikov's butt. 'We go find Commandant, *Zud buro!* Quick march!'

The Russian looked at him for a second, then he shrugged and started to lope along a gallery and down a catwalk which led to the main door of the place.

There was nobody immediately outside and, as luck would have it, the moment they emerged onto the asphalted compound's parade-ground the buglers started again. They sounded nearer than before and The Eagle could now see the scene from the defenders' viewpoint. It certainly felt as if the camp was being attacked by hordes of demons. The buglers' musical talents had not developed and, in their enthusiasm, they were now varying their repertoire by howling like jackals.

Zelikov was bounding ahead again like a rabbit. Adam started across the compound after him.

There were large shadows between the pools of light cast by the arc lamps and the two men skipped from one to another. Anxious to give themselves enough light to supply the guns, the Russians had left on all the arc lights. Adam and his prisoner – or comrade – were ignored, if they were seen at all, by the armourers, who were hastily carting crates of machine-gun magazines in heavy trolleys to the loaders. The latter served the gunners who, crouching behind their steel shields, were firing as if their lives depended on it. Seeing all this, The Eagle doubted that they had yet hit a single one of his sixty maniacs from the Paghman Caves. An Afghan frontier marksman reckoned that it took between one and two rounds to kill a man. These Russian gunners were firing a total of some *eighteen thousand* rounds a minute. The whole place reeked of cordite: a blue haze of gunsmoke rose towards the floodlights.

Zelikov was pointing to a metal ladder which led from the tarmac to the armoured command post above them. The two of them climbed up and into the heavily protected hut-like room. In it, three men were standing looking with night-glasses through slits in the steel plates which served as windows. As Adam and Zelikov entered, the heavy steel doors banged shut behind them.

One of the Russians looked around, casually, as if expecting a runner with a message. Then he gave a cry and the other two officers turned to see what he was staring at. A pair of binoculars fell to the floor with a thud as two of the Russians reached for their sidearms. They were ten feet away from Adam. Using the butt of his assault rifle The Eagle smashed at their right hands, one after the other in a single arc, sending the two guns rattling together to the ground. Zelikov picked them up.

The third man, evidently the Commandant, simply looked as if he had been stunned. He was not wearing a belt and had no gun, and there was no other weapon in sight.

Inside the command post there was complete silence. The Eagle saw, on the wall beside the Russians, a loudspeaker, a large map of the locality, and a very big poster. It was a hugely enlarged photograph of a fierce-looking bearded and beturbaned tribesman, a dagger gripped in his teeth, with lips drawn back in a snarl. The bright red caption screamed in Russian: *Dushman*, bandit.

Zelikov, without any order from Adam, wrenched down a long loop of electric flex which connected several large desk lamps with their wall-sockets, and bound the officers' wrists and ankles, after making them sit in a neat row on the floor. He then bowed ceremoniously to The Eagle and saluted. 'All in order, *Komandir preents*!'

On the table was a microphone, linked to a field radio, evidently a short-range one for giving orders to the machine-gunners below. Adam saw the Commandant's eyes turn towards it, but when the Russian saw that The Eagle had noticed, he dropped his gaze and stared directly back at Adam.

The Eagle assessed the Russian; a tall man, erect, with white hair and very blue eyes in a Slavic face, he had a vaguely unhealthy appearance and was probably not over-intelligent.

The Russian said, in passable Dari: 'Who are you, what do you want?'

'We are from the Afghan Forces of Resistance, Battle-Group Kalantut. We have you surrounded. You are prisoners of war. If you obey you will be treated in accordance with the Geneva Conventions of War.'

The man nearly choked. 'Shoot me, bandit! I don't obey orders from scum!'

'Are you the Commandant here?'

'Yes, and you are a filthy swine. Geneva Conventions indeed! We never signed them anyway.'

'Now look, Major . . .'

'*Polkovnik*, Colonel, son of an animal!'

'Colonel then. I am now the commander here. You are under my orders. I know why you don't sign humanitarian treaties. It is because you want to massacre women and children, like those in the village of Kalantut down the road.'

A vaguely uncomfortable look passed over the Russian's face. 'The men are lonely here. They don't get much mail, the food and water are bad, there are no women, there is no leave. There is insubordination, I admit it. That sort of thing happens in all armies in time of war. I am punishing the offenders tomorrow.' The Colonel was suddenly on the defensive.

The Eagle said, 'Colonel, you will call up your gunners and give the order to cease fire.'

'You know I cannot do that. I would be arrested and shot.'

'You have already been arrested and you will certainly be shot if you do not do as I say, but before I shoot you I'll have you taken to pieces, *tika-tika*. You know what that means, don't you? First a finger-joint, then another, and another, then we move up . . .'

The Colonel said nothing. The other two Russians had gone white. They knew about the torture; the Soviets had introduced it to Afghanistan.

'My friend Zelikov here,' continued The Eagle, 'will shortly cut off your right index finger. Not too far down, so that we can apply a tourniquet: we don't want you bleeding to death too soon . . .'

All expression had drained from the Colonel's face. At that moment the radio crackled and a staccato Russian voice spoke from the loudspeaker on the wall. The Eagle looked enquiringly at Zelikov.

'Radio want to know, "Continue fire or not, Officer".' Zelikov grinned, evidently pleased with his command of Dari.

'So, Colonel,' Adam spoke slowly, deliberately, 'you will order a total cease-fire, and all soldiers are to withdraw to their quarters without clearing up, leaving their guns and other arms where they are. Do it now. If you do not obey . . .'

Zelikov had drawn a long knife, and was whetting the edge on the sole of his felt boot. He gestured towards the wall-poster, put the knife between his teeth, and glared menacingly at his former commanding officer in a close imitation of the Afghan *dushman*.

The radio repeated its message – not urgently, just as if it were a routine call. The note of enquiry, however, was quite clear.

Nobody moved. Then Zelikov went up to one of the officers. Pulling back his head by the hair, with a gesture of mock artistry he cut a shallow groove in the form of a crescent across his throat, following the jaw-line from ear to ear. Blood started to ooze slowly, and the cut looked quite dramatic. The victim closed his eyes as if he were going to faint. Zelikov held the man's tunic open at the neck, displaying his work like a barber proud of a fine shave. The knife, in Zelikov's hand, was only an inch or two from the officer's jugular vein. In his right hand was the pistol that The Eagle had given him, the safety catch visibly off.

'Give me the microphone, Commander.' The Colonel was now a beaten man.

The Eagle handed it to him. The outcome of this whole mad enterprise hung on the next sixty seconds. 'Remember,' Adam said, 'if you try to trick us, all three of you will certainly be dead before any help can get to you.'

'I'll not trick you.' The Colonel's voice was barely audible. He took a small microphone on its long lead and pressed the transmitting button. What he said sounded to The Eagle like a standard phrase, repeated twice. A voice acknowledged the message and the radio went dead.

Zelikov was grinning even more widely. 'Fire Command to gunners. All fire stop, leave guns, go to bed' was his version of the message. 'And guns say, "Humbly obey, Officer".'

'Thank you, Zelikov.' The Eagle took the microphone back.

Zelikov saluted. 'At your orders, *Komandir preents*.'

A moment later all firing had ceased. Peering through an observation slit The Eagle could see the men below leaving their posts as ordered, slouching towards their barrack huts in a haze of gunsmoke. The radio squawked again.

'My second-in-command, on Fire Control,' said the Colonel, speaking very slowly as if the life was going out of him.

The Eagle looked at him, staring him down with contempt. 'Commander,' added the Colonel.

'Tell him to come here, at once.' Adam handed the microphone once more to the Russian.

Two minutes later, hearing sounds on the ladder, Zelikov opened the door, concealing himself behind it as he did so. A very worried-looking major stepped into the cabin and straightaway felt Zelikov's knife in his ribs. He took the situation in quickly enough. After one glance round the room he unbuckled his gun-belt and handed it to the Russian private. Red-faced, short, bald and middle-aged with huge pointed ears, he looked weary, his face streaked with black machine-gun lubricant, his uniform dusty. Evidently an officer who believed in taking part in the action in spite of his age. Perhaps he had been trying to impress his colonel. Wasn't it strange how unsoldierly a beaten man could look?

'You speak Dari?' he asked The Eagle.

'Yes.'

As Zelikov was securing his hands and feet the major let out a long breath and then started to pant. 'I was afraid that your forces would mortar us. Those exposed stacks of shells, mines, ammunition, right in the centre of the compound . . .' He gave the impression of a man more concerned with practical matters than military etiquette – or even personal indignity. At a glance he had accepted The Eagle on the same terms. 'Frankly, I was scared.'

'Scared?' Adam said. 'We were told you were Socialist Heroes. Don't say it's all propaganda? Maybe you should use smelling salts before you go out and kill any more women and children. Sons of Mother Russia! When you people decay, you'll not even make decent manure! You became heroes in the past by fighting amateurs or frozen armies, that's all!'

The major was shaking badly now. He nodded his head, slowly and then fast, but said nothing.

Zelikov dumped the major out of the chair he was sitting on with exaggerated glee.

'You'll never get away, Commander.' The Russian Colonel looked at The Eagle with protruding eyes realizing, even as he spoke, the implication of what he had said. If The Eagle and his men did not escape, he was a dead man himself.

'That's what the villains always say in Hollywood movies, Colonel, but you ought to know that the hero always gets away. But of course you are not allowed to see capitalist films.' He turned to Zelikov. 'How far is the gateway, the main gate, guardhouse, from the bottom of the ladder of this place?'

'From the bottom of steps, maybe twenty metres.'

'Right. I'm going to take a walk now. You, Zelikov, stay here with the prisoners. If I am not back in fifteen minutes, or if anybody fires, you shoot the Colonel quick, and kill him. You understand?'

'I understand. Understand and I *want* to kill, I *want* to do it!' He looked, The Eagle thought, like a weasel.

'You may want to, but *only* if and when . . . you have your orders, understand?'

'Understand, *gospodin.*'

The Eagle took the major's pistol and checked it. It was loaded. He slipped the safety catch off and jabbed the muzzle in the man's ribs.

'What's your name?'

'Major Tarov, Igor.'

'Right, Tarov. I am Kara Kush, Commander of the partisan Battle-Group Kalantut. You will go in front of me and do what I say. If you do not obey you will be shot, dead, with no further warning. I'll do it, however, as painfully as I can. In the kidneys.'

'I'll do as you say.' The man's bald head was beaded with sweat, and The Eagle could smell the stench of fear. He was, perhaps, forty years old. But he was now stooped, like a very old man. Adam bent down and untied the major's ankles and after a moment, thinking of the trip down the ladder, his wrists as well.

'Right, let's go.'

They moved down the metal ladder, along the now empty compound towards the gate. As they neared it the single guard, reading the major's rank from his epaulettes, snapped to attention. Then he saw The Eagle and took in, as if in slow motion, his Afghan shirt and baggy trousers. His gaze moved from The Eagle to the major, then to the gun stuck in his back. His eyes stayed fixed on the pistol, as if waiting for the shot.

'Tell him to open the gate and to keep silent.'

This was the major's chance to become a hero of the Soviet Union. But Tarov was already stammering. It took him what seemed like an age to get the words out, but he gave the order.

The guard, catching some of the officer's fear, rushed to obey, clutching at the iron bar on his side of the barbed wire as he tried to release the bolt. Eventually the gate swung open.

The Eagle took charge of the sentry's weapons and motioned both him and the major into the guardhouse, making them put their hands on their heads.

Then he fired his Verey pistol in the air. Hardly had the red light died in the sky, with the imprint of the curving star shell still on his retina, than The Eagle saw his Paghman horde, their bugles dangling, come running up; sixty men in sandals, shirts and baggy trousers, their turbans at rakish angles and not a weapon among them. 'Not a single casualty on our side,' reported their leader, Zafir Khan. They stood around in groups, chuckling and slapping one another on the back.

The Eagle counted quickly. Thirty machine-guns were positioned round the perimeter, intended for firing outwards. They could be swung round for firing into the camp. He ordered

Zafir Khan to allocate a gunner and loader to each and to take over the guns without delay. When the RPKs had been turned 180 degrees they faced inwards and their field of fire covered almost the entire compound of the camp.

In ten minutes, called by the loudspeakers, a mass of Russian soldiers poured from their huts and were lined up on the parade-ground, hands on heads.

Zelikov, seeing the surrender from the vantage of the command post, brought his three captives to join the bewildered Russians below. He had to untie them to get them down the ladder but felt no danger. The Russians were beaten men even before they saw the scene below. He herded them gleefully into the defeated ranks.

Adam was trying to assess the overall position. These Russians, a large proportion of them officers and NCOs, could, once they recovered from their shock, be a considerable problem even if they were unarmed.

He looked round and saw that the mercurial Zelikov had anticipated that difficulty. He had found a drum of electric cable and was unrolling it across the parade-ground. Zafir Khan had understood what Zelikov was doing. He had found a pair of metal clippers and was following behind his new-found collaborator, cutting the flex into four-foot lengths.

One by one, the Russians, covered from all angles by their own machine-guns, stepped forward to have their wrists tied behind their backs with the flex. The Eagle, hitherto a good deal less euphoric than his band of buglers, began to feel that he had, against all the odds, got the situation in hand.

The Eagle was about to give the order to move the prisoners off when, to his left, his eye caught a movement beside the water-tower. Suddenly a score or more Russian soldiers poured screaming from a barrack hut, some throwing grenades, some firing Kalashnikovs from the hip.

Several of the Muhjahidin went down and most of the trumpeter-machine-gunners had to hold fire, for fear of killing their own men. But the two guerrilla gunners nearest to the Russians had a safer angle of fire and opened up, the rattle of their guns mingling with the whoops of the attacking Russians.

At that short range, some of the Russians were cut in two by the heavy bullets, but the others came on. Adam found Qasim at his elbow holding a shallow box of Russian RKG-3M stick grenades, anti-tank weapons, capable of penetrating six and a half inches of armour-plating. Far too powerful for hand-to-hand fighting: but there was nothing else to use. The Eagle and Qasim snatched up the little bombs by their stubby wooden handles and hurled them, with all their strength, straight at the oncoming Russians, now only some twenty yards away. With a dreadful roar and a hellish burst of flame, the two grenades exploded.

Their half-kilo high-explosive charges gouged a great double hole from the ground, and the shockwave blew the two guerrillas to the ground. When they raised their heads, most of the attackers had vanished, blown to fragments which now began to spatter from the sky, together with bits of belt buckle, rags from uniforms, and metal from shattered guns.

A moment's silence; then the few remaining attackers came on again, skirting the grenade holes, and screaming *Ura Pobeyda!* In the glare of the floodlights they seemed to number under a dozen, and the gunners, ripping into them with their lead and tracer bullets, stopped five. The others came on again – apparently out of ammunition but resolved on a bayonet charge.

The Eagle ran towards the first of them. Attack was his only option if he was to live. Ducking sideways as he reached him, he dealt the Russian the most effective karate blow he knew: low behind the right shoulder and to the left. The man dropped, killed outright. In almost the same movement, Adam turned and snatched up the Russian's gun. Now another man was upon him, bayonet at the ready. But Adam had a longer reach. Kicking the Kalashnikov aside, he slashed with his own, using it like a scythe, aiming straight for the Russian's neck. The man's face, contorted with hate and tension, slackened as he felt the blade cut to the bone and muscle. But he was not finished yet. Blood spurting from his mouth, he lunged again, ripping The Eagle's water-bottle and ammunition-pouch clean in half. But the lunge had thrown him off-balance and he spun, trying to regain his centre of gravity. Adam put the bayonet deep into his side as he fell.

The Eagle raised his leg, stiff and parallel to the ground, planted it in the Russian's side, against the hipbone, and tugged.

The bayonet came free. He had never imagined he could kill like this.

As he looked around, Adam saw that Qasim was fending off the three remaining soldiers. He had somehow disarmed one of them, who was now circling round him, waiting for a chance to pull him down. The other two, evidently out of ammunition, were stabbing and thrusting, trying to get through his guard, in a strange parody of ballet and fencing movements.

Adam went for the unarmed man. Taking the forepart of his gun in a double-handed grip, he swung the heavy wooden stock hard against the man's face, like a cricketer damping down the ball. The impact jarred his arm, right up to the shoulder and the Russian dropped, unconscious.

The Eagle swivelled his gun and was only just in time to parry a thrust from the second Russian, who had leapt in, bayonet in line. Adam saw death a split second away, realized he was off-balance and had no response. But Qasim, almost contemptuously throwing off his last adversary, clubbed Adam's attacker from behind with his rifle butt and then turned, swivelling his rifle and driving his bayonet through the leather jacket of the last Russian. The revolt was over.

Time was now pressing. The Eagle planned to plunder the supply depot of all the useful arms and supplies which could be packed into the thirteen trucks they had found parked behind the ablutions block.

What he couldn't take, or didn't want, he would blow up. His own dead and wounded were loaded first and set off on one of the trucks. The prisoners, still hand-tied, went next, packed into three trucks. Feverishly, Adam's sixty-odd men laboured to load the looted Russian supplies into the remaining lorries; Qasim, Zafir Khan and The Eagle making snap decisions as to what was most valuable and what could be left. When the trucks were loaded there was room for only a handful of the Muhajid Battle-Group Kalantut. The rest were ordered to disperse and find their way on foot to the Caves.

Explosive charges with timers were placed inside all the buildings and beside the stockpiles of arms. With a last look round, The Eagle gave a mock salute to the Field Armoury of the Afghan Eighth Infantry and piled into the last truck with Khizrhayat, Tirandaz, Qasim and Zafir Khan. When they were halfway home the night was suddenly lit with a firestorm: the shockwave from the arms dump exploding was so enormous that it almost sent his lorry lurching off the road.

But it was the hopelessness of the prisoners, as much as the huge haul of arms, which excited Adam. Qasim, bubbling with good humour in spite of the exertions of the night, kept saying, 'Guns, ammunition: now we'll show them, Kara Kush!'

And Adam answered, 'Qasim, arms are vital. But the Russians – did you see their faces? Did you look into their eyes? We're going to beat them, Qasim, do you realize that? We're going to beat them.'

2 'I thank the court for its clemency...'

Guerrilla Headquarters
The Eagle's Nest
Paghman Mountains
North of Kabul

APRIL 29

Six days after the raid on the armoury, the monastery was humming with activity. Abundant arms and ammunition meant that the sixty-five men of the Whirlwind could start serious weapons training. A planning section under Qasim was in being; the trucks, well-camouflaged, had been overhauled; the captured supplies were stowed in the limitless tunnels.

Such was the improvement in morale that Adam was able to get the men working to clear a new secret entrance, formed by water rushing past the place from the melting snows. Now there were two completely concealed ways into the mountain, with the observation posts commanding the broad Paghman Valley which lay at its foot, between the Eagle's Nest and the Russian occupiers' domain.

The prisoners, who had been brought here blindfolded, were housed in the spacious chambers which, with their brightly coloured wall frescoes, were perhaps the Buddhist abbott's luxurious apartments. They did not know where they were; and when they heard the roar of the Soviet search-planes, audible even in the caverns, they cowered into corners, convinced that they would be blasted into eternity at any moment.

For three days after the raid, Russian spotting, transport, attack, training and every other kind of aircraft – even tiny civilian crop-dusters – had whined and clattered above the area. The destruction of a major military installation, not to mention the loss of all its personnel and many of its arms, was no small matter. The Russians themselves did not know what really happened: but The Eagle had good intelligence contacts in Kabul, and he read their reports to the great amusement of the Whirlwind men.

'Only a large and heavily-armed force, trained by professionals, probably American interventionists, could have carried out this raid' claimed one 'situation appreciation paper', a grubby photocopy, made on a Russian machine out of office hours. The GRU, Military Security, had already interrogated Soviet combat, supply and logistics officers of high rank, to determine whether there had been treachery. More and more reports showed how everyone concerned was building up a case which, when reviewed in Moscow, would implicate someone else.

During the week the guerrillas had accumulated a vast amount of fascinating information about the Red Army from the prisoners. Adam had given copies of the *Constitution and Fundamental Laws of Afghanistan* to the Russian Colonel and his fellow-officers, and told them to prepare for a trial for atrocities and war crimes. In the meantime he collected any data which would help in the struggle against the invaders. To the Afghans south of the Hindu Kush anything connected with the USSR was a mystery, in spite of their shared border to the north. The Soviet Army was even more of an unknown quantity.

The more they learned, the more optimistic the guerrillas became. Socialism was not producing the desired effect. Either the Russians were poor material to begin with, or the regime had well and truly knocked the stuffing out of its captive people.

Food for the ordinary Soviet troops and NCOs was very poor. Porridge, noodles, bread, potatoes and a little fish formed the basis of an unvarying cycle of menus. Sometimes, the Russians said, they got meat, but not very often. In the cavern, the Russian soldiers sampled the officers' rations and wolfed the superior food with delight, complaining only that there was no vodka, which seemed to obsess them. They explained that they made an illegal brew called *samahonka*, but they didn't really like it. And they begged for tobacco or cigarettes.

The partisans saw that the unbalanced diet had caused many

health problems. Lack of vitamins seemed to be at the root of the ulcers, boils and night-blindness so common among the men. They were grateful when they were given powdered milk, which they said was sometimes to be had in barracks at home in Russia, but could not be found in Afghanistan.

When The Eagle had asked them whether their poor diet was due to transport difficulties, they said that it was, on the whole, better than they got at home. One gunner claimed that the infra-red night-sighting equipment was not in use because vitamin deficiencies in food had so limited the night vision of ordinary soldiers that the invisible-light projectors and goggles were next to useless.

This close-up view of what had been trumpeted as the greatest army on earth provided facts which took time to absorb. The Eagle, having read and heard so much about the Russians as a military power, at first thought that the soldiers must be lying. Questioning them individually, however, he found that their accounts bore out one another.

A major preoccupation was their pay. On the equivalent of $2.50 a week, a private could not buy extra food or send any money home. Everything went on boot polish, tobacco, shaving soap and blades. And the soldiers had to pay the inflated prices of their canteens. A private's entire pay bought no more than six packets of cigarettes a month. An Afghan conscript earned five times as much.

'They're all paranoid,' Qasim said to Adam after one interrogation. 'They believe that they are surrounded by enemies. They genuinely imagine that all Afghan guerrillas are organized and accompanied by CIA agents. I'm glad the CIA isn't behind us, but in a way it's a pity they aren't, for then they'd get a picture of what the Russians are really like. See that one over there' – he pointed to a sergeant – 'he's a gunner from an artillery regiment sent to the armoury to check the shells. He claims that twenty per cent of them are duds!'

The Russians, to the great surprise of the Muhjahidin, didn't wash much. They said that this was because the army gave them little hot water and few opportunities to take a bath. The purpose of military service, they had been told, was to prepare men for war; and there would be no baths in combat conditions. The 170 prisoners had long ago become accustomed to their corporate smell, but they were an embarrassment to the guerrillas, who bathed every day.

The deserter Zelikov (he preferred to be called a 'defector') turned out to be a good cook and an even better barber. He was a conscript from Kiev and, being in the last couple of months of a two-year service period, was almost due for repatriation and discharge. When Adam asked him why he hadn't waited another few weeks and gone home, he said, 'Once I get back there, I'll never get out again!'

He was delighted to be a guerrilla, though not anxious to see actual combat. He hated the Soviet system, although he knew no other, and insisted that a large proportion of the population in the USSR shared his dislike. This was specially true of the non-Russians, whom he said would soon be in a majority. The stupidity of the Soviet Army, in all its forms, was one of his favourite subjects: especially the remoteness of the officers from their men. According to Zelikov they thought about little except their own promotion. He also said that the officers stole supplies intended for the men. '*Vor* – thief!' he would shout, pointing to one or another of them.

The prisoners were now left unshackled, but were kept hobbled, like horses, on ropes which allowed them to walk in their cave prisons, but not to run. It was a situation which needed some supervision but not much. They seemed to be men without hope and for the first two days of their captivity believed they were going to die. They had been told by official propaganda that the partisans tortured any Russians they captured and even skinned them alive. Many suffered from a strange depressive melancholy and others behaved like chronic worriers. Some were to be seen consoling others in quite a moving way. There was even, they said, a special army word, *nastroemie*, 'mood', for this sadness.

In the *Darbar*, the assembly-hall, as the main cavern had become known, The Eagle convened his court at eight o'clock in the morning on the sixth day after the Russians had been captured.

Mostly rather sullen men, they were unshaven for lack of razors, and of various ages, ranks and ethnic stocks. Two of the prisoners were Afghans, interpreters: a lieutenant and a sergeant. Both had been trained in the USSR.

In addition to the hundred and twenty-eight privates, there were seven majors, eight captains, sixteen lieutenants, ten NCOs and of course the Colonel. This was the usual very high ratio of officers to men in the Soviet Army. The charge was murder.

The huge, vaulted cavern's roof soared like the nave of a Gothic cathedral. Hissing butane-gas lamps augmented the dim natural light. The prisoners were ranged to one side of the cave, sitting on blankets, while the guerrilla community, out-numbered by nearly three to one, sat opposite. On the third wall, facing the great oval gap hung with creepers which was the entrance, sat The Eagle and his henchmen.

The Eagle spoke, in Dari-Persian.

'The legitimacy of the forces of the Muhjahidin, the Strug-glers, is established by the Constitution of the Sovereign State of Afghanistan, promulgated on Mizan 9, 1343, which is equi-valent to October 10, 1964 of the Christian Era, signed at the Gulkhana Palace by King Zahir Shah.' He had been careful to include copies of the laws of free Afghanistan when stocking the fortress. 'I refer to Title Three, Article Thirty-Nine, which runs as follows:'

He paused, and said to the captured Afghan lieutenant, 'You will translate what I am saying, without deviation, into Russian; first saying that, according to the Constitution, there are only two official languages in this country: Dari-Persian and Pashtu. We are using Dari, but the prisoners may communicate, through you or directly, in either.'

When this had been conveyed to the Russians, the Colonel stood up. 'I am Colonel Aleksandr Petrov, of the Red Army of the Union of Soviet Socialist Republics. I demand that this farce be stopped and that I and my men be released immedi-ately. Failure to comply will result in the most crushing conse-quences. You should realize that you will all be hanged if you do not obey, regardless of our own fate.' A rest had restored some of the Colonel's confidence.

As if on cue, or at a signal, one of the guerrilla lookouts came running into the cave and handed The Eagle several sheets of paper. He looked at them, smiled and said, 'You Russians certainly do seem to think alike, Colonel! These are leaflets, supposedly from the Kabul Government, which are dropping like snow, all over the place. They are addressed to us. I shall read what they say:

'"People of the mountains! Deceived Afghans, captives of the anachronistic clergy, the aristocrats, landlords and backward tribal chiefs! Misinformed bandits! This is an appeal from the legitimate, republican and socialist government of our beloved country. The imperialist-Zionists and their lackeys the Pakistanis and Iranians, as well as the Egyptians, the Chinese and other enemies of the revolution and of the people, have deceived you! Lay down your arms and join us in the building of a free, noble, progressive homeland! Kill the British, American, West German, French and all other agents and spies among you! Release the soldiers of the brotherly Soviet Army, here as peacemakers and at the invitation of the legitimate, progressive, benign and homeland-loving, Islam-believing, single and only Government of the Democratic Republic of Afghanistan! Know that the President, His Excellency Agha Babrak Karmal, has announced an amnesty. You will be free to return to your homes, to your crops and animals, to your wives and chidren. Accept the amnesty! Join the joyful New Day!"'

There was a roar of derisive laughter from the assembled Afghans.

The man on The Eagle's left, Tirandaz the sharpshooter, grinned. 'It is quite poetic, Eagle, but they have a long way to go before their poesy competes with that of the great Saadi, Hafiz or Rumi! But it's nice to know that they are trying.'

The Eagle, when the leaflet had been translated to the Russians by the very uncomfortable interpreter, said, 'Babrak Karmal's airborne petition to the Muhjahidin, on behalf of the Russian prisoners and their friends, is dismissed. To continue:

'In accordance with the Afghan Constitution, Title Three, Article Twenty-Six, Paragraph Two, I inform the prisoners of their rights. I quote: "Innocence is the original state: the accused is considered innocent unless found guilty by a final judgement in a court of law."'

The Colonel shouted, 'This isn't a court of law!'

'I hereby declare,' continued The Eagle, 'this assembly, composed of citizens of Afghanistan, to be a court of law under the Fundamental Law of Afghanistan. The charge against the accused is murder, direct murder or, alternatively, indirect by collusion, before or after the event. The penalty for murder in this country, as in Russia, is – and always has been – death.'

Pandemonium broke out among the Russians when they heard the translation of this charge. Some cried out, others tried to run forward and throw themselves on the ground in front of The Eagle and his companions. Only the Colonel remained calm, evidently trying to give an example to the rabble. The Afghans, unused to such excitable behaviour, leaned forward interestedly, eagerly pointing out to one another the more hysterical of the Russians, looking at the scuffles as the terrified men argued among themselves, and wondering what could be the subject of such disputes. All the Soviet prisoners, whether Slavs, Balts, Tartars or Tajiks, seemed equally affected.

Three shots rang out. 'I haven't got a gavel,' The Eagle explained, putting his smoking revolver back into its holster, 'but be careful that I don't shoot someone by mistake. I might, if your restlessness makes me too excited.'

The shivering mob subsided, their eyes fixed on him. Some were wringing their hands in silence, others groaned, or repeated like a litany, 'Lord have mercy . . .'

'Eagle, this is going to take a year, why don't we get on with it?' Qasim was getting bored.

The Eagle turned to the prisoners. 'You must listen, or we'll make you listen. The Fundamental Law, while prescribing the death penalty, provides for mitigation. It states that, in a case of murder, the bereaved may relent, and accept compensation instead of revenge. If any of you are found guilty, I shall ask the assembled people here, the Afghans, who are accepted as the bereaved in the case of the massacre at Kalantut, to pronounce whether they will accept compensation – or whether they still insist upon execution of the death penalty, as is their right.'

The Colonel was still trying: 'I demand liberty, and at once, for all of us!' He shook his fist. The rest of the Russians again intoned, in a deep chorus, 'Lord have mercy.'

The Eagle held up his hand for silence and looked at his copy of the Constitution. 'The accused Aleksandr Petrov will take note of Title Three, Article Twenty-Six, Paragraph One of the Constitution, an abstract of which was furnished him yesterday, together with other relevant papers: "Liberty is the natural right of the human being. This right has no limitations except the liberty of others and public interest as defined by law".'

He turned to the Colonel. 'Aleksandr Petrov: you will recognize this court and allow us to continue, representing your associates yourself or nominating someone else, who may be anyone of your choice, or I shall immediately hand you over, for summary trial by consensus, to the *Jirga*, the assembly of the Afghans present today. The *Adat*, customary law, allows for this as an alternative to your accepting the authority of our court.'

This really interested the Afghan crowd. Cries of 'People without honour' and 'Hand the murderers over to us, Eagle!' filled the air. Turbans were unrolled and waved, and a group began to sing the national hymn:

'. . . *zindabad Qaum: Sar-buland bashad, bairaq-i-Afghan!* Long Live the People, honoured, eminent be, the flag of the Afghan!'

The buglers were practising their own warcry, like a football crowd, shouting it out syllable by syllable: 'The Trumpeters Are Here!'

When order was restored once more, the Colonel said, wearily, 'I accept the jurisdiction of the court.'

'Petrov, Aleksandr, Citizen of the Soviet Union, are you guilty, directly or by association, of the murder of one or more of the people of Kalantut?'

'I am not guilty, in either sense.'

'Is any one, or are any number, of your associates, guilty in either sense?'

'None of them is guilty in either sense.'

'The court regards them as innocent, until guilt can be proved. Qasim Hashemi will now state the facts.'

Qasim rose. 'Respected sir: the entire resident population of Kalantut village, Kabul Governorate, was seen by me and four others, dead, murdered according to a witness, by Russian troops from the Afghan Field Armoury occupied by elements of the USSR's three hundred and sixtieth Motorized Rifle Division. The evidence of our eyes, Russian ammunition, and a witness attest to this, though the witness died of his wounds. Colonel Petrov has admitted the guilt of his men, to our

Commander, when Battle-Group Kalantut was recapturing the Armoury in the national interest.'

The Colonel stood up. 'President of the court! The witness has failed to add that I voluntarily said that I was about to punish the men who had committed the offence.'

'Sit down,' said The Eagle. 'If an offence has been committed – and none disputes that – and if you say that you knew about it and were even going to punish its perpetrators, you cannot plead that your men are not guilty.'

One of The Eagle's men, whispered to Qasim: 'Is our Eagle a lawyer?'

'No, he's a professor of technology, in the Faculty of Science of the University of Kabul.' The questioner looked awestruck at this answer.

The Colonel was on his feet again. 'I was prevented from doing my duty.'

'You mean that you would have tried the men for murder of innocent civilians, women and children?'

'*Gospodin* President! The charges had not yet been framed. You led the attack which overwhelmed us, I had no time.'

'You were overwhelmed by bugles, a drainpipe, the treachery of one of your own men, and by two or three of us, that's all. But never mind that. We'll take your argument into account. Have you anything else to say?'

The Colonel, his face a mask of tension, seemed to have used up most of his reserves of energy in his earlier sallies. '*Gospodin*, sir. You give me some hope. It was a matter of the honour of the Red Army. We *would* have tried the men.'

The Eagle paused a moment, then said: 'We have never heard of any such trials before: but, Petrov, we know of the murders of innocent people by your forces, in our country. Six thousand men, women and children, the entire population of a village called Atrnak, near Kunduz, were massacred in May, 1980. That is only one of your crimes.'

'That is all I can say, *gospodin*. Of course, if the Party or the Security Services intervenes, the sentence is not carried out.'

'Why would that be?'

'On the legal grounds that the men were acting in the interests of overall security, against spies and saboteurs.'

'And you would agree with that?'

'I am not consulted in such matters.'

'We shall take account of that, too. Has the accused anything more to say?'

'Yes, *gospodin*.'

'Say it, then.'

'When you captured the Armoury, forty-two men were in the barrack block nearest to the water-tower.'

'Yes.'

'Those men are all missing.'

'Yes. They died, to a man, when they tried to break out, after the order to surrender had been given. There was fighting. We lost six men there, through their action.'

'President of the court! Those men of ours were in detention, precisely because they were to be accused of killing your compatriots at the village of Kalantut.'

The Eagle was surprised. Either this was true, or else it was a most ingenious idea. Blame the dead. Aloud he said, 'If they were in detention, accused of a crime, how could they get out so easily and attack us, fully armed, and kill six men?'

The Russian shrugged. 'You saw the arms and ammunition piled in the open. They got out of the block and seized grenades and other weapons. That's all.'

'I repeat: how did they get out of detention so easily, Petrov?'

'They were not locked in. There was no need. They knew that if they left the block they would be shot by the guards. There was no hope of escape.'

'If they were under detention, and likely to be punished by your court of enquiry, why were they so keen to break out and help in the defence of the camp when it was attacked?'

'I can only think that they wanted to redeem themselves. If they had helped to defeat the attack, it would have counted in their favour at a court-martial.'

The Eagle looked straight at him. 'Colonel, is it not possible that those men had hoped to arm themselves and get away, perhaps to join the Muhjahidin, as so many Russian soldiers have already done?'

Petrov looked away, then sighed. 'It is possible, President.'

'Another question, Colonel. Is self-incrimination allowed in Russian courts?'

'Yes, it is normal. The courts rely on it.'

'And, lastly, is there presumption of innocence, or presumption of guilt?'

'Anyone who goes before any court in the Soviet Union is presumed guilty. This is based on the contention that no innocent person ever gets as far as a court of law. He or she would be exonerated during the preliminary investigation.'

'Thank you.'

'*Gospodin* President!'

'Yes, Colonel?'

'I said that we were innocent and did not want to recognize your court precisely because, in our country, I would have been admitting guilt if I had acknowledged that I had been arraigned before a properly constituted court. You must allow us time to get used to your ways.'

'Our ways, Colonel, are the ways of the entire civilized world. We have had these ways for thousands of years. You have only had your ways for – what? – sixty years. Your ways are the ways of the dictator, not of humanity. You should not need time.'

Although the Russian's words were being translated, faithfully, for the assembled Afghan multitude, some of the finer points seemed to be escaping them. Qasim nudged The Eagle. 'I think that we should summarize for the people. They are getting restless again.'

The Eagle stood up, the better to be seen and heard, and moved into the space between the two parties.

'Afghans and prisoners! This case is simple, but everyone must know what it means. I shall explain in a few words. Now listen:

'It is admitted that the villagers were massacred. Someone must pay for it. The Colonel claims innocence for himself and for all his men who are here today. The law upholds him, as we have found none who can say that anyone here has committed murder.

'In his own regiment, the Colonel acts as judge. He states that he had no time to put the murderers on trial, so we cannot find him guilty.

'We are also told that the men in detention at the camp were the real murderers, who killed without orders or permission. All those men are now dead.

'It is my judgement that justice has been done, even if only by accident, with the killing of the Russian murderers. Under the law of requital, the blood of the people of Kalantut has been avenged.

'Now we must, surely, acquit these men, for no blood is on them, so far as we know.'

The Eagle at first saw only the poetic justice and the elegance of the solution, as if fate had arranged the whole matter and planned the outcome. But the Afghans wanted blood. Most of them, after all, had not been at the battle, had not seen what was involved and had only heard of the massacre at second hand. It was the non-combatants, deprived of the release afforded by battle, who felt most deeply about justice and revenge.

The assembly drowned the voice of the Afghan interpreter, shouting for revenge. They cried out the names of relatives who had been burned by napalm, who had suffocated in gas, who had been hunted down like rabbits by strafing jets or blown apart by helicopter rockets. They threw sandals, and their cries became one voice, terrible in the echoing vastness of the immense cavern, *Marg bar Rouss, marg bar qatilun!* Death to the Russians! Death to the murderers!

Like every natural leader, The Eagle knew that time would reduce tension if he let them have their say. The shouting went on for ten minutes or more as he returned to his seat, and sat, impassively, waiting.

The Russians, pitiful pictures of hopelessness, huddled in groups, clutching one another, even clawing at the cave-wall, fear in their eyes, a fear made more terrible than those of cornered animals by the human ability to think about the future. They were visualizing torture, dismemberment, a sordid and meaningless death. Zelikov had a word for it. *'Demoralizatsiya, Komondon,'* he whispered.

The Eagle was getting a first-hand demonstration – and it was to be the first of many – of the fragile esprit de corps of the Soviet Army. Adam remembered reading some of the literature. Following the Second World War, all other modern armies had concentrated upon encouraging small bodies of men to form fighting groups. Such men remained together from their early training days and through active service. The result was an army made up of a large number of strongly bonded units, like the hunting groups of man throughout the ages.

The Russians had rejected this formula because, as their own documents, closely studied by the CIA and other Intelligence agencies, showed, they *feared* combinations of people. Men were regularly moved from one unit to another, units were endlessly transferred. 'Bonding' was never given a chance to happen, even by accident. In consequence, units easily fell apart. Captives joined the enemy, especially if the enemy had the camaraderie which the Russians lacked and no doubt craved.

Desertions and suicides were surprisingly frequent, and the rapport between men and officers was not good enough to ensure morale capable of surviving adversity to the extent which most other modern armies regarded as normal.

One reason for the startlingly poor quality of the Russian combat troops – even the best of them – was probably the large proportion of them who were alcohol-dependent. Adam had not read the many accounts published abroad showing alcoholism as a major problem in the Soviet Union; much less the confession of one Russian soldier: 'Even if you are not an alcoholic when you go into the Army, you are when you come out.' But he was now getting evidence at first-hand.

More than half of all the Russian soldiers taken prisoner craved alcohol. Some begged for drink, others showed alarming withdrawal symptoms. Adam, in the past week, had come across another factor which might well contribute to the indifferent quality of the Soviet soldier. Although the Army drew from all ranks in society, his prisoners constantly complained that what they called 'very intelligent' people, as well as those with good contacts, contrived to keep out of the Army altogether, buying successive deferments by bribery or going into higher education.

The storm of Afghan protest at what they thought was incomprehensible leniency had subsided to a mere background murmur, so Adam judged the time was ripe to take charge again. He stood up. 'All this does not mean that our prisoners can get away without some recompense to us. After all, we have worked and taken great risks to acquire them. So I have a proposal to make.

'We ourselves owe a debt, a great one, to certain people whom most of us do not even know, people who, maybe, had hardly heard the word Afghanistan till a year or two ago. But these people, in far-off lands, learnt of our plight and answered the call of humanity. They came here and they tended our sick – many are still doing so – undergoing the same hardships as us, and for no material reward. They eat poor food and have to drink polluted water. They catch diseases, they are hunted by helicopters, and still they come. They are the doctors and nurses of International Medical Aid, *Médecins sans Frontières*, and other organizations and they are saving hundreds of lives. It is evidence of the rottenness of our traitors' minds that Keshtmand, Karmal's Prime Minister, has publicly said that he sees this selfless work as a cover for "other missions". Kabul cannot see the heroism and sacrifice of these good people.

'One of these, a thirty-year-old doctor called Phillipe Augoyard, was captured in January 1983 by the communists while tending the sick. His trial, as a spy, was filmed and shown on television. By this travesty of justice, the communists revealed their own evil better than their worst enemies could. The film was shown here in Afghanistan and released worldwide. It showed the exhausted Dr Augoyard, a broken man, being sentenced to eight years' imprisonment for "espionage". As the cameras recorded the scene, the doctor thanked the court "for its mercy". This was on March 13th, 1983.

'The crime was, in fact, committed by the Soviets: jailing an innocent man. As a result, the name of the Russians and of our country stinks in the nostrils of civilization. Do you wish it to be so?'

The Eagle raised both arms into the air.

'I therefore propose that we offer these Russian prisoners as a part exchange for the unconditional release of the gallant Dr Augoyard. Although he is only one man, he is worth ten times as much as this trash from the New Civilization!'

The Afghans cheered.

When the possibility of their release registered in their benumbed brains, the captive Red Army men again intoned one of their hardly cheering dirges. The interpreter rendered it as '*Rusya, Madar-i-Muqaddas!*' – Holy Mother Russia.

On June 3rd, 1983, it was announced by the Afghan Chargé

d'Affaires in Paris that Dr Phillipe Augoyard had been re-prieved and would leave Afghanistan within the next few days. By June 9th, the French Embassy in Kabul stated that he had been handed over to them. By the middle of the month he reached Paris.

The trial was over and the fate of the prisoners decided. Afterwards, in one of the smaller caves which Adam used as an orderly room, Qasim showed The Eagle a collection of what appeared to be waste paper – scraps from the backs of envelopes, even bits of cloth.

'When they were waiting for the trial,' he said, 'the Nikolais asked that these, their last letters home, might be sent there for them.'

'Letters home?' The baker Nanpaz was eavesdropping and could not hide his puzzlement. 'Are these men or not? Perhaps, given more time, they would have sent home samples of their needlework as well! They kill children, and they write letters home. They firebomb us, and ask us to be postmen.' The baker suddenly gave a great laugh. 'If that's what the Russians are like, Afghanistan has nothing to fear.'

The Russian prisoners of war never saw their socialist paradise again. When they were interrogated by the GRU, it was offi-cially decided that their spell in captivity had produced 'disturb-ing symptoms of bourgeois thinking'. According to information that reached The Eagle's band through their double agents in the KHAD, the prisoners revealed 'taints of sympathy with the Afghan bandits'. Some had stated, defiantly, that the rebels were not counter-revolutionaries but patriots, and one Russian private had said, 'They are farmers and workers like us.'

The Muhjahidin never learned how the Russian hostages and their dangerous sympathies were disposed of. They were very probably shot. They did, however, return to their homeland in an all too familiar form as cinders in the little chromium-plated urns, which now grace so many homes in the Soviet Union.

News travels fast in Afghanistan. Soon the *shabnamas*, 'night letters', passed from hand to hand in towns and villages, were full of The Eagle's exploits, some real, some imaginary. In the teahouses and market-places, in government offices and army barracks, the equivocal name was whispered, in hope or in fury, more and more often, as the Russians became bogged down in their Afghan adventure, and as the spirits of the people rose accordingly.

The Russians, true to type, assumed that he was the leader of a great, countrywide conspiracy, supported from outside and directing an organization of thousands, perhaps hundreds of thousands, of men. Nothing less could dare to oppose them, nothing else could have carried out the exploits, all over Afghanistan, which were ascribed to him.

Abroad, people accustomed to thinking in conventional terms, were delighted that the Afghans 'had thrown up a national leader at last'. But the Afghans, unlike other peoples, did not work in that way. They had always won their wars against occupiers in the past, even with an equivalent disparity of weapons: but never by following a single man at the outset of the struggle.

Adam Durany knew that an Afghan leader, living and fighting amid such a highly individualistic people, must act as a catalyst. The Afghans would, indeed, rally to a leader: but only after he had proved himself, and after they, too, had some gains to bring to the contract. They always enlisted under a leader's banner as equals. For this reason, The Eagle had three objectives: first, to hurt the Russian invader and make him pay; second, to establish his own success; third, to raise the fighting consciousness of other Afghans, and to help them establish their positions as victorious warriors.

When he heard the radio reports of the exiled political men wrangling in Pakistan and Europe, Adam laughed. When, from the same source, he listened to thoughtful but misguided military experts explaining, with copious references to Vietnam, Yugoslavia and elsewhere, that 'nothing important can happen among the Afghans until they rally behind a single, national leader', he shook his head. Experts they might be: experts in anything but the facts of Afghan history.

It was less than a month after the trial of the Russians at Paghman that Adam decided to descend upon another stockpile of weapons. Since the Afghan Army had become so unreliable, their arms and ammunition had been dispersed throughout the country under Russian control, and only issued to Afghan units with the strictest precautions. This, in fact, was only when the Soviet troops pushed them forward to attack rebel strongholds, and kept them covered from the flanks and rear.

The arms store which was Adam's new target was at the Peak of the Standard-Bearer, north of Kabul. He planned to attack it, neutralize the opposition, take away what he could and destroy the rest. Afterwards, making known what he had done – and how he had done it – he would use the exploit to encourage others and to underline his motto: 'Daring and guile!'

Like the Soviets themselves, the Afghan Army were short of trucks. Just as all transport in the USSR is available and earmarked for military use, so the Afghan Army also commandeers anything on wheels when needed. A line of such trucks, seized from firms and merchants large and small, had just driven into the guarded area of the dump, full of weapons and explosives.

The Eagle had reconnoitred the place and observed its routines several times. Today he saw that, as on previous occasions, the vehicles had stopped just inside the high wire perimeter fence, to be unloaded later in the day. Deliveries, he had noted, stayed loaded until the changeover of guard duties.

In another half an hour, just after nightfall, the last truck of the evening would arrive. This one always carried miscellaneous despatches and supplies. He and Qasim withdrew, parallel to the road, to await the final truck.

When it was a mile from its destination, two figures, in heavy sheepskin coats and carrying boxes such as are common among wandering pedlars in Afghanistan, signalled to the driver of this truck that they wanted a lift.

The driver looked out of the cab.

'What's this nonsense? This isn't a bus service for beggars. We're only going up to the military camp anyway. Get out of the way, snake venom upon your fathers!'

'Respected sir: the officers in there have called for us. How can we refuse such a command?' The Eagle's whine was perfect mimicry.

'Called for *you*, idiots! That's impossible. The officers there are gentlemen – they don't talk to scavengers, buffoons, carrion!'

74

'Sir,' said Qasim, rewrapping a greasy turban around his head and scratching for non-existent fleas, 'we are afraid of the *Rouss*, too. If we don't get to see them, they'll be angry with you, as well.'

This did not seem at all likely to the sergeant-driver. But, he reflected, such effrontery from people like this, people of this low class, usually meant that there was something in what they said.

'Who are you? What do you want? If you're not lying, where is your *kaghaz*, your paper?'

'Excellency! Of course I have one. I'll show it to you.'

Adam opened the passenger door and climbed into the cab, pulling his dirty suitcase behind him. Before the driver knew it, a very long, thin knife was nearly in his ribs.

'Just drive on when my friend knocks on the partition behind you, my little nightingale, or your stomach will feel this without your mouth having tasted it.'

There were three distinct raps from the back. Qasim, holding a grenade with the pin out and his fingers on the spring release, was too close to the three soldiers sitting guard over the load for them to want to make a move.

The truck rolled towards the entrance of the camp.

Moments later they were in, past the bored guard at the gate, and parked at the side of the last weapons truck standing just beyond the wire.

Qasim jumped down first, pushing the three terrified soldiers, their knees knocking, before him, into the shadows beside the guardhouse.

The Eagle brought his own prisoner to join them, and all five men stood, silently, waiting, while he went back for his case.

Adam reappeared in a moment, wearing a gasmask, and took over from Qasim, who put on his own mask and produced two strange-looking objects from the huckster boxes.

In another minute the masked men had sprayed, from their Smith and Wesson gas generators, just enough disabling mist to knock out the camp guards, and pushed the prisoners from the truck in among them.

After that it was easy.

Jumping into the driver's seat of the last supply truck, Qasim started the engine, while Adam planted timed explosive charges where they would do most harm, then ran to join his friend. The truck careered in reverse to the main road, and they were away.

They had used only a little of the anaesthetic gas, from the dainty little apparatus, weighing no more than eight kilogrammes, which could produce gas from its pump and tank for as long as forty-five minutes.

They were three minutes away from the Peak of the Standard-Bearer when the depot went up, with a roar and a blast-wave which rocked the hurtling truck, while an orange glare lit the surrounding countryside and illuminated a thick cloud of oily smoke which stood out against the white clouds of the sky.

As the two guerrillas shook hands in mutual congratulation, The Eagle wondered what the American suppliers would have thought of the use to which their equipment had been put. The sample units had been sent sometime before to the Afghan police for riot control evaluation: and had fallen into the hands of desperadoes like Adam and Qasim.

The Americans had been careful enough, at the time, to ensure that the gas generators went direct to the laboratory of Dr Adam Durany, the eminent technologist at Kabul University – a very responsible man.

Next morning, complete strangers in the streets of Kabul were shaking hands and embracing. In Herat, four hundred miles away, the streets rang with the cry 'Victory at Standard-Bearer Peak! Long live The Eagle!'

3 Karima: 'If you push me too far . . .'

Kabul City and Jalalabad
Afghanistan

JUNE 7–8

Karima sharpened the carving knife with a whetstone to what Mr Zoltan had called 'razor status'. He had taught her so many things: even ones that didn't connect with her work, interesting things, knowledge from the outside world, from foreign places. Like the fact that his name, Zoltan, was a form of 'sultan', a name which the Turks had brought to Majaristan, his mother's country, hundreds of years ago. And it meant 'king'. To Karima, Mr Zolton had been a kind of king. Mr Zoltan's second name was Pomakov, and he came from Bulgaria, *Bulgharistan*; and his mother was Hungarian, from *Majaristan*. Those people were, he said, Huns – a kind of Turk – and had settled in Europe long ago, two or three centuries before the time of the Prophet. Pomaks were the Bulgar people who had joined the Turks in the days when the Sultan of Constantinople ruled them.

She looked out of the kitchen window, down into the garden with its neat flowerbeds and gravelled paths. Why did Mr Zoltan have to go away? He was happy here, in the modern apartment, with her as housekeeper and various lads as houseboys working under her. He'd come to Kabul twenty-five years ago, to work as an engineer on the great new highway being built from Kabul to the Soviet Union. Zahir Shah was King of Afghanistan then, and you didn't see many Russians. Czechs, Poles or Bulgars, yes. Very few Russians. Of course, in her village, you never saw a foreigner at all, much less married one like Mr Zoltan's mother had done. Whatever would that be like, to marry a foreigner? Well, Karima was sixty years old now, and she would never know marriage at all. Mr Zoltan, if he was still alive, would now be fifty-seven. Mrs Pomakov, Mr Zoltan's mother, sounded very nice, though. Latifa, her name was. Was she still alive? she wondered. She'd be nearly eighty. She'd sent Karima some lovely carved wooden combs through Mr Zoltan once: when he had come back from leave. All the way to Bulgharistan to go on leave!

That was beyond Iran, beyond Turkey, nearly at the land of the Franks. But the Franks, *Farangis*, were not bad, either; she had seen them in the streets of Kabul. The Farangis were divided into nations – *Fransavi*, *Almani*, *Inglisi*, *Italavi*, Ispanyul. Mr Zoltan had explained a lot about that, too.

How kind Mr Zoltan had been to her. One day, a Friday holiday, he had taken her to see the great new road and the Salang Tunnel which started forty miles from Kabul. You could hardly make it out at first, because of the swarms of Afghan workers heaving and pushing and operating machines. There were even machines that dug; the labourers called them *devs*, demons: enormous things they were; some had buckets on them, like water-wheels, which endlessly shifted earth instead of water. There was a big office there, and Mr Zoltan was in charge of a whole section of the highway. 'That's my bit, Karima, all my own. And I'm well up to schedule with it, too.' He was obviously a big man there, even bigger than she'd thought. There were Russian engineers, but they were always having to ask Mr Zoltan questions, looking at big sheets of white paper with drawings on them, needing his permission to do this or that. Yet he was such a quiet man; she'd never have guessed that he was a *sarkarda*, a chief supervisor.

'The tunnel alone will cost thirty-eight million dollars,' he had said – or was that for the whole road from Kabul to Doshi? When it was finished, the journey took only three hours by truck, instead of several days over the Hindu Kush mountains on horseback.

They had stopped for a picnic on the way back, in the warm spring sunshine, just before they reached the dust of Kabul, which at times covers everything, and always kept Karima busy, sweeping, cleaning and washing clothes. They always talked easily. Mr Zoltan, like many of his Pomak, Turkish-influenced, countrymen, spoke modern Turkish perfectly. Karima, coming from the north of Afghanistan, knew the old Turki tongue, and they could understand each other very well indeed. In Kabul most people either spoke Dari-Persian or Pashtu, and Karima still found these languages, so different from her own, quite difficult to speak, if not to understand.

On that day, Mr Zoltan had spoken of his own country, and she had asked him why he did not have a king.

'We had them once, Karima, but those days are past. Now we have a *jamhuriyat*, a republic.'

'Mr Zoltan, what is it like to live in a *jamhuriyat*?'

'Some are better than others, just like some kingdoms, of course.'

'What is life like in your *jamhuriyat*?'

'It has been improving. We have had hard times, of course. There was a great war, you know, the one with the Alman. They occupied our country, and the Russians helped to drive them out. That was when Afghanistan was neutral. And there is a Russian saying, "It is better to be cold than blind".'

'Yes,' said Karima, 'we had hard times, too. The Alman engineers went away from here, to their war, and we couldn't get anything from them to repair the electric factory or the machines in the workshops they'd built here – oh, I suppose fifty years ago.'

'That's right. Well, we had a new government, in Bulgharistan, and they preferred to have a republic. A party of the people, working folk, organized it.'

'So it is *Shoravi*, communist, like the *Rouss*?'

'That is so.' Mr Zoltan had shaken his head; but Karima knew – he had told her – that that was what Bulgarians did when they meant 'yes'.

'Mr Zoltan, has it improved your land?'

'In many ways, Karima. We do not starve now, as some people used to do. We all have work, and we are working hard. I think that it is the best way for us.'

Karima considered that.

'The Afghans don't really like to work as labourers, especially the men. They say that's why we have the "No Work, No Food" programme. Even peasants, who don't belong to tribes, like to think of war, of dying to defend the country.'

Mr Zoltan laughed.

'Well, we are not really a military people, in Bulgharistan. So perhaps it is easier for us to organize, to work for peace and not for war. That, anyway, is what we like to think.'

'And are the *Rouss* bad people, as we so often hear?'

'*Tetka* – little aunt; the *Rouss* are not bad people. As with the Afghans, some of the people who have power can do bad things to ordinary folk. That will always happen, anywhere. But the *Rouss* people themselves are very nice, and kind and good. They sing, and joke a lot, and they will share their last bite with you.'

Karima gave a little laugh. 'That sounds just like us. There are some terrible officials here as well. In the war, you said, the *Rouss* had driven out your enemy. Did they not take you into their *imperatori*, their empire, after that?'

'Well, Karima, there are no *imperatoris* now, not like there were. The Russians are helping us, and we are helping them. It is a brotherly thing, for we both think alike.'

'Excuse me, Mr Zoltan, but if the Russians *became* cruel to you, what could you do?'

'If anyone tries to push me farther than I am prepared to go, whoever he is, Karima, I shall make any sacrifice to oppose him, once I have found the way to do it.'

Then Mr Zoltan had gone away, and Karima had stayed on in the apartment block, this time working for the Russians who now had most of the important jobs on the Great Northern Road. She looked after a succession of officials and engineers, for the Russians had taken over the whole block, to house their people. In a beautiful part of the New City, the building was one of the best in Kabul. It had telephones, running water, flush toilets and double-glazing; even a swimming pool, and was one of the first to get colour television, though it could only pick up the local station, *Da Kabul Tilivizyun*, so far.

The new Russians had been complimentary about Mr Zolton. 'A great socialist engineer' they called him; and they told Karima that he'd been given a prize or a medal, for his work. Not surprising, really. Who would have imagined that people, or even a million demons, could have punched a great hole straight through the mountains, one and a half miles long and eleven thousand feet in the air, the link between the two halves of the highway?

Karima was there, because of Mr Zoltan's importance, for the opening. The Russian deputy Prime Minister, little Mr Mikoyan, was there too, all the way from Musku. Beside him stood the Afghan King himself, Mohammed Zahir. She noticed that the tunnel, as well as the road, had two lanes. People could drive back and forth, each using one of the twin roads, without ever colliding. And, of course, this brought the *Rouss* very near.

But the King had been there, so all must be well.

Many people still loved Zahir Shah, son of the great hero Nadir Khan who had rescued the country from the Brigand chief Saqao, and before that, as Marshal of the Armies, from the British, even. The Marshal had been ill, in France, and was carried on board the ship on a stretcher when he came back to save the homeland.

Karima, as she left the celebrations in the Russian car driven by her employer, saw evidence of the people's love for the Marshal-King's son. Just in front of them, without any escort or a single armed man, the royal car had stopped. The King stepped out, to kiss the head of a small girl, standing by the roadside. As Karima watched, the little one handed his majesty a furry bundle. It was a wolf-cub, its eyes scarcely open yet, which she had found, abandoned, near her mud-brick home. Then, after a rush of nervous words, she ran away.

There were tears in the King's eyes when Karima went to his side, for Mr Zoltan had opened the car door and said, 'Quick, see if you can help him,' and let her out.

She walked timidly up to him and stood, respectfully, while he composed himself. Then he turned to her, and said, 'Did you see that? Thinner than a toothstick, ragged, and yet she said to me, "Welcome to our village, Majesty. See, I did not come empty-handed. I found this cub yesterday: it has lost its mother. So you should take it: you are its king as well as mine . . ."'

But now the King was gone, living, they said, in exile, in an apartment in Roum, the land of Italya. The radio said, constantly, that he had been an evil man. Some people, too, whispered that he had brought the Calamity on the Afghans by sending young men to Russia to be trained. She did not know which, if either, was really true. People said all kinds of things.

The communist government had taken over, and the sort of Russians who came here had changed too. The nice ones had gone, the newcomers were hard men, cruel, arrogant, dirty, drunken and foolish. These, Karima thought, could not be the ones who had saved Mr Zoltan's country – and yet they were always saying that they had come to save us. From the Americans. Unlike Mr Zoltan, they did not even believe in God. Her present chief, Comrade Kirilyan, was fond of saying, 'Jesus Christ is another name for opium!' The Prophet Isa . . .

People were fighting the Russians now. You heard about it all the time, as in the days of the old wars. People flooded into Kabul from villages, wounded, saying that they had been bombed and machine-gunned, their villages destroyed. People like her. A woman had whispered to her in the market the other day that there had been a great killing in the Salang Tunnel, where Mr Zoltan had worked. A thousand people were dead. An Afghan had set his fuel tanker truck alight in the middle of a Russian convoy, with no hope of escape for himself. The woman had said, fervently, '*Fidai*, self-sacrificer, may Almighty God bless him and give him the Garden of Paradise!' But Karima's life was here, in the apartment block, far from such things.

She had no family now: the whole village had been wiped out by typhus in the old days, well over forty years ago, before they had got the epidemics under control. They had taken her to Kabul, the Women's Welfare Organization, and taught her domestic science. She'd learned to read and write a little, and to do embroidery. Then she got this permanent job at the apartments, originally built by the government for slum-clearance. It was now a paradise for people who had the influence to be allocated lovely homes like this.

When she had first seen it, she had been amazed. Here, people lived like kings. They even had separate rooms for eating and sleeping. And a *room* for washing and bathing in: unheard of in a mountain village. It was almost like having a room to grow crops in. Every man a khan, every woman a khanum. In the kitchen there was a Frankish thing, a machine, which she now used with great efficiency and aplomb, called a *prishur kukar*. It worked by steam, and it cooked things in no time at all. It gave out a scream like a demon, but it was harmless, really. Except, of course, for that time when it had exploded and spat the midday meal all over the ceiling, itself as wondrously white as a Friday turban on a saint.

And she had her own room. It had a string bed, good straw matting on the floor, real patterned curtains and double windowpanes. There were drawers set in the wall, a wardrobe and a large chest. She had never accumulated much, certainly not enough to fill all these things, but they were better than even the chief of her own hamlet had ever had. She had sufficient possessions for her needs, and there was money, safe in the post office, for her old age.

For the past week, since the Event – something that was like a message from the dead – she had worked hard. It was probably the shock of the Event which had brought all the memories flooding back. Anyway, she could not stop them running around in her head. The past, pictures in her head; duty, the need to do something, something which was right. What was it?

She remembered the village, her hard-worked parents, two harvests a year and little food, but good times as well as bad. Her cousin, Lalbaz, whom everyone said she would marry when she grew up. He had always said, 'I'll go to Kabul one day, Karima, and what I shall do there will be heard around the world!' She was fifteen when the typhus came. Lalbaz was two years older and had gone away to work. They had heard he'd had an accident, was dead. He had been killed by a machine which went wrong, in the far west near Iran, they'd said.

Then the Women's Welfare. Now it was called the Institute for the Development and Emancipation of Women. After they had sent her here, they kept in touch. Once a year they sent her a paper in Dari-Persian, nicely printed, saying what they were doing, all kinds of things. She especially liked the reports of the awards they gave to people who had served their country. Mr Zoltan used to translate them into Turki for her. One was about Mrs Safia Bakhshi, and had her photograph with it; a good-looking woman who had had real troubles. She had received a prize for rearing nine children who all did well, though she had been so poor that she had almost nothing to do it with.

When her husband died she had taught herself, from *The Rose Garden* and *The Orchard* of the great poet Saadi, and then she used that wisdom to bring up the nine.

At the age of fifty-two Safia Bakhshi had been declared Mother of the Year. Who could imagine that someone like that, nearly destitute, could rear two university professors, one of surgery and one of political science, a geologist, an army officer, a teacher, a merchant, a mathematician and three other graduates? And yet every year there were several like her. Mr Zoltan had said, 'Karima, if it can produce women like that, your country hasn't much to fear.'

Well, there had always to be people who cooked for officials and cleaned apartments. We can't all be sixteen-year-old Malali, who snatched the flag and rallied the exhausted troops to win their great victory at the battle of Maiwand, near Kandahar. They named a school after her, and made speeches, every year, about her sacrifice. Perhaps there would be a school named after Safia Bakhshi, too, one day. The apartment was spick and span. The accounts for the month, the grocer's bill and so on, were all paid up-to-date. This evening's meal was ready to be served. Everything was clean, bright, ready. Tonight the chief had guests, and he liked things to be correct. Four for dinner, although it was the houseboy's day off. Thorough, the chief, even if he was an atheist. Of course, they'd have to have an atheist as the head Russian of the Afghan Section of the KGB. He was 'Direct from Section Five, KGB/Moscow: supervision of individual Fraternal Foreign Lands'. That's what he'd said, and he made her memorize it.

She looked around again. Everything was in order. The beautiful silk shirts were freshly ironed; and she had even polished his new Japanese hi-fi equipment, the noise-chest she called it, which could wail like a herd of she-camels. Sometimes it gave out the sound of men and women screaming to music – well, some sort of music – while General Kirilyan lay back and drank.

Whisky, Chivas Regal, was what he liked. It came via the Soviet embassy. Funny how those Russians, who spoke all the time against the Franks, loved Western luxuries so. All except for *sagmahi*, fish eggs. Those were their very own, and they had a fascination for them – fish eggs, she thought, must be very common in their own country, and so they craved them, living so far from home.

The whisky was ready. Ah, there was the muezzin, giving the Call to evening prayer. That meant that General Kirilyan would soon be home, probably cursing everything about this lovely apartment, and promising Karima again that they'd soon move into one of those huge villas at Dar al-Aman, that the princes used to own. 'Just as soon as we get some central heating in, *Babushka. Then* you'll know what socialist life is really like!' He looked like an *ifreet*, like the *ifreet* of all *ifreets*, legendary demons: with his huge cigar, shiny red face, and bushy brows, and that nasty-looking blue-black gun never far from his right hand. A violent man. Not like Mr Zoltan at all.

There it was now, the doorbell. He had a key, of course, but always rang to summon her as he came up.

She looked out of the window. The Afghan soldier at the entrance was presenting arms, his hastily thrown-away cigarette still smoking in the rhododendron bush. Karima smoothed her apron and ran to the apartment's double door. The general swept in, without a word, followed by his aide, Major Hamdi, the Afghan who'd grown up in Russia and loved Russian *chaqawdar shorwa*, that soup made from beetroots. Hamdi, who was always boasting about the Russian food at the Khyber Restaurant in Pushtunistan Square, and the picnic boxes they sold you there. But you had to have armed guards at picnics nowadays. After him came a man in a neat Western suit, with big spectacles, and after him a shrimpy one, a male secretary with a small beard.

They sat down at the dinner table, as they always did, before the meal, for a conference. Karima stood respectfully by, waiting for an order: ice, perhaps, or salted nuts, or even to run to the shops or deliver a message.

In the years that she had been in contact with the Russians, Karima had learnt to understand almost everything they said. She couldn't speak more than a word or two of their language, but then she didn't have to. All they asked was that she should follow what they were saying to her, and should do what they wanted, fast. As she stood there humbly, before these important men, she was listening to their talk; and they talked freely. Servants soon become invisible to people who occupy a country.

'This is the nineteen-eighties! We've got to take some account of world opinion and the damage this man can do. Don't you know that Moscow has laid down the line? We have to fight the fight of words, all right, but there has to be consistency, and we have to know what to say.' The general was very angry.

'Comrade General!' said the civilian, 'as deputy director of training of the KHAD, it is not my function to produce explanations as to why the head of my department of the Secret Service should disappear.'

'Lieutenant-General Ghulam Siddiq has not disappeared, you fool! I wish he had. He's in Pakistan, giving press conferences, you lunatic! We trained him in Moscow, in Section Nine: Foreign Training, gave him the best that the KGB can offer, and what does he do? He goes over to the enemy. He's got to be killed, I tell you! When he defected a week ago, the KGB Colonel Semensev was almost unhinged at the thought of the consequences. He shot an Afghan beggar in the market near the Pul-i-Khishti mosque, started a riot, and was beaten by the crowd. We must liquidate, destroy, kill Ghulam Siddiq. That's all you can do with people who push you too far!'

Push me too far. That's what Mr Zoltan had said. Karima's concentration slipped. They wanted to kill someone, a general, an Afghan, who'd pushed them too far. Her mind went back to what she'd heard a week ago, and what she'd seen, the Event: the pictures that had been in her mind, night and day, for a week.

She had been in the Char-Chatta, the Four Arcades bazaar, after buying fresh vegetables for the evening meal, when a ragged man had come up to her, someone whom she vaguely thought she knew, but could not place. '*Ana*, mother, aren't you the daughter of Chakmaq Khan of Kilichkoy?' he said in Turki, the language of her village.

'Yes, I am, but he is dead.'

'I know that, he died, like the others, of typhus many years ago.'

Karima said, 'I was the only one who got away. But who are you?'

'I am your cousin, Lalbaz Khan. I was away, working as a

labourer, at the big irrigation place, in Herat, when the plague struck at Kilichkoy. When I got back to the village, it had been destroyed, levelled and burnt, by the sanitary administration. They said I'd get compensation, but I could never prove my right to it. I thought I recognized you. Well. After all these years!'

He was a stocky peasant type, with second- or third-hand clothes, and a long white scar on his cheek. He must be over sixty now. The man she might have married. He looked undernourished and terribly poor.

Karima made up her mind quickly. 'I have a good job, I am working as a housekeeper, for the *Rouss*.'

'The *Rouss*, the *Rouss*, the sons of pigs!' Lalbaz was shouting now. A crowd gathered and some stallkeepers murmured, '*Chup sho!* Be quiet; stop him: *khatar de* – it's dangerous!'

Karima took his arm. 'It is not safe to talk like that, Lalbaz. Come with me, I'll give you food, and I have money. You'll be all right. You can get work.'

Lalbaz squinted at her, hatred in his eyes. 'I'm with The Eagle, I'm on my way now, to the Heaven-Born! I may be a beggar now, but I have the pride of the Afghan. I spit on the *Rouss*!' At the top of his voice, he shouted, in Turki, '*Yasha Kara Kush!*' Long live The Eagle!

A man stepped forward from the crowd. He looked like a Russian, a foreigner, at least. He drew a gun and shouted in perfect Dari, 'Try spitting now, you scum!' as he fired. In a second, Lalbaz was lying there, blood from his mouth spreading until it was swallowed, as if hungrily, by the thick dust.

That was the Event. A man had been killed, one of her own kin. Killing meant revenge. It started blood feuds among the people of the mountains. Men killed men, and women were left to grieve, with only, as the Afghan song said, the faces of their children to remind them of the men who died for honour. And they brought up their children, too, to die for honour. Their sons, that is.

But, on the radio now, you could hear the women of the New Afghanistan proclaiming the New Day. She had heard them a hundred times now, calling, 'Sisters arise! Women are now the same as men, with equal rights and duties, in our dear land!'

A Russian had killed her cousin, Lalbaz. The murderer was a KGB man, like her boss.

Push me too far . . . any sacrifice . . . when I have found the way.

The general was shouting again. 'How can I explain this to Moscow? I can't. But the Red Army has special long-range diversionary combat teams. They are specifically entrusted with the task of assassination of "important figures beyond ordinary military reach". One of these should be sent out, to hunt him down, and to strike.'

He turned to the maid. 'How long have I been calling you, Karima? Bring some more ice, this whisky is boiling hot, damn you!'

Karima bowed, with folded hands, as she had been taught to do. She went into the kitchen and filled a large bowl from the wonderful ice-maker which dispensed cubes when you pulled a lever. It was from America. Who would believe how the Russian general had got it? He'd said, coming in one night very drunk, 'I got something useful for the flat today, *babushka*. Ice-maker, from the Pamir Room at the top of the Intercontinental. That fool of a head waiter didn't want to give it to me. I had to show my gun to some manager of something. I claimed it as a prize for the way I dance the *gopak*. It'll come tomorrow.'

And it had come, in an Iranian-made Paykan pickup truck ordered by the hotel from Shirpur Char-Rah, and delivered to the door. The general could, it seemed, do anything, get anything, he wanted.

She covered the bowl of ice cubes with a white cloth, and put it on a tray. Then she carried the tray into the dining room, which was full of stale cigarette smoke and argument. There was a small ornamental table by the wall. Karima put her tray down on the dumb waiter and placed the table next to the general. Then she carried the bowl over and placed it carefully on the side-table. She looked at the general's bulky neck, muscles contorted as he roared, leaning forward to emphasize what he was saying. There it was. Cloth off, lean towards him . . .

Taking up the knife, sharp as a razor, Karima said, 'You have pushed me further than I will go, Comrade General,' and – with a single movement – she cut his throat.

As he slumped forward and Karima backed towards the door, the Afghan intelligence chief's left hand was clapped to his mouth. He looked like an amazed child at the circus as he rose, uncertainly, from his chair. Then, kicking it backwards, he sprang at the woman with a curse. Karima, her work-hardened muscles twice as strong as his, pushed him to the ground. While the terrified secretary retched in a corner, she thrust the long, thin knife between the spymaster's ribs, through the soft wool of his vest. As he went slack, she gasped, 'For you Lalbaz, for you!' The knife stayed in. She had to tug hard to get it out.

Major Hamdi still sat at the table, his head in his hands, rocking back and forth very slowly, as though regressed to early infancy.

The secretary was also clearly now in shock, sitting paralysed, bolt upright, like a man made out of stone. Only his bright eyes moved, rolling insanely out of all control.

There was hardly any blood on her. Karima walked into the alcove, through the kitchen, to her tiny room beyond, and changed her apron. She looked at her face in the unframed wall-mirror, and put her brush and combs, presents from Mr Zoltan and his dear mother, into the shopping bag together with her bank book. She took the voluminous, tentlike *burqa* cloak, which covered her from head to foot for modesty, from behind the door, pulled it over her and ran.

Through the kitchen. No, first turn off the butane-gas cooker. Into and then out of the sitting room by the far door. Close it. Then down the stairs and push the swing doors; about to pass the *sarbaz* on guard, the conscript, in his dowdy uniform, only about sixteen years old.

'What's the hurry, mother?' He moved towards her, as if to start a conversation, jerking his head upwards as Kabulis do at the end of a question, and gave his usual foolish grin. His cheeks were hollow, Karima noticed. They really did not feed them properly, in the Army.

No sound from the apartment yet. Karima smiled and moved away, towards the road. 'I forgot something. And now it's all come back to me.'

He couldn't see her smile, through the dense mask of the *burqa*, but he knew her voice. You always had to check, that was orders. The officers were very keen on checking. He gave her a mock salute, 'Order me!' Silly women, heads full of bubbles; of course, they forgot things all the time. She'd forgotten a can of oil, no doubt, and the general was roaring for his dinner. Well, there was men's work and there was women's work, and it had always been that way. Only three hours now to the end of his *naubat* . . .

Ten minutes later Karima was at the Shahr-i-Nau post office to draw her money. She threw up her veil to argue. 'Not at this time of night, mother white-head,' said the guard. 'Come back tomorrow. Inshallah, God willing, you can have it then. Post office hours are nine a.m. to six p.m.' Tomorrow. Tomorrow she'd be hanged – after they'd taken her apart.

There was a grocer's shop near the post office, open until very late. Kabuli grocers, she believed, had all the money in the world. The grocer took her savings book and looked at it. 'You want it all? I can't do that. Money is only worth half what it was when you put this in – it is called inflation – so I can only give you half. And, of course, I'll have to bribe the postal clerk to let me take out someone else's money. Just let me see your name, on your identity book.'

Perhaps it was only worth half, now, she thought. Of course, everything had gone up in price so much. 'Here's my name and fingerprint. Look, I'm Karima Chakmaqi. I work for a general, so hurry up.'

'All right, here you are.' He counted out the greasy notes slowly, lovingly, as if he was parting with letters from his lady-love, thought Karima. But she had to have it: had to be patient. 'Look after your savings always, Karima,' Mr Zoltan had said, 'for they will mean your future safety.' And, all the time she had known him, Mr Zoltan had never, never once, been wrong about anything.

When the fat, unshaven grocer had finished putting down the notes, counting them thrice in case he robbed himself, he looked at her with narrowed eyes.

'What do you want all this money for, *morak*, little mother? And at this time of night, too. Surely you're not eloping, are you – not at your splendid age?' He covered his curiosity with the joke.

'Better late than never,' said Karima, in the same spirit.

What a lot of money it looked, even half of what she'd thought she had was quite a bundle. What she was now holding in her hand must be enough to buy a cow, as her father used to say when he spoke of great riches. She put it away and started to leave the shop.

'And see you buy the general's groceries from me in future, I'll give them to you at a good price!' The grocer smiled like the predator he was.

'With faith in God.'

'I entrust you to God.'

And now? She walked towards the bus station, and spoke aloud, as she worked things out, making up her mind. 'Mr Zoltan. You have led me up to now. But I'll have to go and find The Eagle. He has to be my sultan now, my Mr Zoltan.' Everyone knew that The Eagle was the deadly enemy of the *Rouss*. She knew that even General Kirilyan could not catch him, and had spoken about him more than once, as if he was afraid of him.

Karima slowed down near the Nau-Roz Carpet Shop opposite the Blue Mosque and rummaged in her shopping bag for the permit which officials' servants carried, to travel free, even without question after curfew, on the buses. She found a small sheaf of papers as well. Surely those were the ones she'd seen in front of General Kirilyan, on the table, when she had . . . finished . . . him. She must have picked them up without thinking. Well, The Eagle would find them useful, she was sure. Mr Zoltan had been very particular about looking after papers. 'Karima, papers can be the most important thing in this world.'

In this world. She was passing the mosque. She would not have to go in to say her prayers. People on a journey were excused formal prayer. But she always prayed in some form or other. She would recite the words as she walked.

> *Lead us onto the straight path, the way of those upon*
> *whom thou hast bestowed thy kindliness – not of those*
> *who have incurred wrath – of those who go not astray.*
> Amen.

The Eagle. Cousin Lalbaz's last words had been *Yasha Kara Kush*, Long Live The Eagle. She'd heard that The Eagle had started his fight against the *Rouss* alone, with just one other man. You could do a lot if you tried.

The Eagle, she thought, as she fought her way onto the big Mercedes bus for the four-hour journey to Jalalabad, four thousand feet below Kabul, might be able to use a good cook. Of course, as the radio was always saying, the people in the mountains with him might be starving. 'Only two per cent are fighting against socialism, and will not obey the law. They are starving.' Well, if they were, they wouldn't need a cook. She could do something else instead.

4 Business on the Frontier

*Manchester England
and Istanbul Turkey*

MAY 25–26

Now and again, on British television's networked news, there were reports from Afghanistan. Sometimes these were documentary films, taken at great risk by cameramen and reporters who had trekked across the mountain ranges from Pakistan and actually brought back film of the fighting. Sometimes there was only a map of leaf-shaped Afghanistan, stretching from China to Iran, with a voice-over saying that resistance was continuing, that this or that town or province was in revolt.

Mr Pendergood always followed those pieces of news with great attention. He listened to the radio too, both at home, the luxurious house in the northern English town where he had his prosperous road haulage and other businesses, and in his Jaguar as he gunned it along the motorways to visit one or other of his branch managers.

When he heard that the United Nations had condemned the Russians for the invasion, he had hoped that something would now be done; nothing was. Then he thought that the Soviets would withdraw after the unanimous resolution of the representatives of the Islamic States condemning them. After all, the USSR was supposed to be the champion of the emerging nations and the anti-imperialists. But they did not. Several western nations showed displeasure at the first Russian attempt to conquer a country outside the Soviet sphere of influence since World War II. The USA, for instance, boycotted the Moscow Olympics. But, after a decent interval, trade and cultural relations began to return to normal. Even the wrist-slapping was over.

Pendergood, listening to the radio over his morning cup of

Earl Grey tea one day, heard two scraps of news. The first was that the Geneva Conference, supposed to solve the 'Afghan problem', had collapsed. The second was that the proportion of Afghan civilians already killed was greater than those who might have died in a world nuclear war. Pendergood had made up his mind even before the newsreader came to the item about the alleged use of poison gas . . .

He was single, fifty-three, and had been described in his local newspaper as 'amiable and massively-built, a pillar of the community, Rotarian and transport king'. Mr Pendergood reckoned that, amiable or not, the time had come: enough was enough.

He bathed, did his fifty press-ups, dressed in one of his impeccable, grey chalk-stripe suits, and called his general manager. Then he visited his lawyer to arrange for the sale of his extensive assets, and told his secretary to call the travel agent who specialized in Middle Eastern matters for top people, with efficiency and discretion: Hogg Robinson in London's Kingsway.

Before lunch he was getting a hundred and thirty miles an hour out of the car as he flogged it down the motorway towards Heathrow Airport.

As the English countryside, in all its astonishing neatness, flashed past, Pendergood wondered whether a police patrol would pick him up: he almost hoped they would. Providing he did not refuse to stop, they would not arrest him. They only gave you a summons. And who was going to enforce that, and where?

On the empty passenger seat lay the object he had taken from the wall, inside the front door of his mock-Georgian house, on the way out.

An Afghan dagger with the Seal of Solomon on the hilt, mark of one of the master smiths of the Frontier. Tucked into a slit in the deerskin scabbard was the usual trophy: the scrap of fading, coarse material; cloth from the knife's first victim. From the uniform jacket of a redcoat in the first Anglo-Afghan war.

It had been his grandfather's, and given to Pendergood when he was only ten years old. As a boy he had never looked at the weapon with particular pride: never thought that he, Painda-

Gul, would one day be a United Kingdom citizen, anglicized into the respected Mr Pendergood, company director, who read the *Daily Telegraph* and was from time to time invited to give prizes at charity occasions.

Most of his fellow Britishers, certainly until a few months ago, would not have been able to locate Afghanistan on a world map. But Pendergood, like his ancestors since long before the ancient Greek geographers had reported to the West about his tribe, the warlike *Apridae*, the Afridi of today, knew where it was. And he knew that the people of the Free Land needed him.

Pendergood parked the Jaguar at the Heathrow Long-Term Car Park and took the courtesy bus to Terminal Two. Then he checked in for Flight TK 90, takeoff time 0945.

His neighbour in the jetliner introduced himself as a scientist, heading for Anatolia to advise on soil erosion problems, sent by a major British university.

'I am honoured,' said Pendergood in his agreeable north country English voice, 'and as for me, I am the Khan Painda-Gul Khan, of the Pashtun Land. My name means "Everlasting Flower" in the transborder territory. I have a business matter to attend to.'

'Indeed,' said the academic, turning his grey face, grey-rimmed glasses and grey look upon the swarthy tycoon. 'And what might your avocation be?'

'I have recently retired from commerce,' said Mr Pendergood, 'and my family have trouble with their neighbours over who owns what so I am going back to help them sort it out.'

The conversation lapsed, and Pendergood's thoughts went back to that day – thirty-three years ago – when he had taken a flight to Paris, on the off-chance that he might be able to meet another man, also of Pashtun blood. Two decades before the man's father and Pendergood's had, at the head of the Pashtun armies, stormed the stronghold of the tyrant usurper of Kabul's throne. Now the son's standard waved over the Crillon Hotel. His name was His High Royal Presence King Zahir Shah.

Inside the hotel Pendergood had put on his Afghan cap, of rare golden karakul fur with tiny curls, and sat in the lounge while he watched various people coming and going. He followed some of them, finally, up the broad stairs to the first floor. More people were standing on almost every step and in the corridors, waiting to see the great man. Some had parcels, others letters. One man had a huge and elaborately polished saddle, fit for a king, at his feet. They all looked like Frenchmen, and as if they wanted something badly. Probably money. Pendergood ignored them and pressed on.

Finally he saw a door, and a small group being ushered into an anteroom. Pendergood followed them and, like them, sat down. After a few minutes they disappeared, at someone's beckoning, through a door at the far end of the room. A few minutes later the courtier showed them out. Coming back, he looked at Pendergood and, assuming that he had an arranged audience, signalled him to follow.

In a few seconds, Pendergood was in a large room with two rows of straight backed Louis XIV chairs down the middle. The rows faced one another and only one chair was occupied. On it sat the King: a tall man with black, piercing eyes and an athlete's build. The half dozen courtiers present were standing along the walls of the room where they could not hear any conversation. Pendergood walked up to his monarch, took and kissed his hand and, with the Pashtun's usual aplomb, sat down and began to talk. After all, a king was just a type of tribal chief.

'Painda-Gul of the Pashtuns, from Afridiland, at the service of his Majesty,' said Pendergood.

'You are welcome. May you never be tired. What work are you doing?' The King was wearing a grey, single-breasted suit, and sat very straight. He had a moustache, and he was going bald. He was about forty, Pendergood knew, although he looked rather older; certainly older than his photographs. Still, he'd been on the throne since he was nineteen. His father, Marshal Nadir, was killed by a disaffected student in 1933, and Zahir Shah had reigned since then.

'May it be acceptable to his Majesty! Engaged in commerce in England, and free for any service commanded by the Imperial Presence, sir!'

The King sat quietly. Pendergood said nothing. He had, after all, only come to render homage to his king. He'd used the customary formula but didn't need a job.

'Painda-Gul Khan. You are welcome to come to Kabul, to serve your country. We can find some work for you; there is need of people with experience.'

'Your Majesty has honoured me, and I rejoice that we have such a great king.'

'All my work is for you, for the people,' said Zahir. 'Thank you for coming, Painda-Gul Khan. May your life be long!'

'May his Majesty live for ever!'

Pendergood had taken his hand and kissed it, as the King made the customary modest gesture of snatching it away.

It wasn't the content of the meeting: Pendergood knew that chiefs and monarchs seldom *said* anything of consequence at audiences. It was the fact that he had now met the King. And he had pledged his loyalty to the Afghan Land. The King had, later, not acquiesced in the Russian occupation. From his Italian exile, he had just stated that it was his wish that things could be put to rights. He took no active part, but saw himself as the unifying element. Pendergood understood. Others were trying to form a government in exile: but the war would have to go on.

He was now on his way to see an arms dealer in Istanbul. He would do some buying: after that he would join the fight.

Pendergood thrust Paris and the Crillon out of his mind as the stewardess came past, making sure that seat belts were fastened. Turbulence, she said. Turbulent: that's what the British had always called the tribes. The Romans had called the British that, too, once upon a time . . .

The pilot's voice came over the intercom. 'This is Captain Kayser. In a few moments, at 1605 local time, we shall be landing at Yeşilkoy Airport, Istanbul. Thank you for being with us, and please fly again with Türk Hava Yollari.'

Pendergood had forgotten to fill in his disembarkation card. The woman at the immigration control window said that she would do it for him, to save time. She took his British passport from him. 'No, I'd better do it,' he said, 'I've got a foreign name, you see. It's Gul, spelt –'

She smiled at him. 'You think I can't spell "Gul"? It's one of our own names, too.'

Nobody in England had ever been able to spell his name.

I'll soon be there, I'm halfway home at least, Painda-Gul

told himself as the bus took him through the outer suburbs towards Taksim. At least the Turks were not asleep, he thought, as he passed the huge posters with their slogan: *Crush Communism*! The Russians had been trying to conquer Turkey, too, for centuries.

He would make certain arrangements with the arms merchant in Istanbul, and then visit the gunrunners of the Afghan borderland.

5 A Caravan for David Callil

Inside Afghanistan
On the road west of Chitral, Pakistan

MAY 31–JUNE 8

The straggling line of animals which formed the caravan – donkeys, mules, camels and here and there a horse – crept through the defiles north of the Khyber Pass, plodding towards Kabul. It was not taking the usual lowland route. Nowadays, everything which moved between Pakistan and the Afghan capital by established ways was checked and double-checked; the communist regime at Kabul and the Russian overlords hated 'the colander', as they called the open transborder territory. Too many people, too much news of the outside world and too many guns were trickling into the former God-given Kingdom, now the People's Democratic Republic of Afghanistan.

Daud Khalil hugged his belted fur coat around him as the icy wind from the Hindu Kush seemed to tear at his throat, seemed to scream defiance at everyone. Every now and then there was a miniature avalanche. Boulders loosened by the wind or the melting snow, at some incalculable height above, would roll and thud, blocking the way before the stumbling animals. In this never-ending mountain wind, Khalil had been told, people went mad.

'When you feel both starving and ready to vomit,' the old cattleman had said, 'that is the first sign of the *diwanagi*, the madness. It is partly the height which does it. If there is anyone with you, have him open a vein, to release the pressure of your blood. If you are alone, do it yourself, with a penknife. You may bleed to death, but you may live.'

Khalil pressed his clenched fist down upon the camel's neck, and thought he felt it respond with gratitude. Central Asian

99

two-humped Bactrians, he knew, were sensitive; if badly treated, they often run away. Hardship breaks their hearts. Well-treated, they are the finest mounts on earth. 'We learned kindness,' the cattleman had said, over the fire one night, 'from having to treat the camels well. Then we applied it to people.'

It was the cattleman who had taught him Pashtu, the ancient Afghan tongue, sitting night after night under the stars, encamped under the Southern Cross. '*Afghanistan Zindabad!* – Long Live Afghanistan. There's probably no more than a dozen people in this country, Cobber, that speak Pashtu now, or know much about camels. But it wasn't always like that.'

Even above the shriek of the wind, Khalil heard the now-familiar thunder of an avalanche. It sounded as if it was just above him. As one man, the thirty members of the caravan pushed their animals against the rock wall, covering their heads with their hands and crouching against the grey conglomerate. It was either that or the precipice on the other side of the ledge. Within seconds a cascade of boulders, stripped of their snow and dust by the wind's lashing, hurtled past, within a foot or two of the little group. When the avalanche was over they started moving again. Khalil, nudging his camel forward, thought of Sydney, New South Wales, where he was born.

David Callil he was then, of course, in the Anglicized version of his name, grandson of the Afghan Anwar Khalil of the Yusufzai clan. Anwar had been a companion of the great Dr Allum, known throughout Australia in the nineteen thirties as a wise man and a healer, almost a saint. Khalil still had the clippings from the *Melbourne Age*, with pictures and testimonials of the doctor at work. Before the railways were built in Australia, both Anwar and Allum had learned their camel-caravan skills in just such terrain as this, alternately whipped by wind and rain and baked by the Central Asian sun. The Australians had needed transport, and the Afghans had come, halfway across the world, and made the great trans-continental roads, treading them out with their camels. To settlers in remote districts, the link with the outside world had been the *Gan*. Even when the railways and motor transport came, the trains were called the *Gan*. Then the camels, no longer useful, had been let loose in the desert, had run wild. Now, generations later, they were being rounded up and sold to Saudi Arabia, for a new life in a new land. Dr Allum's name, too, had come to the fore again, as Australians embraced the new vogue for herbal medicines, the remedies in which the ancient Hakim had specialized.

'One day,' the old cattleman had said to Callil, 'your turn may come; your *Afghaniyyat*, Afghanness, may be needed. Listen, I shall recite to you the words of the national bard, Khushhal of the Khattak clan, who roused our nation against the Mogul conquerors, the Mongols from the north. Who knows, they may sweep over Afghanistan again . . .'

At twenty-eight, David Callil was fluent in Pashtu, well versed in the traditions of an ancestral land which was as shadowy as that in any fairy-tale – and assistant manager of a factory in Sydney, making small machine parts. After the Soviet invasion in 1979 and the Russian takeover in 1980, *The Australian* featured something about Afghanistan almost weekly. But Callil could not connect himself, his life and hopes, with this far-off land where hippies used to go, or through which thousands of Antipodean overlanders in battered Bedford trucks, seeking their roots, raced on their way Home, which generally turned out to be London's Earl's Court and a job washing dishes in a pizza parlour.

In 1982, the old cattleman was long dead. Callil was watching the television news when he saw the documentary film made in the Panjsher Valley by the British newscaster Sandy Gall. Commander Mahsud was preparing for a strike against the Russian forces. A line of ragged, bearded men, ill-equipped and thin from hunger, spoke laconically about driving over a hundred thousand well-disciplined troops out of their land. Some of the Afghans had muzzle-loading guns, unrifled, such as had not been used in any real war for two hundred years. There they were, making their own gunpowder, firing at helicopter gunships which dropped explosive charges disguised as toys, for children to pick up . . .

Countryside like this ledge in the mountains, people like that muleteer in front of him, men who were not afraid to die . . .

Five days before, asking questions and hanging around the

bazaar of a tiny frontier town, he had met the caravan as it was assembling. A week before that he had been in Sydney, buying his single ticket to Pakistan. Now he was in Afghanistan: and Pakistan, thirty miles distant, already seemed a world away.

Suddenly the way ahead opened up, and the caravan moved onto a small plateau. On one side stood a massive stone-built and fortified building: the Sarikoh Caravanserai. When the animals had been fed and stabled in a roofed area sheltered from the wind, Callil went into the huge barnlike room which seemed to form the main dining, resting and sleeping space of the *serai*.

Khalil began to doze, less and less aware of the smell and his body, aching all over.

A kaleidoscope of Sydney flashed through his mind. The decision to get to Afghanistan, to see if he could help, even in some small way. He'd gone into a shop, attracted by a poster proclaiming *The Truth about Afghanistan*. The man inside was friendly enough at first. 'Welcome. What's your name? Right . . . No, you can't go to Afghanistan yet, mate, there are too many bandits about. But the Soviet Union will soon help to sort them out.'

He was in a communist office!

'But the Afghans are fighting for their freedom *against* the Russians!'

'Balls! The Russians were called in to help defend the Afghan Revolution against the capitalists and the American imperialists. Look at these photographs of captured Yankee arms and poison-gas canisters . . .'

He'd then gone to see his employers, giving one day's notice. The boss had started to shout and bang his fist on the desk. 'Afghanistan – are you crazy? That's just a load of effing Arabs. Look, no time ago our Deputy Prime Minister lost his job because of a scheme to raise four billion dollars from the Arabs for mineral exploration. It's this bloody Asian connection that's ruining the country! We never had unemployment and inflation before it. Abbos, the lot of them. We've given rice to Indonesia, technical help to South Korea, rehabilitation money to Vietnam, we've helped Indochinese refugees to Thailand. We're up to our necks in a barmy plan called ASEAN, together with a dozen woggie countries. They're worse than the pommie commies who're wrecking labour relations in Australia. I ought to know: it's ruining my business. Keep out of it, son. Arabs!'

'The Afghans are not Arabs. They're Caucasians . . .'

'Oh, get out, bastard!'

The fire was out and the dim pre-dawn light was spreading through the hole in the roof. Suddenly, as Khalil snapped awake, there was a wild cry from the Mulla's sleeping place, a heaving and threshing, while the Hazara beside him jabbered, 'He's been bitten by a scorpion!'

'*Bagir o naman!* Hold him and don't let him go, dog, son of a dog! Swine, child of adultery! Accursed infidel!' The Mulla's voice was raucous, hysterical.

Several men, at the Mulla's urging, took hold of the figure lying next to the man of faith and held him down. One had a long dagger out, its point at the throat of the captive.

'Kill him now!' screamed the Mulla. 'Child of abomination, Russian! *Shoravi*, communist!'

Khalil stood up and went over to see what was going on. The prisoner, until so recently a travelling companion, was spreadeagled on the floor. He was a good six feet tall with a scraggy reddish beard, and his eyes rolled in great alarm.

'How do you know he's a Russian?' Khalil said.

'How do I know? I know, you fool! I was lying there, just about to get up to call the dawn prayer, rehearsing the phrases, "Come to Prayer, Come to Success!" Then I realized this swine was talking in his sleep. Yes, talking. And he was talking Russian. Carrion-eating dog!' The Mulla's forehead was a mass of knotted veins. He trembled all over, and repeated chokedly, 'Godless, godless', as the assorted Tajiks, Pashtuns and Hazaras gazed at him with expressions of fear, respect and delight chasing across their features.

The captive cleared his throat and managed to say something which sounded to Khalil like 'comrade'. '*Roussi*?' Khalil asked.

'*Nein, nein, Kamerad, Deutsch,*' howled the six-footer, his beard covered with spittle.

'There you are, he's talking Russian, slayer of children, eater of filth!' said the Hazara.

'No, he's not, he's talking German, he's an *Almani*, he says.' Khalil suddenly realized that everyone was now looking at him, ignoring the man on the floor. The Mulla pointed his finger dramatically at the Australian. '*Alman, Alman*, is that not in Russia?'

'No,' said Khalil, 'it is not.'

'What's your name?'

'Khalil.'

'Khalil, stand aside, for your evidence may be polluted. We do not yet know.'

He faced the crowd. 'Which of you, swearing by the Four Friends that you are submitted to the Divine Will, understands the language of the Alman?'

Nobody could speak much German. Finally Khalil regained some credence by suggesting that a mixture of French and English be used, since the German admitted to knowing some of each. '*Fransavi! Inglizi, ja, ja*. A leetle. Un peu, kleine . . .'

Khalil, suspicion having been lifted from him, was asked to translate the German's story. It was short enough. He was a craftsman in metalwork from Dresden, fed up with life in West Germany and something of an idealist. He had heard of the war in Afghanistan, decided to go and help, was making his way to the Afridi gunsmiths of Darra who had started a secret factory north of Kabul.

The Mulla led him away, saying, 'Now, brother, repeat after me, "All praise to Allah, Lord of All the Worlds . . ."'

Khalil had an aim now. There would be work for him, surely, at the gun factory.

6 Bright Wolf

The Eagle's Nest
Paghman Mountains
North of Kabul

JUNE 8

'I am a Christian,' said the German. He was taking to Callil at The Eagle's Caves. 'And it was that which made me come here, to do what I can. I did not come here to engage in religious activities, however.'

Callil said, 'I saw you being led away by the Mulla at the caravanserai, under religious instruction, it seemed. What happened next?'

'That did not last long,' said the German, shaking his head slowly.

'Because there are plenty of Mullas, alleged men of Islam, who support the communists: I suppose you told him that.'

'As a matter of fact I did not. I did not know it at the time, though the airwaves are full of Kabul propaganda claiming that Islam and communism are the same,' said the German.

'Well, then. What did you do to get away?'

'When I was jumped in the *serai*, I didn't have a chance to say my piece. I had learnt a portion of the Koran, specially, to explain myself to the Moslems.'

But the Koranic recitation had not worked, in the Mulla's case. He wanted the German to start from the beginning, Chapter One.

The Mulla's attempt to convert the German to the Firm Faith had, however, been frustrated by the lack of a common language, and by his determination to fight tyranny rather than the devil. After getting away from the Mulla, which he had only managed to do by borrowing his donkey without permission, he had fled from the caravan. Now he kept going south west, hoping to find a guerrilla band to join. The worst of the mountains were behind him: but even so his journey to the Paghman Caves showed remarkable optimism and tenacity.

Two days later, passed from one way-station to another, the German was installed in The Eagle's nest, demanding to be trained for battle.

Callil had taken longer to find Kara Kush. In Afghanistan a man who spoke the language but did not know the name of his own tribe, or his ancestral village, was more than a curiosity. Callil was determined, but had to wait until a man was sent to Paghman by his hosts, at one village, to find out exactly who this strange visitor might be.

Adam Durany had welcomed both the German and the Australian into the ranks of the resistance. Now they were trying to settle down. It wasn't easy: the Muhjahidin were itching to fight, chafed at the discipline and the idleness while Adam made plans and awaited specific information and arms for specific projects.

It occurred to Callil that he didn't know the German's name. 'What are you called?' he asked. 'I'm known as Khalil in these parts.'

'Me? My name is Bardolf. That means "Bright Wolf", you know. But I can't be called such a name here; wolves usually stand for unpleasantness south of Turkestan. So they asked me what I should be called, so that people would be able to remember it. I chose, from what I have just recited to you, to have myself called *Shaahid*, "The Witness".'

'What's he talking about?' the blacksmith asked. The others nodded. They wanted to know, too.

'He's saying what his name used to be, in Almanistan.'

The baker laughed. 'Yes, I've heard, I know what it was. It was *Gurg-i-Roshan*, Bright Wolf. It's quite crazy, really. How can you have a *bright wolf*? They don't shine at all. I've seen hundreds of them, and they're always dull. It's like saying "iron wool". Crazy.'

Khalil said, 'But, in the west, they do have a sort of iron wool. It's called steel wool, as a matter of fact.'

'In the west,' said the blacksmith, 'they're all crazy, as the baker said.'

'Crazy enough to drop everything and come to help you,' said Khalil, without thinking.

The blacksmith stood up. 'Help us to do *what*, you dog and son of a dog!' His face was contorted with rage, and his turban was falling off, a cascade of cloth over his right shoulder. 'Help us to fight, to shed our blood? We know well enough how to defend our honour without people coming here and saying that they are helping us. The help we need is knowledge of surgery and medicines; we need arms, we need cartridges, we need technical skills. Where is his help? He did well to call himself "Witness", for what he does is to witness the bravery of real men!' He spat on his hands and paused, looking around wildly, as if to seek more foes.

The German looked puzzled; he wasn't a jumpy man: in fact he was quite slow, both in movement and in speech. All the same, he was very large. He asked Khalil, 'What's he saying?'

'Yes, yes. You tell him. Say it in your own dog's tongue, *wagh–wagh*, that yelping nonsense!' roared the blacksmith, still thoroughly aroused, as Khalil started to translate.

The German said, 'I don't see why he should be annoyed because we want to help them. I don't think I would be . . .'

'But I *do* see,' said Khalil, 'and I'm going to say I'm sorry. It was all my fault. Afghans won't accept help if there is any suggestion that they can't do their own fighting. The fact is that things are very bad for the Muhjahidin just now. When all you have is your pride, you can't stand to be patronized.'

'But they *do* accept help. The tribes sometimes work together, don't they?' said the Witness.

'That's different. If they are allies, one helps the other. If they are not, they make a pact to share the victory. We aren't either. In fact, we are uninvited guests, in their eyes, and pretty strange ones at that.'

The German was shaking his head over this when the blacksmith leapt. His arms caught Khalil on the shoulders, and brought him down, half-winded, to the cave floor. Someone adroitly removed the daggers from the scabbards of the two men as Khalil rose and the two, crouching, circled around, looking for an opening to attack.

The blacksmith was a good six inches taller than Khalil, and had very well-developed arms. But the Australian was lighter, probably fitter, and ten years younger. The smith made a hideous grimace, and flapped his arms up and down, in the imitation of a bird of prey, a gesture of bravado so often seen at Afghan wrestling bouts. Khalil bared his teeth, and the appreciative audience cried out with glee. So far, nobody seemed to be backing either contestant. This was a fight, and it had to be stoked up before they would commit themselves.

The two jumped and sprang, forward and back, until Khalil, tired of the preliminaries and his blood now up, moved back to prepare for a great lunge. Then he realized, as his back hit the cave's wall, that the smith had manoeuvred him into a corner, was closing in. In a second, his great hands had closed around Khalil's throat, choking him; he felt his eyes actually bulging, as people said they did when being strangled.

Khalil did not hear the shouts of the delighted Muhjahidin. He could not feel the blacksmith's breath on his cheek, although the man's face was now only a few inches from his own. He was blacking out, with a sensation like a roar of water in his ears and a dark cloud, rolling across his mind. But, as he fell to the floor, a shot rang out, and the blacksmith threw him aside like a toy, while the whole company swivelled to see who was coming in, through the cave's mouth.

Adam fired into the air a second time, his face expressionless. Walking straight up to the crumpled Khalil, he struck him in the solar plexus once, carefully, with the butt of his revolver. With a great gasp, Khalil started to breathe again, and to come to. The blacksmith and the others stood limply, like small boys caught stealing apples. Kara Kush's calm was worse, they knew, than his fury.

'Gather round.' Adam sat down on his accustomed ledge, while they ranged themselves in front of him to attention, in the military way which he had taught them. He looked at them until they were completely still, his grey eyes boring into theirs, lids unblinking. Then he spoke, deliberately using the rustic Dari, the common speech that they knew best.

'I'm giving you a command now. If, at any time, at any place, anyone starts to fight with anyone else, without my orders, and against a member of the group, both parties will be shot. I shall not shoot them, and neither will there be a trial of any kind. It will be the duty of any and every man who sees a fight start to

shoot anyone else involved, and immediately, without warning.'
He stopped. The atmosphere was crackling, as if there was
electricity about.

'If you accept this order,' said The Eagle, 'raise your arm
and say "Understood and accepted".' He stuck his thumbs into
his belt and stared again, straight at the standing figures.

In a moment, thirty hands were in the air. As Khalil came
to full consciousness the roaring in his ears was replaced by the
shout, 'We understand and submit, O our Chief . . .'

Adam Durany had been working day and night to weld his
men into something like a fighting unit.

The Paghman Caves were the ideal hideout, the people were
keen to fight. At the same time, few of the volunteers had
military experience, they lacked arms and money, and there
was – at first, at least – little understanding of the need for
training and equipment.

Word had been reaching Paghman that arms were to be had
on the frontier, near Pakistan; that a man called Pendergood,
or Painda-Gul, the Abiding Flower, was organizing supplies, a
man who had no truck with the contending factions of exiled
politicians there, and wanted only to help restore freedom.

Khalil had little scope for his engineering skill here, Adam
realized; but on the other hand, he could be useful in a delegation, finding out about Pendergood and his arms. And he
could take the German. It would mollify the blacksmith.

After a discussion with Khalil and Bardolf, and excited talk
about the possibilities of rockets, mines, machine-guns from
the fabled stores of the mysterious Pendergood, the Australian
and the man from Dresden set off together.

Dressed as Pashtun tribesmen they slipped southwards,
through the valleys of the Kunar and Kabul rivers, travelling
by day and night, eight hours walking, then four for sleep.

7 Noor Sharifi, Hostage

Pul-i-Charkhi Prison
Kabul

MAY 2

Hatim Quli looked exactly what he was: cunning, malignant, petty – and dangerous to anyone who fell into his power.

One of the first few recruits to the People's Democratic, communist, Party of Afghanistan, Quli was a total opportunist. He had wormed his way up in life because things like principle did not trouble him at all: and because intrigue for its own sake awakened in him a delight which gave him the energy which seems to underlie all human success.

He loved to do things anonymously, destructive things, and to watch the effects unseen. Even under the royal, and later the republican, regimes, he had flourished. Hatim Quli sought people's weak points, found out who their enemy might be – and sold the information. For twenty years he had been known to the Afghan political police, and especially those of its officers whom he was blackmailing, as 'The Devil's Secret Service man'.

For fifteen years Quli had worked within the party, skilfully surviving the internecine warfare among the comrades. When the Russians entered the country in force, he had come into his own: and now he was commandant of the notorious Kabul prison at Pul-i-Charkhi.

He imitated the Russians in only wearing uniform on ceremonial occasions. Although he felt safer, more anonymous, in European civilian clothes, he chose shirts, ties and the rest which were in such startling taste that almost any westerner would have classed him on sight as an exhibitionist pimp.

The *dirishi*, civilian outfit, which he preferred was a tightly-fitting suit of green and blue stripes with a purple fleck, cut from heavy topcoat tweed. His double-breasted waistcoat was set off by a heavy watch-chain. In his platform-soled shoes he stood all of five foot six. But now, crouched behind his desk, he seemed to the handcuffed girl who was being pushed towards him like nothing so much as a very large, very repellent toad. Even his face was like a frog's.

'Miss Noorjan Sharifi, please, honour me, come in, do! You'll really have to take another name, you know. This is the New Age, we are all equal now. "Sharifi" means of high, princely, rank! This is not Europe, you know. Here hardly anyone has a surname, and those who do are always people with these ancient pretensions.' He had managed to forget that his own father, a thieving grocer who put sand in the sugar, had once tried to adopt the aristocratic surname of Hashemi, because his father's name was Hashem. Quli senior had been chased out of his village for it. He himself had been named Hatim after an ancient hero. 'Besides, the Sharifs are descendants of the Prophet, and we don't really want that nonsense in a free country like this.'

'The country may be free, Commandant, but I am not. Why don't you stop making speeches and tell me when I can get out?'

'I have a file here on you.' He rummaged in a mass of papers which he kept on the desk to make it look important. 'Yes, here it is.' The girl took in his beady eyes and the rolls of fat on his neck, his broken teeth, and shuddered. 'Your father, former Minister Akbar Sharifi, was an associate of Zahir, the former king who hasn't answered our invitation, from his bolthole in Rome, to return to Kabul for re-education.'

'My father served his country all his life.'

'Wrong. He did not serve his country, he served the fascist swine. But *now* he may have a chance of serving his country – if he is sensible.' He gave a self-satisfied smile. At Party meetings he was being more and more noticed for his clever speeches. One day he might become Minister of the Interior, then he could really serve.

'Have it your own way.'

'Luckily I do not have to have a way of my own. I glory in having been given the way, the Way of the Leader, the Great Babrak Karmal.'

'Long live the Revolution,' she said. Quli sidestepped the sarcasm.

'Now *that's* better. People such as you, young, let's see, yes, twenty-four, studied abroad, attractive,' he looked at her auburn hair, green eyes, beautiful hands, for somewhat longer than was necessary for mere identification, 'such people can be valuable to the nation.' She was too tall, he thought. Must be five foot eight in her stockings, and she had that supercilious Sharifi face. He preferred them podgy.

'I have always been ready to serve Afghanistan.'

Quli scowled. 'The kind of service that people of your sort are readied for, my dear, is lying on their backs in silken capitalist boudoirs, or tripping half-naked around swimming pools set with diamonds, showing themselves off to European degenerates.'

'What should I be doing, then?'

'You could be trained, and work for Department Six of the Intelligence. They want people like you, with cosmopolitan backgrounds, international contacts. Why, you must know half the capitalists of the West. Don't you?'

'I do know a lot of people over there.'

'Then you can help us, and you can help your father. If you don't agree, I'm afraid he'll be in great trouble. I could not protect him beyond a certain point. If you are sensible you will be well rewarded.'

See what he had in mind, she thought, it might be the best policy. Think about the implications later. Besides, the food might improve if they thought she was co-operating. The meat was rotten and full of maggots.

'Tell me more.'

So, she was getting softened up, he thought. He had been right after all. He had told the head of Department Six, that fool Zimanov, that he was sure that he could turn these aristocrats. They were all the same, greedy. She was wearing jeans, faded ones at that, but she craved the high life. He was sure of that.

'Comrade Noorbibi. You can get a proper briefing and a real Party education at one of the new training centres. There is a lovely one at Dar al-Aman, with audio-visual aids, brand new from Hungary and the German Democratic Republic.'

112

'But what would I be expected to do if I were sent abroad?'

'I am not sure, but can give you, in confidence, some idea of possibilities, which I have learned from a high quarter.' That sounded better than 'from Zimanov', who used to be doorman at the Yamaw Hotel. He had been sacked for stealing travellers' cheques from Americans, and subsequently claimed that he had done it for political, socialist, motives.

'The foreign press regularly tells lies about us. The West is full of fat lice, millionaire Afghan émigrés who constantly smear us and run down the country. They even say there is a civil war here.'

'But aren't there millions of Afghans living in misery, in huts and tents in Pakistan, and more than a million in Iran?'

'Comrade Karmal has explained that for the British television. I saw it myself on video, here in Kabul. He told the interviewer that they were seasonal workers. They cross the border to help with harvests and so on.'

'I see.'

'Yes. Now, in addition to refuting this lying propaganda, these Zionists and capitalist smears, you will also make contact with others.'

'What others?'

'Well, some of them at least are probably your old school-friends. Young people who have joined the undercover liberation forces in the West.'

'Terrorists, you mean, like the Red Brigades?'

'I said, and you must not distort my words, the liberation forces of the people. Many of their members are from rich families. They do not yet understand our revolution, but they are very useful. They have entrée to the highest quarters. We can link up with them.'

'A lot of people don't want to co-operate with the USSR,' she said.

Quli laughed. 'Have you never heard of the Russian phrase *agent vlyyiyania*, an "agent of influence"? They are to be found all over the world. Few of them *want* to act for us. They include trade union chiefs, politicians, academics, all sorts – even some millionaires. How do we recruit them? Why, we swamp them with praise, lavish hospitality on them, make them think that they are important. We don't recruit them at all. Lenin laid down the line on them; he called them "useful idiots".'

She had never understood before why so many people in free countries seemed to be on the side of the communists. Now she did.

Hatim Quli did not have his way. The girl refused to co-operate, in spite of the threats against her father. But Quli knew, from his training and his experience, that this was not the end of the story. He simply sent her away to be dealt with by Senior Case Officer Nikitin, of the State Security Committee of the USSR: for further investigation and, frankly, blackmail.

Then he turned to the next target individual on his list. It was a very long one.

8 A Formal Case has been Initiated

*The Great Castle
at the mouth of the
Paghman valley*

MAY 4

Three days later Noor, now shackled hand and foot, was pushed forward for another interrogation. This, she saw at once, was to be a much more official kind of interview.

There were three men behind the long table, and the scene was not the smelly office of the odious Quli, though the dungeons from which she had been brought were larger and more primitive. She knew where they were: knew the place from happier days. This was the spacious room which had once been the audience-chamber of the old castle guarding the road to Paghman. Now it was a Russian *fortifikatsionnye*. The khans of Paghman had built the stronghold in ancient times. Beyond it lay the first Paghman valley, the huge fertile garden north of the capital. Farther away again were the foothills, and after them the snow-capped Paghman mountain ranges. It was whispered that Kara Kush, The Eagle, the resistance leader, had his base there . . .

Noor looked at the three men. One was grey-haired and had three stars on his red-and-gold shoulder-boards. A colonel. The second was a captain. Two Soviet soldiers. The third, a civilian by his dress, was probably KGB.

She looked at the captain again. Not a Slav, she thought; probably from one of the USSR's captive Central Asian republics, a southerner to them, a northerner to us.

Captain Azambai was, in fact, a trained fighting soldier, a regular officer in the Soviet Fortieth Army, and he did not like political work. But the KGB was concerned with crimes against the State, and the Red Army was here to enable the Afghan government to control the country: and Azambai was on duty.

He looked back at Noor, and found himself approving. Blue jeans and a shirt, and her feet were bare. A hostage or an agitator? Whatever she was, she did not seem at all afraid.

The Commandant, the KGB case officer and the captain sat facing her, their table strewn with papers. The colonel spoke:

'I am the Commandant, Colonel Slavsky, and this is Senior Case Officer Captain Nikitin of the State Security Committee of the USSR. He is seconded to Afghan State Security, and we are here to carry out a preliminary investigation of your case. It concerns anti-socialist propaganda and treason against the State. Your name is Noor Sharifi, radio producer, daughter of former Sirdar Akbar Sharifi, a State hydropower employee?'

'I do not speak Russian,' she said in Dari-Persian.

The colonel turned to Azambai. 'Comrade *Kapitan*, what does the prisoner say?'

The girl looked at Azambai with a contempt that he could feel, almost like a blow.

'She is saying, in her own language, that she does not speak Russian.' Azambai dropped his eyes.

The colonel said nothing.

Captain Yuri Nitikin, slight, bespectacled, dressed in civilian clothes, shuffled his papers. 'According to our records, she *does* speak Russian. What she means is that she *will* not. We get a lot of these cases. That's what you are here for, Comrade Captain Azambai. You come from the same kind of people, don't you? But you are a Soviet officer.'

There was no doubt that the innuendo was there: Soviet, but not Russian.

'I am from Soviet Turkestan, Comrade Senior Case Officer. My native tongue is almost indistinguishable from Dari-Persian. I understand what the prisoner says.' He could tell, looking from the corner of his eye, that she could follow every word of the conversation.

'Very well. Thank you *Kapitan*. Comrade Commandant, we shall proceed in Russian on this occasion and Captain Azambai will translate for the prisoner. But,' he looked quite pleased at the prospect, 'at our next session I am sure she will agree to speak in Russian.'

116

He turned to Azambai again. 'You will please translate what the Commandant said into Dari.'

Azambai told her, in the Afghan tongue, what the two men had said.

Nikitin looked at Noor over his spectacles. 'Please identify yourself formally for administrative purposes.'

She let Azambai translate.

'I am Sharifi, Noor, daughter of Sharifi, the Sirdar Akbar, former Minister of Mines and Ambassador of His Majesty the King to various foreign courts. Is that what you want, Mr Turkestani?'

'My rank and name are Captain Azambai, and you will address me as such,' said Azambai. To the others he said, in Russian, 'The prisoner concurs with the official identification.'

'Citizen Sharifi,' the KGB man was more comfortable in standard phraseology, 'after considerable investigation which shows that you have been engaged in anti-State activity, slandering socialism, forming a network of accomplices, agitating against the fraternal armed forces of the Soviet Union and many other actions, all documented and attested, I have to inform you that a *Delo Formulyar*, a Formal Case, has been initiated against you.'

He paused. The woman was taking no notice of him.

'Are you listening, citizen Sharifi?' He raised his head to look at her.

'All I know is that Hatim Quli tried to recruit me with cajolery and threats to go abroad as a spy: presumably on your behalf, like you use the Cubans and the East Germans. As a spy and confederate of terrorists. Now, a couple of days later, I find that you are claiming that you have done all sorts of investigations, all kinds of paperwork, making out that I am a danger to you. You're just trying to frame me, that's all. This is my country, not yours. Anti-State activity! What State? It is you who are trying to destroy the Afghan State!'

Nitikin, head in his hand, calmly heard her out. Then he continued:

'The decision has been approved, after due study, by the chief of the appropriate subsection of Afghan State Security, the KHAD, and the signed documents to that effect are here. They are all in order.' He held up a paper.

Azambai thought, She knows it's a sham and that we're out to use her for something. I wonder what they really want her for? There must be some strong reason for this detailed cover of legality – and for bringing in the Commandant. There must be dozens of people in the cells below. They were certainly not all going to be given such extensive treatment. She must be an important prisoner. Of course, she was an ambassador's daughter . . .

The case officer had rifled through a sheaf of papers. 'Citizen Sharifi, silence and lies will not foil the agents of Soviet justice. We know all about you.'

He lit a cigarette and inhaled deeply. What a silly little man, Noor thought. Without his power he would be nothing and nobody. Pathetic.

'Yes, we know all about you. You attended a private school in Ealing, West London, where you also lived, in a privileged neighbourhood?'

'That's right.'

'You were recruited by British Intelligence, overseas espionage, what they call MI – military intelligence – six, sixth section?'

'No.'

'Do you deny that Century House, a tower block of offices on Westminster Bridge Road in London, is the headquarters of British Intelligence?'

'I don't know.'

'Well, it is. We know everything. Why did your family have a house in the same West London area as that of the spy-nest at Century?'

'Westminster is in SW1, inner London, and Ealing is West. They aren't near each other. Westminster Bridge Road is in the south-east area.'

'Sharifi, I note your admission that you know the district where the British spy centre is located.'

She looked at him with astonishment. 'That's not what I said . . .'

He smiled, and bent briefly over his papers, pen in hand.

'Now, citizen. You have travelled extensively throughout the capitalist world, under diplomatic cover, with your father?'

'As a member of his immediate family, I was entitled to

diplomatic immunities. That's not "cover": it's standard practice, worldwide. Part of the international law of diplomacy, contained in treaties. It applies to the children of Soviet ambassadors, too: they're not spies, are they?'

'That's just a quibble.' He made another note, murmuring its contents as he wrote: 'Admits to using diplomatic cover.'

'You contacted many capitalists and other personalities and members of ruling circles?'

'I know a lot of people outside.'

Outside. She caught herself using that Russian term for the free world.

'All quite innocently, of course.' Nikitin smiled more broadly, exposing tiny, pointed teeth.

'Captain Azam-Bai –' she pronounced the syllables separately, to emphasize their meaning, Great-Chief, and she saw that he understood her. He was called Azambai because his ancestors had been rulers, once upon a time, in Turkestan . . .

'Ask the case officer if he has ever heard of George Orwell.'

'This Orwell is your contact, your confederate, your controller?' Nikitin became excited. 'English, American or Zionist?'

'Orwell was a British author. He wrote about someone tortured by a rat.'

'You are attempting to introduce irrelevancies to cover your guilt, citizen. It will not succeed. You do not know what a rat is like, because you have not lived among the starving people in England, where you were a pampered cosmopolitan.'

She said nothing.

'London is swarming with them, though not in your part of it, where the MI6 spy-nest is located. People are half-starved. They are frequently beaten by the fascist police, kept in squalor and teeming in mass prisons.'

'No.'

Noor was wondering whether she was losing her reason, imagining all this. She had to say something. All she could think of was, 'You can easily drive me mad, but only God, whom you think doesn't exist, can make you sane.'

'You are under official legal-administrative detention, and it is forbidden to make speeches in these circumstances. Slanders and political statements in the guise of religious talk are offences in law.'

119

'Nikitin, you fear words because you are a prisoner yourself. You need four walls to keep me under control. But the walls around *you*, you carry those with you all the time. My mind is free, if my body isn't. Your mind and your body are enslaved, because you think and act only at the will of others.'

The colonel was pretending to read something in a file. Azambai translated the words automatically, not allowing himself to heed their meaning. The two Russian soldiers who had brought Noor in were delightedly winking at one another and, indicating Noor, tapping their foreheads. Noor stopped talking. Nothing would get through to these people, if what she said was true. If it had not been she would not have been here.

Case Officer Nikitin was droning on. 'You are under detention for your own good, to prevent the just anger of the people from exploding against you, as it doubtless would if you were at liberty.'

Noor shook her manacles at him. 'I suppose *these* are to prevent people from attacking me?'

He smiled, gums showing above the little grey teeth. 'It should be obvious, except to those who do not want to understand, that you have been put under that restraint to prevent you attacking the lawful authorities.'

'And do I get a lawyer?'

'All in good time. Socialist justice is not the sham that bourgeois law amounts to. We have no "presumption of innocence" because, with us, innocent people are never arrested or charged. Therefore you are undoubtedly guilty. We are determining the extent of your guilt, so that your sentence shall not be too light or too harsh. Your laywer will be there at your trial, and will give details of your repentance, and also explain whether you were led astray or improperly brought up. And if you have named your accomplices, you might get a corrective sentence rather than a capital one. Treason, in Afghan Law – as in all socialist lands – means death, of course. I am only here to investigate and advise.'

'Then what is the purpose of this rigmarole?'

'I have just told you, and there is nothing to add. Now,' the case officer leant forward, hands on the table, 'there is another point. You have only one close relative, your father. Failure to confess in your case would mean that we would have to investigate whether his loyalty is sound. Who knows what the outcome of that might be?'

The threat was so strong that even the colonel, who was trying to show no feelings, turned sharply to look at the man.

'That is blackmail.' She pursed her lips as if she was about to spit.

'That statement will be added to your file, since it constitutes slandering a State functionary in the course of his duty.' He was not annoyed in the slightest by her attitude, Azambai observed. No doubt this sort of thing had happened to him a hundred times before. Nikitin made a note in the dossier before him.

'You are blackmailing me with threats about my father. Are you doing the same to him, about me?'

Nikitin almost purred. 'Citizen, so far as we know, citizen Akbar Sharifi is working voluntarily for the State. If, as you seem to imply, he may need some pressure before working wholeheartedly for reconstruction, it sounds as if he might need investigation. But let me say at this point that we have no reason to suppose that he is not a loyal supporter of your April Revolution.'

'You mean that he has gone in with you?'

Nikitin said nothing. He had found that there was a great deal of truth in the saying, 'saying nothing is always saying something'. Give people time and they could torture themselves well enough to make any other pressure merely additional.

Azambai suddenly began to feel angry. It took all his self-discipline to keep him in his seat. A prisoner of war, yes. Someone who had been captured on the field of battle, yes. One could apply pressure, threats of death even. Presumably such people knew the risks inherent in taking up arms. But a woman? A political prisoner? This was no work for soldiers. Or was the Army just an extension of the Party? He recalled, as if in answer, what a fellow officer, a real Party enthusiast, had once said to him in the USSR: 'Without the Party, Comrade Azambai, there *would be* no Army: always remember that.'

No Army. If there were no Soviet Army, at least the Afghans would be masters in their own country . . . he stopped himself. This was no way to think. He was not married, but he had a family: parents, brothers, cousins, all in the Soviet Union, just a few hundred kilometres to the north.

Nikitin was talking again. 'And such a serious view is already taken of your conduct that you may be sent to Tula, in the Soviet Union, for full confession and rehabilitation.'

Azambai saw it now. Her father must be very valuable to them, and they wanted to keep him at work. That was what it was all about. Sending her to Russia would make sure that he did. Taking hostages and sending them away was one of the most effective methods of keeping people docile that the authorities knew. It was rife in the USSR, an old Russian tradition even before communism. And it was working in Afghanistan almost as effectively.

As an Uzbek, Azambai knew a great deal about hostages. Some of his family had been through that in the nineteen thirties. Now they were tame. He would always behave himself, he realized, because of his family.

The Soviet Union was obsessed by legality and correctness. Was it that bureaucracy, taken to extremes, became oppression? Or that oppression needed the fiction of legality, a craving for the respectability that it could never have?

Azambai was still wondering when, the papers served, they sent the girl back to the communal cells below.

9 Captain Azambai, Soviet Red Army

South of Khaja Rawash Airbase
Kabul Road

MAY 2

Captain Yusuf Azambai. That really stood for something in Uzbekistan. People in Russia often said that the Uzbeks were not warriors – not nowadays at least. They said that centuries of the soft life of Central Asia's most cultured land had made them effete. That their lack of interest in the Russian advance into their homeland for a hundred and fifty years had helped the Slavs to consolidate their empire deep into Asia.

Let them say it, he thought.

The Central Asians, people like Azambai, had ruled European Russia itself for two hundred and fifty years. That was longer than most Europeans had held their own more recent empires. Even in Slavic Russia it was still remembered that those old Russian princes, the stiff-necked aristocrats, traced their ranks and titles from Mongolian – and not Russian – *yarliks*, permits to rule, granted at Saray, the great capital of the Khan. Turkestan was not pacified by the Russians until the 1930s; and Captain Azambai, though a good communist, had heard the tales of the resistance, of the deeds of the *Basmachi*, and in one part of his mind he was almost proud of them.

He was only twenty-eight, a product of the policy of Nativization, assimilation into Slavic culture. His father had remembered the days when their country had been free, as he called it. He always called Nativization 'Russification'.

But the older generation also spoke of their fear of the tortures and dungeons of the old-time Emirs, of the taxes and seizures of their goods, of the forced labour and the uncontrolled epidemic sicknesses. Many of them had found,

123

after the Bolshevik Revolution, that they could survive well enough under the Soviets, and left it at that. It was the foreignness of the Russians, and their monopoly of the real control, which they disliked. But there were many advantages. A man would be left alone if he kept quiet. He had to vote for a certain candidate, but if he behaved himself, would not be flogged just for nothing. The Slavs had a saying which they quoted to minority peoples. 'Why should you care who's holding the goat, if you're allowed to milk it?'

But the curious thing was that the younger people, people of the captain's age and younger, were starting to question Nativization. Some were in prison for 'agitation'. There had been show trials of separatists lately. They wanted more milk, and even part control of the goat.

Yes, something was stirring in Turkestan. From time to time in the papers one saw that bands of Murids, disciples of Sufi spiritual teachers, had been rounded up. Unofficial mosques had been established, and everyone could hear the broadcasts of 'the message of Allah' from the three thousand kilowatt transmitter in Iran. And there was Radio Pakistan, mentioning unheard-of luxuries which were apparently available for ordinary people there. And Soviet Asians had come back from the Great Patriotic War against Germany to tell, in Bokhara or Stalinabad, that they'd seen the Russians run 'both ways': in retreat as well as in attack.

And something was stirring in Captain Azambai, as one of those seventy million non-Slav Soviet citizens that, had they known it, Moscow was already privately calling, 'our Eastern time bomb'. Before the end of the century their birthrate would make them the majority in the Soviet Union.

When he was off-duty, Azambai would put on a civilian suit and a plastic raincoat, perch an Afghan fur cap on his head, and pass the time walking through the Kabul bazaars or sitting in a teahouse, making friends. Doing this really helped; many of the Soviet soldiers, cut off from all contacts except those of the barrack room, were showing unwelcome psychological symptoms. Many had been sent home; the worst cases had even developed delusions; some had become violent. Civilians would not talk to them, pretended they did not exist, or spoke to them confusingly; and shopkeepers, except for the greediest or poorest, would not seem to comprehend even the simplest words in Russian, or even in English or the other languages which all the Kabul traders knew quite well.

Yes, the teahouses helped. Although they numbered a quarter of a million, most Kabulis seemed to know each other, or at least could place anyone after a few sentences. The captain was never quite sure whether the Afghans knew from his accent, his clothes, or his lack of mutual friends or geographical knowledge, betrayed by his conversation, that he was one of the occupying army. Nobody ever said anything about it. But then, nobody ever mentioned the Russians in his presence, either, in the teahouses.

One day Azambai had gone into a café where he had guessed, by the atmosphere, that the regulars had been talking about him. They had all fallen silent and looked guilty as he entered. He even thought that he had just caught the words that the owner was saying: 'He is really one of our own – he'll come home.'

Az khud-i-ma hasten, you are one of our own. That was the phrase that Afghans used to one another, and it showed a deep affection, a bond that made their eyes light up. One could feel the effect, almost physically. So far, however, nobody had said it to Captain Azambai. To them he was what he had represented himself to be, Yusuf the Turkestani, 'an official'. There was an Afghan Turkestan, too, of course. Exactly the same sort of people lived on both sides of the Oxus. Members of families separated by the water would wave to one another at the narrower points.

All over the Soviet Union there was a great yearning for peace and security: but the Party, and most of the highest officials, were obsessed by fear. Azambai was becoming convinced that his rulers feared losing power and had displaced that fear onto the external enemy, the Capitalist Imperialist.

But those who had little to lose, the ordinary people, seemed to fear the West less and less.

Friendship with the people of other countries: not to be an outcast nation; that was what the great mass of Russians wanted. It might take a lot of time, and in the meantime Captain Yusuf Azambai sensed, day by day, a fellow-feeling among the

125

Afghans which the foolishness, as much as the evil intent, of the regime had brought about.

Who would ever know what did it, had made him change his life? He started to wonder, and then stopped; and started to think again. Of course he had thought of getting out, of going to America, perhaps, where you might have your own farm, or a small shop. Even Russians spoke of it. They were all immigrants over there, in the United States, or the children of immigrants, weren't they?

Was it only the shock of how things had changed, that had changed him: or had he intended it all along?

It had just come to him, the plan, as he was driving along the road. He was in an army car, with some sticks of dynamite needed for training exercises. And in civilian clothes: he was off-duty. The two-way radio was on, so that he could be called up by the new commander if there was a crisis, to do his active duty job of spotting *badmashes*.

He had been to the great Soviet Army base, at Khaja Rawash, six miles north of Kabul, to see about the delayed supplies for the fortress garrison. Halfway back to the city, he had felt filled by something, well, like light: that was all you could say about it. Everything seemed changed; suddenly he felt as if he knew the truth.

The Eagle that they talked about *was* right, was the hope, the real man of the time. It was as if a voice was saying, 'Must go to him, must go to him.' But of course there was nobody in sight. A disembodied voice. Could he do it?

His relatives in the Soviet Union would be arrested, made to suffer. His name would be besmirched, used in propaganda as a man who'd taken American money, or fallen prey to Zionist brainwashing, cosmopolitanism. A traitor.

Then the solution, fully rounded, all of a piece, came to him. He saw the scene in the officers' mess. The colonel talking.

'*Died on active service, ambushed by terrorists. A pension for his dependants. Such a promising young officer, a really good product of Nativization, you know. A toast, Comrades, another vodka . . .*'

He stopped the car. There was nobody, not even a patrolling helicopter, in sight. This road had been quiet for some days now, since the last batch of bandits had been wiped out trying to mine it. Usually it was forbidden to travel on it without an escort, but a shortage of spare parts meant that vehicles were scarce. After clearing a road, the army would risk using it for a day or two. Until the guerrillas came back.

Captain Azambai tied together and fused the packets of dynamite which he had collected from Khaja Rawash. Then, removing the raincoat and radio from the vehicle, he drove it off the road and blew it, expertly, into pieces. It made a satisfactory, but not too loud, bang. One heard that particular sound all the time these days. The official explanation was that it was blasting from the quarries in the hills.

It was only a three-mile walk to Kabul from there and the new guerrilla, dressed in his respectable off-duty civilian suit, trudging along the road, looked perfectly natural. There was little petrol to be had these days; salaries were so small that the middle classes, people who wore clothes like these, walked everywhere when they could not get on the crowded buses.

Something was coming from the direction of the airfield. He turned.

'Hoo-raa!' With clenched fist salute and the new Afghan cry of salutation, pioneered by the Party, he greeted the vehicle coming up behind him. It was a five-ton BTR scout car, with the top shut. The standard reconnaissance vehicle of the Soviets, in green and khaki camouflage. Like most Soviet Fraternal Force vehicles, it carried the blazon of the Afghan Army. The teenage driver, a Russian conscript corporal with a Slavic face, opened his hatch and called to him.

'Jump in, uncle, if you're going to town. I'm delivering this to Kabul. We're not allowed to pick up Afghans, but you seem to be a good Party man.' Obviously a Komsomol member, doing his good deed for the day. He spoke in Russian, with a couple of Dari words to help out, in case the Afghan comrade didn't understand.

'Thank you, I don't speak much Russian.'

'Never mind.'

'What was the explosion, off the road, a few minutes ago?' the Russian asked his passenger.

'*Da da, vodka, bravo!* I like drink too much,' smiled the captain. Azambai was overdoing it a little, but the noncom didn't know. He just said, 'Afghanistan very good' in his best

Pashtu, and left it at that. He was thinking about something else. In Kabul he might sell a couple of gallons of petrol, for money to buy himself a ring, silver with lapis lazuli set in it.

They sped on, past the lines of caterpillar-track mounted surface-to-air rockets defending the city against possible capitalist bombers, towards Kabul.

How strange, thought Yusuf, I've been purified, made clean and whole. I am a new man. I was born only today. And, of course, anyone who talks like this is insane. Perhaps it is as well, for the Soviet Union, that they've only lost a lunatic. If I'd been there, they'd have had to put me in a madhouse. It costs the State so much to give therapy to dissidents. Medical treatment is expensive.

Lunatic or not, his surname, Azam, meant 'the great', with the honorific *bai* denoting descent from what the western Turks called a Bey, a governor. Well, Lenin himself was an aristocrat of the noble Ulyanov line. But he might now have to be more like a fox, he thought, to reach the Paghman range or Kohistan, that really wild country of the hillmen, to find The Eagle and his men. He was momentarily startled to find that a part of his mind was working out a programme for him.

It was impossible to walk all the way to the foothills; the transport corporal was only going as far as Kabul, and it would not do to tarry there. And the radio was quite heavy, even though it was one of the new ones. Most of the Soviet equipment was incredibly bulky; the radios had vacuum tubes, which blew or shattered easily but, oddly enough, would be safer than transistorized ones in nuclear war, less vulnerable to EMP, the electromagnetic pulse which followed a nuclear explosion.

They were in the town, rolling over the dusty asphalt. The scout car stopped.

'Thank you, officer!'

'A pleasure, sir, *gospodin*!'

He jumped down from the motor near the centre of old Kabul's crazy jumble of shopping streets, a mixture of open-air market and tiny stores, among the offerings of silks, vegetables, kitchen knives, meat and fur caps, old clothes and auto-parts.

There were no Russian civilians in the street at the moment, though they were sometimes to be seen, in groups and carrying guns, stocking up on blue jeans and scents, karakul furs and Western candies, anything they could not get at home.

The military were being kept off the streets: too many of them had been killed recently by angry Afghans. Only the civilian 'advisers' – there were perhaps ten thousand of them in the whole of this huge country – and their wives and children could walk about with impunity. Despite the cruel provocations of the regime, Afghans still clung to the principle of sparing non-combatants. Yet some of those specialists, Azambai knew, were more deadly in what they could do than any ordinary soldier might be. There were, for instance, the KGB, security, running the Afghan KHAD, the political police, to whom a network of informers gave their information, leading to death, destruction, torture, hostage-taking.

As he was walking, determined to keep moving in case a *zhondarm* decided to ask for papers, Azambai realized that he was in familiar territory. Yes, this was the street of *Banafsha-i-Koh Chaikhana*, the Teahouse of the Mountain Violets, which he often used to visit. There it was. Time for a cup of tea. Almost from habit he turned and walked straight in. There were about twenty people of all ages and kinds, sitting smoking, sipping green tea with cardamoms, gossiping as usual. Just the same as always. He sat down at a table and called for tea.

It was still only eleven o'clock in the morning of the day on which he had got up as a smart and promising captain in the fraternal forces of the Soviet Union. Now he was skulking, like a fox. He would have to accomplish more by sunset. Get to The Eagle.

The tea came, hot and sweet with a dollop of clotted cream swimming on top – a drink that was almost a meal. He fished some coins out of his pocket, waved away the change. The lad smiled thanks. Now a shadow had fallen on his table: there was something between him and the sunshine pouring through the dirty windowpane.

He hadn't got a gun, but he picked up a knife from the table, to be as ready as possible for anything.

But it was only Wasif, a petty official from the Ministry of Frontier Affairs.

'May you not become tired, Mr Yusuf of Samarkand stock. You are early today, *janim*, my life.'

'May you not become sad, Mulla Wasif.' In Afghanistan everyone was addressed by his father's title, if he had none of his own.

Wasif sat down. 'Backgammon?'

'Forgive me, I'm a little tired.'

'Your flocks and your house are well, I hope?'

'Thanks to God. Are you well?'

'Praise Allah.'

'Any news?'

'None.'

Azambai sipped his tea, while Wasif eyed him, rather narrowly, he thought. 'Things are bad among the tribes, you know.' But Wasif was always conspiratorial. He liked to hint at deep secrets, known only at the Ministry.

'I thought there wasn't any news?'

'That's not news, it's going on all the time.'

'Not a revolt?'

'Among the tribes, you can't tell whether they're having a revolt or celebrating a marriage. Kabulis say that when they hear two Pashtuns singing love songs, they think that they're swearing at each other.'

'Yes, I'd heard that.'

Suddenly Azambai felt very tired. It was almost as if someone else was talking as he said, 'Listen, Wasif. Where can I find The Eagle, and how soon can I do it?'

Wasif looked at him as if he'd just disclosed an unbelievable secret. His mouth opened once or twice, then shut. Then he shook his head as if to clear it. Then he gulped a couple of times. Finally he said: 'No, you must be all right. But I always thought you might be a big man in the KHAD.'

'No, I'm nothing like that. I . . . I just want to join The Eagle,' was all that the Turkestani could manage.

'Then who *are* you – what work do you do?'

'Until a few hours ago I was a captain in the *Askari Sowyeti*, the Soviet Army.'

'Unmentionable interior parts of a swine!' Wasif's face was a picture of astonishment. 'Who are you now?'

Azambai shrugged. 'You tell me, my friend.'

Suddenly, and very alarmingly, Wasif was standing up,

waving his arms and shouting: 'O people! O brothers, come here, hear this!'

Azambai grabbed his arms and tried to stop him, to pull him down on the bench beside him. Wasif was laughing though, fit to burst, and the people of the teahouse were gathering around with puzzled but interested faces, peering.

'It's nothing,' was all that Azambai could find to say. He repeated it several times.

The crowd leant forward. It was always something, it couldn't be just nothing. People came to the teahouse to hear things. That is why these places were called the Newspaper made of Bricks.

'Shut up.' The owner of the café, the massive Dilaram (it means Heart Ease) Khan, bellowed from beyond the cooking-pots. 'We don't want the *zhondarm* here.'

'Zhondarm, zhondarm, calamities upon the spiritual teacher of the zhondarm's mother!' raved Wasif, tears of laughter running down his cheeks. He was capering with excitement.

But the crowd demanded more. Seizing Wasif, they insisted on knowing what all the fuss was about. 'Stop screaming, you Tajik! Tell us.' A burly hillman grabbed him by his pyjama jacket, using the name for Persian-speakers which implied scorn in the Free Land.

'All right then, leave me alone and I'll tell you.'

'Well, tell us.'

The Pashtun bared his teeth. 'I am telling you. Guess what?'

Their faces darkened. They clearly did not want to guess. Perhaps the hillman would give him a thump.

Wasif saw this change at once. 'No, sorry, this is the story. You all know Mr Samarkandi here? He's not a spy after all! He's an officer from the Russian menagerie.

'And he's become one of us. He just said to me, *Kuja'st Kara Kush* – Where's The Eagle?'

Everyone looked at him, then at Azambai, and then very quietly they stepped forward one by one, and shook his hand. Wasif kissed him on both cheeks, the awful beard getting in Azambai's eyes.

'How did you know I wasn't a spy?' Azambai asked Wasif, when all had returned to their places to talk over the implications. Heart Ease was serving tea to everyone, free of charge.

'Well, it's pretty obvious, isn't it? Spies don't go about asking anyone, at random, how to find a wanted man, a man with ten million *afghanis* on his head, now do they? Anyone asking "Where's The Eagle?" in Kabul is either one of us or he had better have the protection of a uniform and a gun. Even then we'd probably give him an Afghan Salaam for asking, and not tell him anything.'

An Afghan Salaam. A stick of dynamite inserted into someone from the rear and detonated. It was said to date from the time when a military officer, from another foreign invader's troops, fresh from a rather different experience in a docile colony, had shouted at a hillman, 'Afghan, Salaam me!' They had said it was the rapid and explosive response that had given birth to the phrase. Nobody knew, however, if the act had actually been tried. Among the tribes, of course, anything was possible . . .

Wasif waved for some more tea. 'Are they after you?'

'I don't think so. Not yet. Not unless they get suspicious.' Azambai told him what he'd done that morning.

'Aferin! Well done. But you must be careful: you might be recognized in the town. We'd better get you to The Eagle today.'

'That's just what I want. But listen Wasif, are you sure that nobody will talk, the people here, I mean?'

'I am quite sure. Don't worry. A lot of funny things have happened already, and without a leak, among us Mountain Violets.'

That evening, dressed as a mountain man, former captain Azambai was dropped off a day-workers' truck in the foothills, and sat waiting at the rendezvous, a goatherd's hut looking like a mere pile of rocks, where the guerrillas of The Eagle would collect him as soon as they were sure it was not a trap.

To pass the time, he tuned his stolen army radio to the various frequencies which might carry something about him. Nothing. Routine military traffic. Either he had missed it, or they weren't going to announce his unfortunate death. It did not do to give too much currency to Muhjahid successes. They'd be sure it was an ambush. Killing a captain and destroying military property, and with army explosives, would qualify as such a coup . . .

There was a sound now, outside the hut. In a second someone was inside, and the door slammed shut. A flashlight glittered; in its reflected light Azambai could see a tall figure in hillman's dress.

'Welcome: I am The Eagle. Welcome home.'

Azambai took the hand held out towards him. 'Is there work, master?' he asked in Dari.

'Work enough, and more. Come with me, and bring your tribute.'

'Tribute?' Azambai stammered. Of course, it was customary in the East to give your leader something every time you saw him, or at least when you swore allegiance. A gold coin, usually. But he had not thought that such ancient customs were still carried on. 'Forgive me, my Lord Eagle, but I have nothing . . .'

'Nothing?' The Eagle laughed. 'You have, I am told, something which is worth more than gold to us. A Russian army multiple-frequency radio nothing? Wait and see . . .'

10 The Treasure

Kajakai
Kandahar Province
South-West Afghanistan

APRIL 30–MAY 10

'Cowards weep and cowards work, but fighters go to Paradise . . .' He wasn't weeping now, but he had to work, was too old to fight.

Sirdar Akbar thought of the poem as he sat, slumped over his drawing table, slide rule in hand, in the tiny room which the Administration allowed him. He would have fitted more naturally into a Paris salon or the Assembly Hall of the United Nations, where he had been Afghanistan's ambassador not so many years before. As Minister of Mines, appointed by the Royal Government because of his geology and engineering degrees, he had served his country well. As a diplomat, too, he had been an outstanding success. Diplomacy was in his blood: his ancestors had been feudal lords, courtiers, king-makers, even.

Akbar had been one of the several hundred young men, fervent patriots, chosen by the King in the nineteen thirties and 'forties, to go abroad for higher education, for technical and scientific training. It was the King's own idea; they would return and, instead of lording it over vast estates, the technocrats would transform the country, bring it into the twentieth century. Afghanistan had enormous natural resources: water-power, rich virgin land, coal, oil, natural gas, iron, zinc, copper, chromite, even rubies and emeralds. And it was a large country, the size of France, and with such enormous scope that Western experts, visiting it, babbled about the 'coming Switzerland of the East'. With, for Asia, a tiny population, under ten million.

The new-age Afghan technicians had done extraordinarily

well in the twenty-odd years before the revolution. Hydro-electric power stations lit Kabul and provided the power for the new cotton mills, cascading millions of square metres of cloth; vast quantities of fresh, dried and canned fruit flowed from Kandahar. Coal was mined, manufactures of all kinds started to pour onto world markets. The traditional industries, the *karakul*, 'Persian' lamb, the carpets and skins, were for the first time organized with proper quality control and efficient marketing. Kandahar International Airport, one of the most modern in the world, took shape. Afghanistan seemed set fair for prosperity.

But as the country's world role developed, paradoxically, the skilled people became fewer and fewer. The demand for administrators and for overseas representation drained the specialists from the factories and the land schemes. The ministries were fully staffed; the diplomatic service sucked in technicians to send abroad as ambassadors. People like Akbar Sharifi went overseas, spent years in embassies, shuffling paper, attending cocktail parties, jet-setting around the world to conferences. The country started to slow down.

In the meantime, the Russians, beyond their long land and river boundary to the north, had mounted a plan of their own. They wanted Afghan raw materials for their empire, and they wanted Afghanistan itself as a launch-pad for their drive to the Middle East – and perhaps to India. The plan was to indoctrinate the young people who were replacing Sharifi's generation, and to distribute them throughout the civil service and the army.

Russia watched its red moles, undecided whether to choose a political or a military coup: and prepared for either.

When most of the older generation had retired, they were succeeded by youngsters, far less able. Few of them – perhaps three or four dozen – were actually communists; but they were powerful within a weak and inefficient administration. The Western powers, afraid that a strong Afghan army might descend upon the Indian subcontinent as Afghans had done for centuries to establish their own Raj, refused military aid or training facilities. The rulers of the Soviet Union took all the Afghan military cadets they could, welcoming them with open arms, and indoctrinated them as deeply as they could.

Akbar Sharifi retired early, was no longer a possible threat to the Russians, even though he had a seat in parliament as a senator and was an adviser to the Ministry for Foreign Affairs.

Now he was demoted, probably lucky to be alive, supervising the installation of the new turbines in the giant white walls of the Kajakai Dam. That December, when the traitor Karmal was brought in as 'President' by the Russian Army, many people had been taken out and murdered, even in the public streets. But the Sirdar would never have worked for the Russians merely to save his own life. Brigadier Sahki had anticipated that. The Afghan Secret Police, the KHAD, had been well trained by the Russian KGB in techniques of blackmail.

The old man remembered that perfect Spring day, April 27th, 1978, when the revolution had begun. Certain cadets, trained in Russia under a perfectly normal military aid scheme and completely indoctrinated, had worked their way up in the armed forces for years, until they reached the rank of colonel. This was during the rule of Daud Khan, who had displaced his cousin, the King, and made himself President. On the day of the coup, there had been only a few communists in the whole country, but the Army was trained to obey orders.

The Afghan Fourth (Armoured) Division, led by Colonel Aslam Watanjar, moved into Kabul and seized the small airfield near the Royal Palace. While the Fourth Armoured Division secured strategic points and government buildings, another communist, Colonel of the Air Force Abdul-Qadir, seized a helicopter and flew it to Air Force Headquarters at Bagram, forty miles north of the capital.

The MiG fighter-bombers, at Abdul-Qadir's command, then scrambled and headed straight for the Presidential Palace. Their incessant pounding, with bombs, machine-guns and rockets, broke the resistance of the elite Presidential Guard, who were holding out on the ground against everything that the Fourth Armoured could throw at them. Loyal Air Force units, ordered in from Shindand Airbase, five hundred miles to the west, arrived over Kabul to crush the revolt, only to find that command communications had been disrupted, and they had no idea where, or what, to strike. Running out of fuel, they returned to Shindand, where they were arrested.

Thus the communists won the vital battle for Kabul. Immediately afterwards, Akbar remembered, hundreds of people were murdered, and among the many hostages taken – they included members of the royal family – was his only child, his daughter Noor. He had not been able to contact her since. Thousands of civilians and soldiers were buried in mass graves.

In April, the 'Democratic Republic of Afghanistan', whose birth had been meticulously planned and organized by the Kremlin, was proclaimed. Afghanistan was virtually a part of the Soviet Union. Only the people stood between the government and Russification.

Akbar had been left alone at first. Then, three months ago, a civilian captain in the Secret Police had come to him, just after three o'clock in the morning.

'*Safirseb*?' – Mr Ambassador. People in Afghanistan, after they retired, always retained, by courtesy, the highest title they had held during their careers. 'Please come with me. You have a meeting with Brigadier Sakhi.'

Sakhi. The Butcher, they called him. More recently, too, *Bacha-i-Rouss*, Child of the Russians. Ambassador Sharifi exchanged his pyjamas for a dark three-piece suit.

Ghulam Sakhi looked wide awake, at four a.m., one of those night people, as the Americans called them, who were most alert while others slept.

He sat behind his desk at KHAD Headquarters, chain-smoking. He had a close-cropped head and a Mongolian face covered with pockmarks. There was a nine-millimetre Beretta pistol near his hand. A tiny gun: but at point-blank range like this it could kill instantly. The Sirdar hadn't seen Sakhi for twenty years: since he was President of the *Anjumani Aryanie Afghani*, the AAA, that crazy association whose name stood for the Association of Afghan Aryans, modelled on the German SS. Its members liked to use the ancient name for the country, Aryana, and to feel that they lived in the cradle of the *Nizhadi Humayuni*, the Imperial Race. Sakhi had even lived in Germany. On his Kabul office wall was still to be seen the brown banner of his Hitler Youth unit.

The captain withdrew, with a smart '*Zindabad Inqilab!* Long Live the Revolution.'

Sakhi was grinning, with a false grimace which only made him look the more malevolent.

'Come in, how nice to see you, may you never be tired, Ambassador, have some tea, are you well?'

Akbar took the chair which Sakhi indicated, and folded his neat hands on his lap.

The brigadier leant forward, one arm on his desk.

'You will have been waiting to hear from us, respected sir, and therefore this meeting will doubtless be a relief to you. It is often so, as we have found in similar cases; and I am happy to be the instrument of your adjustment.' A psychopathic killer and a lunatic; that was his reputation: and definitely a fantasist, thought Akbar. He waited. Sakhi picked up a pencil and weighed it in his hand.

'From now on you revert to your proper rank and title of Engineer Akbar. None of this "Sirdar" business. We don't have princes and the like nowadays, you know. One leader, one teacher of socialist reality: that is the . . . Afghan Way.' *Ha, you nearly said 'Aryan Way', didn't you?* thought Akbar.

Brigadier Sakhi tapped the pencil on the desk.

'Engineer Akbar. A lot of people have died, or have gone missing, since the revolution. Many of these have been specialists and technicians. We all know that they were killed by the terrorists, working for Israel and America, or bribed to desert the Homeland, to impoverish it. That is a well-known capitalist economic weapon. Because of this, I am collecting people with technical knowledge and you are one of them. The Kajakai Dam, near Kandahar, is, as you know, one of the largest in the world. The Americans botched the job there, or else it was them and the King's regime. We Afghans lost a hundred and twenty million dollars because of that. Anyway, we need massive electricity generation in that area. You have been chosen to install the new machinery. It is a *shturm* effort, a crash programme.' He used the Russian word, Akbar noticed.

The old man spoke: 'But there aren't any turbines, and anyway, I heard at the Ministry that the project failed because the specifications were badly drawn up. You have, in any case, capacity for 120,000 kilowatts and no industry to use it.'

Sakhi smiled. 'How typical of a blinkered Western-minded lackey! Akbar, have you never heard of the Egyptian High Dam at Aswan? The Americans refused to finance it, Western capitalists said that it could never be done. Abdul-Nasser asked the brotherly Russians and, *puff*, the whole Egyptian desert is green! As for using the electricity, there will soon be an urgent need for all we can make there. We can even export it. Kajakai can be the biggest thing in Asia.'

Akbar sighed and thought: *Export it like the Afghan natural gas, 2,500 million cubic metres, exported to the Soviet Union through a pipeline without metering, so that the Soviets could pay us what they say they have used; is that 'the Afghan Way'?*

'You will have the title of Assistant Chief Engineer. The Chief Engineer is Yilderim Barqi, a good Party man.' Sakhi emphasized the last four words.

'Yilderim Barqi is a garage hand from Karta Chahar, and knew nothing about hydropower up to last week . . .' Akbar could hardly believe what he was hearing.

'He will be in *overall* charge, Akbar. You supply the technical know-how.' So, Yilderim was the boss, because he was a Party man . . .

'Now, Akbar, I want you to work for your country, build it strong, build it great, to become a fitting member of the socialist camp.'

The Socialist three-ring circus, Akbar thought. Yilderim couldn't even change a spark plug. Maybe that was because he was studying Russian texts: 'Always use Soviet electricity: watt for watt it is the purest in the world.' Aloud he said, 'I am obliged by your offer. But I am now an old man, not up-to-date in these matters. I would not understand a Russian turbine.'

'Afghan technicians,' said Sakhi, his eyes gleaming with a hideous malevolence, 'can take a Soviet helicopter, demount the weaponry, find out how it works, and fire it at another aircraft from the ground, using string, hammer and nails as a firing mechanism, and bring the aircraft down. Afghan technicians can do anything, I have observed. If they are bandits and terrorists.'

'Oh yes, I have heard of that,' Akbar smiled. He murmured, 'That's when they are dealing with the brotherly socialist gunships, the best in the world.'

'What did you say, Engineer?'

'Nothing directly relevant, Brigadier.'

'The new Russian turbines have already been delivered to

the site. They are the best in the world.' Sakhi tapped his pencil on the desk again.

'Brigadier Sakhi, I feel that, all things considered, I must decline the offer.'

'Then I have to tell you, Citizen Akbar, something more. Hear it and then give your final answer. Your daughter, Noor Sharifi, has been denounced by a patriot for anti-Party agitation and is now in protective custody, to defend her from the understandable wrath of the toiling people whom she was trying to betray. We expect her confession hourly, of course. I am afraid that she will have to go to the correction centre. You may have heard of Tula.'

Tula! The concentration camp attached to the steel mill, two hundred and twenty-five kilometres south of Moscow. Hundreds of Afghan hostages, including women, were working there. Some had already died, of ill-treatment or inadequate industrial safety precautions.

I am the man who, as a youth, prayed that I might be tested, to show my faith, my resolution. Noor is my only surviving child, born in my old age. God damn you, Sakhi, damn your Democratic Party of the People, damn your brotherly Soviet turbines.

Akbar took a deep breath then pleaded as he knew all along he would have to plead. 'Please don't send Noor to Tula, Comrade Brigadier. Many of the hostages sent there have died already. Let me have her back! I'll work for you, at anything.'

'She is a strong girl,' said the Mongolian. 'If she is assigned to rehabilitative work at Tula, I am sure that she will come out of it refreshed and purged. We need them all, the reformed as well as the enlightened-to-begin-with, in the new Afghanistan. You will take up the post? I'll have a travel warrant issued for you later today. You report to this office, with no more than thirty kilos of luggage, at eight tomorrow morning. Remember, it's much warmer in the south-west, so you don't need many clothes: that ambassador's suit you're wearing is ridiculous. Take overalls: and you'd better meet the production norms that Comrade Yilderim sets, remember? Just remember Tula steel mill, and I'm sure that will help you to solve all problems. Good day Comrade Engineer Akbar. Long Live the Revolution!'

*

Brigadier Sakhi was dead now, gunned down by a patriot outside the Soviet Embassy in Kabul, on April 18th. But that hadn't helped Noor: and Sirdar Akbar was still a captive at the hydropower dam.

Akbar looked at his slide rule once more and did the calculations all over again. They came out the same as at all the other times. It wasn't the specifications; but there was something wrong somewhere. The massive, steel-reinforced concrete at Kajakai was sound, and the dam, standing there since the nineteen fifties, was as firm as a rock. The immense bulk of the dam sat partly within a hollow, blasted from the rocks, like some enormous giant's tooth filling, gleaming white out of the grey. Good enough. When the mass of the matrix, the rock, had been calculated, it was obvious, given the character of the rock itself, that the dam would hold. Now, however, on a tour of inspection of the encircling mountain-girdle, Akbar had found that some rocks were fissured. Earthquakes? No, that had been taken into account. Erosion? Next to no rainfall here, and there had not been time for any significant erosion to take place. Blasting? It could never have produced such effects . . .

Only one possibility occurred to him, a remote one. If the rock were partly of a different consistency from the samples on which the original calculations of their stress-resistance had been based . . . Could the dam burst? Was the $120 million really wasted?

Akbar got up and called his servant. He'd brought the brothers Salik and Samir with him from Kabul. They were the only two people in the world now who cared about him and could help in any way.

'Samir, call the guard. Say I have to inspect the rock-face again. He can bring the jeep and we'll leave as soon as it comes round to the front.'

'By my eyes, Excellency.'

He was back in three minutes. 'I've told the *zhondarm*.'

The internal telephone rang. 'Engineer Akbar? Chief Engineer Yilderim here. Go and look at the rock-face if you must, but you can't have the jeep, the driver is busy.' *Yilderim had sent him off to fetch drink or hashish, or something, that would be it.* 'But there's no problem, Engineer, just take Samir.'

'How about an escort? I'm not allowed out on my own.'

'That's quite in order, just put Samir on the line. I'll tell him something.' *Samir too? Samir as his escort. Gone over to Yilderim, to the Russian side?*

Samir took the handset. '*Bali, bali*, yes, yes. I understand. Yes, by my eyes.' He didn't look at his master as he replaced the instrument on its cradle.

'Why am I allowed out alone, with only you, Samir Khan?' *Better have it out with him now.*

'Excellency! We are allowed out: or, rather, you are, because I am to be responsible for your safe return after the inspection.'

'And if I tried to escape – would you stop me?'

'Yilderim is holding Salik, Excellency, against our return. Would you have him kill my brother?'

'May the right prevail, may the evildoers receive their recompense, whoever they are, Samir. Let's go, on foot.'

Yilderim was almost certainly corrupt, greedy too. But he was still afraid enough of Kabul, of the KGB, to keep a tight grip on affairs at Kajakai.

But if Yilderim had such strict orders, this suggested a possibility: that Sakhi had no real hold on Akbar, that Noor was perhaps free? He could never act on any such flimsy hypothesis, but the thought was a kind of hope, one to keep at the back of his mind where there was none. Like a false coin in an otherwise empty purse.

They tramped around all morning. Akbar looked at the rock. No, there were no inherent weaknesses: it was all of the same type. Now for the fissures. He found one, and clambered down, leaving Samir at the top of a rise. He was in a dry river bed. There was the base of the crack. Measure the length and width of the gap, do some calculations, after estimating the weight of rock, the stress factors.

Here was a boulder, wedged in the fissure. It must have been there some time, for there was moss on it. He looked again. Just like a doorway, in a sense. He felt words going round in his head; the heat must be affecting him. No, it wasn't the heat. He was reciting the words of the old tale, 'And, lo, Alla-addin called out "Open Sesame!" And, slowly the boulder swung aside, and the young man entered the Cavern of Treasures.'

He tugged at the boulder. It came away easily, just as if on a pivot.

The fissure led to a passage, then a cave. Akbar walked inside. This was a honeycomb, a catacomb, in fact, part of the very ancient underground dwelling places, cities almost, which were found all over Afghanistan: and all the way to the Gobi in Mongolia. Generations of troglodytes had lived here millenia ago. That was it! The dam's weight had cracked the rock because it wasn't a solid matrix at all – not at this point at least. It was a mass of passages, linked caves, leading to caverns. Sometimes there were even underground saline lakes in places like this. He would have to make more calculations.

As the days passed, Akbar supervised the unloading of the generator turbines from their immense transporters, and had them positioned near the gullies which would eventually receive them. There was a great deal to do; even moving such weights was a major feat of engineering in itself. The American-built town of Lashkargah, near Kajakai, had been virtually deserted for years, but was now suddenly full of workers, Party officials, nomads and traders. A large space was turned into a market; a mayor and police chief were appointed, a court sat once a week; and even the present generator capacity of the installation was becoming stretched, as demands for power continually increased, for light, for machines, and to supply current for the cookers, videos, food-mixers and deepfreezes. Wherever did all these people, all this equipment, come from? The place was like a boom-town. What an extraordinary transformation!

And Arghandab. Sixty miles to the south-east lay the second of the monster dams, again American-built, with its own town and hydropower centre. This dam, with its huge lake, hardly twenty miles from that other white elephant, Kandahar International Airport, was also about to burst into life. One day, visiting the engineering shops there to get some spare parts, Akbar saw crowds of Russian technicians, Soviet Air Force officers, and the piles of aeronautical maintenance equipment being offloaded from huge trucks. Walls were plastered with posters showing an Afghan soldier, side by side with a peasant, busily defending the Revolution with a gun. People had even unearthed some ancient posters from the American period and stuck them up, perhaps in an excess of zeal. They showed an

143

Afghan in a peaked cap and an American engineer in a turban, both admiring a huge melon. They stood beside a Ford tractor, shaking hands. Underneath was the triumphant caption, 'Water for the Thirsty Land!'

Another rousing slogan, though, had been partly covered in whitewash. Running the length of a long, low, building, it proclaimed, in English: 'Afghanistan, with its proud and ancient peoples, welcomes the new ways of US technology!'

But at Arghandab the usual miserable presence of Afghan Army conscripts was not to be seen. Here, instead, were fresh-faced, well-fed, stalwart troops, well turned out, looking properly defiant. A lot of money and training had been deployed, Akbar could see, to effect this transformation. They goose-stepped around the new Monument to the Fallen Heroes, too, in a very Russian fashion. The guard, like the one at Lenin's tomb in Red Square, was changed every hour, on the hour. Their vehicles bore the blazon of the Afghan Fifteenth Infantry Division.

Back to Kajakai. Akbar, in a series of forays, had mapped many of the galleries inside the mountain walls around his dam. The cracks, he was now positive, had reached their maximum extension and were not going to expand further. Nothing was going to disturb the ancient monastery for some time yet.

But, as he worked on the survey of the place, something nagged his memory, something from the distant past. He knew it was related somehow to the area north of Kandahar. He could not quite capture it. Old age, he supposed, was having its traditional effect. He used to know it, that was sure. Perhaps he'd forget his own name next.

Then, one day, exploring the caves he stumbled on the great tunnel. This, his engineer's eye told him, was of relatively recent date and the discovery of a bolster chisel and a nearly modern-looking hammer confirmed this assessment. About a hundred years old.

Akbar remembered now about the story . . . It said that the Afghan ruler, Amir Abdur-Rahman, at the time of Queen Victoria, had had prisoners working somewhere up here, feverishly and for years, to seek some hidden treasure. Yes, that was it, the Loot of Ahmad Shah, talked about with bated breath as the greatest treasure the world had ever known.

But they hadn't found it. Still, this was a promising place, near enough to where Ahmad Shah – Afghanistan's first king – was said to have diverted the river, and discovered an underground tunnel complex.

The Master Tunnel, as he named it on his sketch maps, was large, dry as a bone and free of moss and fungus. Why had the tunnel been cut at all? Looking at the plan, Akbar projected the line of the passage at its present angle, to the surface. It should emerge there . . .

The next day he was climbing, with Samir, to the vantage-point, the outcrop of rock above and to the north of the dam, officially to continue his 'inspection'.

The view from this point was breathtaking. They could see over thousands of acres – both new farmland and desert – to the forests beyond. On the surface of the dam, a vast expanse of still water, tens of thousands of water-birds of every Afghan variety went about their business, unconcerned about being in a country at war. And here, just a few yards away, what he had thought was an ancient fort was revealed as the ruins of a medieval mosque.

He and Samir spent hours clearing rubble with their bare hands, moving carved marble pillars, stacking exquisite blue tiles, looking for the entrance to the tunnel. It was there all right. Just behind the prayer-niche facing Mecca, as Samir pushed away a pile of rubble from the collapsed roof, a dark hole with steps came into view.

The two men, without exchanging a word, began to climb downwards. Samir, who had few possessions, was proud of his flashlight, which he kept clipped, as a schoolboy might, to his belt. Now it stood them in good stead. The steps were easy to use. The treads were intact, and whoever had made them had taken care that the rises were no higher than even an old man could comfortably manage. Akbar, however, panting with the excitement of the unknown, was relieved that they were going down and not up.

At the bottom of the steps, a tunnel ran into another passage at right angles to it. Then it opened out into a vast passageway, with man-made caves to left and right.

Akbar went into the first cave, knocking over a slab of clay, which toppled from a perished wooden plinth as he brushed past.

It was here, almost as an anti-climax after such suspense, that Sirdar Akbar and Samir found the gold.

At first they thought that they were looking at a wall, with leaves of long-dead creepers hanging down, one over another, covering the three sides of the cavern, from floor to roof. But, as soon as Akbar touched this surface, he realized that the scraps were tattered pieces of ancient, perished leather: remnants of the once-sturdy sacks in which the gold coins, millions of *mohurs*, had been stored.

Samir stood stock still, playing his light back and forth like an automaton as the coins came cascading to the ground, bright as the day they were minted. There was no damp to corrode metal, Akbar realized, and fine gold does not oxydize anyway.

The Hoard of Ahmad Shah. As Sirdar Akbar stood there, senses reeling, Samir stepped forward and pulled at another piece of leather. More coins spilled out, tinkling, then lay like a frozen stream, silent, shining, challenging.

Akbar took the flashlight from Samir's hand and went back into the passage. Immediately opposite the cave which they had just left was another, full of sacks. Walking down the tunnel, the two men counted twenty such caves, until they turned and retraced their steps. When they reached the first cave, Akbar picked up the clay tablet and slipped it into his satchel. It had writing of some sort on it.

'Samir, we must get back to the administration offices, in case they miss us.' He did not caution Samir not to tell anyone of their find; and Samir knew that, after this, neither would speak of it to anybody, at least until they had absorbed the staggering facts.

'Ah, yes, Excellency.' As they climbed the steps to the ruined mosque, Samir said, 'There must be . . . a million . . . coins there, Excellency.'

'Yes, Samir. Millions.'

They were late back at the offices, but Yilderim (which means Thunderbolt in Turki) didn't care. Busily justifying his name, he was jumping about in a drunken frenzy, playfully striking with a stick at some Russian troopers who had drunk orange juice mixed with a can of anti-freeze liquid intended for their tanks. Holding Salik as hostage, Engineer Yilderim had dismissed the old man and Samir from his mind.

When they got to Akbar's room without challenge, passing the sounds of revelry coming from the party in the canteen, the two men slumped into armchairs. Samir had never so much as sat down in his master's presence, let alone sprawled in his best seat, but neither noticed. Then, like schoolboys suddenly given a whole day off, they jumped to their feet and danced, twisting and whirling, in the ecstatic if undignified configurations of the *Atan*, the national sword dance. Then they stopped, giggling, slapping one another on the back, shaking their heads in near-disbelief. Finally, with Akbar shouting '*Mast-i-be-mai* – drunken without wine!', they sat down again. Sirdar Akbar remembered the tablet, and brought it out from his bag. It was small, no larger than an average modern book, and the words on it were impressed, scratched as if with a piece of wood, in excellent Persian calligraphy. He wiped it with his bandanna handkerchief and placed it on the desk under his reading lamp. The words stood out clearly:

'786'. This was the numerical equivalent of the phrase 'In the Name of God, the Beneficent, the Merciful', often used in manuscripts and inscriptions. Then: '*Khazana-i-tila-i-Zat-i-Shahana, Sultan Ahmad Shah, Durr-i-Durran* – Gold Treasury of the Essence of Royalty, Sultan Ahmad Shah, Pearl of Pearls . . .' Then the date: '1171 Hijri – Year of the Flight'. Equivalent, in the Christian Era, to 1757: the year after Ahmad Shah had sacked Delhi and carried away the treasures of the great Moguls . . .

Samir, looking over Akbar's shoulder, could not make out the words: literacy was not his strong point.

'Read, Excellency, read!'

Akbar read the words aloud:

'There are forty-eight caves, and in each cave a hundred piles . . .' Akbar wiped the sweat from his forehead and paused.

Samir, forgetting himself, shook the old man's shoulder. 'Read, read!'

'Yes, I'm reading. The next words say that each pile contains a lakh – a hundred thousand – gold *mohurs* or the equivalent of ingots.'

'Excellency, what is that worth?'

'Wait a minute.' Suddenly fearful, Sirdar Akbar covered the tablet with some papers and tiptoed to the door. There was nobody outside; Yilderim and his friends could be heard singing at the top of their voices. Akbar went back to his desk.

'The inscription continues, "Each pile has one thousand bags of one hundred coins or equivalent gold. Total amount, forty-eight *krur*".'

'"Forty-eight *krur*!" – Excellency, a *krur* is half a million!' Samir's eyes rolled.

'A *krur*, Samir,' Akbar said quietly, 'is indeed half a million according to the Dari, Persian, reckoning. But this writing was done by a Mogul, Indian, scribe or treasurer. In India, a *krur* is exactly ten million. There are four hundred and eighty million coins – or their equivalent – in those caves!'

At first, Akbar had thought that he could do something with the gold: put himself and his daughter out of the hands of the communists, perhaps. Or – crazy idea – give it to the Kabul regime of Babrak Karmal so that they could buy the country's freedom from the Russians. He and Samir sat in the room, at first elated, then dazed, finally discussing eagerly about what gold, on such a scale, could do.

It was Samir who brought them both back to reality. 'There is a saying, Excellency,' he said, 'that "if a cat is rich, the money belongs to its master." We can't use the gold. The moment we tell Engineer Yilderim, or Kabul, or the Russians, we are dead men; and then someone else owns it. The only hope is to get it out of the country so that it can be sold abroad. Then the money could be used to buy arms for the people. If the people don't get guns and rockets soon they will all be wiped out, now that the Russians are destroying the farms and the villages, and slaughtering the population.'

Someone abroad: that was it. The Americans? The British? Akbar's mind began to work. If he had someone to send, he might try anywhere, Japan, Western Europe. He could get the gold to the sea, all right. He had blood-links with the huge Durani clan, whose territory extended from Kandahar to the ocean, to the shores of the Arabian sea. But Akbar had nobody to send. After all, Samir was more of a houseboy than a diplomat. Emissaries in modern times had to negotiate through institutions, ministries and established delegations. Samir the servant would never get an appointment with a high government official anywhere. In ancient times, of course, one simply sent one's messenger – with a token or password – to a single person, a ruler or a prince, who would have the power to say yes or no . . .

Akbar flicked on the radio, a cheap, medium-wave transistor which he had got, though forbidden to own a set, from one of the guards. He had paid for it with his wrist watch, the gold Vacheron Constantin. Radio Pakistan came through loud and clear on the medium wave, the nearest station which gave anything resembling impartial news.

It was time for the news. In English. Akbar had once laughed, as so many others did, at the lilting accent, which people who had been educated in Britain called 'Bombay Welsh'. Not any more. Now it was his only channel to the real world. Nothing about Afghanistan, except that there were now three million refugee Afghans, driven out by napalm, phosphorus bombs and terror, sheltering in Pakistan. Perhaps a quarter of the entire population. Then . . .

'His Royal Highness, Prince Jamal ibn Zaid Al Narabi, son and heir of His Majesty, King Zaid Al Narabi, Monarch of Narabia, the North Arabian Kingdom, will visit Pakistan in six weeks' time, heading a mission to inspect some of the two hundred and eighty Afghan refugee camps in the North West Frontier region. His Royal Highness has especially asked that the mission be regarded as a private one, and in deference to his wishes there will be no State welcome.

'He is expected to arrive in Peshawar on June 12th and will be accompanied by only a small personal staff, though these will be individuals of high rank. The Governor of the North West Frontier Province has intimated that it would be regarded as a seemly gesture if, in their private capacities, the people of the region were in evidence in the streets on the day of his arrival, perhaps with Narabian flags, to express brotherly greetings to the representative of our fellow Islamic country. After the news, there will be a talk entitled "Narabia, today and yesterday".'

149

Akbar jumped up, ignoring the twinge of rheumatism which sudden action always produced in his leg. 'Samir Jan. We've got it! That's the answer. I see it all now!'

'Excellency?'

'Didn't you hear?'

'I don't understand all that English. Frankish tongues sound like dzz, dzz, nothing more, to me.'

'An Arab prince is visiting Pakistan soon, Samir. He will be in Peshawar city, no distance from here, just over the border.'

'Excellency?'

'He is the son of King Zaid, may his good fortune continue! You were there with me for three years, Samir, while I was Ambassador at his court. His Majesty knows me well. He has oil money, billions of dollars.'

'I remember, Excellency, I can still speak Arabic.' Samir still did not understand what his master was driving at. Like a good servant, he waited.

'He'll buy the gold from us, and bank the money in Switzerland. Then we can contact the freedom fighters, who are being slaughtered for lack of guns. They could buy rockets, everything. Our country might yet be saved, Samir!'

Samir nodded, slowly. 'May I be your sacrifice, Excellency. You know better, of course, but you can't go to the prince, you're under close supervision, arrest in fact. And how could we transport the gold from here to Pakistan?'

'Transport is easy, Samir. We are in the country of the Durrani Clan, and it stretches from here, through Pakistan, to the Arabia Sea. They have been smuggling from there to the Gulf, in dhows, for centuries. They'll do it.'

Akbar's eyes were gleaming, and he tugged at his neat goatee excitedly.

'As to who will go to the prince, Samir, there is only one person who would do it, and do it at whatever cost. Someone who has seen the gold and knows Narabia. That person is you, Samir.'

With that optimism which, over the centuries, has unseated as many Afghans as it has supported, Samir immediately said, 'Yes, I could do that, Excellency. But I do not remember the prince.'

'That's not important. He was studying at Oxford when we

were at Hadiqa City, but you can prove that you have been there if you talk to him, and you can show him samples of the gold. Then he is bound to take the message to King Zaid.'

Samir considered it. '*Mumkin* – it's possible.'

The old man smiled and touched Samir on the shoulder. 'Good. I'm tired now, Samir. Let's leave it at that for today.'

In the morning, again getting permission from Yilderim by offering Salik as a hostage, the two men went back to the cave. At the entrance, the old man slipped off his sandals and went down into the shaft. There was no sign that anyone else had been there: piles of dust which he had left, craftily positioned, the last time, were intact.

The pair of them did not stay long: only long enough to collect, in the haversack which he carried on inspections, a hundred or so of the gleaming mohurs. It was on this visit that Akbar noticed that there were smaller passages, and air vents, in the treasure-cave. He would be able to use those, he thought, to bring cables, to install lighting in the warren of passages. That would be useful in the shifting of the hoard.

He had already worked out that the treasure, estimated roughly by the number of almost perished sacks piled up in the tunnels, had a present-day value of something like four hundred billion dollars. It didn't look like it: gold weighs heavy, but takes up remarkably little space. It was a sum equal to the entire monetary reserves of the oil countries: more gold than any single country on earth possessed. Nearly three times the entire external assets of Saudi Arabia.

It would not do to send Samir yet; they would first have to work out some scheme for getting the treasure out. Transport to the coast would be easier: Durrani trucks. Then smugglers' dhows to the Gulf.

All that day Akbar surveyed the site. Yes, he thought, that was it. It would be quite possible to remove the coins through the hills, via the ruined mosque, since, although it commanded a view of much of the countryside below, it nestled among features which sheltered the route from observation.

This must have been in the mind of whoever hid the gold, or whoever built the mosque. A treasury with a way to get in and out without being seen.

Then Yilderim announced that an inspection team, Afghan

and Russian, was visiting the site, 'for evaluation', in three weeks' time. This was both good and bad, Akbar realized. It meant that Engineer Yilderim would start frenzied activity, having the place cleaned and painted, working out wall-charts of progress, and generally demonstrating his value. It also meant that Akbar would be left more to himself, and could get on with the wiring of the lights in the treasure tunnels. But it meant, too, that he could not yet risk sending Samir to Pakistan. His disappearance might make the Russians decide to strengthen the guards, or arrest Samir's brother – any number of possibilities. Akbar was prepared to meet problems as they arose if he had only Yilderim to deal with, but not if he was faced by the tougher, ultra-suspicious, socialist rescuers from the north.

Going to and fro, being in and out of the treasure caverns so often, may have made Akbar and Samir careless. Just after the Russians had made their inspection and left, the old man and his servant climbed to the ruined mosque for a final check, without maintaining their usual vigilance. When they came out of the mosque and sat in the shade of a wall, resting after their climb, they saw the spy. He walked past without seeing them, at a slightly lower level, and then paused. He had found Akbar's sandals, pointing to the entrance to the steps. They recognized him; a police agent from Kabul ostensibly concerned with security, but probably posted here to keep an eye on Yilderim. As they watched, he went down the steps leading to the treasure cave. 'You let him get out of here alive,' said Akbar, his ageing face as hard and desperate as anything Samir had ever seen, 'and our country is finished. Afghanistan is dead. The Army and the KGB will destroy us as they destroyed the rest of Central Asia.'

'Excellency, I promise. By my head and eyes. He is a dead man.' The lithe six-foot figure of Samir slipped away like a wraith.

Former Minister Akbar made a little gesture of despair and turned away, shoulders hunched. He sat down and lay back in the shade. Everything depended on Samir.

Samir's body tensed with total concentration, as he tiptoed along the tunnel towards where the spy was now standing, flashlight in hand, absorbing the incredible truth.

Suddenly there was a click and the shaft was flooded with light, bright as high noon. The spy had found the switch operating the lights which Akbar had so laboriously installed.

The two saw each other at the same moment. Samir sensed rather than saw the Browning in the spy's hand. There was a slight bend in the passage which would intrude on the gunman's line of sight, so Samir threw himself against the wall. Then he started forward as the first shots rang out, ricocheting off the hard rock of the tunnel. The firing stopped. The man would shoot again, Samir knew, but perhaps later rather than sooner. He would have deduced by now that Samir did not have a gun and would probably wait until a minimum distance separated them.

Only a few yards to go now. Something hit his toe and he reached down. It was the spy's flashlight, which he had dropped when he reached for his gun. Samir picked it up and threw it as part of the same movement, straight at his adversary's head. It missed by an inch and crashed in pieces against the wall. The place was full of cordite fumes and the spy's face emerged from the smoke, grinning evilly.

Samir dived for the man's ankles.

As he launched himself forward and down he was aware of the spy's confident crouch, aiming the gun at him as calmly as a man with an aerosol of insecticide, about to destroy a bluebottle.

Oh God, it shouldn't be like this.

Again, a shot, and in the same moment a thump on his shoulder, like a giant's punch. The sick, sick feeling as he doubled up; then a great gasp, a reflex, as if his body screamed to heal itself with air.

Samir lay still. He heard groaning and realized the sound came from himself. He looked up and saw his adversary's face wet with sweat but gleaming with triumph. The man was pushing another cartridge clip into the gun-butt. Samir felt death seconds away. So this was how it happened. It was not at all like in the films.

In a second or two now, he knew, the spy would bend down, hold the automatic pistol close to his ear, and fire a single shot. Something buzzed at the back of Samir's head and became a man's voice, the voice of his village preacher, the ancient sage and Mulla, Mulla Jan. '*Ya Hafiz, Ya Hafiz*, O Protector, O Protector,' it said. The Mulla had taught him to say that when he was afraid.

And he was afraid. Too afraid to ask for mercy. Too afraid to think.

Now the spy was ready to deliver the *coup de grâce*. There was his face, there was his breath; the gun barrel would be coming down right this moment: unless . . .

Suddenly Samir felt as if he was watching the scene, with himself in it, from a distance. Something extra was working in his brain, at a speed the rest of his mind could not register.

He'd fallen sideways, against the wall, jammed against it, like a twisted tree trunk. His right shoulder was throbbing, and his shirt was soaked with blood. His left side was pressed to the wall, the arm bent, the elbow in a depression, one of the niches which, centuries ago someone had hewn out to hold a lamp.

His fingers were moving now, feeling, clutching. They closed over something round, hard, and sharp. It was the beaked part of a Greek or Roman baked clay lamp.

As the spy bent down – quite slowly, as though savouring the moment – Samir, using his left shoulder as a lever, his elbow as a fulcrum, the beaked lamp in his head as a dagger, swung around and jerked himself upward. Gasping with pain, he struck straight at one of those infernal eyes.

After that, it took only a few seconds. The spy was blinded and in no condition to fight a man of Samir's build, even with a bullet in his shoulder.

'My turn, Comrade Kabul swine,' said Samir. He picked up the spy's gun and shot him, cleanly, through the back of the neck.

Samir's shoulder wound was bad, but not really dangerous, Akbar decided when Samir stumbled into daylight. But he would now have to get away immediately, Akbar realized, before anyone got to know about his injuries, and linked it with the disappearance of the spy.

In considerable pain, Samir set off within the hour, on foot, his wound covered in cotton waste and bound by a thick turban-length of cloth. A few miles out of Kajakai he stopped in a village. There the blacksmith, accustomed to such problems and asking no questions, dug out the bullet and cauterized the wound with a piece of red-hot iron. His surgical instruments were a knife and a pair of pincers.

Yilderim, as it happened, chose to visit Sirdar Akbar a few minutes after he had cleaned the blood of Samir's wound from his office floor. He looked up at the sound of the thunderous knock and wondered, as the communist engineer lurched into the room, whether Samir had been caught. In spite of his anxiety the old man could not help feeling a rush of anger at the sight of this drunken fool, his chief engineer, who knew nothing about anything, but held authority because he was a good Party man.

The former garage hand, with a bottle of vodka in his right hand, stumbled across to an armchair and slumped into it, fixing the old man with his bloodshot eyes.

'Ex-Ambassador, former prince and general scum: *khar-kuss-i-padar lanat* . . .' The obscene oaths died away into a mumble. He closed his eyes and broke wind noisily.

Yes, thought Sharifi, this is it. Had he found the gold or the dead man, or both?

He reached into his pocket and took out a pinch of snuff. He gave a thunderous sneeze, which brought Yilderim back to life.

'I'm lonely, you old fool! It's wrong for people to drink alone. Here, have a shot.' He offered the bottle, but Sharifi shook his head.

'All the more for me, then.' Yilderim hiccupped, and looked at him morosely.

'Come on, I only want to talk.' Yilderim was looking at Sharifi anxiously, his mood changing under the influence of the drink. 'Tell me something about your life. Yes, that's what I want to hear. We might become friends, who knows?'

So, thought Sharifi, he doesn't know anything about the gold – or the spy – yet. I might as well keep him occupied while Samir gets away. If I go on talking, perhaps he'll drink himself into a stupor.

He blew his nose on a huge red bandanna handkerchief.

'All right, Yilderim. I'll tell you what I was thinking about.'

Yilderim nodded, grinning, and settled deeper into the easy chair.

'As you know, there is always a holy fool who lives in the sacred place near here called the *Chihil Zina*, the Forty Steps.

When one dies, another always appears to take his place. And I feel that it is nearly time to spend the rest of my life in contemplation.'

Yilderim made for the door. 'Well, whatever you do, install the turbines first. I'm off to bed. This damned vodka isn't what it used to be. Upsets my head and stomach.'

'Samir is gone?' Yilderim was sprawled on the couch of his luxurious studio apartment when Akbar made his report. His head was throbbing from the excesses of the night before. 'Why should I care, Engineer? I don't know how people can have feudal things like servants in a socialist country. Comrade Karmal will ban such exploitation as soon as he gets round to it. Let him go. People's servants are always running away. He's probably got into some trouble with the local villagers.'

'But shouldn't we report it?'

'To whom and for what? The Revolution has far more important things to concern itself with than looking after former aristocrats' lackeys. Tell you what, though.'

'What?'

'Since I can't hold one or the other of the servants as a precaution against your desertion, from now on you'll have to take a guard with you when you go out.'

'Certainly, Chief Engineer. I only wanted to make sure that you had the report, that all was in order.'

Thank God. No police interest in Samir. So he would have a good chance of getting through: although he still wouldn't know whether they were after him or not.

Quite a lot had happened since they had found the tunnel. Akbar had worked out that Amir Abdur-Rahman's miners had missed the hoard by inches, and that it had only been revealed when a part of the inner wall, weakened by their burrowing, had fallen down. Akbar had installed electric light, and had even found a tunnel which passed close to his own office. Samir had made a secret entrance to it, so that it could be reached without going outside and making the long climb up the hill to the old mosque and then down the steps to the treasure cave.

Akbar had coached Samir well in what he had to say to the prince – if he ever reached him – in Pakistan. It would need an experienced diplomat, with credentials and long-term planning, to deal with any modern chief of state. But to send a man to a traditional absolute monarch, or the son of one – people whom one knew on equal terms, and under such medieval circumstances as those prevailing in Afghanistan and Narabia – that was easy. And Samir was exactly the kind of man to do it, the faithful retainer, a type recognizable anywhere in the Middle East. It could not happen in the West, nowadays; Akbar smiled as he thought of it. But this was not the West.

In spite of his throbbing shoulder, Samir made excellent time on the sixty kilometres of road from Kandahar to Qala-i-Jadid on the Pakistan border. Plenty of trucks, driven by wild Pashtun tribesmen, ferried everything from machinery to tobacco along that route; the all-weather highway built by the Russians stopped there. Northwards, it ran nearly to the Soviet frontier, was suitable for the heaviest motor vehicles, including tanks. Even thirty years ago the neighbourly Soviet roadbuilders knew what they were doing, and why.

Samir slipped across the unmarked border into Baluchistan, and took the road for Quetta. From there he had no difficulty in getting a ride in a truck, all the way up to Peshawar.

There was no problem, either, in finding the Afghan camps. Three million refugees took up a lot of space. Samir soon found a small room in Peshawar, and settled down to await the coming of the prince.

Peshawar was more than a Pashtun city of twenty-five thousand houses; more than a frontier town; more than a place near which millions of Afghan refugees, accustomed to the cool mountains, sweltered in desert camps. Even when the British had ruled India and severed this area from Afghanistan, the town had been a listening-post for Russian spies. Now more than ever it was a centre of Soviet Intelligence. And here, before Prince Jamal's visit, Samir was to meet one of the Kremlin's most dangerous agents – and, innocently, to regard him as a friend.

Peshawar City was teeming with refugees, expatriates, sympathizers of the rebel cause: Samir felt safe there, among his own. He was, however, very much alone, unable to confide in anyone. And he had weeks to wait until Jamal's coming. It would be necessary to sell some of his gold coins to pay his way.

Thus it was that after a week of walking through the bazaars and finding himself down to his last few rupees, Samir approached a goldsmith with two of his mohurs: two-thirds of an ounce of fine gold.

The man tested it with acid, weighed it and offered the Afghan the gold price of $2000. Obviously one should not accept the first bid, Samir thought; he would see what others might give. Apart from some derisory offers of a few rupees, made by people deceived through greed into hoping that this untidy figure might be completely stupid, the price seemed fairly standard. There was one exception. A man in an antiques shop took one look at the coins, then two looks at Samir, and placed sixty thousand rupees, worth three thousand dollars, on his counter.

Samir accepted at once, and – innocently – became quite attracted to the genial antiquary, with whom he soon found much in common. To be fair to Engineer Akbar's servant the goldsmith, Rind by name, was a highly skilled operative. Anyone who had two gold mohurs of the Delhi minting of 1677, he guessed, might well have more of them. Everyone in Peshawar – like almost everyone in the rest of the subcontinent – dreamt of finding treasure: and not without reason, hoards were always turning up.

Rind was not only a Soviet agent: he made a great deal of money buying antiques from the ignorant. The strategy with gold coins was practised and effective. If someone found coins, he would take them from one goldsmith to another to have their value assessed. Then he would return to the highest bidder and sell at least some of them: probably not too many, to avoid suspicion. Rind's practice was to make sure that he offered the highest price, to ensure the man's return. When he came back, he could be tracked to his home. More often than not, the gold was there, buried in the earth floor. A knife in the night, and the gold was Rind's, for nothing. The system had produced many successes and no unfortunate consequences. People who found buried treasure almost always did two things: they moved it to their own houses, and they kept their mouths shut. For the police, therefore, the murder would always appear to be some kind of revenge killing, and the file would be closed for lack of information.

Rind, who had developed almost a sixth sense for a really good haul, today invited his customer to the Café of the Green Roof for tea and talk. Although wary, Rind thought, Samir was undoubtedly lonely; and loneliness was the mark of a man with a secret in a town where it was never difficult to make friends, and very easy indeed if you had money to spend.

Samir, though, was careful. The various men sent by Rind to follow him home reported after three of his visits that he had given them the slip in the maze of alleyways of the old town. Samir had not yet offered Rind any more gold, but he was clearly a man with something on his mind, so the spy decided to cultivate him.

Samir was quite flattered by the attentions of his affluent friend, and by his suggestion that they might work together, dealing in antiques. Rind was not impressed by a couple of mohurs and besides, he had shown himself to be a fervent anti-communist.

They had many things in common. Samir had spent three years in Narabia with Sirdar Akbar, and Rind spoke Arabic too. He had learned it in Moscow, but he did not mention that to Samir. He spoke with a Gulf accent, which was an added bond.

Rind was biding his time, certain that Samir would invite him to his place of residence one day soon, when the Afghan suddenly forestalled him. It was their mutual knowledge of Arabic which had given him the idea, and the words, prompted by the burden of his responsibility, came tumbling out.

'Mr Rind, you might care to help me with something I am working on. I am afraid that I might fall ill, or have difficulty in carrying it out. It would be wise to have a friend, so important is this matter.'

'My dear friend,' the spy showed his delight with a great smile which Samir took for friendliness, 'I will help you in any way you wish, *ba sar o chashm* – on my head and eyes.'

Whether it was from fear of illness, or the narcotic *charas*, hemp resin, which the Red agent had put in his water-pipe, Samir told the whole story to his new friend: and signed his own death warrant.

The following day Samir was dead, stabbed through the heart in Rind's garage, his body buried in a disused graveyard.

Before he got rid of Samir, Rind had a complete picture of the situation; he knew all about the find of the treasure, and about the target, Prince Jamal. It would be easy to impersonate Samir in the negotiations with the Arab. He even knew about the Swiss bank arrangement: and a letter from Akbar on Samir's body gave the code-word: 'Goldenbird', with which money would be accepted or given out by the bank without any questions. Any guerrilla organization, or KGB man, could draw, when the deal was struck, up to four billion dollars.

Rind would report to Moscow Centre. They would, he was sure, allow the treasure to go to Narabia, since King Zaid would be buying it with his own and other oil states' funds. The USSR would then be heir to the accumulated riches of the Gulf – without having to fire a shot, suborn a leader, or even organize a political party.

It was testimony to the power of Soviet secret police training that Rind dismissed, almost instantly, the temptation to usurp the whole four billion and make it his own. The Russians, as they always boasted, looked after their own; and Rind's chief – the man in Moscow whom they called The Snail – would reward him well. After all, it was the coup of the century: perhaps the greatest coup of all time. Besides, he reflected, the KGB left no operative in doubt as to what happened to traitors.

That same night, the message – a report in detail and his own suggestions for action – went out through the automatic encoder of Rind's special radio hidden in the dusty antiques shop in Peshawar. The radio's dish antenna was directed towards the geostationary satellite of the Soviet *intersputnik* network twenty-two thousand miles above. This relayed west Asian KGB reports to Moscow, transmitting in ultra-short bursts, and operating on randomly changing frequencies. The high-security transmission equipment was a triumph of electronics engineering, next to impossible to locate. The transmissions were so short that nobody would pick them up, the Russians were sure of that. After all, their new *Molniy*, 'lightning', system was an adaptation of the Motorola rig made for the CIA in Scottsdale, Arizona, acquired by the KGB from American infiltration agents captured in Eastern Bloc territory.

BOOK 3

Halzun, the Snail

'My spirit will stay in Afghanistan though my soul will go to God. My last words to you, O my son and successor, are: never trust the Russians.'

King Abdur-Rahman Khan of Afghanistan

1 Nurhan Aliyev, Uzbek Librarian

Tashkent
Uzbek SSR
Soviet Central Asia

MAY 24

Just before midnight, Rind's message reached the high-frequency section of the Communications Special Service Directorate on the fourth floor of the Committee for State Security's building at No 2, Dzerzhinsky Square, Moscow.

The duty cypher officer's eyes widened as he looked at the prefix for the second time: classification 'Total', the highest rating there was. Such a signal must be communicated only to the big man himself, to Halzun, The Snail. And instantly. One 'Total' a year was the average.

The officer lifted a red handset and alerted Highest Circles Liaison: Halzun's number was restricted. Moments later the telephone rang in Halzun's luxurious apartment half a mile away. The Snail listened, then hung up without comment. He stood for a moment, staring straight ahead. Halzun had intuition: a sixth sense born of a lifetime in intelligence. He rang for his car – a gleaming, black-and-silver ZIL Model 4104 monster with a twelve-foot, eight inches wheelbase, the ultimate in Soviet status symbols – and five minutes later was in his own office on the first floor of the KGB headquarters.

The red light went on, above his outer door. Little short of a nuclear war would justify intrusion while that light was on.

At 4.00 a.m. Halzun was still at his desk. He had underlined two lines in Rind's decoded message: 'Request permission to negotiate sale of coins, impersonating representative of Sirdar Akbar.' Beside the single sheet containing the message were

163

three thin files, each with a bright red stripe and a multi-digit Communist Party membership number on the cover.

Over and over he turned the dossiers around in his hands, reading and rereading their contents, seeking inspiration to match the information content; assessing and reassessing his agents' suitability for the task.

Finally, he made his decision, rose, and put the files away carefully in a small filing cabinet. After locking it he attached his personal seal to the drawer, switched off the red light and rang for his secretary.

Night shift secretaries were men, and Halzun studied the expression on the ascetic face of the tall young Ukranian who stood impassively before him. The signal which had brought The Snail into the building in the middle of the night was, he could see, already a matter of office speculation.

'Take a letter, Comrade Sivilskiy,' said Halzun. He dictated briefly. 'Send that to Tashkent, immediately, by air courier. And wait a moment.'

Swiftly he encoded an answer to Rind, in Peshawar: 'Project authorized up to final negotiations with Arab king. But physical delivery of consignment subject to modification as we have a superior plan and am sending representative with full powers to organize transportation phase. HALZUN.'

It was now 5.00 a.m. Halzun sat for a further hour at his desk, thinking about ancient artefacts, about metallurgy, about Ekranoplans: the new Surface Skimmers, which could transport enormous loads for great distances, the Navy's 'war-winners'.

He would get in touch with the people connected with these things later in the day. His modification of Rind's plan was, he knew, a masterpiece.

Two days later Nurhan Nureivich Aliyev, Librarian and Chief Museum Curator, sat at his desk in the mock-oriental building of the Academy of Sciences, Uzbek Soviet Socialist Republic, Tashkent. The title had a fine ring about it, Nurhan had thought, when he was appointed seven years ago: in recognition of all his work in the art of ancient calligraphy. 'A true artist, unsullied by religious superstition', the news item in *Pravda Vostoka* had called him at the time. Most of those who cared about the old arts – poetry, ceramics, manuscripts and miniatures – had died:

after all the Revolution was sixty years ago. Or else they had been polluted by the degenerate values of the oligarchs overthrown by Marxism-Leninism. Now there was a new Uzbekistan, the most progressive of the Central Asian Republics. There was a museum in Samarkand, showing how miserable people's lives had been in the old days. Nurhan was thirty-six, strongly-built and almond-eyed, and intelligent. Yes, he'd made something of himself under socialism. His father had been a camel-driver. Under the old regime Nurhan, too, would have been a camel-driver.

It hadn't all been easy, though. A librarian and curator of the museum had to be a man of the pen and of the book, and a man of the desk. During the first two or three of those seven years, Nurhan had resented the constant ideological training, the military service – and the unarmed combat, the constant testing of those abilities which the Party had decided he possessed and should develop further.

Ultimately, of course, he had come to understand the pattern and had fitted very comfortably into it. First, the KGB sought and found people with talent, young ones. Then they assessed them for other capacities. The latent abilities were brought out, developed, and eventually the many-sided Soviet Man began to appear. They had discovered that he had one unusual and unsuspected skill – that of killing – and when this had been perfected, he had understood the real meaning of achievement, as explained by the Party. 'Once you can do something supremely well, and you can place that at the service of the Great Cause, you will ache to express yourself in the correct way, the Soviet Way of the Party, the People, and World Socialism.' How true the words of the ideologists had been. He could feel the truth of it, enveloping him like a warm cloak on a cold night. The KGB did not waste people: it taught them, trained them, kept their details on file, or sleeping on a computer disk, but ready nonetheless.

And just a few kilometres to the south lay feudal Afghanistan, where some deluded people simply did not understand socialist reality. Until a few years ago the place had actually been a monarchy! Now it was under a socialist government, but only Soviet expertise could tap the real potential of the people, help them modernize and form the link to the Far East; to Pakistan and India, beyond which lay the oil of Arabia and the Gulf. It should not be too hard for the fraternal helpers from the USSR who were now in the country. After all, the Afghan *lingua franca*, Dari, was almost exactly the same language as they spoke on the other side of the Oxus River. And *Pravda Vostoka* had explained, in long articles, how most Afghans were welcoming their liberation and exulting in their freedom.

Today, however, on his desk was a long white envelope, the top left hand corner emblazoned with the emblem of the Soviet Union. He read the words on it, neatly typed in capitals: COMRADE LIBRARIAN NURHAN ALIYEV. URGENT. IMMEDIATE. Below that, in smaller letters, he saw the magic words: 'Central Committee of the Communist Party, *Uzbekskaya Sovyetskaya Sotsialisticheskaya Respublika.*'

It had come. The summons to the office of Comrade Gamidov, the First Secretary.

Nurhan walked across the road, deserted except for the donkeys and buses, each moving as lazily as the other in the summer heat. He climbed the steps of the massive multi-storey building whose architecture he rather liked, although it had been described by a visiting western scholar as being of the 'Brutalist School'. He showed his red-covered, official *propusk*, internal passport, to the sentry at the door. The man saluted and directed him to the porter's window.

'Comrade Aliyev? You are expected. First floor, Room 191.'

Aliyev patted the white dust from his trouser-legs and straightened his tie. In the outer office a pretty secretary in a black dress with a large white collar, properly dressed for administrative work, led him to a large cool room, with a fan whirling in the centre of the ceiling. The First Secretary, a tall man with slant eyes, rose from behind his desk.

'Nurhan! How nice to see you, Comrade. We haven't met since cousin Halide Akhmetova's wedding! What a day that was!' He fished in a box and brought out a huge Upmann Havana cigar. The girl appeared with a silver tray. On it was a bottle of dry *shampanskoya*, the very best, and two glasses.

'Prince Goltisyn established this brand before the Revolution, on his estates in the Crimea,' said Luty Gamidov; 'and the USSR will soon be the largest champagne maker in the whole world.'

'It is an honour to be here, Comrade Gamidov.' Aliyev was, it was true, a distant relative of the First Secretary, but he hardly thought that he merited this kind of reception.

'Socialist, Cuban cigars are the best in the world, like our *Sovyetskaya eekra*, or what foreigners, for some reason, call caviare,' Gamidov went on. 'Soon there will be nothing, even in the West, which we don't have in a better form than anyone else in the world.'

'Yes, Comrade First Secretary.'

'Oh, call me Luty, Nurhan – anyway in private. And don't feel too overwhelmed. I have news for you now, good news: but I am also happy that today I have heard that I am, finally, a Candidate-Member of the Politburo.' He raised his glass.

'Comrade Luty, warmest congratulations to you for a well-deserved promotion and to your continued good health and long life.'

'And to you, with thanks, and to the tireless Toilers of the East.'

They drank, and the secretary brought in another chilled bottle. They must have a huge refrigerator here, Nurhan thought. His own, which he considered quite a prize, was tiny. And always breaking down. 'This comes from the Highest Quarters,' said Gamidov. He held out an envelope, large and grey, with a number stamped on it: Z/22/133S Moscow Centre.

Nurhan took it. The flaps were sealed with red wax. The symbol was not the usual hammer-and-sickle. It looked like a *halzun*, a snail. The Russians, of course, had no letter 'h', unlike the Central Asians, and would call it 'galzun'. Which was why Hamidov, there at the desk, was Gamidov to the ethnic Russians: much as the Nazi monster had to be Adolf Gitler, or Khitler.

And Halzun was the code-name (was it his real name?) of the man at the Foundation for Traditional Arts, near Moscow, for whose message he had been told to wait. Aliyev was a 'home sleeper'. Ordinary sleepers were people sent abroad under deep cover until they were activated at a prearranged command. Nurhan, as a home sleeper, carried on a useful ordinary job in the USSR while he awaited his summons to special duty.

'Ardent revolutionary greetings,' said the First Secretary,

and stood up once more to show that the meeting was at an end. He knew that Aliyev was aching to read his instructions.

The envelope did not give him much information. It contained an Aeroflot one-way ticket to Moscow and a telephone number. The enclosed note, typed on an old-fashioned, manual Cyrillic machine, said only, 'Telephone Halzun on arrival'. Moscow 221-0762 is the number of the central switchboard of the KGB, manned around the clock.

Nurhan Aliyev was on his way.

The big Ilyushin IL-62 jet from Tashkent to Moscow that Thursday morning was crowded with Uzbeks hugging baskets of fruit, bundles of rugs, embroidered hats, slippers and watermelons. One, who called himself Buyuk Shikarchi, The Great Hunter, even had a miniature deer with him. All these things were being taken by the Uzbeks to be sold by their compatriots in the Union capital's free-market stalls. It was not easy to get a permit to live permanently in Moscow, but some of them, perhaps as many as three thousand, had done it. Each one had relatives left behind in Central Asia. There was no barrier to a brief visit to Moscow – one could stay there for up to three days without a permit – and it was safer, much safer, to carry the merchandise oneself from the Uzbek family plot than to entrust it to the State Railways. People travelling by train, or those working on one, had plenty of time on the five-day journey to rifle its cargo. The newspapers even carried reports of whole trains disappearing into thin air.

Nurhan hadn't been to Moscow before. As a good Party man he hoped people there were better socialists than his fellow Central Asians, most of whom had worked out a method of living with communism without actually embracing it. The Uzbek traders were chatting in the aircraft's gangway, lighting up while the *No Smoking* signs were on, and showing general high spirits.

He'd always felt that the Uzbeks were soft and stupid. If they'd been prepared to become nativized, more like the Russians, more of them would have been entrusted with high positions and special missions, not just rural jobs; they would have qualified for work such as The Snail had now undoubtedly prepared for Nurhan Aliyev.

The Uzbeks, Nurhan reflected again, were – like the Georgians, the Azarbaijanis and a dozen other nationalities within the Soviet Union – adapting the system to their own purposes, instead of developing into proper Soviet Men, as they should.

He winced at the sight of his fellow-countrymen, embroidered skullcaps and turbans awry, bargaining and bartering as they sat in the giant jet, a proud achievement of the Revolution, of which they seemed completely uncaring. Because they had tipped the cabin crew lavishly, they thought they owned the aircraft. The banter, flashing of gold teeth, tabla-playing – it was almost scandalous.

They treated Aeroflot like a camel-caravan: a way of transporting their smelly bundles of foodstuffs from one place to another. The cabin crew, according to the Uzbeks, had sold all the in-flight meals to 'speculators' in Tashkent. His compatriots, however, fed Aliyev on cheese, nuts and raisins.

2 The Artefacts Department

MAY 26–30

'Comrade Aliyev? Welcome and warm greetings. I am Halzun.'

The Snail rose from behind his massive desk, ten times more impressive than Gamidov's in Tashkent. A huge man, middle-aged, built like an all-in wrestler with a touch of Tartar in the eyelids, Halzun was dressed in a beautifully cut, undoubtedly foreign, suit. He motioned Nurhan to a comfortable chair, and sat beside him on another. Nurhan noticed that his nails were manicured, and the scent which came in wafts from him must have been bought in Paris. The Grecian statue of an athlete in the corner was of museum quality.

They were sitting in the same first-floor office where two nights before The Snail had burned the midnight oil. *Nachalnik* – Chief Director – Halzun came directly under the Chairman of the whole KGB organization, a post held for many years by Yuri Andropov, later effective dictator of the Soviet Union and a personal friend of Halzun. Aliyev could almost smell the aroma of power. He recalled the statistics from a briefing, years ago, at the training centre in Tashkent: the KGB's budget was three billion dollars a year. It had a hundred and ten fulltime officers controlling – worldwide – literally millions of agents of all grades.

'This is a great honour, Comrade Director. I have waited long for this bright day.'

'You have good references, Nurhan Aliyev. Too many of the Central Asian people are content to let the Russians run this great country of ours, this Federation. It is always a pleasure to meet someone who understands the importance of Marxism-

Leninism, and who can thus contribute to the onward march of history.'

Halzun, Nurhan remembered, was an Eastern word. Comrade Snail himself must be one of the examples of successful Nativization: *Korenizatsiya*, that was the ideal. Individuals chosen from the most promising youth of the ethnic minorities could by this process be admitted – eventually – to 'equality through harmony' with the Slavic Soviet population.

'Comrade Aliyev: you have been selected, as you no doubt realize, for a special and highly important mission.' The Snail gestured to him to take a cup of coffee, an unusual refreshment in modern Russia where the drink is scarcely ever to be seen. He squeezed a quarter lemon into his cup and Nurhan did the same. It tasted foul. Still, coffee was a great luxury. Even people who didn't like it knew that.

'Your training is complete, and has been kept up-to-date. Your mission will involve going to Pakistan and you will have the cover of an Afghan. This is the best possible infiltration policy at the moment. Many Afghans are leaving their country these days.'

'Yes, Comrade Chief Director.' An overseas assignment was almost unbelievable. It was almost like hearing that you were off to the moon. And Halzun had said it just like that, as if people went abroad every day of the week. Next it might be America. The very heart of the capitalist-colonialist enemy. A man could really serve the socialist ideal there. Right in the centre of world imperialist plots . . .

But why were so many people leaving Afghanistan? Nurhan wondered. Surely they were happy that the Soviet Limited Military Contingent had come to help safeguard their Revolution?

The Snail seemed to read his thoughts. 'You understand, Comrade, that the people leaving Afghanistan are only the malcontents, the exploiters and the lackeys of international capitalism. In their dying throes, the members of the ruling circles of Washington and Wall Street excite these people – who may be rich or poor, young or old – and beguile them with the false allure of the façade of their trumpery pretensions.'

Yes, of course. That was it. The Party knew why such things came about. It was scientific historical determinism.

'There is some fighting, of course, against bandits – and the Americans have made much of it. Naturally they have forgotten how much fighting there was in Vietnam.'

The Snail continued: 'So. You will be sent to Afghanistan by military transport. Once in Kabul, however, such is the depth of your cover, you will have to arrange your own *legenda* – story – and documentation. We cannot trust even the Afghan socialist authorities where documents are concerned. Spies are everywhere. If the Americans, for instance, have infiltrated penetration agents into the Kabul records departments your cover could be exposed. For this reason I want you to keep your identity secret even from the Islamabad *Rezident* of the KGB. You may contact him – his name is Zakarov – through the Soviet Embassy in Islamabad, the Pakistan capital, only in circumstances of extreme peril or emergency. And remember, the Pakistan security agencies watch our Islamabad Embassy, even our ambassador, Vitaly Smirnov, like hawks. Nearly a hundred and fifty "legals", agents posing as Soviet diplomats, were expelled by countries around the world in 1983. "Illegals", on the other hand, are hardly ever caught. But only because we warn them as I am warning you.'

'So I am to be an "illegal", Comrade Chief Director?'

'Yes, illegal. That is why your repersonalization, your new identity, must be known only to us, here: Department 8, Directorate S. Even if Rezident Zakarov encounters you, under normal circumstances, in Pakistan, he must not know that you are one of our operatives. And you must also keep away from the Afghan Consulate in Islamabad. Mohammed Hakim Sarboland, the Consul-General, is a traitor to socialism. He has defected. The consulate is believed to be suffering from bourgeois pollution.'

'Understood, Comrade Chief Director.'

'Good. Now, Aliyev, you will be working with a Pakistani firm, in Peshawar, established by us and operating for many years in the antiques field.'

The Snail refilled Nurhan's cup. 'Peshawar is very important to us – and to the West. For Pakistan, it is their most vital frontier town, capital of the North-West Frontier Province, full of ethnic Afghans. It is an ancient Afghan city: indeed, it is the ancestral home of the recently deposed Afghan royal family.'

172

The Snail frowned. 'You may remember the first of May, 1960, over twenty years ago. That was the day when the American spy Francis Gary Powers was shot down, in his U-2 reconnaissance plane, over the Soviet Union, near Sverdlovsk. He got ten years. I saw him myself at both Vladimir and Mordovia prisons . . .' Halzun sat up, very straight, and looked Aliyev full in the eyes. 'Of course, Powers did not have to serve his whole sentence. He was detained for less than two years. That was the time it took to arrange his exchange for our Colonel Rudolf Abel, in Berlin. You see, we always look after our own, Aliyev. You will bear that in mind, won't you?'

There was no mistaking the message: we look after our own. Nurhan nodded. 'Yes, Comrade Chief Director.'

'Good. Now, I was talking about Peshawar. It was from the great American spy-base there that Powers set off on his mission. And we arranged for a magnetized screw to be inserted in the mounting of his aircraft compass: that's how he flew off course, you know. That operation was a triumph of KGB/Peshawar, and there are even better things to come from them.

'Now, as to your own role.' Halzun stretched, and smiled. 'Your specialist knowledge of calligraphy will be of value – inscriptions, writings, lettering on coins. There is a good market for Middle Eastern artefacts throughout the world, and these days especially through the USA, Egypt and Switzerland.'

Aliyev was puzzled. 'But, Comrade Chief Director, Peshawar is a frontier town of intelligence importance in Pakistan. Is it also a centre of the antiques trade?'

The Snail smiled. 'In recent years it has become so. There always was a fair amount of stuff sold there: but now, since the Iran difficulties, and with the influx of Afghan émigrés, some bringing works of art, it has become important. You know, of course, that most of that kind of Islamic material is eventually sold to the Arabs, who have hardly any historical documents or artefacts of their own?'

'Yes, I have heard that, Comrade Chief Director.'

'Very good. You will be given further details, and communications information, by the Special Technical Section. Tomorrow I shall take you to the Arts and Artefacts Department myself, you will find that interesting. I have always found it useful to establish a personal connection with agents, and to make sure that the right feeling is transmitted from the source of direction to all departments with which they will be involved.'

The following morning, having spent the night in the Dnyepr Hotel, where the KGB maintained suites for its senior operatives, Nurhan was taken by limousine, the driver ignoring all traffic signals, to the director's office.

There, after a brief wait, he was joined by The Snail and driven to a large complex of buildings to the north of the city. From outside the place looked like a drab industrial site. Indeed, the sign outside said, in large letters, RED STAR BELT, BUCKLE AND WALLET FACTORY NUMBER 23.

Once inside, Nurhan was at a loss to know how the place might be described. They were welcomed by the Department's director and given drinks in a very beautiful office, decorated with works of art. Then, in a lightning tour, Aliyev was shown where perfect replicas of priceless ikons were made; the furnaces and the forges working on bronze and other statuary; the air-conditioned studios where master calligraphers were producing documents and books which had all the appearance of being centuries old.

'Of course, comrades,' the director was saying, 'the East Germans have a forgery factory, too, in Prussia. But we pride ourselves that we are better. After all, the German centre is well known in the West – some of its work has been identified by museums and dealers. But we have no record of work produced *here* ever having been traced back to the Soviet Union.'

'What is the purpose of the activity, Comrade Director?'

'It came about through the marriage of two factors. Originally, State Security concentrated on exports of ordinary items – chairs, toys, chess sets, radios and so on – made in the Corrective Labour colonies. Four million people still work in our camps. Currently these products earn fifteen billion dollars a year from sales to the European Community alone. The capitalist West screams about cheap labour, but is glad to shut its eyes when there is a bargain to be had.

'Plentiful and cheap, sometimes specialized, labour was the first element. Then there is the Third Special Section of the KGB: Illegal Documentation. This is devoted to the manufacture of foreign passports, the forging of identity documents,

174

share certificates, anything for use by our operatives in the West.

'Over and over again our agents in the West reported the great demand there for works of art, initially used by our people as bribes. Put the two together: talent and artworks – and you have a major earner of hard currency. It contributes to the USSR's budget: and it helps in the funding of the KGB itself.'

What a brilliant idea! Nurhan was impressed; and he became even more so as he looked at examples of his own specialities. There were Islamic ceramics, and metal or enamelled plates and ewers from the Seljuk, Ottoman, Mogul, Egyptian Fatimite and Abbasid periods. Even to his expert eye they could well have been made in Isfahan, in Kuthaya, in Bokhara, in India.

'But surely some of these can be detected as replicas?'

The director smiled. 'Yes, some of them, but the vast majority cannot. We have outlets and individuals to supply what collectors like to call 'provenance'. As long as a piece has what seems to be a good history, it is seldom given sophisticated scientific tests. Naturally, things sometimes go wrong. Recently, a lot of supposed Islamic artefacts, exhibited in Japan, were found to be false. But, since they were only traced as far as Iran, everyone thinks that they were forged there. In fact, we had infiltrated them into Iran through our southern borders, by way of Azarbaijan. The confusion of the Khomeini regime actually helps in this, along with the fact that the Iranians are desperate for money for their war with Iraq, and ask few questions.'

'So the Iranians co-operate, in spite of the hostility of their regime to the Soviet Union?'

'My dear Comrade Aliyev!' the director laughed, 'the Devil himself would co-operate with us, or anyone else, if there were enough money in it. In your specialist field alone – manuscripts – we have developed the market so thoroughly that everyone seems to be imitating us. It is my opinion that our success even stimulated that man in West Germany to forge the so-called Hitler Diaries recently.'

'And the outlets?'

'They vary, from reputable – or greedy – businessmen in Switzerland to unwary dealers in Cairo or Damascus. Our agents in the Islamic and eastern countries have been able to plant many a priceless artefact where its presence alone is thought to be its own provenance.'

'Why,' the director giggled at the memory, 'even the Hermitage Museum in Leningrad tried to buy one of our Central Asian pots "from the time of Tamerlane", which was on offer in India, until we stopped them.

'Metal,' he continued, 'is our speciality. As you know, you can't date it at all by scientific methods, unless you analyse the metal content of an alloy. Then, if it is of a different composition from that traditionally used in a certain place or at a specific time, it becomes suspect. Our solution: we simply imitate the formula of the original alloy – brass, copper, silver, gold. That defies even spectroscopic analysis.'

'What about artefacts still being produced: are they always of poor quality? Much of the stuff we get in our own Bokhara or Samarkand is really appalling.'

The director rubbed his hands. 'That is another branch of a fascinating subject. We obtain "Roman" glass from the small workshops of Damascus, and "ancient clay lamps" from the potters of Iraq, which are no different from the real thing. The art has not died out. Nobody can tell the difference. Pottery, ceramics or glass, like metal, can't be carbon dated.'

Back in The Snail's office, Nurhan was handed the report from Rind at KGB/Peshawar, and told to digest it thoroughly. Gradually the whole fantastic plot came alive for him.

'You are to take local charge of this operation, Aliyev,' The Snail said; 'and supervise Rind when he meets the Narabian prince. Jamal is to think that he is dealing with Sirdar Akbar's people.'

'You have captured Akbar's network, Comrade Chief Director, I can see that,' said Aliyev; 'but what about getting the gold out? The transport alone is a major operation even without the security aspect.'

'First,' said The Snail, 'we shall take the treasure away to a safe place. Don't worry about that. Your task is to get the coins to Narabia, in accordance with our instructions. As for Akbar, he is under close supervision. There is no chance that he will be able to communicate with the Arabs.'

'Then why not kill him?'

'Simply because he may be more useful alive. We may need

him, to "authenticate" something, perhaps a message to the Arab king. He is to stay alive, if possible, until the transaction is complete. After that, it doesn't matter.'

'Understood, Comrade Chief Director. And are there any special instructions about this Peshawar *Rezident*, Rind?'

'You shall never forget for a moment that, together with you, he possesses knowledge which can make or break this operation. Keep him on the tightest possible leash.'

'I understand.'

'And remember, Nurhan Nureivich, this matter is one which is to be dealt with by this office only, and by me personally. Nobody else, even in the KGB, is to be involved at any stage.'

'Fully understood, Comrade Chief Director.'

It was now time to put other wheels into operation. As soon as Nurhan Aliyev had bowed his way out of the office, Halzun reached for the telephone. He dialled 206-2511, the Moscow number of the all-powerful Central Committee of the Communist Party of the USSR. When Extension 5-5191 answered, he said, 'Halzun to Network A: activate Plan Goldenbird.'

Nurhan spent the next few days studying every aspect of The Snail's remarkable undertaking, and the many special briefings which would prepare him for his mission. At the Balashika, Department Eight's training complex fifteen miles east of the Moscow ring road, they seemed to know every detail of life in Pakistan and Afghanistan.

The night before he was to leave Moscow, his colleagues from Directorate S gave him the customary farewell party, at one of Moscow's best restaurants: the Uzbekistan. He was touched by their comradeship, the warmth of their concern for him, and their dedication to their 'life task', as the KGB called it. None asked any details of his mission.

The Uzbek found himself at Moscow Airport the following morning, dressed in military uniform, with a ticket and papers identifying him as Anis Madrunovich Urokov, rank *serzhant*, assigned to Afghanistan for 'linguistic duties'.

As he walked to the check-in desk he heard a voice and saw an attractive, blonde woman-member of the Aeroflot ground-staff standing beside a pillar, smiling at him.

'This way, please, *gospodin* Major.'

Nurhan frowned. He had indeed been promoted to major: the day before, in fact. But this was either a trick or a very serious failure of security.

'*Niet*. You are looking for someone else. I am Sergeant Urokov . . .'

The girl in the trim blue uniform nodded pleasantly and came closer. 'Well done, Comrade. Just a check.'

'*Spasiba*, thank you.'

'*Pazhalsta*, not at all.'

He felt himself swelling with pride. They were testing him to keep him alert, so that he would not make mistakes under active conditions. People told tales of the chivalric knights of long ago. They were mere exploiters. But this, the KGB service, this was a true elite.

The Uzbek checked in and sat down in the departure lounge to wait for his flight. Aeroflot never announced delays or cancellations, so it might be several hours before the next flight to Tashkent, although it was scheduled for departure in thirty minutes' time.

He was inhaling deeply on his fifth unfiltered Byelamor cigarette when a bent old *babushka*, wielding a brush and clucking at him for spilling ash all over her marble floor, spoke into his ear.

'Comrade, there is much temptation, in the outside world, to be seduced by capitalism. Some have succumbed. Just remember that, just as I could kill you now, you would never be safe if you deserted. Your closest Western friend, or your American debriefing officer, could well be a *Chekist*.' It took all Nurhan's training not to goggle at her. The thought of defection had never occurred to him; but now he saw very plainly – and was glad – that for traitors there was never any real escape.

The crone held her hand over his head as if in blessing, gave him her own version of a friendly smile, and limped away, wiping her nose on her sleeve.

A *Chekist*. The KGB used to be called the *Cheka*, and the half-million present-day members still used this term for one another. Again the feeling of pride came to Nurhan. His organization left nothing to chance. After all, if he had had any ideas about deserting to the capitalists, this experience would have straightened him out. The Committee for State Security was, in reality, a fatherly entity. He doubted whether, even for the rich, the capitalist West had anything equivalent, any strong reassuring sense of communion, to offer its elite.

3 A Passport for Tezbin, Carpenter

Moscow/Kabul

JUNE 2–11

Nurhan Aliyev flew to the huge Bagram Airbase near Kabul, in one of the great Antonovs of the air bridge which shuttled between Logistics Command near Termez in the USSR and the Afghan capital. The KGB, he noted with admiration, had drilled him perfectly and had avoided giving him any special facilities.

As a sergeant he had some privileges; better gruel than the men and an inflatable mattress instead of straw. But he still had to line up for hours at a time: first to board the transport and then for his documents to be processed at his destination. But none of the real sergeants seemed to realize that he had been 'in the army' for no longer than three days. The crash-training was perfect.

At Bagram his movement order was stamped and he was assigned a place in a military truck for Kabul. Once there, he was decanted, still in uniform, at the Pul-i-Khishti Bridge. It was exactly as it had been described at the Balashika Training Centre. It took him only half an hour to part-exchange his uniform, for two hundred *afghanis* and a shabby civilian outfit, with one of the Afghan old-clothes men standing there. At first the sight of so many Soviet soldiers selling equipment unmolested puzzled him, but the Afghan hawkers obviously regarded it as normal. They showed no suspicion about him which, in present circumstances, was all that mattered.

Still, all those Soviet soldiers, peddling things in the street . . . The Uzbek was looking too closely at one young conscript, who mistook his attention for customer interest. He called out to Nurhan in broken Dari, brandishing an army belt.

'*Pryazhka*, buckle, friend?' Nurhan shook his head. The soldier turned to a man with a basket, 'Two eggs for belt and buckle? Have you *frukt*, fruit? Give me *tabak*, tobacco . . .'

Another member of the Fraternal Limited Contingent sidled up to Aliyev, opening his greatcoat to show a pair of excellent army field-glasses. '*Binok, binok*, see far with *binok*, Afghanski?' A tall Pashtun glimpsed the glasses and pushed forward.

'*Militar – armiya –* are they military, from the army?'

'*Da, da! Ookraddyenniy –* stolen!' He added, to Aliyev's amazement, '*Soovyeneer*, souvenir.'

This could not really be true: the gallant, all-conquering troops of the Soviet Red Army selling equipment, desperate for eggs and tobacco. And the KGB's secret centre, Balashika, instructing Nurhan to trade there. The Uzbek concentrated hard, until the explanation came to him. Of course: they were all agents. Very clever; the Army had obviously sent them out to trap black marketeers. No doubt all these thieving Afghans would soon be behind bars. Nurhan felt better now, and decided to have a cup of tea.

Not far from the bridge he found a small café, and sat down beside the huge samovar. At the same table was a Russian private, talking to the café's owner in fairly good Dari. 'Not only are we badly fed, hungry, but the officers have stolen all the vodka that was supposed to be stored for the Great October Revolution celebrations on 7 and 8 November, five months away. That's why we are trying to get a little money in, tovarish . . .' Nurhan closed his eyes. This was palpable nonsense. Everyone knew that the men were well fed in the army, and that the officers were good men. Obviously he was another *agent provocateur*, entrapping a suspect. The soldier seemed to be overplaying his part, but perhaps it was because the Afghans were unsubtle, stupid . . .

The café proprietor gave the man a hundred *afghanis* and took a handful of what looked like Kalashnikov cartridges from him. When the soldier had gone, he looked at Nurhan, shrugged, and started to talk. 'They're getting worried, friend. They haven't got over the matter of the poster yet, and that was three days ago!'

'The poster? What poster?'

'If you haven't heard, you're the only person in Kabul who hasn't. Where have you been?'

Nurhan spread his arms. 'I've just arrived from the north, looking for work.'

'Ah, that explains it. But the poster was one of the funniest things in years. Want to hear about it?'

'Yes.'

The Afghan sat down opposite him. 'Well, four days ago a *shabnama*, a clandestine leaflet, came out. It said "*When you see a Nikolai vehicle with several men in it, shout the following phrase, which is Russian for 'you can't park here'. They may not understand your accent, so throw a grenade inside, and they'll get the point of the joke!*"'

The Kabuli tittered, then shook with laughter, wiping the tears from his eyes. Very crude, an incitement to terrorism, Nurhan thought. Not even funny. But he remained silent.

'Now, my friend, comes the good part,' the man continued. 'Because one of the leaflets fell into the hands of Nikolai GRU, Army Intelligence, their counter-atack was to put up posters all over Kabul saying: "*It is forbidden to tell any Soviet soldier that he must not park his vehicle!*" Everyone wanted to know what it meant, and so those who had seen the *shabnama* told those who hadn't! The funniest thing for years.' He slapped his thigh and went over to the samovar to get Nurhan another cup of tea. 'Here, northerner, have this one on me!'

He took a crumpled piece of poor quality paper, evidently the leaflet, from his pocket and read out: '"*Zdrastvoytye* – hello in Russian".' Then : '"*Stayanka zdyes zapryeshena* – you can't park here!"' He was almost helpless with laughter now.

Nurhan threw some money on the table and walked out. He didn't want to be found here when the police raided the place. Word would surely soon get around that there was a capitalist-imperialist agent and agitator running a teahouse in this area . . .

Following the Kabul River upstream, Nurhan saw a knot of youths twenty yards ahead, dressed, as he now was, in baggy trousers and waistcoats over long shirts. They might direct him to a lodging house. As he came closer to them, he noticed that they were carrying guns. They looked arrogantly at him as he came abreast, and one of them spat. As if in answer to his unspoken question, one of them shouted 'Guardians of the Socialist Revolution! The Militia of the Fatherland Front!'

He wrinkled his nose. Undisciplined, dirty, jeering, disorderly. That was no way for a true socialist to behave. Still, there had been a saying in the old days, during the forced collectivization. 'The road to paradise must first pass through hell.' He passed his ideological brethren with face averted.

The street widened, and Nurhan stopped to buy a mutton *kabob* from a street-vendor.

'Brother, I'm from Turkestan, looking for work.'

'*Aw*. Yes.' The skinny imp presiding over the charcoal took the five *afghani* piece and tested it with his teeth before dropping it into his sleeve pocket.

'Where can I find somewhere to stay, a bed?'

'First on the right, you'll see a huge modern avenue, Jady Maiwand. Walk right down it. Don't be misled by the big shops. Behind them is a warren of streets. They're full of doss-houses.'

It certainly was a warren: a part of old Kabul built by minority Shia sectarians as much for defence against their orthodox Sunni neighbours as anything else. They would welcome one of their own. Nurhan stopped at a dilapidated building made of adobe, obviously a rooming-house, and noted with satisfaction the spray-painted slogan on the wall: 'Long live Ali the Martyr, murdered by the Sunni dogs!'

Inside the door, a man sat on a prayer-mat. Beside him was a clod of earth on a tray – a souvenir from the Holy City of Kerbala, ready for his forehead to touch in prostration.

Nurhan took off his worn shoes. With a piece of chalk which he picked up from the rickety table, he wrote on the leather soles the names of the first two Caliphs of Islam: Abu-Bakr, Omar. Many Shias liked to walk upon the names of those they considered usurpers. It was as good as a password.

The hook-nosed landlord grinned and held out his hand. 'Welcome.'

'I'm from the north. Need a room.'

'No rooms. Got a bed. Good clean straw.'

'*Kho*. Good. How much?'

'Twenty *afghanis* a night.'

'Give you ten.'

'*Kho*. Three nights in advance.'

'Here you are.'

'*Namit* – thy name?'

'*Kalb-i-Ali*, Dog of Ali, Turkestani.'

'*Kho*.' The man spat out a stream of tobacco juice.

The house had held a dozen transients, small artisans for the most part, looking for work in the capital. In a dirty first-floor room they lay on straw palliasses, each with its chalk lines to mark the individual's territory. The place reeked of goat, mingled with the smell from a tannery somewhere deeper down the alleyway.

The Uzbek soon made friends with a carpenter, Murtaza Tezbin, from Andkhoi in the Afghan north, also a Turkestani. Nurhan, according to his cover-story, came from Khanabad, hundreds of miles to the east of Tezbin's village, so they would have no mutual friends.

Tezbin, with little prompting, told Nurhan a mass of details about his family and home town. His ambition was to find a job as a carpenter in the big city.

After several days of this friendship, when he thought that he knew enough, Nurhan suggested a walk to a place he had already marked down as suitable. There he killed Tezbin – with a single blow, as he had been taught. He disposed of the body in a deep but dried-up well beside the ruined house where the two of them had sat down to talk.

Armed now with the carpenter's papers, Aliyev went to the passport office, whose procedures he knew from reading a study made by KGB agents. It was in the Ministry of the Interior, and the process was simplicity itself.

He studied the form. No criminal convictions. No political record. Yes, he had the deposit against his 'behaviour when abroad' – Tezbin's life savings alone would more than cover it, and they were in cash. Confirmation of his identity from his local police or gendarmerie office? That was something else . . .

The clerk at the hatch was in no hurry. 'We'll send it to Andkhoi by post. Come back in about a month.'

A month. Far too long. 'Respected sir, that is a long time.'

The shabby Kabuli took a pinch of snuff, sensing a bribe. After all, the man had cash . . .

'Haste comes from the Devil.' Clerks were full of these tags, they used them as a substitute for education.

'Mr Chief Clerk. I want to go to Pakistan . . .'

'Everyone wants to go to Pakistan.'

'But sir, I beg to say, there is work for me there.'

'They all say that. All the Pakistanis have gone to the Gulf oil countries to work, and ragamuffins like you have taken their jobs.'

'Sir, I have friends and relatives in Pakistan – they can get me work, but I have to go very soon, or they'll find someone else.'

'Well, what do you want me to do, *Jan-i-Masum*, by the life of the Immaculate One? I am a man of importance, I can't spend all day with you, Turkestani loafer!'

'Anything which your wisdom indicates.'

'Listen. I have two jobs. When I am finished here, in the afternoon, I have to go all the way to Parwan for my second job, and stay there late into the night.'

'Yes.'

'Why, four hundred *afghanis* wouldn't compensate me for staying in here and contacting your local police by telephone. And the bandits may have torn the lines down again.' He looked the Uzbek straight in the eyes.

'*Sarkatib seb*, I'll have five hundred left after the deposit. As I would be going to a good job, you are welcome to four hundred.'

The man held out his hand, and Aliyev gave him the money. In two minutes the clerk, in a better humour, was speaking to the chief of police at Andkhoi.

'Forgive the trouble, Komondon. Ministry of the Interior here, Passport Department. Could you please check the details of an applicant? Registration book AND-7797/J. Name Tezbin. Yes, he's over forty, so he has a conscription deferment card. Thank you.'

He held his hand over the mouthpiece and turned to the Uzbek, anxious to share his triumph. 'He's checking. A police major, actually doing it himself! But they always jump to it when we call them. We're Kabul, the capital, to these provincials, and the police come under this Ministry. I may be only a passport clerk, but Major Fuzul up there doesn't know where the query originated. It might even be from the Minister himself . . . Here he is now.'

He puckered his face as if that would help him pick up the voice from Andkhoi above the crackling on the line.

'Yes. Turkic stock, black eyes, wheat-coloured face, no pock-marks. Has he people there? Good. Then they could be guarantors for his political reliability? Fine. You'll confirm by mail? Thank you, Major, so long.' He deliberately used an over-familiar manner.

'There you are, Mr Tezbin. I'll just make out your passport for you.'

Ten minutes later, the booklet was ready, proving that Nurhan was not only Murtaza Tezbin, Carpenter, but that he was a citizen of the Democratic Republic of Afghanistan. The passport officer was in an expansive mood now.

'Mr Tezbin, I feel that we are now old friends, and I'll prove it by giving you a piece of advice that is worth more than the passport.'

Nurhan bowed. 'Thank you, sir.'

'It's about how to avoid conscription.'

'I'm over age, and besides I have a deferment card to prove it: here it is, see, "Murtaza Tezbin, not liable . . ."'

The clerk laughed. 'Things must be ordered better in the north, you poor thing! Haven't you heard of a snatch-squad? They have quotas, they've got to get so many men a day for the New Democratic Army. They range the streets and shanghai anyone they can find who isn't deaf, dumb and blind!'

'But the deferment . . .'

'They ask for your papers. They love deferment cards: soon as they see one, they tear it up and puff! You're in the back of the truck. The whole of the original army has deserted to the terrorists. Your country needs you. For the New Democratic Order.'

What a way for his mission to end . . . Nurhan grabbed the man's sleeve. 'What do I do?'

'Find out the time of the bus you're taking to Pakistan, and stay indoors until it's nearly time for it to leave. Then go straight to the bus station and get aboard, that's what you do. Even then, the *pishkis*, conscription squads, may waylay the bus. If they do, give them all your money and they'll let you go – until the next time. It's easy.'

Taking a bus down the A-1, the American-built road from

Kabul to Peshawar was easy, too. The passengers sang a song based on the ancient classic, *The Lights of Canopus*. Nurhan joined in the chorus, although the underlying meaning, which delighted the others, escaped him:

'Thy foe was but an ant – a serpent now is he!
And on this ant-turned-serpent take sure vengeance now!
For this snake will else a mighty dragon be:
If you, through delay, him to live allow . . .'

The Pakistani border guards were lenient. They glanced at the Uzbek's new Afghan passport but did not object – if they noticed – that he had no visa. The Balashika briefing officers were up-to-date on Pakistani immigration procedures, as on everything else.

That afternoon, in the back room of the antiques shop which was now his headquarters, Nurhan applied his calligrapher's skill. It was easy to change, with two strokes of a pen and a razor blade, his passport description. *Najjar*, Carpenter, had become *Tajir*, Merchant.

Aliyev smiled with satisfaction. Prince Jamal, son of Zaid, would soon be here, walking into the trap.

BOOK 4

Hail Jamal, Son of Zaid!

Mulla Nasrudin went to the office of the People's Democratic Party. He asked the man at the information desk:

'Where is Comrade Amin, our first Socialist leader?'

'He's dead, Comrade.'

'And where, Comrade information officer, is Comrade Chairman Tariki, our second Socialist leader?'

'He's dead, too, Comrade.'

'And our fraternal Russian KGB chief, General Viktor Paputin?'

'Dead. But why are you asking all these questions?'

'Because, Comrade, I do so enjoy hearing the answers!'

Night Letter of Mazar, Occupied Afghanistan

1 'This is your mission Jamal . . .'

The Airport
Hadiqa City
Narabia
Arabian Gulf

JUNE 12

There were over a hundred Cadillacs, 'stretched' Mercedes limousines, bullet-proof Rolls Royces and Range Rovers with special bodies parked on the tarmac, as Prince Jamal drove up to his private 707. The turnout might have been larger. Everyone knew that one always saw off and greeted one's relatives, fellow members of the Royal Family. On the other hand, Jamal had had more than his share of it himself, turning up at all hours of the day and night, driving hell for leather to the huge airport from the capital along the kingdom's beautiful, but only, eight-lane highway. It was almost obligatory to kiss the hand of Uncle this and Aunt that, or Cousin someone, as they returned, often reluctantly, from Europe or America, where the need for urgent medical attention so often took them. Especially in the dreadful summer heat of Hadiqa City, when a cooler West beckoned.

He stamped on the brake-pedal and opened the doors of his favourite Ferrari, a 512 BB, by pressing a single button. Tawfik, his secretary, tumbled out of the passenger seat, his stocky form cramped, the flabby face twitching with fear. Prince Jamal liked to cover the twenty-four miles in twelve minutes. The stupid but useful little man actually panted with distress when Jamal played little games to worry him, like ostentatiously painting over the speedometer. After all, flat out the car could do a hundred and seventy-two miles an hour. The fastest of its kind in the world.

Jamal tossed the car keys to Snowflake, one of the Nubian slaves, and smiled at the respectful throng.

The usual, practised cry – signalling either welcome or farewell – went up from the assorted millionaires, princes, princesses and Bedouin chiefs, the hangers-on, servants and drivers who were clustered at the foot of the embarkation steps. Jamal waved to them, and turned as Tawfik tugged his sleeve to draw attention to the guard of honour which he had to inspect, to the strains of the national ode.

The Narabian colonel, black-bearded and beetle-browed, with naked sword held upright, escorted Jamal back to the steps as the women in the crowd started their shrill ululation, the *walwala*, as indispensable as a salute in the East as carols at Christmas in the West. Jamal silenced them with an upraised hand, and spoke: '*Sidi Aqid!* Colonel, brethren! I go in the service of the Nation. *Allah ma Narabia!* God be with Narabia.' This was the formula, which never failed to produce a tear. It had been provided, at very great expense, following a million-dollar study by a top Madison Avenue public relations firm; as was, too, the statutory answer, equally moving to the hearts of the people: 'God be with you, too, Our Lord Jamal. Long life to Jamal, Son of Zaid, the Narabian!'

Jamal paused for the photographer of the *Narabian Times*, after Tawfik had adjusted the gold circlets of his *agal*, and twitched the *kaffia* headcloth so that it formed a tiny peak, the sign of a prince, at the hairline. They went into the aircraft and the door, with its golden crescent moon and black scimitar emblem, banged shut.

Over the Arabian Sea, heading for Pakistan, Jamal took off his robe, belt and jewelled dagger. He felt better in the Savile Row suit, of specially woven white sharkskin cloth. Educated in the West, virtually brought up there, he liked to think of himself as a citizen of the world and a son of Narabia. And his public school in England, rounded off by Oxford, had certainly sharpened his mind.

Time for a conference. He admired what the papers called his lithe form and hawklike features briefly in the full-length bathroom mirror, and called the others: the secretary Tawfik, Court Minister Hafiz and the Military Adviser, Colonel Yahia ibn Yusuf (Eton and Sandhurst) to the conference table in the main lounge, the Diwan, of the great aircraft.

'History of Afghanistan, please, Tawfik.'

The secretary rustled a piece of paper. 'Size of Texas, Highness, mountainous, shaped like an oakleaf, wedged between China, Iran, the USSR and Pakistan, which latter was formerly part of India. Fierce independent people, ninety-five per cent Moslems. Part of the ancient Arab conquests under Caliph Haroun El Rashid. The British and Russians have vied with each other to gain power over it for a hundred and fifty years. The British called this struggle "The Great Game". Live Long, Highness.'

'Thank you. How about the Russian invasion?'

'Ten years ago, Prince Daud sent his cousin the King into exile and set up a dictatorship. The government, then as now, only controlled the towns. Life continued as before, mostly under feudal chiefs, mostly tribal. Five years ago a band of malcontents, mainly half-educated communists, seized power, killing dictator Daud. Successive Red administrations, if you can call them that, followed up to end 1979, December 27, when – sliding into anarchy – the terrified Reds called in the "fraternal Russians".'

The Prince said, 'How did the governments change, one after another?'

'Just by one party boss killing another. Daud, the republican prince, was killed by the communist Taraki, then Amin killed Taraki and became boss. He then called in the Russians, and their puppet, Karmal, killed him.'

'And Karmal is still in power?'

'Yes. His faction had Amin smothered with a cushion, and gave out that he'd died of "galloping diabetes", suddenly, during the invasion.'

'That seemed to bring things up to date. But how about the guerrilla war? Colonel, what are the military implications of the Russian presence?'

'May the Emir's life be extended!' Colonel Yahia stroked his neat beard and inclined his long head. He looked regimental, even in civilian clothes. 'With a strong military and guerrilla tradition, Highness, the Afghans are not like their neighbours. Everyone is regarded as a soldier. The Russian Army's objective is to secure the country as a base for further expansion, and to open the way to India. They have at least 105,000 troops in place; one airborne and six motorized rifle divisions, plus tank divisions, but this is not enough. Against that, the Pashtun Durrani tribe alone can put almost a quarter of a million fighting men into the field, if properly armed.'

Quite a copybook soldier. He spoke in clipped sentences, but had done his homework.

But Jamal wanted to know the present situation. 'Sidi Aqid Yahia! What's happening now?'

'The people, Highness, have been subjected to devastating attacks by heliships and airborne commandos. Most of the old regular Afghan Army has joined the rebels, in the mountains, which form the major part of the land surface. All the larger towns have had uprisings from time to time. The best intelligence estimates are that the Russians have lost 10,000 men and four hundred aircraft – some of the most modern in the world – felled by guns and missiles, captured by the rebels from the Russians. The puppet government reckons the damage done by guerrillas to their installations and facilities at four to five hundred million dollars, and have announced that officially.'

'Can the rebels hold out: could they even win?'

'Highness, they are learning. But the Russians are learning, too. There are reports, for instance, of some Soviet forces being sent out disguised as rebels, operating in the mountains against the Muhjahidin. Nobody can yet say what the outcome will be. The guerrillas are fighting, in widely separate groups, under local commanders. They are unlikely ever to combine into a single movement. This is because of the nature of the terrain and the fact that they are of many different ethnic stocks. It also means they can't be easily crushed.'

'Are they getting any outside help?'

'The Russians and the communist regime claim, of course, that they are. They can hardly admit that the ordinary people are fighting for freedom and have few arms. So they blame Egypt, China, Pakistan and the United States. In fact, such aid is minimal, if, indeed, there is any at all.'

'And the refugees?'

'Driven out by bombing and terrorism, their fields are barren, deliberately devastated. There are nearly four million refugees.

There are two hundred and eighty camps in the Pakistan border area alone. Refugee support costs over one million dollars a day, for bare subsistence. Half of the cost is met by Pakistan, a poor country, in a magnificent effort. Half comes from international agencies, and hundreds of millions from Islamic countries.'

'The Western response?'

'Much shouting, Highness, anti-communist rhetoric. Dutiful printing in their press of the fact that five thousand people a day, two million a year, are fleeing from terror attacks . . .'

'"Verily, when God seeks the downfall of a man, he first makes him blind!"' the Prince quoted.

'Eminent Highness!' It was the suave, courtly Minister.

'Speak, Alim Hafiz.'

'You have honoured me. The situation, may my words find agreement from you who know better,' Hafiz could not cure a lifetime habit of flowery speech, 'the situation is complicated and, may it find favour, needs close attention.'

The Prince was getting bored. 'You are a learned man and speak well, but I need facts, and I want to sleep.'

'May I be the sacrifice for the life of His Royal Highness!' The Alim started his compliments again, but caught himself just in time. 'The facts are these: although called in by a minority government which only came to power by coup and murder, the Russian presence is legal. Any sovereign state can call in troops from anyone else.'

'Even to butcher their own people?'

'Regrettably, yes. That is the state of international law, the legal basis. It explains how the Soviets keep their hold on their satellites: Poland, Czechoslovaia, and so on. But to continue. This means that we can't easily denounce the communists.'

'Right.'

'It also means that Your Royal Highness will have to be careful in making contacts with political figures of the Resistance. There are several groups of them with offices in Pakistan. Added to this, some may be – probably are – penetrated by Red agents. Nobody can be sure.'

'I see. Now, what are the rebels called?'

'*Muhjahid* is the name of the warriors: "Struggler". Traditionally it is translated in the West as Holy Warrior, like the

Crusaders of the old days. The plural is Muhjahidin. News commentators from abroad think that Muhjahidin is the singular, though.'

'Thank you, Alim, perhaps we are getting a little too detailed. "Speech short and work long", isn't that the proverb?'

'Your Royal Highness's patience had emboldened your loquacious subjects to prolong their ramblings, my Lord . . .'

'So, *I'm* to blame for what you do, is that it?' Jamal liked to make the courtier cringe, because he was more than a little annoying, even if he had a crafty brain.

Jamal addressed the whole group. 'His Majesty has sent us on a special mission. Overtly, I am going to Pakistan to visit the refugee camps, to bring some comfort to three and a half million of our brothers and sisters. I shall be touring the camps in the Peshawar area. In one sense, however, I am your cover. You will collect all possible military and political information, to enable the Throne to decide how to deal with the Russian threat. Make sure that you do your utmost. Our survival may depend upon it.'

All nodded. The meeting over, Prince Jamal retired to the luxurious bedroom and slept, to be fresh for his reception in Pakistan.

2 Highness, I am Samir, servant of Akbar

Peshawar
North-West Frontier
Pakistan

JUNE 13–17

Prince Jamal, staying at the luxurious Peshawar Intercontinental Hotel, went out daily to see the refugees in their camps a dozen miles away. He was not well prepared for the horror of it. Three and a half million people, mostly women and children, the survivors of relentless bombing raids whose purpose was to drive them into destitution, make their land barren, and deny refuge, food and cover to the patriots who still fought in the mountains. He saw people without eyes, with shattered limbs, lacking medical help and sometimes even food.

But he also saw a proud people who, when he stood in the back of his Land Rover throwing them hundred-dollar bills, cried: 'Prince of Arabia! Give us guns!' And as he watched, astonished, while the ragged multitude ignored the money and still called for guns, the reporters and photographers, some from highly reputable news media, already earning huge salaries, fought each other for the fluttering notes. Are we all mad? he thought, were we born for this, is the whole world insane?

Jamal sat down on the hard bench in the back of the open-top Land Rover, neat packets of banknotes beside him, the shouts of the people ringing in his ears.

A towering Pashtun, who had walked for twelve days through the mountains from the northern battlefields of Afghanistan, fought off the armed police and jumped onto the vehicle. There was practically no flesh on his bones, and he was dressed in rags. His eyes burned red as he sat down beside the Prince.

The policeman sitting opposite Jamal struck out at the newcomer with a *lathi*, a brass-bound stave. The hillman seized it, broke it in two, and gave the Pakistani three strokes over the shoulders. The little sergeant screamed with pain and rage and drew his gun.

'Stop that,' said Jamal, and the policeman subsided into a sullen heap.

The Land Rover continued its slow progression as the Pashtun spoke.

'Son of a King! Your ancestors and ours fought side by side on the battlefield and they won their wars. Today, people who call themselves our leaders sit on silken cushions and beg from you, who skulk in your marble palaces, afraid to fight. We, the fighters, go without.

'Son of an Arab! The weak, the women, the children, are tortured and dying because of your neglect! God will requite you! Show me your palm.'

Jamal, without knowing why, held out his hand. The Pashtun looked at it, as if reading the lines.

'O Prince, whose ancestors were eaters of desert locusts and became noblemen: you will become dirt!

'What a beautiful, what a soft hand, O Prince! How sad to realize that one day, perhaps soon, it will burn in hell!'

Jamal shuddered. The man was right. The Arabs were full of talk and sometimes handed out money – but often to the wrong people and usually because they did not want to be thought stingy. The Kuwait and Saudi clinics serving the camps were good, but small. The Pashtun was talking again.

'Prince of the Arabs! You have thousands of young Emirs, princes, and wonderful weapons, the best. We are fighting with our bare hands, in the freezing mountains and scorching deserts. We are starving while you are overfed. We sleep on rocks and you doze in satin. If one, only one, of your princes were to come to us, to fight side by side, it would say more to the world, and to our people, than a thousand of your majestic visits!

'Don't put it out of your mind, noble Arab!'

Jamal's orders, from his father, the King, were to see and to be seen, while his entourage collected the information which the old man needed. The refugee question was – not secondary, exactly: after all, he had brought money to hand out, and to give the people at least some hope. There was little that an individual could do. Surely it was mainly a political problem, surely one should not get too involved with distress which one could not remove? The United Nations Refugee High Commission was swamped by the problem; so was Pakistan, so were the International Red Cross and the other agencies. Dr Bruttin, the IRC surgeon, was at full stretch, doing seven amputations a day.

At another camp, Prince Jamal raised his camera to take a picture of a group of children when they screamed in terror and ran away, falling over in their panic.

The camp commandant touched his arm gently. 'We forgot to tell you, Highness, that the last time anything was pointed at those children, it was a gun, and bullets followed, killing their parents. Look at their eyes, Prince.'

Jamal could stand it no more: not for today, anyway. He went back to his hotel suite and lay on the bed, listening to the racing of his heart.

Then he heard another sound, a tapping. A ragged figure had climbed onto the ledge outside his window and was trying to gain his attention. His first thought was to call the guard and have the man arrested. But Rind had already hissed, in Arabic, through the half-open sash, 'Prince, I am from your father's friend: I am Samir from Afghanistan, from Sirdar Akbar. Let me in!'

He spoke with the intonation of the Gulf. Jamal opened the window wide.

Once inside, Rind bowed, and touched his head, eyes and heart. 'Homage, Highness!' he said. The Arabs might, privately, call him *ajami*, 'one of the dumb', in spite of his knowledge of Arabic; but Rind had no doubt that he could outthink this locust-eater, and was convinced that he would pull off his deception.

Now for the next phase: a bit of romantic chivalry, theatre. He seized Jamal's robe and hung onto it, saying at the same time the ancient desert phrase of one who seeks protection, '*Dakhilak*, O Jamal, son of Zaid, Lord of the Anaza tribe. I am in your house!'

'Enough – you have my protection!' Jamal was half-amused, half-impressed, by the old-fashioned approach. He had seen hoary-headed ancients do it to his father in Narabia; but generally only when they wanted a camel, or to be sent to Harley Street for the treatment of some imaginary disease.

'Peace upon thee, Emir.'

'And upon thee peace. Come and sit here. Will you take some refreshment?' Jamal noticed that the man was staring at a very large bowl of fruit, embedded in crushed ice, which had just been sent up. Jamal signed to him to help himself. Rind's clothes were clean, but torn. On his head was a mountaineer's Chitrali wool cap, and he badly needed a shave. Nurhan and Rind had worked hard at the details of the disguise.

'Thank you. I am Samir Kandahari, and my chief is Sirdar Akbar Khan, Sharifi. I was with him in your Hadiqa City, when he was Afghan Ambassador there. I have also kissed the hand of your father, the King.' The Afghan said no more for a time. He was too busy demolishing the pile of fruit.

'What help do you need? Perhaps some money. Life is bad, I know, in poor Afghanistan.' The Prince was speculating: a couple of thousand dollars should set him up in some sort of business in a place like Pakistan – repairing bicycles or something. 'And how is His Excellency the Ambassador?'

'Money?' The Afghan laughed. 'We don't need money. We have more money than anyone else in the entire world!' He threw back his head and roared with laughter, his eyes streaming, until Jamal was almost sure that the poor fellow was deranged.

'You must have been through a great deal of trouble, since the *musibat*, the calamity . . .'

'Your Highness, my master told me to show you these.'

The spy took from his waist a roll of cotton cloth, heavy with coins, and handed it to Jamal. The Prince poured the gleaming pieces onto the table. 'Mohurs,' he said. 'They are hundreds of years old. You have many of these? If you want us to buy you arms, we can't do that. The international repercussions . . .'

'Highness. Let me explain. The Ambassador is well; he is in Kandahar Province. Now I beg you to listen, with patience, though what I have to say is indeed amazing. We have found the huge gold hoard of Ahmad Shah.' Rind paused to let this sink in. 'Sirdar Akbar Khan calculates it's worth over four hundred *billion* dollars, all in gold coins. We want your father, the King, to buy them from us. We can send them, via the Baluchistan coast, by the old smuggling route to the Gulf, in dhows. When you have received them, and not before, all he wants is for you to pay us in dollars.'

Jamal leant forward in his chair as the meaning of the words became clear, wondering at the same time whether he could trust his own ears. Rind now spoke more slowly, partly to help the Prince to catch up, but also to show that the innocent 'Samir' had difficulty with complicated plans.

'The money is to be placed in an account in . . . that country . . . yes, *Swissera*, Switzerland, in a bank account at the Credit Central. The Afghan freedom fighters will then be able to buy all the arms they need from the international arms men. The Afghans will then defeat the Russians, and our country will be free. And the threat from the *Rouss* to your land will be removed.'

Jamal said nothing: his mind was still reeling.

Rind looked at the bemused expression on the Prince's face and continued.

'O Prince! Can you not see that destiny has brought us together and kept the hoard safe until this hour, so that in one stroke all the evils will be banished? But the greatest speed is necessary if the arms are to get to us before the Russians wipe us out.'

Jamal said, '*Jalib*, interesting. But how would you get the money out of the bank, without opening an account with a signature? How soon after we got the gold would we give you the money? How would you know that you could trust us?'

Rind smiled. 'It has all been explained to me so many times that I know it by heart, Highness. First, you open the account with a nominal sum, ensuring that money can be put into it by the use of a single word: "Goldenbird". We can all remember it because it alludes to an ancient tale of great significance. Second, when we land the gold, when you have inspected the consignment, you will be in touch with your embassy in Switzerland, by satellite link-up, from the landing beach, and signal them to deposit the dollars. Third, we will be checking, through our own people, the precise moment when the account is credited with the dollars, by the use of the "Goldenbird" password.'

Jamal raised his hand to stem the torrent of detail. The man seemed to have everything worked out, but there was something else that had to be understood first. 'Mr Samir, you must remember that nothing could possibly be settled until I have told my father all this. And, of course, we would have to test the gold.'

'We know that. As for testing the gold, take all you wish: here are fifty of the coins. And when the Magnetic Pole, your father the King, has agreed, as we know he will, you can place an advertisement in a Pakistani newspaper. This one you have on your table will do well.

'Say, simply, "*I love the golden bird*," and our representative will contact you, using that phrase "Goldenbird" for identification.' Rind smiled and took the Prince's hand. 'Thank you for your hospitality, sir. I shall go now; with faith in God.'

'Would you like to leave by the stairs?'

'Thank you, I am quite comfortable climbing down walls.'

The Prince, taking a deep breath, wrote in his notebook the words, 'Goldenbird, ancient tale. Sirdar Akbar Khan, Kandahar. The hoard of Ahmad Shah. Worth over $400 billion.'

After that, there did not seem to be much to do other than to go to bed. Tomorrow he would tell his pilot to get the aircraft ready. After he'd checked on the tale of the Goldenbird. If the Afghans got their arms, Narabia might not be threatened after all.

Next morning the Prince called for his car and was driven along the Khyber Road to the ancient part of Peshawar City, where veiled women and burly, swaggering frontier men made way reluctantly for the Mercedes. Jamal believed in omens. It was time to find a story-teller.

At the Jail Bridge the crowds, mini-vans, donkeys and goats were too jampacked for the car to move. Jamal left the driver there, stepping out into the smell of coriander, kabobs and sandalwood.

A party of huge Pashtuns from the borderland, plodding along with saplings which they had cut for walking-staves, saw his desert headdress and shouted, equivocally, Jamal thought, 'Live until death, Prince of the Arabs . . .'

A tiny, wizened rickshaw man was tugging at his sleeve. He

jumped onto the seat while the man got between the shafts. 'Qissa Khwane' Jamal told him.

They went into the Khyber Bazaar and down to the T-junction, where the man pointed south, through a winding street. Jamal left the rickshaw man gazing bemusedly at a fifty-dollar note, his share of the oil money of Arabia dreamt about by everyone. Nearly 1500 rupees . . . In a few minutes Jamal was in the Qissa Khwane: the Market of the Story-Tellers. Did stories hold a clue, not only to history, or to human hopes, as some believed, but to the very meaning of life, as the sages said?

First came the china stalls, then copper, then shawls. A man tugged at his sleeve and offered to show him the Pipul, the bo-tree descended from the one under which Buddha had taught.

Though he had spent so much time in the West, the roots of his own ancestral culture were in the most ancient East. Prince Jamal began to feel like a part of the scene rather than a mere playboy visitor.

There were no story-tellers in the main bazaar. Jamal took a right turn.

In the warren of streets, he scanned the name-boards of the tiny shops, there seemed to be everything except story-tellers to be found. Pharmacies with human skulls and stuffed lizards hung from the ceilings; a crippled man, even his head awry, sat among a billion beads, stringing numberless rosaries for telling the Ninety-Nine Beautiful Names; he saw shoes, slippers, glass bottles, clay pots; butchers, basket-weavers. And here were 'guaranteed Arabian Perfumes', just as he had seen 'guaranteed Peshawar perfumes' on sale in his own city in Arabia. Import and export was a funny thing . . .

Then he saw it, took it in, passed – and turned back. The almost illegible, painted sign, in sensuously beautiful calligraphy, which said, 'Hasan Mirza, *Da Qissa Khazanachi* – Prince Hasan, Treasurer of Stories.' Jamal pushed aside the bead curtain and bent to step inside.

A small man, perhaps sixty years old, finely boned, dressed in a blue, double-breasted suit and wearing a trilby, his features not unlike those of a south Italian, with curly white hair and a small moustache, and moving very silently towards him. 'Peace on thee. Art thou strong?' His smile was familiar, mannered, like those on the faces of the courtiers in the palace at Hadiqa City.

Jamal's Pashtu wasn't up to much. He wondered whether the man spoke English, which he was very comfortable in. But it always paid to start with Arabic, he had found. People hardly ever knew it hereabouts, but it had prestige. And his father had told him that, in the East, it was always important to get the first blow in oneself.

'And on you peace. Are there books of the narratives in your shop, may you live long, lord?'

The Mirza looked at him and answered in English. 'I can *read* Arabic, of course, sir, but Persian is my mother tongue. I expect you know English language, though?' He spoke it well, though it was certain from the cadence of his voice that he'd never been in an Anglo-Saxon country.

'Yes, I do. Thank you. I'm from the Gulf, and I want some stories for my children.'

'We have all the stories here; those which are not in the books are in my head. I could even have them written down for you. You have come to the right place. Have some tea.'

He clapped his hands and a small boy with a shaven head ran in carrying two glasses. As he was ushered to one of three big, worn armchairs in the shop, Jamal saw that he was in a largish room, completely lined with shelves full of books. Could all these be books of stories? They sat and smiled at one another for a minute or two.

Jamal said, 'Have you the story of the Goldenbird? I think it must be from the Classics, or it may be an Afghan tale.'

The story-teller nodded. 'The Goldenbird, *Zarin-Parinda*, is what the Afghans call the hoopoe with the crown of gold. He is the leader who takes the Thirty Birds to find their destiny, their Leader, true reality.'

'And have you got the book?'

'Only in Persian. It is the *Mantiq al Tayir*, Speech of the Bird, the famous classic by Attar. Some people call it the "Parliament of the Birds".'

'Is it a long story, and what are its chief points?'

'It is quite long, but it can be summarized. I'll have it written for you in Arabic, in a fine Naskh hand, and posted to you at

204

home. It should arrive in a month or two.' Like a made-to-measure suit, Jamal thought; what a good idea. But he wanted the information at once.

He said, 'Take this, and here is my card. Send me the book. But, in the meantime, I would like to hear the story, if you would be so kind.'

The Mirza took the ten hundred-dollar notes and, without a glance at them, handed them to the boy hovering at his elbow. His suit was shiny and very threadbare, and he was certainly in reduced circumstances, but his behaviour was patrician. To Jamal he said, 'To hear is to obey. I am the treasurer of tales, and I shall certainly tell you about the Bird. This youth, however, is my own treasurer of funds, and he will know best what to do with the money.'

'Forgive me, Sidi Mirza, I didn't notice your man standing there.' These Persians had been practising courtly manners for thousands of years and they always liked to score off an Arab. 'But I am travelling: and although myself an Emir, who does not like to handle money any more than you, I have to get things done.' He felt quite petulant.

The Mirza beamed. 'Your Highness. As a man of nobility the tale of the Goldenbird is exactly right for you. I shall summarize it.'

He started without further ado. 'One day the representatives of the birds of the world decided that, like all other forms of creation, they should have a king. They agreed to seek one, and they found the hoopoe, *hudhud* with his golden crown, to lead them in the search. He knew the Way, for he was in the service of their Celestial Monarch.

'They had many discussions, and they travelled through mountains and valleys, through happiness and perils, always, of course, led by the Goldenbird. They had many crises, and again and again the hoopoe had to correct them, raise their spirits, keep them moving forward.

'Finally they reached the curtain which concealed the throne of their king, and prostrated themselves in awe and fear. Then the veil parted and the birds, as they looked up, saw that there, in front of them, was a huge mirror. Their king, they realized, was none other than the reflection of them all.'

Mirza fell silent, and folded his hands.

Jamal asked him. 'Is this story a good omen?'

'It speaks of man, of course, and of the fact that it is the unity of human souls which totals absolute divinity and truth, from which we are ordinarily separated.'

The Hoopoe, representative of the Great King Solomon the Wisest. Himself a king, wearing a golden crown, like the *agal* and *kaffia* headdress of the King of Narabia, leading his people to their high destiny. His father's role.

Jamal embraced the Mirza, and stepped out of the shop into the dusty alleyways once more.

3 Send for Yunanian, the Chemist

The Palace, and
The British Embassy
Hadiqa City
Narabia

JUNE 18

King Zaid of Narabia and its Dependencies sat in his reception-hall and thought about his life. He was, indeed, a king to the outside world: but, to his people, among whom kingship was actually proscribed as alien to Islamic thinking, he was still the Sheikh. In fact, by Bedouin custom, the sheikh of all sheikhs was known by the plural: *ash-shuyukh*, the sheikhs. That was the nearest to a king they would allow anyone to be. Traditionally, kings were their enemies: the ancient ones, of Egypt, Persia or Rome.

Other desert kings – and sheikhs – had four wives at a time: he now had none; Zarifa had died twenty years ago, and he had not remarried. Other desert kings had as many as two or three hundred sons. He had only one: Jamal, of Oxford – and California, places where he often preferred to spend his time.

This multi-million-dollar Hollywood-style palace had been designed by perhaps the world's greatest, certainly its most expensive, architect. King Zaid's zoo was the biggest in the world, bought as a package from a German firm. His underground nuclear shelter was enormous, and the very best. His fountains, over there beyond the pillars in the marble hall, flowed with rosewater, as had those of the great Caliph Haroun el Rashid of old, but Zaid's money was in Zurich, and his slaves, effectively, included highly sophisticated top executives in business corporations around the world.

Arabia, he reflected, was now full of rulers like him. One or two generations ago, their forebears had been high or low: some desert chiefs, others only poor fishermen, on the Gulf, over yonder, which the Russians in Afghanistan had nearly reached. As chiefs, of course, the kings had claimed the most imposing ancestry, descent from the Queen of Sheba, from Abraham, from other people whose names sounded strange, and were largely unknown to most of the world, but which, in the ears of a hundred and fifty million Arabs, conjured up pictures of pure magic. The magic of long ago.

King Zaid had tried to balance the needs and rules, the customs and the requirements of the old and the new, of Arabia and London, of camel and Cadillac. In conformity with Islamic law, he wore no silk or gold; he did not drink alcohol or smoke; he would not have recognized a pig if he had seen one, and he said his prayers five times a day. When the oil wealth came pouring in, especially after the two huge OPEC price rises – which the West had called blackmail – he had tried to use it wisely. Now his capital, Hadiqa City, had the best of everything.

Nobody starved, nobody even went hungry for a day, unless by choice in the fasting month of Ramadan. There were eight colour television channels, showing soap operas of life in New York or Blackburn, in all its rich intensity, to an often baffled audience of two million people, most of them still unable to read or write. His army was equipped with weapons so modern that they were not even in service with the countries which produced them. Their armies could not afford the sophisticated gadgetry until their governments had got the money from Narabia or its like to pay for them. His fellow kings were, generally, much alike. Only that morning he had received a call, on the satellite link-up between his palace and that of the king of Naranjia. 'My wives have just bought a new 'plane for a trip to Paris,' the Naranjian had said; 'They want to load it up with diamonds, or something, there: and a new dress designer from Haiti will be in France, too. Is there anything they can buy for you?'

A servant, a huge, fat Nubian eunuch, with a gold sash and curly-toed slippers, was suddenly at his side, 'Majesty, His Royal Highness presents his homage. Returned from El Bakistan, he seeks an audience. The matter is urgent, says the Prince, O Majesty the King!'

'Kafur, tell the Prince that I am here, in the Diwan.'

The old man leant back on the sofa, tucked his feet under him, took out his rosary, and called for fresh coffee flavoured with ground cardamoms.

What Prince Jamal had to say drove the last, beguiling thoughts of a desert life completely out of the King's head. The Russians' SS 20 missiles, in their silos at the Caspian base in the USSR, could not reach his country. Now, the immense military build-up in southern Afghanistan, with the preparation of missile sites in the Kandahar area, only a few hundred miles away, put his entire country at their mercy. The way to Arabia through Pakistan might not yet be open to the Soviet ground forces, but from Afghanistan they could hold the Arab world to ransom. And the oil produced in the USSR might be exhausted by the end of the decade, according to American estimates. Would the Russians move into Arabia?

It was true that President Carter had stated, years ago, that anyone trying to control the Gulf 'would be repelled by any means, including military force'. But what if the Russians used surrogates, or puppets, as in Afghanistan? In Asia, Africa and the Americas, Soviet policy was to use local people as their Trojan horse.

And the Afghans? They were anything but a spent force. Three years after they had been all but written off by the West as a nation hopelessly lost to the Russians, the people were still fighting: so effectively that the guerrillas controlled 99% of the country, and the Russians even had to dive-bomb the cities to regain control.

The Russians, of course, were far from being beaten, but they were taking a military and propaganda hammering such as they never had before. The West, on the other hand, was not helping the Afghans. And yet – perhaps to represent themselves as saints – the leaders of the developed world had actually said that they were sending arms. They had the best of both worlds. By not supplying arms and saying that they were doing so, they avoided annoying the Russians, since the Kremlin knew what was, and what was not, getting through. At the same time, all the peoples of the East who sympathized with the Afghan freedom struggle now believed that the West was whiter than white, and active in the struggle. The Russians gained on all counts. They had a place to test weapons, and, with luck, could convince their own people – and some others as well – that the 'Western interventionists' were trying to fight the Soviet Union through Afghan guerrilla surrogates. And, as long as the non-aligned nations thought that the Western powers were giving arms to the Afghans, they would not do anything themselves to help.

The only losers in this game of bluff were the people of Afghanistan itself. It was hard to believe, but those were the real facts. The increased supply of arms was due to Afghan patriot, not to foreign, effort.

And now, almost incredibly, the Afghans had produced this story – or this fact – that they had found the ancient hidden treasure of Ahmad Shah, billions of dollars worth, and had offered it to King Zaid. To buy arms, to free themselves, to get the Russians out, to remove them, some distance at least, from Narabia and the other oil states.

'Jamal.' Zaid had made up his mind. 'This is your mission. I want you to go to Europe, to America if necessary. Search among the libraries there, ask scholars. Is there any truth in the tale of this treasure, and what is its quantity? This sort of information, as everyone knows, is not easily to be found in the East. Even if it is here, it would take us years to dig it out. The scholars and the libraries of the West have centuries of information on the East.'

'By my eyes, Father.' The Prince bowed.

'I shall have these coins tested, Jamal, to make sure that they are not counterfeit. I shall have it done locally, to avoid any interest if they are sent to the West. The press there get hold of everything, and we could have the Russians after us in a matter of days. If the coins are genuine, you shall leave immediately.'

'Your lightest wish is my command.' Jamal inclined his head.

The King ticked off his instructions on his fingers. 'Make the arrangements for the stocks and other investments to be liquidated at my signal. Keep in touch through our consulate in Zurich. We can trust Consul Ali Husseini there. I have a direct radio link with him from the palace. When you have confirmation or otherwise about the treasure, radio me in the *Mas-haf* Cypher.'

210

'By my head, eyes and heart.' Jamal gave the salute: touching his forehead, brows and breast.

The King looked at the glittering *mohurs* once again. He and his old friend, Ambassador Akbar of Afghanistan, had played many a game of chess, gone on many a hawking expedition together. They had watched camel races, had vied with one another in the composition of poetry, had even been adjudged equals in calligraphy. His friend was in trouble. That counted, too. Even if the gold turned out to be counterfeit, he would try to do something for him. And the price of gold was going up: some said that it would double within six months.

The friend, the gold, the SS 20s . . . What a combination. First it was recalcitrant camels which had been the bane of his life. Then oil people and diplomats. Now he was haunted by friendship, treasure and missiles. Well, perhaps things had got so bad that they could only improve from now on.

'Gold? Testing gold is simplicity itself, Majesty. Methods have been known for centuries, and new ones are being added all the time.' Artran Yunanian, the Armenian chemist, bowed with every word he spoke. He had known the King for decades, and feared him; but Zaid had always been good to him, and whenever he called for Artran, there was some commission or some reward never far away.

'Artran. What do you make of these?'

Yunanian gasped as the fifty pieces, bright as from the mint, were poured out of a bag onto the table.

He took one up and bit it. 'It's soft enough to be real, Majesty. Perhaps you have found a hidden hoard, somewhere near the palace? I could get you a good price. These are collectors' pieces, you know, very ancient.'

'No, I was sent them by a friend.' They might be of interest to collectors, but millions of them on the market would destroy their scarcity value. 'I want them properly assayed and I want it done at once, and I do not want anyone else to know.'

The podgy chemist looked at the monarch with an expression which combined servility, delight and injured innocence. 'Instantly, Majesty, properly and secretly. How could it cross your noble mind, the noblest of all minds, that I, Artran Yunanian, father of Sagdasht Artranian, on whose beloved head I swear,

211

Majesty, that I could ever betray a confidence? Why, I'll kill my wife and child . . .'

'That won't be necessary, Artran. Just test the gold. How old are the coins, by the way?'

Artran squinted at them. The lettering was in the Arabic script. Like thousands of Armenians in the Arab world, mostly shopkeepers, he had never learned to read it, although he could speak the language fluently enough.

'Oh, they must be one or two thousand years old, Majesty . . .'

'I hope that your chemist art is better than your history, Artran. How do you assay gold, anyway?'

'Sire, there are several methods. In the streak test, you draw it along a hard surface and compare the colour and softness of the streak with that made by a known quality of gold. That's the simplest, but there are alloys which are equally malleable, so it is not much use nowadays. Then there is the acid test. Certain alloys defy acids, but they are generally those made in advanced countries, and, as this gold comes from the East, the acid test would probably suffice.'

'I want a conclusive result, Artran!'

'In that case, Majesty, I would have to find the specific gravity. This test is foolproof. All metals and alloys displace a different and distinct quantity of water. By measuring this, we can positively determine if the coin is gold.'

'That is the test you shall do. When can you report the result to me?'

'This evening at sundown, Majesty.'

'Very well. Take these coins and go.'

'May the life of the greatest King, Shadow of the Almighty on Earth, be everlasting . . .'

'Get out, Artran, and take that packet over there with you.'

Yunanian the chemist scuttled out, clutching the package wrapped in a fine Kashmir shawl which he knew, by custom and experience, contained a fat bundle of currency notes, payment for his trouble. A king, in the East at any rate, always gave people presents which corresponded with his own dignity and importance, not with theirs.

Throughout the day, the King faithfully fulfilled his obligations.

He read State papers, said his prayers, visited the new dry dock. He also received several relatives who wanted to set up profitable enterprises, such as flying in frozen chickens from California or building ten new hotels. These would add to the thirty which already stood, monuments to man's inhumanity both in aspect and content, dotting the panorama of bleak hills amid which the capital sat: the highest point on a huge and arid plateau, best suited to Bedouins' flocks and oil rigs, sweeping down to the great flat beaches beyond which was the Arabian Sea – and Afghanistan.

The hotels, the ambassadors, the docks and the chamberlains – and the oil wealth – might come and go, the King reflected, again and again during that day. But the Bedouins, his people, would go on for ever.

When Yunanian had counted his bakhsheesh, and found it to be no less than five hundred *dinars*, worth over a thousand dollars, he took the coins to the little laboratory behind his shop and tested them. Yes, there was no doubt that they were gold, and fine gold at that. The King had got hold of gold. There had been about fifty coins. Why was he so keen to have them analysed? Surely because there must be more, and very many more, somewhere. Otherwise he would never have troubled himself to call in Yunanian. A hundred mohurs like this, would be worth, let's see, at a thousand dollars an ounce – say about $44,000. Peanuts, though, to such as the King, who already had hundreds, perhaps thousands, of millions of dollars in cash, investment and revenues.

Yunanian was sure that the King was up to something. But what? What else had he said? Nothing. Except to keep it secret. He would go back to the King, taking his report, and try to find out more.

As the sun set, Yunanian was sitting in the palace courtyard, waiting to be summoned by the inner guard. He could have got as far as the ante-room where people with business with the King usually waited: but that would have cost money. The guards and ushers knew their services were worth something, and made sure that visitors knew it, too. But Yunanian realized that Zaid would call for him in any case, and the guards and the courtiers would have to find him, double-quick. So he waited. Perhaps there would be another reward, a further bundle of notes, for doing the assay.

Someone tugged impatiently at Yunanian's sleeve. It was the palace guard. 'Hurry, *Armani*, Armenian! Our Lord the King commands!'

The interview was brief.

'Well, Artran, are they genuine?'

'Perfectly, Majesty.'

'Good.' The King was relieved, and it was this sensation which may have caused his guard to slip. 'By the way, have you ever heard of a king, an *ajami*, a Persian, called Ahmad Shah?'

'I have, of course, Majesty.' Yunanian, like many others in the East, always said that. 'I do not know,' after all, is something said only by ignorant people. He had in fact never heard of Ahmad Shah, but it did indeed sound like an *ajami* name. *Ajam*, the Dumb. What the Arabs called people who did not know the Arabic language, especially Persian-speakers.

'What do you know about him?'

'That he was a king.' That was safe enough! He must be a king.

'What else?'

'I may need some time to remember, Majesty.'

'Did you hear that he had a treasure?' The mistaken belief, that Yunanian was trustworthy and that he might really have known something about Ahmad Shah, had overcome King Zaid's natural caution.

The Armenian stood silent for a moment, wondering what to say. Then, recovering himself, he poured forth such a farrago of nonsense, produced from an overheated imagination fuelled by a desire for information and reward, that Zaid soon saw the familiar pattern.

'All right, Yunanian. That will be all. Tell nobody. Keep the five gold pieces I gave you, for yourself. Now go. I have important matters to attend to.'

Yunanian bowed low and backed from the royal presence.

Once outside, his mind began to work again. Five gold mohurs, over fifteen hundred dollars worth in gold value. As collectors' pieces, who knows? They were very old. Perhaps worth twenty-five thousand dollars the lot. Not a bad day's work. But there was something else that might bring him even more. The treasure of King Ahmad Shah. That was it. Zaid was a silly old fool. Once a Bedouin, always a Bedouin. He had found a treasure. More likely, someone else had found one and he knew about it.

'*Majesty, perhaps you have found a hidden hoard?*' '*No, I was sent them by a friend . . . Is it gold? Are they genuine . . . A Persian-speaking king . . . Did you hear that he had a treasure?*' It must be a really big treasure: that was certain.

Yunanian did not know of any Persian-speaking kings who had been anywhere near Narabia. And he could hardly go to Iran or anywhere like that to seek the treasure: especially with so little to go on. No, unfortunately, there would be no progress in that direction. Anyway, the gold had already been found: King Zaid's possession of the coins was proof enough of that. So Yunanian would not be likely to get his hands on any more of it. That left him with that other commodity which he knew was often as valuable as any merchandise, though more perishable than any: information. 'News, like fish, must be sold before it stinks.' That was the old saying. He would get onto it tomorrow morning.

Roger Lowther was Third Secretary and Visa Officer at the British Embassy, Consular Section, Hadiqa City, Kingdom of Narabia. That, at any rate, was what it said on his office door. In fact, all the visa work was done by the intrepid and officious Miss Hilda Spencer-Starman, technically his deputy. His own title, like that of many another minor intelligence officer in British diplomatic stations around the world, was as improbable as the size and hideous colouring of the immense plaster Lion-and-Unicorn coat of arms which surmounted the entrance to the Embassy's Chancery inside the walled compound. Lowther often winced as he passed below this monstrosity: the size and shape dictated, no doubt, by some London functionary whose desire to impress foreign natives matched his lack of taste.

There hadn't been any news for days. Lowther had done *The Times* crossword, and even the one from the *Illustrated Weekly of India*: once the parish magazine of the Bombay expatriate Memsahibs and now often barely literate, though clearly aping the manners and actions supposed by this generation to have been those of the former elite.

Lowther shook his head, to unstick his straw-coloured hair from his sweating forehead. He had switched off the air-conditioning and opened the supposedly bomb-proof window to get some air, however full of sand and flies it might be. He had sinus trouble, and the chilled air made it worse. He was typical of the dozens, perhaps hundreds, of young men and women who filled the lower echelons of the Foreign Service, in London and abroad, and he knew it. He had met too many of them to think otherwise.

A Third Secretary, a dogsbody, fetching and carrying for the ambassador, and sometimes only the counsellor. Spending countless months, sometimes years, in 'just brushing up your knowledge of Siam, I mean Thailand, my boy', of not being able to join his father's London club because ambassadors belonged to it, and it would not be seemly for them to meet him on equal terms. 'Sitting in' on allegedly important meetings which seemed to have a beginning and, mercifully, an end, but no middle and no easily discernible purpose. Discussions, briefings, situation papers, the same old offices, the same kind of chairs. 'No, of course, at your level you can't have a Persian rug on your floor. I don't care if it is only a Turkoman saddlebag. Why, even Ministers . . .'

Lowther's clerk Halabi affected a sickly sort of familiarity with him because they were both British subjects (and, as the passports put it, citizens of the United Kingdom); Halabi, who had been born in Aden, now came into the room. He was carrying a cup of tea on a saucer which also held a sodden gingernut. It must be eleven o'clock.

Lowther had passed examinations in Arabic, though he had an execrable accent and hardly knew any of the language, to the great wonderment, respect almost, of all the Arabs who met him. When he had first arrived at the embassy, three and a half years ago, Lowther had asked Halabi to speak to him in Arabic as often as possible and, infuriatingly, Halabi had turned this request to his own advantage. He regularly said sentences, in Arabic, to Lowther, but in the same appalling accent that was Lowther's own. It gave him great satisfaction. Besides, nobody else really understood what passed between them. The rest of the British staff assumed it was some obscure Arabian dialect that was involved, while many Arabs imagined that it was an especially polished form of English. Halabi had fostered the latter impression.

Halabi now moved forward and adopted a conspiratorial posture, pursing his lips and leaning, too close, towards the Englishman.

'*Jar all jar sows all Armawny, bee kidmatic*,' he drawled. He was quite proud of that. Anyone with less experience of Lowther-speak would probably have said, '*Ja al-jasus al-Armani, bi-Khidmatak*.'

He was trying for effect, too. It worked, as usual, setting Lowther off like an alarm clock. He leapt from his chair, looked wildly around, and shook his fist at the man from Aden. 'Halabi, how many times have I told you not to say "The Armenian spy is here"? Mr Artran Yunanian is a British subject who comes here from time to time to see about visa and other matters.' He struck out, petulantly and without effect, at a fly which was slowly circling the biscuit in his saucer.

Halabi shrugged. He nearly said that nobody else understood their patois anyway, but that would have annoyed Lowther further. One knew when to stop.

'And put on a clean *galabiya*. You look terrible.' Lowther gazed at the billowing, ankle-length nightshirt with distaste.

Halabi withdrew, again bowing in that way which Lowther always suspected to be some private joke. Or copied from an American film, set in Algiers.

Lowther gulped his tea and then pressed the button of the intercom. 'Halabi, tell Mr Yunanian I'm on some urgent work, and would he kindly wait.' He started to nibble his biscuit, displacing the fly.

Lowther had his own style with Yunanian. Once the man had, he believed, been on the point of blackmailing him. Certainly he had behaved with undue and oily familiarity when speaking about certain unusual videotapes for Lowther that had been delivered to his pharmacy by mistake.

When he had heard the chemist's story, Lowther's first reaction, as always, was to check it against three things. First, was it true? Second, was it useful? Third, if true and useful, what was it worth? One couldn't waste taxpayers' money.

'I don't think that this will be of any interest to us, Artran.'

Yunanian had been afraid of that. He had spent several

minutes trying to get a price for the information fixed before he revealed it. He had even gone so far as to suggest that it was something that the French, the Americans, the Italians, even, would give a fortune to hear, if he were just to drop in on their embassies, no distance away. Lowther wasn't buying that, and Yunanian had had to tell him all.

'Now look here,' continued Lowther, when he had heard the story, 'it is of no concern to Whitehall if the King has found gold, or if this gold is treasure, or if this treasure belongs – or belonged – to a man called Ahmad Shah, who sounds like some kind of a Persian. But he might be an Indian, Pakistani or Afghan. They all come under the South Asian Department. We're responsible to the Middle East Department.'

'Respected Mr Lowther! Everyone knows that your great White Hall can use information. Who am I, a poor chemist, to know more about such matters? But I do know, Mr Lowther, that I have brought you important news in the past, and you have thanked me for it. And anything that the King is doing is always interesting to everyone in embassies. We both know that. And, after all, I am a poor man, Mr Lowther, I have so many small children . . .'

'I thought you only had one child?'

'Well, yes, but you know what I mean, Mr Lowther. Now, you will get promotion, and the White Hall will be pleased with you. And there isn't much else that you can tell them, because nothing ever happens in Hadiqa City. I will throw in some information about the North Koreans, who have a big plot to undermine this country, Mr Lowther, and also something about the cement contract, that I have learned from my brother-in-law, which might go to a British company. All I need is a small amount.'

'Like what?'

'Let us not talk about money, Mr Lowther. But, if you insist, let us say a thousand dinars . . .'

'I'll give you twenty dinars; take it or leave it. Not for information, you understand. *Ex gratia*, distress allowance. Now, Mr Yunanian, I have a lot of work to do.'

'Make it twenty-five.'

'Done.' Lowther scribbled a chit. 'Here you are. And forget about the North Koreans. You sold me that story last week.

London doesn't believe a word of it. Take the chit to Mr Halabi.'

'I know where to take it. Thank you, honourable Mr Lowther. I hope that it gets you promotion, and you are soon made ambassador. In Paris.' Yunanian was out of the office like a shot. After all, he had a lot of embassies to visit before they closed for the day. Gold and kings were of interest to everyone. He might sell the story three, four, perhaps even five times that day.

Sir Leicester Browne was depressed. Her Britannic Majesty's Ambassador to the Court of Narabia sat in his study, reading *The Heraldic News*. Narabia was, in the Foreign and Colonial Office classification, a 'hardship nation'. That meant extra money and better leave. True, there was no hardship here as ordinarily understood: indeed the Ambassador, lacking private means, had seldom lived so well. But there were some things one missed: certain interesting amenities of London's Shepherd Market and Soho for instance.

Now what was on the agenda for today? The First Secretary brought him a sheaf of papers. 'London decrypt of the overnight telegrams, Your Excellency.' Tiresome fellow, Hoskins. He loved words like 'decrypt'. What was wrong with 'Here are the telegrams which the Cypher Room has decoded?'

'Yes, Hoskins?'

'And sir, the Russian tanks.'

The Ambassador sat bolt upright. 'Russian tanks? What are you talking about, man? The Russians aren't here yet, are they?' It was just possible, of course. The FCO message had said 'Experts agree world oil and natural gas may last no more than forty years but USSR's only twenty years. Russians are long-range planners so may try to capture mideast oil sooner and Narabia vital . . .'

Hoskins gulped as the Ambassador stared fixedly at him. 'No, sir. The Russians are not here yet. But you will recall that the Narabians bought some old Soviet military hardware from Egypt after the Russians were kicked out by Sadat, and the Americans wouldn't supply Narabia in case they used US arms against Israel. Well, a British firm is repairing the Russian tanks, and supplying spare parts . . .'

Yes, of course. It all came back to Sir Leicester in a rush. 'Just a little joke, Hoskins, sense of humour and all that. Quite a useful sideline for British engineering in these hard times, isn't it? Us and the Chinese, supplying most of the Third World with spares for Russian armaments.'

'Yes sir, exactly. Well, you have to see the engineer-in-charge, Ramsbottom he's called . . .'

'He would be. Yes, I remember him: Lowther calls him "the Yobbo".'

'. . . and get the specifications from him. He's doing a reverse engineering job.'

'And what might that be?'

'Reverse engineering means taking existing machinery and making blueprints from it, so that our people can see the state of the Russians' art . . .'

'Art, Hoskins?'

'Technology, sir.'

'Well?'

'Well, Your Excellency, these are confidential documents. You have to take possession of them personally.'

'In case the Russians see them?'

'Yes, I suppose so.'

'So, you think that they don't already know how they designed and built their own tanks?'

'Those are the orders, sir.'

'I see, Hoskins. All right. London must have its reasons. Send this fellow Plushbottom in.'

Another of those days.

Then Lowther came rushing in. 'Ambassador. I have something to discuss, from the Palace.'

The Palace? Perhaps it was a sounding about Sir Leicester's KCMG: Knight Commander. He only had an ordinary knighthood at the moment.

'Do come in, my dear fellow. Buckingham Palace, eh?'

'Hadiqa Palace, sir.'

'Oh, all right, then, hurry up, will you? I've a lot of things to do before the Diplomatic Golf Tournament.'

Lowther told him, nasal from his swollen sinus.

'Can't make head nor tail of it, meself.' The mention of the Palace had unsettled the Ambassador. He sat with half-closed eyes, trying to think about the problem of the Persian gold. Instead, a picture of Hobgoblin Pursuivant, an official of the College or Court of Arms, or Heralds, or whatever it was, swam before him.

Lowther was speaking. 'So I think we'd better turn it over to Mosaic, sir.'

'Mosaic? You mean a pattern of small tiles? Why should you? Are there any around here?'

'Not that kind, sir. "Mosaic" is the code-word for what we usually call "Jigsaw".'

'Stop playing games and get on with your work, like me, Lowther. I've got to, er, play golf . . .'

'Not the *game*, sir. "Jigsaw" is the man who puts things together. Intelligence information. If we have something perplexing, something that we think might be important, we can telex it straight to Jigsaw in London, and he marries it with other inflow and makes a picture for the Secretary of State.'

Marries it with inflow: a picture for the Secretary of State. Where did London *find* these idiots?

'If that's the procedure, Lowther, why don't you get on with it, man? Why all this fluttering about with games and tiling?'

'I need your permission, sir. FCO instructions clearly state that Mosaic can only be contacted direct with an upthrust.'

'Which means?' Inflow and upthrust. Things were getting worse since that circular about 'Use Standard Terminology Only'. To be referred to as 'USTO', of course.

'Upthrust is the code-word for "authorization by the Head of Mission", sir.'

'I authorize it, then. Will that be all, Lowther? Don't just stand there snuffling.'

'Yes, sir. I'll get on to it right away.'

'Don't get on to it – get on *with* it!'

The fool was scampering off now. Thank goodness. Upthrust and inflow. What was telexing called? Almost certainly 'outflow'.

'Right.' The Ambassador pressed the button on his intercom. 'Miss Triptych, let me know when Mr Ramsbottom arrives. I am reading the London decrypts – I mean telegrams.'

'Yes, Your Excellency.'

He picked up the first printout. 'London to all Stations . . .' Sounded like a railway announcement.

Still, there might be something in this Afghanistan business. Two tours of duty ago, Sir Leicester had been HBM's Ambassador in Kabul, so he knew – and liked – the Afghan people.

They'd give the Russians a run for their money, just as Mrs Thatcher had reminded people their warriors had done in the case of the British. Although she could have put it more diplomatically.

A strange country, though, full of all sorts of communities, different from one another, but all fanatical Afghans. The Ambassador remembered explaining this as best he could to an open-mouthed Minister of State on tour:

'There're many communities here, you see, Minister, all with their own land, flocks, customs and histories. In United Kingdom terms you might almost say that the Tajiks are their Saxons, the Pashtuns resemble the Scots, the Turks are sort of Vikings and the Arabs are the Norman conquerors. The Nuristanis, of course, up there in the wild mountains – they're the Irish.'

Quite a neat summary, he had thought. But the visitor, primarily a politician, of course, had only refilled his glass with port from the decanter and said, lamely, 'Of course that's a great simplification, I suppose?'

'Yes, indeed, quite a simplification.'

The Minister had been more interested, the Ambassador remembered, in the size and scale of the huge British Embassy at Karte Parwan: the most imposing in Asia. It was built by order of Lord Curzon, to impress upon the locals – and the Russians – that the Empire was something to reckon with, that the British were the champions of The Great Game, the struggle for Central Asia.

4 Thank you, Dr Anddrews

Oxford
England

JUNE 20

Prince Jamal flew to London by Narabian International Airlines; featured on the passenger list as Mr Kazim bin-Abdallah, also the name on his brand new passport. Narabian-Int was discreet. There was no point in attracting attention to himself by using his private jet, he thought. Perhaps he had little native Bedouin caution left, but he did have some idea of what four hundred billion dollars meant.

He spent the night at the Savoy: like so many of its patrons, he could not resist the exclusively English cooking of its Grill Room, where nothing so ordinary as French cuisine – *nouvelle* or *ancienne* – was permitted. The following morning he went by rail from Paddington to Oxford. It was Monday, and the Intercity train was full of university dons, returning from London where so many of them maintained useful contacts with the media, with government departments and with the other attractions of the capital.

He had no appointment, but took a taxi straight from the station, looking like an advertisement for plastic food, straight to St Saviour's College, where his old tutor, C. E. G. B. Anddrews, was sure to be found. The porter at the lodge recognized him at once.

'Prince Jamal, sir! What a pleasure to have you back with us.' He'd bought a cottage out of the tips which he had got from Jamal alone, so he would hardly forget him.

'Great to be back, Mr Williamson. Lovely weather, isn't it? Have you seen Dr Anddrews today at all?'

'Yes, sir. He's in his rooms. You know the way, don't you?'

'I know it all right. All those essays and tea and crumpets.'
He wrinkled his nose and the beefy Williamson laughed, as if at a joke.

'Right-ho, sir.'

Jamal climbed the stairs, worn by centuries of under-graduates, which led to the tutor's rooms. It had hardly changed. Slightly run-down, the walls scuffed, the smell of wet raincoats and something which might be liniment: St Saviour's was noted for its Rugby men. He knocked. 'Come.' Yes, that was old Andie's voice all right.

'Please forgive the intrusion, sir.' The short, thin form of the ageing scholar was hunched, as always, over a mass of papers at the table in the corner. Probably writing a review, a hatchet job, for the *Times Literary Supplement*, Jamal thought.

'My dear Jamal. This is a welcome pleasure!' Anddrews stood up, dwarfed by his visitor, and clawed his distance glasses from his cardigan pocket. 'You look fine! How is life in Narabia?'

'Everything's great, doctor. Things seem to be just the same here.'

'Yes, not very different.'

Jamal decided to plunge straight into his story.

'It's luck for us that you are a specialist in Middle Eastern history, because we need your help. Wc have to have some information, on a matter of the greatest confidence.'

'Anything I can do . . .'

'I need information about King Ahmad Shah.'

That evening a routine-looking message pulsed out from the radio room at the Royal Narabian Embassy in Kensington Palace Gardens, London.

It was sandwiched between two long commercial signals, and it was in clear: too short to need the economy achieved by using Narabia's usual five-digit commercial cypher.

The listeners at GCHQ, Government Communications Headquarters near Cheltenham, looked at the intercept. Nothing special here. The reference prefix was, routinely, put through the computer which interpreted Arabic word-roots, and the watcher peered at the screen. Prefix *KHJL*, *KHaJaLa*, in Arabic, he noted, might mean 'tangled' (plant); 'luxuriant' (valley); 'full' (garment). It could also mean 'timidity', 'bashfulness' . . . No, nothing there. Not an Arabic word. Just a reference to earlier correspondence. He filed the message.

Addressed to the Ministry of Commerce, Hadiqa City, Narabia, the message caused a flurry as soon as it arrived. The cypher officer knew what *KHJL* meant: it was a contraction of the phrase '*KHususi – JaLalat al-malik*. Special: King's Majesty'. A despatch rider, siren wailing, was at the palace with it, within minutes.

Rising from his evening prayers, King Zaid looked at the printout:

MINCOMMERCE HADIQA REFERENCE KHJL UNIT PRICE TWENTYEIGHT POUNDS SEVENTYSIX PENCE SECOND COMMODITY SIXTYONE AND THIRTEEN PENCE NARABEMB LONDRA.

Jamal, reporting from London. The figures would be in the *Mas-haf* cypher. The *Mas-haf*, of course, was one of the names used for the Koran. Every Koran in existence had an identical text: none varied by as much as a dot, so the chapters and verses were always constant. King Zaid reached for his copy and looked up chapter twenty-eight, verse seventy-six: 'Such were the treasures we had bestowed on him that their very keys would have been a burden to a body of strong men.'

Good, Jamal meant that the immense treasure's existence was confirmed.

Now for the second extract. That should tell what he thought of the outlook. See chapter sixty-one, verse thirteen: '. . . help from Allah and a speedy victory; so give glad tidings to the Believers.'

Support the Muhjahidin. Thank you, Jamal. I shall proceed with the transaction. Now, how did one go about putting an advertisement in a Pakistani newspaper? Better send for Court Minister Hafiz, he would get it done . . .

BOOK 5

A Mirza in a Mulberry Tree

PARTIZANS – (Guerrillas). National volunteers, who fight against occupation forces on territory usurped by the enemy, and who rely upon extensive support from the local population.

The Soviet Dictionary of Basic
Military Terms, Moscow

1 Hang the Bandit Scum!

Kabul and Panjsher Valley
Afghanistan

JUNE 9

'Comrade General, this Afghan assignment is the most interesting experience of my life; there's much of detailed value to us, here. Far more, even, than I saw in Egypt.' Major Bakunin's eyes gleamed behind his spectacles. Here, interest and policy, reality and ambition, blended: he was able to tell the truth and at the same time to remind the general of their long association. He had been waiting far too long for his colonelcy, and this might be his chance at last. Perhaps his final chance.

The major had been with the weapons evaluation team which carried out an assessment in Cairo following the Six-Day War. The general was his chief, then, and the Russians had learned a great deal from this field-testing, in real war, of some of their arms. They had, in spite of the disaster to Nasser's arms, also managed to acquire from Cairo a few examples of new Western military hardware, and technical lessons had been learnt from those, as well. Major Bakunin had been commended, by both President Podgorny and Marshal Zakharov, when they went to Cairo and agreed to replace up to eighty per cent of Colonel Nasser's lost equipment. In fact, it was Bakunin himself who had done most of the research work, and the general had got all the credit. And he could be useful to General Boris Kishniyev, Inspector-General of Ordnance, again. The opportunity of promotion had made him forget his rancour.

'Of course, Major Bakunin, this is a very different kind of war, more like the one carried out by the Americans in Vietnam.' The general had only been in Kabul for two days. He obviously did not know very much about the Afghan operation, which put Bakunin, as the expert weapons man on the spot, in a strong position. He had been studying the campaign against the guerrillas.

'In a sense, Comrade General, you are indeed right. But I would like to suggest that this is far more a war of small ordnance, and that flame-throwers, mortars and light and heavy machine-guns plus auxiliary equipment will be the decisive factor.'

This interested General Kishniyev, as Bakunin had known it would. He said, 'But everyone in Moscow claims that it is the helicopter gunships which will do the job, as we learned from their tactical use by the Americans, against the Vietcong.'

Everyone in Moscow. That meant the people who supported 'wings against stings', the air lobby which was always struggling with the gunners for primacy. Bakunin had prepared himself for this one.

'Tactical supremacy does not win wars, Comrade General, as I believe you once said, in that important speech at the Polish Military College which was afterwards published in *Krasnaya Zvezda*.'

Bakunin was rather a creeper, thought Kishniyev, and he did not get his facts quite right. Still, he might be useful in getting the Afghan anti-bandit weapons evaluation report done. And he did read *Red Star*, the Ministry of Defence newspaper; and remembered what he read: which showed that he was keen.

'Bakunin, at that time I also said that smaller weapons, mortars, automatic rifles, grenade-launchers and flame-throwers did not win wars, but had to be harmonized in operation with the overall plan.' Bakunin had been sent on ahead to do the basic study. How did he relate it to the general's doctrine?

'With respect, Comrade General, I was coming to that, for I think that it is your primary contribution to the moulding of strategic thinking.'

Primary contribution? Well, he might have an idea, let's hear it, the general thought. And the lunch at the Military Mission's mess was not bad at all . . .

'You do rather a good borshch here, and the bread is delicious. Have another drink and tell me all about it.' No point, the senior officer thought, in letting the fellow imagine that he himself had no idea how an inspector of ordnance could actually influence strategy.

Bakunin raised his glass. He had deep-set eyes, a mop of black hair, and the olive complexion of his trans-Caspian forebears. 'To the victory of the Socialist Camp and our fraternal aid to the peoples of the Marxist-Leninist nations!' They drank.

'In the evaluation of the disastrous outcome of the Six-Day War, your summary, Comrade General, insisted that short-range, wire-guarded missiles should replace heavy guns for the tank-killer formations of the Egyptian Army. The Egyptians pinned their faith, and based their strategy, on this doctrine. The result, though not a victory, was a significant loss of Israeli tanks, caused by the Egyptian Special Services and Seventh Brigade.'

'That's true. The thirteen-centimetre wire-guarded missiles did really well. This *is* excellent bread.' No point in looking too keen.

'The bread is made from Soviet wheat, Comrade General, supplied to the Afghan Government on the personal order of the President of the Presidium of the USSR.'

'*Soviet* wheat? But, Bakunin, this country is a rich cereal-growing one. What's Soviet wheat doing here – especially when we're having to buy grain from America?'

Bakunin searched his mind for a moment, arranging the correct words to explain. 'A lot of the standing crops have been destroyed in, er, operations. Farmers took up arms. They had to be punished. They are like our Kulaks, rich peasants who hated socialism, who had to be liquidated. Then, of course, er, terrorists have burnt some fields, to interfere with the land-redistribution programme.'

'Then what do the people eat?'

'A lot of the enemies of socialism starve, I understand. I certainly hope so.'

The general was a professional soldier, who had been in the army since the Great Patriotic War against Hitler, since 1942 in fact, and remarks like that brought back painful memories. He sighed. 'Carry on with your report, Major.'

'Comrade General. The ground-to-air missiles and the MiG fighters and fighter-bombers are for national defence, against invaders and so on. So is the heaviest artillery.'

'Yes, I do know that, Major.'

'This leaves among the rest, the tanks and helicopters, which in Afghanistan have a well-established role. Tanks can only move along certain kinds of terrain, and many get bogged down or cannot manage the mountain tracks; they are, therefore, of limited value. And there are separate reports for these two items, in any case.'

'Right, but continue.'

'Now, we know that helicopters can be used against all kinds of targets, but, as all armies have found out in counter-insurgency operations, at the end of the day the infantry must go in and flush out the enemy, man to man: or, at least, with relatively short-range weapons.'

'Exactly, Major.'

Bakunin was now getting into his stride. 'When, as in this country, the bandits move around and change their locations all the time, we use flame-throwers, light and heavy machine-guns, mortars and grenade-launchers and the like: all close-contact arms. Initially, when the Soviet Limited Contingent entered Afghanistan, during December 1979, they brought with them hundreds of tanks and large aircraft. Experience has shown, however, that we can best root out terrorists by a swift descent upon them, using the smaller weapons.

'The formation of small combat groups is the answer to the Afghan situation. We are busy forming these now. They will change strategic thinking. We have already produced good effects in counter-terrorist actions.'

'Yes, of course.' The general was pleased. 'I would like to see something of such operations, in the field. Could this be arranged?' Then, he thought, he could use a telling phrase in his report, 'as I observed in the field'.

Bakunin hesitated, though only for a moment. 'Every-thing can be arranged, Comrade General, and it will be my pleasure to do it. But it may take a day or two. The reason for this is that the political people do not like high-ranking officers, even anyone of field rank, to be too near a scene of action. There have been losses – senior officers killed, includ-ing fifteen generals – and this makes good propaganda for the enemy.'

'Damn the political people! I'm here to do my job. I have a

piece of paper from even bigger political people, saying that I must be given "every facility to complete my task".'

'Yes, Comrade General. I shall bring this to the attention of State Security at the highest level. Colonel Sementsev is the man. Then of course, we have to deal with Operations Command and Control.'

'And what about them? They're soldiers, aren't they? They carry out the operations, I watch them. That's all there is to it. It's perfectly normal, almost routine. I'm not trying to sleep with their wives, you know.' Even fighting soldiers, he thought, seemed to be behaving like bureaucrats nowadays.

'Understood, Comrade General. But we have had difficulties in the past. This is because Operations does not like non-combatant personnel near a scene of action . . .'

The general's face went purple. 'Non-combatant personnel! Son of an animal! Just you tell those fancy boys that I, Kishniyev, holder of the Order of the Red Banner and a dozen other medals for gallantry in action, was a fighting soldier, killing Germans, when they were pouring out liquid from both ends of their bodies in their cradles. Operations! They don't know what an operation is! I'll show you something, little father!'

The general unbuttoned his tunic and pulled up his shirt.

'What do you think this is, a love bite?'

He showed the scar of an old knife-slash, or bayonet-wound, stretching from his collarbone to his navel. 'This was done to me, to Doris Kishniyev, outside Kiev, in 1944, by a Nazi panzer grenadier. And it was I, even with my guts hanging out, who turned that Germanski bastard into good-quality fertilizer. Operations!'

'Homage to the heroes who saved our Mother Russia,' stammered the Major. 'I'll make sure that Operations knows of this.'

The following morning General Kishniyev, Major Bakunin and a captain attached to them by Operations, were standing on a hill overlooking one of the gulleys which commanded the entrance to the Panjsher Valley, north-east of Kabul. The armoured personnel-carrier was parked a short way off, with a black-haired, thickset, smug-looking officer in it. He had been introduced as Colonel Sementsev, and he made sure that everyone knew he reported direct to the State Security Chairman. 'I am reluctant, Comrade General,' he had said when he joined the group, 'to dignify a fly-swatting operation like this one, against *khuligans*, hooligans, with the presence of a man of my rank. I speak only of the dignity of the rank, not of the man, you understand. But I admit that the instructions are quite in order.'

The general disliked him on sight. Still, he knew the type: politicals dressed as soldiers – and they called them colonels, even generals. Moscow was crawling with them, and crawling was mostly what they did, when they weren't bullying. But they had power, and could only be handled with an equivocal joke. And if that didn't work, *kaput* . . . And what about his own, very senior rank, anyway?

'It is a great advantage to have you here, Comrade Sementsev. I agree that things like this are a bore, and must be doubly so for a man of your distinction. Still, we all have to do things that we don't like. It's the penalty of honourable service. Let's just look upon it as a day out, like partridge shooting.'

Sementsev relaxed a little. He was a terrible snob and he would be able to tell his wife that evening that, on a special mission, he had been hobnobbing with General Kishniyev, Hero of the Soviet Union. He might even get the great man to lunch with them. That would be quite a coup. At the same time he remembered with satisfaction that he was, in a sense, actually above the general. He had been told by Moscow to keep an eye on him. When people reached the rank of general, they sometimes said unwise things. Rank went to their heads, probably. There was that major-general who had defended the Crimean Tatars, saying that they had been unjustly decimated and exiled by Stalin. Pyotr Grigorenko, that was his name. They'd had to put him in a lunatic asylum and fill him with drugs. That was the KGB, they had the power. And then they'd slung Grigorenko out of the country, out of the USSR. That was the KGB, too. And all that remained of the entire Crimean Tatar nation was still in exile, somewhere in Soviet Asia.

Now Grigorenko's voice was heard on the terrorists' Radio Free Afghanistan, slandering the Soviet Union. That proved he was a traitor.

The four men were now looking through their field-glasses

at the countryside below. Panjsher, which means 'Five Tigers', had been one of the playgrounds of Afghanistan. Its beauty was such that people came from all over the world to see it, to swim in the rivers, to ski in the winter. Now it was the home of the infernal bandit Mahsud and his ruffians. The huge valley in the Hindu Kush slashed through Afghanistan in an arc, from almost Pakistan to above Kabul. It was used as a guerrilla base, and, as Bakunin's frank and indignant briefing put it, 'insolent interventionists and spies abounded, doctors from France were actually treating the Afghan terrorists there. And making films about it, and showing them in the West'.

But, the night before, men of a Soviet motorized rifle division had treed some of the tigers. In a small group of caves near the town of Gulbahar – 'Spring of Flowers' – commanding the valley's mouth, an advance party of Mahsud's guerrillas had established a look-out post, to warn of any approach into Panjsher by their enemy. The Russians, and a contingent from the Afghan Army, were dug in here, trying to seal the Panjsher off, to protect Kabul, only sixty miles away.

There were twelve of them, sent there by Commander Mahsud to gain experience and to constitute his outermost patrol. This was part of their two-weekly stint, after which they went to a remoter part of the valley for rest and relaxation, and some more basic training. Huddled in the caves, with no food, scanty ammunition and no radio to warn their chief, the guerrillas looked down on the Russian troops below, and knew that they would never get away. They had, it is true, left a sentry at the bottom of the cliff where the caves were, but he had been surprised by a Russian picquet of the airborne division in rubber boots and camouflage uniforms, who had then called up the riflemen.

'There're three caves, and we estimate about three or four men in each,' said the Afghan lieutenant who, for appearance's sake, was in command.

'How do you propose to deal with them?'

'We're going to make this a *letuchka*, a short training exercise, Comrade General, to give as many men as possible experience of how to do these things. Starving them out would take too long, and using heavy artillery would be a waste of expensive shells. So we'll use mortars.'

'Right. Carry on when you're ready.'

Lieutenant Ablagh saluted and did a smart about-turn. Until a week ago, he had only been a senior corporal, but, with the desertion of more and more Afghan soldiers, promotion was very quick these days. Anyway, he was a Kabuli and it was better to go into the Army and get somewhere than to be snatched from the streets by one of the pressgangs and kept in the ranks until a Muhjahid bullet got you. Or a knife in the back from some teenager in an alleyway.

The Soviet troops had drawn back three hundred metres, and a scruffy Afghan Army mortar crew, some of them only sixteen years of age, shuffled forward, reluctant, dropping things, spitting and cursing, looking at the Soviet general like dogs might at a vicious master, half-fawning, half afraid of him.

In the caves, the twelve men, three old, five middle-aged and four who were little more than boys, had dug through the limestone, working all night, and connected their burrows. Now the three small caves were linked they might just be able to think of something. Nobody knew what. But the digging had been something to do. For one thing, they needed only one look-out now, and the rest of them could take it in turns to sleep.

The limestone had been quite soft, and the back of the largest cave was big enough to contain the material which they had dug out. The evening before they had thought that they might climb out in the cover of darkness. It only took a few minutes to discover that this was impossible. Flooding the rock face with infra-red light and using special goggles and image-intensifiers, the Russians had been able to see any movement almost as well as if it were day.

At dawn they had assembled, leaving one man on watch, in the largest cave, while Feroz, their leader, served as prayer-leader, facing in the direction which they supposed was that of Mecca.

They took comfort from the familiar words of the congregational prayer:

> '*Glory to thee, O God! And thine is the praise and blessed is thy name and exalted is thy majesty: and there is none to be served besides thee . . .*'

Then they went back to their places, lying on the cave-floors, waiting for the attack.

'All ready to fire, General, sir.' The Afghan lieutenant was back.

'Right, carry on.'

Three mortars, three caves. The aim was so bad that sixty rounds produced nothing but holes in the cliff and powdered limestone. Emboldened by the conscripts' blundering, the guerrillas poured a concentrated hail of AK-47 fire towards them, putting them to flight, although at that range and angle the soldiers were in very little danger. A runner came up to the general, a piece of paper in his hand. 'Sending in the armour now, if you agree.' He signed it 'yes', and went back to his binoculars.

Below them a specially-adapted T-62 battle tank, its turret closed, edged forward towards the cliff-face. In place of its 115-millimetre cannon, it carried a strange apparatus, ending in a very ugly spout. The Kalashnikov bullets glanced off the thick armour-plating, striking sparks and giving the group in the cave little comfort.

Feroz said, 'Hold fire. We only have one thirty-round magazine left. Let's see what they are going to do.'

Fifteen yards away from the cliff, the Ognemetnyy tank stopped. Slowly, the long snout moved upwards, to an acute angle, until it was pointing directly at the centre cave. Then, by telescopic action, it was elongated, became thinner, tapering to a point. A distance of thirty feet separated the snout from the cave.

Feroz could see it clearly: the greatest of all horrors . . . *Atish-pash!*' he shouted, and started to take aim. Before he could fire, however, the *atish-pash*, the flame-thrower, like some obscene hose-pipe of hell, belched burning liquid death. Within a quarter of a minute, eight of the guerrillas were reduced to smouldering ashes. A pall of oily black smoke drifted over the cliff-top.

The other four, standing in their cave-mouths and waving unrolled white turbans in surrender, and coughing, retching, climbed down the cliff-face as prisoners. While virtually every other army in the world had discarded the flame-thrower, the Russians still had uses for it.

'Well done,' said the Soviet major, who had not taken any active part in the operation. 'But I wouldn't have started with such a raw mortar crew. They need practice. Of course, I'm only here as an adviser.'

'Fascinating,' said the KGB man, 'let's see the prisoners now.'

The general watched the captives being rifle-butted forward, but said nothing.

The four captives, three of them old, one very young, were ordered to sit on the ground as an interpreter appeared. The oldsters were wearing traditional Afghan dress: shirts over baggy trousers, with turbans on their heads. The youngest, Aslam Jan – who was fifteen – wore sandals, jeans and a zip-up windcheater. He looked like the schoolboy he had been only a month before. They were all dirty, thin and quiet; their eyes glowed, with fear, hatred and exhaustion.

'Have they said anything?' asked the general.

'Nothing much.' The interpreter, a thickset townee, wriggled in his ill-fitting suit. He hated the job, but it was all he could get. Anyway, his wife and children would have suffered if he had refused to serve the Army. It was a pity they had discovered that he spoke Russian. His parents had escaped from the USSR at the time of the Bolshevik Revolution and settled here.

One Afghan prisoner spat, as best he could with a dry mouth. The others did the same. Then they started to chant, slowly, enunciating the words carefully, looking straight at the Russian general.

'And what does that mean, Interpreter?'

'Nothing much, *gospodin* General.'

'It must mean something. Is it a religious hymn?'

'They are only dogs, filthy ones, *muzhiks*.'

'And they are saying?'

'They are saying, *gospodin*, "Death to Socialism, Long Live Free Afghanistan".'

'What are you going to do with them?' The general turned to the KGB man.

'I think they'd look nice hanging from that big tree over there, don't you, Comrade General? A sort of warning and an information-piece. We used to send captured bandits to

KHAD-i-Panj, Afghan Secret Police Office Five, but they always died under interrogation there.'

'They don't have any rights then, as prisoners, Comrade Sementsev?'

'They are not soldiers, they are criminals. Hanging them from a tree is justice. Assembling with arms is a crime under the Constitution of Afghanistan, and revolt against the State is a capital offence. State Security has a blanket instruction covering all such positive cases. All is in order. A proper report will be made out, of course.'

He spoke quietly and patiently, almost soothingly: in much the same manner as a humanitarian official in the West might to an old lady who was objecting to the destruction of a rabid dog.

The words of the official document of the Ministry of Defence of the USSR ran through the general's head. 'The Soviet Armed Forces shall be ready at any moment to inflict a shattering, repelling blow against imperialist aggressors . . .'

The Soviet group lunched at the Sementsevs' large, sprawling villa, a frenchified one built in the reign of King Amanullah Khan, in the nineteen twenties.

Natalia Sementseva plodded back and forth, carrying bowls of fruit, shashlik, yoghurt, bottles of wine and loaves of bread from the kitchen to the dining-room. They had three servants, but she was more accustomed to looking after the entertaining herself. She was as fat as Vassily Sementsev was hefty: but that was why he had married her. She came from the Ukraine, where men, she thought, tended to be rather crude, and she was pleased that she had landed such a sophisticated husband. 'I'm pretty high up in State Security already, Natalia,' he'd told her when he was only a fairly junior clerk, 'but I have prospects, you know.' In addition to being a perfect civil servant, he had an uncle who supplied many of Moscow's high officials with fresh fruit and other delicacies from Azarbaizhan.

It was a good meal, but the general had taken a little too much Georgian wine. His face became flushed and he looked morose.

Never mind, thought Natalia, as she watched him sitting there glowering, we are getting guests corresponding to our status at last, even if we are stuck in this mudhole called Afghanistan.

'I see a man,' the general was saying, in a deep, growling voice, 'a man with long hair and tattered clothing, covered in lice, howling at the enemy as he rushes upon him, a long knife in his hand. He is little better than an animal, with eyes blazing and murder in his heart.'

'Comrade General, you have described these beasts, these murdering Afghan savages, perfectly,' breathed Sementsev, delighted at the picture and revelling in the distinguished company he was now keeping.

General Kishniyev wagged his forefinger at the KGB man. 'I have seen these men, Comrade State Security Committee Director, seen them many years ago. I saw them when I was serving at the front, in the Great Patriotic War, when we drove the Germans back. I was eighteen years old then, in the Red Army, fighting for the Motherland.'

Sementsev was slightly confused. Perhaps the general *had* drunk a little too much. 'Saw them? But surely there weren't any Afghan savages on the Russian steppes?'

'No, they were not Afghan bandits, Sementsev, they were our own Russian partisans, our own guerrillas fighting for our land. And the fascists consumed them with flames, incinerated them with flame-throwers. They took many of them prisoner, too, and then they hanged them, hung them on trees. People come to resemble their enemies, Sementsev.'

Natalia was biting her knuckles. She wasn't over-bright, but even this suburban housewife, who had just heard the recital of an encounter with evil terrorists, and then heard this equated with the heroic Russian resistance, knew that something dreadful must now happen. She braced herself, as if to meet a blow.

Sementsev leapt to his feet, panting. His eyes were staring, his composure gone. For one wild moment he wondered whether this was a provocation, a test of his own loyalty. You had to be careful, after all. Recently the police in Moscow had been tested, by Andropov's personal order. Squads of *provocateurs* had broken traffic laws and offered vodka to the police when caught. Almost all the vodka had been accepted, and no charges were made by the police. But then all the policemen concerned were jailed, to concentrate the minds of the rest.

No, this wasn't anything like that, he was almost sure. The KGB's Third Directorate was responsible for army loyalty and for identifying disruptive elements. He must act now, even if it was only a trick.

He took a deep breath. All present, his wife, Major Bakunin and the captain, were goggling at the general. But the older man's eyes were looking straight ahead, fixedly, as if watching some far-off scene. He hardly seemed to be there at all, as he repeated hoarsely, 'Yes, yes, yes! Tactical superiority over the fascist enemy!'

'General Boris Kishniyev!' Sementsev's voice was hysterical. 'You are under arrest. The charge is treason and slandering the people of the Soviet Union. You know as well as anyone else that we are not fascists and do not oppress the toiling masses of Socialist Afghanistan. In Soviet Law, all members of the Armed Forces, of any rank, are answerable to the KGB for any political statement.'

The general, looking at nobody, very slowly removed his belt with the gun in its polished holster, placed it on the table before him, and held out his arms, as if for manacles.

He looked up, his eyes mild as a baby's. 'Comrade Officer of the Committee for State Security, I feel happy now, contented. Better than I have ever felt since the liberation of the Motherland after the Great Patriotic War. Do you, Comrades, also know what it is to feel freedom and contentment: to have found a chance to do your human duty?'

Two hours later, his wrists in irons, General Kishniyev was led to an aircraft and flown to Soviet Military Headquarters, Tashkent, en route for Moscow. Once there, he was sent for treatment to the Kazan Special Psychiatric Hospital, to become the two hundred and sixteenth major dissident in mental care.

When he saw the stamp of the Directorate of KGB Surveillance and Special Checking on the general's dossier, the head physician immediately filled in his diagnosis in the space provided. It read 'Formal diagnosis: Schizophrenia caused by philosophical intoxication.'

Massive doses of haloperidol, specific for schizophrenia, are the standard treatment for this condition in the USSR. In normal people, it causes fear, insomnia and physical rigidity. Those who have suffered its effects seldom recover from the horror derived from its generic name: 'Butyrophenone madness'.

'Son of a pig! Spit that out. You are not allowed to eat before you are hanged!'

The ancient guerrilla, Anwar, a porter in earlier life, smiled quietly, and took no notice.

The Afghan security agent, there as a witness, so that all the forms would be correctly filled in, struck him on the head.

The oldster smiled again, and asked, 'Does the brave policeman envy me my chew?' He did not have many teeth left, at seventy-four, and had been working on this morsel since he went into the cave, two days ago. He had had nothing else, except some water, in his mouth.

The security man wrinkled his nose in disgust as the starving man, thin as a stave, spat out a piece of motor-tyre.

The official report said, 'None of the terrorists would admit guilt and, all documents being in order, they were hanged at precisely three o'clock.'

2 Compassionate leave for Mr Khan

New Delhi
India

JUNE 8–14

'You have taken a lot of leave already this year, Mr Khan,' said the head of the department. He was not enjoying the heatwave in the Indian capital. And he had to spend far too much of his time dealing with applications for time off from staff who usually did not deserve it. They also generally had ingenious and less than candid reasons for asking for all this free time.

'Besides, Mr Khan, there is a lot of work coming in, and we need your linguistic skills.' He leant back in his chair and looked belligerently at the broken air-conditioner jammed against the window. Mr Khan, he reflected, looked every inch a prince; courtly, very tall, muscular and dignified as well. But after all . . .

'I know, sir. But you know, too, that I have always done my duty.' The Mirza Ilyas Khan knew that he had to go through this bureaucratic palaver. It wasn't as if he really needed a job. He could live without it. But, having been brought up knowing several languages, in a family with the equivalent of the Western work-ethic and an intense sense of duty, he could not, at nearly fifty years of ago, change his approach to life: nor did he want to. It had served him well. So he worked where he could be useful.

'Of course, I do realize that family affairs must be attended to,' said the director, thinking, although he did not say so, that the Mirza was indispensable to the department. Coming from forebears in Afghanistan and Turkestan, his connections and inside knowledge were international and important. That was in addition to his linguistic abilities. These things still counted for a great deal in the East. They probably always would, the director reflected. After all, he was not exactly a peasant himself. Mind you, India was a democratic and free country, but still . . .

'And we do, of course, appreciate your dedication to your work, Mr Khan.'

'Thank you, Shree Director. Of course, Director, you will have noted that I have, in fact, had less than half the time off that anyone else has had. And mine is, I assure you, a serious and delicate family problem. I am fully prepared to work my forthcoming holiday period, all of it, if necessary, in lieu.'

'That will not be necessary, Mr Khan: though we shall expect you to do whatever extra is involved in the upcoming workload of this Department. I shall allow you the required time off on this occasion, then. But please do try to abate your demands upon our patience in future.' After all, one had to keep some kind of rein on the staff.

The Mirza cleared his throat. 'Sir, I am most grateful. You can have no idea how much your generosity means to me in this vital matter.'

The director looked up at him, surprised at the intensity of the Mirza's words. Something really was worrying Khan. He began to feel sympathy for this slightly mysterious man. Mr Khan came into the office, worked hard and well, and went away again, day after day, year after year. He was a man of culture, of education, from a world that the director only dimly perceived; a world which somehow included poetry and horse-racing, ancient warriors and kings, courts and nobles of the old days.

He stood up.

'That's settled then. But you can only have from next Wednesday morning until the Friday afternoon. Two and a half days. You will not be paid, and I can't yet say whether it will affect your pension entitlement.'

'Thank you, sir.' The Mirza bowed, hand on heart, and left.

It was Thursday. That left the Mirza a little time to settle a few small affairs. Over the weekend he went to inspect the family property, near Delhi. He was the last trustee of the estate to reside there, and his thoughts were solemn as he walked among the tombs of his ancestors who had lived and died in India. And there were other things to consider. He made his will, and spent more time than usual with his wife, Salima, and son, Amin Jan, telling them tales of his ancestors, of chivalry and bravery, of victory and defeat, and of his own youth.

The Mirza's family had settled in India following the last of the many Mongol and Afghan conquests, before the British took over. His own life, as well as being rooted in the ancient traditions, was influenced by a public school education, by service in the army, and by his fame as a considerable chess player, an athlete and a crack shot. He spent much of the weekend with his rifle at the club range. He was preparing, as all the members knew, for the interdepartmental shooting championship.

On the Monday, he went to the Air India offices in New Delhi to get his ticket. The price was 2,866 rupees; $300 – nearly three years' income for an average Afghan. The weekly flight at this time of year left Delhi Airport at 08.25 on Wednesday, Flight IC 451. It returned on Friday, leaving at 09.25, arriving in the Indian capital just after midday.

The Afghan tourist visa, valid for a week, was no problem. Karmal's government liked to encourage Indian citizens, as a counter to the Pakistanis next door. It was even said that the Afghan communist chief had once tried to pressure Mrs Gandhi into a visit, expressing the hope that a friendship between India and Afghanistan would make Pakistan like meat in a sandwich.

'You're not a journalist?' the clerk at the Afghan visa office asked.

'Oh, no.'

'Good. We don't let them in. They only write lies. But you are welcome. I'm glad you're not going to cause trouble.' Three photographs, seven dollars, and he had his visa.

On Tuesday the Mirza sat at his desk, looking at documents and rows of figures, at letters and files, at memos and printouts. He got through his work, but he thought of Aslam Jan. Fifteen years old, and he was dead: the child of relatives of both his father and mother, the same blood as his, the same genes. The boy's parents were dead too, murdered, it was said, and God alone knew who else. He had heard about Aslam through a diplomat in Delhi, who had received a letter via the diplomatic bag, from someone in Afghanistan. All it had said was, 'Mirza. Your cousin Aslam Jan, an orphan, has been killed by order of the enemy.' In Persian, the message contained only fifteen words, one for each of Aslam's years.

3 Account paid

Kabul
Afghanistan

JULY 14–16

Compared to Delhi, it was cool at Kabul International Airport, with the morning breeze sweeping southwards from the Paghman ranges, and the snow-capped Hindu Kush standing sentinel beyond.

The Mirza had no problems with the customs officials, but he was kept waiting while people rushed about, looking for the immigration police. There were Russians everywhere, shouting and running about: nothing like the controlled efficient machines of popular fancy. Their frustration was not helped by the attitude of the Afghan officials, never known for their urbanity, who were plainly disgruntled and showed it at every opportunity.

The whole effect was unusual, almost quaint. It could well have been the performance of a very bad play, he thought, written and directed by someone who was trying too hard to imagine what a Central Asian country under Soviet domination might be like.

It was midday before he got to the city centre, and half-past twelve when he found his kinsman, the retired Colonel Sakafi, at his house near Tiger Gate, on one of the two hills which cut the Afghan capital in two. The Mirza had taken great care to make sure that nobody was following him.

The old colonel was sitting in a chair, swathed in an eiderdown draped over a low table, underneath which hot air blew from an electric fan-heater at his feet. He didn't mind when the power failed. It meant that the guerrillas had sabotaged the power lines again.

The colonel showed delight, but no surprise, at the arrival of his guest. He'd sent the message, after all, and had known there would be some kind of answer soon.

The Mirza embraced him, and took a place beside him in the sandali.

'Aslam Jan is dead, killed by the *Rouss*?'

'Captured in Panjsher valley mouth with other guerrillas, tortured and hanged. We buried him, of course, but . . .'

'But he has yet to be avenged?'

'Yes.'

'"*Verily we are from him, and to him we must return!*" Since this is a matter of *badal*, blood feud, we have to know who was responsible, so that I can do my duty.'

'We do know. The Muhjahid commander sent us word that we could have the right of retaliation, in accordance with tradition. We have to deal with a Colonel Vassily Sementsev.'

'Who is he, and where is he to be found?'

'Russian KGB, Colonel, State Security. His office, well guarded, is in the city, not far from here. He also killed another Afghan, named Lalbaz, of Turkestan, in the street a week ago. Without penalty. We'd have executed him anyway, for that.'

'Where does he live?'

'He occupies, with his wife, a large villa on the Bagram road a mile or so out of town. It was built by Zaki Puladi.'

'I know the house. We'll have to reconnoitre the area, though.'

'We can do that very quickly. How long are you here for?'

'Colonel, I must catch the Air India flight to New Delhi, leaving Kabul Airport on Friday morning at 9.25, your time.'

'Mirza: that means you've only got tomorrow! It will be hard to discover his routine in that time, almost impossible I would say.'

'We'll have to do what we can. What gun have you got? I'd like a long-range rifle.'

The colonel smiled.

'Oh my brother, I have a lovely one, all ready for you. Follow me and I'll show it to you now.'

The old man led the way to his woodshed in the garden behind the house. Inside it, a camouflaged door swung aside when the colonel pulled on it. 'I keep a small heater in here, to make sure all is dry and ready,' he said.

The shed had been built against a small cave, which was full of weapons. The Mirza didn't like the look of the bundles of dynamite sticks so near the naked lamp flame, but he said nothing. Pulling a long package wrapped in plastic sheeting from a wooden box, Colonel Sakafi presented it to the Mirza, holding it out on the inside of his forearms, palms upraised. It was the gesture of the armourer offering his weapon to the Crescentader, the Muhjahid, of old. Both smiled. There was hunting to be done.

Back in the house, the Mirza looked at his new gun. New it was, all right: it had hardly been used. A Soviet SKD, a Samossarjadij Karabin Dragunow, a beautifully-made, sniper's carbine.

It was well greased, and there were five ten-round magazines with it. 'Fifty shots, 7.62-millimetres long,' he said, counting them.

'That's right. Isn't it enough?'

'Plenty. However did you get hold of it?'

'The Russians are corrupt as all hell,' said the colonel. 'Believe it or not, this gun was sold to someone I know by a Nikolai officer who offered it for foreign currency. It cost us $500. On the frontier it would fetch $5000 from a Pashtun chief.'

'Foreign currency buys comfort in the USSR,' said the Mirza. He was cleaning off the storage grease.

'But guns buy death in occupied countries,' said Colonel Sakafi, 'just look at that telescopic sight. High-precision. That's why it's called a *snayperskaya*, sniping, rifle, by the Russians.'

'You know a lot about it.' The Mirza was interested.

'I have always liked guns. After all, I'm an old infantryman. You cavalry people are always lurching about: how can you take aim from a horse's back? You don't really know what shooting is.'

'I can shoot all right,' said the Mirza, 'although I admit I learned most of it on the range and tiger hunting. But give me some more details. I don't know these guns at all.'

'Right. What do you want to know?'

'Ammunition? Range?'

'Special ammunition for maximum accuracy. Accurate to about 1300 metres. The weight is about four and a half kilograms, or ten pounds to you Anglo-Saxons.'

'Anglo-Saxon *trained*, if you don't mind. What's the muzzle velocity?'

'Of the order of eight hundred metres a second: say about 2600 feet per second. Better than the Kalashnikov, and equal to most heavy machine-guns.'

'Excellent,' said the Mirza.

They discussed transport. 'What's the most unobtrusive vehicle we can get for a short field-survey?' Mirza TimurKhel was not well up on Kabul conditions under the Russians.

'A motorcycle. The Nikolais hardly ever stop and check people on them.'

'Can we get hold of one?'

'Yes, we'll call in Halim. He lives just down the road.'

'Can we trust him?'

'Completely. We have worked together before.'

While they sat drinking green tea with ground cardamoms, Anis, the houseboy, slipped out of the house to call the man with the transport.

It was a large, gleaming BMW, the R65 model, brought by a grinning youth with the 'European', red-haired, freckle-faced looks which have always surprised foreigners who imagined that all Afghans are swarthy. He worked for Afghan Tour, the semi-official Kabul agency which once organized sightseeing trips around the country.

'Halim's seen Sementsev several times,' the colonel said, 'so he can tell you what he looks like.'

The Mirza questioned Halim.

'Well, he looks very ordinary. Just like a Russian. Medium height, I suppose. I've only seen him sitting down, in cars and restaurants.'

'Halim Jan, can't I get just a look at him, somehow? Or see a photograph?'

'No, Mirza *seb*, there's no hope of that. These people always rush from one place to another, never lingering anywhere. You never get a good look at them. You could only see him at the office, and that's too dangerous. Otherwise, he'll be at the house or at one of the prisons or interrogation-centres.'

'Could you do me a sketch – or do all Russians look alike to you?'

Halim tried. It wasn't very successful. 'It's not that they look alike. It's just that this man is so *ordinary*. Like a man behind a desk, a minor official, quiet. Doesn't shout or wave his arms, or anything. I'm sorry, Mirza.'

'It's all right, Halim. He's a KGB colonel; does he wear uniform?'

'No: none of them do, except on special or social occasions.'

'No limp, spectacles, broken nose, bald head or anything?'

'No. He must be about forty, and he has a Slav face: you know, blue eyes and high cheekbones. A lot of them look like that.'

That would have to do.

They had a meal, and then the Mirza, with Colonel Sakafi riding pillion on the big motorcycle rode out along the excellent highway to look at Sementsev's house. They cruised around, the huge machine burbling beneath them, noting trees, wells, culverts and the like.

They went to pay their respects at the grave of Aslam Jan. The Mirza placed a token handful of earth upon it, and made his pledge of requital.

Just before the sunset curfew, they rode back into the city. Nobody had taken any interest in them. This, they agreed, may have been because almost everyone riding a motorcycle these days, especially a powerful one, was an official or in the police.

The Mirza worked with the rifle, cleaning and getting to know it, even speaking to it. It had been well protected, wrapped in oiled cloth and the barrel plugged. Its box had been part-filled with sawdust to absorb moisture. The colonel had packed the ammunition in silica gel, guarding against condensation, the worst enemy of the rifleman. The Mirza field-stripped the weapon with the greatest care, studying the mechanism and the electrics of the sight. After admiring again the scooped-out butt, which so effectively reduced its weight, he placed the gun in a secret hiding-place under the floorboards of the study, had a light meal of tea, bread and soup, and went to bed.

He had decided not to take the rifle outside to try any ranging shots, to get his eye in. Someone might hear. Besides, trying to kill with a gun he'd never shot with was Mirza the hunter's way of giving the Russian just a little better chance.

*

Thursday morning was clear and slightly sharp at first, with very little wind. As the sun rose, the Afghan Tour Land Rover, a long wheelbase model with a soft top, driven by Halim, arrived at the house to collect the colonel and the tourist from Delhi for a sightseeing trip. They drove around, scouting, looking again at the lie of the land, for two hours, and breakfasted in a wood six miles from the city. They slowly formed their plan, going over the arrangements again and again in the greatest possible detail.

When the Land Rover next appeared on the road where the KGB chief's house was situated, the business-suited tourist was no longer to be seen. Mirza, sitting beside the driver, now wore the garb of a Pashtun hillman; voluminous shirt, baggy trousers, turban wound over a conical skullcap.

Eight hundred yards from the target, Halim stopped the vehicle and the Mirza, thanking him volubly in rustic Pashtu for the lift, took his sacking-covered bundle from the back and started to walk along the road. Halim accelerated away with a wave and a shouted 'Happy hunting!' A massive Pashtun tribesman, somewhat down on his luck and therefore having to work for effete Kabulis, bearing a heavy pack with his tools in it, was the most natural sight in the world to those who passed him as he trudged along.

The houses, standing for the most part among trees, were each of two or three storeys, built in late Victorian style in the 1900s. Each was surrounded by a wall and usually guarded by a night watchman. There were many trees thereabouts, and the Mirza, during his reconnaissance, had marked down the perfect one for his purposes. It was a massive mulberry, with just the right kind of branches for a *machan*, the hide which he or his *shikari* had prepared in north India so many times in the past. Sitting in such a tree, with a goat tethered in the killing-zone, the hunter waited until the tiger, on the prowl, came for the captive animal. When he had killed and was eating the goat, one shot could be quite enough.

The mulberry stood alone, but in such a position that, by climbing upon an orchard boundary wall, he could reach its lower branches without being seen from any angle. How useful that Afghans had walled orchards, far from any house.

It was more difficult to climb, the trunk was smoother, and

the bundle with the rifle heavier, than he had thought. He was also less agile than he used to be. A man of fifty in the Afghan glens is usually still very active, but in the softer life of Delhi one tends to put on weight.

Now he was up. As he had guessed, the tree afforded perfect cover and a clear line of sight to the house he wanted, which must be – he squinted at the first storey, level with his seat – must be about 650 yards away. There was no wind.

He unwrapped the bundle and took out the rifle, a hammer, a large nail and a magazine, already charged with ten 7.62-millimetre shells. At this range, a bullet would take under a second to cover the distance to the target. He would be firing at only half the maximum effective range of the gun, so its accuracy would be that much greater.

He hammered the nail into the branch at his side, and hung the sackcloth from it. He snapped the magazine in and felt the gun assume the configuration and balance which had been designed into it.

Using the knurled wheel of the sight, he brought the front door of the house into focus and read off the scale – exactly six hundred metres. Six hundred metres is six hundred and fifty yards. Good guess.

He set the range into the elevation knob, and squinted at his target, using the point of the top chevron as his aiming point. The horizontal scale was obviously for wind correction. There was no wind at the moment: but if one sprang up later, he might need more than one shot. On the other hand, at this relatively close range, the wind might not matter. He'd know when the time came.

The Mirza was a good enough shot to drill a hole in the centre of an object two and a half inches by three and a half, at this range: and that was precisely what he was proposing to do. The size of a man's forehead.

He looked at his watch. Eight-forty a.m. Sementsev might have left the house by now for his office in the city. If he were still at home, he would probably leave soon, and this would not allow much time to kill him and make the final arrangements for his escape. If he could get to his chosen hideout in broad daylight. That would be very dangerous indeed, but the Mirza, thinking of Aslam Jan hanged from a tree, was not concerned about that. The main thing would be to keep young Halim and the colonel out of trouble. If the Mirza himself died – well, he'd had most of his life anyway.

Now for the house itself. He had done well to choose this tree and not to try to get any nearer. The place was surrounded by barbed wire. He could see the drive and the front of the house, and there were at least two, no, three sentry-boxes and a dog patrol. There were signs that a metal-girder tower was being built, and what looked like parts for an observation platform, and a demounted searchlight, lay on the ground beside it. Tools and sandbags, too: they were about to turn the place into a fortress. He was too far away for the dogs to be a problem; after all, there must be plenty of other people passing within this distance of the house, and the animals must be trained to disregard them. The dogs were German shepherds, really vicious-looking ones. Their handlers were Russians, in grey fur caps, Kalashnikovs slung across their backs.

There was no radio mast on the roof, but twin telephone wires ran on poles from above the porch towards the main road. Presumably they joined the ground cable at that point.

So far, it was obvious, the place had not been proofed against long-distance attack, against shelling, mortars or a sniper. There were bars, but no sandbags and probably no toughened glass, in the windows. They had just rigged up a defence against a fairly weak frontal attack. Quite enough during the first months of the occupation, of course, since most of the active snipers of Afghanistan were to be found in the south, towards, or on, the Pakistan frontier. Anyway, few of them had precision rifles effective over really long distances. Perhaps later, thought the Mirza, they will wake up and cut down this mulberry. But that would be helpful, one hoped, only to Sementsev's replacement.

Still no signs of Sementsev. The garage doors were shut; no car was visible. Did transport call for Sementsev, or did he drive himself? Anyway, it was time to check the other line of sight.

Over to his right, just under a kilometre away, was the second house. It was higher, standing on a mound, and it had three storeys with large windows. On the long, flat roof, too thin for him to see at this distance, there was a very long washing-line. He could see its white-painted poles.

254

The Mirza took out a matchbox and opened it. He unwound a long, thin wire attached to a tiny instrument, a mass of fine, soldered wires and transistors mounted on a scrap of circuit-board, with a built-in miniature microphone: a matchbox-sized VHF/FM transmitter, powered by a nine-volt battery. The wire was the transmitting antenna, and the range was 1,218 metres. The washing-line was – he measured the posts with the range-finder – 900 metres away. Excellent. The module was preset for sending on 100 megaherz, in the VHF band. It could be heard on any ordinary VHF receiver, the kind that thousands of people had, even in Kabul. It could also be picked up, of course, in the Sementsev house: if anyone was listening on 100 megaherz. But that would hardly matter, even if they were. Very short transmissions, under three minutes in duration, couldn't be located, so let Sementsev hear if he liked . . .

He placed the wire carefully, so that there was no tree, no building between it and the house with the washing-line. What was the time? Just coming up to nine o'clock. He was to check in every hour, on the hour.

At a few seconds to nine, the Mirza connected the battery to the tiny set to activate it and started to speak. 'No report. Show now if receiving.' This was short, and equivocal enough. Someone who just happened to be receiving on 100 megaherz at that moment might miss it, or would assume that it was a military or test transmission.

He disconnected the battery and looked towards the washing-line. It was fluttering with white sheets. Colonel Sakafi had heard, knew that the hunter had reached his *machan*, and had nothing to report. Communications were working perfectly.

The Mirza stowed the radio back in the pocket of his Pashtun shirt and looked towards the KGB man's house again. Still no movement. The tiny set which the Mirza carried had been brought back from London, two years ago, by a student, who had bought it for amusement. He had soon tired of the little toy, and it had quickly found its way to the Resistance when the Russians banned all non-official transmissions and equipment in the country. It had only cost four pounds in England, and it ran for sixty-five hours on a battery, the colonel had said.

It was a perfect shooting day: calm and quiet, crisp and clear. But where was Sementsev?

Mirza tried to visualize his prey: Russian, forty, 'ordinary'. Not exactly a classical villain. Perhaps it was just as well that he didn't have a grotesque description to contend with. This was, after all, to be an execution. But if he'd seen him, there would be less chance of killing the wrong man.

Now that was where a tiger-shoot was easier than a manhunt. When the tiger arrived, you knew your target. You didn't shoot a jackal which happened to be prowling around, instead. And, of course, you had the goat. But where was the goat in this case?

The question turned around in his head. Find the goat to Sementsev's tiger. If he could solve that one, there need be no mistake.

Put it into the back of your mind, Mirza told himself, and let your brain solve it. He took out some food: white cheese, bread and walnuts, pickles and a gulp of water from his flask. Hunting sharpened the appetite.

Colonel Sakafi sat by the washing-line on the flat roof of his old army comrade's house, waiting for the signal. He had the keys to the building, and it was so well protected, with iron bars and shutters, that Jasmine House needed no watchman. The colonel went in, from time to time, to see that all was well. Akram, who owned it, was always in Jalalabad at this time of year, where he had relatives and business interests. It was warmer, more comfortable down there. Akram had said, 'Use the place for whatever you will, my dear brother, a man cannot be in two houses at once: "the opportunity is dear", as the saying goes, "and time is a sword".' This proverb, therefore, had been chosen as the basis of the code which the Mirza would use to signal when he was to be picked up.

The place they had already arranged: a large, single-segment drainage pipe positioned by the main road, dry at this time of the year. The pipe was intended to carry the runoff from the slope above it to prevent the carriageway becoming a river when it rained.

If the Mirza finished the present matter quickly, he would have to be picked up soon after, and at great risk.

If he had to wait until darkness, or even stay all night at his post, he would have to be collected in time to catch the plane to Delhi which left Kabul Airport at 9.25 the next morning.

Twenty-four hours left, as of now . . .

Colonel Sementsev sat in his office and looked at the transistorized clock on the wall opposite. Nine a.m. He had left the house early that morning to look in at the prison, to see how the *stukachis* were getting on. These were the paid KGB informers, some of them prisoners, some guards and the rest officials, who provided him with a useful stream of information. He was an expert in this field, and also in planting *agents provocateurs*, an ancient KGB tradition. He had suggested to the Moscow people, when that old fool General Kishniyev was repatriated, that he might be put in a ward full of *stukachis* in the mental hospital. The result? Kishniyev had named, in conversation, several Red Army officers of high rank. They were 'sick of the brutality of the occupation forces in Afghanistan', as he had put it: in typical bourgeois capitalist jargon, of course.

Sementsev had been commended by the Comrade Chairman personally. Well, in a letter of course. That was pretty well the same thing as seeing him personally. 'Outstanding zeal in defence of socialism'. What melodious words. It could mean promotion.

There were things to attend to. He lifted the handset and telephoned his wife.

'Natalia. Is everything in order?'

Natalia Sementseva was breathless with excitement.

'Everything is fine, Vassily. All the food is in, all the drink; and the music is arranged.'

'Excellent. And everyone is coming?'

'Yes, everyone who is anyone. I am so excited.'

'Well, Natalia, just to confirm. I make it thirty officers of the administration – that is, rather, the fraternal advisory groups helping the Afghan Government. Some of them are high-ranking *apparatchiki*, permanent Party officials, you know.'

'I know, Vassily. You really are wonderful to get them. Of course, after the Comrade Chairman's message –'

'Yes, people are beginning to recognize our contribution at

last, after all this time . . . Well, we start eating at nine, and after that we'll have the music and dancing.'

Sementsev was rather good at the tango and foxtrot: the latest dances in his circle in the USSR of the eighties. None of that rock and roll, of course: the Chairman didn't like it. So far 'The Birdie' was not frowned upon. People flapped their arms on the dancefloor and clapped their hands as they hopped. But the Soviet Deputy Minister of Culture had just warned that Western music undermined youth.

'Of course there will be speeches and toasts and some moving patriotic songs,' the colonel told his wife. It was Sementsev's forty-fourth birthday. Entertainment always helped to cement contacts, especially when people were away from home, serving the Motherland in distant countries.

'The guests may leave by midnight: but you realize, don't you, that these important occasions sometimes continue into the small hours?'

'Oh, yes, I know: that's just fine! But you won't be late, Vassily? You'll be sure to be here to receive the guests?'

'Of course I shall be, my little pigeon. Home by about a quarter to nine. I have some very important interviews and so on: State affairs you know.' He broke off. One mustn't talk about official matters to one's wife, or on the telephone.

'Is the hot water system repaired yet, Natalia? It is? Good. And remember to have the servants put the red bunting up across the chandeliers. Well, I must go now, there are some important visitors to see . . .'

Sementsev put the instrument back in its cradle and shouted into the hall. 'Boy! Bring tea. And make it Indian tea with lemon and a lot of sugar, not that horrible green Chinese stuff!'

There were dozens of files to study. Moscow believed in keeping people busy. He leafed through the papers: reports on foreign infiltrators. He knew that none had been caught, or even really suspected: but the Kremlin had announced that foreigners, CIA men, were helping the Afghans; it would be a feather in his cap if he could find even one. He put that file aside for urgent attention. Then there were all the forms to fill in about former Russians, émigrés, resident in Afghanistan, and about suspect Afghans, people who had been abroad or who hadn't been seen lately. Give those to Prem Lal, that stupid Hindu in Afghan State Security, the preposterous fool who thought he should have the Order of the Red Banner just for working thirty years undercover for us in the police in Kabul . . .

The morning wore on. At midday, Sementsev called for his big Chaika and driver to take him out to the Intercontinental to lunch. Kabul was warm, but the cool breeze from the Paghman mountains made it very pleasant.

From two p.m. until the office closed at four-thirty, Sementsev did more office work, but mostly mused about the important prisoner he'd got in the bag. It was a woman, an *Afganka* who had been educated in Europe, an official of the Afghan Red Crescent, raising funds from charity sales and luncheons among the diplomatic wives, that kind of thing. Her name was Halima Iskandari, and she had been married to a former professor at Kabul University, who had disappeared. Almost all the academic staff, of course, were traitors: three months after the occupation, over eighty per cent of them had fled from the socialist regime.

This woman hadn't fled. When her husband disappeared – into Pul-i-Charkhi Jail, in fact – she had organized demonstrations by the families of the suspects, at the gates. When she was arrested and added to the catch, she had talked. Not directly, but foolishly. She had confided to another woman, one of Sementsev's prisoner-informers, that she had information that the Russians wanted more than anything else. She knew, she said, the exact location of The Eagle's headquarters.

And now, Sementsev smiled confidently to himself, she would tell him. The informant had been very clever, in two ways. She had pretended to cry and had constantly wailed that if only The Eagle were there, he would help them: and she had had the sense not to say anything to the Afghan guards, even to the commandant of the prison. She had reported the news directly to Sementsev. Too many Afghans were *turubchas*, 'radishes' – red outside, but white, non-communist, inside.

One of the reasons The Eagle and his band had got away with so much, Sementsev was sure, was that even the senior members of the Afghan Security Services were traitors. Or, at least several of them must be. Well, this time the KGB's equivalent in Afghanistan, the KHAD, would know nothing about it; not until The Eagle was caught, anyway.

Then, perhaps, Sementsev's promotion would come through. He'd already been told by his mentor in Moscow that something might be done for him, if only there were some fact, some achievement, to back up a recommendation for a transfer to a more pleasant spot. 'Frankly, Vassily Petrovich, though I have influence, there has to be something concrete to reward. I got you the posting to Kabul, remember, to enable you to distinguish yourself.'

Well, he'd provide something. The capture of The Eagle, the man that all Kabul looked upon as their hero.

He sat back in his chair. It was too soon to interview that Iskandari woman: they hadn't finished softening her up. They could be very tough, those Afghan crones . . .

Yes, a posting to somewhere really comfortable, really pleasant. Paris? Rome? Washington? The head of the German Democratic Republic's police mission in Kabul, now reorganizing the Afghan political police, had told him and Natalia wonderful tales of the life in the United States. He'd been there, operating under cover, undetected, for years.

A burst of wild, wailing music broke into his thoughts. Sementsev frowned. *And* he'd get away from all the physical danger that was getting worse in Kabul by the day. And from the incessant, hideous Indian film music, played day and night from the next-door building. There, the 'Pakistan freedom movement', the Zulfikar Organization had their offices. The Red Afghan government had given them sanctuary, when they stole a Pakistani aircraft. When the office closed, Sementsev had himself driven to a villa, formerly King Amanullah Khan's, at Daral-Aman. It had been built, sixty years before, in Afghan-baroque style: a mixture of Saracenic and French-bourgeois. The general effect was of a wedding cake gone wrong.

This was the secret headquarters of his interrogation unit, the Special Information Service, the *Khimama*.

The house stood alone, in the middle of five acres of landscaped garden: one of those breathtakingly beautiful Afghan gardens which successive, astonished English travellers had admitted surpassed even those of their own homeland.

But, up the marble steps, beyond the Grecian pillars and inside the iron-studded olive-wood doors, the place was a prison. Much of the interior, the graceful reception rooms, the cool passages, the study and billiards room, had been removed. Inside the gutted shell there were now only barred cages, cells, interrogation rooms, and one or two offices for the administration. The staff were mainly Russian, with a few Afghan and Central Asian interpreters and guards.

He made his way to his comfortably furnished office, with its Daulatabad rugs, panelled walls and great Jacobean desk, and called for vodka: the Ukrainian kind, Gorilka, with plenty of red pepper, and some sunflower seeds. This was, after all, cocktail time in the West; and he was preparing himself for the gracious life over there.

His assistant, *Kapitan* Anatoli Smirnov, had the file ready.

'Anatoli Grigorevich, how is the prisoner Halima Iskandari?'

The lanky, dark-haired youth shrugged, pushed out his lower lip, narrowed his eyes.

'Not quite ready, Comrade Colonel.'

'What treatment has she received?'

'Chemical and "hot" physical treatment. It's all in the report.'

Sementsev pursed his lips and flicked his eyes across the paper. Castor oil, sodium pentothal, the truth drug, beating with whips and rubber truncheons. He noted that the document was not signed. This was an internal reference paper. It would be destroyed as soon as he was finished with it. Things like that didn't go into the files.

'All right, let's go.'

He gulped his vodka and picked up a handful of sunflower seeds. Opposite the desk, on the far wall, was a padded door. The two men opened it and walked down three or four steps into the interrogation chamber.

It was not as well equipped as the Operations Room, the notorious torture chamber in the Afghan Interior Ministry's basement, Sementsev reflected, or the Central Interrogation Office at the Prime Ministry, the *Sedarat* – but it produced far better results.

In the middle of the floor, shackled to an iron chair, sat a tall, thin, middle-aged woman, wearing what remained of an expensive jacket and skirt, in light tan cotton. She had a face that had been beautiful. Her black hair had been dyed: it was now growing out, showing white at the roots. She'd been stripped and beaten: stripes of blood showed through the fabric of her outfit, in front, on the thighs, across her back. Her eyes were red and bruised, and she was filthy dirty. She had a long nose and arched eyebrows, and she scowled at the two men as they entered.

The uniformed Soviet soldier, standing below the windows, saluted.

Two Russians, dressed in the standard Moscow heavy black suits of outmoded cut, stood up. They had been sitting on a padded wooden bench which was bolted to the floor.

The whole place was bathed in blinding white fluorescent light, from a dozen long tubes fixed to the ceiling, protected by armoured glass.

Sementsev sat down and spoke to her in Dari. He already knew that she did not, or would not, speak Russian.

'Good evening, my lady. Are you ready to talk?'

She spat, though there was no saliva in her mouth. Sementsev smiled. He rather enjoyed this kind of thing: you might almost say, he reflected, that he had a taste for it. A little violence did a man good. A pity Natalia didn't share his interests: but, even then, he did manage to knock her about a bit from time to time. And it was a good old Russian custom, wasn't it? Every Russian worth the name would admit that.

'Mrs Iskandari: we know that you know where the man called "The Eagle" is to be found. You are going to tell us, and then we shall frame the charges for your trial. What you say now will determine whether you get a light or a heavy sentence.'

'I don't know what you are talking about! I have told your men that I did not say anything to that woman in the prison! She's imagining it, or she's insane!'

Her voice was a croak, and she felt unutterably weak.

Sementsev sighed, apparently with annoyance, in fact with pleasure. What a pleasant little apéritif to his evening's entertainment.

'What you do not realize, Halima dear, is that people *always* talk, *always* confess. You have read, and heard, no doubt, that "so-and-so was tortured, but would say nothing". We who are actually involved in such things know that this is simply not

262

true. There comes a point, if the police officer knows his job, when the suspect *must* talk. The mind and body, or one or the other, simply demand it. Oh yes, it makes a good film, makes a good tale, this "and he did not speak". The only circumstances in which people don't talk is when something has been bungled, or where the operator has lost interest.'

This was a long speech for him, but he had used it dozens of times, and liked it. Besides, in his experience it was true. The only truth he had not told her was that some people who tried to hold out went raving mad.

'Bring the Scorpion.' He hardly turned in the direction of the Mongolian-faced jailer, one of the two in civilian clothes, as he gave the order.

Two lengths of electric cord were clipped to the metal chair. They led to a box with a glowing dial.

At a signal, one of the men switched it on. The woman jerked in convulsions. By the eighth shock she was screaming, as the amperage was decreased and increased, to prevent her getting used to it.

They threw a bucketfull of cold water and carbolic disinfectant over her. When they stopped, all she wanted was a cigarette. But she couldn't have stood much more, and the Russians knew it.

Sementsev smiled again. No point in making it too easy. Besides, he still had one or two other little tricks to use. He stood up and took his assistant back to his room for a few more vodkas: Wyborowa, from Poland, this time, his favourite.

The two guards had taken the Scorpion machine out, leaving the soldier to watch Halima. He sat quietly, looking at her. Grasping at straws, she thought that she might, even at this stage, manage to outwit the Russian beast. If she did not, she feared that she would talk. If not now, then under more drugs, and if not that, they would have something else.

He looked like a Turkestani. Perhaps there was a chance.

She spoke to him in colloquial Dari. 'Are you a Moslem?'

He lifted his big, close-shaven head and turned red-rimmed eyes towards her. It was forbidden to talk to prisoners, but he usually took risks when he felt like it.

'I am an Uzbek.'

There wasn't much time. She knew he had a Caucasian

dagger, very sharp, in his boot. She'd seen it during the last beating. 'For God's sake, brother, kill me, now!' She couldn't talk if she were dead.

'Why, lady?' He was not surprised, only curious.

'What does it matter?'

He said nothing.

'My relatives will give you a hundred gold pieces.'

The Uzbek was looking interested. They'd certainly flog him, but he could say that she'd looked like breaking loose, or something. He'd get his gold. It was a wild hope but it looked as if he might really do it. He was certainly not too squeamish.

But when the Uzbek stood up, as if to walk towards her, Sementsev and the lanky Smirnov came back into the room.

When they had shut the door, the Uzbek saluted again. Well, that was that. The last hope gone.

Sementsev snapped his fingers. 'Now, madame, we shall continue. Will you speak?'

She shook her head. 'Burn in Hell!'

He laughed. This was going to be good. 'Bring the man in.'

The man must have been in the corridor just outside. Within a few seconds he was hurled into the room, fell sprawling onto the floor and was dragged across to lie between Sementsev and his victim.

'Farid!' She had thought her son was safe, among the guerrillas somewhere, after he had been reported missing, three months before. Now he lay there, a once-massive twenty-five-year-old reduced to a bundle of rags, caked with blood, one arm broken, one eye missing, moaning and half-dead. Her baby, Farid, a captain in the Guards, champion marksman, best athlete in his regiment, father of her grandchildren. This rag doll.

'Water.' At Sementsev's command the Uzbek splashed the captain back to consciousness.

He sat up, saw his mother, and tried to reach out to her.

Sementsev rubbed his hands together. This was better than the theatre.

'He doesn't know anything, I promise you!' The woman shouted in her agony, her eyes were beseeching Sementsev to show some mercy, praying that something might save her son.

'Now,' said the Russian, 'I shall have this traitor's throat cut in front of you if you don't talk. It took a great deal of trouble, and much of our blood, before we caught him. He should die anyway, for his treachery to socialism, to his country and to his soldier's oath.'

He looked at her with an obscene sneer, the excitement rising inside him.

'Unless, that is, you care to tell us where The Eagle is. In that case, his trial will result in, shall we say, only about twelve years' rigorous imprisonment. And that is light. The *Russians* we retrieve from the terrorists – they die.'

'Can I speak to him?'

'Say anything.' He made a mock-courtly gesture.

'Farid Jan, can you hear me?'

'Yes, Mother.' He tried to smile, but his contorted face would not obey. It looked terrible. Before he was handed over to the Russians, Guards Captain Farid had been tortured by the Afghan KHAD–*i-nizami*.

'Farid, you are an Afghan soldier. Be ready for death.'

It looked more like a smile now. He mumbled, 'I am ready. I entrust you to God.'

Halima Iskandari bared her teeth. 'Russian, lower than a monkey! You are not human beings! If you wish to do so, kill this man. Because he *is* a man, he is ready!'

Sementsev was slightly sensitive to the criticism that he lacked human attributes. Indeed, as with many Russians, it was the pointing out of the obvious which annoyed him. Uncultivated Russians, for example, as Halima knew, usually became enraged at being called uncultured. Halima reflected that this, in many cases, was like being angry if you said that someone had a nose on his face. Sementsev lost his temper. He'd show her. This should break her.

'Cut his throat.' The soldier took out a very large spring-knife, snapped it open, and slashed at the young man's jugular, as Farid murmured the last words of the phrase 'Verily we are from Him, and to Him we shall return.'

The blood gushed onto the floor. Within four or five minutes, the body had been removed, and the place neatly scrubbed by two shivering prisoners with buckets and brushes. The smell of carbolic again filled the room.

Sementsev recovered his temper when he saw the mother

shuddering uncontrollably at what she had seen. He looked at his watch. Plenty of time for the next scene.

He gave an order. A small table and a fresh bottle of vodka, with a small glass and salted nuts and raisins, *kishmish*, was put before him.

The woman was moaning like an imbecile, but Sementsev was glad to note that she had not entirely taken leave of her senses. The next item on the programme would undoubtedly provide a fitting and successful climax.

She did not look up when the door clanged and another battered figure was thrown at her feet.

Sementsev waited. Women were always curious. All it needed was to arouse their curiosity a little.

'Mrs Iskandari, who do you think we have here? I wonder if you can guess?'

Sure enough, she looked: slowly at first, then with a jerk of the head. It was her daughter, beautiful Roshana, brilliant artist, a noisy but fascinating girl, with her mother's looks and her father's personality, people said. Eighteen years old.

Their eyes met, and Halima Iskandari felt as if something had died within her.

People spoke of the fires of Hell. Was there a hell worse than this?

Sementsev was watching, alternately throwing back tots of white spirit and chewing nuts and raisins, a fixed smile on his face. He had looked into Halima's eyes and he had seen just what he wanted. He had won, as he'd known he would.

'Mrs Iskandari, you will either talk, now, or you will see what can happen to a girl, with all the possible variations, performed in front of you, starting with these idiots here, and followed by, oh, shall we say, twenty or thirty others.'

'"I call you to the judgement of God, before tomorrow's dawn!"' Without knowing what she was saying, Halima screamed the words from the Classics, '"Have fear of the cry of the oppressed!"'

The Russian laughed, really enjoying himself.

'Yes, yes, *Afganka*, I'll remember that. God's going to call me for a little talk about sulphur and brimstone and demons with pitchforks, before the sun rises once more. Very poetic, old witch. But you will talk now, won't you?'

He knew the answer before she said it.

'Yes, I'll talk. May God destroy you and all your people, as he has destroyed the evil ones a thousand times before!'

Sementsev could hardly stop laughing. What a comedy for an atheist, to see these wretched creatures relying on something that did not exist.

Sementsev sent the other men out of the room. Security would have to be absolute: the secret – and the credit – would be his alone.

He stood before her and, after a moment, nodded, as though signalling the exact instant when she should speak.

Halima Iskandari told him about the caves, deep in the Paghman mountains where The Eagle, Kara Kush, was to be found.

Sementsev slapped her face. 'You realize that if you have lied, you and your daughter will have to pay even more than you already have?'

'Yes.'

He was too good an interrogator to doubt that she had told the truth.

Then he handcuffed the girl's wrists behind her back and raped her while her mother watched.

When he had finished, Sementsev got up from the floor and walked to a hook on the wall, from which he took down two wooden handles connected by a piece of piano-wire. Slowly, with an entranced expression on his face, an expression which made him look almost benign, he strangled both the women. Security was complete. It was a very satisfactory feeling: especially as he still had his birthday party to look forward to.

'Dead before tomorrow's dawn', indeed! Dead? He was just beginning to live.

Absolute security. The woman was dead. He'd got The Eagle's location and would report it personally to the military in the morning, verbally. By tomorrow afternoon The Eagle and his band would be wiped out or in prison.

Now it was time for a good hot bath, a shave and a change into uniform. After that, a pleasant drive home to dear, plump Natalia and the birthday party which she was preparing at this very moment.

He chuckled all the way to the house, at the memory of the

curse. 'Hello, God! I've come a little early, but you see this crazy *Afganka* woman summoned me to appear before you before tomorrow's dawn . . .'

It was cold, now, in the tree, and the Mirza hadn't brought a warm coat. The quarry was undoubtedly away, at work. That meant he'd have to wait until six, at least. No sign of life from the house: nobody had been in or out for – how long? Nearly six hours; it was now three o'clock in the afternoon. There had been so little movement around the place that the Mirza, at first thankful that all was so quiet, now craved almost any stimulus, any sign that would connect him with his enemy. Only the busy helicopters, on observation missions, had disturbed the silence of the day.

The workmen who must be involved with the improved security, the tower, the light, had not appeared. Just as well. Time to check in now. He called the colonel, sticking to the agreed wording. The washing on the line twitched in answer. Surprising how long a day could be if one was doing nothing . . .

Suddenly, the Mirza stiffened. A delivery truck, its canvas hood strapped down, had arrived at the door of the Russian's house. The driver got down, stood by the barbed-wire fence gesticulating, and seemed to be shouting. Within a few seconds, the patrol appeared. Either there was nobody in the sentry-boxes, or they were asleep. Anyway, the Mirza hadn't seen any guard-change yet. Holding the dogs back, the guards, two of them, opened the gate in the fence and beckoned the vehicle inside. It was driven to the back of the house, out of sight. Well, nothing much there. It didn't look like Sementsev coming back, unless he was taking extreme precautions, a possibility which the rest of the picture did not bear out. Besides, the truck wasn't guarded or armed so far as one could see. And why would Sementsev be returning in mid-afternoon? A few minutes later the truck appeared again and, waved through by the same guards as before, rolled along the drive and disappeared in the direction of Kabul. False alarm.

The Mirza reflected, at 6 p.m., that in only fifteen hours he'd have to be at Kabul Airport, heading for home. Time was his luxury.

*

It was going to be even colder tonight. If he had to wait until then, the Mirza was prepared to do the job at close quarters. Somehow, in that case, he'd have to get through that barbed wire. Not over it: the height was more than fifteen feet. Evade, or deal with, the dogs and the patrol, and any other guards who might appear. Find where the quarry was, and deal with him. And then get out and away, if that were possible. If not, Colonel Sakafi would get the news back to Amin. He was only ten years old, but he was already a good shot and spoke the two chief Afghan languages, like all the family. It might be, say, four years before Amin could undertake the task, but that he would do it, and avenge his father, the Mirza was certain.

Eight-forty. It was time for the sunset prayer.

Eight-fifty p.m. There was a car coming, its engine drowning out the wail of the distant Kabul curfew siren. A large Chaika, the Russian model which looked like one of the flashy old Packards, without an escort, coming in very fast, off the main road. This must be him. There were lights on in the house now, and a bright one illuminating the front entrance. Why no escort? Because it was probably safer to look anonymous: a car could be ambushed on the road if it had a telltale escort of motorcyclists.

The men of the patrol had opened the barbed-wire gate before the lumbering, twenty-foot long Chaika reached it. They could be seen, dimly, standing to attention just inside. The Mirza suddenly cursed. If he had known more about the conditions, *that* would have been the perfect place for the ambush. They hadn't surveyed things properly, any more than he had. Of course, he'd had no time, but they had had plenty. There was a clump of bushes where he could have hidden, and a couple of grenades would have done the job from there. People on guard, standing to attention, were ridiculous under alert conditions. All very well when you were playing soldiers, on a parade ground or 'standing guard' somewhere for ceremonial purposes.

Too late for that now. The car swept into the drive, headlamps on full beam, and stopped at the front door. A rectangle of light flooded out. The man who was opening the door looked like a soldier. Mr Sementsev's wife was wise not to greet her husband herself. Or perhaps she was busy with the dinner arrangements. No chance to shoot.

The KGB chief – or at any rate, a man of medium height – entered the house, and the car was driven to the back. There must be another garage there, or perhaps the driver was going to the kitchen for a snack and a smoke.

More lights in the windows. Yes, that must be the main reception room. Ground floor. It had long curtains, filmy ones, which showed up the heavy iron bars. Looking at the windows through the telescopic sight did not help much. The gauze of the curtains fuzzed everything in the room beyond. Except some moving figures. No, what would have been useful was an infra-red sight or telescope, to sweep the immediate approach to the place, to learn of any movement around the house, in case he had to go into the close-quarters mode. Some infra-red sniperscopes intensified even starlight, made the darkness almost as bright as day . . .

The thought suddenly struck him. Infra-red, of course! For all he knew, everything he did was being watched, from the house, by infra-red. Then he remembered that the Dragunow had a sophisticated infra-red detector. He could check.

The Mirza felt for the detector switch. There it was, at the top left of the 'scope, three-quarters of the way along. Flick it on. He moved the range drum to setting '4', for infra-red, and looked through the sight. No sign. Now sweep from left to right, slowly. If an orange-red blob appeared in the telescope, it would mark the point from which he was being observed. He could hit such a source in the dark, by aligning the reticule on it, but the muzzle-flash of the shot would give away his presence. No coloured light. No infra-red. He relaxed.

Time to test the night-firing procedure. The Dragunow had a battery-operated shielded lamp which lit the sight needle when a switch on the gun barrel was turned. Yes, it worked perfectly. Just as well the battery hadn't run down. The Mirza could see the glow of his sight perfectly.

That about completed the technical work. Time to do some more dynamic exercises, or he wouldn't be able to run when the time came. And, of course, the finger and knuckle exercises, to keep supple for the trigger work.

Nine o'clock. The Mirza checked in on the mini-transmitter. Too dark to see the washing on the line now. The colonel would turn on the bathroom light to signify 'received your message'. Yes, there it was. Strange to think that his lifeline was a yard of flimsy wire.

He turned back to his quarry's house just in time to see the first cars approaching from the main road. There was a whole string of them. Several were those outdated five-seater Zhigulis, Russian copies of the old American Plymouth. They cost $12,000 and were greatly coveted by high officials. As automobiles, they were rubbish; but as Soviet status symbols they were second only to the top car, the luxurious Zils, imitations of the Lincoln Continental. The cars stopped, to be checked and admitted through the security gate. As each car deposited its passengers, it drew to the side and did not immediately leave, allowing the following cars to let their occupants out. Then, when there was a gap, the car turned, went down the drive, passed through the gate, and headed towards the Kabul road again. So, Sementsev was giving a party.

As each guest arrived, the Mirza could see a man in the warm glow of the front door with his hand extended. Sometimes a formal handshake, sometimes an embrace with both arms, sometimes a real bear-hug. There was no doubt that this thickset figure was Sementsev, the quarry, the tiger. And he was only about five feet seven inches tall. Good. And the guests? No doubt, either, that they were the bait which had brought him out.

Sitting in his machan, looking at his tiger, Mirza Timur-Khel chuckled to himself. There it was. He had lacked a lure, the customary goat. But he had not had to bring his own. The tiger was providing a whole herd of them.

The guests did not start to leave Sementsev's house until well after midnight. The Mirza had counted the hours, keeping himself awake with difficulty. In such cramped conditions there was a great danger of falling asleep. He had been here for fifteen hours now: no tiger ambush ever lasted more than nine or ten hours, at the very most.

Here they were, at last; guests leaving, cars picking them up, affectionate and slightly drunken farewells, floodlights on. With luck, he might get the man, though only as a silhouette.

That was rather a problem. Every marksman has fired at sometime or other in the dark, of course: but always at a lighted target. Whenever Sementsev came to the door to speed a guest he was not in the light. The bulb shone behind him, outlining his head almost like a halo. Would that affect the aim, mislead the retina, cause the bullet to go wide?

The Mirza had counted some thirty people going into the house, and had not had a single chance to shoot. At least ten times he had started to squeeze the trigger when, through the magnifying telescope, he had had the host's head in the middle of the crossed threads. But always he had moved away, almost as if he knew that he was in the sights.

So there were thirty who would be going home, and, not all of them at once of course, so there should be several opportunities. He knew nothing about Russian parties. How long did people stay? Were they all seen off by their host?

In the event, the guests left in ones and twos. Sementsev came out each time to say goodbye. They were drifting away now at quite nicely spaced intervals. They must have telephoned for their cars, which were always waiting when the door opened.

Seven people had left so far. There were now less than six hours left. That raised another question. Would it be better to wait for most of them to go, or to strike as soon as he had a perfect opportunity? In the first case, there would be less people available for pursuit. In the second, he could start his escape straight away, while he still felt like it. Because there was an itch in his mind which suggested that he might shoot Sementsev and then, instead of retreating, finish off a few more of them, just for the sport of it. But no, some might be innocent; he was here as an executioner, not a murderer.

He had wedged the gun on an improvised rack, nailed to the branch in front of him, so that he could use it, like the ancient musketeers, to take the weight and prevent the trembling which came from muscle-fatigue.

The rifle now lay at the perfect angle, its butt against his cheek. It was pointed directly, and slightly downwards, towards the place where Sementsev's head was usually to be seen when he came out of the door. It was a self-loader, of course.

The Mirza sat still, breathing slowly and evenly, with every muscle slack, his eyes glued to the rubber moulding of the sight. Tension caused wobble. At this range that could be a real problem. He did not want to loose off shot after shot, like some cowboy in a movie, however satisfying it might feel. He was a trained sharpshooter: professionalism almost demanded that he should do the job in one shot.

The door opened a crack, then stopped. He noted with satisfaction that his breathing was not affected; the pulse-rate perhaps, he could not tell, but the breath was perfect. He was glad that he did not smoke: shallow breathing was the best, but it had to be in long, even breaths.

Was Sementsev never going to open that door?

The time dragged on. Two o'clock. Five hours to airport check-in.

Now the door-crack was opening wider. Sementsev and his friend must have been having a last-minute word, or perhaps it was a drunken handshake. The guests who had come out last were staggering slightly, and one stumbled and even fell. An extra bonus.

The door was wide open now. There he was, the tiger, moving forward. If he came any farther, he'd be too woolly, less than a shadow, and it wouldn't be worth trying. Now here was the man Sementsev was seeing off. Good, there was no confusing them: the other man was very short and slim, and Sementsev looked almost tall beside him. Yes, both were moving slowly, swaying slightly.

They were still talking. The guest stepped almost, but not quite, beyond the range of the light. Better still. Through the magnifying lens of the 'scope, the hunter saw Sementsev move forward. Now: he was the perfect target. Stay there, murderer, while sentence is carried out . . . he fired. The recoil compensator was so good he hardly felt the weapon lurch.

A tremendous urge to run, to get out of the tree, even to fall out, to run forward and attack or else to run away, away to safety, began to take hold of him. He could feel it spreading through his whole body, like the craving for a drug. One word came rushing to the rescue: discipline. The Mirza's army training had not been wasted, or forgotten. He sat stock still. This feels like an age, he thought, but *I must wait until I see him fall*.

It must have been less than a second, for so far the man had not moved at all. Then, as if hit by a tremendous punch, Sementsev spun sideways, into the lintel of the door, arms upraised, knees stiff, body curving. It was like slow-motion, and the Mirza could see his every movement as he fell. He was too experienced a hunter not to know when the quarry has been killed. No, Sementsev had not been merely wounded, however badly. He was, clearly – and cleanly – dead.

As the Mirza gathered up his rifle and equipment, he could see that the people at the front door were milling about, like ants when their nest is disturbed, their very movements speaking of their puzzlement. He kissed the warm metal of the gun.

He had expected to be exhilarated, and he was. But he had not reckoned with the euphoria which now made him want to stop, to go straight home to his wife and child, like someone who has been to an entertainment in town, and now wants only to rejoin reality, perhaps to talk it over in a warm room, sipping a cup of tea and munching tiny sweet almond pies, with the curtains drawn against the winter . . .

The floodlights had gone out, and there was some firing, though not in his direction. Perhaps a panic-stricken Russian had imagined that they were being attacked by guerrillas from the road. Good, they still did not know what had really happened, so they would not know what to do. Perhaps they needed a good NCO, someone to take charge. 'I'm sorry,' he said aloud, to the picture of Sementsev's family in his mind. 'But it was a debt, and it is not seemly that a man should owe.' To Sementsev's shade he said, 'You hanged a child, and we gave you a soldier's death.'

Now he was down from the tree. No cramp. Lucky he had remembered to do static exercises. Well, perhaps a bit stiff. That would soon wear off. No time to talk to the colonel. But the old man must know that something, good or bad, had happened, since there had been no call at two o'clock.

Over the wall, on to the ground. Now down the road, up the slope. Hard to see in the dark. He followed the road, though quite slowly, by dragging and tapping a stick which he had picked up. Moving incongruously like a blind man at a trot, the tap of the wood telling him when he was off the tarmac surface. The smell of honeysuckle was now very strong. There was a bush of it directly beside his destination.

There it was now, the honeysuckle. To the side. Yes. The

shape of the huge drainage pipe, well over two metres in diameter, just up from the road, concreted into the rocks on the slope. Full of brushwood, nice and dry.

Into the pipe. Hunter turned hunted. He arranged the brushwood, at the mouth of the segment of pipe. Not too densely now: that might encourage someone to investigate. There were a lot of these pipes, set starkly into the hillside. Could they, would they, search them all? Sometimes, of course, they were full of scorpions. The Afghan black scorpion was the most deadly on earth. He shuddered. Still, this was the best idea that they had had when they had made their plan.

If a pursuit party came along this road and looked into the pipe, they'd have him for sure. With his teeth, the Mirza tore open a plastic bag and started to smear its fatty contents all over his clothes. There was no time to take them off. Then he applied the stuff, liberally, to his hands, face and head. Snow-leopard grease. For centuries the Pashtun tribesmen had used this when on a raid, to approach a house or pass through towns. Dogs were mortally afraid of the leopard smell, and would not go anywhere near it. In fact, when they got wind of it, they fell silent, probably prompted by some ancestral fear.

He must be less than seven hundred yards from Sementsev's house now. On the main road, like every kind of a fool. But he had refused to make his way to where the colonel was waiting. If there was a house to house search, and that was possible even in this place of scattered dwellings, old Sakafi could well be compromised. It was the colonel who had thought of the leopard-grease, when he had reluctantly agreed to the Mirza's hiding in the pipe.

Now he could hear the dogs, and smiled. They were on the right trail, but he guessed that it was most likely to be because whoever was in charge found it easier to hare down a surfaced road than to scramble across country, through parks and gardens, streams and lakes, in a prosperous suburb which was half a rocky wilderness, than for any other reason. He must be an old soldier, probably a senior sergeant. That was how they always thought. Still, he would also be doing some real hunting, even if only because there would be other men with him, who would observe his zeal or otherwise.

The dogs were getting closer, barking furiously as they ran; and men's voices were mingled with them now.

It was strange how one thought, under stress. The barking now actually sounded to him like the words 'come out, come out'. He remembered that someone was supposed to have said to a squirrel, 'Why don't you come out in the winter time?' The squirrel had answered, 'Look how they treat me in the summer, why should the winter be any better?'

Now they were very near, say about a hundred yards away. No, even nearer. There were the beams of their flashlights, actually probing through the loose brushwood of his shelter, getting in his eyes. Now there were tackety boots turning, slowing down. They were coming close to the drainpipe. He could hear voices, could make out their speech. Russian. He couldn't understand a word. He kept absolutely still.

The dogs had started to whine, then fallen silent. Now the guards were cursing them, urging them on.

Maybe one of the men would come and check the pipe himself. Just room enough to aim this rifle from the hip, like a cowboy with a shotgun. Yes, that was it. He would take some of them with him. Nine rounds left, probably more than enough to go round. In the dark, though, he'd have to shoot at point-blank range: remember to aim just above, and to the right, of the flashlight's bulb. For the heart. Of course, if the Russian had the light in his *left* hand . . .

No, they were going away. The sound of boots, receding down the road, the dogs barking again. Everything normal. Thank you, heroic and kindly snow-leopard. I'll call my next son by your honoured name.

The time now? Just before three o'clock. Four hours to airport check-in. Could that lifetime have lasted for less than an hour? Colonel Sakafi would now be listening all the time.

He could call in now. The Mirza arranged the transmitting wire so that it was outside the pipe, with no obstacle between it and the Jasmine House, and connected the battery. 'Is that you, my *bulbul*, my nightingale? This is your Majnun, pining for his Laila. Opportunity is dear, *job done successfully*, and time is a sword, *I am well and holed up as arranged*.' He added, 'As arranged, beautiful lady, six kisses at your boudoir window.' The code for *pick me up here at six in the morning*.

There was nothing more that he could do. No way to get confirmation that the message had got through. The only thing now was to wait. It would be suicide for them to try to collect him during curfew, which didn't end until 4.30 a.m., even without the hue and cry for the killer of the KGB man. Three hours to go. Funny how tired he felt: the adrenalin must all be used up. He packed up his things as neatly as he could by touch, and lay back instantly asleep.

The revving of a Land Rover engine woke him. It was backing off the road, its rear end coming towards the entrance to the pipe. As it touched the circular concrete rim, the Mirza tore the screen of brushwood away, and saw Colonel Sakafi, grinning from under the soft-top canopy. 'Well done, warrior hero! Six in the morning. No Nikolais in sight.'

He was wide awake now, the bundle had been thrown into the back, the colonel was making room for him. Halim finished the imaginary task under the bonnet which had covered the embarkation, and they were off.

On the way to the airport the grease-ridden Pashtun became the Indian tourist again, taking his suit from the case which the colonel handed him.

There was a roadblock on the highway, but the tour agency car was waved right through by the bored trio of guards: one policeman, an Afghan corporal and a Russian private. None of them could read the Roman letters of the English text, or the Sanskrit of the Hindi on the Mirza's Indian passport, anyway.

At the airport the Mirza described the events of the night. Nobody seemed to notice, at the entrance gate, that the guard-dogs tried to strain away from the residual whiff of snow-leopard still on the Mirza. Halim flashed his official card, and managed to get hold of a soldier to guard the Land Rover. The night before he had caught someone unscrewing the petrol cap, while in his other hand he had a packet of sugar, already opened. It was a complicated life, working for both sides.

The Mirza shook hands with his friends as the announcement called passengers to check-in for Flight IC 452.

'What are you going to do with the gun, Colonel *seb*?'

'Keep it, of course.'

'Supposing they search the wagon on your way back to Kabul?'

'They usually don't search semi-official transport, except in curfew hours. But, in any case, I like to take a little risk now and then, it seems to keep one young.'

They embraced. 'Thank you for your hospitality.'

'You have honoured us.'

'It was my duty.'

'Safe journey.'

'I entrust you to God.'

They might have been any ordinary people, seeing off a friend after a short and refreshing holiday, a midweek break.

There was unlikely to be any complication now. The Mirza checked in and picked up his hand baggage. Through passport control. Now the departure lounge. 'Boarding please' . . . Air India stewardesses in saris, smiling passengers. On the plane.

By two o'clock that afternoon, Mirza Ilyas Khan was going up the steps of the office building near Connaught Circus.

The *chaprasi* on duty at the door came to attention and saluted with that imitation of the British gesture which is still standard in independent India. Unlike the westernized office staff, who preferred to use English, he spoke in Urdu. '*Apka mizaj?*'

'*Thik, mehrbani*. Well, thank you.'

'*Koi khabar?* any news?'

'*Hech*. None.'

As he walked past the open door to the room where the head of his department sat, ever-watchfully, he heard the familiar voice, and braced himself for the stilted officialese.

'I am glad to see that you are back in station, Mr Khan. It is gratifying to me that you are not late, also.'

The Mirza entered the room and bowed. The heat was stifling after Kabul, and the air-conditioner was still on the blink.

'It is to be hoped that your family members are well now?' The director smiled mechanically.

'Yes, sir. Everything went well, and within the time which you so kindly allotted.'

When they had seen the Air India plane take off at Kabul, Colonel Sakafi and young Halim headed homewards.

The Land Rover stopped on the way, beside the grave of

their kinsman, the Muhjahid Aslam Jan, and they got out.

The colonel slipped something from his pocket and pressed it into the still soft earth, in the midst of the flowers at the gravehead. It was a single, empty 7.62-millimetre brass cartridge case.

'It is done, *shahid*, martyr, Aslam Jan,' he said.

While the Mirza returned to his office nearly a thousand miles away, a messenger was shown into the cave where Adam sat, secure within the Paghman Mountains.

'A verbal despatch, by relay runner, from Colonel Sakafi, in Kabul, Komondon Kara Kush.' The man stepped forward, kissed Adam's hand, and stood, with hand on heart.

'Very well. Give the message.'

'The message runs, "The execution of the murderer Sementsev, in retribution for the death of the Muhjahid Aslam Jan, took place this morning before dawn outside Kabul, in accordance with the traditional Law. Sentence was carried out by the warrior Mirza Ilyas Khan, of the Timur Clan."'

BOOK 6

Daughter of Daniyel

The Afghans themselves proudly believed themselves to be of Israelite origin and their own historians, as men stating an established fact, refer to them as Ben-i-Israel – the Children of Israel . . . There were indeed a number of resemblances between Afghan customs and physical characteristics and those of the Jews, and certainly the Afghans displayed towards their foes a ferocity equal to anything to be found in the Old Testament.

Patrick Macrory: *Signal Catastrophe* – The Story of the Disastrous Retreat from Kabul.

1 Prem Lal, KGB *Rezident*

Kabul
Afghanistan

JUNE 8

Karima had never heard of Prem Lal, and even if she had, she would not have recognized his car as it passed her on the road to Shahr-i-Nau, the New Town, as she was starting her life as a guerrilla. And Prem Lal, for that matter, did not even notice the plodding, veiled figure heading for the bus station. If she had known that he was the chief of an important section of the Afghan political police, she would have paid the little Russian Zaprozhets car more attention. If he, on the other hand, had had any inkling that the old woman was carrying some of the most important documents in the country in her bag, he would have abandoned his plans for the evening there and then. As it was, each figure continued towards its destiny.

Prem Lal, although an Afghan intelligence man, had been Russia's Secret KGB Resident in Kabul for nearly thirty years. It was through him that Babrak Karmal, who then had had only about five or six supporters, had found his way to power. Lal had shown that he could muster hundreds of collaborators, many in key positions, when the time came for the Russians to rush Karmal out of his East European cold storage after the earlier Red coups had collapsed. Prem Lal had spent lavishly from his Russian money, to build up a network of agents and to convert disaffected people to communism – or what they thought was communism – in those three decades.

The Afghans in general were supposed not to be fond of Hindus, but Prem Lal's father had nurtured the hope of high office for his son. Hindus, in spite of what people said, had risen to high office in Kabul: Chaman Lal (no relation) was actually head of the national bank and was said to control far more than the country's finances. Young Prem was brought up to aim high, though the family was poor. By the time he was eighteen years old, something happened which convinced him that he was destined for great things.

It was at the beginning of 1941, and a sidelight of world history was touching Afghanistan: something which might have ended with Prem Lal attaining high office.

Britain was at war with Germany and Afghanistan was neutral. Prem Lal's father came home from his evening job as a clerk at the German Legation accompanied by an Indian, a Bengali, who was introduced as 'a family friend'.

The friend was none other than *Netaji* – Great Leader – Subhas Chandra Bose, the Indian nationalist who had escaped from Calcutta, where he had been under house arrest. His aim was to reach Berlin and to work from there, rousing the people of India against British rule. Those were the days of the Nazi-Soviet Pact, and Bose was waiting for permission to travel through the USSR to Germany.

The journey took some time to arrange. In the meantime Bose, a man of charismatic personality, fired young Prem with tales of heroism and India's fight for independence. Before he left the Lal household, Bose advised Prem Lal to leave the backwater of Kabul, to go to Bengal, where Bose would meet him one day, and would be glad to have him as a henchman.

In April, as the snows were melting, word reached Kabul that Subhas Chandra Bose had arrived safely in the German capital via Moscow. Hitler had even given him an inscribed cigarette case. Prem Lal took leave of his family and made his way to India, to Bose's home province of Bengal, working underground. It was there that he joined the communists.

Two years later, Prem Lal was chief of Nationalist Intelligence in Calcutta when the thrilling news came. The Leader, Subhas Chandra Bose, had arrived, by German submarine, back in Asia, and reached the Japanese-occupied area of Burma. He was now Commander-in-Chief of the INA, the Indian National Army, composed of 45,000 former British Indian Army fighting men captured at Singapore. Lal's message from Bose included these words: 'I have not forgotten you, Prem Lal. Prepare yourself for power!' Heady stuff for a twenty year old. Within a few months, Prem Lal was sure, the Indian

Nationalist and Japanese armies would sweep through Bengal, adding India to the Greater East Asia Co-Prosperity Sphere. Prem Lal would be Minister of Internal Security, of the Republic of India . . .

The Indians had Imphal surrounded: it was due to fall in less than a day. Then fate stepped in once more. Suddenly the monsoon broke, the Japanese air force was grounded, the British brought up more armies, Bose fled to Saigon, then to Taiwan, where his aircraft crashed and he was killed.

Prem Lal found Calcutta suddenly too hot for him: someone had betrayed the Movement, and he escaped to Kabul with the British-Indian Criminal Investigation Department at his heels. They did not know his real identity, however, and he then returned to India to work for communism for six dreary years. He came to realize that there was no hope for communism in Nehru's independent India, and said so to the KGB *Rezident* in the Soviet Embassy in New Delhi. This man, after consulting Moscow, had Prem Lal groomed for work in Afghanistan.

By 1952 Prem Lal was back in Kabul, with excellent, if forged, certificates showing that he had not wasted his time away from his homeland. He had been recruited by the Russians as a mole and trained, first in Moscow by Section Ten of the KGB, and then in Prague, where he had done his field-training. The documents which he was able to display to the Afghan authorities, however, 'proved' that he had been awarded the BA degree of a small Indian university, followed by a scholarship in police work to an Austrian institute of higher education. Moscow, naturally, made sure that the documentation looked right. They knew that all certificates offered by candidates for employment in government offices in Afghanistan went to the Kabul Foreign Ministry for verification.

The officer there who was responsible for confirming qualifications was on the Soviet payroll. His job was to contact the Afghan embassy nearest to where any educational certificate originated, to check it. Instead, he passed Prem Lal's 'qualifications' to the Soviet Embassy who, already briefed, sent them on to Moscow. Once at number two, Dzerzhinsky Square, Moscow (better known as the Lubianka, from the name of the prison in the same building), the papers were soon at the Third Special Section, responsible for all KGB illegal documentation.

Within two weeks they were returned to Kabul, via the USSR Embassy, accompanied by the necessary certification, apparently stamped on them by the appropriate Afghan consular officials in India and Europe, testifying to their genuineness.

Prem Lal was given a job in Kabul police international intelligence. This involved hardly any work at all: Afghanistan was a backwater. And the Hindu was aware that he would never rise much higher under King Zahir Shah. But as the KGB man in Kabul, well, that might well come to something in the years ahead. After all, he was only thirty years old.

The communization of Afghanistan at that time was not one of the Kremlin's priorities, however important it may have seemed to Prem Lal. But, obeying his instructions to the letter, he spent the next decades doggedly finding mail drops, converting dissident students and idealists, who opposed the favouritism which they felt had invaded every aspect of official life and employment, and choosing likely candidates for leadership of the Afghan Communist Party. Because communism, in Afghanistan, meant totalitarian Russia, the party was called, instead, the People's Democratic Party.

This Party must have been the slowest-growing one in history. For no less than twenty years it had only six members. By the time Prem Lal was fifty, there were at the most three hundred. These were split into two factions: the 'Flag' *Parcham*, who were mainly Persian-speakers, and the 'People' *Khalq*, who used the other national language, Pashtu. Since Prem Lal was of Indian origin, neither a Tajik nor a Pashtun, both coteries looked on him with suspicion and disdain: but he held the purse strings, and much Moscow money flowed through his hands to the leaders of both groups.

The communists, using a tiny but deeply indoctrinated band of army officers, seized power in a military takeover in 1978, and made Taraki – Prem Lal's first choice in his secret despatches to Moscow – President of the Republic.

Within a year, between three and seven hundred communists had come into the open or had been converted: most of them were probably opportunists. That may well have been the high point of their power. Thereafter, each faction's murder gangs hunted the other's assassins in city streets, and eventually hundreds of 'anti-Party' communists were jailed and hanged as first one element, then the other, gained the upper hand in government: that is, such government as there was.

Prem Lal was not now popular in Moscow. He had exaggerated the power and unity of the Afghan communists.

The Russians, as was admitted by some of their policy makers who visited Kabul, had blundered into the Afghan adventure for several reasons. Henry Trofimenko, a leading expert on East-West relations, claimed that the occupation was attempted because the Kremlin feared an American invasion of Iran. 'We felt ourselves to be under pressure,' he said.

The military and the geopoliticians, however, felt that the country would make an ideal springboard for extending Soviet power into the oilfield of the Gulf; and to pressure China with the implied threat to India. The Soviet Communist Party pressed for the invasion on genuinely sentimental grounds: to go to the aid of their beleaguered Afghan brothers, faced with counter-revolution. Some circles (such as the KGB) wanted a buffer against Islamic propaganda, now threatening the USSR's Moslem population. Anyway, Afghanistan's minerals made it potentially one of the richest countries in Asia: which interested the heavy spenders among the Soviet ministries.

There were three Red Afghan dictators in three years. Amin had followed Taraki, and now Karmal was in charge: and he was KGB-trained. The Soviet Army had actually brought him into the country from his exile in Prague. Prem Lal's work shrank to next to nothing. Karmal was developing his own organization, Afghan State Security, the KHAD. If it took over, there might be no Soviet *Rezident*: or else one would be sent direct from Moscow, a Russian, working from the Soviet Embassy. Prem Lal badly needed an achievement, to convince Moscow that he was both active and successful.

Pondering these facts, Prem Lal had an idea. Moscow said that Zionism was behind the counter-revolutionary forces, and claimed that Pakistan was infiltrated by Zionists. Prem Lal would find a Zionist nest, a Jewish network.

And where to find such a thing in Kabul, Moslem Afghanistan? He knew. Nobody else, though, had yet thought of it. He smiled to himself.

Ministry of the Interior figures showed that there were now six hundred Jews in Afghanistan, mostly in Herat and Kabul.

There was, for instance, the daughter of that Bokharan magnate Isakhof, who was the son of Isaac of Bokhara. Prem Lal had been compiling a dossier on her for some time now. She behaved like a Westerner, wore slacks, smoked, had a flash, modern apartment in the New Town, spoke foreign languages, and mixed with diplomats. Everyone knew that diplomats were spies. Spies always had accomplices, as did traitors and saboteurs . . .

He drove past the imposing new buildings, the mansions, embassies, apartment blocks. Then he was there. One of the best apartment blocks in New Kabul, in the whole country, in fact.

'A quick check' was KGB jargon for a meeting which should produce a private advantage for the officer involved.

'You are not an Afghan at all, you know,' Prem Lal said, as he placed his worn leather despatch-case on the table. 'We keep an eye on all you people.' He stared at her.

He had just sat down at the dining-table in the apartment of a highly attractive girl, just as he had seen his superiors do, back in Prague, when out on training exercises. Every job had its perks, its fringe benefits. Frightening young women into providing companionship – and more – was one of them.

He looked around the well furnished room. This could almost be a home in Europe. Plenty of pine panelling, a tidy kitchen glimpsed through an archway, open-plan, with the bedroom over there, next to the bathroom. Posters advertising pop groups on the wall, everlasting dried flowers in a Victorian vase, striped tribal rugs. She must have picked up these ideas from the foreign colony in Kabul. They had loose morals, of course, everybody knew that, even though they professed to despise the hippies and other drug-takers, who were their fellow nationals.

The girl said nothing. She was wearing her hair in a bunch, gathered on the top of her head, well washed jeans, and a fisherman's sweater over a rollneck sweatshirt. Her nails were lacquered bright red and she was smoking a cigarette, probably a foreign one, Prem Lal thought. She certainly was attractive. And only twenty-six.

'I said, "You're not an Afghan at all, you know."' He was

relishing this experience. Ever since he had found her card and photograph in the files of the Security Police, three days before, he had known that he would.

There was plenty of time. 'It is only my duty, you understand, as an officer, and I am a Grade Six officer of the KHAD, to root out and identify those who might prove to have irregularities in their background or associations.'

'I was born in this country, of parents who were also born here, in Kabul,' she said. Better not say any more or any less than this odious creature demanded. He was fat, middle-aged or older, oily, his breath smelt of garlic, and he wore patent leather shoes, a bright check suit of shoddy cloth, and carried no less than five flashy pens in his handkerchief pocket. His hair was dyed a startling black.

'There is a saying, "If a dog is born in a stable, that does not make it a horse",' said Prem Lal. He was pleased with the phrase, which he had been saving for such occasions as this, occasions which would doubtless become more and more frequent now that the right people were in charge of the country. He hadn't shown her his identity book, which would have told, by his name, that he was of Indian origin; and he had a Hindu name.

He had been born here, too, and his father, Raman Lal, as well as his grandfather, Moti Lal, had been servants of all the Afghan governments since the turn of the century.

In any case, he was going to change his name to Prem Ramanov. That would sound good, almost Russian, in Moscow. Meanwhile, here in Kabul, he had plenty of power.

'I have here a file which says that you have not been abroad; yet you live like a foreigner, I notice. I would like to see your identity book.'

She rummaged in a striped canvas holdall and brought it out. He opened the stiff blue covers of the little booklet with a sniff. It looked as if it had been shaken up with the earth from potatoes, which no doubt it had, in the bottom of that shopping bag. Some people had no respect for documents. When Afghan identity books had first been issued, under the previous regime, people had opened stalls on the outskirts of the cities, hiring them out by the day or the week. The customers were peasants who might be asked for them on the streets after they had come in from the countryside. But as neither the peasants nor the police were very literate, the whole operation petered out.

No, she hadn't been abroad, or it would have said so here. But the document recorded that she did speak three foreign languages, and Western ones at that. An educated girl, capable of intellectual conversation no doubt. That might well mean that she was some kind of a socialist, too. Still, one had to be careful; there were so many fakes about, Maoists, Trotskyists and so on, deviators, degenerate scum.

He returned the booklet.

'You are the daughter of Daniyel of Bokhara?'

'Yes.'

'And, of course, your parents did not support Israel? You see, we do know a thing or two. We do know that you and all your family are Jews, *Yahud*. Now, anyone can believe anything he wants to in Afghanistan. But if that belief causes him to harbour thoughts detrimental to the wellbeing of the country, well, that is a different matter, isn't it? If that belief caused him – or her – to do anything against the State, that would be a dangerous belief.'

'The flap of your suit jacket is torn,' she said, suddenly.

Prem Lal sat forward and frowned, at first taken aback, thinking that she was changing the subject, then realizing that such a remark was too absurd to have such an intention.

There could only be one other reason. She was hinting that she might mend it for him, might be prepared to be friendly.

Prem Lal said, 'The Great Leader, Babrak Karmal, has said in an interview with a correspondent of *The Times* that General Zia, President of Pakistan, has planned, as a Zionist and Israeli agent, to invade this country of ours. So those who believe in Zionism, like Zia, are our enemies, and they must be dealt with.'

This might be the right time. 'But, reverting to your remark about my jacket pocket: yes, you are right, it needs mending. I caught it on the edge of a metal filing cabinet last week. I have no woman to look after me. You may care to repair it, now. Or I could bring it to you, in prison, and you could do it there. People have a lot of spare time, you know, while their cases are being investigated.'

'Cases?' She wondered what she had done, or could be alleged to have done. After all, she was an architect, not politically active or engaged in crime of any sort.

'Miss Maryam, crimes against the State, as I shall define more closely in a moment, often take the form of economic sabotage.

'You see,' said Prem Lal, 'we keep an eye on you people.'

Then he said, 'It is surprising how often illicit things are found in Jewish houses. We can always find what we want to find.'

Yes, of course, Maryam thought. It's easy to plant evidence.

Prem Lal sat back in the chair, savouring the possibilities.

He might take her to a restaurant: the police could get free meals almost anywhere. Not, of course, to the 'Twenty-Five Hours', in West Shahr-i-Nau Park: that was Chinese. They might be secret Maoists. The Blue Club, now that had a striptease show . . .

'I'll sew it up now,' she said.

He took off his jacket, and she brought her sewing basket. Yes, thought Prem Lal, she does look attractive, sitting there. She could do more than mending for him, all right.

She was frightened, he could see that. Yes, he could have a fling. After that, she could be his first Zionist agent.

She was searching in the basket now, as he watched, for needle and cotton. Like her shopping bag, the thing was untidy. It even had pieces of paper in it, all kinds of odds and ends.

Things were so much neater in Prague, places like that. Women there took real pride in their sewing . . .

Where did she get her clothes? She didn't make them, he was sure. Probably at the Apollo Boutique, near the Blue Mosque. They had things there from West Germany, Italy, France. Capitalist goods, of course, but pretty things. He could go to the boutique with her. Or to a tea dance, at the IC, the Intercontinental Hotel. Five to seven p.m. That cost only fifty *afghanis*, about seventy-five cents. After that, take in a film: one of those Indian musicals, at the Timur Shahi Cinema. Even the artistes of the Tajik Dance Ensemble, the *Lola*, 'Tulip', group, had done that. They came from the Soviet Union, led by the great choreographer, Walamat-Zada. You couldn't see Indian films in the USSR, they'd said.

She had found the needle and thread and looked tense now, worried, as she bent over her sewing.

'How about something to drink?' he asked quite mechanically. The Russians always insisted on drinks, although Prem Lal had no head for alcohol.

Maryam put down the jacket and brought him a glass of wine, the thick, red, sticky stuff those Italians made and sold at Tritons, just off the Daral-Aman road, the only wine makers in the whole of a country famed for its seventy-two varieties of grapes. Well, it was sweet, didn't make you gasp, not like that dreadful vodka . . .

He drank it, she finished the small repair, and Prem Lal, well pleased with his day's work, took his leave.

'I shall visit you again tomorrow, Maryam Jan, at about this hour. You may care to have a meal ready; something like lamb koftas with aniseed. I may be able to protect you, but can give no guarantee.'

An hour later, following an anonymous telephone tip-off that Prem Lal was carrying enemy money, a US hundred-dollar bill, sewn into the flap of his pocket, he was garotted in the torture chamber of the KHAD's headquarters at Shashdarak. His end was tidied up with a death certificate which said, quite accurately, 'died from sudden inability to breathe, followed by heart stoppage.'

The call was traced, since even automatically dialled ones were logged in Kabul these days. But the trail ran out at the switchboard of the subscriber to Kabul 31851 – the Intercontinenal Hotel. The operator could only say that it had been placed by someone using a public call box in the lobby.

Maryam knew that sooner or later someone from the Afghan KHAD, or from the Russian KGB, or even from GRU, Military Security, would see her dossier, the one that Prem Lal had had with him. Then they would be after her. Especially if he had left a report or memorandum.

Early next morning she went into town, without any real plan. There was nobody to help her, nobody in Kabul whom she could trust. Young intellectuals were either taken in by the regime, which promised so much and said the present terror was 'an interim measure', or had no contacts among the ordinary people of the country. Westernized city folk had disregarded everyone else for too long. In any case, Prem Lal had said, 'We keep an eye on all you people.'

Some other town might be better: nearer a border, perhaps. Mazar was too close to Russia, Herat only led to Iran. Kandahar might be too far from Pakistan, their nearest neighbour. Where else was there? She looked in the window display of Bakhtar Airlines, the Afghan internal carrier. 'Fly in the new YAK-40s, the Soviet wonder-jets! Fly Bakhtar to Mazar, fifty minutes, to Herat, seventy minutes, to Kandahar, to Kunduz.' Kunduz! On the military road to the Soviet bases. 'Twenty-seven passengers, in amazing comfort, flown by Afghans, at over 8,000 metres up in the sky!' Those YAK-40s, passenger aircraft, had been adapted for war. Kandahar, Mazar and Herat, when the people rose against the Russians, had been bombed and strafed. The terror bombing had killed perhaps twelve thousand people. Half of each city was in ruins. And those places led nowhere.

Anyway, as she could see through the plate-glass window, intending passengers were now required to produce their identity books, whose numbers were noted by the ticket clerk.

She looked at shopkeepers, beturbaned grocers who peered back enigmatically, seeing only a Western girl, or perhaps a Russian or a Cuban, nothing to do with them. In the more modern shops she saw people in fashionable Western clothes, but now, as never before, Maryam thought, there was something closed-in about their faces. They did not smile, and had that wary look which meant they would not confide anything that they might know about a hope of escape, of freedom, to someone they didn't know. People drew back from the Russians, Czechs, East Germans, strolling in the streets. Many of them, even men out shopping with their wives and, occasionally, children, carried slung Kalashnikovs, or guns in holsters. The Afghans were mingling with the representatives of a new empire. New, but with the very ancient and specious pretension that it was here for the good of all.

Maryam was now looking into the window of the Kabir Boutique, at Ansari crossroads, reading a sign. It said: 'Best Afghan handicrafts, made by the Bani-Israil. A new consignment from Jalalabad.'

That was it! The Bani-Israil. She would go to the caravanserai of those people, near Jalalabad, in the southland where the

Pashtun warrior tribes lived, the People of Israil. She could take the fast Mercedes bus. It made the trip in less than three hours.

They were not asking for permits, on the buses: not yet, anyway.

2 Fazli Rabbi, Innkeeper

Jalalabad
Afghanistan

JUNE 8

That night Maryam slept in the women's section of the Jalalabad caravanserai. She had a bed next to a muffled figure who had also recently arrived.

In the morning the woman said, 'Madam, excuse my impertinence, my name is Karima. I am looking for a man called Kara Kush, The Eagle. Do you know where I might find him? I know serais always have information. There isn't one near Kabul now.' That was what, people whispered, the Muhjahidin called their hideouts.

In Karima's home village, she remembered, people always went to the Serai, the local halting-place and inn for travellers, if they wanted information about anything or anyone. Now she could only remember having heard about the one at Jalalabad, a hundred and forty-five kilometres from Kabul, and had taken the bus there – in the opposite direction from that of The Eagle's headquarters.

Maryam looked at the other woman, trying to work out what she meant. The Eagle? Well, there were plenty of dotty old dames ranging up and down the country, and they said the strangest things.

'No,' she said, 'I'm afraid that is something I have never heard of.'

The timid, bundled-up old woman, and her young, sophisticated sister, seemed to have nothing in common. Yet each had had the experience of sending an enemy of their people to his death, and their paths would cross again.

Karima called out, almost in anguish, 'Oh, how can I find

the great Eagle, my sisters?' The other women, sitting or lying in the dormitory, simply looked at her, expressionless.

Then one of them, who had heard the servant's first words to Maryam and had scuttled away, drawing her veil across her face, was back, tugging at Karima's sleeve.

'Who are you, mother? Never talk before strangers about The Eagle. It is dangerous.'

'I have to find him. I am Karima, from Turkestan and Kabul. He does not know me. But I want to join him.'

The other woman, who had the wiry frame and weather-beaten face of a mountain shepherdess, said, 'You stay here. It may be for a day or two. If he wants to see you, he'll send a message. Just stay in the Serai; and listen – *never mention his name*. If anyone asks, say that you are a traveller, looking for work.'

'Thank you, sister,' Karima said. 'I understand.' She turned away and started to make her bed.

The other woman touched her arm. 'Are you in trouble?'

'*Mumkin*, possibly. I have killed two of the *Rouss*, important ones, *shuravis*, communists . . .'

'That is enough. Never mention that to anyone. If you have problems, ask for Inayat, the proprietor's wife.'

She ran out. A moment later, Maryam saw her through the window, hurrying away, perched on a tiny donkey.

Maryam had a bath, put on her jeans, T-shirt and tank-top, and went in search of information. She found a door marked *Daftar*, office, knocked and went in.

The owner of the Serai, a huge, middle-aged, muscular frontier man, greeted her affably in his office-cum-sitting-room, bare of all furniture except for a rifle, some rugs and a couple of long sofas. He was sitting in the middle of one, back to the wall. He gestured to the place opposite, inviting her to sit. It was much hotter here than in Kabul, and somehow the whole atmosphere was different. It was Pashtun land.

'May you not be tired.' The ancient greeting.

'May you not be sad.' The standard answer.

He looked at her without curiosity, like a benevolent brigand, which she was quite prepared to believe he was. Pashtuns usually take people as they come.

'*Dodai* – bread?'

He offered her a piece of unleavened bread, torn from a selection of elephant ear-flaps nailed haphazardly on the wooden wall behind him, and gestured towards some cheese and salt. Then cup after cup of sweet green tea, made from water boiling in a huge samovar. Maryam decided to confide in him.

She took a small piece of bread, sprinkled salt on it, divided it into two as he watched, and handed one half to him. He took it at once, held it for a moment as if making up his mind, and then chewed and swallowed it.

'Very well, we have shared bread and salt. What help do you want, maiden?'

The bread and salt bond was inviolable. From now on, the Pashtun was bound to defend her, even at the cost of his own life. She would have to be treated exactly as if she was of his own family. *Namak-haram*, unfaithful to one's salt, was one of the three worse epithets which could be hurled at an Afghan. It ranked just below *haramzada*, bastard, and just above *kafir*, infidel. Such an insult could be wiped out only by blood.

The Pashtuns look down on people from effete Kabul, and Maryam's accent told that she was from the capital. Although the innkeeper had accepted her salt, she would do well to establish an affinity with him too; but obliquely would be the best way.

'I am from Kabul.'

'Things are bad there.'

'That is why I am here.'

'What do you need?'

'I need help, to get across the border, to the Pashtuns there.'

'What is your tribe, and what is your name, and whose daughter are you?'

'I am a traveller.' The phrase is used by people in the East to denote a reluctance to explain themselves much further.

The innkeeper was not, however, content to accept the traditional formula.

'A traveller. Is there *purs-o-pal*, questioning and searching, for you? And what Pashtuns do you seek?'

'The Yusufzai, the Joseph-born.'

'You are of the Yusufzai?'

'I am of the Bani-Israil.'

'But, light of my eyes, so are we all. That is what the Afghans are.'

Maryam had laughed, many years ago, when her parents told her that the Pashtun people swore they were the direct and legitimate descendants of the people of Israel. That was when she was about nine or ten. By the time she was fifteen, she had become deeply interested in this history, or legend, or whatever it really was. She had, in fact, done seven years' study on the question since then, for her own personal interest.

She had started at the Library of the *Pohantun*, Kabul University, where she had surprised the librarian by asking to see the *Jewish Encyclopaedia*. She had looked up 'Afghanistan', in Volume I of the edition of 1901. There it was: the history of the Pashtuns, according to their own lore.

'Afghan tradition traces their descent from the lost Ten Tribes of Israel. The *Tabakati Nasiri* says that the Bani-Israil settled in the country of Ghor, south-east of Herat, carried there by Bakhtannasar (Nebuchadnezzar).'

And there were plenty of graves in the area of south-west Afghanistan with Hebrew inscriptions, even if they were later than Nebuchadnezzar. The people had long locks of hair, they named their home mountain range the Sulaiman, Solomon, Mountains, and there were still Jews, practising ones, in Herat and elsewhere in the country.

The fact was that some ten or twelve million people, many of them bearing Old Testament names – Isaac, Israel, David, Sulaiman and the rest – make up the Pashtun tribes. They form the majority of the people of Afghanistan itself, and to the east their territory extends from Kashmir in the north to the Arabian Sea in the south.

They insist that they are the descendants of one Afghana, commander of the armies of Solomon, son of David. Their oral traditions are recorded in the standard work, *The Afghan Treasury*. A very large number, probably a majority, of the Pashtuns would cut the throat of anyone who expressed absolute disbelief in their claim.

Since the Bani-Israil descent is rooted in the complex but detailed genealogical charts which show both the origins and the relationships of the tribes, the whole question is still an extremely live issue. To deny anyone's ancestry is unthinkable – or fatal.

Maryam had read both the *Treasury* and the many books, often written by Westerners who had served in India, supporting or opposing the theory. Most of these, largely British, writers, were as fanatically for or against the story as the Pashtuns themselves were addicted to it. For Maryam, something which seized the imagination to this extent was in itself a source of wonderment.

'I am Fazli Rabbi, of the Mohmand Clan, and we are cousins of the Yusufzais. I shall take you myself to the Khan who is a direct descendant of David the King of the Bani-Israil, in the transborder country of the mountains.'

'Thank you, my name is Maryam, and I seek sanctuary and protection with the people of David. I am oppressed by the *Rouss*.'

'*Har Firauni-ra Musa*, for every Pharoah there is a Moses,' said the Pashtun, 'but it is not seemly that we should travel alone, a man and a woman, whatever they may do in Kabul and places like that.' He disappeared through a door into the rooms which made up his private part of the Serai, and came out again with a tall, handsome woman of middle-age, dressed in a waistcoat, woolly jumper, and baggy trousers with a green skirt over them.

'This is Inayat, my wife. As you know, "Inayat" means Blessing; and she will be a blessing to you as she is to me. She will teach you the language of the Real People.' Maryam took her hand, and laughed. The Real People spoke Pashtu, of course. So far, she and Fazli Rabbi had been speaking Dari, which had only a small number of Pashtu words in it. Inayat handed Maryam a silk outfit, like her own.

'But who will look after the Serai? And how will we get over the Pakistan border? I have no passport.' Maryam could still hardly believe that all this was happening. She had heard of it, of course, but actually living through it was different. Here was a total stranger, leaving his home and business, breaking the law, to take an unknown person into tribal territory just because she said that she needed help. Maryam shook her head, as if to clear it.

'Passport – massport!' He used the Eastern derision-rhyme

to show his contempt for small details. 'I have never even seen one. Never mind about that. Border? We don't recognize the border, we are a free people, and that British-drawn border cuts the Pashtun land in two. As for the Serai – Serai-maray – I'll show you.'

Fazli Rabbi put two huge hands to his mouth and shouted 'O Asil! O Palang!'

Asil and Palang, who came running, rifles in hand and turban-ends across their mouths, were two strapping youths, over six foot tall: Fazli Rabbi's sons, who might have been any age from seventeen to thirty. Like their father and mother, they had massive, muscular frames and grey-green eyes. The Mohmand warriors were among the most feared on the whole frontier. Together with the redoubtable Afridi clan, they dominated the Khyber Pass area.

Fazli Rabbi explained that he was initiating his sons into the mysteries of the catering and hotel business, as practised in the Fazli Rabbi Caravanserai on the Jalalabad Road.

3 To the Castle of the Yusuf-Born

The Path of Flight
Smugglers' Route
Jalalabad to Pakistan

JUNE 9–19

Next morning, when the three travellers set off at dawn, on horseback, Fazli Rabbi relaxed his medieval and Pashtun manner to disclose that he had been planning to visit the Yusufzai leader for some time and also that, in spite of his apparent indifference to affairs other than those of the Serai, he had detailed knowledge of what was going on in the country.

'There is a very large Russian military force quite near here,' he said. 'Their headquarters is at Jalalabad City, and they come from the two hundred and first Soviet Motorized Rifle Division. They support what is left of the Eleventh Afghan Infantry, most of whose men have deserted to the Muhjahidin. Recently, the Nikolais called in helicopters to pursue some guerrillas into Pakistani territory, over there,' he waved his hand in the direction of the frontier, 'and the Pakistanis shot two of them down. Now the *Rouss* are quieter. They used Hind helicopters and fixed-wing aircraft. That reminds me. Don't pick anything up from the ground. The *Rouss* drop explosive grenades designed to maim; may dogs defile their graves!'

Fazli Rabbi's interest, and his very detailed facts, even the numbers of the divisions and the data on the aircraft, made Maryam realize that this was no ordinary Pashtun, or even innkeeper. 'Hind', for example, was the code-name used by NATO to denote the Mi-24. They were called that in Western short-wave news broadcasts.

Inayat, also, had a sharp eye for weaponry, and she once said, 'SAM-7s are the medicine for those,' as a Russian helicopter passed overhead. Even Maryam only dimly remembered from the radio that the SAM-7 was a shoulder-launched rocket. 'They are heat-seekers, you know,' continued Inayat, 'with a device for locking onto the exhaust of a hostile aircraft. They are useful against tanks, too.'

On the other hand, she worried more than her husband did about 'the boys', left to look after the Serai. 'You know,' she said to Maryam as they rode side by side into the hills, 'Fazli Rabbi insisted on calling them Asil and Palang. That means "Noble" and "Leopard". He is fond of leopards, and thinks that they are noble. But are these the right names for people who will run a business? Many people believe that people try to follow the meaning of their name. What do you think?'

'I am sure they'll manage all right,' was all that the girl from Kabul could think of, so she said it.

'Well,' said Inayat, 'I suppose they will be all right. After all, "Zabardast", my husband's surname, means "violent", or "powerful", and yet he has made a very good thing of the Serai since we took it over ten years ago. Before that, he was in the Army, you know.'

North of sub-tropical Jalalabad, with, for mountainous Afghanistan, the amazing sight of palm trees and citrus fruits growing, the road follows the Kunar River, the ancient Choaspes, flowing down from the snow-capped mountains of Kafiristan, land of the Infidel.

Fazli Rabbi led his party northwards, at first, following the route probably taken by Alexander the Great on his Indian campaign. Through smiling fields, past ancient Buddhist monuments, into walled towns with medieval forts to guard them, this was, at last, the real land of the Pashtuns. Everywhere they went, herdsmen with flocks of fat-tailed sheep, farmers opening their irrigation channels for the day's watering, children hurrying to the Mulla's school, called out the inevitable '*Starai ma she*, may you not be tired!' Those with more time to spend would invite the travellers into a teahouse or a walled garden, where soft fruits – peaches, apricots, plums – grew. 'Are you strong?' 'Are you happy?' 'May faith be thy daily bread.'

Every man carried a gun, some of them the long, muzzle-loading *jazails*, handmade perhaps a century or more ago, others perfect replicas of British Lee-Enfield .303s, made in the trans-border armouries of the Afridis. They were perfect copies, even to the stamp 'G VI', King George the Sixth. The empire which owned more than a quarter of the surface of the earth had struggled, ineffectively, to add this territory to it, when the Pashtuns had declined the honour.

As Maryam and her escort moved deeper and deeper into tribal territory, there were Kalashnikovs, rockets and the new Soviet grenades. When he can, the Pashtun warrior tries to keep up with developments in weapons technology. Once Maryam saw, silhouetted against the evening sky, a huge clansman on a horse, his grenade-launcher on his back, scanning the darkening sky for helicopters. Behind him on a donkey, like the squire of some knight of long ago, came his disciple, a boy of perhaps ten, carrying a back pack of the latest Russian rockets, ready to hand them to his master the moment there was action.

The international border, the Durand line, had been drawn through the middle of the tribal lands. On one side was Pakistan, inheritor of the British Raj, on the other Afghanistan, master, until so recently, of its own destiny. As the party moved further northwards, the going became harder, the trail passing north and east through stark mountains, where beetle-browed warriors of the Tarklanris saluted them gravely with an upraised hand, then went back to their ploughing, rifles slung across their backs, more often than not with a red rose stuck in the long ringlets behind their ears.

On the whole, the Pashtuns were magnificent specimens, which some attributed to the fact that infant mortality was very high, and only the toughest survived. They were darker than the average Afghans, usually tall, with hooked noses and long, often straight black hair and eyes which varied from grey to deepest black. Again and again, as if from nowhere, sentries would appear and seek the travellers' credentials, usually by a brief exchange of words:

'Peace on thee.'

'And on thee peace.'

'Where from and where to?'

'From Jalalabad to the Yusufland.'

'With faith in God. May thou become great.'

'I entrust you to God. May thou be blessed.'

Without the deep valleys cut into the mountains by the rivers flowing here for uncounted millennia, it would have been impossible to get through these mountains. Fazli Rabbi and the two women crossed the international border without knowing it. Both the Afghans and the Pakistanis, following tradition, left the tribal people to their own devices. If they had tried to put up fences or barbed wire, they would have been torn down. This was the Rahi-Gurez, the Path of Flight, used by refugees and smugglers moving between the Indian sub-continent and Central Asia.

They stopped, the first night, at the fort of Malik Miskin Khan, a friend of the innkeeper from Jalalabad. He was all of six foot seven inches high, an ancient warrior chief who commanded nine thousand fighting men. He was allied, by blood, to the Yusufzai innkeeper, and he proudly showed off his family tree, mounted on the wall of his bare reception hall in the clay-brick fort. It traced his family back to the great Qais, of the Bani-Israil.

'Lady,' he said to Maryam, 'we Pashtuns have three parts to the code of the Pashtun, called *Pashtunwali*. They are: hospitality, safe-conduct and "exchange". The last means that we exact a life for a life, insist on requital for misdeeds. But,' he drew himself up and gulped some green tea from a china cup, 'in practice, ancestry is the most important thing for the Bani-Israil. It is so important that it is not mentioned in Pashtunwali, in fact. It is taken for granted.'

The following morning, when they were about to leave, Maryam made the mistake of offering to pay for the night's hospitality. The old chief at first bristled, looked as if he was going to do something violent, and then laughed. 'It pleases the Pashtun to know that he can outdo others in hospitality,' he said, 'and so I am glad that I can teach you something.' He illustrated this double-edged compliment with a tale, which he insisted on telling, even thought it meant delaying the start of the day's march.

'You will know,' he began, 'that there is now in Kabul the presence of the *Rouss*, the eaters of filth. Not long ago, a Pashtun notable of the *Musa-khel*, the Moses tribe, who hailed from the far south of here towards Baluchistan, was turned out of his house. His name was Ibrahim Khan, and his house was wanted by the *Rouss* for the family of one of their officials. As you also probably know,' he made a gesture of contempt, 'Kabul people do not help their neighbours, and they have little or no clan feeling. So Ibrahim had nobody to support him against the tyrants, and thus he became, in his old age, destitute. He had to sell shish-kabobs in the street.'

The ancient stroked his beard. 'Among us, even though we are warriors, commerce has no stigma, in fact it is a blessing: for all the prophets engaged in trade of one sort or another.'

He paused for a long time, and then looked at the travellers, as if seeking encouragement.

'What did Ibrahim Khan do?' asked Maryam, genuinely interested.

'Ah, what could he do? He sold kabobs, and he waited. Then, one day, someone shot the Russian who had taken his house. Perhaps it was Ibrahim Khan; perhaps word had got back to his people, who sent someone for *badal*, "exchange".'

'So he got his house back?' Maryam asked.

'Patience, child. That is not the point. My intention is to tell you about nobility of spirit, about honour and taking things from women.' The old man made everyone sit down and called for tea.

Then he resumed. 'Although the Russian was dead, his wife still lived in the house. Ibrahim could not touch her, for it is *sharm*, a dishonourable thing, to harm a woman. He waited for a chance to show his Pashtunwali, his chivalry.

'It so happened,' said the old man, gazing into the blue haze of the mountainside where the track which Maryam would ascend ran, far into the distance, 'that one day the wife of the Russian came upon Ibrahim Khan selling kabobs in the street.

'She said, "Are you not the man who once owned the house in which I live?"

'He answered her, "I am Ibrahim Khan, of the Musa-khel, and my dwelling is the one known as Flower Fountain!"

'She said, "Yes, that is the house. Can you help me?" He said, "What help do you need, woman of *dimokrasi*, from a kabob-seller in the Kabul streets? Your people say that they rule this land, and they should help you if you seek it. Are you not *nufus-dar*, 'one who has people?'"

'She said, "Yes, I have people, but I cannot trust them. My husband is dead, and I have no money. I shall soon be sent back to *Rousiyya*, and there I shall be poor. But I have heard that there are jewels buried somewhere in the Flower Fountain garden. Do you know this legend from long ago? Can you help me find them? If you do, I shall reward you."

'The elder of the *Musa-Khel* said, "Let it not be said that someone asked Ibrahim Khan for help in vain. I shall come with you, lady."

'To summarize. He went to the house and took up a spade. Then he asked himself, "Where would I hide jewels in this garden if I had any?" His instinct answered him. He began to dig and presently he unearthed a large clay pot, filled with wonderful gold and jewelled ornaments, which had been buried there at the time of the second British invasion. He gave the treasure to the Russian woman.

'She said, "Ibrahim Khan, you and I are now rich. Take as much of the treasure as you wish, and my thanks with it."

'And Ibrahim Khan told her, "I am Ibrahim, son of a chief and a man of the Musa-born. I answer the cry of distress of a woman, and I help her. Shall it ever be said of me that I have profited from the misery of a woman?"'

The old man gave the travellers, one by one, a penetrating look. 'And my answer to you, Maryam Jan, is just the same.'

'Well said, Son of Qais!' shouted Zabardast. 'And I, on our journey, shall see that the lady knows the tale about the man, his guest and his horse, for she may not have heard it yet.'

'With faith in God.'

'I entrust you to God.'

They went on their way again.

The northward journey from Jalalabad to the stronghold of the Yusufzai chieftain was no more than a hundred and twenty miles as the crow flies. Across these mountains, however, and through these deep valleys, at times almost as desolate as a moonscape, it was half as far again. The little party forded rivers, their horses splashing gratefully through the crystal waters, while the June sun beat down upon them, and the dust-laden, singing wind sprang up, viciously scouring their faces and hands, then dying, suddenly, into an eerie silence.

Maryam found, in Fazli Rabbi and his wife, an infinite

source of folklore, general information, songs and stories – and contemporary knowledge. As they rode, Maryam adapted slowly to the outdoor life of the Afghan borderland and they talked continually: about everything under the sun.

She soon saw that this was no country bumpkin and his woman, wayside innkeepers interested only in gossip and profit. Nor were the pair merely relating things that they had heard; they knew a great deal, in depth, and Maryam was soon sure that Fazli Rabbi and Inayat were deeply involved in the freedom struggle.

'It is obvious,' the Pashtun said when they were sheltering from the midday sun on the fourth day in the wilds, 'that you are an Afghan. But you are a *shahri*, a city-dweller, and somewhat soft. This journey will correct that: you are already riding your horse like a veteran, not like someone out for exercise because she has eaten too much *pilau* the night before!'

She was getting used to the Pashtun raillery, the half aggressive, half humorous way in which these people treated one another. Fazli Rabbi was including her in his community by speaking like that. It was, she supposed, something of a compliment.

Did he know how the border people felt about the puppet government? There had been rumours that the tribal chiefs were being bribed by the Karmal regime to keep quiet, to let Kabul rule the settled parts of Afghanistan. Maryam felt well enough established with her host to sound him out.

The huge Pashtun's face cracked into a smile. 'The tribes, collectively, are both part of Afghanistan and not part of it. Part of it because most of the people in the country are Pashtuns. Not part of it because we were here before there was an Afghanistan, and millions of us live outside, in the Free Land, between Afghanistan and Pakistan. Millions more live in what is now known as Pakistan. When you meet more of us, as we get deeper into our free territory, you'll see other differences.'

He gave a huge, bellowing laugh, which so alarmed his horse that it whinnied. 'You see, we don't like being "administered".' He spoke the word with a scowl that would have wiped the smile off the face of a plaster saint. Pashtuns being administered was obviously a very serious matter.

'The British came here, as you know, armed to the teeth.

307

They drew a line on a map and had a conference with the Kabul government. The parties agreed –' he lapsed into direct speech – '"this is ours and this is yours."'

Fazli Rabbi stared at Maryam's eyes and bared his teeth. 'They said, "On this side is Afghanistan, and this side – India." They made one serious mistake. And what was that mistake, Maryam Jan?'

Maryam said, 'They cut the Pashtun land in two.'

'Yes, Maryam, they did: but only on the map!'

He looked at her triumphantly. 'You see, neither the Afghans nor the British actually ruled the area. Perhaps this is the first time in history that people, probably through vanity, took into their territory a nation whom they did not – could not – administer!'

'How could that happen?' Maryam asked.

'Very easily. The Afghans of Kabul were afraid to say that they could not rule the tribes. The British were the same. Sir Mortimer Durand was their man. The two got together and could not admit to one another that neither of them could rule the clans. So they drew a map. Drew a map! And the line was called, still is, "The Durand Line".'

Fazli Rabbi laughed and shook his head. 'Drew a map . . .

'Maryam Jan, that was about ninety years ago. The Pashtun tribesmen had always descended into India, in search of loot; their own land was often poor, mountain ranges and near-desert. You know the saying about why India was there?' He pointed his finger at Maryam.

'Yes, Fazli Rabbi. We've even heard it in Kabul. It runs, "If Allah had not intended the Pashtuns to have fat money-lenders to rob, why would he, in his wisdom, have placed them so near at hand, in India!"'

'Well said, girl! But there is more to it than that. The Pashtuns always used to enter the service of any conqueror, including their own leaders. You have heard of the Pashtun kings of Delhi, our own *Raj*, haven't you?'

'Yes, of course.'

'Well, more recently, the British were afraid that the Russians would foment the wildness of the tribes and persuade them to descend on the British domain in India. And the Kabul Afghans feared that the Pashtuns would attack them. In fact, of course, the Pashtuns have always fought to preserve Afghanistan. So long as they were on the southern and eastern flank, Kabul was safe against invasion.'

'But,' said Maryam, 'the Kabul rulers have always had to keep the tribes sweet. That is the talk of Kabul. People are always complaining that they send food, clothing, money and arms to the Pashtuns.'

'Certainly, and the British did exactly the same. The Pakistanis do it, too. But remember, we do not call this bribery. It is tribute from weaker peoples!'

Fazli Rabbi gave another huge laugh. Maryam had heard some of this before. The names of the warrior clans, and of their ruling families, were as well known, and as feared or respected in Asia as any elite elsewhere. Their war cries, usually the clan surname, echoed through the hills – Afridi, Waziri, Orakzai, Khattak, Mahsud, Shinwari, and a dozen more.

'It is natural,' Fazli Rabbi was saying, 'that when Babrak Karmal was brought from the communist lands into Afghanistan as a Russian puppet, he should be mortally afraid of us, the ten million Pashtuns.

'Karmal continued sending the customary presents: money, trucks, radios, food. The money from Kabul was known as the "watch and ward allowance", and was paid out of the policing budget of the Ministry of Tribes.'

Maryam said, 'Did Karmal's money pacify the tribes, or reconcile them to the communist regime?'

'At first, I do admit,' Fazli Rabbi scratched his head, 'we kept out of Kabul affairs, as we always do. But, when murder without reason, atrocities – acts beyond anything sanctioned by law and custom – carried out by Russian miscreants, became widespread, we thought again.

'We gave sanctuary to the refugees, and allowed them to go down into Pakistan. We welcomed their fighting men and their army deserters, when they started to come to us, and to form guerrilla bands. But, my girl –' Fazli Rabbi shot a glance at Maryam to make sure that she was absorbing the lesson '– many Pashtuns are vain, like so many other people. Karmal knew this and at first doubled his bounty and sent men to "explain" that the refugees were malcontents, the deserters criminals. I myself saw the beautiful air-conditioned buses, loaded with gifts, which came to the *jirgas*, the assemblies, of the people presided over by the chiefs.'

'But it was not enough?' Maryam could see the picture: the greybeards taking the presents but increasingly objecting to the regime.

'It was not enough. Karmal then invited a selection of chiefs and greybeards to Kabul, for a conference. He proposed to explain to them how he, and the "New Order in Afghanistan", was to save the country and its people from "Zionism and the Chinese, from America and Britain, from Pakistan and India". Practically the whole world, it seemed from his message, was about to descend upon the Afghans.

'Well, the Maliks (which means "kings", you know: our leaders are as important as that) either went in person or sent influential representatives. They were regaled with huge feasts, taken to see the wonders of the great city, filmed for television.

'A select number of Pashtun leaders were accommodated in the Kabul Intercontinental Hotel, with its soft beds, marble floors, chandeliers and coffee bars. I was there myself, and I noticed that this tourist paradise impressed some of them less when they saw, mounted on the walls, muzzle-loading muskets of the kind which their clansmen had stopped using fifty years and more ago. Telling them that these were there just for decoration only made them laugh.

'Eventually the "delegates" were settled in the large conference hall, film cameras whirring, to hear the harangues of the New Men of the Party, explaining why it was best that Afghanistan should embrace socialism.

'The immense portraits of the man known locally as Korl Morks had been removed. He was too obviously a foreigner.

'After a few warming-up speeches, recited from texts prepared by the Ministry of Information by officials who seemed, to the huge fighting men, to be of suspiciously paltry physique, there was a stir of interest. Members of two or three Pashtun clans got up and spoke, fervently and at length, on the good things of the Karmal regime. In accordance with custom, none of those listening showed any reaction, but they were certainly memorizing faces! Decisions, of course, are not made at assemblies like this. Much consultation had to take place between the elders and the ordinary members of the tribe.

310

'As a final touch, Babrak Karmal, surrounded by armed security men, stepped onto the platform. He was short, even in his platform shoes, plump and shifty-eyed. He seemed reluctant to look directly at any of the two hundred and fifty men sitting there, silent and appraising. He probably felt a bit like a Christian in a Roman arena, unsure if and when the lions were going to spring.

'Journalists present have said that they actually felt the hair rising on the back of their necks as these warriors and elders looked at the man who was claiming to be their leader. They knew that both his puppet predecessors had been assassinated; and in the past two years, at that.

'Comrade Karmal had given a good deal of thought to his speech. He regarded these men as politically immature: they would not respond to the kind of phrases which he was accustomed to using. He had been trained in Eastern Europe, and knew that many people there – as in the West – responded to meaningless clichés which had somehow acquired magical force: in their ears, anyway.'

'How did you know that?' Maryam felt compelled to ask. Fazli Rabbi fascinated her.

'I have seen a copy of the speech, in draft form, sent from Moscow. And I remember the text, remember it very well. We are, on the whole, a verbal and not a literate people. That means we have very retentive memories.

'Well, Maryam Jan. That kind of talk would only be likely to "raise the consciousness" of the ten million tribesmen to the fact that the time was nearly ripe to kill him as one of the *malahida*, the atheist infidels.

'His speech, in contrast to the gibberish he regularly gave to the tame Party men, or the patronizing sneers he bestowed on the unconverted, was a model of courtesy and tact. Afghanistan was threatened by terrible enemies, as in the past. She was independent, Moslem, hopeful of progress. She had a future as great as her glorious past – a past which was largely due to the ancestors of the Pashtun warlords assembled here. "Give me your help against the Zionist-Imperialists, and I shall give you everything!" he concluded, and his assembled platform claque cried their customary HOO-RAA! The Hoo-Raa was just a little subdued, for their eyes were fixed, not on the

Leader, but on the unblinking lion-gaze of the frontier men.

'Malik Asaf, one of the most important of the tribal over-lords, stood up first, as was his due. All eyes turned to him, and Karmal bowed, wondering whether this man would support or reject him. Everything depended on the next few moments.

'"There is one question to ask," he said. He was over seventy years of age, six feet four in height, with a hooked nose and a large white turban, crossed bandoliers on his chest, and a voice like the sound of boulders rumbling down the mountainside.

'"Please ask it, *shaghali* Malik Asaf Khan!" Karmal managed a smile.

'"Mr Karmal, as you know, I represent my people. If they want to know something, I must see that it is asked. It does not have to represent my own views."

'"Of course, respected Malik."

'"In that case, as this is a fraternal meeting as you have said, I request that it be put by the man who asked it. He is here, beside me."

'"Please continue." It must be some important associate of the Malik, Karmal thought. This might be a good sign; perhaps the Malik was bringing in a friend with influence, to prepare the ground, or to test the water.

'"In the deliberations of the Pashtun and Afghan people," roared the Malik in what he thought was a soft voice, "all, even the lowest, have the right to speak. It must be the same, of course, in your *dimokrasi*. So, with pleasure, I call upon Yusuf, son of Suleman, who helps in the kitchens of my fort."

'The silence seemed to become even deeper. Karmal squirmed, his face wet, both from the heat of the television lights and from anxiety. The Malik had trapped him. He had given permission for the voice of *dimokrasi*. To deny it now would not only be against *Pashtunwali*: it would be an insult to the Malik. Even to scorn, publicly, a pot-scrubber, who was also a member of the Malik's tribe, could start a war. He stood for a moment, then sat down, hard, on the plastic chair behind him on the platform.

'Yusuf, son of Suleman, stood up as if this was his own house; Pashtuns are hardly ever shy. "Mr Karmal. I want to know when the Russian Army, sons of noseless mothers, will leave Afghanistan."

'Karmal recovered quickly and reached for the stock answer, prepared for him in Moscow. He had repeated it so often that it now sounded quite plausible. "The Limited Contingent of the Red Army will leave Afghanistan when foreign intervention has stopped, and when our borders are secure."

'He looked around, and resumed the oily smile which had become a reflex.

'The chiefs were slumped in their upright plastic chairs, many of them with eyes half-closed. Most were accustomed to sitting cross-legged, and Karmal had in any case ordered too much food for them in the middle of the day. Nobody paid much attention to the youth who stood up again, a young Pashtun of no important rank. Yusuf waited for Karmal to sit down before he spoke. "Your answer reminds me of a tale told among the Pashtun people. Mr Korl Morks might care to hear it, too. Perhaps you could repeat it to him sometime. This is the tale: There was once a fisherman, who caught such a huge and wonderful fish that he thought he must take it to his king. When he was given an audience, carrying his fish, the people of the court were amazed. They knew that the king would have to give, in exchange, a really wonderful present to equal such a gift. As you know, Mr Karmal, a king must always return a gift with something of similar value.

'"The king was delighted, but perplexed, because he was covetous and stingy and a puppet of his vizier, the prime minister. The vizier, as always, was standing behind the king to counsel him in whispers, and the king leant back somewhat to hear what the advice would be. The vizier, whose thoughts were always quick, told the king to ask whether this fish was a male or a female. This the king did."

'Everyone was absorbed in the story now. The Eastern habit of using parables to make a point was something they almost lived by. Many of them knew the tale, but they wanted to deduce what meaning the kitchen-boy was suggesting for it.

'"But," continued the youth, "though without power, the fisherman was intelligent. He reasoned that the king and the vizier were trying to fob him off. Whether he said it was a male or a female, the king would tell him to go away and catch its mate, which would be impossible, because there never was another such fish. Thus, he thought, the Court would save themselves the reward, and he would lose face when he failed. By this trick the king and the vizier would appear wise to the courtiers."

'So he answered, "Majesty, this fish is neither – it is *narmada*, a hermaphrodite!"

'There was a roar of applause from the assembled chiefs, and Karmal, nonplussed, declared the meeting closed. That evening, everyone in Kabul knew the story. Before curfew time, the *shabnamas*, night papers, passed from hand to hand and printed by the Resistance, said, "Karmal is a puppet king, and his Red Afghanistan is a hermaphrodite. Pass it on. Signed: The Fisherman."

'There have been no more meetings of Pashtun clan chiefs in Kabul since that day. This may have been because of the hostility which Pashtuns always feel towards the hirelings of foreign powers. It may have been due to the story of the hermaphrodite fish, told by the kitchen-boy from the borderland. Or, it may, indeed, have been because those chiefs suspected of sympathy with Karmal were found dead, shot or stabbed, in their homes, within weeks of that conference.

'So, Maryam,' Fazli Rabbi concluded, 'you will now better understand the kind of people in whose land we are, and whose chiefs we are about to meet. These tales are recited, from village to village, by the travelling bards. They call them "Tidings of the Folk".'

It was ten days before Maryam saw, against the deep blue sky, through the heat-haze, the imposing outline of the Pashtun castle which was their goal.

It was battlemented and built of the same kind of boulders which littered the terrain, cemented together. Its walls, all of twenty feet thick, were patterned with loopholes. Parts of the walls had been chipped by the heavy artillery shells used against it in one or other of the campaigns – against the men of the Free Land. It had never been conquered: even when forty thousand British troops had been thrown into battle against a single clan, the Yusufzais, a century ago.

Three massively-built Pashtun warriors, their hair in ringlets and turbans worn askew, with that air of insolence which appeals to some and infuriates others, came striding down the road which led to the main keep.

'Peace!'

'Peace.'

'I am Fazli Rabbi, nephew!'

'May God give you salvation! You are one of our own.'

'Is there permission to enter?'

'Honour us!'

The great wooden doors swung open and a group of men who had been sitting around in the courtyard beyond, rose to their feet and formed a double row in honour of the visitors.

A tall, thin man, with bushy beard and long robe, came out from the cool darkness of the inner colonnades, and embraced Fazli Rabbi Khan, amid the ritual shouting and noisy exchange of compliments which makes so many strangers think that Pashtuns, when they meet, are about to start a fight.

He was about thirty, Maryam guessed. His clothes were costly, the robe of brocade, with gold-embroidered slippers on his feet.

'Maryam Jan, this is Daud Khan, son of the Chief of the Yusufzai, our host, the Lion of the Frontier!'

The Lion turned to her, and smiled, showing perfect white teeth. '*Pa khair raghle*, you come with happiness! Transport your honourable self in this direction!' He spoke courtly Pashtu, of an archaic kind, and used the language gracefully.

They went into a long, high *diwan*, reception hall, inside the castle, carpeted with precious rugs, hung with valuable ancient Bokharan tapestries.

Seated on bolsters, before mounds of spiced rice and chicken, Daud explained that his father was away, but that he was anxious to be of any possible help to his new guests.

He had business with Fazli Rabbi, too. Crate upon crate of shiny new machine-guns littered the hall, their tops open, the stencilling which might have shown their origin covered with daubs of black paint.

Daud gestured towards them. 'As you see, my Khan, we are ready to speak with you.'

Maryam offered to leave the two men alone to discuss business, but Daud said, 'Maryam Jan: the British, in their time, used to drop leaflets over here, saying that they had an empire with six hundred million people in it. I gather that the Russians only have two hundred million or so. *Goyim barkapiran* – filth upon the infidels! We shall manage them, so we don't waste time here with what some call "security".'

That was that.

Maryam gathered that Daud Khan was some kind of agent for a Pashtun called 'Painda-Gul', Everlasting Flower, who had consigned the arms to him. Fazli Rabbi was to arrange their transfer to guerrillas operating in the Kunar Valley area, and Daud would pay for transport.

She was intrigued to learn that this Painda-Gul, from England, was spending his entire fortune, earned during a lifetime in commerce, on weapons for the guerrillas.

The two men included her in their conversation. They took Painda-Gul's contribution so much for granted that she found herself saying, 'But isn't this a rather extravagant gesture? What is he going to live on, after this?'

They both laughed. Then Fazli Rabbi said, 'Daud Jan, I promised the old man, Miskin Khan, at Alucha, that I would let Maryam hear the famous tale of the Pashtun and his horse. So far, I haven't told it to her. Perhaps you'd like to do so, then she'd understand what our people are really like.'

'Certainly,' said Daud. He made a sign to the various fighters, courtiers and others in the hall to gather round. All of them, including servants, formed a ring on the floor. When water-pipes had been brought, he began.

'There was once, among the Suleman people, a tribesman who always adhered to the principles of hospitality and honour, to Pashtunwali. He owned a beautiful horse, of high pedigree, worth a great deal of money.

'But he fell upon evil days, and lost all his money. He still refused to sell his horse, which he managed to feed and keep fit, the last vestige of his opulent past.

'A man who had long coveted this animal decided that the time was ripe to try to buy it from this man, Ismail Khan, and he went to his house to open negotiations. When Ismail Khan saw him coming, he arranged for his wife to prepare a meal for the guest.

'The other man arrived at the door, and as is the usual way among us, the two of them talked for a long time about generalities, and then they ate.

'When the meal was over, the would-be buyer asked Ismail

Khan whether it would be possible to buy his horse, and that he would give him a huge price for it.

'"My friend," said Ismail, "you are too late. That stew which you just ate was made from the flesh of that very same horse."

'You see, he had nothing else to give his guest.'

Daud Khan pointed his finger at Maryam. 'Sister, when there is a guest, or when someone needs help, the Pashtun will make any sacrifice. What I have just told you is a legend. But what you have heard about Painda-Gul is a fact. Do you think he cares what happens to him financially as a consequence of his sacrifice?'

The following morning Maryam descended from her cool room, lined with cedar wood, in the upper floor of the castle, to find a bulky figure, a man of fifty or more years of age, poking about in the packing cases which were still strewn about the main hall.

'Peace,' he said.

'Peace.'

'I am Painda-Gul. I arrived late last night. May thou never find adversity!'

Life was getting more and more like a fairy tale.

An hour or two later, a fusillade of shots rang out. Maryam ran to the window of the sitting-room where she was resting, to see two men entering the castle grounds. They were Muhjahidin, wearing Afghan shirts and baggy trousers, crossed bandoliers and rough wool hats. The Yusufzais embraced them like long-lost brothers; the shots which she had heard were in welcome, not hostility. David Callil and Bardolf, from The Eagle's nest, had arrived to arrange the smuggling of their share of the weapons.

'Welcome! Are the men strong?'

'Strong! The Almighty be with thee!'

'Prosper!'

'Be blessed!'

BOOK 7

Ataka! Ataka! Ataka!

VOYNA – [WAR]. Wars may be divided into unjust (predatory) wars and just wars. Just wars are waged to protect the interests of the working class and the toiling masses, to liquidate social and national oppression, and to protect national sovereignty against imperialist aggression.

The Soviet Dictionary of Basic Military Terms
Moscow

1 Nanpaz the Baker

The Castle
Paghman Valley

JUNE 5

Dildar Nanpaz the baker, early each morning, drove his rickety old truck to the fort, now full of Russian troops trying to keep some sort of grip on Paghman, key to Kabul and last bastion against the Tigers of Kohidaman and the equally infuriating *Margjos*, 'those who sought death' of the Hindu Kush. Beyond that lay Panjsher, and Commander Mahsud, twenty-eight-year-old engineer and military genius, who had driven both the regular Afghan Army and the Soviet tanks out of the domain, killing the governor, forcing Kabul to withdraw its entire administration. In one battle, which lasted a month, he had destroyed thirty Russian tanks and, in hand-to-hand fighting, had shown that the Russian infantry, though better armed and highly trained, was no match for his men.

The Russians, with their own sense of humour, called the Tapa, the great castle, 'The Kolkhoz', the collective farm, because it was stacked with fruit and grain, vegetables and dried fruits and all kinds of delicacies from the Paghman valley beyond. The garrison seldom had to eat from cans.

Nanpaz himself was part of this local economy, for he supplied bread, as his ancestors had always done, to the people of the castle.

His own house had been destroyed three times by Russian bombardment, during the fierce battles with the partisans in the valley. Everyone had helped to rebuild it, even women and children carried the stones. His bakery, however, had always survived, and the Paghman people, including the leaders of the resistance, had insisted that he continued to supply the castle.

Someone had said that they might, one day, poison the loaves; others that they wanted Nanpaz to stay in business for some other, future stratagem of an even more refined kind. Nanpaz didn't know what, but he was glad that he could stay in business. He would have left it, of course, at once, if he had been asked. But nobody asked.

He sounded the horn as the truck came close to the main gate, and the guard, a Central Asian who was joking with his fellow, opened it and waved him through. They were getting rather slack; didn't they wonder if he had a bunch of Muhjahidin in the back of the covered truck?

Nanpaz drove up to the cookhouse area within the great courtyard. The sergeant-cook was there, and two soldiers whose job it was to check and unload the loaves.

'*Khush amadi*, welcome! *Bekhair ye*, – are you well?' They always spoke in a mixture of Persian and Pashtu. Perhaps they got it from those little books they all had in their uniform pockets.

'Thanks to God.'

The Russian held out a packet of cigarettes and he took one and lit it, politely. They tasted very nasty, like devil's dung, he thought, and had strange cardboard holders. Perhaps they were handed out as a punishment. That could be a joke. He'd tell the lads in the bakery later. 'I was *punished* with a Russian smoke today.'

'They're good,' the Russian said. '*Kazbek* brand.'

'*Sar-Khubbaz-seb*, Mr Chief Baker,' they used such funny words, partly classical, would-be formal, as if they were self-educated idiots like so many of those village louts who went to Kabul and came back with odd phrases which they thought impressed people.

The Russian pointed. 'There's a field-kitchen over there. Get yourself a cup of tea. We haven't got the voucher to pay you yet. I'll go up for it while these men unload.'

'What a great kindness, Your Hallucination.'

'Be strong.'

The baker walked across the space and a corporal handed him a mug of good tea made from a samovar, a giant one, set on the carriage. 'Thank you, captain-seb. Are your roots treacly, or is there a pitcher in your brain?'

322

'I don't understand Dari very well.'

Of course he didn't. That was what it was all about. This was a joke the Afghans often played on Nikolai.

'Oh, forgive me. I'll teach you some. Now, repeat after me. This is a . . .' He pointed to his elbow, and then said a filthy word. 'And this means "I love you".' He uttered another. 'Thanks for the tea.'

He gave the mug back to the corporal and looked around. The field-kitchen was being towed away now, out of the gate. Nobody checked it. Always useful to keep your eyes and ears open.

Then Nanpaz saw the ten-ton truck.

It was covered with tarpaulin, camouflaged in dusty green and yellow-brown, and carried a sign on the side: *Khidmati Dosti Wa Hamkari – Friendship and Co-operation Service.* These were the trucks which were to be seen on all the main roads now. The radio said that they carried medicines and food for the suffering masses. Peeping under the cover, the baker saw metal boxes filled with ammunition. Well, well! The Nikolais were so afraid of being ambushed that they were disguising military vehicles as welfare trucks. Quite a good sign. Must tell the Muhjahidin.

There was no driver in the cab, and the keys were in the ignition lock. A Russian soldier came up to him, sauntering, but scowling at his interest. 'Death to America and its bastard children, the Zionist Pakistanis!' said Nanpaz, loudly and clearly. He had heard this on the radio, and quite liked the rhythm of it. It was funnier, even, than the nonsense rhymes that people in Paghman were so fond of.

The soldier gave the clenched fist salute. The Afghan comrade must be all right, he probably thought, and turned on his heel, after warning Nanpaz: 'Danger – *miny*.' Mines.

When the Russian was inside one of the doorways within the encircling wall, Nanpaz climbed into the truck's cab. Nice feel, quite new, bulletproof windscreen. Nice grenade, a fragmentation one, hanging easily to hand.

Start the engine, into first gear. Rev the engine, handbrake off.

In a few seconds he was driving the great ammunition-truck out of the gate and down the road; and without any reaction from the guards. Obviously, anything going out was seen as all right.

Nanpaz began to realize why he had done it. The Eagle, talking to him in his shop one day, had said, 'Nanpaz, mines are what we need. The Russians have plenty, and we want them, to mine the highways, to keep their trucks and tanks off the roads. I wish I could steal some mines. Then we'd show them . . .'

And here he was, Nanpaz the baker, with a truckload of, as the soldier had so conveniently told him, mines. He'd better get the lot under cover somewhere, and tell The Eagle. He'd burned his boats now, of course . . .

Stealing a Russian truck – death. Stealing munitions – death. Loss of the bakery, and transportation of his wife and children, a kind of death for them, too. *Niet millosti*, no mercy, for anyone. Russian words. The Russians knew that he had done it: so, whether he got the load to The Eagle or not, he was now, like it or not, a guerrilla, one of the Muhjahidin. The baker laughed. And to think that he had felt so humble about the warriors for such a long time, wondered why and how they could challenge the Russians, who had such power. Now he knew. It was easy. You only had to try.

He laughed even louder when he passed a huge, if primitively drawn, poster. It showed a group of guerrillas, with the caption, a masterpiece of the Red Afghan propaganda department: '*Sharm bar Qatilun!* – Shame upon the Killers.' He rather liked the look of them. One was almost as fierce, he thought, as his own father who'd fought in the 1919 war.

The baker was gone: the searchers found the bakery blown up. There was no sign of his family, either. Even their house had been gutted of anything portable, and his assistants were nowhere to be found. The commandant of the castle, Colonel Slavsky, had had apoplexy and recovered from that: but not from the shock. Several Russians – the sergeant, the chief of the kitchen, the main gate guards – were under arrest. Russian military punishments, in Afghanistan at any rate, were reverting to those of pre-revolutionary days: the knout. The prisoners were stripped and the torturers were called. The commandant watched as the unfortunates were pegged down to the parade ground upon the order 'Stretch them out'. Then came the words feared by so many generations of malefactors and innocents alike, 'Thrash with whips! Without mercy! Start now!'

The sight did not make the commandant feel as much better as he would have liked, even when the blood flowed and soaked the whips. Raided by a baker! He would have to answer, to Army Security, the GRU, for the lost ammunition if he did not get it back. Soon.

The fixed-wing reconnaissance craft and the helicopters were out, careering all day in the skies. The scouting parties swarmed over the countryside; informers were offered double, treble the usual money for any whisper. For three days there was no trace of the truck or its mortar bombs, essential for the defence for the castle at Paghman.

Then, as quickly as it had been lost, the truck turned up again. It was standing, only five kilometres from the castle, partly covered in straw and amateurishly half-hidden behind a loopholed breastwork. The wind seemed to have blown off some of its makeshift camouflage. Evidently the guerrillas had not yet been able to move it to a better hideout. Helicopter Pilot Leonid Federov, of Air Reconnaissance, whooped when he saw it, and called in through the radio network, direct to the castle's command.

Colonel Slavsky was so delighted that he spoke directly to the flier, shouting into the microphone. 'Comrade *Leytenant* Federov! Warmest thanks. I'll get you a medal when there's another engagement that'll cover it.' He could hardly propose an award for the finding of the truck and cargo, which would be followed by an enquiry as to how and why he had lost it in the first place.

The Russian recovery team found everything intact. Every mortar round, every road map, even the driver's wallet stuffed with the new Afghan notes. Those terrorists really must have panicked, thought Slavsky. Of course they probably did not know that without this load there would have been no ammunition for the mortars in the castle, and only rifle-fire to defend it. And the marksmanship of the Soviet soldier was generally admitted to be poor. Each platoon shared a single sniper's rifle.

Although it was an excellent Dragunow SVD, the training in its use had not proved to be sufficiently good.

'Primitives, bandits, that's what they are,' Slavsky told Major Vasilev, his second-in-command. He issued the mortar bombs and ordered a secret watch, day and night, to be put on all approaches to the truck. The terrorists might be planning to come back, perhaps with someone who had a knowledge of munitions, or with their own transport. Intercepted on the way to the cache, there could be some good hunting, and no butcher's bill.

2 The Whirlwind to see Colonel Slavsky

Below the Castle
Paghman

JUNE 19

In the event, nobody came. It was two weeks before the advance picquets reported that the Paghman force, wearing the green caps of The Eagle's unit, *Girdbad*, the Whirlwind, were approaching the Tapa Castle in some strength. It was just after first light, on a perfect June day.

When the Russians had first entered the valley, the resistance fighters had stopped them, shooting down five helicopters and destroying several tanks and APCs in what was known to the Muhjahidin as the First Battle of Paghman, in July 1981, and the Soviet troops had withdrawn. Now the bandits were actually coming straight at the fortification.

They could not hope to take it, of course, Slavsky thought; though, in addition to rifles they were seen to be carrying what might be Russian *dashkas*, heavy machine-guns which had been captured or handed over by Afghan deserters from the Red regime. These were the weapons which were, at last, bringing down the helicopters, sometimes with only a short burst of fire. They were the great prize, when they could be removed from immobilized armoured fighting vehicles and carried off.

Slavsky ordered the aircraft to stay on the ground. 'We'll not need air support for this one,' he told Strike Liaison, briefly. 'We'll show the scum what ordinary guns can do.' Here was a chance for a little hunting, in armchair comfort. He missed the regular slaying, of bears and boars, that he and his fellow officers used to enjoy in the Russian forests at this time of the year. A little blood out here might make up for his deprivation.

One of his Central Asian officers was on forward observation.

A Mongolian with a sense of the dramatic, he was delighted that the guerrillas were coming out at last. He should come through, over the air, at any moment now.

The radio in Slavsky's room crackled. 'Forward observation to Commander: *Khun-Khur*, Blood-Drinker here.'

That barbarian would insist on using, as his code-name, some dreadful native word. All messages had to be in standard and authorized terminology; but, unfortunately, for security reasons, local call-signals could be left to private enterprise. 'Commandant to Blood-Drinker: come in, then.'

'Blood-Drinker reporting, two hundred to two hundred and fifty terrorists advancing towards killing ground. Lightly armed, parties of ten to twelve, no good targets yet. Now approaching at 1,750 metres.'

'Heard and understood, Blood-Drinker, Commandant off.'

Slavsky turned to his radio operator. 'I'm going to the Command Post now.' The man followed him up the steps to the turret of the castle, stuffing a piece of mould-proof black bread into his pocket. He had developed a taste for Afghan-style bread during Nanpaz's time, but alas it was now back to Army tack . . .

There was an armchair in the turret, and Colonel Slavsky settled himself in it. What a view! You could see almost the whole valley. The chair idea was copied from a film he had seen – shown for briefing purposes only, of course – an American production. It had shown a tough Yankee commander in Vietnam, directing operations from just such a perch as this. And he had been attended by his faithful radio operator as well, just like Slavsky.

The radio squawked: Blood-Drinker was coming in again. Slavsky guessed, by the interference, that other units, hearing that something was happening in his sector, were breaking into the artillery communications network to eavesdrop. Well, he'd show them how things were done. Let them listen.

Yes, it was the forward observation post. 'Blood-Drinker to Commander. Attention, *badmashes*, villains, closing, advancing under natural cover, range a thousand metres and moving.'

The radio operator was gesturing to him that someone else was trying to get through. Slavsky acknowledged Blood-Drinker and looked enquiringly at him.

'General Zeitsev asking to come in on our frequency, sir.'

Zeitsev! That comedian! The old drunk would not keep out of anything, would he? Promoted far beyond his competence, just because people were saying that air support was the coming thing.

'Put the general on, Signaller.'

'Zeitsev to Slavsky: are you there, Comrade Colonel?'

'Listening, Comrade General.'

'I've noticed that you have a little game going on over there, in your castle, eh?'

'That's right. And, Comrade General, I am in the middle of dealing with some bandits, if you don't mind.'

'That's just what I want to talk about. They seem to have got very close to you, and you perhaps need ground attack by aviation: *Shturmovyye deystviya aviatsii*, SDA, which I control. You know about it, of course.'

Of course Slavsky knew about it. He even knew the relevant passage from the textbook by heart: 'SDA = attack by air from minimum distance against visible targets, using various destruction methods and means.'

'Comrade General! I know all about it, and I have already declined air support. I can easily deal with this rabble, and we are under orders not to waste supplies, as you perhaps know.'

'Comrade Colonel, I understand completely. It was just that I hoped nothing had slipped your memory.'

Insolent fool. Still: 'Thank you, Comrade General. I am returning to my attack situation. Slavsky out.'

Time to speak to the people who would actually engage the enemy, the Mortar Unit.

'Commander to *Pervyy Eshelon*, First Echelon. Hear now. Object of imminent engagement is neutralization of enemy. Situation estimate already made. Prepare for operational orders.'

This was going to be a copybook exercise, just like those which he had studied again and again during his three years at the Frunze Military Academy.

Mortar Control was coming through clearly, terminology very correct.

'Mortar Control reporting: Mortar Control to Commander.

First Echelon mortars deployed in maximum density, and listening.' Good.

The Colonel had worked out a plan for just such a situation as this: dealing with a terrorist attempted assault on a DFS, a permanent fortified structure. The mortar sub-unit of his motorized rifle regiment was already drilled, in impeccable military phraseology, for such a situation, taken direct from the book, *Organization of Fire*.

Time for the next step. 'Commander to Mortar Control. Confirm readiness for automatic or barrage fire.'

Slavsky had set up the system himself: the latest in electronic linked and synchronized fire, so that the whole augmented battery of forty weapons could fire simultaneously. From the book, of course.

'Mortar Control to Commander. Confirming mortar battery ready for concentrated fire, barrage or automatic.'

Now the spotter, Blood-Drinker, was coming in again through the artillery network. 'Commander from Blood-Drinker. The enemy is now at 750 metres and closing. Shall I fall back to prepared defensive position, query? Hear and respond. That was Blood-Drinker to Commander.'

All was at combat readiness. There was no need for the forward observer now. Slavsky answered: 'Commander to Blood-Drinker. Affirmative. Fall back, fall back. Do not engage the enemy. I am taking command initiative.'

'Blood-Drinker to Commander, heard and understood. Transmission ends.'

Slavsky turned to the radio operator. 'Combat alert!' The message went out.

The klaxons sounded, and the non-combatant troops clustered around the forty mortars. That was a good sign, showed that the men were keen, Slavsky thought, as the loudspeakers echoed through every corner of the castle.

'Combat alert! Combat alert!' Then: '*Ataka, Ataka, Ataka!* Attack coming. This is a combat alert.'

The advancing men on the plain below him were clearly visible through Slavsky's field glasses now. 'Artillery Watch, attention! This is the Commander. Take over spotting of approaching bandits and confirm.'

'Artillery Watch to Commander. Message heard and understood. Enemy in our glasses. Estimate numbers: two hundred and fifty men. Lightly armed, parties of ten men each, closing in, now at five hundred metres.'

'Commander to Artillery Watch. Understood. Continue observation.'

Slavsky was going to let the Muhjahidin get as near as possible, to minimum mortar-range. Then he was going to butcher them. Every mortar linked, each firing at once, at precisely the same moment. If the Afghans didn't break up their groups and go into individual attack formation very soon now, they would all be annihilated.

Now to get the range, to the last millimetre. 'Commander to Artillery Watch. Take range and bearing from Plan Position Indicator and supply to mortars.'

'Artillery Watch to Commander. Taking range and bearing for supply to mortars from *Indikator Krugovogo Obzora*.'

'Commander to Mortar Firing Central.'

'Mortar Firing Central listening.'

'Take range and bearing of target.'

'Mortar Firing Central understood.'

'Commander to Mortar Firing continues message . . .'

'Mortar Firing Central listening.'

'Commander to Mortar Firing.' Slavsky almost rubbed his hands together. This was the life. 'Precise Firing Procedure will be followed.'

'Mortar Firing Central acknowledges. Fire Procedure will be followed.'

Colonel Slavsky took up his glasses again to have a look at his opponents. He could see them very clearly now. So these were the famous Whirlwind warriors. They picked fancy names like that, he thought, because they were such a hopeless rabble. Like children playing at Indian chiefs, like beggars imagining that they were kings.

The Eagle looked around to see that his men were correctly deployed, and beckoned to his second-in-command, Qassab the butcher. A useful man. Of course, he was used to blood, but he had also passed the guerrilla battle course in thirty days instead of two months. He had shown distinct command ability, too.

'Qassab. They haven't fired a shot. They're either calling in air support, *halikuptars*, or they're holding their fire until we get closer. Which do you think it is?'

'Holding fire. Maybe they're afraid of the *dashkas* we've got set up. Helicopters don't like heavy machine-guns. Anyway, why should they fire until we get really close, so long as we are still advancing?'

'Right. I think so, too. So far, so good.'

'What do you mean, Eagle? We'll never kill anyone in the castle from the ground with rifles: they're safe in there, and we are very exposed out here. I'd have liked some information, or orders more specific than "Follow my flag signals."'

'Security, Qassab. Perhaps you talk in your sleep. Ever thought of that?' The butcher was the butt of all the Whirlwind men, since he had formed the habit of falling asleep when he was a reserve during fire-fights; though he would wake up, completely alert, in a split second, if called upon. Firing never bothered him: it was the strangest thing, thought his commander. The butcher said nothing.

In the castle, the robotic procedures were grinding on. 'Mortar Control, this is the Commander. Acknowledge my signal . . . Good. Stand by to fire when sighting completed. Firing to start when the enemy reaches one hundred metres and not before. I repeat, one hundred metres. Ignore any enemy fire. Keep behind parapets. Confirm if understood.'

'Mortar Control to Commander. Understood.'

'Commander to Mortar Control. Once mortars are sighted at minimum range, aim at bandit groups when they reach one hundred metres. Each double mortar position to take one bandit group. Starting from left. Left most bandit group will be for mortars one and two. Complete this ranging and report.'

After a few moments Mortar Control confirmed the arrangement.

'Commander confirming that mortars shall not fire at random and that all fire is electronically synchronized. Mortar Control to confirm.'

'Mortar Control confirms for Commander.'

'Commander confirms instructions. One hundred

metres . . .' The check-list litany droned on. Finally, 'Fire will be continuous at twenty-five rounds per minute until counter-manded.'

The Mortar Control operator confirmed.

'Commander to Mortar Firing. Stand by to fire. Keep radio channel crystal stable 444 open.'

'Standing by. Channel open.'

Crouching behind his boulder, The Eagle spoke to the butcher. 'We're nearly at their mortars' minimum effective distance, Qassab. This is more than the "killing ground": it's like the "total liquidation ground".'

'*Nichevo*, no matter, Eagle.'

'Right. We're at a hundred and fifty metres now. Signal orange flag to our whole Battle Group, for "Increase pace of advance".'

'They've seen it, Eagle. Battle Group advancing.'

The Eagle felt the sweat running down the back of his neck, like a man would in a steam-bath. 'A good commander does not expose himself unnecessarily,' it had said in the field manual which he had been studying. But this was going to be a gift. He had to test himself, to have been there, right in front. Certainly the men expected it: Afghans had never shown an inclination to be led from the rear.

There were only a hundred metres to go now. If they went any nearer to the castle, the mortars or machine-guns would certainly fire, since at closer range their mortars would be less accurate.

'Qassab: we are now one hundred metres from the target. This is the minimum effective distance for Russian M-37 mortars. Raise the green flag.'

'Green flag up, to signal "Prepare for Battle". The Muhja-hidin combat group signallers have acknowledged.'

The snouts of the 82-millimetre mortars, their barrels almost vertical, were clearly visible to the guerrillas. They could im-agine the Russian mortar-men, bent over their sights, the 3.3 kilogramme rounds ready to drop in.

Each one of the two hundred and fifty raiders had stopped. All were unwinding their sashes.

*

In the castle's command post the radio was screeching. 'Artillery Watch to Commander. Bandits have stopped at one hundred metres.'

Slavsky was glad. He had been on the verge of ordering 'Fire!' at the moving men, before their impetus brought them too close. 'Commander responds: you can sign off now, Artillery Watch.'

What was that they were doing? 'Comrade Colonel!' The radio operator was excited, 'they're making turbans of their white shrouds, wrapping them around their green caps. This is a suicide attack.'

'Damned barbarians, that's what they are, Ivanov! Their religion, you know. What an ideology! They think they'll go to Paradise, just for being killed by us.' Still, the cold menace of the thing made him feel uneasy. Surely there could not really be people with no fear of death?

The guerrillas must be kept still at all costs now, The Eagle thought. 'Blue flag up, Qassab.'

'Blue flag up, Eagle, for "Battle Group stand firm".'

Seeing the flag, the baker said to himself, 'I hope my hands are shaking only because of the desire to kill. But I don't know: I'm only a beginner at this sort of thing. I'll have to remember to ask Komondon Eagle when we get back to the Caves.'

In the Command post, all was in order. Slavsky intoned, 'Commander to Mortar Control. Stand by for firing.'

'Mortar Control to Commander: standing by.'

This was going to be as easy as any exercise, probably easier. Those guerrillas were crazy, waiting to be killed. They'd be done before lunchtime. Colonel Slavsky was sure that he'd enjoy his meal. Some of those excellent *kalbasa*, pink Moscow sausages, had arrived, and he liked them very much. He reached for the microphone. Here goes.

'Commander to Mortar Control: I shall now count down to firing signal. Fire synchronizing buttons at the count of ONE.

'Now countdown begins. Ten, nine, eight, seven, six, five, four, three, two, ONE!' There was always a thrill in giving the actual firing order to the artillery oneself.

The forty mortars, all sighted on their targets, unmissable, static targets – two mortars with their high-explosive shells due to hit each guerrilla combat group – fired.

With a combined roar and a surge of flame from two score weapons, with rock and steel flying in all directions, the bombs, doctored by The Eagle's skill to fire prematurely, exploded in the mortar tubes, blowing the guns, their crews and the spectators crowded around them indiscriminately, to smithereens. For at least a hundred men it suddenly seemed, and almost instantly was, the end of the world.

From the turret high above the mortars, *Komendant* Colonel Slavsky saw the carnage among his men, and stared in disbelief at the whooping Muhjahidin below, less than a hundred yards from the castle walls. He struggled to his feet from the cushioned armchair, only to fall back into it, neatly picked off by an expert guerrilla sniper, Maher Tirandaz, as the men of the Whirlwind withdrew under covering fire.

To the side of the castle, a second explosion and a column of smoke showed The Eagle's observers that the mine placed at the weakest point of the wall had done its work. For the men in the castle, shocked and confused, trying to organize first aid, this sound, and even the smoke, made little impact.

As the wall was breached, the second attack unit of the Whirlwind hurled themselves into the fortress, through the dust, fumes, falling rocks, spraying the few defenders at point-blank range with Kalashnikov rapid fire, killing most of them and driving the rest into headlong flight.

In the deep underground ice-chambers, the prisoners, suspects and captives intended for deportation as hostages to Russia, were found crouching in the far corners of their huge communal cells, as they had been warned to do by The Eagle's message the night before. None was injured.

Within ten minutes the entire group of captives, some fifty people, was scrambling up a rock face, guided by the Muhjahidin who had been trained for this phase of the operation. Both the hostages and the Whirlwind attack force had reached safety before, at last, the helicopters came overhead.

'Not a scratch on anyone,' said The Eagle, as they celebrated their victory. 'It was as good as one of those raids right into Kabul City, the time we blew up the gas tanks and got clean away. If you rememeber, not only did we not lose anyone, but several people joined us, right off the streets.'

He hugely enjoyed telling his men, most of whom had been kept in ignorance for security's sake, how he and a small group, instructed by Captain Azambai, had doctored the mortar shells in the parked truck, and simply left them for the Russians to collect.

'If the Nikolais had still been eating my bread, instead of that unhealthy baked brown leather of theirs, their brains would not have been so addled as to fall for your ruse, tampering with their mortar bomb fuses. Anyway, that kind of fiddling can be dangerous. We could all have been blown up.' The baker grinned.

The Eagle laughed. 'Nanpaz, you are a better baker than you are a linguist. You didn't know, did you, that the Russian word *miny* means "mortar bomb" as well as "mine". It means that, though we didn't get any mines, we did get, thanks to you, the little amusement we've just had.'

'Thank you, Eagle.' The baker had had his recognition at last. 'After all, they do say, "A ruse is worth a tribe".'

'Long live the Revolution!' said the butcher.

'Shame on the killers!' said the baker.

'Hurrah for Victory!' said The Eagle.

After the baker had had his share of glory, The Eagle let the Muhjahidin into the secret he had held back thus far. They cheered Captain Azambai to the echo when they discovered that it was his radio which had eavesdropped, on the castle's special frequency, revealing that all the mortars had been linked, electronically, to fire at the same time. They insisted on Captain Azambai teaching them the word for it, which they sometimes called him by, as a title: '*Radiovoyna*' – electronic warfare.

BOOK 8

Nest of the Eagle

> As to fanaticism, well, if we in England found a foreign army, for no reason that we knew of, invading our country and blowing up our homes and public buildings, etc., I fancy we would do our best to wipe them out, and call ourselves patriots, not fanatics.
>
> George B. Scott
> *Afghan and Pathan*

1 One hundred and fifty-eight – and volunteering

Eagle's Nest
The Buddhist Monastery
Paghman Mountains

JUNE 19

Colonel Slavsky's abrupt treatment of Helicopter Ground Support meant that General Zeitsev had taken his pilots off standby. It was some time before the scouters came over the Paghman foothills looking for the Kara Kush band, Battle Group Whirlwind. By that time, three hours after the mortar explosions, the freed hostages – and some booty – were safe in the ancient monastery's tunnels.

A few of the hostages were suffering from malnutrition, some were half-blind from being kept in the dark: for weeks in some cases; but there were no serious cases of sickness.

Adam Durany called Qasim into his 'orderly room'.

'The Russians had all those people ready for deportation. They won't, therefore, have planted spies among them to collect *our* secrets. But we've got to weed out any agents who have been trying to collect information from the real hostages. As soon as everyone has rested, we'll set up an interrogation system to deal with this problem.'

Whilst they were discussing the details of this necessity, three armoured personnel-carriers manned by Afghan regular troops had drawn up at the Russian roadblock on the Kabul-Paghman highway, twenty miles south of the Caves.

The men at the roadblock had seen the castle, three miles south of them, under threat, and heard the firing and explosions when the mortars went up. They had not been informed about the action, however. As far as they were concerned, it was just another Muhjahid raid, beaten back, probably with the usual high casualty list for the Afghans. None of their business, anyway. Most of them just wanted to get back to the Soviet Union and safety.

Several tanks were dug in by the roadside, hull-down, commanding the road with their heavy guns and automatic weapons. An Afghan Army captain sat at a table in the middle of the road. A Russian officer, the two small stars and narrow red stripe of a second lieutenant on his khaki shoulder-straps, sat smoking on a deck chair beside him.

Stoi! – Halt. Two Russian privates trained their weapons on the cars, pointing to the red and yellow Traffic Control board by the roadside. From the leading personnel-carrier an Afghan colonel jumped down and, accompanied by two NCOs carrying the latest model Kalashnikov 74s, strode up to the captain, as the Russian guards presented arms.

'Where are your papers? You cannot proceed without orders from the High Command. Paghman is full of bandits, didn't you know that, colonel? You'd never get ten kilometres, not with those cars and only thirty men. Show me your movement order.' The captain held out his hand for documents.

The colonel looked at him coolly. 'First, stand up when you speak to me, unfortunate one! Have you forgotten how to salute?'

The captain struggled to his feet, red-faced and apologizing.

'Excuse me. I am only an administrative officer . . .'

'How long have you been in the Army?'

The captain looked uneasy. 'Two months.'

'Why are you in the Army?'

The man appeared to consider this for a moment. 'To serve my country. To safeguard the April Revolution.'

'Ever heard the word "sir"?'

'Forgive me, sir.'

'Captain: I am on my way to Paghman, and so are these men with me. My movement order is in the guns of my men. We have work to do there. If you don't give us passage we'll do the work here – by blasting a way through you and your Russian dog-friend here.'

The captain, instead of being frightened or annoyed, snapped to attention and saluted. 'Colonel *seb*! You have the very best of movement orders. I don't need paper or lead bullets. All I need is to know that someone is still prepared to fight. That is what we call *Afghaniyyat*, "Afghanness".

'Just pretend to show me papers and I'll let you through. These Russians don't understand a word of what we're saying.'

'Thank you, Captain. You seem a very patriotic man for someone who is taking orders from enemies. What's the explanation?'

'Colonel *seb*: I am only a clerk from the Ministry of Economy. I was forced into the Army, but I still have a sense of honour.'

The colonel shook his hand. 'Captain, you are one of our very own!'

The captain signalled to his men to lift the striped red and yellow road barrier. Before the cars moved forward he walked to the door of the first one where the colonel sat, opened it and bent down. Then he kissed the instep of the colonel's boot.

'Kill some Russians for me,' he said, 'my family have been taken hostage.'

The colonel saluted him. 'By my head and eyes, brother,' he said.

Half an hour later, scouts reported to The Eagle that three of the latest Soviet armoured personnel-carriers, BTR-70s, were making their way towards the guerrilla stronghold. One of the advance picquets had noted that they were flying the old flag of Afghanistan, the vertical black-red-green tricolour, and not the socialist emblem.

A group of wild-looking hillmen signalled to the vehicles to stop. Everything, from primitive matchlocks and ancient Martini-Henry rifles, real museum pieces, to new Russian Kalashnikovs and shotguns, were levelled at the newcomers.

The commander, Colonel Barakzai, clambered out of the lead car, and held up his right hand in greeting. Uruzgani, a wizened warrior with a rocket-launcher over his shoulder, who was known as *Tonkkhor*, the Tank-Eater, moved towards him, levelling his weapon. At that range, two or three yards, it was extremely dangerous.

The colonel shouted: 'Peace! Tell your leader that Colonel Akram Barakzai, Thirty-Seventh Commando Division, is here, with vehicles and thirty men. To join the fight.'

As the APCs were being hidden under piles of brushwood,

Adam went down to the cliff face to welcome the newcomers. 'This is the first regular army unit we've had come over to us, so you are doubly welcome,' he told the colonel. 'How did you find us?'

Barakzai smiled. 'It's quite a story, but, as you'll see, there's no security problem.

'I was dining with old Colonel Sakafi a few weeks ago, and telling him that I had about three dozen men ready to take to the mountains, but that I wondered how to contact a suitable guerrilla group. Sakafi said, at once, "You must go to The Eagle, Kara Kush: but plan your move well. Get all your families to safety first: then act swiftly. Use effrontery!"

'I asked him, "Where exactly could I find him, though?"

'He said, "Years and years ago, when I was hunting in the Paghman Mountains, way beyond the valley, I saw a young fellow who'd fixed himself up with a cave in an old Buddhist monastery. I tracked him, just for fun: I'm an old hunter as well as a warrior, you know. Well, that fellow is Adam Durany, Sirdar Akbar Sharifi's friend. I know them both well. And the caves – I'll draw you a map."'

Everyone laughed. Adam said, 'But how did he know that I was The Eagle?'

'I asked him that,' said Colonel Barakzai. 'He said, "He may be a fine engineer, but I've been in military intelligence as well as in a fighting unit. When The Eagle sent me a note asking me to inform the Mirza in Delhi that young Aslam Jan had been murdered by a KGB man called Sementsev, I read it very carefully. First, I recognized the classical quotation he used: it was one of Adam's favourites. Second, I remembered that I knew the Mirza and that he was Aslam's only relative."'

'Just as well the Russians haven't got you on their side,' said Adam. 'Hundreds, perhaps thousands, of people know how to get in touch with us, but only through a long line of inter-mediaries. Very few can get here without going through the sieve.'

The colonel leant back in his chair. 'Yes, the strength of the Afghans is that they are at last getting security-minded. So many people have to stay in their jobs because there isn't anything else for them to do. If they take to the mountains, their families suffer. If they don't, they can always do their bit by helping the Resistance. Even under the occupation, this gives some spice to life.'

'Colonel, I am working on two main concepts,' Adam said. 'The first is that we must have a lot of exploits, punishing the Russians and showing that everyone can do something, that even a small force can hurt.'

'Yes, Adam: keep up morale and hit the enemy; excellent military principles.'

'But we have to do more, you know . . .'

'Organize, unify, prepare to drive the invader out!' The colonel's eyes were blazing, his Pashtun blood stirred.

Adam laid a hand on his arm. 'Yes, all that, but we have to do it the *Afghan* way: use the character of the people and the nature of the terrain and our history. At the moment, everyone is fighting his own war, large and small bands scattered through the whole country. If we form large armies, the Russians will wipe them out, or else they will not be able to operate in rugged terrain without being destroyed from the air. Small bands, guerrilla actions. And the key to success here is in two principles: information and co-operation.'

'I agree with everything you say,' the colonel said. 'We can get high-grade information from the KHAD, the secret police, even. But do you get co-operation from other bands?'

'Yes we do, colonel. In fact, only last week we were attacking a Russian transport section when another group approached and helped us out. There was only one problem there.'

'And that was?'

'They wanted to do it by themselves! You see, for the size of the convoy, either of us could have dealt with it. We'd both got the same tip-off from the Afghan logistics people. Duplication of effort.'

'Adam, what you need is centralized information, not centralized command. Then you can share the operations out.'

'Exactly.'

'I think I can help you there. If you like I'll work out a plan for Pan-Afghan intelligence and operational liaison.'

'That's just what we need. And, in the meantime, let's start with the problem which Qasim and I were puzzling over when you arrived. You can help us there, too.'

'Glad to. What is it?'

'Screening the hostages, to sift out any informers among them. The prisoners we've just rescued from Slavsky's castle. And you can train one of my men in interrogation methods: Qasim would be good.'

The colonel was pleased. 'Great, Adam. Soon as you like.'

'Fine. Have some food and then you and Qasim can begin. We haven't had time to check the hostages at all, except to see whether anyone is injured or ill.'

Half an hour later the interrogation began.

Qasim watched as the first batch – all men who were volunteering to join the Muhjahidin – were brought in, one by one. It seemed to him that the colonel's methods were altogether too gentle. He had expected interrogation to involve, well, bullying at least.

But Colonel Barakzai had told him, 'Simply observe and learn.'

A beefy, beetle-browed man in his early thirties, well-developed physically, with an intelligent face, stepped forward.

'Abdullah Wardaki, from Kabul Province.'

'Welcome, Mr Wardaki. You look as though you have seen some military service. You hold yourself well.'

'I have been an officer in the Kabul Fire Brigade.'

'Excellent! For long, and how recently?'

'For five years, and until three months ago.'

'That must be very interesting. How many of the new fire engines have you got there?'

'Nine, sir.'

'I heard that you had three of the large water tankers, too.'

'That's right.'

'Where is the Central Fire Station in Kabul, again?'

'In the compound of Kabul Police Headquarters.'

'Did you find that it was easier to deal with fires quickly, after automatic telephone dialling came in?'

'Oh, yes. Very much easier.'

'I thought so. There was a fire near my house, in the Mikro-rayon block, the modern one, at Nadir Shah Maina, you know. The people there were nearly all foreigners, so they didn't know what to do. I found a distraught woman at my door, saying, "My apartment is in flames! What number do I dial to phone the fire brigade?" Of course, I was able to tell her it was 777, and your people were there in no time at all. Do you remember that fire? It was about two years ago, people called Martin, I believe.'

'Yes, I think I do. I am not quite sure, though. What time of the year was it?'

'Autumn.'

'I may have been on leave then. I went to Europe for training.'

'Eastern Europe?'

'Yes. Hungary. Terrible place. Communist persecution; tyranny everywhere.'

The colonel smiled, and continued in his conversational tone. 'Well, Mr Wardaki, we have your particulars. Please step outside and I'll make arrangements for you.'

The man bowed, and went out of the room. Colonel Barakzai looked at Qasim. 'What did you think?'

'I don't know. He sounds all right.'

'Qasim, you haven't done any intelligence work, have you? What's your background?'

'University of Wyoming, through its programme with the Afghan Institute of Technology, Kabul, sir.'

'I see. Well, listen. The Central Fire Station is in the middle of Kabul, near the Ministry of Mines. Did you know that?'

'No, I thought it was where he said it was.'

'So do lots of other people: but not firemen. It was moved from Police HQ some time ago.'

'So he's a phony?'

'Let's say for the moment that he's not a fireman. He thinks you dial 777 for "Fire!", but it's actually 13.'

'Did he get anything right at all?'

'The number of new fire engines, and that's all. He agreed that they had three new water tankers. Actually they have four.'

Qasim scratched his head. 'But if he *is* a plant, why didn't they train him better?'

'Because, my dear friend, you can fill a man full of facts to make him seem plausible, but you cannot make sure that he will remember them all, especially under stress. And you can't be sure exactly what facts he will be asked. When you have a job, there are thousands upon thousands of little details that you absorb and remember. You can't programme all that into a spy.'

'But colonel, what about all the agents who are trained especially to fool interrogators?'

Barakzai laughed. 'You've been reading too many spy novels, Qasim. The fact is that cover stories only work, in general, when the interrogator has less first-hand knowledge than the subject.'

'What's going to happen to Mr Wardaki, or whoever he is?'

'He'll have to go before a Resistance court. It's up to them. But bear in mind that if they let him go, he may have gathered information which could be useful to the enemy.'

The questioning went on.

'What is your work?'

'I'm a fur tailor.'

'Where is Faryadi's Fur Atelier?'

'In Shahr-i-Nau, the New City, opposite the Pakistan Embassy.'

'Where are you from?'

'Jalalabad. I am an archaeologist.'

'How interesting. Tell me what the Jalalabad "Fish Porch" is.'

'It's the unique stucco mosaic scene of the Buddha meeting the God of the Nagas.'

'What's its importance?'

'Considered to be one of the most important pieces of ancient Buddhist art ever found.'

'I am from Kandahar.'

'Work?'

'Restaurant hand.'

'What restaurant?'

'Salimi's.'

'Did you ever work at the booking desk?'

'Yes.'

'What is the telephone number?'

'Kandahar 3455.'

*

'Farmer, from Ghaza, near Paghman.'

'Why did you leave?'

'The place was bombed to pieces in an unprovoked attack by Russian aircraft.'

'How many died?'

'Nine out of ten.'

'Date?'

'The night of August 11th, 1983.'

Barakzai told Qasim to have all the volunteers' names checked by the *turubchas*, partisans ordered to continue working for the KHAD as double agents.

Desperate to break the growing Resistance movement, the Russians were planting spies whenever they could. They had also raised the reward for the capture of insurgents from $3,000 to $10,000 a head, paid in cash, and in dollar notes.

Their last interrogation subject was so extraordinary that after a few questions, and hardly able to suppress their smiles, they sent him to see The Eagle.

A small, bowed figure shuffled into Adam's 'orderly room', sunken eyes still bright under a small turban, white beard neatly trimmed. He raised his right hand and gave a smart salute, hand at the regulation position on his headgear. He looked all of eighty years old.

'Private Ghulam Husain, from Shunbul District, reporting for duty in the army of Kara Kush!' His voice was strong enough, even if he spoke through toothless gums.

'I know I have arthritis in my legs, but my arms are still strong,' shouted the ancient. 'Give me grenades, and I'll throw them further than anyone else . . .'

'Yes, I'm sure you will, father, but . . .'

'I've trained all my boys, and their boys, too. There's over a hundred of them, and we've got to join the war.'

'How far have you trained them to throw?'

'Give me one of the little *Roussi* things, bombs, *Ragad*, Fives, and I'll show you. I'll hurl it twice as far as anyone else.

Ragad, that must be the Russian initials, RGD, with vowels added, Adam realized. He went into one of the adjoining caves and came back with a Russian RGD.

'This?'

'That's it.'

'Right,' said Adam, 'let's go outside and see what you can do.'
The old man stumbled after The Eagle through the connecting
passages to the open hillside. He put the bomb into a fabric
pouch, pulled the ring and began to whirl the thing around his
head. Adam started to count and when he had got to 'two',
flung himself on the ground. After all, it only had a four-second
fuse.

As he watched, the grenade left the sling and flew what
seemed an incredible distance, before shattering a rock sixty
yards away. Spent metal fragments scattered over the watchers.

'All right, that's enough. You can use slingshots. You're as
cocky as the old fellow of Bamiyan who'd be a hundred and
sixty now, if he were alive.'

Ghulam Husain grinned toothlessly. Then, from the inner
pocket of a waistcoat inside his padded jacket, he took out a
wallet. Slowly, like someone performing a conjuring trick, he
extracted a piece of yellowed paper and handed it to The
Eagle.

Adam looked at the heading: *The Kabul Times*. Underneath
he saw a full page headline, '145-year-old Man Recalls Past
Life'. Just below was a photograph, and it bore a remarkable
resemblance to the slingman. The caption said: '145-year-old
Ghulam Husain posing for a photographer near the wall of his
house'.

'But,' said Adam, searching for words, 'that would make you
– let's see – one hundred and sixty years old.'

'No, I'm not 160, only a hundred and fifty-eight!' cackled the
ancient, stowing the clipping away. 'And I'll tell you some
more. I know the Russians. When I was ninety, those devils
actually came into Afghanistan. It was in the north and they
got forty miles into the country, pursuing a guerrilla leader who
had taken sanctuary with us. We saw them off the premises,
Eagle! I've got experience of the *Rouss*, don't you see! I'm a
useful man. Most of these silly children here don't know how
to fight, don't know their enemy.'

When he was ninety . . . Adam remembered that there had
been such an incursion, in Stalin's time. The old fellow was
getting even more animated.

'We'll shove their Victoria back down their throats . . .'

He ended with a rolling, obscene, untranslatable oath: '*Gohimadaripirishanbadani-jaddishaitan* . . .'

'All right, *Ghazi*, warrior hero: Queen Victoria's dead. It's the Russians now. You're in. Now, if you'll excuse me, I have other people to see . . .'

When Barakzai had seen all the volunteers, accepting some and referring others for further enquiry, he and Qasim began work with the other hostages. The information which they brought, from all over Afghanistan, was not only of astonishing variety, it also helped to fill out the picture which the Resistance could use in planning co-operation between town and country, between Turk and Tajik, Pashtun and Nuristani.

So far, nobody in the Resistance had collated the material.

2 Silahdar Haidar, Weapon-Bearer, reporting, Komondon

Eagle's Nest

JUNE 20

In Kabul and the other large cities of the country – in Kandahar, Herat, Mazar, Jalalabad, Maimana and Khanabad – resistance was impossible to stamp out. No sooner did the Russians and their Afghan communist allies stop one outbreak than another started. The cities of Herat to the west and Kandahar, to the south, were dive-bombed again and again. In town after town, civilians suddenly appeared from nowhere and stabbed Russians to death in the streets. Women rushed up to off-duty soldiers and threw their arms around them, blowing both of them to shreds with hand-grenades. Some of these very same bombs had been sold to the Afghans by Russian infantrymen, or exchanged for hashish, for which they were developing a marked taste.

Russian deserters who got out of Afghanistan told the world's television audiences that the Red Army now compelled them to sign a paper saying that, if captured, they would kill themselves. In the event, none did.

People told of red-hot chillies, sold to the Russians as sweetmeats which the underpaid Soviet soldiers insisted on eating, the tears running down their cheeks, and saying, when challenged, 'I paid for this – I am eating my money!'

A party of guerrillas, coming upon a village in the mountains west of Kabul, demanded food. When the people brought them bowls of inedible gruel, they spat it out, and threatened to beat the peasants. Crying with shame that they had nothing better to offer the warriors, the people of the village admitted that what they had brought was boiled and puréed grass: all that they themselves could find to eat. Their fields had been ruined by phosphorus bombs dropped by the Russian aircraft. Some of the narratives bore out reports which had already appeared in the world's press.

It took ten days, with tanks and flame-throwers, to crush a single uprising in Herat. At one time, fifteen thousand people were imprisoned in a single Kabul jail, the notorious Pul-i-Charkhi. The elite Afghan garrison at the great fort, the Bala Hissar in Kabul, rebelled. Some men fought their way out. Most of them were shot by Russian firing squads, according to other deserters.

But if oppression produced heroism and resistance, it also encouraged other characteristics in a minority, the self-seekers. Although the treachery and settling of old scores, the false denunciations and the cowardice of some fell far short of the picture of 'the faithless Afghan' once promoted by some writers – there were enough dishonourable acts.

Some Afghans joined the Russians. Some 'fled' to Pakistan posing as refugees, expecting to gain sympathy and to live a life of idleness. A good many managed to live in luxury in exile, earning the name of 'Gucci Guerrillas', and pretending to organize opposition to the communists from safe havens. The Russians spread the word that there was no point in the West helping the Afghans as they were so divided: and pointed to the assortment of competing émigré groups in Pakistan.

A great deal of information about the world reaction to the Russian invasion continued to filter back to the Afghans: through smuggled letters, returning fighters, radio broadcasts and through blundering admissions by the red Afghan regime's press.

Afghans all over the world did what little they could to alert foreign opinion: but the fact that the Afghans were fighting back seemed to have had an adverse effect on world sympathy. People, it seemed, felt that the Afghans were managing to hold their own, needed no outside help. As one hostage put it, 'If we had been totally helpless, the outside world would have been stirred more deeply, I believe. Listening to the overseas broadcasts, we hear how heroic we are. Nobody asks where we can get the arms . . .'

Afghans demonstrated in front of Afghan and Soviet embassies: in Washington and Tehran, in Paris and in New Delhi.

Afghan diplomats defected in a dozen capitals. The press and television gave them, on the whole, brief – almost dismissive, coverage. Many overseas Afghans slipped into the country from the Iranian and Pakistani borders and joined the guerrillas. Others sent money to relatives who managed to buy the trickle of guns which were getting into the country.

Geography – and ethnic and other differences – made it difficult for guerrilla forces to unite: but, paradoxically, this made it all the harder for the Russians to deal with them. Destroying one Resistance group did not affect any of the others.

The Resistance owed much of its strength to Afghan Army desertions. No less than seventy thousand men – three-quarters of the Army – were with the patriots in the mountains. Most took their weapons with them.

As the stories unfolded, some of them at enormous length, the line of people waiting to be questioned pressed forward, as if by this action they could hasten the process. One man, however, sat silently aside, as if wrapped in thought, waiting his turn but yet refusing to stand in line, speaking to nobody.

When his turn came, he was seen to be a rugged-looking northerner, who spoke Persian with the accent of the people of the Oxus, and held himself as if he had been accustomed to authority. He had been picked up by the Russians the previous day, for having no papers, and was awaiting interrogation when he was released by the attack on the Paghman castle.

'Sir: I have waited until you saw the others because I have a special message for The Eagle, and I can give it to no other.'

The colonel could not shake the man's resolve. Adam came in response to his call.

'If it is an operational matter,' The Eagle was becoming quite professional, 'you should have seen someone about it at once. Who are you?'

'I am *Shahrdar*, Mayor, Haidar, Weapon-Bearer to the Lords of Sher-Qala, near the Russian frontier. I bring news of my lord the *Noyon* Juma, who is dead, a martyr. He died fighting the Russians and killed many, blowing up a *halikuptar*.'

'Welcome, *Silah-Dar*!' Adam bowed, hand on heart. He knew how rank-conscious the descendants of the ancient Mongols were. 'You have honoured us. And what is your message?'

Haidar sat down on the seat indicated by The Eagle.

'Commander. The treasures of Afghanistan are being taken to Russia. Large quantities of the rubies of Badakhshan and of the lapis lazuli of Jurm, and emeralds and gold, too, have been collected near the port of Qizil Qala. They are then transported to the Soviet Union, across the Oxus River, on the gunboat *Jihun*. There is talk, too, of a great treasure which has been found and which will go by the same route.'

The Eagle raised an eyebrow. 'And the message?'

'My lord Juma had heard of you. He wanted to capture or destroy the treasures, to deny them to the Russians. To do this he needed the help of a great commander and a group like yours. There is much confusion in the north. We are either untrained or else the roaming bands are not to be trusted. He sent me to you to say that the treasure, if we got it, could be used to buy arms. We had only one rifle and a few old guns at Sher-Qala. And these were shared by the experienced fighters.'

This information matched something that The Eagle's agents had reported from Kabul. General Kirilyan, a high-ranking KGB officer, had been murdered by his woman servant, and some important papers, relating to the transfer of treasure to Russia, had disappeared. Could they be connected to the Oxus hoard?

'General Kirilyan,' he said, half aloud, 'had some papers dealing with an Afghan treasure . . .'

'*Aghai* Kara Kush! – Mr Eagle.' It was the old woman, Karima, who had come here, in a long detour, all the way from Jalalabad, after getting away from Kabul. She was now the chief housekeeper at the Caves. 'May I say something?'

He motioned her to put down the tea-tray she was holding and spoke kindly enough, although he was thinking about the treasure and did not relish the interruption.

'Sir, I wonder if the papers of General Kirilyan which I gave you when I came here, might have something to do with what you were talking about . . .'

She hadn't mentioned Kirilyan's name to the guerrillas in the Caves before.

'But weren't those just some papers of yours, given to us for safe-keeping?'

'No, sir. They were papers belonging to General Kirilyan. They were in front of him, on the table, the day I . . . finished him. You see, Mr Zoltan always said . . .'

So one of the men whom Karima had killed was Kirilyan himself! And his papers, the missing documents, were . . .

The Eagle was already on his feet and running from the cave, into the storehouse. He found a mound of documents of all kinds, anything but well organized by Zelikov, who should have filed them. Within three minutes, knowing things by sight rather than by content, as is the way with people who look rather than read, Karima had found the sheaf of documents. 'These are the ones, sir.'

They were, of course, in Russian. Who could translate them? Azambai the Turkestani was away on a scouting mission; Zelikov was hopeless for anything more than simple interpreting. The Eagle sent Qasim to find out if anyone among the new arrivals was thoroughly versed in Russian. 'Try to find someone educated, Qasim!'

In four or five minutes he was back, followed by a tall, slim girl dressed in jeans, battle-top and cartridge belt.

'I know Russian very well, commander.'

He looked at her, half-absently, wondering whether she really did know Russian, whether the papers did really contain anything of value. Then she said, in English, 'Do I call you Eagle, or since we know each other, could it be Adam Durany?'

She held out her hand, quite formally, as if to show the degree of familiarity that she expected.

Adam stared at her and tried to say something, and somehow, the words, he knew, would be all wrong. 'You're . . .'

Noor Sharifi said, 'There is an old fairy-story, where the witch says, "If you don't know my name, you can call me grandma!"'

'Noor!' That had been her favourite fairy-tale . . .

Then they just stood there, clasping hands, and laughing until the tears rolled down their cheeks, so that they could not even see each other. 'Noor Sharifi,' Adam said.

Karima said, 'If this is the daughter of the great Sirdar Sharifi, I'll get some fresh tea.' She bustled off to change into a clean apron. In fact, the tea she had already brought was still perfectly good.

Noor started to work on the Russian documents.

According to General Kirilyan's secret papers, Afghanistan now owed the Soviet Union no less than one billion dollars for military aid in the war against the guerrillas and for 'general policing'. One million dollars a week had been allocated for the Kabul government, since little was being collected from taxes, and other revenues were almost non-existent. Rebels had destroyed two hundred million dollars worth of government property.

The Afghans had undertaken to supply the Soviet Union with natural gas through the existing pipeline, and to allow extensive development of the oilfields in the north. Sheep and cattle, hides and skins, rugs and carpets would also go to the Soviet Union to offset the debt. Rich in minerals, the country would also send tin, copper, chromite, zinc, lead and manganese, even salt, in 'fraternal assistance contributions'.

As the world's only source of the semi-precious stone lapis lazuli, Afghanistan would give the entire production – some three tons a year – to the Russians. The rubies from the famous Jagdalak mines were also part of the contract.

It was estimated by the Russians that the treasures from archaeological sites, the lapis lazuli and the rubies, when marketed abroad, would fetch about ten billion dollars. The Russians were getting a good bargain.

This despoiling of the country had become General Kirilyan's job because, interestingly enough, the whole enterprise came under the KGB.

'This is obviously too devious a matter to leave to the internal affairs ministries of the USSR,' said The Eagle, as Noor translated the documents to him. 'And it also helps to destroy the Afghan economy.'

'Hold on,' said Noor, 'there's much more. Look at this: "The KGB is legally responsible for all precious jewels and metals in the USSR. Because of the special nature of the Afghan materials, however, their handling will come under Halzun, Dzhanmagometov, head of the Second Main Directorate of the KGB."' She stopped.

'I can see that the secret police should be looking after Russia's gold reserves and other precious metals, as a matter of security,' said Qasim; 'but what is this Second Main Directorate, and why should they care about artefacts and things like that?'

Noor leafed through the papers. 'Here is something that might connect with it.' She read out: 'Extensive activity, throughout the world, by the organisms established by the Second Directorate have made it possible to obtain significant amounts of *valuta*, foreign currency, by the judicious placing of works of art. There is a large collectors' market in the capitalist world for such things as the jewelled artefacts found in Afghanistan, while the price of lapis lazuli, a precious stone, may be controlled and encouraged upwards by a monopoly of it. Pakistan is to become a major source of "ancient" artefacts.'

Adam could not help smiling. 'A capitalist monopoly of the treasures of ancient kings, operated by the Kremlin!'

So the Russians were selling collectors' items, worldwide, through the KGB. Afghanistan was certainly one of the world's great storehouses of such things, as the French, Italian and other archaeological missions had discovered and reported.

He stopped smiling. It would not be easy, might well be impossible, to prevent this rape of the country's wealth and heritage. Noor had stopped reading aloud, and was scanning yet another document. Adam began to turn over possibilities in his mind.

'My father!' Adam jumped from his seat at the girl's cry, unable for a moment to understand what she meant. He and Qasim stared at Noor, while she in turn, face almost bloodless, stared at the paper in her hand.

'What is it?'

'Adam, this is about my father. It says: "Engineer (formerly Sirdar) Akbar Sharifi, of the Kajakai electrical generating complex, Afghanistan, is working closely with the Soviet authorities. Through his instrumentation, the treasure hoard, known as the gold of Ahmad Shah, was made available to us."'

She looked wildly at the two men. 'Working with them? Then they were right when they told me he was a traitor!'

Adam and Qasim looked uncomfortably at one another. What was one to say?

Adam said, 'Look, Noor: your father is my friend. We need not believe any of this unless we hear it from him. Forget about that. What about the gold?'

'It says,' she went on, dully, 'a first consignment of ancient gold coins, worth in melting value, as bullion, some $28 million but perhaps ten to thirty times that much in collector-value, is to be held at Qizil Qala, on the Oxus, to await transfer to the USSR.'

Qazim clapped his hand to his head. 'The gold of Ahmad Shah! That's the treasure that everyone has been looking for since the sack of Delhi, two hundred years ago! People say it's worth billions. How did he find it? Why did he tell the Russians? Can this be true?'

'I think it *is* true,' said Adam. 'The first Afghan king of modern times, who looted both the Peacock Throne and the Koh-i-Noor diamond, the "Mountain of Light", now among the British Crown Jewels, had a vast treasure which he captured from the Persians.'

Noor said, 'At least I know where my father is: he's at Kajakai. But if he's gone over to the Russians, there is nothing more to be said.'

They studied the papers for hours. Kirilyan certainly had been efficient. There were details of the gunboat *Jihun*, to be used in the transfer, of the unit of border troops which would protect it and its disposition, and of the likely date when the accumulated treasure, with a guard from Moscow, would be moved. The date was six weeks off.

'We must go and investigate, you know,' Adam said, when they had made a written summary of all the information. 'This even tells us exactly where the treasures will be kept, and which unit will guard them.'

'But,' Qasim was more cautious, 'supposing, after losing the papers, the whole plan has been changed? After all, they may know that we have them.'

'We have no means of knowing that,' said Adam. 'But I'm ready to try, anyway.'

Adam sent word to Afghan contacts in the secret service, asking if there was any news about General Kirilyan's papers. The answer, brought by courier within three hours, was a huge bonus. It was a photocopy of a telex message, before encoding, from Kabul KGB Residency to Moscow Centre. It stated: 'General Kirilyan's papers relating to the Afghan treasures now established as destroyed without falling into enemy hands.

Security is therefore intact.' Obviously Kabul KGB were terrified of being held responsible, and were trying to lie, or hope, their way out.

With the colonel's help, Adam and the others began to work on a plan for an expedition to the north. As Barakzai told them, it would be extremely dangerous. Nobody could travel to Turkestan by the only good road system, for this was the main means of entry and exit for the Soviet forces. Also, it went through the Salang Tunnel, carefully controlled and patrolled for fear of sabotage.

'We have no good maps, and never have had in this country. The Russians have some, as they have carried out a complete aerial survey of Turkestan. These maps haven't been generally issued, even to the Red Army, though. So we can't hope to get hold of one. Then we have to remember that the overland route is across some really tough mountains. In places there are ravines; elsewhere only goat tracks: so we couldn't use vehicles. Getting over mountain passes at ten thousand feet is no joke.'

'Furthermore, we have no friends at the other side,' said Adam.

Shahrdar Haidar was on his feet at once. 'We have all of Turkestan on our side, if we can get in touch with the guerrillas. There are the Wolves, the Turks who have been fighting since long before the Russians invaded. They declared war on the communists after the original coup, years ago. And I have heard of many army deserters there, most of them originating in Turkestan, who are fighting very well.'

'That's true, Shahrdar. But we still have to contact them.' Adam could see that there were more problems than he had thought.

'Remember,' Haidar said, 'I have just covered that exact route. I came across the Hindu Kush alone, so I know that it can be done. It was difficult, but there are people in the mountains to help, and food can be had. There are fertile valleys. There are few Russians at ground level: they mostly patrol the region from the air, and not very frequently at that. You have a guide, at least, in me.'

The colonel said, 'There are, in fact, ten ancient caravan routes across Kohistan, to the north. That is, after we get over the Paghman Mountains, just beyond here. We can take the

Ghorband, instead of the Charikar, road, and this will avoid the main highway. That means following deep river-beds, for the most part, as these run through the valleys, of course.'

'If we ever managed that,' said Adam, 'would that not bring us out too far to the north-west? We want to emerge directly north, or north-east of here.'

'No.' The colonel was positive. 'I have flown over that area. Once you have got across the Paghman Mountains into Kohistan, you can use one of the ten caravan trails. You can work your way straight north, or anywhere you want to go.'

Adam asked, 'What sort of heights would we be travelling at?'

'Two to four thousand metres. Of course, there are peaks covered with glaciers and perpetual snow, but the trails themselves are nothing like as high.'

'And after Kohistan, Land of Mountains, we still have the north-west Hindu Kush range. How do we get through that?' Adam wanted to know.

'That's the least of our troubles. The main highway that we are avoiding follows the Charikar River plain. We do the same, but keep out of sight of the arterial road itself. And, in that area, we are sure of local help and advice. By the time we get to somewhere north of Doshi, we'll be in the river area, heading north.'

'Colonel, what is the actual distance?'

'I suppose it might be two hundred and fifty miles, Adam. But that doesn't really tell you anything. What counts is the terrain. One mile up a mountain can be worse than a hundred on the flat. And we have three mountain chains to cross.'

This was roughly the route which Haidar, the Turkestani, had travelled, carrying Captain Juma's message. It had taken him just under three weeks, on foot or riding with friendly peasants, on horseback, on donkeys, sometimes in a cart.

It was now June, one of the hottest months of the year. Such a journey could not be made after September, and should be completed by the end of August. Even the petrol froze in the tanks during the winter on the main roads through the mountains.

It took a day to obtain a French army map, dated May 24th, 1901. It was on the scale of one to one million, and actually used by a Russian unit. This document showed several routes through the northern mountains, but it covered only the region from Kabul and Paghman to Pul-i-Khumri: about half the route they proposed to follow.

'Still,' said Colonel Barakzai, 'it confirms my memory. And it does cover the worst part: the most mountainous area. Though I cannot say whether a map, even a military one, which is over eighty years old, is likely to be very accurate.' Still, as Qasim pointed out, it was correct in all the places that they were able to check from their own knowledge.

'Here's to the *Service Geographique de l'Armée*,' said the colonel, reading from the map, 'even though the whole idea, given that the treasure may not still be there, is crazy!'

'Not only that,' said Noor, 'but we have forty-two days until the treasure is moved. It took Haidar three weeks to get here; so if we want to make it, we'll have to start almost at once. That leaves twenty-one days for equipping, for training and everything. What does the mayor think about speeding it up?'

They all turned to Haidar. 'Could the journey be done quicker?' Adam asked him.

'Eagle, I heard that there was a shorter route, but that was after I had come most of the way. The mountain people say that, with guides, the journey can be done in fourteen days. That is, with a caravan, though you can only use animals at certain stages. And I had no money at all, so I was dependent on charity.'

'What do you do with the animals when you can't go any further?' This was Qasim.

'I know about that!' Noor had been on several mountain journeys, into Nuristan and in the Paropamisus, north of Herat; 'You hire them, with their owners. Then, when the going gets too hard, you pay them off. When you get to another stretch where pack animals can be used, you hire some more.'

'I suppose you want to come along, Noor?' The Eagle was not sure whether this was a trip for a woman, but she had done more mountain travel than he had . . .

'Of course I do. Whether you like it or not!'

'If we decide to go, of course you can.'

While they were talking, a young man dressed in the office suit and karakul fur cap of a Kabul city-dweller came rushing in, shouting, 'Where's The Eagle?' Two armed guards were following him closely.

Adam looked up. 'Who's this?'

'That's Halim Jan, from the Afghan Tour Agency, that I was talking to you about. Friend of Colonel Sakafi's,' said Colonel Barakzai.

Halim was out of breath. 'Quick! Look at this!'

Adam took the piece of paper and read it. 'Where did you get this?'

'A friend of mine brought it to me from the Nizami KHAD.'

'Halim, have you transport?'

'Yes, but if they start to ask questions afterwards, I'm going to have to get out and come here.'

'You'll be welcome.' Adam spoke to the others, who were trying to work out what might be happening. 'Read this paper. I'll be back as quickly as I can.'

He took off his gunbelt and snatched up an old felt cloak. When he had put it on, it covered him completely, from his shoulders to his heels.

As the colonel reached for the piece of paper, Adam and Halim were scrambling down the cliff-side.

Perhaps they would beat the KHAD and save Kalan.

3 Time to move on, Big One . . .

Eagle's Nest
  Kalan's Farm
Near Kabul

JUNE 20

They called him Kalan, the Big One. He might not have seemed such a giant in the Pashtun borderland country, but here, near Kabul, where people were wiry rather than massive, he was really big.

Kalan ran the restaurant, the trading post and a workshop for simple machinery repairs, just off the northern road. If you wanted a cup of tea while your irrigation pump was being fixed, you could get it there; and admire a range of rugs, or a new line in kerosene lamps, while you drank it.

Kalan had been in the area for years. Nobody around there really knew where he came from, and nobody cared very much. He was useful and he was popular. Some thought that he must be a man with a past; others, satisfied with their own community, believed that it was the most natural thing in the world that a man would want to settle in a happy, quiet and prosperous area of fruit-trees and good farming land.

Today, Kalan called his assistant, Hashim, to take over while he went to look at a pick-up truck that had broken down. It belonged to a farmer some four kilometres away, always a good customer for the miscellaneous services of Kalan's establishment. He took up his shotgun and pulled on a pair of beautiful red leather, curly-toed Bokharan boots that he was breaking in. In his jeans and loud check shirt, he looked like a farmer from the American Mid-West. In fact, he had been, until ten years previously, a shipwright on the Pacific coast. Then he had got wanderlust, and had wanted a place of his own, work to do, but something which he could control, among the kind of people he could get on with. He'd started wandering, and ended up here. Now he was forty, and he liked the life.

Kalan waved, 'Couple of hours should do it, Hashim; repair job at Shirinab,' and climbed into his beaten-up 1976 Chevrolet, the service kit in the back and a nodding donkey mascot in front. When the Chevvy truck turned off the main road along the gravelly track which led to the farm, something caught Kalan's eye: something had moved, he was sure of it, in that tree, over there. A lone bandit? There were several loose in these parts; but Kalan thought that he was well enough known not to be attacked. Bandits were some of his best customers, for cartridges, food supplies, information.

A Muhjahid on the run? Kalan, like the rest of the people in this flat, fertile area, kept out of trouble as much as he could. One gunship could destroy the whole place in minutes. But everyone would help a rebel – if he could do it discreetly. He stopped the car and opened the door, shotgun at the ready. A man was grinning, no, laughing, and waving to him. Tall, dark-haired fellow, looked quite tough. Dressed like a guerrilla. No gun though: not that you could see, anyhow. Kalan sat there, while the other man jumped out of the tree and came running up. Kalan called to him in Dari.

'*Chi gup as* – what's up?'

'*Chi hal dari* – how are you?'

'*Fazl-i-Khuda*   I'm well, thanks to God . . . Where's the busted pick-up truck?'

Adam spoke to him in English. 'There isn't one. I sent the message. It just struck me,' said The Eagle, 'that you might be able to help us. And we could help you, too. We're thinking of a trip to the north.'

'Adam K. Durany! That Kabul professor. Haven't seen you for years. How's the University? Why are you dressed like that? What's all this about?'

'Thrown in my hand. I'm a Muhjahid now.'

'Is that right? Any future in it? Pays well, does it?'

'Listen, Louie,' it was the first time that Louis Palmer, of Seattle, Washington, had heard his own, real name for years, 'if you care for a trip, we could take you on – and you could help us, too.'

'Gee, I don't know. Got a pretty good little business going

here, now. All this Robin Hood stuff is all right for some people . . .'

Adam sat down beside him, in the passenger seat. 'Don't let this influence you too much, Louie, but one of the reasons I stopped by was to tell you that I've just heard, from a good source, that the KHAD are onto you. They have been asking around if that "big American" was still running a store somewhere round here. If this wasn't such a crazy country, they'd have had you in the bag months ago. You're registered with the Aliens Office, you know.'

'Gosh, if that's so, I'll certainly have to make plans.'

'Not plans, friend, tracks. The KGB could be at the *Karkhana* any moment. Turn over the store to your manager and come on a trip.'

'What is all this about a trip? Where to, and for what?' Louis was interested.

'To the north, to the Oxus at Qizil Qala. And to blow up a boat, that's what for.'

'I'll be darned. The Afs have only one crazy little boat, the *Jihun*, in the whole country – and you want to blow it up?'

'That's right. It's working for the Nikolais now, and it is an important job; and –' Adam's voice became more serious '– I think that you, with your maritime experience, could be useful.'

'What the hell? Sure, I'll come along.'

'Great. *Haraka* – Let's get moving.'

Kalan would be a useful addition to the expedition: Adam had, in fact, thought of him before the tip-off through Afghan Tour. The day before, word had come that the Russians were pressing the Kabul authorities to round up stray Americans and people educated in the West. Just as journalists, barred from entering Afghanistan in their professional capacity, could get there by simply asking for tourist visas, so too, dozens of Westerners were living in the country without restriction. Russian efficiency had flagged when faced with Afghan casualness.

And The Eagle had moved just in time. Hashim, Palmer's friend and assistant, left in charge of the café-workshop, received a visit from a Soviet snatch squad within twenty-four hours. He told their leader that Kalan had gone.

At The Eagle's Nest it was decided to leave Qassab the butcher as Adam's deputy, to work in joint command with Colonel Barakzai's training group to organize the community and train everyone in the various functions which would make the Whirlwind a better fighting force. For the first time, logisitics, liaison with other resistance groups, intelligence and communications were being put on an efficient basis. The Eagle's aim was a group which could now absorb and train almost any number of new recruits.

Karima, listening to the plans but saying little, now put in her bid. 'Eagle *seb*! I have to come with you to the north.'

Adam had been waiting for this. Karima always spoke tentatively about anything that might be challengeable: but if she thought that something was right, she used positive words, and somehow she seemed to get her way. But surely, a woman of over sixty, however big and strong . . .

'You could be very useful to us, here, Karima. You know how much we depend upon you for housekeeping and so on.'

'There are other women here, Eagle, who can do everything just as well. We have got it all properly arranged.'

'Karima!' Adam felt that he must stamp this out at once. 'Let's look at this logically. As you must know, it's going to be a terrible journey, up and down mountains, in snow and ice, and we may well have to fight from time to time. We might all be killed.'

Karima said nothing. Perhaps he was impressing her.

'Every man or woman on this trip must be able to do things which are necessary and which are useful to everyone else and to the mission. If you can tell me how you would fit in, I will consider it.' That, he thought, should clinch it.

Still she did not speak. She was giving up the idea, no doubt.

'Is that decided, then?' He looked at her.

'No, Eagle, I was waiting for you to finish, so that I could answer.'

Here comes the tortured reasoning, Adam said to himself.

'Very well, Karima. You have your say.'

'How many reasons do you want to allow me to go with you?'

'Reasons? Well, let me see – give me six reasons, six good ones.' That should settle it.

Karima stood upright, her hands folded respectfully. Then she said:

'Commander! I offer you six reasons: first, it is unseemly for Noorjan Khanum to go alone, without another woman, among so many men. Second, it is unbecoming for her not to be accompanied by someone to look after her, as she is a woman of rank. Third, I am strong and can carry a pack much heavier than the twenty-kilo ones that the Muhjahidin wear on their backs and complain about. Fourth, I am from the north and I speak Turki, so that will be useful: many people wouldn't understand even you up there. Fifth, I can organize the eating arrangements and buy food without attracting suspicion. Sixth, as a woman I would not be suspected as a spy if you needed information, and I could get it from other women and even children, while armed men could not.'

Adam was flabbergasted. He sat at the table, wondering what to say.

The colonel said, with a wry smile, 'Commander, if you want a seventh reason, it is that she has out-thought you!'

Everyone laughed. Adam said, 'You can come. But I have to know one thing. I thought that you always went by instinct. How did you produce a list of arguments like that? Not by instinct, surely?'

Karima smiled, something that she very seldom did. 'Commander, it was instinct that told me that you would demand strong and simple reasons. After that, it was easy.'

Inwardly she felt a quiet satisfaction. It wasn't really so hard to think, not if you'd seen it done as often as she had. Many a time, in the old days, Mr Zoltan had shown her. 'Now, Karima. I know, intuitively – that means inside me – that I have to widen the road a full two metres here, where it is marked, on this map. What I have to do, however, is to find five or six good reasons which will satisfy the Russian Chief Administrator. He does not believe in feelings, only in facts.'

Thank you again, Mr Zoltan.

Forty-one people were selected. Adam, Noor and Karima, plus Captain Azambai with his Russian and Turki knowledge, all made lists, to compare with those of Colonel Barakzai. Zelikov was included, because he could, if need be, impersonate a Russian soldier; Qasim, as second-in-command; and Nanpaz the baker and Halim from Afghan Tour, who had had to leave his employment in a hurry, were strong and useful in many different ways. Twenty other guerrillas, including Louis, and twelve of the newly recruited Afghan Army defectors made up the total: roughly equivalent to two guerrilla battle groups.

The expedition, in accordance with Resistance custom, was given a name. At Haidar's suggestion, remembering the fort of his dead chief, the partisans named themselves 'the Sher-Qala Commando'.

When all was prepared, Colonel Barakzai wrote a message to the Russians, to be broadcast over Radio Homeland, the Kabul clandestine station:

> From an Afghan soldier to the Russian colonisers! It is an historical fact that we are still here when all our invaders are little more than encyclopaedia entries. The Greek, Persian, Mongol and other empires are gone. Reflect, how much is left of the domains of the Zoroastrians, the Buddhists, the Hindus and the Arabs and all the others who came here: either to 'help the people' or to make this land their own? History, dear Russians, offers you no chance at all, and yet you talk about the 'historical process'. It offers even less than the supposed Law of Averages – and *that* is non-existent!

Guerrilla preparations for the expedition to the north were well advanced when the Russians decided to wipe out the Resistance in Paghman. Its valleys and mountain ranges had always harboured dissident fighting men. Unpopular Kabul regimes had never reduced the independence of its people. Strategically, as well as tactically, Paghman threatened the capital. And, somewhere in its higher mountains, the Russians knew, was the headquarters of Kara Kush, the leader whose power was growing by the day.

They had tried before to bring the region under control: seizing hostages, poisoning wells, bombing villages. This time they were determined to conquer it, to teach the Paghmanis a lesson they would never forget. And to show the rest of Afghanistan who were the masters now.

4 The Fourth Battle

Valley Entrance
Paghman

JUNE 24

The Fourth Battle of Paghman began at dawn. Sayed Wazir
Shah, until recently a medical student, now a partisan, lay in
his foxhole on the curve of the road. It was sixteen kilometres
north of Kabul, at the approach to the Paghman valley, and he
had just taken over highway observation from Ustad Najib, the
middle-aged schoolteacher.

Najib had been the only man to escape from the massacre of
everyone in his village, on the other side of Kabul. Six thousand
people had died there. The place had been levelled, on suspicion of harbouring guerrillas, by air attack. Afterwards the
Army had come in and shot all those they found still alive. The
bodies were burned with napalm, the ruined buildings set on
fire.

Najib had escaped by what seemed a miracle. Early in the
attack, the schoolhouse had collapsed, burying him, unconscious, in its debris. His dog had sat by him all night, whining,
but ignored by the troops. In the morning it had partially freed
his face and neck by digging. Grasping its collar with a hand
which he had worked free, Najib had told the dog – *Kahraman*,
'Champion' – to run. Champion, understanding, it seemed,
what he had to do, had pulled his master from beneath the
wreckage. Afghan hounds could kill leopards, for all their effete
looks. Kahraman showed that they could do other things,
too . . .

Suddenly, Najib was back at the foxhole, his dog at his side.
A small urchin, pushing a bicycle, was with him. It was Wali
Jan, from a mile down the valley: the son of a smallholder.

'Respectfully reporting, sir!' Wali, at eight, was eager to imitate the warriors. He saluted.

'What is it, Wali?'

'They're coming. The *Rouss*. Very many of them, with tanks and much armour: *houz, houz* – clank, clank!' He was out of breath, panting with excitement.

It was too early to put up the signal flag: nobody would see it in the pre-dawn haze, the false dawn that was only just starting to pick out the mountaintops behind them. But The Eagle had to be warned. There was no radio, and his Caves were some kilometres away. 'Have you got a Verey cartridge, Najib?'

'No, the nearest person I know who has one is Haji Suleman. He's at Sang-i-Surkh, two kilometres from here.'

Wazir Shah took a flashlight from his pocket and scribbled a message. Wrapping it in his red handkerchief, he tied it to the dog's collar. 'Now, Najib, tell him to go to The Eagle, fast!'

Najib stroked the dog's long mane. 'Go home, Kahraman, quickly home!' The ash-grey hound was straining at his collar: then he was away.

'Do you think he'll make it?'

'I don't know. I expect so. He'll go to Roman first. He's never missed a titbit yet.'

No Verey lights, no rockets. Not much of anything, in fact. Of course, the Russians scarcely ever ventured out at night. They had infra-red equipment, but they needed air support, and you can't attack guerrillas with helicopters in the dark. That's why the flags had always been sufficient – before this.

'Wali Jan, go home. Lie low. This is no place for you.'

Wali turned and rummaged in the saddlebag of his battered bike, taking out a Fanta bottle. 'If you send me away, I'll only go down the road and use this on a tank, as they come up the hill.'

Wazir hesitated. Then he shrugged. 'You should be out of the battle, *chuchim*, kiddie.'

'I am supposed to be too young to fast in Ramadan,' said Wali. 'But I'm not too young for this.' He inspected the rag-fuse stuffed into the bottle's mouth, and fixed a box of matches to his wrist with a rubber band. 'I'm out of that, but,' he drew himself up, and repeated a common Afghan saying, '*Afghani-*

yati khudra chitor tark kunam? How can I abandon my Afghanness?'

'None of us can, but take care, Tiger.'

There it was, now: the rumbling of caterpillar tracks. Tanks and armoured personnel-carriers, approaching in some strength. They moved to the outside of the bend in the road. Yes, there they were. They had their headlights on, too.

It was a good vantage point. The road went through a rocky patch, with boulders on either side; boulders which rolled down the mountainside and had, at times, blocked the highway. The Construction and Maintenance Unit, from time to time, brought men and machines along here, to clear the road. They pushed the boulders just off the carriageway, at places piling them up so continuously that they looked like *sangars*, rough defensive embrasures, which the hillmen had always used for sniper refuges.

Behind one such natural breastwork, the three checked their weapons and looked at the column snaking its way towards them, like a Chinese dragon of the night, studded with headlamps, stretching back for several kilometres.

'Wazir, there's thousands of them, Russians!'

'*Dorogh na gufti*, you're not lying.' Wazir counted his magazines. Ten. That was three hundred rounds, just over seven minutes' continuous firing. The Kalashnikov, one of the best guns in the world, derived from a German design and developed by captured Germans in Russia after World War II, was the most successful of all modern infantry weapons. And in the foxhole, buried in loose earth just below the surface, there were a dozen RKG/3M stick grenades. They could penetrate six and a half inches of armour. They might get a tank or two.

The men crept back to the foxhole and scrabbled the grenades out of the ground.

'If they are T-54 tanks,' said Najib, 'these will do. These grenades will penetrate 165 mm armour-plate. But if they are, say, T-10s, the real heavies, well – they've got eight-inch armour. Too thick.'

'Right;' Wazir was making three piles of the stubby weapons, 'but if we can't get at any vulnerable places, like the side, just under the turret, then let's concentrate on the personnel-carriers, they're much weaker.'

'I know. Four to six inches.' It helped to talk shop, to repeat what they had learnt from the stolen textbooks. This must be why, in military training, there was so much jargon, Najib thought. It helped to fill your mind, make you interested in something other than the dryness of your mouth, the strange new stiffness in your knees, the growing sense of unreality. The approach of death.

The rumbling was getting louder, and in the early morning mist the three watchers could now see the long file of death, snaking up the mountainside, lights still on, raising a cloud of dust. *Khaki*, the word as well as the colour, that the British had adopted from their Afghan campaigns.

'How many rounds have you, Najib?'

'Five magazines. A hundred and fifty shots.'

'Wali?'

'Three Fanta orangeade bottles, sir!'

They were right by the road. Wazir handed the others four grenades each, and took four himself. When they had clipped them to their belts, they took up their ammunition and crept from one boulder's cover to the next, to a rise some twenty feet above them. Far better cover.

Kahraman the hound bounded into the cave where Roman Zelikov, who often fed him, was shaking himself awake from his sleeping bag. He'd been dancing until late the night before, learning the whirling Milli Atan, which the Pashtuns danced to whip themselves into the right state of fervour before an attack. The tune, *Youth into Battle*, was still running around in his head.

Kahraman licked his face and buried his muzzle in the Russian's furlined sleeping bag. Was he looking for a morsel to eat? the man wondered.

There was a piece of red cloth tied to the dog's collar. A paper in it. Zelikov, unable to read Dari-Persian, looked at it, guessed its message must be urgent and jumped up, naked, rushing to the cave where The Eagle sat, eating oats, yoghurt and raisins, the usual Afghan breakfast. An illustrated Russian book on military tactics lay open before him. He couldn't understand the text, but the diagrams told him a lot.

Adam took the paper. *Enemy advancing in force: already*

reached Safedpul. Heavy armour. Perhaps hundreds of tanks and APCs. Wazir.

Zelikov read it from Adam's face. As The Eagle buckled on his gun belt, the little Russian, still stark naked, ran to the cave mouth and was already beating out the rallying call on the giant drum. DA, DA, DA *DA*! DA-DA-DA!

'*Haraka, haraka!* – get moving!' The call ran through the honeycomb of caves.

As the drum-beats reverberated through the hills, the answering flags went up in the Paghman valley. In relays, scraps of cloth appeared, like petals scattered in the dawn, and other drums took up the call: DA, DA DA *DA*! DA-DA-DA! As the early breeze swept down from the Hindu Kush, more and more flags appeared. There were the standards of Paghman, of Karez-Mir, of Shakar-Dara, of Bezadi, of the Lord of Bezak. Now the huge drums of Koh-i-Daman answered, the purple banners of Kohistan joined the flags of Begtut, of Sabzao, and the triangular pennants of Qala-Muhjahidin.

'Come to the battlefield!' The chant went up from a thousand throats in a hundred caves and cottages. People snatched up guns, knives, even spears, and started to sharpen their long Khyber swords.

'DA, DA DA *DA*! DA-DA-DA!' Men, women and children, all of those who had survived three devastating Russian campaigns against them and could still walk or run, streamed from rocket-blasted houses, from shacks, farms, tents.

'To the battlefield!' A blacksmith picked up a new, very evil-looking scythe and sprinted to his appointed place. Butchers brought out their knives and cleavers, the irrigation men seized their long-handled spades.

'DA, DA DA *DA*! DA-DA-DA!' Modern weapons were still scarce in Paghman and, beyond it, in Kohistan: but most of the fifteen thousand Russians who had already died in the Afghan mountains had been surprised at what could be done by the rebels, even when they had only rocks in their hands.

The old people and the walking wounded, not yet recovered after the earlier attacks, were being marshalled, with the children still too young to fight, into the deep caverns. '*Ajala, ajala*, hurry, hurry, the Nikolai helicopters will soon be overhead . . .'

*

The two men stood with the boy at the valley's mouth and saw the green pennant of the *kashshafi*, the advance scouts, go up. The drums thundered louder as it was joined by Paghman's ancient orange battle-flag, with its black eagle emblazoned in the centre. The message had got through. '*Shabash*, Kahraman – well done, Champion!' Wali jumped up and down with joy, until the schoolmaster pulled him down.

The advance guard of the invaders was now less than six hundred yards away, swathed in dust. The tail of the roaring, clanking convoy was invisible now, so great was the cloud raised by the vehicles in front, mixed with the fumes from the groaning, five hundred horsepower engines.

It was still too early to fire. The AK-47's effective range was three to four hundred yards; and the grenades could only be used in really close-up fighting. If, as often happened, one or more of the tanks broke down, this would slow down the advance. There was not much room to get a tank off the road, and even less to bring a heavy recovery vehicle up parallel to the column. The Russians, obsessed by the vast plains which formed most of the Soviet Union, had not yet learnt much about mountain warfare.

They were still coming.

Suddenly, young Wali pulled at Wazir's jacket. 'They've got scouts. Look.' He pointed downwards, towards the road below them. Sure enough, four men were crawling into the foxhole which the guerrillas had just left. They were wearing Afghan Army grey uniforms and full webbing equipment. Numerous hand-grenades, tank-killers, were clipped to their shoulder harnesses.

Ustad Najib was craning over the rocks and looking down too. Then, to Wazir's amazement, he beckoned, carefully, to the newcomers, to climb up and join him.

For a moment Wazir thought that Najib was a traitor. Or that he was trying, rather foolishly, to lure the men up so that he could shoot them as they approached. Then, as Najib grinned, he put his gun down and recognized, climbing towards them, Colonel Barakzai, the Afghan Army defector.

Wali gave the Pashtun cry of delight, but quietly. 'That evens things out a bit.' In a moment, the colonel and his small party were beside them.

'We were out on a training patrol,' said Colonel Barakzai, 'when we saw the flags go up.'

'"Luck is not sold in the markets",' Wazir quoted, as they all shook hands.

'Who's in command? How many men have you got?' The colonel was very professional.

'Nobody in command. Three men,' said Wazir.

'How many grenades have you got?' the colonel asked.

'Twelve, anti-tank,' said Wali.

'Good. We four have six each. Our task is to delay the enemy, try to destroy or at least to detrack as many vehicles as possible, preferably tanks, and the bigger the better. Do you know about the fuel tank weakness?'

'No.' They all leant forward.

'Right and left of the front, Russian tanks have fuel containers which are not heavily armoured. If we are in luck, they will not have sandbagged these. All tanks are now being modified to protect the diesel, but there is this design fault and for the moment the best they can do is to tie sandbags over them. Go for these soft spots. With luck we can roast a few of them.'

'That'll even things up a bit,' said Wali, once again.

'Perhaps. Now, we are on an incline here; the road slopes upwards behind us. The best place to attack a tank. We'll set off now, four on one side of the road, in the rocks, and three on the other, in spaced lines. Each man will be ten metres from the next. Each pick a tank or, if you can't, an APC. If they fire first, I'll either throw one grenade or fire one green smoke flare into the sky. If you see that, throw. Do you all understand?'

'Understand.'

'Wait.' He looked around a rock towards the enemy column. Something unusual was happening. The seven rebels looked at each other: the enemy vehicles had ground to a halt.

They were under three hundred yards away. The freshly stencilled insignia of the Afghan Army were clearly to be seen on the leading machines.

'They're not expecting an attack yet. The turrets are open.' Colonel Barakzai whispered to Wazir.

As they watched, some men, dressed in Afghan tank-crew gear, got down from their turrets and walked back from three of the lead tanks, evidently looking for someone, perhaps a senior officer. Seven or eight vehicles back, they halted beside a scout car. 'Mark that one, it's a colonel or above,' said Barakzai; 'he must be in command.'

Nine men were talking, gesticulating, shaking their fists. The crews of the three lead tanks, minus the drivers.

Suddenly, as they watched, the guerrillas saw two men stand up in the rear of the scout car, aim their automatic rifles, and shoot at the tank-men with a hail of rapid fire. The nine men went down.

Mutiny? The rebels looked at one another, grimaced their puzzlement, and shrugged.

'Now!' It was the colonel. 'Something is going on, but it does not matter to us. It's too light to cross the road, so we'll file down this side of the highway and carry out the plan I gave you. Are you ready?'

'Colonel *seb*!' Wali had his hand up.

'Boy?'

'We must name our battle group.'

'All right, name it.'

'I name it Kahraman, Champion.'

'All right. Now get on with it. *Haraka*, March!' The convoy had not moved. The seven guerrillas, each with a grenade ready in his hand, crept silently towards the array of guns, men and metal, each determined to disable at least one tank.

It took them a quarter of an hour, eyes down, to avoid dislodging even a pebble, before they were in position, each behind a boulder or a pile of rocks, each standing stock-still, opposite and above his target. Looking through the lacy leaves of a rock-plant, Najib saw that many of the tank commanders were now standing up in their places, turrets open.

The colonel had led his men past the first dozen tanks, and beyond several personnel-carriers crammed with troops, all in the Afghan field-grey. His intention was to cause havoc towards the middle of the convoy. The rear vehicles might then reverse, and those in front could be left to the main body of the Muhjahidin when they arrived. Seven men could make quite a mess, strung out like this; he was sure of that. Cut the dragon in half: always sound tactics.

He squinted down at the shoulder-strap on the summer

uniform of the tank commander whom he had chosen as his own first target. He was about twenty metres away, sitting there, looking bored. Two small stars on a red stripe, two more on either side. A captain. The Soviet must be sending officers in for training. He crept forward. When he got to within ten metres of the man, who was now lighting a cigarette, the colonel remembered that he was a Pashtun, of the Barakzai clan, and could not attack a man without warning. Now and again, famous in history, this kind of bravado possessed the frontier men.

He shouted, at the top of his voice, '*Gospodin Kapitan!* A Barakzai is here!'

A grenade went right past the astonished Russian's shoulder as it curved, falling into the bowels of the tank, as Barakzai threw himself behind the rock which he had already marked down as his shield against the blast-wave.

There was a moment of total silence, and then a roar as the impact fuse set off the half-kilogramme high-explosive charge. The tank was buckling: then it exploded with a sound of screaming metal which blended with the crash of six other tank-killers, as the weapons of Kahraman Battle Group came into play.

The mangled remains of a heavy machine-gun, torn from its mounting, fell with a thud that he first thought was a shell, only feet from where the colonel crouched.

He could not see how many hits they'd scored. There was firing; automatic weapons, bullets from a dozen carbines whipped past his head, chipped his sheltering rock as he lay there, scrabbling in the hard ground, instinctively trying, like some lizard, to dig himself in.

Now men were swarming all around him, men in Afghan Red Army uniforms, in full battle-kit, with carbines, fixed bayonets, grenades. In a few moments, he thought, I shall be dead. But I got my target. He unclipped a second Russian grenade, gripped it by the polished yellow wooden handle, and jumped up, prepared to rush upon another tank.

The turrets were all shut now, and the soldiers had scrambled from their carriers, up the slopes on either side of the road. One of them pulled him down; as he was about to smash his grenade on the man's head, blowing them both to pieces,

Colonel Barakzai recognized Arif Qamrudin, the brightest officer-cadet at the military college, and a relative of his as well. He could not kill him . . .

Barakzai handed his grenade to the young man with the fixed bayonet, in a token of surrender, and lay back on the uneven ground, hands behind his head. Afghanistan, the Homeland, had come to this. Arif had come to Paghman to kill his own people. The bayonet was so close he could see its blue-black, serrated, wire cutting, edge.

Shooting, screaming and explosions became more intense, and louder, as the colonel waited for the bayonet thrust. It didn't come. He looked up. Arif was standing, steadying himself against a rock, firing towards the enemy convoy. Barakzai struggled to his feet, slowly realizing that the cadet was on his side. He unslung his AK-47 and took his stand beside the younger man, aiming for the red and yellow epauletted figures, the Russian officers, who were trying to rally groups of their own men as the Afghan cadets, three hundred of them, turned on their supposed allies.

Barakzai and his three men worked their way down the convoy, throwing grenades until they had no more, firing their guns into the knots of howling Russians who, betrayed and perhaps surrounded, fired in all directions, at whoever seemed to be the enemy.

Dense clouds of black, oily smoke were rising from crippled tanks, trapped men were screaming in the blazing battle-monsters, dying amid the orange flames, while ammunition exploded all around them. The acrid, burnt cordite fumes made the colonel cough. It was a strange sight, he thought, surveying the scene as he snapped his hinged bayonet into position. Hand-to-hand fighting, some shouting orders, some howling with battle elation, even though blood gushed from wounds they had not felt. Barakzai looked around for someone to attack, just as a Russian, a six-footer with a huge moustache, a caricature of a Caucasian bandit, came for him with an automatic carbine spitting fire. His lips curled back to show a new sight for an Afghan. Common enough in the Soviet Union, here the stainless steel teeth, top and bottom sets, looked like something from the nether regions.

The bullets were whipping wide. In his excitement, the Russian had forgotten to correct his aim. Kalashnikov 47s, because of a design fault, always fire high and to the right.

Even before the colonel had time to react, another man came hurtling at the Russian from behind. He was a small, thickset figure in shirt and baggy trousers, with a rolled-brim, soft wool Nuristani hat pulled down, almost over his eyes.

His knotted arm muscles stood out as he clutched the long-handled, sharpened spade, swinging it like a flail. Its edge glittered in the early morning sun as the guerrilla brought it down at an angle onto the Russian's neck, just under the ear. The paratrooper fell, blood gushing from his mouth.

Reinforcements had arrived.

The irrigation ditch diggers, the terrible *belchis*, spade wielders, were here.

Sergeant Rybakin was a veteran of several battles with the Muhjahidin, and had learnt many of their tricks. As he had told his men, that was the only way to survive, once you got to the hand-to-hand stuff. He was a Ukrainian, but a good Soviet soldier nonetheless. Beckoning to his section, he jumped from his transport and led them into the thick of the fight. They fought in twos, as he had taught them, back to back, putting short bursts of AK fire into every bandit they could see, cleanly, effectively, like executioners: no bullet wasted.

The tactic worked – until the Russians met the Kohistanis, massive mountain men who took three, four, five bullets and still came on. Rybakin's kit was shared out among the surviving sergeants in his barracks that very evening.

A swarm of small girls and boys, village children of the valley, suddenly came running through the band of warriors, skipping and dancing, heading for the Soviet fighting vehicles, zigzagging as they ran.

They carried, in both hands in front of them, containers made from gallon oilcans, half-filled with some substance, each with a burning slow-fuse on a stick strapped to the side.

Incredibly, their figures too small to register in the soldiers' eyes as attackers, these children – some forty or fifty of them – got within a few yards of the invaders before being seen.

Then, almost as one single individual, they whipped the

smouldering, wax-soaked cord-fuses from their straps, plunged them into the cans and hurled them at the Russians.

Dense clouds of smoke, blown by the morning wind, drifted over the tanks and made the Russians choke, as their eyes filled with tears, visibility obscured.

Zubeida, daughter of Pir Samander, led her friends in a wide circle, to attack the Russians towards the end of the convoy, where no guerrillas had yet penetrated. Zubeida's fighters had been practising, with a weapon that had seldom been seen in Afghanistan since the time of the Mongols, seven hundred years ago. The Russians were wearing flak-jackets: but the women's arrows found the heads and throats.

A bunch of Russian soldiers, standing back to back on the top of a great, six-wheeled truck, had turned it into a fire-point of devastating power. The truck must have been crammed with rifles and ammunition. As each of the paratroopers emptied his magazine into the attacking Afghans, he threw the weapon to another man squatting at his feet, a loader, who handed him another AK-74 complete with fresh magazine. These new guns had a killing range a hundred yards better than the standard Kalashnikov. The firing was so continuous, the action so rhythmic, that there was almost a poetry in the sound, the movement brought about by the sheer professionalism of the firing of these superbly trained soldiers. Each Soviet tank battalion had its special parachute company, for deep penetration and arduous missions.

A pile of bodies mounted up, like a barricade of flesh, around the sweating, cursing, straining Soviet strongpoint. Again and again the Afghans came on in waves, but were always beaten back, dragging and carrying their wounded, men with star-fractures caused by the new, tiny 5.45-millimetre tumbling bullets which made wounds which would not heal. The modern form of the outlawed dum-dum bullet.

There were twelve Russians firing, and at least as many loading their guns for them. In between attacks they changed places, the fighters getting some rest from the intense concentration of continuous automatic weapon firing.

Abdul-Ghani Khan, son of a peasant, formerly manager of

a textile mill and now a mechanic with the Resistance, struggled to an outcrop of rocks, two kilometres from the fire-truck. His rocket-launcher had five times that range. If he fired soon and scored a hit, he might save the lives of a group of some fifty fighters whom he could see about to make another suicidal assault on the Russian paratroopers. He unshipped the launcher from his back and put a SAM-7 into the tube. With the sight dead on target, he fired his one and only shot. In seconds, the twenty-pound missile had hit the back of the driver's cab; after the orange flash, nothing moved.

Abdul-Ghani whooped with joy. The launcher and four rockets had cost him $2,000 – two years pay at his old job. Money well spent.

Wazir Shah was perched on a rock beside the road, his rifle set at 'single shot'. He was picking off, for preference, every man he could see with the bright epaulettes of an officer. Russian troops, the Afghans had soon discovered, became bewildered in combat if not given constant orders by their officers. Wazir inwardly blessed the name of Stalin. It was he who had reinstituted the broad, flashy Czarist shoulder-boards which made it easy to recognize – and deal with – a Russian officer in battle. The rank and file of the Red Army called these huge shoulder-boards 'Stalin pancakes', someone had told Wazir Shah. He was totally exposed to enemy fire, but had no sensation of danger.

It was a dissociated feeling. Now and then, he became aware of the din of battle, even the stench of blood and sweat and guts. It was like a slaughterhouse which he had once visited: the smell was the same.

Looking at the absurdity of the scene, at people who – if history had been otherwise – could have been friends, trying to maim and destroy each other, he remembered what he had seen a week ago in Kabul, less than twenty miles away. He'd sneaked into town on reconnaissance.

Standing on the pavement of the newly-surfaced main avenue, the Jadi Maiwand, near the smart shops, he had been waiting to cross the road. A woman was in a hurry: alone, apparently, among the silent crowds standing patiently while a seemingly endless Russian convoy of heavy military trucks,

ZIL-131s with fearsome mounted rocket-launchers, streamed past them.

The woman was pushed back by a military policeman as she made to dart across the road. Turning on him, she screeched, 'Is *this* communism, Nikolai?'

A tall, fair man, to whom Wazir had been talking a moment before, smiled. He was a timber expert, brought by the Russians from Latvia, another Soviet-occupied nation, on the far Baltic Sea. He, at any rate, had seen all this before. 'Yes, madam citizen,' he said. 'That's *exactly* what it is.'

Najib threw away his empty, useless rifle and ran, drawing his long Afghan knife, into the middle of a knot of struggling men. A group of Russian soldiers had surrounded three Kohistani hillmen and were jabbing, slashing, lunging at them with their bayonets, panting and screaming in turn. The mountaineers, armed only with thick staves, were desperately holding the attackers off, but only just. The bayonets were too short to reach the Afghans' vitals, but the rebels would soon flag, as they tired.

As he came within six yards of the whirling mess of figures, the balding schoolmaster, gasping with the unaccustomed effort of the battle, saw and snatched up two green-painted grenades lying in a hollow in the ground. He wondered, briefly, if they were duds, then hesitated. If he threw them now and they exploded, he would kill five or more Russians – but three guerrillas would die, too.

Like many Afghans, Najib had a loud and penetrating voice. And his was immensely powerful. At this moment, above the roar of battle, his words came over, clearly, to the embattled Kohistanis. 'Brothers, run!'

There was a distinct pause; even the Russians slowed down their attack. Then the hillmen took to their heels, without knowing why, but sensing something imperative in that order, and scrambled up the hillside.

The Russians turned to meet this new challenge and then came at him, bayonets at the ready, their faces contorted, a picture of grimy demons with deep-set eyes and button noses . . .

Najob turned around and ran, fumbling with the ring-pulls

of the RGD-5s. Four-second delay fuses, that's what they had. For a few moments he was outdistancing them. That should be time enough. He turned and tossed the grenades right into the bunch of them, throwing himself on the ground at the same time. His pursuers disappeared in the terrible explosion; the blast-wave crushed the breath from Najib, but he survived.

A huge Russian, demented with fear, rushed behind a tall rock and came upon an Afghan, Shola Khan, whose brother had been roasted on a spit by Soviet soldiers: they had wanted him to give away the position of a partisan band. Shola was in no mood to receive a surrender or to take a prisoner, though that was the Russian's hope.

Colonel Barakzai made as if to raise his bayonetted gun once again, to run forward, when he noticed that something was amiss. His right arm did not work. Grinning reassuringly, a spadesman led him, quietly, away from the fighting, to a hollow where several other casualties were sitting or lying, being given water by some village women. Their wounds were dressed with the liquid from boiled willow bark and tar: the nearest thing to first aid that the rebels knew.

Barakzai saw Qasim loping past, almost casually, carrying a large, shiny, button-type anti-tank mine. He shouted, 'Where's The Eagle, Qasim?'

Qasim pointed. 'Over there, on the ridge. Machine-gun post.'

Barakzai struggled to his feet and found Adam manning a Russian Pika machine-gun, with Noor steadily feeding the heavy, two hundred and fifty round belts of cartridges through the acceptor-gate. Several more belts were coiled in a box beside her.

The gun, accurate up to a thousand yards, was earning its keep at a quarter of that range: the heat from the barrel could be felt at two or three feet. Adam was keeping separate the two parts of the enemy force, where the colonel's group had attacked, so that the various partisan *dastas*, five-man sections, could cut the Russians into still smaller units and finish them off.

Suddenly, out of the corner of his eye, the colonel saw a Russian soldier, a tiny, neat tank officer with black uniform and padded crash helmet, gasmask and hand-grenades, climb over the crest of the natural parapet in front of them, and start to unsling his rifle. He must have scaled an almost sheer cliff, and Barakzai knew a moment of admiration for the courage of the man. He could have been picked off at any moment if a single guerrilla with a rifle had looked up from the road. But he had taken the risk, to stop the murderous fire of this single machine-gun, which was methodically riddling one group of Russians after another as they ran forward, or sought cover, or tried to get away.

Instinctively, almost, Barakzai reached for his pistol. It wasn't there and, besides, his arm was useless. And Adam hadn't seen the Russian.

As he was about to throw himself between Adam and the Russian's line of fire, Noor, from her sitting position to his left, picked up a heavy, jagged piece of rock and hurled it straight at the Russian's face. It struck him a glancing blow on the forehead. Unbalanced, he gave a scream as he fell back, dropping into the fighting swarm below.

Adam had just realized what had happened. He turned his grimy, sweat-streaked face towards the girl and smiled his thanks, with a rueful shrug. There was no time for anything more. Besides, he felt sick at the sight of the slaughter.

The colonel could not resist standing up to take stock of the situation: nobody, anyway, seemed to be taking any notice of the little group with the machine-gun.

The picture was now fairly clear. In the small valley with the road snaking through it, the Russian convoy was well and truly bogged down. Barakzai could see, too, that the Afghan cadets, who had been put in front of the Soviet forces to bear the brunt of the attack, were instead fighting side by side with the men and women of Paghman and Kohistan. As he watched, he saw that the confusion of battle, and especially the defection of the Afghan cadets, had caused the Russians to attack each other. One Soviet infantry platoon counterattacked a Russian para-troop section as he watched, mowing down almost all of them.

He counted thirty tanks destroyed or out of action. Some Russian officers were shooting at parties of their own men as they prudently ran away, their rifles empty, from fresh waves of guerrillas who at times outnumbered them by as many as twenty to one.

In the end, the Russians managed to get sixty tanks away, while the helicopters – which had been unable to attack the swirling mass of men for fear of killing their own – systematically strafed guerrilla reinforcements still swarming down from the hills.

The Molotov cocktails and the grenades had run out, and the rebels were down to their last few rounds, when the Russians broke and ran. Their tanks were black with troops clinging onto any projecting surface, having abandoned their own trucks and ACPs, most of them burning or severely damaged.

Back at his headquarters, The Eagle reviewed the gains and losses. Of the three hundred cadets who had been forced, at gunpoint, to spearhead the attack, seventy were dead. Two hundred joined the guerrillas and the rest were missing, probably in Russian hands. Just over a hundred guerrillas, men and women, had died, and fifty-three were wounded, some very seriously, with no proper medical service to help them. One helicopter had been downed, ten trucks were captured. Thirty tanks were burnt out. Guns and ammunition were looted from the Russian vehicles, though this was not easy; the helicopters bombed and rocketed them to prevent their use by the rebels. The Russians killed their own wounded as they lay in the trucks, with fire-bombs and high-explosives, which were dropped from the hovering choppers. And they abandoned their dead, seven hundred in all.

Qasim had two tank kills, the colonel one, the boy Wali one tank and a truck, and The Eagle had brought down the scouting helicopter with his heavy machine-gun, as it flew, too low, into the valley.

Najib and Wazir Shah were found among the dead. Their names were given to two new battle groups formed by the Afghan officer-cadets.

The Fourth Battle of Paghman was featured in the world's press, through the many accounts given by cadets, Russian prisoners and even leaks from Russian Army Headquarters.

Paghman is so near to Kabul that even the Afghan newspapers had to make some mention of the event. They could not say, of course, that a full-scale battle, involving no less than ninety tanks and seven thousand, two hundred Russians – one tank regiment and one motor-rifle division – twenty helicopters and a squadron of fixed-wing attack aircraft, had been outfought by poorly-armed guerrillas. Not when the rebels had won. As Colonel Barakzai pointed out, the outcome would have been in doubt even if two equally matched armies had fought the action.

So the *Kabul New Times*, for instance, had to content itself with the words that 'a major operation against bandits' had taken place in Paghman.

Two days later, hundreds of thousands of leaflets were dropped by Soviet aircraft over the vast Eagle domain of Paghman, Kohistan and Koh-i-Daman.

They offered amnesty to any guerrillas surrendering, and a guarantee of their safety. Anyone who brought in the 'so called Eagle', would be given fifty thousand dollars and a free pass out of the country.

As Noor put it, 'American money and a chance to get away from Socialist Afghanistan! It shows you what the Reds think is really valuable.'

The Russian soldiers did not relish it when small boys started to shout after them, in the Kabul streets, 'Trapped by a dog, Nikolai!'

The Soviet troops who took part in the action fought well enough, but revealed more of their shortcomings than Russian pride could bear. Their word for that battle is the short, express-ive one that their parents still use to describe Stalin's reign of terror: *koshmar*, a nightmare.

BOOK 9

Across the Hindu Kush

Our 'heroic' representatives, politicians in exile, should have this message about their two duties: stop criticizing each other, and come here to do some real fighting.

Guerrilla from Koh-i-Daman, when asked for a message for Afghans abroad.

1 An Izba in Nuristan

The Koh-i-Daman Foothills

JULY 3

The Sher-Qala Commando, bent on finding and capturing the battered old treasure ship on the far Oxus River, set out on July 3rd from the Paghman Caves. Less than a half day's march into the Koh-i-Daman foothills, fate played a card: and the future of the expedition fell squarely into the hands of a twenty-one-year-old helicopter pilot, *Leytenant* Yuri Nikodemov.

Afghanistan, even under alien occupation, was crisscrossed by a myriad of caravans like The Eagle's; there were some on the spanking new roads of the Great Circle of highways which engirdled the country: but there were thousands more, at any given moment, following the ancient cross-country routes. Nikodemov, on routine patrol, usually paid little attention to these travellers: his job was to look for trouble. One third of the whole population, it was said, was on the move at any one time: you couldn't bother with them all.

This bright July day, Nikodemov in the air and The Eagle's band on the ground, both felt the uplifting joy of the early Afghan summer. The Russian, looking down from his huge Mi-24, glimpsed and dismissed as harmless the small party of no more than forty people – traders, no doubt. A motley assortment of mules, donkeys, even camels, probably heading for Turkestan before the autumn snows trapped them there for the rest of the year.

Here in the foothills the trail wound through the enchanted countryside, whose meadows, orchards and streams, hoopoes and nightingales, had moved Afghan poets to compose some of the country's best-loved odes. But there was no cover against air attack, nowhere to shelter, no crags or valleys, where people

389

could hide or melt into the background. The Eagle and his friends looked up from time to time at the helicopters, on watch and ward duty, seeking infiltrators from the north. There would be no hope if the gunships attacked.

As Nikodemov passed over, swooping down to get a better look at the caravan, the vista seemed one of calm and peace. His eyes dwelt on the flocks of sheep in emerald pastures, the quail, the rabbits; he could even see timid white deer standing nervously not far from the trail.

There was nothing suspicious about the caravan. But someone must have known its composition, someone connected with the Russians, and alerted them. The radio crackled in *Leytenant* Nikodemov's ears:

'Base to Nikodemov, attention, attention! Notorious bandit nicknamed The Eagle and his band, believed attempting to break out beyond Paghman disguised as caravan, heading north. White horse in front, black one in rear. Find and destroy, repeat destroy, these bandits.'

Automatically, the lieutenant acknowledged the message and went back to have another look at the plodding beasts below. He took the helicopter lower, its great bulk swooping just a few hundred metres over the line of animals. Yes – that was it! Positive identification!

As he completed his pass over the meadow through which the caravan was passing, Nikodemov caught his breath at the beauty of the place. Trees, just enough of them to relieve the flatness, rushing streams and the brows of the distant mountains, the haunting blue-green of the Afghan upland light. His craft had swooped so low that he could even smell the richness of the forest leaves . . .

One part of the pilot's mind was running strictly to routine. Signal to helibase: 'Bandits sighted, going in to attack.' Then circle once, to manoeuvre into a correct sighting position, while alerting the bomb-aimer and machine-gunner. Must give them time to prepare. Then – attack! Two or three passes should be enough: gunfire, high-explosives and phosphorus bombs to finish off the enemy, the so-called Eagle . . .

Then another thought intruded, started to take over, and Senior Lieutenant Yuri Nikodemov's mind was filled with another scene, a scene of nine months before.

It had been in Nuristan, the mysterious part of the country to the east, where he had been on a reconnaissance mission, in another Mi-24. In those high mountains, Nikodemov had swerved a precarious route through a gorge, and come too near to an out-jutting rock. Half a metre too close.

That was the length of the main rotor blade sheared off by the rock. The craft shuddered, yawed, steadied for a moment. It held just enough lift for the pilot to put it down, preciously, on the very edge of a cliff face. He could see the sheer drop an arm span from the aircraft's nose, and he threw himself through the door onto a ledge, even as the giant gunship tilted, slid forward and then toppled, into the deep valley, pieces flying off as it was battered against the jagged rock-spears jutting out from every side.

From his ledge, Lieutenant Nikodemov saw the machine, with the rest of the four-man crew, come to rest at the bottom of the valley. Soon afterwards there was a loud report as the fuel tanks exploded: then a dense cloud of oily smoke. Finally, the entire wreck was encircled by roaring flames. Nobody could have survived that.

He clawed his way off the ledge onto the cliff-top, shocked but unhurt, and lay, panting, on the ground. When he felt better, Nikodemov looked around him. This place might have been on another planet. Huge cedar trees, high mountains stark against the sky, eerie silence. Nuristan, 'Land of Light', renamed a hundred years before, by the Afghan king Abdur-Rahman Khan who disliked the old name: Kafiristan, 'Land of the Infidels'.

He climbed down until he came to a small valley hemmed in by rocks, a hundred feet or so above the valley proper. It was tree-covered in places, bare in others, and – like a garden – well supplied with bushes and flowering plants of all kinds, all designed by nature.

Nikodemov, through some process which he, briefly, thought of as a return to the mentality of some remote ancestor, began to think of this place as his very own, and of himself, the former city-dweller, balletomane and dashing pilot as – 'the man'. The man who belonged here, the man for whom this place had been waiting.

*

Two months went by. No Russian aircraft had passed overhead. The year was turning, the leaves yellowing in the forests, though there was still food to be gathered. The man collected mulberries, found pine kernels, dug up roots, tried various leaves and flowers to vary his diet. He was in good enough health, but in these high mountains where the air was thin, he tired easily.

He had thought, many times, about getting away. North of where he had built what he called his *izba* – no more than a Russian peasant hut roofed with branches – there was nothing but a huge, sheer mountain wall, with the snowline almost daily descending, as it became cooler, as if it was eating away at the valley in the high ranges which he shared with the wolves, a few deer, birds, hedgehogs and a multitude of other small animals whose names he did not know.

To the west, as he knew from aerial maps, there were more mountains, clad in tall pines, their cliffs so perpendicular that none could climb them, to reach the next valley, without ropes and pitons. And the next valley beyond that: what if it were just the same? This was the Hindu Kush, the Hindu Killer Mountains, and he was an outcast, lost in the wastes of the ancient Kafiristan, one of the least known lands on earth.

The east or south: those were the options. Day after day he thought about the problem. But there was something about the mountains, the altitude, perhaps, or the food – or even about his own nature – which made it harder and harder, with each day, to come to a decision. Besides, if he left the *izba*, would he always be sure to find food? Would the mountains be even higher, the snow line lower, the glaciers larger, the ice cliffs more menacing?

It was these thoughts which soon took him over, even when he had tried walking towards a possible escape route. He always returned to the *izba*, to his home.

At first he had thought a great deal about his real home, about his family. He had also feared that if he stayed there, his enemies, the Afghan bandits, would get him. Or that he might fall ill, perhaps with appendicitis; simple to deal with when there was a doctor, but a killer when you were alone.

Then these matters had seemed more and more remote, unreal. He had started to wonder, instead, whether he should enlarge the *izba*, make some sort of weapon to use for hunting, collect seeds so that he could grow his own crops, especially those delicious sunflower seeds, or perhaps more berries. There were wild onions, carrots, mulberries by the ton. And there were so many fascinating plants, edelweiss, even: who would have imagined that? And rhododendrons everywhere. Masses of pomegranates. He might catch fish: there were many in the streams.

But autumn was coming, and this would be his first winter here. First of how many? And what was happening in the world? The world, because this place was not in the real world at all. Two months was all it had been, but that was enough to tell the man that, when you were alone, you became someone else, someone different. Someone you would rather be.

As he sat at the entrance of the *izba*, looking down over the valley, his own valley where, perhaps, no man but he had trod for years, another thought struck him. Of course: it was the rest of them that were trapped. He was what people were like once, what everyone really should be like. Free of desires and free of discontent.

Unknown to Lieutenant Nikodemov, there was a transverse cleft between the mountains, and it connected his valley to another, where people lived. One of these people was Shtasu Zijik the hunter: and Shtasu was very angry at what he had just seen.

He touched the hilt of his ancient ceremonial dagger for luck, and ran out of his wooden house which was perched, like an alpine chalet, on the mountain near the town of Kamdesh. Like most Nuristanis, he did not concern himself with strangers over much, although he was always polite to them. If they behaved themselves, that was. But this, he thought, as he took his shotgun from the decorated wooden rack at the doorway, was too much.

A strange looking vehicle, of the kind he would soon know well enough as an assault helicopter, had made three sweeps over the little town, and had dropped something; something which burst into flames and had even set the butter and cheese shed on fire. He could imagine Mas Wousop and his men trying to put out the flames, and wished that he had been there to help him. But perhaps he would be able to do something just as good instead. Deal with this intruder.

The rotor-craft had turned again, to make another pass, and by that time Shtasu was ready. Steadying the gun on a rock, as he would when stalking an approaching snow-leopard, he waited silently. The gun did not have a very long effective range: seventy-five metres, but it was loaded with heavy shot which would stop a deer, a big black buck, or a bear, dead in its tracks. He willed the aircraft to come a little closer, 'Come on, *kakiwar*, big bird, whoever you are, and you'll get something special here.' Suddenly, as if in answer to his invitation, the helicopter, to get a better look and to take photographs, careered towards him.

Shtasu had never been out of Nuristan, the strange country of blond, blue-eyed mountaineers whom people had thought to be the descendants of the lost armies of Alexander the Great. Shtasu spoke only Nuristani really well, and he wore the red, black and white woven headgear and long wool cloak of the country. The British, a century ago, had believed that the Nuristanis shared the same ancestry as the Europeans, partly because of their looks, and also because they sat on chairs and ate at tables, instead of on the floor. The simple, open-handed Nuristanis, when they first saw Westerners, had also described themselves as 'Brothers of the Franks'.

Shtasu knew about guns; and because of his twenty years as a hunter was known as *Achchy*, the Eye. His present weapon, moreover, was semi-automatic: one of the best, made by Luigi Franchi of Bescia, in Italy. It had been a gift from a big-game hunter for whom Shtasu had shot several snow-leopards and an *ovis poli*, the great wild sheep whose huge curved horns were so much prized by collectors. Naturally, the foreign gentleman would now be able to say that he had felled them himself. A Frank called Marco Polo had, apparently, told the West about these animals.

Here it was, then, the big *kakiwar*. It must be three hundred metres away and was closing very fast.

The helicopter was coloured in swathes of camouflage paint; and to the hunter it looked like some monstrous, batlike tiger of the skies, diving towards him. He took aim.

It still came on, unaware of the single man in the red goatskin boots and black cape, squinting along the Browning-type barrel, on a crag in the middle of nowhere.

As it came nearer, the Nuristani gently squeezed the trigger. Easy, now . . . He could see a gun barrel in its nose. A big one. This was a hostile *kakiwar* all right.

But this would not be more difficult than killing a really big black bear. After all, *they* closed in and clutched you.

The helicopter had moved its angle of approach slightly, and was heading for him almost sideways. That was a pity; he would not, after all, be able to get it in the nose. And it was travelling faster than he had thought, unused as he was to estimating distance with such game. Flying sideways!

He would have to strike it from behind, as it passed below him through the valley. In that way he might wound it, anyway.

As it roared past with a great wind, Shtasu panned his gun on the rock, and fired. What the hunter did not know was that the huge Mi-24s were patched, in vulnerable places, with armour, which could easily withstand the heaviest shotgun ball. Armoured, that is, with titanium steel to protect the pilot from below, from the sides – but not from behind or above. The Soviet would learn that lesson later: when they'd lost enough of them to snipers.

The big bullet crashed through the glass and went through the back of the Russian pilot's neck, coming out at the other side, and crashing to the cockpit floor, stopped only by the inner surface of the bulletproof glass windscreen. Range sixty metres.

The helicopter had been diving through the valley two hundred feet away and twenty feet below him, when he fired.

Kara? Where was it? He peered down. There it lay, a mass of burning wreckage, in a river at the bottom of his valley. Four hundred feet below. There should be some useful pickings there, when it cooled down. That might help Mas Wousup's butter makers to pay for the damage. Some of it was metal. Useful for the blacksmith.

The hunter Shtasu, the Eye, looked over to where the dairy people were running about near the sheds, looking less like agitated ants now. Good. They'd got the fire out. Like a mad sky-elephant, that *kakiwar*: smashing something that had nothing to do with him. Well, he'd heard about mad elephants; they had to be killed.

He'd go to see Wousup now, and visit the *kakiwar*'s carcass later.

Yuri Nikodemov had seen the helicopter swoop, had heard the crash of the explosion when it bombed the Kamdesh butter shed, had seen it return. And, when he heard the report of the shot from Shtasu's gun and saw the Mi-24 fall, he realized that the war had caught up with him.

The Russian put on his flying jacket and jackboots, picked up his stick and started to scramble down the mountain, towards the wreck. Why, he did not know: as he got near, the blast of the exploding shells, cartridges and bombs threw him into a crevasse. By the time he had struggled free and found the way again, all was silent.

As he approached, he saw that the fire was out: whether burnt out or blown out by the explosions, he was not sure. The framework lay like the skeleton of a gigantic whale. There was no sign of a survivor. There was no point in staying here. Best to get back to the *izba*.

Nikodemov started up the slope again, finding what looked like a bridle path. He had only taken about thirty steps when he saw, coming from the opposite direction, another man.

Wousup hadn't needed the hunter's help, and had signalled to him across the crags that all was now under control. As he made his way towards the wreck of the helicopter, Shtasu saw, coming up the path from the opposite direction, a man. Strange: first a big false bird, like a carriage in the sky, and then a man coming from it. Had he been inside? Perhaps he was one of those men who rode sky-carriages. Yes, of course. Shtasu had heard about them. Everyone in Nuristan was proud that it was one of them, a Nuristani, who had gone to Kabul, and had become *Komondon-i-Tiyara*, 'Commander of the Fliers'. They had roaring sky-carriages, it was said.

The two men stopped and looked at one another. Shtasu saw a Frank, a man in *faranki* clothes, at any rate: but with a full beard and carrying a stick, otherwise unarmed. Like one of those foreign hunters who used to come here, years ago. Perhaps he was an Afghan of some kind, an *Awdali*.

They were only a few metres apart now. Shtasu decided to try Pashtu: he knew a little. '*Starai ma she* – may you never be tired!' he said.

The man shook his head.

Shtasu pointed to himself. 'Shtasu.' He indicated the sky and the sun. His name meant 'starshine'; surely this man would understand that?

There was no response, so he tried sign language. The people of Nuristan used it all the time because, at a distance, the roar of the waterfalls drowned speech, even shouts. No, sign language didn't work with this stranger.

The Russian looked at Shtasu. He'd never seen anything like this apparition before. Wearing Nuristani breeches, a black cloak of fine wool, with blue eyes, fair hair – and carrying a very modern automatic shotgun, a powerful one.

Shtasu tried again, this time with the only Persian phrase he knew, which the *Awdalis* said to one another: '*Manda nabashen* – may you never be tired!'

Then, '*Kara kakiwar* – where's the bird?' Didn't he understand anything?

The other man was looking at his gun. '*Stwa* – four shots,' Shtasu explained. Better reassure him, '*wrorim*, my brother.'

The Russian spoke now, in his own language, telling him he didn't understand. '*Ya ni gavaryu Nuristanski.*'

He must be some kind of an Atghan, thought Shtasu. Foreigners surely didn't ride about in *Kakiwars*.

'*Tushish Awdali*?' He pointed to Nikodemov. Then, touching his own breast, he said, '*Mam Nuristani.*'

The lieutenant understood. Nuristani, of course. '*Mam Russki,*' he said.

Russki? What was that? Shtasu wondered. Some kind of Frankish person? He spoke again.

'*Tushish Faranki*?'

'*Franki, da, tovarish.*'

He *was* a Frank, after all. Anyway, the *Faranki* was unarmed: he should be welcomed. The Nuristani took some dried apricots from his leather pouch. '*Yaw*! eat!'

Understanding the gesture, Nikodemov accepted the fruit,

and offered Shtasu some *jalghozas*, pine kernels, from his pocket. Shtasu took two or three, as a token of goodwill. The Russian gestured to him to take more. Shtasu wasn't hungry: besides, the niceties had been sufficiently observed. He smiled. '*Mam awzhekh* – I have already eaten. *Kuja-st aamou*?' Where was this stranger's house?

He had to draw a hut on the soil with a twig before the Russian understood. The man was asking about his *izba*. Nikodemov pointed up towards the small valley above them.

Together the two men climbed up to where the little shack rested against a rock. Now Shtasu understood. This man was some kind of a traveller, and as such he was his guest: protected by the sacred laws of hospitality. But he could not stay here, it was going to be too dangerous. Little by little, he managed to convey that, however nice this place might be at the moment, it would not be long before it was impossible to survive there. '*Aaw*, water – *dash* – rain – *zeym* – snow.' Shtasu gestured, showing how the snow line would come down, how rain would fall, how snow would pile up, three metres high, in spite of the sun throughout the winter. Best to get away.

'Come to my house, brother, you are welcome.' With signs and a medley of words in the Dari-Nuristani *lingua franca*, the hunter took his new guest to his own home.

There was no airstrip in all Nuristan, and the Afghan governor and officials had defected from the communist regime, most of them taking refuge in nearby Pakistan. Nuristan had been cut off from Afghanistan for a year, and was only occasionally patrolled by reconnaissance aircraft.

Salt and small manufactured articles like needles were now difficult or impossible to get. Nuristan was returning to its ancient, medieval, self-sufficient economy.

Things were to remain very much the same for a few months more – until the Russians tried to conquer the ancient land. When that happened, the Nuristanis put up such a fight that both the unwilling Afghan troops, sent ahead, and the Russian soldiers, untrained for mountain warfare, were wiped out or put to flight in one engagement after another. The Russians fell back on mass air attacks on civilians, bombing every town and any village they could find, with fire and high-explosives. Still they could not demoralize the Nuristanis, and the fight continued. The people who had defied the armies of Alexander the Great were not impressed by their new enemies, with or without modern technology.

But that was later. In the meantime, faithful to their age-old code of hospitality, the Nuristanis looked after the Russian lieutenant well, and arranged for a party of men to take him to the Afghan administrative border, where he was handed back to the Soviet authorities.

When Nikodemov had asked people who knew Nuristan the meaning of the word, *banna*, which the people of the mountains had said to him so often, they had said, 'It means *wror*, in Pashtu, *baradar* in Persian: "brother".'

That had been nine months ago.

With the call of the forest in his mind and the hospitality of the mountain villagers in his heart, with the picture of Shtasu the hunter holding up his hand in farewell clearly before him, Nikodemov now wheeled the rotorcraft away, towards his distant landing pad. He would not defile his honour. He would return one day guiltless to the *izba*, his home among the tall cedars of Nuristan.

The lieutenant flicked the transmission switch.

'Nikodemov to helibase. No sighting of a terrorist caravan. The upland valley is clear of suspicious figures right to the mountains. I repeat. No sign of bandits.'

'Helibase to Nikodemov. *Nichevo*, never mind, Comrade *Leytenant*. Must be a false alarm. Resume normal duty and return to base as scheduled. Helibase out.'

Nobody else in the helicopter seemed to have seen the caravan: so he had not really taken much of a risk, the lieutenant thought, as he covertly checked the crew's behaviour.

Some day, Lieutenant Nikodemov was sure, he would return to Nuristan. But not in a *kakiwar* like this, not in a uniform, not as a foreigner. Just now, of course, he had to carry on. He had relatives in Leningrad to think of – and his oath as an officer.

He was not ready yet.

He grinned to himself. The Eagle must be feeling good. Good luck, *banna*, brother, Eagle. You are still free.

2 The Wild Ones of Murad Shah

The Lower Paghman Range

JULY 5

'*Teeo pang!*' Adam faced the huge man dressed in a cloak of fox and lynx skins who held a long, thin knife at his throat, while two others held him fast. It didn't look as though he would be able to talk his way out of this ambush.

No journey to the north now. He'd probably be dead in a minute. The caravan was resting. Adam had gone down the mountain slope to talk to one of the patrols, and had almost reached their brushwood hideout when, as if from nowhere, three men had leapt upon him. Big men, in belted furs, with strange faces quite like Europeans, grey or green eyes, straight noses, fair and red hair.

They had whisked him away from the patrol's hideout so fast that the three guerrillas sitting inside had not heard a thing.

It was mid-morning, and the sun was hot. These men were dressed for a colder climate than this. One of them unwound a length of rope from around his waist, rough rope that might have been made from creepers, and tied The Eagle's ankles and wrists with it. Another man took up a long pole and the three pushed it between his arms and legs and lifted him, as people do a dead or captured wild animal, and carried him uphill, away from where the guerrilla caravan was resting.

He could now see that the men were wearing strings of pierced crystals around their necks, their hair was long and matted, and their feet padded along with the tread of mountain folk. Each one wore a beautiful silver-mounted dagger in his belt. As they walked, they chanted softly, '*pang! pang!*'

Adam struggled and started to shout, hoping to attract the attention of some of his guards. Instantly the men stopped. One of them picked up a rock, and almost casually, but with great precision, struck the captive at the back of the neck. The Eagle blacked out.

He came to with a searing headache, and found himself still being carried, still uphill. He gave a cry as the jogging pace of the men jolted his spine, the pain shooting up into his head. Quietly the leader took up a stone and indicated, by signs, that if he did not remain silent, he would be struck again. '*Amou, laysat,*' he said.

Pang? Amou laysat? He wasn't Russian, anyway.

He lost consciousness again. When he came to, someone was splashing cold water on his face.

He was in a cave, with a brushwood awning just covering the entrance. Inside, a fire was burning, fed by some dry material which gave almost no smoke. Around him, lit by torches of resinous wood stuck at an angle from holes in the cavern walls, he could see shapes hanging. Human? No. They were pieces of animals, smoked and drying.

The man handed him something and made motions to show that he should eat it. His hands were still bound. Adam took the food with both hands and tasted it. It was a sort of bread, made of barley or lentils. It tasted gritty, and had pieces of charcoal embedded in it. Then the man lifted a clay pot and held it to his lips. Adam drank. It was good water.

The fifteen or twenty other men in the cave crowded around him, making welcoming signs. Adam indicated that they should untie him, but the leader laughed and shook his head.

There was nothing to do but wait.

They had emptied Adam's pockets and were amusing themselves, examining their contents. Passed from hand to hand, they looked at, shook and even tasted the various objects. They liked the watch, the pocket compass and the knife. They seemed baffled by the comb, the money and the notebook. Finally they put everything in a neat heap and covered the pile with stones.

Some hours later they brought him soup, of meat flavoured with herbs. It was delicious. '*Yaw, pang!*' they said.

Evidently he was *pang*. '*Yaw*' undoubtedly meant '*eat*'.

His head still hurt. It must be late afternoon. They had not killed him, but what did they want? And what would happen to the caravan?

He was sitting, still bound, on the cave floor with his back to a rock. One of the wild men had, with a kindly gesture, put a fur blanket under him, and made a cushion from a bundle of straw for him to lean against. He watched as the men went about their business.

Two or three of them were cleaning weapons. There was a pile of knives, one or two modern guns and an automatic pistol. They showed that they knew what they were doing, using the oil and the pull-throughs expertly, squinting down barrels for traces of dirt, emptying and refilling magazines to check for possible jamming. Armed, experienced fighters.

Two men were operating a strange type of mill, a conical container into which they put large seeds. When they had satisfied themselves that it was full enough, they fixed a heavy, angled wooden stick into the centre of the mill. One man was then blindfolded, for all the world like an ox on a water-wheel, and, taking the stick in his hands, he moved round and round. The other man inspected the result of his labours: a thick oil dripping into a bowl from small holes in the base of the earthenware cone. When the bowl was nearly full, one of the men took up a pot and filled it with the liquid.

Across the cave from this scene, three others were carefully laying long strips of dried meat on boards covered with cloth. Wooden mallets were used to pound the meat until it became a powder. This material was then put, in handfuls, into cotton bags which were weighed in the hand and then sewn up. Concentrated food rations, no doubt.

This was all very interesting, thought Adam, but what about his own people? They would be worried, and might send out a party to search for him. And yet, if they did, it was unlikely that they would find this place.

The men were now talking together in low voices. They were discussing something and pointing to the cave's opening. They did not seem interested in Adam at all. Every now and then they would stand still and listen. Adam could not hear anything, but they probably had far better ears than his.

They must have had a scout outside: a man came into the darkness, running, and repeated something three or four times. It sounded to Adam like *Marut*, which was not reassuring. He remembered that this was the name of a fallen angel from

Islamic lore. Marut taught men magic, and he was suspended in a rocky pit on Earth as a punishment for his sins . . .

Marut. Suddenly the dwindling light from the cave's entrance was briefly darkened and a tall, thin figure, dressed in some tight-fitting garment, lifted the awning and slipped inside. The cavemen surrounded him. With cries of welcome they offered him something to drink, and then pointed out the captive.

The newcomer unslung an automatic carbine from his back, and walked over to Adam, sitting down on the ground in front of him. Adam saw that he had a full beard like his captors, but was darker, more like an Afghan, and was dressed in a grey Afghan Army uniform without rank or other badges. Perhaps thirty years of age, he had very dark eyes and extremely white teeth, which flashed as he smiled.

Before he said anything he reached forward with a knife in his hand and cut the bonds from Adam's limbs with two quick movements. Then he sat back, cross-legged and took off his Pashtun sandals, massaging his feet. Apparently satisfied with this, he said in Dari: 'Welcome. We shall be eating in about an hour, when the lads have got the food ready.'

Adam felt distinctly annoyed. 'What is this all about? I have been attacked and kidnapped, and I don't want to eat with you, whoever you are!'

Once he'd said it, he felt slightly ridiculous.

The man laughed. 'I'm sorry, but now you know where we are, we'll have to keep you here until we move on. This is our *karar-gah*, our resting place.'

'Who am I going to tell, you idiot! Who cares what a bunch of madmen are doing and where they are? You'd better let me go. I suppose you've told these apes that you are the accursed demon Marut, and got them to work for you . . .'

'Marut?' The other man seemed surprised. 'Oh, you mean my name. I am called Murad Shah. These are my Nuristani lads, from the north-eastern mountains, you know. That's the way they pronounce "Murad". I don't suppose they have ever heard of Marut . . . Marut, me . . .' He started to laugh. 'I've been called some things, but never Marut. Who are you?'

'I am called *Teeo pang* by your men,' said Adam, 'but I am The Eagle.'

'Kara Kush – The Eagle?' Murad was on his feet. 'I had no

idea. I'm very sorry.' He held out his hand and Adam took it.

'*Teeo pang*,' said Murad, 'only means "You're a foreigner", in Nuristani. You are foreign – we all are – to these men.'

'What are you doing here?' Adam wanted to know.

'We're fighting the Russians, like you.'

'Where is this place?'

'Three kilometres north-west of Baghabad, "Land of Gardens", in the foothills.'

Adam wanted to know where Murad was from. 'And where did you collect these goons? They're a long way from home.'

'We are all from Sayed Khel.' Murad sighed. 'We are the only survivors of the battle last January. If it hadn't been for these men, my bodyguard, I'd be dead.'

Six months before, The Eagle knew, the Russians had attacked one of the strongholds of the Resistance at Sayed Khel, the place named after the Sayed family. The defenders had fought for eleven days, with light arms, against the most powerful weapons of the invading army. Even the outside world's newspapers had heard of the battle. It had been a disaster for the Muhjahidin. Sayed Khel no longer existed.

'There were nearly four thousand of us, not counting women and children,' said Murad; 'and they had tanks and aircraft. Our rifles had no more effect on them than peashooters, and we were short of ammunition. We fortified every house and dug tank traps in the road. At night we burned the fields and the orchards where they were bivouacked with kerosene, roasting many, but destroying our own land. We made bows and arrows when the ammunition ran out. We made holes in the ground and lay in them until they overran us. Then we rose out of the holes with sharpened sticks and stabbed them. But they still kept coming.'

'What were your casualties?' Adam asked.

'Over one thousand killed, though we estimate that we killed or wounded twice as many of the enemy. Two thousand six hundred of our men were captured.'

'What happened to them?' Adam could guess, but he wanted to know just the same.

Murad shrugged. 'Four hundred or so were lined up and shot. About two thousand, many of them wounded, were taken away in trucks. Kabul radio said these had been put into camps for "re-education". They will, I think, try to force them into the Army, because men are so short and the Russians are always pressing the Afghan Army to do more fighting. Of course they'll only desert to the Muhjahidin.'

'How did you get away?'

'I had been hit two or three times and fainted, I suppose through loss of blood and so on – shock, pain, I don't know. These fellows you see here, "the goons", are what's left of my *halqa*, my bodyguard. They had originally fled to Sayed Khel over the high eastern mountains, when their villages were destroyed by air attacks. They carried me here and looked after me. They are great experts in survival, and they know how to look after wounds.'

A mountaineer brought two mugs of tea and *kishmish*, dried fruit.

'And you have set up a miniature village in this cave?'

'That's right. As you see, they know all kinds of arts and crafts. Herbs, cookery, hunting, making things. Their fur coats would fetch a fortune in Western Europe, I expect. Not to mention those handmade harps slung on their backs.'

'I think,' said Adam, grinning at the simple faces of the cavemen, 'the time has come that you came to us and taught us a few things.'

'I was hoping you would say that, Commander,' said Murad.

Captain Azambai, in charge of the caravan, had sent some men to scout, others to collect forage and rations, and had set the rest to carrying out exercises, weapon cleaning and the other boring tasks which had to be done.

Adam had been missing for five hours. Azambai knew there was no real prospect of finding him if he had got lost or been captured by bandits, for the hills were riddled with caves and in places covered with thick brush. Small valleys filled with cedars, mulberries, mountain garlic and a dozen different kinds of flowering shrubs gave perfect cover, both to men and to the wildlife. It was said that the mountain tigers had their haunts there, too, though they only attacked people in the winter when hunger forced them to prowl around the villages.

In spite of Noor asking him to send out more patrols,

Azambai decided that they must wait. Just as she was about to go off on her own to look for him, Adam appeared, surrounded by a ferocious flock of Nuristanis, carrying gifts of oil, honey, and snow-leopard skins.

Murad was introduced to the captain.

'This isn't good enough, you know,' Azambai said, after welcoming him briefly. 'Your men ought to be better disciplined than they evidently are.'

Murad gave him a mock salute. 'I'll try to fix them up with uniforms, general.'

'Captain. No, there aren't any uniforms. We'll get local clothes from the villagers. And I'll try to find one or two of our own people who speak your men's language. We'll never be able to talk to them if you get shot, and they might do anything. This really is not very satisfactory.' Azambai the soldier couldn't say how delighted he was that Adam was safe, after all. But his emotions had to come out somehow.

Murad saw the point. 'Sorry, captain. Yes, I'll co-operate in any way you wish. We'll even go back to The Eagle's Nest, if you think that we'd be more useful there.'

Azambai softened. 'That would be the best thing, of course. But I quite like the look of these people. We'll just have to try to turn them into *askars*, soldiers, as I'm trying to with the other Muhjahidin. It will be difficult for them, but discipline will see us through, you know that.'

'I know that.'

The following day, as the caravan continued towards the high Hindu Kush, the climb became more and more precipitous. At the first halt there was a small inn where the plodding Nuristanis, who had been taking turns at riding and walking, were able to hire small, powerful Kataghan ponies with the money which Murad, usefully and surprising everyone, produced from a leather bag. Gold sovereigns, with the head of King George V on them. Murad explained that they had come from a hoard, buried since the 1919 war with Britain, and donated by the man who had captured them from an Indian Army war chest sixty years before. He had been an ancient, wizened fruit farmer, who only had enough cherry trees to keep body and soul together, but he had never thought of using the gold for himself. 'I thought, "It'll come in handy,"' he said. Murad had come across him quite casually and had said that he was a Muhjahid: nothing else; and was presented with the sovereigns.

Louis Palmer, unexpectedly, was found to have a working knowledge of the Nuristani language. It had interested him for years, and he had had several men from the secret land working for him from time to time. He soon became the chief of one *dasta*, and Murad's second-in-command. He sang their songs to their own harp music, and even seemed to enjoy the dried meat which they cooked, mixed with herbs and water, and served with melted butter and sprigs of fresh rosemary at each midday halt.

He even taught them long strings of words in Dari-Persian and Pashtu; something that they had not wanted to attempt before.

3 Land of the Living Prince

Beyond High Serai

JULY 11

Upwards into the Paghman Mountains, the narrow road led, at two thousand feet, through flint-strewn defiles and across gorges spanned only by rope bridges, often with a drop of several hundred feet. Hardy wheat actually grew at these heights, in fertile patches, and villages, built of stone, clustered against the towering mountain walls. Some peaks were snow-capped in midsummer, soaring as high as twenty-five thousand feet. The camels, now unable to stand the conditions, had to be sent back. The caravan, both animals and people gasping for breath in the rarefied air, at times could move only at a snail's pace.

'*Bala, bala!* Upwards, upwards . . .'

The melting snow on the lower ranges was the worst cause of landslides at this time of year. Often the fallen boulders were piled so high on the rock-hewn ledges that it took hours to manhandle them out of the way. Meeting another file of animals, coming in the opposite direction meant, again and again, one or other backing along the ledge until it came to a place where the path was wide enough for two horses to pass at once.

It was six days into the journey, and everyone was blistered with sunburn from the ultraviolet light, in spite of the mixture of grease and charcoal which they smeared on their hands and faces. A day beyond High Serai, where the villagers had treated the people of the caravan well, with meat and drink and even applause as they left, the mules moved more and more reluctantly. Hired, with their muleteers, from the Serai, they were not accustomed to the northwards journey, and the increasing altitude now troubled them.

'*Bala, bala!*'

Viciously, one of the mules kicked at its owner, who was trying to urge it around an especially difficult curve in the path, studded with slippery, cobble-like stones. The man lashed at the mule, losing his temper, just as they reached a spot where the path widened. In a second, the animal had turned and snapped at the man, its eyes rolling and its lungs gasping for breath.

Its teeth sank into his shoulder, going right through the thickly padded mountain coat, into the flesh, and held on fast. The mountaineer, screaming with agony, flailed about, while the mules in front and behind started to buck and kick.

Before anyone could see exactly how it happened, the mule and the muleteer were over the edge, bumping and rolling to their deaths in the valley floor, five hundred feet below.

Adam edged his way past the remaining animals to see if anything could be done. Nothing could. The man and the mule lay, some distance apart now, with no possibility of rescue or of climbing up. As Adam and the others watched through their binoculars, the badly injured man, knowing what his fate would be, rolled over slightly, and drew his gun. At the first shot, the mule jerked and lay still. The watchers turned away before the second report echoed from the rocks.

Azambai had joined Adam now. His face was taut. 'Which mule was that?'

'Mule number five, sir. Akram Abbasi's,' said one of the mountaineers.

'Adam,' whispered Azambai in The Eagle's ear, 'we have lost not only a man and a mule – we've lost all our money.'

'What, both the gold and the reserve?'

'That's right. I wanted it to be secure, so I put it in the panniers of the best mule, and placed the most reliable men front and back. I should have dispersed it, I see that now.'

Adam was not pleased. 'You are in charge of loading, and we must not fall out, whatever happens. But I don't like the idea of being completely penniless.'

'We'll just have to manage,' said the captain.

They could not buy any more food or weapons now. They would not be able to pay for the lost mule and the hire of the ones they still had left. They would not be able to bribe their way out of trouble, or reward anyone for services. There would be no way to buy information . . .

That day they had covered seven *parsangs*, each *parsang* the distance a horse could travel in an hour. 'Let's call a midday halt when we get to a cultivated spot,' said The Eagle. Azambai agreed, feeling his way along the rock face towards his place at the head of the convoy.

'*Bala, bala!*'

Always upwards, the caravan inched forward, the air getting thinner by the minute. The travellers began to feel mountain sickness, which made them want to lie down and sleep; some with hallucinations and a constant drumming in their heads, the 'torture of the mountain-demons' which even acclimatization does not overcome. At one point the muleteers refused to go any further, and had to be threatened with guns.

As the sun was declining, mercifully, the road began to descend, passing through surprisingly lush but uncultivated land. Wild pomegranate, pear trees and cedars, lower-growing vegetation, replaced the eternal pines. The animals sensed the improvement first, and started to quicken their pace, in spite of the treacherous, gravelly stones underfoot.

Then, as if to dash their hopes, nature produced another trick. A wide, rushing torrent, fed by the melting snows of Yellow Mountain, crashed straight across the mountain ledge along which the travellers were picking their way, completely blocking it. It was nothing less than a huge waterfall, and to the less experienced seemed an impossible barrier. Noor, towards the middle of the caravan, saw the captain arguing with the guide sitting on a black horse behind him, and the file of animals stopped. Surely they would not be able to get past this?

Then she saw one man after another turn and pass a message to the one behind. Soon, the Nuristani in front of her said, in broken Dari, 'Back up, we have to rush it. Pass it on – *haraka*, get moving!'

Slowly, painfully, the whole string, some sixty animals, retreated along the treacherous ledge, until Azambai's horse, in the lead, had a space of about twenty feet between it and the foaming water gushing from above and disappearing into the valley to the right.

Azambai, as the others watched, kneed his horse and urged

him forward, gaining enough impetus to plunge into the broad fall and to carry him through without being swept away. But supposing beyond the waterfall the road narrowed, or turned in a hairpin bend? Noor covered her eyes. When she looked again, the Turkestani, and his horse, had disappeared.

Now it was the turn of the second man, the Turkoman guide, who had been this way before and had obviously advised Azambai what to do. Without a moment's hesitation he patted his horse's head, pulled on the reins and then pushed them forward, the signal to leap. Instantly, the beautiful Kataghan pony, long golden mane flying, launched himself towards the foam. As Noor watched, he vanished, as in a scene from a folktale.

Slowly, one by one, the people of the caravan passed through the water curtain, emerging on the other side soaked through, but safe and sound. Even the mules were prepared to make the leap, sensing, perhaps, that there was no other way. As each rider passed through this unprecedented baptism, the sensation, the shock of the icy water and of going into the unknown seemed to last for an age, though it could only have taken a fraction of a second.

Beyond the waterfall, and hidden by its stark white sheets of water, plunging like an eternal veil, lay a small, neat, valley, with black tents pitched, sheep quietly grazing, children playing, and a group of women preparing a meal for the herders of the tableland. Steam rose from men, women and horses as they plodded, almost automatically, towards this community, human beings drawn irresistibly towards other humans, without reason or plan, feeling both misery and relief.

An old man, limping from some injury or disease, came towards them, and spoke in the rough Dari of the mountain.

'Welcome! May you never be tired!'

'May you be strong!' Azambai said.

'May you live forever. You came well through the falling waters.'

'May you find salvation! We did not know any other way to do it!' The captain grinned, recovering his good humour. 'Where are we, friend?'

'This is Tutabad: Place of Mulberries – look,' he indicated thousands of mulberry trees, some very large, which covered the hills around his valley. 'We are the people of Zinda-Mir, the Living Prince, and those are our tents.'

They had meat, but it was for sale. They could not afford to give any of it away; everything was measured, accounted for, in a frugal way which astonished the other Afghans, generally given to hopeless extravagance. But they soon realized that anything less than the most careful husbandry in this part of the mountains could lead to starvation, at least of protein.

Qasim and the Nuristanis, however, having dried their clothes, went into the trees beyond the sheep meadows and came back, an hour later, with the carcasses of two fine white deer. There was food for both Muhjahidin and nomads. The herdspeople brought out green tea, salt, beans, barley and dried apricots.

They had no guns themselves and – unusually for mountain folk – did no hunting.

They had obviously organized their lives around mutton and wild fruit and vegetables, bartering meat and wool for other things which they needed. Hunting did not appeal to them. 'Most of the animals here are foxes, lynx, wild cat,' they said, in answer to Adam's questions. He felt that it would not be polite to point out that they had seen herds of mountain goats, grouse, partridges and plenty of the white, as well as brown, deer. 'We all have our own ways and customs,' he said, and the twenty or so shepherds gravely agreed, rubbing the mutton fat into their beards as they sat around a fire, made from brightly burning cedar-wood.

There were no Russians in these parts, nor did the writ of the communist People's Democratic Party of Afghanistan run here, either. The people were not nomads, for they had villages lower down the mountain. This was their summer pasture-land; where they camped for months at a time, since it was too far from their houses to bring the sheep up every day. They had heard something about a change of regime, but only that it was not popular. Yes, caravans did sometimes come through from the north or south, but people did not stop to spend time or to talk with them. Caravan people always seemed in a hurry to be on their way.

The shepherds showed little interest in The Eagle's plans: to them, a caravan was a caravan, a body of people carrying on their own way of life, like the sheep people had theirs. They would take nothing for allowing the animals to graze on their ground, but bartered their delicious cake made of pounded walnuts and hazelnuts with honey for a few boxes of matches: a real luxury for them. Ordinarily, they explained, they kept a fire or two burning all the time to provide such heat and light as they needed. Adam fell asleep that night, thinking how idyllic a life it would be, to become a sheep farmer in the high mountains, to build his own house, to hunt and fish and live on hazelnut bread and yoghurt, forgetting the disaster of the lost money, and the not very good prospects of a small band like his trying to attack the might of the Russian Army at its great base of Qizil Qala.

It was light when Adam woke. A man was leaning over him, holding a knife to his throat. Instinctively he reached for his rifle. It was gone. He sat up, cautiously, and two more men came up and looped a thick rope around his body, trapping his arms. Everywhere he looked, other men, the muleteers and guides, were immobilizing his people.

Nobody said a word.

As Adam watched, the muleteers dumped all the arms, rifles, revolvers, grenades, even swords, in a pile with two men to guard them. They herded the shepherds, who were completely unarmed, into another group and set guards on them. Then they started to rifle the baggage of the caravan. Either they were bandits or else they had realized that they would not now be paid, and were going to plunder the caravan instead. It is hard to conceal anything from anyone on a caravan journey. Adam realized that these men probably knew that the gold had been on the lost mule in the ravine.

There did not seem to be any hope. Adam caught Captain Azambai's eye. He was sitting up, too, some distance away, looking wretchedly at the systematic, practised sorting of the goods and chattels. He rolled his eyes and shrugged. Even if he had been near enough to talk, there was not much to say.

Now the thieves were methodically searching everyone's pockets and taking watches, any money they could find, and small personal possessions. The burly Nuristanis growled as

413

their crystal necklaces were taken away, but they were helpless, too.

Adam could not see where Noor was. At the angle at which he was sitting, trussed like a fowl, he could not even move to see what might have happened to her, or to Karima.

The sheep people were sitting quietly, philosophically, almost, on the ground, under the guns of their guards. They had probably learned, over the centuries, that it was best to acquiesce in situations like this. They would either be killed or set free. Either way, it was the will of Allah. In any case, there was, surely, nothing that they could do . . .

There was a Persian saying, '*Na ba zar, na ba zor, na ba zahr* – Not money, not force, nor poison.' Well, they had no money, no force, certainly no poison. That seemed to be that. They would probably be killed.

The leader of the muleteers, known for some reason as *Hairan*, 'the bewildered', was small, and bent, almost hunchbacked, with a low voice and an unassuming manner. Yet somehow he had become a leader, and the other men, some of them huge and villainous-looking, followed his orders without question. Adam found himself hoping that they would quarrel over the spoils; though how that might help him and his band he could not tell. In story-books, of course, that was one of the possibilities.

It took an hour or more for the looting to be completed, and for the booty to be collected, in neat piles, on the green grass of the meadow. It was all done so quietly, so professionally, that Adam was sure that these robbers had done the same thing many times before. Even if they had not originally been attracted by the gold, he felt, the thieves would almost certainly have tried to rob the caravan.

And the guards, four of them, posted the night before and due to be relieved every four hours, had not raised the alarm. They must have been silenced, somehow. Had they been killed? Adam could not see any of them, or any dead bodies, either, from where he lay.

Hairan had come to some sort of arrangement with the shepherds, who were nodding their heads: the two men guarding them were withdrawn and joined the rest of the robbers, now surrounding their leader. Then Hairan was climbing onto a pile of saddles and boxes, arranged like a platform, around which the loot was neatly stacked. His men positioned themselves in a circle around him, sitting cross-legged on the ground. Evidently the shepherds had promised not to make any trouble when the guards joined the leader's audience.

Hairan stood, now atop the improvised platform, and addressed his men. He was making quite a long speech, in the archaic form of Dari which was used in these mountains, as Adam could tell from its cadence. But he was too far away to hear what was actually being said. Now and again the listening men laughed, sometimes they shouted.

In the middle of one such shout, rising from the ever more animated leader of the robbers, from whom Adam's eyes had strayed, there was a rattle of rifle-fire.

It came from a clump of trees, some hundred yards from where Adam was lying, and a hundred and twenty from the robber group.

When he looked back to where the band had been sitting, Adam saw that they were sprawled in heaps, some evidently dead, others struggling on the ground, some tugging at the butts and barrels of rifles from the arms pile, trying to get them free to shoot at their attackers.

He looked back towards the trees again. Some twenty men, dispersed in open array, were running, very fast, towards the robbers, stopping every now and then to fire into the mass.

Nobody from among Hairan's men had been able to get a shot in before the newcomers were among them. Rapidly they formed a circle around their prey, first shooting at them and then covering them with their guns at the ready, as all those who were on their feet – and some lying on the ground – raised their arms in surrender.

The raiders were dressed in furs and leather trousers, with wide leather belts and crossed bandoliers. On their feet they wore soft, curly-toed Turkoman boots, and three or four of them, who seemed to be the leaders, had wolfskin, Mongol-type caps with flaps on their heads.

Adam was trying to work out the meaning of this event when he felt a hand on his shoulder. He jumped, half turned around and was surprised to hear Noor's voice. 'Stay still, or you'll get hurt.' He felt her knife slash through the ropes which bound his arms.

He stretched himself, wondering how she had done it – and what to do next.

Putting his finger to his lips, he signalled her to be still, in case the new arrivals saw her.

She laughed. 'Don't worry! They're friends of mine.'

'Friends?'

'Yes.'

'What do you mean, friends? Where are they from? Who are they? How do you know them? What's been going on?'

'One thing at a time.' She was enjoying the moment. As Adam stood up and tried to get his circulation going again, Captain Azambai came up, rubbing his wrists. With him was a tall, Mongol-capped figure.

Adam shook the grinning newcomer's hand, almost automatically, as he said, 'When is someone going to tell me what is going on?'

'I just went and collected these men to help us,' said Noor.

'Where did you find them, and anyway, how did you get away from the camp?'

'Last night I couldn't sleep. I saw Hairan giving a hot drink to the watch, after stirring something into it. He gave some to all the men on guard. I guessed it was either poison or dope. I was scared and made quietly for the trees, to decide what to do. I ran into some of these men. They turned out to be friendly.'

'You're obviously the only intelligent person among us!' said Azambai, perhaps relieved at not being the only one to have blundered. 'Those fellows shouldn't have taken the drink. Must have had *chars*, hemp, in it.'

'Why did you wait until dawn?' Adam asked.

'To catch them at a moment when they were distracted.'

'I am Tourzan, which means "brave" in Pashtu,' said the leader of their rescuers. 'That's the name my parents gave me.'

'He prefers to be called Farid,' said Noor.

'We are most grateful for your kindness and owe our lives to you and your men, *shaghali*, mister, Farid,' said Adam, remembering his manners.

'It is my duty,' said Farid, happily. 'We live beyond those

trees, there, in a group of villages. These simple folk don't have much to do with us, as we collect taxes from them, for the Zinda-Mir, the Living Prince, our chief. "Living", of course, also means "very great". That is his title.'

'Well, who are these robbers?' the captain wanted to know. 'They seem pretty experienced to me.'

'Oh, yes, they are indeed. The Mir has been after them and others like them for years.'

'Did you say years?' Adam asked.

'Yes, years. They are professional thieves. Their ancestors were known as the Assassins. They are sort of licensed killers. Legend has it that they originally followed a terrorist chief called Hasan, son of Sabah, in Persia. He sent people out to kill, for political reasons. They sometimes call themselves "People of Truth". The founder, and his successors, are supposed to be incarnations of a deity, a sort of god.'

Azambai said, 'That was the Old Man of the Mountains, wasn't it, *Shaikh al Jabal*?'

'That's right. There are still pockets of them in Afghanistan, though not all of them are killers. A lot of them are respectable grocers and bakers, things like that. Some believe in murder, others say it's a heresy started by a splinter group centuries ago.

'I'll tell you more when we've had a little food.'

Farid led them to a spot beyond the tree-screen where his men had spread a feast such as the travellers had not seen for a long time. The villagers had brought out loads of cooked meat, fruit, cheeses, any number of vegetables and sauces.

'What are you going to do with the robbers?' Azambai asked.

Farid said, 'That is nothing to do with me. Our men have already taken them to the Prince. He may kill them or let them go, or do anything he wants to. We must leave things like that to him.'

'No trial, or anything?'

Farid looked at him as people do when someone has made an improper remark. 'Perhaps there will be a trial. Perhaps not. It is for the Living Prince to decide.' That obviously disposed of that.

'As to the killing and robbing by these Assassins,' Farid said, 'it is all very simple. Their leader, the great Imam whom they follow, is the incarnation of deity in their eyes. Therefore everything on earth belongs to him. If you or I have anything, it still belongs to him. So his followers can take possession of it.'

Adam knew that branches of the Assassins were said to have terrorized whole nations in antiquity, but this persistence of their nests in Afghanistan was new to him. He said, 'People like that are undoubtedly a pestilential nuisance, to put it no higher. But what a weapon, used against the Russians.'

To Adam's surprise, Farid took this seriously. He touched Adam on the arm. 'You ought to be a politician! I'll certainly mention it to the Prince. He might well agree to your suggestion.'

'But how could you keep control over them, if you let them loose among the people again?'

'Use the Russian method, of course. Take and keep hostages. Why, High Serai is full of people we could pick and choose from. It's just that for all these years we did not know that they were Assassins.'

'It's definitely something to think about.'

Desperate remedies for desperate circumstances? Adam was glad that he did not have to make the decision.

4 We must cross
Black Mountain...

Qala Kavi
Central Mountains

JULY 12

The Living Prince's palace, beyond the screen of trees which surrounded the lush pasture of Tutabad, clung to a mountainside which at first seemed like a sheer wall. As the travellers approached, however, they saw that the wall was a mass of natural terraces, perhaps carved by glaciers. The grey fortifications, walls, turrets and embrasures, all rested on stone: no different in texture from that of the mountain itself.

At the foot of the mountain, amid running streams and cherry orchards, protected by the huge castle above, lay the group of villages where Noor had found Farid, the chief of the Prince's advance guard.

'The Prince,' Farid said, after a man had approached, riding a splendid Turkoman-Arab horse, and spoken in his ear, 'would like to see you. We had better go at once.'

'What about the animals, the baggage, and the Assassins?' Noor asked.

'I have already given orders that your goods be brought to the castle in carts,' Farid told her. 'As for the robbers and their animals, that is for the Prince to decide, if you remember. They are under arrest.'

Farid, riding between Adam and the Turkestani captain, told them about the palace. 'It is called Qala Kavi, and was built as the central stronghold of the Arabs who came here over a thousand years ago. They say that the great conqueror, General Kutaiba himself, designed it. The idea was to hold, from here, the entire mountain area of the northern Hindu Kush.'

'I suppose that the word *kavi* comes from the Arabic for "strong"?' Azambai asked him.

'Wrong. *Kavi* is the ancient Persian word for a mystic priest, one who knows secrets, mysteries of the other world. These people were often kings as well. You probably know that Zoroaster started one of the great religions in Balkh, to the north-west of here, parallel to where you are going, in Afghan Turkestan. It spread through Iran, and influenced many other religions. Well, Zoroaster made his start when he converted a *kavi*, about two thousand five hundred years ago.'

'So this place dates from that time?'

'According to legend, the castle was taken from the followers of Zarathustra, which was his real name. That means in the ancient tongue, by the way, "camelman". We still use the word. The building was probably only enlarged by Kutaiba.'

The castle was entered, like so many in Central Asia, by tunnels, with large quantities of rocks piled in shelves above them, which could be rolled down, blocking the entrances, in time of war.

The horses, clearly knowing the way, walked straight into the large openings and plodded up the long inclines, lined with boxes and barrels, stored supplies, which were stacked on either side of the long corridors hewn from the rock. 'The passages twist like this,' said Farid, 'so that they can be defended easily. If anyone got through before we could block the entrances, each passage could be held by as few as three soldiers.'

The whole way was lit by rushlights, projecting from the walls.

Eventually the horses emerged into broad daylight. Adam and Noor, followed by the captain and then the rest of the caravanners, blinked and peered at the unexpected sight of a garden, full of flowers in full bloom, with fountains playing. Twenty or thirty men, dressed like Farid, were sitting and standing in groups, as if waiting for something.

The entire garden was built on an enormous parapet, a ledge with crenellated walls, jutting out from the mountainside.

Farid led them to the edge, from which they could see the orchards and the villages through which they had passed earlier, hundreds of feet below.

'This garden,' Farid told them, 'is quite artificial, in the sense that all its soil has been carried up here and is several feet thick. Beneath that there is only rock.'

A giant's window box, Noor thought. It must have been the size of several football pitches, with a pavilion at one end, climbing roses, jasmine, fig trees growing in barrels, and the smell of flowers everywhere.

They walked along a marble path, with fountains on either side, to the pavilion, built of honey-coloured translucent stone, a type of alabaster which is not uncommon in Afghanistan. There were some strikingly beautiful carpets on the floor, and incense was burning in a golden-domed censer, studded with semi-precious stones, the smoke rising through small star-shaped holes in its upper surface.

A semi-circle of long, fat cushions was arranged before a red and green lacquered wooden throne. Farid motioned to the three – Noor, Azambai and Adam – to sit. The rest of the party, craning their necks like yokels at a fair, were seated at a greater distance from the area of authority.

They were served with a drink of rosewater and musk, and handed small agate bowls containing sugared almonds, tiny green raisins and nuts. Farid passed the time, while they were waiting for the Prince, by telling them about the principality.

The Prince was a great landowner, and also had enormous herds of sheep, horses and cattle. This place, Qala Kavi, was nothing less than an independent domain. It was the centre of a series of valleys and fertile tablelands, two to five thousand metres above sea level. Noor realized, remembering her geography lessons in England, that the valleys themselves were as many as fifteen times as high as what would qualify as a mountain in the West. Fifteen mountains high . . .

Farid did not know how many people there were in the principality, which covered more than three days' journey in any direction from the castle. He was the *wazir*, chief minister, of the sovereign, but this involved more than ceremonial tasks: supervision of the army, collecting taxes, judging law cases and keeping the Prince informed about 'everything of importance'.

As they talked, green tea was served, made from water boiled in a samovar. In this thin air, it took over half an hour, and a great deal of glowing charcoal puffed with bellows, to get the water hot enough.

They must have been sitting there for over an hour when Adam, accustomed to the ways of feudal chiefs, recognized the soft, slowly rising beat of a single drum which signalled the potentate's approach. He could see, looking down the marble pathway, people rising to their feet, guards raising unsheathed swords, and a general air of expectancy as more drums took up the rhythm.

A small group of men, courtiers young and old, dressed in wide-sleeved robes of the padded, bright coloured Bokhara kind, filed in and arranged themselves behind the throne.

Two or three minutes later, preceded by a herald with a massive, gold-bound stick, the sceptre of office, the Prince padded softly into his pavilion.

He was between forty and fifty years of age, tall, with typically Afghan features: an aquiline nose, black eyes and long head. His curly hair was cut short, and his head was bare. Over trousers of white cotton, and a long blouse secured by a red sash, he wore a long woollen robe of dark blue, closed in front by a gold sword-belt, studded with smooth diamonds. There was an immense polished Badakhshan ruby gleaming on the buckle.

The Prince mounted the three steps of his throne and sat down, smiling at the bowing courtiers, and took the sceptre from its guardian.

Farid stepped forward.

'May the Lord's shadow never become less! I beg permission to introduce our guests.'

The Prince inclined his head.

'Magnetic pole of the Earth. The Lady Noor Sharifi, *Agha-i* Adam Durany, *Shaghali* Captain Azambai.'

The Prince handed his sceptre back to the courtier and stepped down from his throne. 'Welcome. Approach.'

He held out his hand to each in turn.

The captain, recalling a passage from the Classics, spoke for them all: 'Rendering homage to the Presence of the Monarch is an honour for his slaves.'

Just as Adam realized, with dismay, that they had not performed the *nazaria*, the ceremony of offering gold and precious jewels or sweet spices and perfumes to the potentate, he saw that Farid had not forgotten. He lifted a piece of red velvet from an inlaid brass tray carried by a splendidly dressed servant and revealed three large gold coins, *ashrafis*, and some silver boxes, such as are used for amber, incense and the like. In accordance with custom, the Prince touched each object in turn, signifying acceptance.

He led the three to the curtains behind the throne. They passed through, into a kiosk build of cedar-wood and fretted with geometrical patterns, where three sofas were ranged before a low table loaded with an astonishing variety of dishes.

'You have come far?' said the Prince, taking up a leg of spiced chicken and smearing it with yoghurt.

'From Paghman,' said Noor, adding, just in time, and just in case, 'Majesty.'

'My name is Rajab,' said the Prince, 'and you may call me that.'

'Hearing is obeying,' said the captain, to set the tone; 'but, *Jalalat*, Majesty, we are in the habit of calling people by their proper titles. You will forgive us if we relapse into that habit.'

'All right, then,' said the Prince, obviously pleased, 'if you persist in these archaic ways down there in Paghman.'

'Thank you, *Hazrat*, your Presence.'

'Are the Russians giving you much trouble?'

'Quite a lot.'

'Durany, you bear a famous name. Are you getting rid of the invaders?'

'*Hazrat*, we are doing our best. That is why we are here.'

'Indeed?' Prince Rajab looked at Adam sharply.

'With your permission, I can explain, Living Prince.'

'Explain, *Agha*.'

Adam told him, briefly, about the war and the purpose of the Sher-Qala Commando.

'Well, my friend, you're halfway there already. You will have trouble with the glaciers to the north, since you can't use the icefree road that the *Rouss* have seized. But I don't see why you shouldn't manage it. Stranger things have been done.'

'Thank you.'

'I can help you, too.'

Adam said, 'Any help is in the cause of the nation.'

'It is my duty, as you are reminding me, young man,' said the Prince. He added softly, almost as if he was speaking to himself, rhyming the lines, 'Let them not say, "We went to Rajab and he sent us away."'

Suddenly he looked up. 'Yes, you need help. Do you know how to make smokeless fires, so that you don't get seen by the enemy?'

Adam and the others shook their heads. Such an art might be useful, Adam thought, but what about supplies, money, weapons?

The Prince looked at him, excitedly. It was obviously something he was very interested in. 'Then you shall learn. As a matter of fact, not many people do know about it. Here's what you do:

'Cut your wood – bamboo is the best – into very small pieces and then into thin strips. Slice these strips into shavings, which must be carefully dried. Light a pile of the shavings. As soon as it is flaring well, put charcoal, piece by piece, on top. When you've got this going, it will burn without any smoke for many hours. You can use such a fire for cooking and for keeping yourself warm.'

He sat back with a smile of great satisfaction. The secret had been imparted.

'*Pakiza*, perfect,' said Adam; 'I'd often heard of the smokeless fires which the mountain bandits used, but nobody ever seemed to know exactly how they were built.'

Prince Rajab scanned the faces of his listeners, one after another. Noor wondered whether his interest in trifles was a pose, a usual one among the many aristocrats who had visited her father's house in the old days. It was said that such people behaved like this to avoid committing themselves when pressed. After all, a prince was not supposed to refuse anything to anyone: his only defence might be to retreat into eccentricity. 'His Highness is having one of his turns,' might then be his salvation; or 'He can't concentrate for a moment, you know. His father was just the same.' Peasants, too, she remembered, practised the retreat into near-imbecility as a form of self-protection. She'd even seen it done in Italy.

'Friends, I told you about the fire because I am superstitious. I believe that when something comes into one's mind it has to be said, as it may originate from a higher level of the mind.'

Rajab looked around, as if expecting an answer. Nobody

could think of anything to say. The Prince frowned. 'Where was I? Oh yes, we live in a time when many changes are taking place, when each must do what he or she can, when effort is effort, but such things as knowledge, equipment, gold even, are forms of effort, concentrated power, like the power locked in petrol . . .' He called for tea and stroked a long-haired white cat with blue eyes, which had appeared from nowhere and was rubbing itself against him.

To the captain he said, 'This is the *Jihad-i-Muqaddas*, the Sacred Struggle. I cannot spare any men, because we have to prepare for when, God forbid, the Russians try to come here. But it is written that those who help and equip the *Muhjahidin* in a just war are equal to those who actually engage in that war. You can have anything from me. I have horses and pack-animals, gold and weapons, even agents in Turkestan.'

'God bless you, sir,' said Azambai.

'That's settled, then,' said Prince Rajab. The Prince rose, to show that the audience was over, and the travellers were led to their sumptuous quarters, for the afternoon siesta.

5 Kara Dagh is Icebound

The Great Pass

JULY 14

'Trust in God – but make sure that you tie your camel, too!' Living Prince Rajab embraced the travellers warmly, as he escorted them next day to the caravan trail beside the mulberry meadows.

'And go in safety to your next halting-place.'

The quotation from the Sayings of the Prophet was especially appropriate, Adam thought, as he gingerly mounted the small and skittish Bactrian camel which Rajab had given him. This was his first time on such an animal; but at dawn on the high plateau he already felt warm, sitting between its double humps.

Azambai preferred the job of caravan-master, after the 'aristocratic courtesies', as he called them. Being born in the Soviet Union, even if one was of noble descent, did not exactly give one a taste for the mixed blessings of a court. Hospitality there might be, but there was also an air of sophistication that he found unsettling. He preferred the directness of the Nuristanis, who weren't at all affected by the castle's pomp, or the behaviour of the Afghan soldiers, who had their own, more direct, ways and conversation. After all, he was a professional military man.

The Prince sent a guide, Razan ('Resolute') Khan, with the company. Razan was a wrestler, specializing in the ancient form of the sport popular with the Central Asians. Its exponents covered themselves with olive oil, flapped their arms like birds when approaching their match, and had to be able to perform a complicated dance as well.

Razan was bulky, but very muscular, short and barrel-chested like many Hindu Kush mountaineers, and he spoke several of the many languages of Afghanistan. He also carried a heavy leather bag, containing big gold coins of the minting of the old Bokhara amirs, from which he paid, at every halt, for all the expenses of the party.

The Eagle was hardly in a position to object: but when he did demur, more for the look of it than for any other reason, Razan grunted. 'The Prince could not have guests paying for anything while they were still in his country.'

There were more serais and teahouses on the road, as they travelled through the area which was now more Turkic than Persian. Here, at several thousand feet, the neat, vine-covered wooden buildings offered shade, refreshment and conversation of a kind which, in other countries, would have spoken of extreme refinement.

The road, if that was the right name for it, still passed through gorges, skirted ravines with foaming rivers rushing through them, and meandered between fields of oats and barley, clover grown for fodder and wild turnips. In some of the villages, people made baskets and leather goods, cloth and silverware. They sold these items to merchants, travelling in caravans, who passed this way once or twice a year, trading salt, trinkets, and manufactured goods from northern Turkestan.

The people, slant-eyed and broad-faced, brought out bowls of mare's milk, pieces of embroidered felt, bunches of wild parsnips, mountain garlic, and beautiful gaddi sheep, whose ewes lambed twice a year. The travellers drank tea with salt instead of sugar, to replace the saline in their blood, which they had lost in the exertions of the mountain trail. Noor passed many an hour – stolen from her rest time – learning the precise way to soak the delicious bread in the tangy tea, to milk sheep and goats, in trying on wild-cat jackets, bargaining for strange jewellery or deerskin boots. One did not really need money, for the people delighted in barter, and would consider anything as a possible article of trade. Even if one bought nothing, bargaining was expected. 'Later, if God wills,' brought smiles. Adam tried, once or twice, to say 'I am at war, I don't buy trinkets.' It didn't work. The area seemed utterly isolated from the war.

At Cedar Gorge, a village perched on the escarpment of the southern Hindu Kush, the village chief pointed with pride to the rolling meadows and flower gardens, but warned Adam of the dangers of the climb that was before him.

'To escape the *Rouss*, you will have to take the ancient way, directly north from here,' he said, 'but that means that you could easily lose your way if there are too many landslides, ice avalanches, even. I do not recommend it, sir.'

They could read the problem, written by nature into the very landscape. They could see the cedar and oak forests, about two thousand metres above. Then, further up the mountain, the tall pines began, and continued, becoming sparser, to a height where perpetual ice was visible. Just below this wound the road, round and round, gaining a few feet every hundred yards, up to the great pass: no more than a cleft between two blue-white glaciers, the gateway through the Hindu Kush, the road to Turkestan.

Here, at Cedar Gorge, they were not much more than sixty kilometres to the west of the Russian north-south road, which was constantly patrolled by Soviet aircraft, to keep it clear of 'bandits'. For the first time since they had escaped from the Kohistan foothills, they saw, as well as heard, Russian helicopters, the big ones, Mi-24s, on reconnaissance.

'Nobody has come through the pass for the past two weeks,' said the village chief. 'That worries me, because traders always want to come here at this time of year, and we generally get one caravan, sometimes two, big and small, every week.'

'So you think the high pass may be blocked?' Adam asked him.

'Either that, or else one of the smaller ravines, through which the road passes, is impassable, on the northern side. You cannot tell from here.' He shielded his eyes against the glare, and looked towards the looming mountain.

'Well,' said the captain, 'we have already done our share of clearing rocks from the road wherever we found them, thus far. Perhaps someone coming the other way will do the same for us.'

They set off as soon as the sun was warm enough, saying goodbye to the once taciturn Razan, who now bear-hugged everyone and seemed genuinely sorry to see them go. When the caravan was a hundred yards up the incline they were to follow, Adam looked back and saw Razan still standing there, beside his beautiful Indarabi horse, flapping his arms up and down: the ancient victory signal of the great wrestlers of the mountains.

The south face of the mountain had no villages, but there were, here and there, rough resthouses of undressed stone, with wooden doors, into which people and animals crowded as soon as the sun went down.

The drop in temperature was rapid and frightening. One moment the travellers were savouring the last rays of the sun; the next, it seemed, they were huddling deeper into their furs. Shivering, they coaxed their animals, who always themselves wanted to shelter as soon as it became as cold as this. Upwards they climbed to reach the miserable – but yet unutterably welcome – hovels which would save them from freezing to death. And this was summertime.

'*Haraka, haraka* – on, on.' The chant was almost continuous now. Above 2,500 metres, eight thousand feet high, the road was too slippery to give the animals any foothold. The sun, which warmed them just enough to make the daytime journey endurable, also affected the icy ground underfoot, making it so glassy that the horses' hooves often could not get a proper grip. Their grooms claimed that, at this height, only yaks could climb higher.

As they rested on the third day out of Cedar Gorge, the insistence of the grooms became impossible to resist. Threatened with firearms, they would not budge. Adam refused to pay them, but they only answered that they would rather have nothing than die by falling off a cliff.

Shahrdar Haidar, who had come this way to join The Eagle after the death of Captain Juma, swore that he had been with caravans which had managed to cover even worse ground than this. Everyone found it hard to believe him. In the end, the hired men and their animals were paid off. Shouldering their forty-eight pound packs, stripped of luxuries and unnecessary weight, the guerrillas struggled on. Unaccustomed to walking, it took them two more days to get into good enough condition to make any real progress.

Here and there, mercifully, and to their great surprise, the trail was clear. Something, and nobody could work out what, perhaps underground hot springs, made the path icefree for quite long stretches of the way. Sometimes, therefore, they were able to make good progress.

Nevertheless, it seemed as if they had been on the road for months, years even. In fact, by then it had been only eleven days.

They got through the high pass safely enough. It was like something from a film about exploration in the region of the North Pole. The pass itself, formed by a fissure between two mountains, was nothing more than a cleft with peaks on either side, peaks of ice, with ice underfoot, ice ahead, everywhere the blue glare of ultraviolet glinting from a thousand ice-faces.

There was no sign of any other caravan, or of an icefall which would have blocked the road. Once or twice they found great humps, making the road like a switchback, undulating for miles. These were caused by avalanches which had been partly cleared or had half melted, making it just possible, with great effort, to climb up the small hill and slide down the other side, ready for the next, inevitable mound.

Beyond the pass they had expected to see a scene like the one from which they had come, the pines shading down to the cedars, then the oaks, and then perhaps smiling valleys and pastures, herds of goats and sheep, villages and friendly faces.

In fact, all that they could see, with the trail winding away into the distance, was a deep fissure, without snow or ice, a gouge like the brown of an iced cake showing through the frosting, running for some hundred yards, until it ran out – at another wall of ice.

That was why there were no caravans, no travellers. The road was blocked.

When they reached the wall, Adam and the captain at once realized that this was not something that they, that anyone, could clear away. There had been an ice-fall: not just an avalanche, but the subsidence of a small, partially melting, glacier. Or even, perhaps, a small earthquake. A piece of ice, solid and weighing thousands of tons, had slid down from a plateau above, and shattered into the cleft through which the road formerly went. Then it had re-frozen.

There was no doubt about it: they had a mountain to cross. 'This,' said Haidar, 'is Kara Dagh, the Black Mountain. It is snow and ice on the other side, too. The only good thing we can say about the situation is that this is the last barrier between us and Turkestan. If we get over it, we shall have reached some sort of safety.'

On more close inspection, the ice-encrusted walls on either side of the ice-fall were neither sheer nor completely solid. Here and there one could see what looked like goat-tracks. Perhaps later in the summer, say by late August, it might even be possible to traverse it without too much difficulty. So, although possible now, it would be very difficult indeed. And they were too heavily laden.

They would have to abandon their arms.

Sorrowfully, they collected their weapons and ammunition, piled them in stacks and covered them with snow. This lightened each man's load by more than thirty pounds. Estimating that the crossing should take two days at the most, they shed all food except what they would need for that time. They kept, too, grease, a kettle and butane gaslamp, and a few medicines, for each group of five. Then they started the climb.

They had reckoned without the absence of shelter huts, and the fact that some of the party were better climbers, younger, in better physical condition, than others. They had no climbing gear, no ropes, no proper boots. None of them had any experience of mountaineering. In that first day they reached the top of a peak, to find that it led nowhere. As night fell the sixty huddled together, keeping one another just warm enough to survive, their faces covered with blankets, breathing painfully and dozing fitfully in the thin air.

The next day, seeing a path below, they split into four parties to test the ground, since the ice was often cracked, with fissures covered, in places, by only a thin layer of crushed ice. It was as if the whole mountain was surfaced with an ice whose brittleness was of an unusual order.

The third day, as they were skirting an outcrop of black rock, along a wide ledge of ice, twenty men, without a sound, disappeared into a fissure which opened up ahead of them suddenly at the same moment that the whole ledge on which they stood collapsed. With a rumbling like rolling thunder, thousands of tons of ice came sliding down the slope above them, like a diabolical mechanism, something from a nightmare, and slowly, with uncanny finality, sealed their grave.

The men and women of the Commando struggled on, tears freezing on their faces, so numbed by the disaster that they did not know if they felt fear or horror more strongly, shaken by uncontrollable shivering, some seeing evil spirits or – in Qasim's case – the leering faces of fat, well-fed Russians, in big warm fur caps, looking down from the sky.

On the third and fourth days they had no food at all to eat. Water was thawed from the ice, after what seemed an age: the pressure in the butane gas cylinder had almost gone. Every half-hour they had to stop and exercise, rubbing their swollen eyes to get the small muscles to work again, reeling from snow-blindness, retching from mountain-sickness. Then they plodded on again.

They moved in pairs now, a stronger helping a weaker one, until they found that it needed three people, and then four, to maintain any kind of progress. Those who had the strength spoke encouragingly to others; people who had any power left in their arms pummelled those who lay down and asked to be left to die. Several seemed to have a sort of fever, a trip-hammer thumping in the back of their heads, noses bleeding. They were all chewing anything made of soft leather, to get some nourishment, or, at least, some sense of eating.

On the morning of the fourth day, a whole *dasta*, five of the Nuristanis, holding onto one another, fell over a yawning precipice onto jagged ice-rocks, three hundred feet below the trail. The survivors looked over at them, helplessly: were almost relieved to see that there was nothing that they could attempt to do. The men were undoubtedly dead, smashed on the ice.

'*Haraka, haraka. Bala, bala*. Move, move. Upwards, upwards.' Every step, every breath, was torture now.

Just before mid-morning, struggling to the top of a bank of snow, Captain Azambai, limping from a wound where a boulder had hit him as it rolled down the mountain just after the high pass, looked over the ridge. There, beyond a rolling, downward incline, he saw, unbelieving, a screen of small trees, then some larger ones, then, rising from the snow and ice, a mountain, and a valley carpeted in green.

They had conquered the Hindu Kush.

BOOK 10

The Wolves of Turkestan

'One of the immediate tasks of Soviet power in Central Asia is to establish proper relations with the peoples of Turkestan, to prove to them by deed the sincerity of our desire to uproot all vestiges of imperialism.

– Vladimir Ilyich Lenin
*Letter to Comrades
Communists of Turkestan.*

1 Like lice on a dinner plate . . .

The North Slope of Kara Dagh Mountain
Afghan Turkestan

JULY 16

'*Nishanchi* – Sharpshooter!'

'*Bayim* – Sir?'

'What do you make of that?'

Lieutenant Ghalib handed the man on watch his field glasses, and pointed at the group of darkish dots struggling down the icy slopes of the Black Mountain.

The clumsy figures, moving slowly even on the steep incline, looked like things he had once seen weaving about on a microscope slide. There seemed to be about thirty of them, straggling in a line abreast, some alone, some bunched together. They could not be wolves or bears: they were men all right.

The Nishanchi handed back the glasses. 'They may be hostile, Nikolais, *efendim*.'

The group was within a mile or so of the high, outcropping crags where the main body of the Turkestani former soldiers were bivouacked, on a reconnaissance mission, two thousand metres up on the Black Mountain.

Survivors of a Russian air crash? The remnant of some mountaineering expedition? The rebel patrol was small, and if this was a trick, it could be wiped out.

Lieutenant Ghalib ran to the foxhole in the snow where his commander, Major Yildiz Han, lay fast asleep. He had been up all night; the unit always kept one third on alert, the remainder resting or out on patrol, ceaselessly prowling in the permafrost. The enemy might be anywhere: anywhere, that is, except on the slopes of the impossible Kara Dagh, Black Mountain, opposite, where nobody could survive for long.

'*Bimbashi bay*!' Ghalib tugged at the collar of the Major's wolfskin coat, sticking out from the top of his sleeping bag, 'Wake, *Bayim*!'

The major was alert in a second, feeling for his revolver, deep inside his fur pocket to keep it from freezing solid.

'Report, Ghalib!' He struggled to his feet.

'Reporting, sir! Party of men approaching at approximately eight hundred metres.'

'Good God! Alert the men.'

Ghalib gave the order to *Chavush* Chelik. 'Sergeant, alert all men for possible hostiles, eight hundred metres at eleven o'clock.' Chelik saluted and was off at a trot.

'Where exactly are they, Ghalib?'

'That's just it, sir. They're coming down Kara Dagh.'

'North slope? *Buyuk Tenri*, Great God, that's impossible! Nobody could mount an attack from there. The lowest pass is at four thousand feet.'

'*Bayim*, take the glasses.'

'I've got mine here.'

The commander pulled his blanket over him like a cape and gasped as the icy air knifed his lungs. After the fug of the foxhole, this was always a shock; one never got used to it. His breath froze in the air, and the crystalline snow crackled underfoot.

Sergeant Mahmut Demir was already at the advanced observation point with the artillery telescope. He came to attention when he saw the major.

'Amazing! Like lice on a dinner plate, *Bimbashi efendi*!'

Yes, that was just what they looked like. The greyish figures, some of them crawling on all fours now, were still advancing, making for the lower ground just in front of, and below, the strong-point.

Did they know that they were being watched? By the look of them, they would not even care. People in that condition were as good as dead. They were moving as if by a common will, part of a single organism, which told them one thing: if they moved, they lived, if they stopped, they died. The watchers could almost sense that will, like an invisible clock which had been wound up and was forcing the common body, like a clock's hands, to move, move, move.

People were usually found at a later stage than this. Lying, frozen to death, the snow drifts covering them, gently offering nature's murder, then her burial. Nature, thought the major, who rears and comforts us, and is trying to kill us at the same time.

But were they Russians?

'We could pick them off from here, sir.' Sergeant Demir's people came from Soviet Turkestan. His whole family had been wiped out by the Russians, for resisting *Ruslashtirma*, 'Russification' as the Turks called it, in the USSR three decades ago. And that was after the famine, in which a million had died.

The major looked at the crawling figures, then up to the birchwood flagpole which stood on the heights behind them. Sergeant Chelik, a stickler for tradition, had just raised it, uncaring, now that action might be near, whether a Russian scout came that way or not.

The war flag, the banner of the three yak tails, was the *sanjak*: the battle ensign of the ancient chiefs. The tails hung from a cross, the emblem of conquest which had made the Crusaders, when they heard of it, believe that Gengiz Khan was their imagined Christian ally, Prester John, sweeping from the East to save them.

'Chelik. Get the rifles out, but keep them in the hot-box.' The firing mechanisms would freeze unless the guns were kept warm when they were not being fired. On the other hand, they had to be kept ready. Hence the hot-box: a wooden chest, lined with hay and with heated bricks to provide a constant warmth. What some people, in more comfortable lands, knew as a slow cooker, using it in their quiet winters for the evening stew.

'Prepare to fire on command, Chelik.'

The figures were likely to be lost deserters or else a Russian trap. The Russians were wily, and they had been trying to trap and destroy the Yildiz Group for two years now.

'Fire at will at any hostile movement, Chelik.'

'Major *bay*. Perhaps they are a Nikolai unit, decimated by the Muhjahidin?'

'I don't think so. There aren't any Muhjahidin on the mountain: and, if things are so bad on the other side of the Hindu Kush that Nikolais have to struggle over the high passes to get back to Russia, then the war is over.'

The major looked again. Most of them were still crawling, but more slowly, as if the sight of the screen of trees had actually eroded their will, made them less, not more, able to carry on. Paradoxical, but he had seen that happen, too.

Or they could be acting a part.

'The rangefinder measures them at six hundred metres now, *bayim*.' Sergeant Demir put the tiny optical instrument back in his warm inside pocket.

The major shrugged. 'My guess is that they will never make it to the trees. But let's watch them for a little longer.'

The Turks were the only highly trained guerrilla band operating in the frozen mountains of the Baghlan area, south of the Oxus which formed the Soviet border. Major Yildiz had collected them from a crack unit of the Afghan Army, all Turkestanis, shortly after the large-scale desertions began under the communist government, just before the Russians moved in. A professional soldier, Yildiz was not politically-minded, but he considered the Red coups to be banditry, not politics. There had been no elections, no campaigning, no consulting the people. On the contrary, helpless civilians had been shot, strategic points taken, fawning puppets of Moscow installed in power. Treason, to Yildiz, was what the men of the Kabul gang, as he called them, were engaged in.

When, even before the invasion, the Afghan Chief of Staff, General Abdul-Karim Mustaghani, had refused to acknowledge the communist regime and had taken to the mountains, Yildiz had made up his mind. The general had mustered his troops north of the Hindu Kush, and Yildiz, answering his call, organized himself independently, choosing the Baghlan area, the far north, as his own area of operations. The major and other rebel commanders had been very successful. Over one million Tajiks in the north of Afghanistan were in revolt, battling against eight hundred Soviet tanks and clouds of aircraft.

Yildiz was in command of Resistance for this area in the mountains, where Soviet mountain and arctic forces, hastily summoned from the Finland border, were reported to be operating.

Yildiz and his men watched the approaching figures for an hour. During that time, they covered only two hundred yards.

They were moving even more slowly now, and – five hundred yards from the soldiers, they had apparently not seen them yet.

They wore no identifiable uniforms, no badges. Only furs.

'There aren't enough of us, to risk an attack on them if they're armed; and if they are not and they stop moving, they'll all be frozen to death before we can either kill or rescue them,' said the lieutenant.

Kill or rescue. Which was it to be? Should he flip a coin? Major Yildiz Han would have to make a decision soon. If it was a trap, the newcomers would have grenades, ready to throw and to blow up their rescuers as they ran to them. They could, just might, be Russians, dropped by a helicopter out of the Turks' line of vision, who had worked their way along the ridges to appear here, giving just the impression of a stranded band that they did now.

'*Bayim.*' It was the lieutenant. 'If this is a trick, are the Nikolais not taking too great a risk? If the roles were reversed, they would shoot us without any enquiry. Exposed as they are now, we could kill all of them as soon as we liked. I don't think that anyone would take such a tactical decision.'

'Perhaps you're right, Ghalib.'

'What do you say, Demir?' Take a second opinion and then make a command decision. Command was what officers were for.

'Major *bay*. On reflection, I wish to volunteer to go forward and see whether they make any treacherous move. We could also send small parties, well dispersed, to approach those of them who are walking or lying singly. In that way we would risk less casualties if they have grenades.'

'Yes, I can see no sign of any weapons. As you say, it would have to be grenades. Very well, sergeant. Go and look at one who seems really feeble. We'll watch you through our glasses. If there is a false move, keep your head down. We'll kill the lot immediately. Dig into the snow if you hear a shot.'

'*Bayim!*'

The burly sergeant saluted, tightened the buckle of the massive belt over his fur-lined white parka, clipped five Soviet Army stick grenades to it, and ran forward into the snow, zigzagging like a fox.

The grey figures had not seen him yet. Major Han took a

rifle from the hot-box and wrapped it in a blanket. He tried to squint through the optical sight. It was already frozen, covered in ice. He gave it back to the armourer. 'Light a fire with some plastic explosive and keep this warm. If anyone attacks Demir, I want to get him first.'

In each of the foxholes, little bits of plastic were already flickering. The men did not need orders to warm their guns: there were so few options in their lives that they carried on, automatically, doing what they could. In this way, they worked as individuals. But their discipline was such that any independent action was only in anticipation of an order. Nobody would fire without one, or unless his superior was killed, and no order could be given. This training was what had made the Turkish troops the most successful, man for man, of all the nationalities in the Korean war.

Louis Palmer at first thought that the big man in the white snow smock and Kalpak wolfskin hat, who wriggled up to him on the frozen ground, must be another member of the expedition. But who? No, it must be a Russian: clean-shaven, with grey eyes, slightly slanting ones. Well, without a weapon, with no strength left, he was a dead man. An American, fighting with the rebels, a mercenary, a bandit, as the Russians had always claimed. Who would believe that he was a volunteer?

The newcomer turned Palmer over where he lay on the ground, satisfied himself that he was not armed, looked around at the other staggering figures of the Commando, and picked the American up. Carrying Palmer across his shoulders, Sergeant Demir strode back to Major Han.

The survivors of the Sher-Qala Commando had reached safety in Afghan Turkestan.

2 Guerrilla City

Kurt Burj 'Wolf Redoubt'
Reed Forest
Afghan Turkestan

JULY 17

Old, she was feeling, very, very old and weary: an old woman – there was no other word for it. Noor half sat, half lay on the bunk and very slowly looked around, at first without much interest. There was a hanging kerosene lamp on a ceiling hook; racks for rifles, rough-hewn wooden walls. A long table stood in the middle of the hut. The windows were shuttered, but a cold breeze was coming through them, stirring the long bead curtains. It seemed to be nighttime.

She was lying on a Turkoman rug, with a straw-stuffed pillow covered in coarse cotton material, at the head of the bed. Beside it, sitting on a stool and holding a jug and bowl, was Karima, gaunt but attentive.

'Noorjan, have something to drink.'

She swallowed the soup. It was warm, with a flavour of meat and herbs. Then she remembered the mountains, the ice, the journey across Kara Dagh.

'Where are we, Karima?' She felt a little better now.

'Mistress, we are with the Wolves.'

'Wolves?'

'The Wolves of Turkestan. Turkoman guerrillas, from our Royal Army.'

'Beyond the mountains?'

'Beyond the mountains. In Turkestan.'

'Are we safe?'

'We are safe, mistress. This is a halting-place in a wooden town hidden by huge reeds. It is called Kurt Burj, "Wolf Castle".'

Adam. Where was he? She was still terribly thirsty, but so weak that she wanted to lie back and sleep. She asked, hesitantly, 'How are the others?'

'We have lost many men . . .'

'Where is The Eagle?'

'He is with us. I'll tell him that you are awake.'

At that moment Adam, with Qasim and Zelikov, threw open the door and walked into the hut.

The Eagle was wearing a long silk Turkestani robe, multicoloured and padded, and still had a week's growth of beard. There were black shadows under his eyes.

'Noorjan.' He just stood there, looking.

'Are you all right, Adam?'

'Yes, I'm all right.'

Karima shooed him out of the hut: 'The mistress needs rest, *komondon*. Leave her alone now. I shall look after her.'

Adam left the hut. The major and Sergeant Demir were waiting outside in the moonlight.

'They are well, *komondon*?'

'Not well, but recovering, thank you, major.'

They walked through the trees in the forest clearing to a second hut, cunningly camouflaged against air surveillance. The whole camp was protected by living creepers, growing like a roof among the poplar and other trees which grew thickly in this part of the Oxus River plains.

The Wolves' base had been hacked out of the *taiga*: thick undergrowth above which creeper-clad trees towered. The place was some two thousand metres lower than the heights of the Black Mountain. The Eagle and the survivors of his band had been brought here, in darkness, tied like sacks of grain across the saddles of the Mongolian ponies which the rebels used for mountain travel. They had then slept for eighteen hours.

'The Russians think that there are only tigers and wild boar in this *taiga*,' said the major, 'and they only have patches of it on their own side of the river, but ours is all of seven miles square, and crawling with bandits – us!'

He led the way into the hut. There, slumped in various attitudes of exhaustion, were the rest of the expedition's survivors.

'They'll be all right in the morning. Nobody has frostbite: they're just starving, that's all.' Captain Babanur was the unit's medical officer. He added, 'I'm glad you are keeping Zelikov with you: some of our men wanted to rough him up when they found out he was a Russian, and I'm short of sutures for sewing on any pieces that might get cut off!' He was a large, beefy man, with the very white face that is often seen among Tartars, and had a stethoscope dangling, like a badge of office, from his neck.

'They have all had glucose and vitamins, a non-voluntary contribution from the Soviet Army medical branch,' the doctor told Adam, 'and we'll have to keep the lot of you here for two weeks at least, to recuperate.'

'That's not possible,' Adam told him, 'we'll all have to be back on our feet in less than a week. We have important work to do.'

'All right, call it five days. I'll give them meat stew and yoghurt three times a day and plenty of exercise.' The doctor sounded resigned. He added, 'I don't know why it is that you people are always so keen to be patched up so that you can go back and get your heads blown off. In industrialized countries, where I have worked, the least headache or cut finger and they want a piece of paper saying that they must have a long rest, on full pay.'

'Ah,' said Adam, 'the difference, doctor, is that in our kind of business, "full pay" *is* getting back into action. That's all the pay we get. So you mustn't stand in our way.'

They all laughed.

The scorching heat of the Oxus plain was a complete contrast, except for the chilly nights, after the terrible glaciers of Kara Dagh. The Turkestan operational area seemed like another world.

The forest petered out into groves of immense tamarisks and huge reed-beds in the marshes which followed the course of the great Oxus River, to the north. It was full of game: teeming with pheasants, marmot, jerboas, and giant fluffy bustards which could hardly fly. The *jairan*, graceful gazelles, nibbled at the green shoots of the grass and flowers which covered the jungle's floor. The Turkish soldiers even kept flocks of sheep, which grazed on the natural hay formed by the parched summer grass whose roots were still alive. There were crops for people, too, wild liquorice, sugar-cane, fruits and vegetables.

The live-off-the-land plan organized by General Mustaghani, the overall Resistance commander of the north, had turned the forest settlement into an extraordinary place. The major showed Adam the workshops and storehouses first. Here, in addition to repairing and servicing weapons, the soldiers had actually set up a munitions factory. 'We obtain, from local deposits, the sulphur and nitre which, mixed with charcoal in the proportions of two, fifteen and three parts respectively, makes excellent gunpowder,' said Major Yildiz Han. 'And,' he added, with all the pride of the pioneer, 'we get all the lead we want from an outcrop of rock near here, and make our own bullets.' Fires were built on the rocks, melting the lead from the veins. It was then taken to the moulds, where the bullets were easily made.

Parts of the forest, which had once been clearings, were overgrown with immense beds of reeds, sometimes standing twenty feet high, their roots deep in the marsh which underlay the leavy loam. The Wolves, following the pattern of the marsh people, had built enormous halls, *muzifs*, entirely of reeds, great structures which soared in arches, reminiscent of the cathedrals of the Middle Ages. The buildings were closely patterned on the dwellings and near-palaces of the marsh people of Iraq. Indeed, this part of the world had been colonized by people from there, over a thousand years ago, after the Saracenic conquest.

Log cabins, reed houses and even tents were covered with fast-growing vines, forming a matted, perfect camouflage. Even where there were bare patches in the forest, creepers had been trained to break up the surface pattern and to provide walkways, safe from aerial reconnaissance.

'It took us over a year to get right,' the major said, in answer to Adam's question.

Eight hundred men lived and worked here, going out on sorties for three days at a time, and returning to be replaced by fresh troops.

That such a place, with a school, library, garages, hospital, volleyball court and machine-shops, could exist, within forty miles of major Russian military installations, was astonishing.

'Supposing,' Adam asked Major Han, 'you were betrayed, or the Russians decided to destroy the reed-beds or the forest with napalm, which they have been using in the south?'

The major tapped his nose. 'As you must know from your Kabul experience, there are hardly three thousand communists in the whole of this country. On the other hand, almost everyone else working for the Nikolais is prepared to help the Resistance. They fear for their families, or they wouldn't be working for the Russians at all. We get all the information we need. We can't easily be taken by surprise.'

The settlement was only sixty kilometres south-west of Qizil Qala port, their destination. From there, the Turks explained, they were able to get all kinds of things which the Russians, unloading supplies, stole and then bartered with the local people. 'They take gold and silver, which we get from the Badakhshan mines, in return for petrol, kerosene, even electricity generators,' Lieutenant Ghalib said, as he proudly showed off his lathes, blacksmith shop and flour-grinding mills. 'This Soviet equipment is often not the best – it's very basic – but it does the job, and some of it wears well. Their motor fuel is, for some reason, dyed green, and is of very poor quality, low-octane, but it serves the purpose.'

'Is there anything that is difficult to get?' asked Adam.

'From time to time you can't get things that would really be useful. At the moment we can't get antibiotics. But then, the Russians are plagued by shortages themselves. And sometimes, of course, the opposition gives us problems.'

'Who's the opposition?'

'Well, independent operators, people who are trying to carry on Resistance work on their own. There was a case a month or so back. Some people from the industrial city of Kunduz arrived in carts loaded with good quality grain marked "Gift of the people of the United States of America". The Russians "bought" it for a stack of uniforms, which we eventually got hold of ourselves.'

'What's wrong with that?'

'Nothing.' The lieutenant laughed; 'except that the Afghans had refilled old sacks and added a lot of purgative plant material to the flour, so the Nikolais soon wanted their uniforms back.

Apparently the effect of the purgative rather ruined their clothes!'

'Weren't they furious?'

'At first they were, but the Afghans explained that American wheat always had that effect on normal people, very different from good Soviet flour!'

The people of north Afghanistan, living so close to what was in fact – though not in theory – the Soviet empire, knew a great deal about its strengths and weaknesses. 'The flour story,' Lieutenant Ghalib told The Eagle, 'tells us a great deal about totalitarian regimes and how to deal with them.'

'In the first place, since the enemy – America – has been presented as a bogey, many people in the USSR will believe almost anything about it. Hence, "The Americans are demons, and so their flour must be horrible".'

'But the Russians, the people, must one day get out of this warped way of thinking?' Adam asked. 'After all, a time is bound to come when they just won't credit the propaganda.'

Ghalib rubbed his chin, reflectively. 'That's something which will take time, I would think. In any case, there's nothing that we, fighting a war, can do about it. I was talking about the weaknesses in Soviet thinking which come from such distortions, not about the remedies. I suppose it's up to the Americans, and the fair-minded Russians, to solve the brainwashing problem.'

'Have they brainwashed the Turkestan people on their own side of the border?' Adam wanted to know.

'Some of them, but not the majority. The chief problem there seems to me to be that the Soviet Turkestanis don't know much more than what the Russians feed them. Mind you, they don't like the Russians, and that has nothing to do with socialism. They have a saying, "A Russian rat is a rat who is a Russian."'

Adam said, 'I heard that there were masses of Uzbek and Tajik soldiers among the first Soviet troops to enter Afghanistan, in December 1979, but that they were withdrawn because they became too friendly with the Afghans.'

'That was an experiment, which failed,' Ghalib said. 'You see, the *Russian* Army, which is what the Soviet Army really is, makes sure that members of the ethnic minorities are distributed throughout its units. The Soviets never had locally raised regiments. The Central Asians are a seventeen per cent minority in most army formations.'

'Then what was the "experiment", Ghalib?'

'Well, since the education and training of Central Asians is deliberately kept at a lower standard than those of the Slavs and even the Balts, the annual conscript intake always contains a large number of men who are not suitable for learning technically advanced tasks. They are channelled into support troops – transport, logistics, mine-clearing and so on. But these are never posted to Central Asian depots.

'They go to the Ukraine, the Russian Soviet Republic, to the Baltic States, and so on. It was some of these that the Soviet High Command tried out in Afghanistan. They deserted in large numbers. Mainly, however, they are not fighting material.'

Major Han had made a careful study of the Kremlin's Afghan campaign, absorbing the contents of captured documents and listening to military radio traffic. He outlined the position for the Paghman guerrillas.

'The Soviet Union is split up into military commands. Logically, it is the Central Asian military districts – Turkestan and Central Asia – which should have taken on the Afghan campaign. Their territory borders ours. But the two of them quarrelled: Tashkent wanted to be in charge, and so did Alma-Ata.'

'And how did they solve that one?' Adam asked.

'By creating another, completely independent command: Afghanistan. A marshal of the Soviet Union was put in overall control, and no less than twenty-five Russian generals were put under him.'

'A marshal!' Adam was impressed. 'And why so many generals?'

'Yes,' said the major; 'of course, any other army would have had only one or two generals – five at the most – for a "Fraternal Limited Contingent to pursue bandits and counter-revolutionaries", as it is called. But the Russian hawks, the War Party, are very strong, and they spend most of their time lobbying for things to do.'

'And, I suppose, there are decorations to be won?'

'Naturally. The Soviet Army is top-heavy with officers, too, of all ranks. They have to do something.'

'Who is the marshal?'

'Marshal Sergei Sokolov, First Deputy Minister of Defence. He was appointed when the "handful of rebels", in early 1980, started to kill too many Russians. It was he who authorized the communist Afghan admission that there were a million resisters in Afghan Turkestan alone. That was to explain why the Red Army had so many casualties.'

Within three days, the members of the Sher-Qala Commando were moving around the camp, being put through drill and familiarization courses by the Turkestanis, and generally getting the feel of the power and confidence which everywhere marked the ever-strengthening national mobilization.

With a large network of information-gatherers, and more and more agents among the Afghans working for the Soviets, the Wolves were able to provide Adam with a ready-made organization to plan and assist the descent upon the treasure.

'I have to know,' The Eagle told the Wolves' commander, 'whether the treasure is still in this area, and whether it is aboard the gunboat or not; and if not, where it is. In either case, if it is in this area, we need a plan to capture or destroy it.'

'You'll have to give me two more days,' said the major. 'This is Tuesday. Shall we say Thursday?'

'I really like Afghanistan,' said the Russian Zelikov; 'in Moscow, it would take two days just to find out what day of the week it was.'

'Don't try to be too clever, son,' Major Han advised him; 'because you and Captain Azambai here are going to be among the people who'll do the finding out for us. Get ready to go to Qizil Qala within an hour.'

3 The Gunboat *Jihun*

Qizil Qala
Oxus River Port
Afghan-Soviet Border

JULY 21

Thirty years ago, Gaidardost the Uzbek had been a Soviet citizen; with the risk which went with it, of being accused – as he was – of economic crimes against the state. He had owned thirty sheep for private profit. He could not have lived without the flock, for the administration at the cotton mill where he worked was corrupt. It recorded that he had been paid double what he actually received; but this was not stated at his trial.

His sentence was five years in a heavy labour camp, in Western Siberia. When he was released, Gaidardost found that he had been allocated a job in the Kara Kum Desert irrigation project. He collected his ticket to the town of Kerki, in Turkmenia, where the labour battalions were based: only sixty miles north of Afghanistan. The next weekend, instead of taking his Sunday rest, he started to walk southwards. Eleven hours later, after climbing a mountain, swimming a river, evading the border guards and crossing a mine-sown strip of ploughed earth guarded by watch-towers, he was free. In Afghanistan.

Now he lived near Qizil Qala, and he had a flock again. But the Russians, six years later, seemed to have caught up with him.

He shook his fist at the military convoy as it forced him and his sixty sheep off the broad tarmac of the northern road, covering him with dust, sending the animals into a field of lucerne from which they would have to be patiently retrieved.

'Death upon the spiritual teacher of your Lenin and Karl Marx! Defeat to the Infidel!'

The splendidly turned out Soviet officer in the lead car, a

Russian GAZ-69 field vehicle like a light jeep, with the aircraft and parachute insignia of the elite Soviet Airborne Troops stencilled on the side, made an obscene gesture back, and shouted an unrepeatable insult. Then he turned to his companion.

'Every little helps, to stoke up the hostility, you know,' Yusuf Azambai said to The Eagle who sat beside him, newly promoted to paratroop colonel by courtesy of the Wolves of Badakhshan.

Yusuf was a colonel too, now, thanks to Noor and Karima sitting up all night stitching stripes and stars, and arm patches showing parachutes and aircraft – not forgetting hammers and sickles – on the field-dress shirts acquired from the purgative flour transaction.

Behind them rumbled an impressive line of Russian BTR-60 PK armoured personnel-carriers, huge, boat-shaped amphibious ones. They had eight wheels for land travel, and, in their water-crossing role, swam powered by water-jets, driven by their rear twin engines. Now, they breezed along at fifty miles an hour, filled with guerrillas wearing the proud khaki and blue of the USSR's Airborne, the most admired of all Soviet formations. The splendid military highway had been built by the Afghan Construction Unit's engineers, using thousands of labourers from the Food for Work Programme.

It would take them only half an hour now to reach the port, the gunboat and the treasure.

Major Han's intelligence work had paid rich dividends. In the two days' research time which he had asked of Adam, his organization had found out that the treasure was still at the Oxus port, already loaded onto the gunboat *Jihun*. His 'Special Duty Group' had acquired Airborne insignia, eight personnel-carriers, a scout car, and a selection of top-priority identification documents like those used by LRRG's: the Long-Range Reconnaissance Groups of the Soviet Army – and a fair knowledge of the way in which such units are run.

Although originally formed to collect information, these units had been upgraded. Now they were designated as special formations, ready to carry out any task. Each group had twenty-seven men, six of them officers and the rest sergeants. Self-sufficient and armed with sophisticated weaponry and communications equipment, they were regarded with awe by the rest of the army. Best of all, from the point of view of the guerrillas, they were seldom seen by the rest of the troops. If Adam and his men made mistakes of behaviour or routine, most people – even Russian troops – were not likely to have standards of comparison.

In the back of the half-ton scout car sat young 'Major' Qasim. Beside him was Major Yildiz Han, the Paghman group's host until this morning. Each of the personnel-carriers contained nine men, half its possible complement. Short on sky-blue paratrooper berets, helmets and jackboots – the Wolves had been unable to obtain enough of them in the time available – The Eagle's force had to make do with paratroop goggles. Each man had a gas mask. Those who did not speak Russian were to put one on at once if Russian troops or officials looked like questioning them, and display a standard army 'chemical decontamination' sign.

Each vehicle carried three small packing cases, whose markings – *Gelignit* – gelignite – had been painted out. Carbolic disinfectant fluid splashed on the boxes masked the explosive's tell-tale smell of marzipan. The reconnaissance men considered the ship to be so heavily guarded that there was next to no chance of stealing the treasure: it would have to be blown up. And they had enough explosive to shatter the gold coins and scatter the pieces far and wide over the vast expanse of river, to be lost forever in its treacherous, swirling waters. Not for nothing was the Oxus styled 'the insane river' by the Arabs when their armies first encountered it.

The sun was sinking beyond the distant Iranian border, when the convoy reached the first of the roadblocks on the main road from Kunduz to the Qizil Qala port area. At the sight of the red and light blue pennant on the lead car, the Russian soldiers on duty leapt to attention, while four Afghan conscripts man-handled the heavy log, which had been rolled across the road, out of the way. Giving them an airy wave of his hand, such as seemed appropriate for a dashing paratroop commander, The Eagle sailed past.

'Very good,' said Major Han. 'We'll make a soldier of you yet, Adam.'

'Nice of you to say so, major. I always was good at amateur theatricals . . . How far are we from the port now?' Adam checked the striped T-shirt which the paratroopers wore under their jackets.

The major looked at his watch. 'Five minutes to sunset, five minutes to the main gate of the harbour.'

It was a pity, Adam thought, that they weren't going into action in full daylight. Their vehicles and uniforms were so impressive, it was almost a waste. As for the faces of the men, the Soviet Army itself was composed of conscripts of such diverse origins that the Afghans looked appropriately miscellaneous.

He only hoped that none of the personnel-carriers would break down. They had no recovery vehicles, spares or equipment to service them.

Another roadblock loomed in the distance. This one was more professional, with two sentry-boxes, floodlamps already on, a portable generator thumping, and twin Afghan and Soviet flags hanging limply in the airless gloaming.

Stoi! Halt. A tall, slim and elegant lieutenant stepped carefully into the road and raised one arm, in a textbook version of 'an officer stopping an advancing convoy for identification purposes'. Adam flashed his headlights in acknowledgement and came to a stop.

The Russian NCOs at the barrier were, unusually, neither lounging nor smoking. They stood alert, obviously annoyed at the presence of this young sprout, who nevertheless outranked them. The lieutenant's boots gleamed in the scout car's headlamps as he pranced up to the vehicle. He looked as if he was going to speak to Adam, who hardly knew a word of Russian.

Before he reached the driver's side 'Colonel' Yusuf Azambai stood up in his seat and roared, in his best regimental manner, 'Get off the road, *gospodin leytenant*, while those sons of animals let us through, will you?'

The lieutenant stopped and stood stock-still. To Adam, he seemed on the point of unslinging his Kalashnikov: but perhaps it was his imagination. Then Azambai shouted, 'I am Colonel Mazhdurov, the *komandir* of this special force, 105th Guards Airborne Division, on special duty, and I am in a hurry!'

The lieutenant saluted. 'That's better, *leytenant*, the Guards like a keen man.' Azambai thought that the best thing to do was to keep talking.

The lieutenant came up to him.

'What's your name and unit?' Azambai asked imperiously.

'Federov, *Leytenant*, 360th Motorized Rifle Division reporting, *gospodin* Colonel!'

'I see. That's General Melik-Bekov's lot, isn't it?'

'Yes, sir.'

Azambai smiled. 'I know him well.' He had, in his Red Army days, actually met the aristocratic Melik-Bekov, the Azarbaijanian terror who lived like a prince, in the USSR. 'You are the fellows who did some good work over in Wardak Province, didn't you? Seen a bit of action, I suppose? Of course, we have been punishing the *badmashes* ourselves, down Khyber way . . .'

'Yessir. Er, no sir. I wasn't there. I have only just been posted here. I am a replacement.'

'Well, Federov, you did well to stop us. But you don't think we're bandits, do you? Get your men off the road, because I want to get this special job over so the men can get a little *kasha*, gruel. We haven't had anything all day.'

Federov was nearly ready to open the barrier. His brow wrinkled slightly as if he was wondering how to ask for movement orders from this elegant senior officer of paratroops, Guardsmen at that. Better keep talking, thought Azambai.

'Pickled herring, sardines and cheese, that's all I've had myself, since yesterday. Something to do with this new chemical defence affair, our task is. You know all about that, I suppose?'

'Not exactly, sir.'

'Well, you do know, I take it, that there is a chemical defence unit stationed down the road, at Kunduz?' Chemical defence usually meant 'gas attack'.

'Yes, of course, *gospodin* Colonel.'

'That's where we have been. Then old General Tairov – he's my uncle – got it into his head that we should do a special exercise, slip in to fool about here: protect this gunboat you've got up at the port. What's it called?'

'It is called the *Jihun*, Colonel,' shouted Major Han, in his most military voice, from the back of the scout car. His Russian was good enough, and he thought that he could lend some verisimilitude to the proceedings. 'That's what it says on the orders. But we're running behind time. I don't know what the general is going to say.'

'Yes, we'd better be getting a move on. Can't stay here gossiping all day. I'll tell the general you assisted us, Federov. Every little helps, eh?'

'Er, yes, *komandir*. Many thanks.' The young officer turned to his men, waving to them to remove the barrier, '*Bistro!* – hurry.'

'*Spasiba, leytenant* – thank you.' The major acknowledged the salute.

They were through. Only the dock gates to deal with now. It was already getting dark.

The dock gates loomed, large, new, made of steel bars, festooned with barbed wire. The car stopped on the shiny new asphalt, extensively floodlit with carbon arcs.

The armoured personnel-carriers drew up in line behind.

'Colonel' Azambai, accompanied by Adam, jumped down from the car and strode across to the guardhouse.

Outside was a large notice, red lettering on white: *The Shipping Administration of Central Asia. Headquarters at Charjui*. Charjui was in the USSR. The Russians were behaving as if this Afghan port was already in their own territory.

Inside the hut, sitting beside a large samovar which they were feeding with charcoal chips, were two Russian sergeants. They stood and came to attention when they saw the officers.

'Colonel Mazhdurov and unit, on a special mission, for the gunboat *Jihun*. I am in a hurry, sergeant!'

The older sergeant, a middle-aged man with jackboots which some first-year conscript had undoubtedly spent a long time polishing, clicked his heels. '*Dakumyent*?' he said.

Documents. Well, there *was* no movement order. Best to try the Airborne pass. Azambai reached into his pocket and took out the red booklet with its gold hammer and sickle embossed on the front.

'There you are, my man. Urgent chemical defence work. The *Jihun.*'

'*Spasiba*, thank you.' The sergeant glanced at it and saw the Guards badge on the Turkestani's right breast. He clicked his heels again, and pressed a button, 'The gates are open now, *gospodin Colonel.*'

Carefully obeying the sign which said *maximum speed* 10 *kph*, the convoy rolled along the concrete surface of the broad roadway to the docks. This was the old part of the port, just a small jetty; and suddenly there she was, the *Jihun*, tied up fore and aft.

The gunboat was brightly lit by floodlights, and lying low in the water, obviously heavily laden. She looked dirty, rusty, had undoubtedly seen better days. A sergeant who had been lolling on a pile of sacks, stood up in the glare of the headlights. Azambai got out of the car and went up to the man as he snapped to attention.

'Who are you?'

'Sergeant Bichak, beg to report, sir!'

'Good. Now, sergeant, we're here on a special mission, as you must realize. Chemical defence exercise. Who is on guard and who's on board, and what are your orders?'

'*Gospodin* Colonel! On shore: myself, ten men in that hut,' he indicated a guard hut some twenty feet away, 'and a special detachment on the ship, nobody to go on board without a permit.' He spoke with a Tartar accent.

'And quite right, too. Make sure that you don't let anyone, anyone at all, on board. Now, I'm cancelling the order about the permit, on my own authority. That means that nobody else, even with a permit, may go on board. Danger of chemical contamination, toxic agents, *khimicheskoye oruzhiye*. And confine your men, for safety, to that hut. That is imperative. Understand?'

'Understood, sir!'

'Now, sergeant. What other ships are in dock here?'

'None, *gospodin* Colonel. The *Jihun* is isolated at this wharf. Orders from GHQ.'

'Good. Who and where are the men on board?'

'They are a detachment from the Intelligence Section of KGB troops, sir. Captain Nazarov, Lieutenant Gritkin and twenty-eight men, seven of them sergeants, on this watch. I don't know exactly where they are. The officers allocate the guard duties.'

'When is your watch over, sergeant?'

'Same as theirs, sir, two a.m.'

At that moment a Red Army officer, in camouflage over-jacket, came out of the wheelhouse and stepped to the rails, fifteen feet above them. He peered into the pools of light and darkness caused by the floodlights mounted high on the boat. The rumbling of the armoured vehicles must have alerted him.

He was wearing a steel helmet, and carried one of the new Kalashnikov 74s. He levelled it at the pair as soon as his eyes became accustomed to the light and shade pattern on the dockside.

'Hands up!'

Attack is the best defence, thought Azambai. He called out, 'Comrade Officer: how do you like it here?' in as jolly a voice as he could manage, though his throat was dry.

'Who are you, what do you want?' The officer levelled the gun, sighting it straight at the Turkestani.

'I'm Colonel Mazhdurov, 105th Guards Airborne, special duty, chemical defence,' Azambai called. 'Are you Nazarov, or Gritkin?'

'I'm Lieutenant Gritkin, sir. You'd better come aboard and be identified. I'm on special duty, too. As the Colonel knows, this is a high-security matter.'

Azambai held up his red and gold booklet. 'Here you are, *leytenant*, this should be enough for you.'

'Not enough, I am afraid, Colonel.' He sounded old for a lieutenant, probably promoted from the ranks. Such men were often difficult, sticking to the letter. Their general aim was, of course, to exercise whatever power they could. Paying people back for all those slaps as rankers . . . And he was, after all, a KGB soldier, not an ordinary army man.

'I'm not a bandit, you know, *leytenant*!'

'No, *gospodin* Colonel. Of course not. Advance and be recognized.'

Now Gritkin had been joined by three more figures, sergeants by the look of them. There was nothing for it, Azambai would have to go aboard.

'All right, Gritkin. I'm coming.'

Azambai signalled to Major Han to stay where he was, beside the guard sergeant, and covered the length of the gangway in three or four leaps. Up a flight of iron steps, then another, and he was on the bridge-deck, holding out his identity book. The lieutenant saluted and took it, looking back and forth between

Azambai's face and the photograph on the document. Then he said, 'That seems to be in order, sir,' handing it back; 'and now may I see your written instructions?'

'For what?' Azambai raised his eyebrows.

'For boarding this ship. The shore-guard must have told you. From *Shtad-Kvartyra*, Headquarters.'

'There never *is* anything in writing concerning chemical defence matters. You should know that, lieutenant.' Azambai put an edge into his voice. He sensed the suspicion of the three sergeants, who were moving closer. Surely they wouldn't dare to defy a full colonel? Poison gas warfare was a crime, and the Russians never admitted to having any more than 'defence measures' for gas. In reality, the Red Army had plenty of gas.

'There is nothing *written down* about the nature of the warfare, Colonel,' said Gritkin, his Ukrainian accent becoming more pronounced with strain or emotion, 'but there is always some authorization in general terms. Such as "This person may board the *Jihun* for such-and-such a defensive purpose." That is what I want; State Security demands it. *Spravka*, proof, that your mission is authorized. You should know that already.'

That seemed to be that. Gritkin was so suspicious that the major knew that he could never shift him with mere bluster. He mentally rifled through the possibilities, his mind working at top speed. Shoot all four Russians? No, that would bring the house down. Explain? No, that would look bad.

He said, 'We're guards and paratroops, and a special reconnaissance group, Gritkin. That means we're unorthodox. Personal verbal orders from General Tairov. We have to provide chemical defence for this ship.'

The other man was unimpressed. 'Yes, Colonel.'

He couldn't be faulted. He stood straight, shoulders back like the good NCO he had probably once been, heels together. He was not being insolent or incorrect to any degree. Merely doing his duty.

'Yes, Gritkin. Now, have you a radio on this boat?'

'We are not allowed to use the radio except in emergencies and for raising the alarm. For instance, in case of theft.'

Azambai managed a chuckle, though he felt more like grinding his teeth.

'Stealing, yes; running off with old lifebelts I suppose.'

'I'm not talking about *blat*, Colonel.' He was hinting that there was something more here than the small-time thievery which everyone in the Soviet forces knew about and practised to some extent. He stopped talking, abruptly. He obviously knew about the gold; he had now almost suggested that this was a plot to seize it. He'd be shot if that happened. Azambai reflected that the KGB had been clever. The NCOs on the gates, and probably those in the hut too, almost certainly knew nothing at all about the treasure in the ship. That was the way to keep security. They had even left a fairly light guard on it. But Gritkin and his sergeants were a different matter.

'And *I* am talking about protecting your ship, against *blat* or anything else, lieutenant. *Blat* is as much an anti-State activity as anything else.' Let the lieutenant think that he was a priest, at heart, if that would help.

'If you can't use your radio, use mine.' He'd just had a brain-wave.

'I'm not allowed to leave the ship until relieved. That would be irregular.'

'Lieutenant, if your superior – Captain Nazarov isn't it? – is awake, tell him that Colonel Mazhdurov would be glad to have a word with him.' He turned his back, ostentatiously, and looked as incuriously as he could down onto the quay.

As if relieved at the decision, Gritkin was away and back in a moment with a tall, thin, slightly drunken captain, smelling of vodka and smoothing his field uniform shirt. He came to attention when he saw the 'colonel'.

Azambai explained the situation. The captain was impressed. 'Yes, Colonel, of course. Come with me to the saloon and have a drink. Gritkin can go and verify things on your radio, and I am sure that all will be in order.' He seemed apprehensive, aware that he was not quite sober, and afraid that the 'colonel' would report him.

That would not do. Azambai would have to go with him, or the trick wouldn't work. He thought fast.

'Thank you, Captain. But I'll have to take Gritkin down to the quay myself. My radio operator will not accept any orders without me. That's the way we do things in the Airborne.' He gave an arch smile to indicate his pride in the endearing little ways of his lads: doing their duty to the letter.

The captain saluted. 'Certainly, Colonel. I'll await your return. I'll have the vodka ready. It's the best.'

Together Azambai and Gritkin went down to where the APCs stood, silently, full of very tense men, waiting for something to happen. Azambai knocked on the turret of the first carrier. Zelikov opened it and looked out. '*Gospodin Colonel*?'

'Captain Gritkin, from the gunboat,' Azambai said, in his best, clipped military Russian, 'wants to verify our orders, sergeant.' He turned to the captain. 'From whom do you want the authorization, Gritkin?'

'From Movement Control, North Command.'

'Yes, of course, that's the best. Everything should be filed with them.' Azambai was sweating, even in the cold night air, but thinking, fast. 'Sergeant, raise Movement Control. You will remember that, on our high-security network, it has the prefix *ooksoos*, vinegar.'

Zelikov was quick on the uptake. 'At once, *gospodin* Colonel.' He remembered that *vinegar* was the call-sign for the third personnel-carrier in their convoy.

'Right, then, I'll leave you to it.' Azambai moved away slowly out of Gritkin's line of vision, then sprang rather than walked the fifty feet or so to the third APC, tapping on the turret as he came level with it.

'When you get a message, in the next few seconds, in Russian, from a Nikolai, just say, "Wait, please, we're checking,"' he told the radio-man. The man nodded. He was one of the best Russian speakers among the Turkestanis. That was why Azambai had chosen his vehicle.

It seemed like only a second before the radio squawked, with Zelikov's voice asking for Movement Control, for Transport Information. The Turkestani replied with the answer he had been told to give and put the caller on hold. Azambai then spoke rapidly. 'When Lieutenant Gritkin comes on, say that our visit is authorized at the highest level, but that it is highly secret and he is to give us all co-operation.'

Within three minutes it was done. Azambai walked back to the slightly chastened Gritkin and fell into step beside him as they made their way back to the ship. 'Well done, lieutenant. I like a man with zeal. Let's have that vodka out now, shall we?'

When they rejoined Captain Nazarov, Azambai underlined the importance of his work by refusing a drink. 'Gentlemen,' he said, 'I have things to do for my Homeland. I cannot drink.'

After a few quick shots of vodka, 'bought from Moscow's best liquor store: 4 Gorky Street,' the captain staggered off, and Azambai explained that he and his men would have to be given a free hand to set up their chemical protection system on board the *Jihun*. Gritkin, very politely, borrowed his forged Airborne pass, photographed it with a Polaroid camera, and locked the print in a flat grey box marked ALTINKUSH. *Altinkush* in Turkic languages meant 'Goldenbird'.

Adam posted two personnel-carriers side-on, with their gun ports facing inland, near the dock gates to discourage visitors. He also arranged for one of his Russian-speaking 'sergeants' to sit with the Soviet guards, in case of problems. Then the rest of the men started to carry the gelignite boxes on board the *Jihun*.

Louis Palmer's days as a shipwright had not been wasted. One look at the battered gunboat and he recognized it as a type which had been popular, for prestige, among second-rate rulers in the nineteenth century. It would be very vulnerable to modern explosives. Forty years ago, it had been brought, in pieces, across the Caspian Sea to Krasnovoksk, and thence shipped overland and down the Oxus River, to be sold to the Afghan government. Even then it had been almost a museum-piece.

Palmer and his group set the charges and primed them, while Adam, with Qasim and Zelikov, wandered through the gloomy, foul-smelling bowels of the ship, looking for the gold. First they found the guards, playing card-games, cleaning their weapons or brewing tea in the large second-class saloon aft. Forward were the two officers, one drunk, the other, satisfied that he had no special responsibilities until the change of watch, studying for promotion examinations.

But where was the treasure?

Qasim had just stubbed his toe on a projecting board in the floor of the main cargo hold, which seemed very small and low, when he realied that the whole floor was composed of wooden boxes. He was actually standing on the cargo, which filled half of the total height of the hold.

Qasim hissed to attract Adam's attention. When he came over, Qasim asked, 'What does "thirty noto" mean, Adam?'

'I don't know. Why?'

'There are dozens, or hundreds, of boxes here. They've all got that stencilled on them.'

Zelikov crept up to them. 'That not "thirty noto"! That *zolata*, Russian word, Cyrillic alphabet. Means *Gold*. This is IT, *gospodeen*!'

Adam went over to where Azambai was conversing in a low voice with Palmer, about something to do with detonating the gelignite.

'Yusuf: we've found the gold. Tons of it! Let's get it out, instead of blowing it up!'

'You must be crazy! Something could happen at any moment. We got on board and we've got the explosives set. Now, for goodness sake, let's get out while we're still alive. Suppose they see us taking things away from the ship? Bringing stuff on board, after all, isn't the same thing.' He didn't feel like a hero, somehow, at that moment.

'I'm going to do it, Yusuf, say what you like. We could use that money to buy arms, to look after the wounded, to get proper medical attention. People are dying from starvation and lack of medicines.'

Azambai paused, then shook The Eagle's hand. 'You're right, Adam. I'm with you.'

The boxes were not very heavy. They weighed about twenty pounds each, and their tops were nailed down. 'I estimate,' whispered Adam, 'that there must be about a thousand *mohurs* in each box. Ten boxes and we'll have one and a half million dollars. A hundred boxes would be fifteen million dollars!'

Fifteen million dollars . . . ten million pounds sterling . . . thirty-two million Swiss francs! Stuck in the bowels of an ancient gunboat full of KGB men, guarded by the Soviet Army a stone's throw from the USSR. However plausible the story of this chemical warfare unit might have been, Adam knew that the tale wouldn't cover the theft of the gold. 'Excuse me, Gritkin, we are just carrying this treasure away to decontaminate it . . .'

A bluff, that's what he needed. Something that would enable

his men to get the boxes onto the quay, into the personnel-carriers, and away. Not while all those Russians were watching, surely? Of course not . . .

Quickly Adam surveyed the rubbish in the hold, and saw a drum of worn electric cable. Not far away there was a pile of old rubber sponges. He stabbed a hole through the centre of a handful of these and threaded them onto the cable.

Azambai looked on in amazement. 'Have you gone crazy?'

Adam quickly explained. 'There are seven Russian sergeants in the saloon aft. Round them up and tell them that we need help, from responsible people, for part of our work. Say it'll only take a few moments. But get them all into the forward saloon . . .'

'You think they'll fall for that?' Azambai's eyes were wide with amazement.

'Better men than them have fallen for it. You see, you know what's happening and they don't. In that situation people will do almost anything they're told. Gritkin probably wouldn't be so easily fooled, and we can only hope he's too busy to leave his office. The captain's too drunk to bother, wouldn't even notice an air raid.'

Adam sent Zelikov to brief his men in the personnel-carriers. Each man was to walk to the gangway and descend to the hold. Then, like robots working in perfect sequence, the guerrillas were to shoulder the boxes and ferry them to the deck, from there to the gangway, and then to the vehicles. Very rapidly: not one step missed, not one moment lost.

When Adam got to the forward saloon, he found Azambai there, surrounded by Russians, all looking attentively at what he was doing. 'Chemical protection,' he was explaining, 'has to be very carefully calculated, with reference to local background humidity.' He shook the flex, with its dirty bits of sponge dangling like an illustration of how to use a washing line.

The Russians nodded their understanding.

'Now,' Yusuf Azambai continued, 'if you will just hold this end . . .' In a moment he had the seven sergeants holding the flex tightly against the panelling. He made them move until they were equally spaced around the saloon.

'Note carefully and with complete attention: the cable must be taut and the sponges must be in contact with the wall. That's fine, you're learning. It needs only a few minutes for the rubber indicators to absorb moisture. I'll be right back with the electronic meter to take a reading. I'm most grateful to you all. No, don't let it sag. Fine!'

Azambai was now at the door; together he and Adam slipped away. The two raced up the companionway and across the deck to see the last of the gold porters disappearing into the darkness of the quay, beyond the floodlights.

Fifteen million American dollars, Adam thought – as the alarm klaxons started to blare.

4 Leninised

On the Oxus River

JULY 21

When the alarm went, Palmer had just connected his firing plunger to the charges. The shock of the raucous braying of the klaxons, mounted on poles every few yards along the quay, made him lose his balance. He only just saved himself from falling on the plunger, activating the induction coil – and killing everyone in the port area, including himself.

The Eagle, rushing to the main saloon, saw Lieutenant Gritkin at the radio, earphones on his head, left forefinger jabbing the klaxon alarm-button. He must have had second thoughts, and contacted his headquarters.

Gritkin grabbed for the grey enamel box on the table, the one marked ALTINKUSH, as he saw Adam. Acting in reflex, Adam seized the box and drew his gun, and turned to face the revolver in the Russian's left hand. They were both panting like fighting dogs.

A dead heat. As Adam stood wondering whether he could risk rushing the man, staccato shooting broke out on the dockside below. For a fraction of a second, Gritkin's concentration broke. His eyes started to move to the left, came back again – and Adam shot him through the heart.

The noise of automatic rifle-fire was more intense now. Adam smashed the glass in the central saloon's large dockside window and looked at the scene below. The lights were still on. Fifteen feet below him the Leopard Man, Cadet Arif Qamarudin, was jabbing with his bare hands, stiffened in karate style, at two Russian sergeants. One was wielding a wooden pole, the other had stepped back to punch a fresh magazine into his gun.

Holding the box by its strap in his right hand, Adam jumped. He landed on the neck and shoulders of the Russian with the gun. For a moment both lay there, winded, on the concrete. Adam felt the sticky warmth on his hand which told him that one of them was wounded. As he sprang up, he saw that blood was seeping from a bayonet wound in the Russian's side. He had fallen on his own gun.

The other Russian was looming now. Where was Arif? No time to look. The pole came swishing down, hit him a glancing blow on the cheek.

The next thing he knew was that he was in the leading personnel-carrier, being propped up on the hard seat by Zelikov. Arif, felled by his opponent, had recovered and jerked the man's legs from behind, when the man was momentarily off balance. Zelikov, coming up, had dragged Adam back to the carrier.

Adam fought the little Russian off, and plunged back onto the quay. A whirl of struggling figures, just outside the guard-hut, was milling, swirling and moving like a grotesque ballet scene. The Nuristanis and the other Afghans were dealing with the shore-guards.

The klaxons were blaring again. Over by the guardhouse, Adam could see that the two armoured personnel-carriers which he had left to guard the entrance were fighting off troops who had obviously been rushed to the entrance. The Nuristanis had moved all the vehicles side-on to the gates, so that they could not be crashed through. It enabled them, too, to fire through the gunslits from inside, in comparative safety.

The *Jihun* was overrun with brawling, struggling figures. Major Azambai and the Turkestanis, as soon as the alarm went, had, as arranged beforehand, made straight for the KGB men aboard. Confused by the Soviet uniforms of their attackers, the Russians had, at first, run in all directions, pursued by the Wolves, who were now dealing with them with knives, guns, bare hands, belaying-pins and jackboots. Most of the Russians were fighting back. Men soon lay sprawled everywhere: on the decks, on piles of canvas, on half-open hatches. One, with a broken neck, was wedged, grotesquely, upside-down, on an iron ladder, as if arrested in full flight.

Adam shot three of the KGB men as he ran from fight to fight, helping the Afghans who seemed most hard-pressed. In four or five minutes it was over. Even the alarm no longer wailed. All was quiet, on the ship, apart from the groans of the wounded.

Azambai ran up to The Eagle. 'What's next?'

'Get your dead and wounded to the APCs, Yusuf, and stand by,' Adam said. He had seen that the Russian shore-guards were flagging. The Turkestanis would soon have them under control. The main gate still held. But soon the Russians outside would bring up heavy guns, and probably rockets.

He scrambled to the dockside once more, colliding with Arif, who was running towards the men fighting near the hut. Stopping him, Adam picked up the document box, still lying there beside the two dead Russians, and told the Leopard Man to take it to the first APC.

Then he saw Palmer, with a bayonet slash in his leg, staggering towards him, the long yellow electric line of the detonator between his fingers.

'Leave it, Louie, too dangerous!'

They couldn't blow the ship up, now, or they'd all go up with it. As the last of the resistance of the shore guard was crushed, Palmer sat down groggily on a bollard. Bullets from the Russians outside the gates whizzed past, ricocheting with an ugly whine. He took no notice, gathering his strength.

Two minutes later Major Han came running up. 'There's no way into this area except through those gates. Everything else is blast-proof concrete. Everyone is defending the gates now. All other resistance has been overcome. What are the orders for withdrawal?'

'Right.' Adam looked around. The major, Qasim and Palmer were waiting.

He turned to Palmer. 'Louie, how wide is the river here?'

'About half a mile.'

'That's the way we go, then.'

They all looked at him. 'Swimming?' asked Qasim, incredulously.

'The APCs are *amphibious*. We'll sail them out. Get all the drivers ready. The quay slopes down to river-level over there, to the left. Abandon the scout car, of course. *Haraka*, move!'

Everyone scattered to the armoured vehicles, as the Russians outside the gates stopped firing. A voice, speaking in Dari-Persian, came from a loud-hailer.

'I want to speak to your leader.'

It was repeated three times.

'Zelikov, get that bullhorn from the guard-hut,' said Palmer, whose leg was being bandaged by the little Russian.

Zelikov brought it, and Adam moved carefully towards the gate. He put the megaphone to his lips.

'What do you want, traitor?'

'*Agha-i-Mukarram* – honoured sir!' The voice was oily and frightened. Some miserable semi-literate clerk, typical of the scum that were fawning at the Russians' heels, thought Adam. They'd been given important jobs, in name, but their Russian 'advisers' had the real power.

'What is it?'

'I am Nasim, harbour master, and I want to have a dialogue with you.'

'A dialogue?' One of those new jargon words, like 'norm' . . . Adam could play for time.

'Yes. We realize that you have some sort of grievance. I am authorized to say that we shall listen to it, and you have a guarantee of safe conduct and an amnesty if you come out and give up your weapons. Rebels have often been misled by revanchists.'

'Well,' shouted Adam, 'I'll have to think it over, and I'll talk to you again when I have consulted my associates.'

'Yes, by all means,' said the voice, after a pause, no doubt to discuss matters with his Russian superior. 'I am authorized to say that you have five minutes.'

'Make it ten.'

'Just a moment.'

Then, 'Very well, ten minutes. But after that we are coming in with tanks and heavy rockets and you'll be blown to pieces.'

'Tell Nikolai I don't like your threats.'

'Ten minutes, honoured sir.'

Adam walked back to where his commanders were standing.

'We've got ten minutes. Do the drivers know how to transfer the engine drive from the wheels to the amphibious mode?'

Azambai said, 'Yes, it's easy. There are diagrams, on the dashboards.'

'Good. How many men have we left?'

'Sixty-six. We've lost ten, dead. All the wounded can fight, so I've included them in the total. There are thirty of those.'

Adam turned to Palmer. 'Louie, can we set off the charges without going up, too?'

Palmer smiled. 'I haven't been wasting my time, Eagle. It's all hitched onto radio detonation now. We can fire it from as far away as three miles.'

'Great. I'm going to keep them talking, while you get the APCs ready to swim. The command will be the Afghan proverb about the pigeons and hawks, which you will hear through the loud-hailer. Have all drivers informed.'

'Right.'

As Adam walked back to the corner from which he had spoken to the harbourmaster, he heard the distinct rumble of the huge T-10 tanks, heading for the docks. At their top speed of twenty-six miles an hour, they could overrun the Commando very quickly indeed.

He raised the transistorized hailer to his lips and shouted, 'Harbourmaster!'

'Yes, honoured sir. Are you surrendering?'

They weren't going to offer any amnesty. It was simply a way to gain time. Better get out before the tanks crashed in.

'I have this to say,' Adam shouted, *"Tis always a kind with its kind will fly: pigeons or hawks, up in the sky!"*

Adam did not wait for an answer. He threw down the loud-hailer and scrambled aboard his personnel-carrier as the line of vehicles shot forward, over the concrete, down the ramp, into the water, and away.

They headed upstream for a quarter of a mile, nosing through the darkness, with their infra-red searchlights full on, and unmolested. 'Let's have the firework show, Louie,' The Eagle said; 'I expect there are lots of Russians on board the *Jihun* by now.'

Seconds later, they heard the roar of the explosion, and instinctively ducked as the pieces of wreckage, some very large, came thudding and drumming down onto the thick armour-plate above their heads. The roof stopped them seeing the explosions, but at least they were safe.

'I'm so glad it was the modern BTR-60PKs we managed to get hold of,' said Major Han, 'because the ordinary '60s' only have soft tops, you know. Some of that debris is really danger-ous.'

'If I wasn't so pooped,' said Palmer, 'I'd run over and have me a visit with the Russkis on their home ground. You do realize, don't you, that this is the frontier, and there's nothing but water between us and the Workers' Paradise?'

'Don't send me back to the USSR,' said Zelikov, in mock terror, 'because I like it in the woods. I don't want to be outnumbered by Turkestanis.'

Everyone realized that a joke helped to relieve the tension, even a poor joke.

'There's worse things than Turkestanis, lad!' The Turkestani Azambai was only half joking.

The APCs, engines throbbing heavily in the fast waters of the Oxus, headed steadily westwards as Zelikov fiddled with the Russian army radio, trying to raise Dushanbe, the powerful transmitter in Soviet Turkestan. There it was, now, on 1143 kilohertz in the medium waveband:

'*Inja Dushanbe* – here is Dushanbe.'

Then Dushanbe, a hundred and fifty miles away, announced the evening news. It was all about how in neighbouring, frater-nal Afghanistan, the workers were glorying in their new-found freedom. Of course, said the silky voice of the speaker, true Afghans deplored the acts of the two per cent, the insignificant but shameful minority, the trouble-makers, egged on by inter-national capitalist warmongering circles, who had made them think that they could 'reverse the tide of history', which Lenin had demonstrated could not be done.

'The Great Lenin . . .' Dushanbe was saying, though even the Turkstani commentator now sounded as if his heart was not really in it – and Zelikov switched off.

'Well, we certainly Leninized them today,' said The Eagle.

5 March South . . .

Wolf Redoubt

JULY 21

The amphibians nosed ashore, twenty kilometres south-west of Qizil Qala Port, on the hard desert sand where a break in the reed-beds formed a broad salt beach. They had been on the river for two hours. They were now only fifty kilometres due north of the Wolves' headquarters at Kurt Burj, and there was still no sign of any pursuit.

On their vehicles' radios, the guerrillas had heard the frantic messages from the military at Qizil Qala, and the answers from Khanabad HQ, which showed that the Russians were convinced that a paratroop unit had mutinied, either at Kunduz or Talaqan, and they were trying to find the fugitives upstream or else on the other side of the Oxus. Reports had poured in, claiming that the 'Russian mutineers' were trying to reach the USSR, to desert, and also that they were trying to join some disaffected infantrymen to the east of the port, where the Russians had had trouble with their own garrison before. The KGB, or military intelligence, must have decided that Azambai was a real Russian colonel, pretending, for some reason, to be a guerrilla.

Adam, sitting beside Major Han in the cramped amphibian, asked him how the Soviets could have become so confused.

'Ah, well you see, we have a good radio system back at Wolf Castle, and some pretty good disinformation men, too. I've already informed them that the escapees are going north or east, and they have broken into the Russian radio network to report it for us.'

The Eagle smiled. 'You think of everything. So where shall we head now?'

'Home. We could even make it to the city of Mazar-i-Sharif,

two hundred kilometres from here, along the sand dunes: we've got enough fuel. But it's safer to get home before dawn, and to get immediate treatment for the wounded.'

There was no road from here to the reed-beds, but the APCs had big tyres, centrally pressurized, and power-steering. They were able to travel overland, and, in a zigzag, the convoy found the surface firm enough to complete the journey in under two hours. At three o'clock in the morning they were rolling beneath the creepers at the eastern entrance to their hideout.

They had not even had a puncture. Soviet vehicles were not only rugged but they had few of the frills which other armies usually consider necessary, and that made for reliability and less maintenance.

Warned by radio, the Wolves' hospital was ready for the casualties.

As the fighters climbed down from their vehicles, they slapped the bullion boxes for luck, and poured, cheering and hungry, into the messhall where a feast was waiting for them.

Noor hugged Adam as he came in. 'And that's not because of your millions in gold,' she told him.

In spite of the journey, the tension, the battle, nobody slept that night.

When the casualties had been visited and pronounced to be 'in a stable condition', the leaders held a meeting to discuss the loot. In terms of arms purchases, fifteen million dollars would buy no more than ten thousand automatic rifles. On the other hand, such money, to the impoverished guerrillas, meant medicines, arms, and some relief for the victims of the Russian terror. In the end it was decided to send an equal amount of the gold to each of the twenty-eight provincial commanders of the Resistance, to spend as they wished. The equivalent of six hundred guns for each province was at least something.

Then Adam broke open the captured document case.

One of the papers in it dealt, in detail, with the transfer of the treasure of Afghanistan to the Soviet Union. The gunboat was to be used, since there was no air freight capacity available: the Army monopolized it. And it was to be guarded by a large KGB contingent. The direct route from Termez railhead, across the Oxus, was too vulnerable to guerrillas, hence the choice of Qizil Qala. This involved a long trip along the Kara Kum

Canal, detailed in wearisome pages of orders, itineraries and explanations.

'Pirates who are also bureaucrats must be the most tedious combination on earth,' complained Noor, as she skimmed the documents.

At the bottom of the case lay a thick book, marked ALTIN-KUSH. Noor opened it and read: 'Operation ALTINKUSH. Highest Secret Classification: *Committee for State Security*, KGB.

'GOLD SPECIE. Obtained from Kajakai (Engineer SHARIFI), hoard of Ahmad Shah. Coins to the bullion value of $30 million approximately, consigned via Qizil Qala to Moscow KGB. Attention: HALZUN, Dzhanmagometov, for Traditional Arts Foundation. Transportation Orders in Document KGB/6/765/ 00987 "Afghansky".

'After the transfer of this consignment to the USSR, the remainder of the Kajakai gold in Kandahar Province will also be known as ALTINKUSH, and comes within the control of the Operative ALTINKUSH.

'It constitutes gold specie of the sixteenth century and earlier, minted in India, Iran and elsewhere, to the face value of $400 billion, repeat $400,000,000,000, four hundred billion American dollars.

'Signature of Amount Confirmed . . . (Uvarov).

'The treasure, now at Kandahar, is to be transferred abroad under the orders of ALTINKUSH, in the Caspian transports and all aspects of this activity are to be subject to the greatest secrecy. The reference numbers for communications, security, and so on are as follows . . .'

'Four hundred *billion* dollars' worth of gold coins?' Noor repeated the sum and looked at the others, sitting around the table in the messhall.

'Are you sure?' Adam craned his neck to make out the figures.

'I'm sure, and even the Nikolais could hardly believe it, since they repeated it and had the confirmation signed by someone at KGB HQ,' Noor said.

'Your father found the hoard of Ahmad Shah, and only a part of it is what we've captured,' said Yusuf.

'The rest of it is still there,' Noor said. She looked stunned.

Major Han needed a moment to get used to the idea. 'I know

I'm slow, but I find this kind of information hard to absorb,' he said.

Qasim said, 'We can hardly go to Kandahar and capture the gold. We'd never manage it, would we?'

'Wouldn't we?' asked Adam. 'Four hundred billion dollars, is about equivalent to the total assets of all the Gulf oil states. If the Russians had that, they would be out of their financial problems in one bound. There's no knowing what they might be able to do. Of course, if they put it all on the market at once, the price of gold would collapse, and with it, perhaps, world trade. On the other hand, if they spent it slowly, on development, food and arms, they could rival the United States itself. They have always been poor. With such reserves, they really could compete. The way they do things, and with the people they have in power now, there'd be very little hope for the rest of the world.'

'OK,' said Palmer, 'that means we've got to do it. But you realize that Kandahar is right the other end of the country, fifty or sixty miles from the Pakistan border, almost on the Arabian Sea, don't you? We'd have to cross the Koh-i-Baba range, go right through the high Hazarajat uplands – hundreds of miles of country that people never traverse.'

'But they do,' said Karima, 'that is the route taken by the *kochis*, the nomad people. They've been doing it for hundreds of years. They used to come, in trading caravans and selling sheep, to our village. Many of them were from Kandahar itself.'

They looked at the documents again. There was no sign of any date, no hint at all, as to when the treasure might be ready to be moved. Only that it seemed still to be there, pending 'finalization of export arrangements' by ALTINKUSH.

'All right,' said Adam, 'let's go and find Altinkush.'

As the days passed in the Wolves' redoubt, the excitement of the expedition caught everyone's imagination. Major Han, with his near-perfect organization, sat day after day with Adam, Azambai and the others, planning the route, discussing the likely conditions, putting together the necessary equipment. Food, medication, water, clothing, animals, radio communication, arms and ammunition: Major Han had – or could find – the answer to them all.

Ten days after the capture of the *Jihun*'s gold, when it was already on its way by courier to the provincial commanders which the Turkestanis had located, most of the wounded guerrillas were either recovered or well on the mend. The exception was Louis Palmer. His bayonet wound, though reopened and cleaned by Dr Babanour, became more and more septic. The bacteria were resistant to the weak Russian antibiotics which were all that could be obtained: day by day Adam and the others watched as the infection became generalized. Two weeks after the attack on the *Jihun* Louis Palmer died.

It was with heavy hearts that the guerrillas took part in the simple burial service. In the words of Major Han:

'*Ghazi* Kalan, the Big One, the American who came to this land and made his life here, was the opposite of those of us who were born Afghans, whatever our physical stock. He took this Afghanness on, of his own free will. He took it on, and he died for it, for freedom. As he has given us so much, may the All Highest give him peace.'

BOOK 11

Southwards to Kandahar

If Russia put a million troops into the country, ten times the initial number sent in, the Afghans would simply wait them out. Sufficient outrages would occur to keep the populace in a properly hateful frame of mind.

A war is fought to a conclusion. Disorders may go on for hundreds of years . . . Disorders are fought, with whatever deadly force is handy, plus the legendary hearts and minds.

James F. Dunnigan
How to Make War

1 Ride and Die!

High Hazara Land,
Central Afghanistan

LATE AUGUST

When Karima had suggested that the only practicable way to cross the high plateaux of Afghanistan to the Kandahar desert region in the south was with the Kochi nomads, Major Han had at once set about finding a suitable migrating caravan.

Malik Aziz's people, totalling almost two hundred, were ideal. They were healthy, friendly, straightforward people, they knew the way, and they were known for their reliability and astuteness. To them, the high mountains and the desert were their own, natural world. Although not warriors, they knew that the guerrillas must be helped in any way possible, if their country was to be saved.

They had no false pride, did not flinch from the description, sometimes disparagingly used of them, *khana ba-dosh*, 'those with their house on their back'.

Indeed, although they walked rather than rode, they carried no burdens: there were plenty of animals to do that. Since the motorways, linking the main cities, had been completed in the past few years, the Kochis' value had increased. They provided transportation through areas where there was no road, they competed with the road hauliers, and they brought news, goods and gossip to the thousands of villages which the new, macadamed highways had bypassed. And the Kochis, some two and a half million of them, were often far better off than the peasants of the settled lands, or even the gun-toting Pashtuns who lived at subsistence level as trade-despising herdsmen-warriors.

The Eagle's party numbered thirty: eight from his original caravan, ten Nuristanis, and the remainder composed of

Afghan Army deserters and three Turkestani soldiers supplied by Major Han. In Afghan terms, it was quite a formidable force, especially since absurdly small parties of Afghans, with local knowledge – once they had battle experience – had shown that they could easily deal with Russian formations several times their size.

For a week the caravan had moved westwards, through the province of Balkh, home of the 'Mother of Cities' of that name, the 'Place of High Banners' of the ancient Parsee scriptures. Then, amid both the desert and the sown land, the column struck southwards into the high central massif. Here they moved through boulder-strewn river valleys of austere beauty, passed great forests of pistachio trees, and climbed towards the great mountains of the Koh-i-Baba, the Father Mountain Range.

Then the caravan plodded farther west, still on the long road to Kandahar and Pakistan, skirting the valley of Bamiyan, from where, in Buddhist times, the message of the Eightfold Path was carried to China, Japan and other great centres of the Far East; and where, more recently, the Russian tanks had been expelled by the Afghan garrison, which had risen against the puppet governor and his Soviet advisers.

South of Bamiyan the caravan rested near the arterial road which bisects central Afghanistan, running from Herat, on the Iranian side, to the east. Here, not far from Chakcharan, in the district of Ghor, the supposed first home of the Bani-Israil in their Afghan diaspora, The Eagle received a message.

The head of a monastery of dervishes, men who had preserved their military tradition since before the times of the Crusades, when they had sent their cavaliers to join the great Sultan Saladin in Palestine, was preparing his men for another war against the infidel.

He had heard, even in his remote fastness, that there was work to be done, and that *komondon* Adam Durany was passing through his territory. Would The Eagle care to come and see the commissioning of a group of his men, who, following the news that Russian tanks might again invade Bamiyan, were preparing to do battle?

Adam, together with eight close friends from the Qizil Qala expedition, followed the guide sent from the dervish settlement, while the Kochi caravan, having declared a two-day halt to do some trading, waited for their return.

It was a three-hour ride to the site of the monastery, hidden in the jagged mountains south of the Koh-i-Baba. Soon after midday, the travellers reined in their horses on the outskirts of a Hazara village, a rock-built, fortified place below a crenellated medieval keep: the main entrance to the dervish stronghold.

Adam followed the other guerrillas into the monastery complex through a tunnel hewn out of the living rock. From the outside, the place looked like – and was – a mountain; but the interior was a honeycomb of passages and chambers. The massive entrance which he had first glimpsed was not now used.

Sometimes the passage led into great storerooms, lit by candles or flaming torches. Sometimes there were great dark gaps to the left or right, with the sound of trickling water or what might have been the scuffling of bats, disturbed by the footfalls of the party.

It was cool inside the mountain, it smelt musty, and the passages were only dimly lit by tiny lamps.

Suddenly they were at the entrance to a lofty hall, somewhere between a cave and a cathedral. The scene could have been right out of the Middle Ages. Burning pitch torches flickered in wrought iron sconces, jutting at an angle from the whitewashed walls. The chamber could have held upwards of two thousand people. A low humming sound came from the very centre of the place.

There, sitting cross-legged in a circle, each on a white lamb-skin mat, with heads closely shaven and wearing baggy breeches and white cotton caps, sat thirty-three men. The torches brought out the glow of their terracotta-coloured, sleeveless tunics. Five candles, in giant, intricately patterned, brass holders, stood before them on the floor. At the centre of the circle sat their leader: eyes half-closed, a green turban on his head, rosary in hand. He had the air of a magician, or of a vizier or paladin from *Thousand and One Nights*.

One of the escort motioned Adam to sit, making a sign denoting silence. The humming rose to a crescendo, following and imitating, though without words, the phrases called out in a melodious voice of the central figure.

The man sitting beside The Eagle whispered to him.

'This is the Sheikh of the *Tarika*, the Order. The disciples are dressed in the sleeveless *haydaria*, the tunic designed by Ali the Lion, Companion of the Prophet and founder of the *Futuwwa* – the first order of chivalry – a thousand and a half years ago. After this benediction, the men will go to join the war.'

A file of men, dressed like the grooms of those regions, in round felt hats and belted, long white shirts over baggy trousers, came soundlessly in soft deerskin boots, into the hall. Each carried a bundle of items which glinted in the torchlight. Each, as he reached one of the sitting warriors, placed his burden behind him, and lightly touched the border of his *haydaria* as he did so. Then they padded out again.

Adam's companion said, into his ear, 'That is their equipment, dug up from its grave where it has rested since the Third War with the British, sixty years and more ago. Taken from its oiled silk and grease, repaired and polished, it is ready.'

Suddenly, everyone rose. The grooms had come back into the room, this time carrying banners and large oil lamps, which they placed on the ground.

The men on the lambskins rose and turned to their accoutrement, while Adam was taken forward to shake hands with the Sheikh, who motioned him to sit on a fur just beside his own, small prayer rug. As they watched, the knights pulled on shirts and coats of fine chain mail, then soft Bokharan boots. The *haydaria* tunics, which they had taken off, were then put on as surcoats. Finally, as Adam gazed at the scene in stupefaction, each man placed a round steel helmet, peacock feathers in its slots and a fringe of chain mail around the neck, upon his head, and took his place, arms folded, standing to attention before the Sheikh. A perfect replica of a Saracen knight perhaps: but no threat to the soldiers of a modern army . . .

One by one, the men stepped forward to kiss the hand of their mentor. As he took each hand, the divine spoke the watchword which had been issued just before the desperate but decisive Battle of Hittin, by Saladin, almost eight centuries ago: 'Ride and die!'

Adam followed the elegant procession of knights and the motley guerrilla band back along the maze of passages. Before they left the castle, however, the Sheikh allowed his men to continue along the path, and drew The Eagle and the others into a different tunnel, leading away from the main thoroughfare. A few moments later the passage turned at a sharp angle, and, almost at once, they found themselves blinking in broad daylight.

The passage had led to a wide ledge halfway down the hill, which formed part of the castle-monastery. From here they looked down, over ancient embrasures, upon the stronghold's main approach. It was one of many perfect vantage points, an outpost for the defence of the main complex. Such a place could only have been planned by a military architect of great genius.

As The Eagle and his group watched, the dervish warriors lined up. The grooms brought their horses, magnificent Arab-Mongol crosses with white manes, covered in rich trappings. They helped each man to mount, handing him his round shield and long curved sword.

The setting sun glittered on their helmets and picked out the white lettering on the green and black banners as the doomed men kneed their horses eastwards along a narrow defile to their rendezvous with the Russian tanks: and death. The dervish mentor smiled. 'We call them, here,' he said, '*shah-gun*, the kingly ones.'

Both Adam and his companions knew Afghanistan too well to believe that they could intervene, could tell this holy but misguided man that he would never see his knights again, that the country would not benefit from senseless sacrifice, however noble it might seem. Even as a demonstration of the unquenchable flame of the human spirit to inspire others, their sally would be useless: Afghanistan, Noor thought, already had enough tales of glory, from a hundred wars.

As in so many Eastern lands, the dervish system, based on the teachings of the Sufi mystics who preached understanding and enlightenment, had fossilized into an intriguing, sometimes exciting, often admired formalism which produced and lived on emotion, wrongly imagined to be spirituality. It must, Adam reflected, have taken a similar path to that of the Western monastic orders of the Middle Ages, until the form and the feeling almost completely overcame the content. Even a thousand years ago, the classical writers were bemoaning this, as they wrote of the many allegedly Sufi schools which were then publicly known.

2 The Mulla and the Water of Life

Baghran Town
Descending towards Kandahar
South-Central Afghanistan

LATE AUGUST

The caravan travelled southwards, to the town of Baghran, high up in the central mountains of the Hazarajat, and camped nearby. They felt the influence of Kandahar now, and signs of the Red Afghan presence were everywhere: in posters, on local radio programmes. 'Shun the Bandits, support the Revolution.' The clatter of helicopters, the miserable-looking Afghan conscripts, their families hostage for their good behaviour, probably aching to desert.

The Kochis tethered their animals and, leaving some of their number in charge, went into Baghran to trade.

'Bandits, interventionists, imperialists will all be killed!' The voice went on and on, screeching from the cracked loudspeaker mounted on a lumbering, battered Party truck. 'Alexander the Great came here to find the Water of Eternal Life! The Water of Life and the Programme of the Party are one and the same!'

The truck stopped in Baghran's great flat *maidan*, which had been cleared of its market stalls, leaving a large paved space for the local citizens of the world's newest communist state to assemble and drink of this wisdom.

The Eagle's band, disguised as Kochis, watched the scene with interest.

The truck's door opened and a young man, a Party activist, fresh from the Ideology School at Dabalkhar, climbed out and onto the cab's roof. He unfurled a red flag and looked nervously around, to make sure that his escorting armed *zhondarm* was in place, automatic rifle at the ready. He was there; bored and smoking a smuggled Peter Stuyvesant cigarette, and thinking about women of all shapes and sizes, but he was indeed there.

'The Water of Life!' screamed the activist. The crowd rustled with interest. Yes, he thought; the Ideology Department was right: see *Red Wisdom* – chapter 7, page 233 – 'Always link the Revolution with ancient values to pre-empt their use by the feudalist-romantics.'

'The Water of Life, comrades, workers, peasants, intellectuals and fellow Afghans! The Water of Life means the New Age, the New Man, the reaching of a new height, the attainment of a goal, the fulfilment of a dream!'

A towering figure, a real Kandahar mulla, beetle-browed and hugely turbaned, pushed his way through the crowd, his stick plied to right and left with that dexterity which speaks of much experience. The townspeople recognized him: Mulla Azimi, from the Shrine of the Prophet's Cloak in Kandahar.

For a moment the activist was afraid of this clerical intervention. These abominable priests were always poking their noses into things which did not concern them.

As Azimi reached the truck, the activist noted with satisfaction that he was wearing a very large, red, cardboard hammer and sickle badge. This must be one of the comrade mullas who had joined the people's struggle. They were useful in keeping the people quiet; they would be dealt with when the Revolution had triumphed. Labour camps were the answer.

The mulla held up a hand, and the activist automatically helped him aboard. The man was so immense that he dwarfed the little intellectual. Indeed, he pushed him into a sitting position and took over the meeting with the accomplished air of a man who has spent his life spinning sermons of enormous length from a single catchword.

'The Water of Life,' Mulla Azimi was roaring, in a voice that needed no amplification; 'come and listen, comrades, for I shall tell you what the Water of Life means, exactly what it signifies and why tireless strugglers like this, our visitor, the activist delegate of the Party and the Leader Babrak Karmal, seek to bring it to us!'

The activist lit a cigarette. No need to keep a dog and bark yourself, he thought; and settled down to reflect on how he would wind up the meeting. There were several matters to consider, announcements as well as agitprop functions, handed down from the highest quarters.

'The Water of Life, O beloved ones,' the mulla was saying, 'is, as we know from the Histories, the real reason why the Great Alexander, the Lord of the Two Horns, came to our land. He journeyed to the farthest east, to Beluristan, Land of Crystals, where, in a cave, he finally found the water which gives eternal life. One drink is enough. This was what Alexander desired, and it was this which he duly found.

'He saw the water, issuing from a spring in the cavern, and he knelt to scoop up a palmful of the limpid liquid. Then, suddenly, he heard an anguished croak. What was it? Yes, you all know the legend, but is it legend or is it fact? The croaking came from a bird, whose beak was decayed, whose feathers had all dropped out, whose talons were scarcely able to grip the ledge on which it perched.

'"Stop, Alexander!" cried the bird. "And, before you drink, reflect that I myself, a thousand years ago, found this miraculous spring and drank from it. And, for the last nine hundred years I have been praying that someone or something would, could, put an end to my life. Eternal life I have, indeed; but it is a life of total misery and sickness, the unbearable exhaustion of old age. None can kill me now, and I am doomed to stay in this state until the end of time!"'

'And that,' roared Azimi, 'that is the life which the Party wants to bring us all. Allow them to do it, and you will exist in total misery like everyone else who has sipped of their infernal water . . .'

'Shoot him!' screamed the activist, purple in the face at the betrayal. The burning tip of his cigarette seared the flesh of his clenched fist where he had frenziedly grasped it.

The gendarme gasped, his head reeling. His orders were not to fire first, but only to protect the Party man. He fingered his gun nervously. The mulla, at the same moment, ripped the communist emblem from his breast and spat on it. Someone threw a stone, hitting the activist on the face. He started to scream with anguish and fury. A murmur, low at first, rose to a menacing climax, from several hundred throats: '*Kus-i-khuk! Kus-i-khuk, Kus-i-khuk!*' The ultimate insult, hideous even to a liberated Kabul intellectual, describing him as one of the most intimate parts of a female swine, drove the little man into a worse frenzy. Snatching the carbine from the guard, he slid off the safety catch and waved the weapon wildly at the crowd.

The mulla reached over, almost casually, and plucked it from his hands. He looked at the mechanism, altered the setting from 'automatic' to 'single shot', by rotating the safety selector as far down as possible. Then, turning towards the activist like a demonstrator at a trade fair, he pushed the barrel of the gun into the other man's open mouth and, carefully pressing the trigger, blew the back of his head off.

The crowd erupted, throwing turbans and shoes into the air. The mulla, after peering briefly at the corpse which had spun onto the ground behind the vehicle, transferred the gun to his left hand and, placing his right over his heart, bowed in a courtly manner, and pointed chivalrously towards a fat lady who had been giggling throughout.

Then he raised his hand for silence. 'Make way for the lorry, the *luri*, to be driven by these sheep back to their shepherd. We want them to report what we think of the Water of Life in this town, at least.'

He jumped down into the crowd.

Amid frantic cheering, the terrified gendarme and the driver, faces white, careered away through the path cleared for them by the exulting rejectors of the benefits of the Great Good News of the Soviet Water of Life. The body of the activist lay, crumpled, where it had fallen.

The mulla held onto the assault rifle. 'It must be worth at least fifty thousand Afghanis,' he murmured. 'I think, my little one, there'll be much more work for you, in days to come.'

He turned to the crowd, again. 'Brethren! The calamity is here! We need vigilance, we need supplies and arms, we need to bear great burdens and to learn new ways. And we must remember this:'

He recited from Sura II, verse 255 of the Holy Book: the potent Verse of the Throne,

> '"*God! There is no deity but he,*
> *The Living, the Ever-Abiding One.*
> *No slumber seizes him, nor sleep.*
> *His is all that there is in the heavens and on the earth.*

Who may intercede with him, but by his leave?
He it is who knows all that is before, after and beyond.
Nor may they compass any of his knowledge, but what
he may allow.
His throne extends over the heavens and the earth:
And, in guarding and preserving, he is burdened not
at all:
For he is the Most High, the Supreme".'

That was how Mulla Azimi, one of his staunchest supporters, came to join The Eagle.

BOOK 12

Ekranoplan, the Sea Monsters

Encouraged by rich peasants, poisonous Zionists and international imperialists, isolated incidents should not be mistaken for opposition or ingratitude towards the fraternal, neighbourly, peace-loving and democratic USSR.

It is untrue to say that there are only three hundred socialists in Afghanistan. All the toilers of the Afghan Democratic Republic are socialists.

Spokesman of the Ministry of the Interior, Kabul

1 Wild Horses

Southern Hazarajat

AUGUST – SEPTEMBER

From the cool uplands of the Hazarajat, home of the people supposed to be descended from the hordes of Genghiz Khan, The Eagle and his companions descended into the blazing autumn heat of the Helmand river valleys.

At the town of Sangar, fifty miles north of the great Kajakai Dam, they met Hafiz Buyukbay, War Chief of Koh-i-Sangan, the Stony Mountain, whose peak scraped the sky at thirteen thousand feet. He was undisputed leader of thirty thousand warriors.

He received The Eagle's party in a long, low black tent, whipped by the constant wind, sustained only by wooden poles and carpeted with sacks. Before the Russian invasion, he had owned half a million sheep and his home had been decorated with Persian rugs and Sèvres china. That had all been sold, for weapons. Today, he was a white-bearded eighty-seven-year-old, who carried an Austrian Mannlicher eight-millimetre rifle slung across his back. He was short, stocky and pugnacious, a farmer-turned-guerrilla with more than a dash of the robber baron in his dress: crossed bandoliers, turban-end across his mouth, long, close-quarters killing-knife in his belt.

Everyone addressed him as *Harb-Bashi*, War Chief.

His military adviser, far from being a Western capitalist-interventionist, was a Russian prisoner-turned-Muhjahid: Antoli Mikhailovich, formerly a lieutenant in the 346th Soviet Motorized Rifle Division, captured when the city of Kandahar had last changed hands, as it did eight times in 1981/82.

They sat drinking tea and looking down at the Helmand Plains as Antoli, at a sign from the war chief, told of his change of heart.

'It's those bunglers in Moscow,' he began, pursing his lips and screwing up his pale blue eyes. He was from north-western Russia, and could not get used to the heat here, sometimes reaching 112 degrees Fahrenheit.

'I don't know whether the general staff or the civil servants are the worse fools. They blame Stalin for not opposing the Nazis when they first invaded us. He couldn't believe it! But I think that misperception of an opponent is their characteristic.'

He loved the word *characteristic*, and used it all the time.

'When I was briefed, they warned me to be prepared for the monsoon in Afghanistan. The monsoon! There isn't such a thing here. Then we had a session with a geographer, who seemed to think that this is a land of coolies and steaming jungles. I've read some books about American top-level bunglers, but ours can beat them every time!'

The Eagle laughed. 'Well, even in the USA when I was there, when I told them I was from Afghanistan, people said, "What state is that in?"'

'That may well be,' said Antoli, 'but I bet they did not say "upcountry" as if we were in Africa. Why, our people thought that the Afghans ate Indian curry, ran in terror from "white sahibs" and were good communists into the bargain!'

Noor asked him, 'Why did you desert?'

'Desert?' The Russian turned to her with a snarl. 'I'm twenty-four years old and a professional soldier. I didn't desert. I rejoined the human race! I am a *Russian* freedom fighter. Afghanistan was free. The USSR is not.'

He was an earnest young man with an athlete's build, in a neat Soviet uniform, from which he had removed all the badges.

The old chief grinned. 'You see,' he explained, 'he complains a lot about the people in Mosku. But I keep telling him that they know a lot more about us now . . .'

'Yes,' agreed Antoli, 'in some ways they know far too much. The bungling of the political people and the ordinary army commands has brought the GRU, Military Intelligence, to the fore. And what have they done? Established a huge, new secret army, the Spetsnaz Force, modelled on the British SAS.'

'What can they do that isn't being done already, to destroy the population?' Adam asked.

The war chief answered. 'They now have efficient units

operating behind our lines. That's to say, they roam the mountains disguised as guerrillas, and destroy Resistance forces. First they ingratiate themselves, then they swoop. We've lost many men that way.

'Then they fire on refugees and destroy villages. This makes the people think that the Muhjahidin are murderers.'

'Very clever,' said Noor.

'Clever!' shouted Antoli; 'do you know what they did in October last in Kabul? There were several hundred young students, with placards, protesting against communism at the Jashn Grounds, the park in Kabul. Fifty Spetsnaz men, dressed as Afghans, appeared and fired fusillades into the crowd. Among those killed were almost a hundred young girls.'

The *Buyukbay*, Adam realized, was biding his time. He would not commit any of his 30,000 men to battle until they were well enough armed to beat the Russians. Small-scale raids was all he could manage. The caravan moved on.

The guerrillas descended from the heights of Zamindawar towards Kandahar city, seeing more and more aerial activity each day. Russian fliers were on constant patrol, looking for guerrilla concentrations which they could blast from the air before they reached the low-lying land to attack Soviet installations.

If there were only some ground-to-air missiles, SAMs, Adam thought, as he saw the enemy passing overhead unmolested. What was the use of one rifle to twenty men? The encounter with the war chief, commander of tens of thousands with only a few light weapons and his men thin from hunger, and the sight of these aircraft; this told the whole story. Without massive support from somewhere – the war would be lost, another country doomed, sucked into the Soviet empire.

The south-west of Afghanistan is a land of deserts as well as fertile plains. With Iran to the west and Pakistan to the south, the huge area watered by the immense rivers Helmand and Arghandab has as its centre the ancient city of Kandahar, founded by Alexander the Great during his thrust India-wards.

The Eagle knew this region better than just well. He had been born here, thirty-three years ago. The Americans had built a modern town for the people who worked on the giant hydroelectric and irrigation projects of the Helmand Valley Authority.

Adam Durany, he had been named by his father, one of the Authority's top hydrologists: a name which could be used either for an American or for an Afghan, and few would have been able to tell which he was. 'Durayney', as the Anglo-Saxons said it, was quite a possible name for either of them. He might be from Idaho or Maine. And 'Durraani', said in the Afghan fashion, was the name of the great Pashtun tribe of the area, the one which had given Afghanistan its first king in modern times.

Adam loved the place, majestic Kajakai, and especially the great blue, artificial lake in the Arghandab, surrounded by high, upright terracotta crags, the beauty of the ancient city of Kandahar.

And there was a strong bond between this desert place and the cool, mountain uplands of fair Paghman, near Kabul, where Adam was to start his guerrilla career. The rulers of Paghman were ancient allies of the ruling family. Indeed, in the Koti Landani mansion at Kabul, Adam had heard a great prince of the royal house, Sirdar Mohammed Yusuf Khan, holding forth, often and at length, about how the Jan-Fishanis, the Paghman people, with their legions, had saved the Yahya Khel family, and hence made modern Afghanistan possible, as he put it.

Such alliances, and tribal, family and spiritual loyalties were, and are, the fabric of Afghan life. By some mysterious alchemy, over the millennia, the Afghans had retained a clear identity, though they had seen changes such as few people ever have.

As the country which linked east and west, China with India and Persia, the European north with the Asian south, carrying the Silk Road which stretched, a year's full march, all the way from Peking to Rome, everything had come to, or through Afghanistan.

In the most recent, the Islamic, period, the Afghans had forged the strongest bonds. The Khans of Paghman were descendants, in direct line, from the Prophet Mohammed. And the cloak of the Prophet reposed in Kandahar itself. When the first king of Afghanistan was crowned, it was a member of the Prophetic Family, Sabir Shah, who crowned him. There were many other links, and young Durany eagerly soaked up the tales as the grizzled elders and tribal story-tellers recounted them. Their duty was to make sure that the lore was not forgotten, and that their listeners, even those youngsters who were yawning late into the night, were word-perfect in the history and the legends.

It was at this focal point of history, some miles north-west of Musa Qala – Moses's Fort – in the foothills and within striking distance of Kandahar and Noor's father at Kajakai, that the nomads and The Eagle's band fixed their base camp.

There were trees here, and water, as well as forage for the animals. The latter would have to be fattened up a little before being offered at the city's cattle market. The Kochis, like the guerrillas, never showed themselves in their full strength in 'foreign' territory, always keeping their goods, and their young men under control in their own camp.

First to Kandahar, The Eagle thought, to collect information, and then there might be some hope of rescuing old Sharifi, who must be living, under guard, somewhere near the Kajakai Dam, sixty miles away.

2 Kandahar in disguise

The Oasis of Panjtan,
Kandahar Province

MID-SEPTEMBER

Adam, with Noor, Karima and ten men, set off, disguised as
nomads, with a Kochi family as cover, for Kandahar.

Nobody tried to stop them as they followed the camel-track
running beside the great asphalted motorway, part of the Asian
highway from Herat, and they entered the dusty city without
incident.

The nomads made their way to the cattle market, while
Adam, Noor, and Qasim, with Karima, walked around the
town, leaving the remainder of their force, split into two smaller
groups, to collect information.

The battles of Kandahar had razed vast areas of the best
buildings in Afghanistan's second city. Public buildings had
been rocketed, parks were full of the homeless, crippled men
and women were everywhere. During the day, however, no
Russian or Red Afghan dared to show his face here, except for
the occasional patrol, which swept in and then out again,
nobody quite sure why. Were the Russians in occupation or
not? It was difficult to tell.

As the four sat at a table in the street outside the Lalazar
Café, a swarm of motorcycle-troops with machine-guns in their
sidecars swept past. Adam looked enquiringly at the café's
owner. He shrugged. '*Shoravis*, communists. They have a
general who wants to look at Kandahar himself, but he daren't
come alone.'

More guards, armoured personnel-carriers filled with troops,
went past. Adam noticed that the two files of men in them were
facing inwards, unable to reach their weapons if attacked: and
in the wrong position for firing.

'Why are they sitting like that?' he asked the Pashtun café man.

'It's an unwritten agreement. They mean to say that they are here to inspect, not to fight. They won't fire first: and, of course, we'd not attack them if they sit like people in a bus.' He grinned. 'We'll get them later, though, when the next fight starts.'

When the first modern Afghan King, Ahmad Shah, had buried his colossal treasure near Kandahar, the whole area of south-west Afghanistan, formerly the garden of Asia, had been desolate for five centuries. Genghiz Khan the Mongol conqueror, destroying the irrigation system, had seen to that. Three immense, snow-fed rivers, the Arghandab, Turnak and Arghistan, roaring down from the great mountains in the north-east, had been diverted and used to irrigate immense tracts of fertile land.

Adam Durany, sitting on a hill between three deserts, which had once been rich farmland, focused his field-glasses on the immense white concrete mass which was the Kajakai Dam. Somewhere around there Sirdar Akbar, hydropower engineer, was a prisoner.

The guerrillas were camped in an oasis, under good tree-cover, less than a mile from Kajakai. To their south was the great highway to Iran. In the opposite direction, it cut across the Helmand valley area to cross the Pakistan border, no more than a hundred miles to the south-east.

The second massive dam, the Arghandab, also lay to the south-east, upstream of the river from which it took its name. Twenty miles south was Kandahar, whose citizens had not long ago driven off the Soviet Army's 40th Army, supported by no less than 240 massive helicopter gunships and the Mig-25, missile-armed 'Foxbat' warplanes.

The Eagle panned his glasses to left and right. The Russians had a well-devised defence system here to protect the dam from the air and keep ground attackers out. Anti-aircraft guns, mobile S-20s, were standing on the perimeter, ready to be wheeled into action. Adam could see guards standing ready at the batteries of surface-to-air rockets, whose crews, no doubt on call, lived in a series of wooden huts dispersed around the main buildings. The approaches were guarded by two dozen camouflage-painted tanks, old and new.

But the many rocky outcrops, covered in trees and bushes, with old goat-tracks still visible, showed Adam that there were still ways to get into Kajakai. He would, in the meantime, send Noor's father a message.

'Your Excellency has made a serious mistake,' said The Eagle; 'and I have come here, at very great risk, to see what we can do about it.'

Akbar sighed. He had been a minister, an ambassador, too, a member of the Afghan Cabinet. Whisked about in a Cadillac, marched along ranks of men to inspect troops, given ovations at the United Nations Assembly in New York. The Eagle was thirty years younger than he, and he'd sat Adam on his knee as a child, fed him with lime-drops, forbidden by his parents in case the green colour meant that they were laced with arsenic. But, of course, he was not a soldier . . .

'Are you sure that we are safe here? It seems rather exposed, and the guard is sitting in the café, just down there.' The old man pointed to the dusty road below the tree-covered hill where they were sitting.

'I sent you a message to start taking walks, always to the same place, and to do it every day at daybreak. As I thought, the guard came to the top of the hill for a week, and then he let you go the last part on your own. He's a communist, and he's lazy. Seeing you saying your prayers embarrasses him. So he stops at the teahouse for a smoke. Besides, I've put a young girl in there. She is decently hidden in the kitchen, but she's allowed to talk to him over the pots and pans, and he's been smitten for days. That's how we knew you were still a prisoner, and hadn't just gone over to the Russians.' The Eagle tapped his binoculars. 'And I've got picquets posted to watch. If he looks like coming up here, they'll fire from three directions. Then his little red feet will go tip-a-tap, Excellency.'

Akbar pondered this for a moment. The guard was always boasting . . .

'He told me that he had one of those new rifles. The kind that fire high-velocity bullets. They pass right through a man, destroying tissue so that it can't be mended, even with an operation. If they hit bone, the force is so great that you die of shock.'

'And I have two men who can put a bullet through his earhole before he can raise his supergun.'

The Eagle crouched among the bushes. 'That's enough about security, except that they have you carefully guarded and we're going to have a job getting you out of here.' He looked at his watch. 'I must talk fast. First, Noor is well. She is with us, not far from here.'

Akbar Sharifi looked as if he was going to faint, and started to say something.

'Never mind talking: listen. You let the Russians get the gold and we had to blow up one lot of it, on the Oxus. We've come here for the rest.'

'Rest? They've taken it all.' Akbar spoke listlessly. 'They followed me and found it. Then they took it, all. Please, tell me about Noor? Can I see her?'

'She's fine, you can see her soon, when we get you out of here. Where have they taken the gold?'

'To the airport. I've heard they are transporting it on the Caspian Sea Monsters.'

'Caspian what?'

'Sea Monsters. They are giant surface-skimmers, huge hover-craft built on the Caspian Sea by the Russians. Something entirely new. Carrying almost a thousand men or a huge weight of materials, they can cover over land or sea a thousand kilo-metres or more. They go over minefields, under radar: they are the latest weapon. The Russian officers in this area have been boasting that they'll win the next war with them. I suppose the treasure is being sent to the USSR.'

Adam's thoughts went back to the treasure.

'Why did you not inform the Resistance that you had found the gold, and arrange with them to get it out?'

'My dear brother, I'm stuck out here. I can't trust anyone. Who are the Resistance, and how would I get to them?'

'And so?'

'And so I sent my man Samir to Peshawar, in Pakistan, to see Prince Jamal. I know his father, the King of Narabia. I asked them to buy the gold and put the money in Switzerland. My plan was to find the Muhjahidin somehow and tell them how to get the money. I had no time to think further. I had to act.'

Adam nodded. 'Then what happened?'

'I have heard nothing from Samir. And the Russians, following me, found the gold. They took it.' He sighed.

'And they still let you walk about, didn't arrest you?'

'Short walks. After all, I can't do much harm to them. I'm not likely to find any more gold. And they need my engineering skills.'

A branch began to creak in the tree overhead. 'One of my men is tugging a string tied to that,' said The Eagle: 'so it is probably your guard coming up the hill from the café. Go down and meet him. I'll stay here for a bit and then slip away. Don't worry, we'll get you out.'

3 Council of War

The Oasis

MID-SEPTEMBER

At the oasis, the guerrillas held a council of war. The gold, as the Sirdar had told Adam, was gone, to Kandahar airport. 'And then, naturally, it would go to Moscow – where else?' said Azambai. Stop the shipment, try to capture it, release the old man: those were the problems. Those and one other. The Kochis had reported from Kandahar that the Russians and the Afghan Fifteenth Infantry Division were likely to attack the city soon. The Resistance in Kandahar sent messages, welcoming The Eagle's force, but warning that there might be an air attack at any moment.

'We can't do much for the city with at most a hundred fighting men – and that is if the Kochis stay with us and don't wander off to trade in Pakistan,' said Qasim. 'I say it's go for the gold first, and try to rescue the Sirdar afterwards.'

'Can't we do both?' Noor wanted to know.

'Let's hear what the scouts have to say about the strength of the enemy defending the skimmers,' suggested Adam.

Qasim produced a piece of paper covered with pencilled figures. 'I've been working it out. Did you realize that if the treasure is the size we think it is, what it will weigh? How could we possibly capture it, store it, and move it to Pakistan, with a hundred men and no transport?'

'May I make a suggestion, sir?' Cadet Arif stood up and held himself at attention.

'Go on, Arif,' said Adam.

'We need more men, more arms, transport and probably more information. Kandahar will probably be attacked soon, perhaps at any moment. I suggest that we help in its defence, and then, if successful, get the Kandaharis to help us with the gold problem.'

'That's all very well,' said Azambai. 'But that would mean, first, that the skimmers might get away before we could stop them. Second, that the Kandaharis could get to hear of the gold, and that – make no mistake – would cause real problems. Gold does funny things to people.'

They all looked at the cadet.

'Yes, captain *seb*. But, first, we could send patrols to assess the likelihood of the skimmers leaving soon. Patrols,' he recited the formula as if from the book, 'have the purpose of ascertaining the enemy's position, strength and intentions . . .'

'That's enough, lad: I'm glad you know what a patrol is for.' Azambai was abrupt. 'But what about the security aspect? The Kandaharis might take the gold from us.'

'Permission to answer, sir! Everything is risky. We must take the risk.'

Adam presiding, a vote was taken. Arif's suggestion was adopted.

It was about twenty miles to the airport, and the captain was wondering how to lead his reconnaissance patrol there without transport, and thinking that only a gift from heaven would solve his problem, when a man came running into his brushwood shelter, under the trees in the oasis, shouting, 'Alert! Commander sir: there's dust!'

Dust. Approaching vehicles. Adam held up his hand.

'*Mlater:* fighting men! These are your orders. Pass the word to let them enter the oasis, don't fire on the first truck if there are more than one – cut any convoy in two.'

The man ran off, rifle at the ready.

Yes, it was dust all right. Zelikov came scrambling through the bushes and said, '*Roussi* truck.'

'How many, Zelikov?' The Russian cocked his head to listen. 'Sounds like five. Maybe six.'

That could mean a couple of hundred men. All around, from behind rocks and trees, Azambai could hear the bolts of rifles click in readiness for firing.

Adam wriggled his way up to Azambai. 'They're heading

straight for us, from the direction of Grishk, downriver on the Helmand.'

Azambai grinned, and snapped a plastic magazine into his new Kalakov AK-74. 'Well, Adam Jan, it's your Paghman river, so maybe it will help you win.' He knew that the mighty Helmand, dammed at Kajakai, rose in the glaciers of the Paghman mountains at 12,500 feet, and crossed the whole country to peter out in the far marshes of Seistan, 625 miles from its source.

The throb of the noisy Russian engines was louder. Not a blade of grass moved as the convoy of six trucks, rugged, cross-country ones, swept into the oasis, along the cattle-track which led to the watering-place beside which Adam, Azambai, Zelikov and Qasim waited, peering through a thin screen of scrub.

The lead truck stopped so close to him that Adam could smell its engine oil. He looked at the symbol on the Ural's radiator. A red triangle, enclosing a circle and head of wheat. Afghan Democratic Army. A young man, dressed in combat grey, jumped down from the cab. He had a lieutenant's insignia and was in full battle-array, even to the steel helmet. Around his neck, oddly, was a small green scarf.

Adam nodded to the others. They covered him as he jumped, pulled the man down and dragged him back into the bushes, the point of a glittering Afghan stabbing dagger held against his jugular vein.

The lieutenant gasped, gagged, managed to say, in a strangled voice, 'Muhjahid – freedom fighter.' He struggled free, dusted himself down and came to attention, his thumbs in line with his trouser seams.

'Beg permission to report, sir! Senior Lieutenant Tura of the Fifteenth Infantry Division, Army of Afghanistan, with six Russian Ural trucks and one hundred and eighty men, thirty-six of them sergeants and the rest privates, all in good order, at the General's orders for liberation, sir!'

The gift from heaven!

Azambai held out his hand. 'Well done, my boy! I'm not a general – I am Captain Yusuf Azambai. This is our commander, Kara Kush, from Paghman.'

Tura saluted. 'At the service of the commander. These green

scarves are our current combat recognition sign. But we're still the Afghan Army!'

Adam took his hand. 'Thank you, Lieutenant. Get your trucks camouflaged. How did you know we were here, and are the Russians after you?'

Tura gave the order to a senior sergeant, who saluted and went off at the trot.

'My father-in-law, Neknam Khan, is a Resistance leader in Kandahar. He sent a message to me in our commissariat truck. We are on manoeuvres, preparing for the attack on Kandahar, sir! No Russians will be after us for eight hours or so, commander.' Tura saluted again, and stood at ease.

'We're certainly short of men, Tura Khan,' Adam said; 'and maybe you're just what we need, though the Russians always attack with really overwhelming forces: that's their philosophy.'

The Afghan defectors were armed to the teeth. They had three of the new Soviet automatic AGS-17 grenade-launchers, devastating weapons which had been used to terrible effect against guerrilla formations. Their trucks contained modern, minimum-recoil automatic rifles, plenty of ammunition, and even a number of shoulder-fired rocket-launchers and rockets.

Now Azambai had his men and transport for his reconnaissance. A thought struck him.

'Tura Khan: what do your written orders say?'

'Beg to report, sir! I have them here, in Russian, Dari and Pashtu. They permit us to operate on manoeuvres, within a seventy-mile radius of Kandahar City.'

'Could you go to the airport without arousing suspicion – where these new Soviet surface-skimmer things are located?'

'Certainly. We have been there many times.'

That was it.

'Tura,' Adam said, 'how is it that a man of your rank, only a lieutenant, is commanding what amounts to a battalion?'

'Desertions, sir: the whole army is falling to pieces. Our original *paltan*, regiment, hardly exists now.'

'Why didn't you defect before?'

'Neknam Khan was arranging for our relatives, kept hostage in Hajikhel Camp, to be rescued first.'

'Where are they now?'

'Most of them died in the attack on Hajikhel. I think that

some reached Bangidar Refugee Camp, in Pakistan, but that was bombed by Russian planes, and we don't know what happened to them.'

'People close to you?'

'Sir. My mother, my wife and two sisters among them.'

Captain Azambai, disguised in the uniform of one of Lieutenant Tura's sergeants, led the reconnaissance. Two trucks, with thirty men, enough for a patrol and even to fight their way out of tricky situations, rolled away within half an hour of the defectors' arrival at the oasis. They bluffed their way, with Tura's movement orders, through the roadblocks of the Soviet 357th Motorized Rifle Division, guardians of the approaches to Kandahar.

They were back in four hours, well pleased, bringing an Afghan mechanic, one of the maintenance personnel at the skimmers' base. He was anxious to defect, and full of information. There were no less than thirty of the skimmers sitting on a special site after their long journey from Krasnovodsk, their home base on the Soviet shores of the Caspian Sea, north of Iran.

And they were soon due to transfer a secret cargo, 'machine parts', already loaded, in heavy wooden cases, on a flight which was estimated to be 'a thousand kilometres'. A skimmer looked like a half-aircraft, half-ship, was powered by immense engines, and could fly, skimming land or sea, at six hundred miles an hour. The Russians, who expected to use them anywhere in the world, were hugely pleased with their performance.

Some details, said the mechanic, had leaked out to the West: and he produced a photocopy, given to him by a Russian technician, of a page from the current edition of a British reference book, *Jane's Surface Skimmers*, with pictures. What the West did not know was that the Monsters were in such large-scale production.

Adam was wondering how to attack the transports and get the gold away when Engineer Sirdar Akbar Sharifi, discoverer of the gold and the father of Noor, ducked into the brushwood shelter and embraced him.

'Ambassador!'

'Adam Jan!'

Adam was flabbergasted. 'Amazing. I was working on all sorts of plans to rescue you. How ever did you do it?'

Sharifi smiled, and pointed to Zelikov, who was pushing his way into the shelter. 'Ask your Russian friend.'

Zelikov drew a long dagger from his boot and started to pick his teeth with it. 'Nothing, *Preents*. I borrow a Ural truck from *Leytenant*, take five Afghan soldiers, and Mulla Azimi show me the way.'

Adam clapped him on the back. 'We don't normally award decorations, Zelikov, but the next time we capture a Soviet soldier with the Order of the Red Banner, I'll present it to you!' He shook his head, slowly, from side to side. He could hardly credit that the exploit had taken place, and was rather glad that the Russian hadn't spelt it out in detail: he was sure that he wouldn't be able to absorb it.

Then he remembered.

'Did Zelikov tell you where Noor was?'

'No. Is she all right?'

'She's fine. And she's *here*. Zelikov, take the ambassador to Noorjan.'

Almost before he had finished speaking, the old man was scrambling out of the shelter, through the bushes, to meet his daughter.

Adam went back to his sketch maps. Now, if the Russians attacked Kandahar from the north, where they were massing . . .

BOOK 13

Into the Abode of War

Da seori nakhl na nisi ratb
(Keep your palm tree in the shade
and you will get no dates).

Pashtu proverb

1 Target: Kandahar Airport

Pendergood's Army
In the Free Land
Pakistan-Afghan Border
and Moscow

SEPTEMBER 15
Late afternoon

The Soviet High Command was indeed furious that the Red Army had been thrown out of Kandahar, again and again and with ignominy, by its people, mere bandits. But there was another reason for their decision to make the city safe for socialism: the presence of Kara Kush and his Commando.

Halzun, The Snail, aiming for supreme power over the Council of Ministers, was determined that Operation Altinkush, his treasure plan, should succeed. As a chess player, he saw two threats to it developing.

The information came from his trusted agent, Aliyev the Uzbek, diligently working from KGB Peshawar Centre, Pakistan. His network of spies extended, now, from Quetta, hundreds of miles to the south-west, to Chitral, abutting Afghan Nuristan. Aliyev worked on a mosaic, collecting, collating, inferring.

Adam Durany would have been surprised at the accuracy of Nurhan Aliyev's message, one of two which lay on the desk before The Snail at Moscow Centre:

SUBJECT: Dangerous counter-revolutionary leader, war-name KARA KUSH, real name unknown. Message begins: Armed group led by Kara Kush, having fought Soviet and loyal Afghan forces in Paghman and blown up Oxus River gunboat JIHUN has struck southwards and now believed nearing Kandahar. Possible threat treasure transfer feared. Message ends.

507

Halzun, deleting the last sentence from the decrypt, marked the despatch 'Immediate', and sent it to Soviet Afghanistan Command, via the Ministry of Defence.

The second sheet of paper would have surprised both Adam and Pendergood:

> · SUBJECT: Force led by arms smuggler from England, sou-briquet PENDERGOOD. Message begins: Suspected presence of above bandit and supplier of war materials to Kara Kush /see last message/ with large tribal force of paid Pashtun lackeys reported heading northwards through un-administered tribal territory unconfirmed. We lack access to this savage region. Message ends.

Much less substantial than the first signal, Halzun thought: there was no point in alerting the Army on that one yet. He rose from his chair and walked through the double doors of his office into the conference room: it was electronically shielded against surveillance.

The five men sitting around the green baize-covered table rose, sat down as The Snail waved a hand, and waited. Halzun reached out a paw for a bottle of Narzan water, poured a glassful, and began to speak.

'Comrades, the War Party has been a great threat to our plan to acquire power and to establish competition, not confron-tation, with the capitalist world. Achieving production of the large Ekranoplan – surface-skimmer – fleet five years ahead of schedule was a blow to us. It also impressed the Party so much that we had to take decisive action before some general or marshal actually took over the USSR. That was the agreed background. Now, Comrade Semyenov, at what point did we end the last meeting?'

The little man across the table rose and spoke fussily, pre-cisely. 'Comrade Chief Director, Comrades. We decided to research the vulnerability of the skimmers, and left the matter of the huge financial resources needed for competition with the West for further consideration.'

'Exactly so,' said The Snail; 'in other words, we were at a loss. There seemed little chance of dealing with these two great challenges.' He struck his right hand into his left palm. 'And I have asked you to come here today to tell you that I, I Halzun, have solved both problems.'

There was a gasp of surprise from around the table.

'A gold treasure was found in Afghanistan, and it fell into our hands . . .' Halzun grinned.

'Comrade Chief Director,' said one of the men, 'that gold was lost to us, by enemy action. The so-called Eagle blew it up.'

The Snail raised his hand. 'Patience, Comrade Kaganovitch! It was indeed lost. But in any case it did not represent a spectacular amount, and would not have paid for our programme. No, we needed billions of dollars for that.

'The Afghan engineer who found the gold, however, miscalculated its value. He thought that it must be worth billions, and offered to sell it to the Arabs. That's what gave me my great idea. I intended to have the hoard brought to the Soviet Union, and our agents penetrated the engineer's network. Engineer Akbar offered the gold but could not deliver. So we stepped in, to oblige.' He interrupted himself with a long chuckle.

'Now we had only minor problems. The British, through Arabian and other contacts, found out the planned deception: that I wanted to forge "gold" coins of the right date and pass them off. The USSR leads the world in both metallurgy and counterfeit artefacts, you know. We have an alloy whose falsity can be detected only by the most sophisticated tests. We only lacked advanced technology: computer-controlled, continuous-process stamping machines. The British supplied those.'

Halzun paused, five pairs of eyes riveted upon him. Then he laughed. 'The Americans will be what they call sore when they find that, with all the resources of Arabia, we are as rich as they are!'

Kaganovitch said, 'And we'll deliver the coins by surface-skimmer?'

'Exactly. Once we have the money, we'll use a certain plan to get the skimmers sabotaged, so that the Central Committee decides that they are useless. It is the last link in the chain. The gold plan, confided to the Committee, has already gained me the as yet undisclosed position of Chairman of the Council of Ministers.'

The five men goggled. Chairman. Effectively ruler of the whole USSR . . .

'Comrade Chairman,' Semyenov was unable to resist asking something which had been nagging in his mind. 'Why should the English have helped us? Didn't they even want a share of the money – they haven't got any of their own!'

Halzun shrugged. 'In international matters there is always a trade-off. The Americans might have got us out of Afghanistan through an ultimatum, as in the case of the Cuban missiles, two decades ago. They didn't try that, because we would have told them to get out of Central America as the price. For the English, a guarantee of peace would mean eliminating their crushing defence burden. And then, of course, we paid well for the stamping machines: and they stand to get cheap oil from the bankrupt Arabs.

'All is ready for the biggest coup in history, Comrades. Our agents are in place in Zurich, to empty the bank account when King Zaid's message comes through, confirming delivery.

'There is a little trouble near Kandahar to take care of, bandits, but we're keeping an eye on that matter. The outlook, we might say, is good.'

'Suppose the Arab king has spies in Afghanistan who could discover the truth?' one of the men asked.

'I have allowed for that. We have planted spurious movement orders all over the place, saying that we are transporting genuine gold coins from Kandahar. That's why we are staging the counterfeits from Kandahar instead of direct from the Soviet Union.

'That will be all, Comrades. I have to go now, to seek confirmation or otherwise about this rumoured attack, by some ridiculous revanchist called Pendergood. He appears to think that he can invade Afghanistan from the unpoliced, Pakistan frontier.'

Pendergood was indeed preparing for an all-out attack on the Soviets in the Kandahar area. He and Callil, with the Free Pashtun Army of their creation, were camped in the Free Land, which nobody in all recorded history had successfully administered. They had already crossed the Toba Kakar mountain range from Pakistan, north of the city of Quetta, and were within a stone's throw of the line on the map which was supposed to be the international border: and Afghanistan. Kandahar Airport was within striking distance: no more than sixty miles to the west.

Around Pendergood's mobile command post – an International truck – was a forest of supplies and vehicles. A mass of tents, originally white, now cunningly camouflaged, was invisible on the hard, flat sand. Clay and pulped grass, daubed liberally but at random, made the camp blend into the terrain, if viewed from the air.

More than three hundred vehicles, ranging from ancient jeeps to brand new Mercedes and American trucks, were dispersed in case of air attack. The six anti-aircraft guns were Dashkas, captured from the Russians and refurbished by the peerlessly competent gunsmiths of Darra.

Darra – Darra Adam Khel – had been on their route from Chitral, when Pendergood had travelled south, collecting his warriors. He, Callil and Bardolf the German had done good business at Darra: the bizarre arms centre of the Afridi frontier men.

Here, in 1897, the Afridi clan had negotiated an unique pact with the British, then ruling India. The imperial power was not strong enough, even in its heyday, to crush the Pashtuns, and knew it. In an unprecedented *de facto* recognition of Pashtun independence, Britain agreed that the clansmen could have their own arms factories. This obligation was inherited by Pakistan when Britain left the country.

Forty minutes drive from Peshawar's frontier bustle, the Pendergood group, avoiding the volleys of gunshot being fired from shops in the main street where intending customers tried out Darra-made rifles, had found almost all the military supplies they needed to complete their army's preparedness.

Until recently, the Pashtuns had been making perfect replicas of traditional weapons: British Army rifles from the Second World War were the most modern ones.

With the war in Afghanistan, however, a flood of weapons, captured by the Muhjahidin or sold to them by penniless Russian soldiers, came on to the market. These the gunsmiths bought, tested and refurbished, selling them again with their own guarantee.

The frontier smiths had their own sense of humour. Their copies of British rifles used always to carry the United Kingdom's imperial symbol, often 'G VI' – King George the Sixth – and a copy of a British proof-mark. Now, with the Russians claiming that Soviet-type equipment was being supplied by their hated enemies, the Red Chinese, to the Afghans, the Darra technicians added Chinese markings to the guns, copied from the ones which were laboriously smuggled from Peking over the high Karakorum Highway into Pakistan. They called this 'getting the Bear by the tail'. It infuriated the Russian agents who mingled with the genuine customers, and saw the 'Chinese' markings being applied. And the markings gave foreign journalists, also present in strength but often less perceptive, copy for their papers, about 'Chinese influence'.

'*Rahla, Rahla!* Onwards,' said Pendergood.

There were about six thousand volunteers, men from several of the Pashtun tribes, in the *lashkar*, the private army, which Pendergood had assembled during his progress from the north to this wild spot. He did not believe in doing things by halves. His machine-guns and mortars had arrived from the Gulf, ordered from Zurich by his contact in Istanbul. His men had all been properly enrolled, outfitted and drilled, photographed and assigned functions in battle groups. The Russians were going to hear, see and feel something of the dragon's claws.

If the Afghan dragon's heart was its men, the claws were its armaments. Pendergood had scraped his resources to the bottom of the barrel, and bought everything he could afford from the Darra smiths and the middlemen of Zurich. Maryam had become his unofficial lieutenant, as Noor was to Adam. Her eyes were round as she looked at the lists of arms and materials, checking supplies.

A thousand Russian anti-tank stick grenades. Some of them had been captured by the Israelis and then sold and resold by dealers; some sold by the Egyptians, others raided from the Afghan stores of the Russians themselves. Grenades, fifty dollars each, cash on the nail. Replica Kalashnikovs, locally known as animals, $1,125 each; machine-guns from Darra, £525. Ammunition, two dollars a round. Rifles, six hundred thousand dollars, ammunition, fifty dollars a magazine: small arms, ammunition, equipment and transport, ten million dollars.

She turned the page. Communications equipment, food, medical supplies, explosives, field-glasses, oil and gasoline, knives. Allowances for families at £25 each, $150,000.

Including the small artillery pieces and grenade launchers, the bill came to just over eleven million dollars.

Not bad, for one man's contribution. 'You're a remarkable man, Pendergood,' she told him.

'Because it's so much?' Pendergood laughed.

'Well, yes. Partly that.'

'Look at it this way,' he said. 'It's my total assets. Now, if my whole fortune had been ten dollars and I'd spent that, nobody would think it was any big deal, would they? So, if you get it in perspective . . .' He quoted the Pashtu proverb, 'First sharpen your sword, afterwards await the call to arms.'

That was the Pashtun talking, the soft-hearted, generous, ruthless Pashtun. Still, that mentality wasn't only useful in the mountains; it had earned him millions in England, Maryam reflected.

'But what happens when all this money is used up?'

'We just don't know. I'm trying for a big blow. There aren't many people who can afford to finance a private army. I could, so I'm trying it. But I'll show you something else. I'm not the only one making sacrifices.'

He reached for a despatch case and pulled out a bundle of envelopes.

'This is what I picked up from my PO box today. I asked my friends in England to pass the word around that we need money to help free Afghanistan, and that I'm using up all my own. This is their answer.'

He brandished the envelopes and selected one. 'I've written the latest list on the back of this letter. See, money is coming in – as little as one pound and as much as a hundred thousand dollars. From people who know me and people who don't. From tycoons and pensioners, even from children. Say what you like, Maryam, our former enemies, now good friends, the British, have hearts.'

Time and again, Kandahar had fought and driven off the Russians. Time and again they had come back. In 1981 the

Soviets, pushing the luckless Afghan conscript Army before them, had besieged the city for five months, from May to September. It was partly a matter of Russian pride. The Soviets occupied Kabul, it was true, but Kandahar was the true Pashtun capital of Afghanistan, and it commanded the flat land to the south: the way the Russians would have to roll if they decided to go for Pakistan, India, the Arabian Sea or the Gulf. And the people in the outside world always knew what was happening in Kandahar: Pakistan was only sixty miles away. This time the Reds were determined to get into the city and to hold it.

Pendergood, now known as Commander Painda-Gul, had sent a radio man, disguised as a farmer, into Kandahar, to keep him informed. Since the Russians were planning not only to capture the city but to activate the big power stations at Kajakai and Arghandab to provide electricity for the immense military base planned for the area, Pendergood and Callil – now Commander Khalil – were going to blow up the lot.

They had consulted civil engineers in Pakistan, who gave them little encouragement. No, it was next to impossible to destroy modern dams by guerrilla action. They were too massive. And dams of the kind near Kandahar were situated between mountain gorges, which supported the reinforced concrete. The engineers suggested that they try something easier. Even Professor Mahmud, the Afghan Minister of Water and Power, kidnapped by the guerrillas, knew nothing about any weaknesses in the dams.

Pendergood sent for a copy of the famous Swiss Army guide to guerrilla operations: Major H. von Dach Bern's *Total Resistance*. It was full of fascinating material of great value: but it did not encourage the blowing up of dams. Then he spoke to mining engineers and finally to past and current members of Pakistan's military, sappers who should have had the necessary knowledge. Quite properly, these men refused to discuss such matters with 'unauthorized persons'. There wasn't anything useful in encyclopaedias, either. Callil suggested going to America to find the people who had built the dam. Pendergood overruled him. 'Cal, can you see someone who built things like that, triumphs of engineering, helping to destroy them? Did you know that, during the last war, one of the British pioneers of radar resisted combating German radar, because he had such a pride in the phenomenon itself?'

They became short-tempered, even with each other, as they went about their business of preparing the arming of the great Pashtun army that was Pendergood's dream.

Sitting in a Peshawar café one day, the two Pashtun leaders broke into English when referring to the technicalities of the operation. Maryam, sitting with them, whom they never consulted about anything, began to get the drift. She was a Dari speaker: her Pashtu was still weak.

'You want to blow up Arghandab and Kajakai: is that it?'

'That's right.' Pendergood stretched, reluctantly including her in the conversation. 'But those fool engineers say it can't be done. You have to know the design, to find the weak points. You also have to know its geology. There's no hope of finding a geologist and a set of plans of the two dams, either here or even in Kabul. I'm sure.'

'You never know,' said Maryam, mysteriously. There was no harm in letting them wait; after all, they had made her wait all those months before discussing things with her.

'Oh, don't be silly, Maryam,' said Callil, automatically. He was annoyed: the more especially because, with his technical knowledge, Pendergood had imagined that he could work out any problem. In fact, he only knew about light engineering. Blowing up dams was something they hadn't taught at his institute in Australia.

'Silly, am I?' Maryam teased him. 'Not as silly as you imagine I could do it, you know, as easily as winking.'

Pendergood sat bolt upright, beginning to think that she did know something, after all. He glared at her. 'All right, then. Tell us.'

'I'll tell you, as long as you realize that I'm just as good, just as useful, as either of you. No more male chauvinism.'

They looked at one another.

'Yes,' said Pendergood, at last. 'You're just as good. I never said you weren't.'

'You thought it, though; promise not to think it again?'

'Promise.'

'Callil?'

'Promise, Maryam.'

The two men leant forward.

'Now,' said Maryam, savouring her triumph in advance, 'I am an architect – if you haven't forgotten – worked in Kabul, trained in Kabul.'

'Yes.' Pendergood *had* forgotten.

'Can you imagine any architect, in a country which has two of the most important dams in the world, designed to provide power and water for millions of people, to restore fertility to the soil for the first time since the thirteenth century, not being anxious to know everything about such dams, from the technical point of view?'

Callil said, 'I've heard that Kariba, in Africa, is the really big one. It features in all the reference books . . .'

'Kariba!' Maryam skidded the heel of her hand across her forehead. 'Just listen to this and I'll give you no more statistics. Kariba Dam has a hundred and thirty thousand acre-feet of water; Arghandab alone has three hundred and fifty thousand. Arghandab cost over a hundred and twenty million dollars, when dollars were really dollars. Call it at least 350 million today. The area which it is due to irrigate was once the most fertile, and one of the largest, gardens in the world. It could be again. And that's not to mention the enormous kilowattage from thirteen hydropower plants due to be fed into a national grid.'

'Whew!' Callil wiped his face, and not only because the temperature was 112 degrees in the shade. 'We never heard about all that in Australia.'

'Or in England,' said Pendergood. 'But you do realize, don't you, that we've been planning to destroy Afghanistan's greatest asset, which could give life to the barren land?'

'Life? With a million dead civilians in under four years?' Callil exploded. 'The Russians would use the power to destroy the rest of the people, and the Helmand river valley to feed their own. Apart from the military base they're already building. There's only a small generator working there now. We could wreck that, and black out Kandahar, but the people won't mind . . .'

'Yes, all right. Let's get back to Maryam.' He turned to her. 'Okay, Maryam Jan. You are the expert here. What's the information, and where is it?'

She threw back her head and laughed. 'For seven years of my life I studied, ate, slept, almost worshipped, Kajakai and Arghandab. I have every detail, including strengths and weaknesses, all here.'

She tapped her forehead.

'And can the dams be blown up, either of them?' Callil wanted to know.

'Either or both. All you need is explosives and access. I can show you, Commanders.' She emphasized the last word. 'And, I think, in future you'd better call me "Commander", too.'

That conversation in Peshawar seemed a world away now as, four hundred miles nearer their objective, the three commanders, one of them a woman, sat in the desert twilight, waiting for news. If none came by tonight, they would strike deep into Afghan national territory and establish a battle base within easy reach of the two great dams. They would need all their men to capture and hold the dams before they blew them up.

It was cool in the desert twilight, and the waiting made for reflection, memories. Maryam's thoughts went back to the scenes at the refugee camps in Pakistan, now far behind them. Soon, perhaps, she would meet, in battle, the men who, in the name of an idealistic creed, had put the people there. She remembered the babies horribly burnt by napalm, jellied petrol, the sightless women, the men without arms and legs. All without land, homes, clothes, food, sympathy . . .

Once she, like many other young people, had been attracted to the idealism of that same philosophy, whose leaders had ordained this; had read its books, had learnt its songs. Now she had seen its actions.

As she watched the lines of hunted, staggering people, some even crawling on hands and knees, going into the miserable camps, the words of that rousing anthem, the *Internationale*, ran through her head.

Arise, ye prisoners of starvation . . .

Yes, they were starving, all right. Ragged, miserable, stumbling and lying where they fell. Many had been eating grass.

Arise, ye wretched of the earth . . .

It described them, perfectly. When she looked into their

517

eyes, she saw no hope of redress for the crimes which had been committed on them. How did the next line go?

For justice thunders condemnation . . . Justice!

It was only then that she finally stopped feeling sorry for herself, swore to help bring succour, even if it meant her own death. Aloud, she shouted the final, triumphant phrase:

'*A better world's in birth!*'

Pendergood and Callil looked at her, nervously.

'It's very hot on the frontier in this season, especially before three in the afternoon,' Pendergood said. 'I'll take you where we can get a long, cool drink and a rest, away from this awful place.'

Maryam was suddenly jolted back to here and now. The battle. The two radio men, Daud and Zakaria from the communications truck, came running, shouting.

'Commanders, it's starting, we'd better alert the men!'

At the beat of the rallying drum, the men mustered before their clan chiefs. With long ringlets, hawk-faced, broad swordbelts, desert sandals on their feet, each was the epitome of Pashtun valour. Men of the Suleman mountains, thirsting for battle. Young men in their twenties, typical of the Sons of Qais, of King David of the Bani-Israil.

Pendergood and Callil listened to Zakaria as Maryam got out the large-scale ordnance maps.

'The radioman signals that all telephones in Kandahar have gone dead,' Daud gasped. 'This always happens when an attack on the city is imminent. Also, he learnt that the communications system for the allied Afghan-Soviet Armies in the south is now centralized at Kandahar International Airport. He suggests we knock it out. Kandahar Radio, on 864 kilohertz, has just gone off the air.' He and Zakaria were still out of breath.

Pendergood looked at the map. 'The airport is eighteen miles from the city, on a tarmac road. It's now seven-forty p.m. If we strike north-west from here, we should get there in two hours at the latest. Let's try to cripple their communications, destroy as many planes as possible, and then help fight off the attack on the city. Agreed?' The others nodded. The Arghandab and Kajakai dams would have to wait.

At that moment, called by the siren of the radio truck, the

chiefs of the Pashtun battle groups lined up in front of the commanders. There were ten of them, each the chief or a son of a chief of the tribe to which his men belonged. Every *ghund* of six hundred men was composed of twenty smaller units, fighting teams, and those into small, *dastas*, handfuls. Collectively or otherwise, these men were something to be reckoned with.

'Tigers!' said Pendergood, 'the plan is this: we drive across the country, following the hard sand tracks of the nomads, keeping off the Kandahar-Quetta arterial road, which is usually patrolled. Make sure that the *ghunds* are dispersed so that they don't get bogged down in sand dunes, stopped by minefields or decimated by air attack. Light no fires, show no lights. No smoking. So far the enemy hasn't seen us. Let's keep it like that.'

'When do we attack, Painda-Gul?' asked Talib Khan, a six-foot-six, barrel-chested ancient, the chief of the Isa-Khel contingent.

Pendergood raised his finger in warning. 'You'll be told when. No attack without a command, orange flag by day, green flare by night. We are going for the airport, this side of Kandahar.'

He went on briefing the chiefs, describing the roles of the various contingents. Half an hour later the *lashkar* set off, without lights, heading into the territory of the Afghan Democratic Republic, known to the Pashtuns as *Dar al-Harb*, the Abode of War.

2 The Russians are coming

The Eagle's force
North of Kandahar City

2100 hours

The Russian attack came, as Adam had thought it would, from the north. Kandahar lies just above the point where the Arghandab and Tarnak rivers meet, and south of it is the Registan desert, the Land of Sand. To come that way would mean the Soviets using bridging equipment where the Arghandab forms a U-bend with its sister river. To the north, however, is the spur road branching from the Kabul highway, along which the tanks and troops could pour more easily, as they had done so many times before.

The Eagle's band, now numbering some three hundred fighters, had already moved across country from the Kajakai area towards Kandahar when Azambai started to pick up greatly increased radio traffic on his stolen Russian receiver. As the trucks raced eastwards he took off his earphones and told Adam, sitting beside him in the Afghan Army transport, 'They're shaping up for a night raid on Kandahar.'

'Any details?' Adam shouted, as he bounced between the seat and the roof.

'I am listening.' He went back to the receiver. Then: 'Yes. They always attacked in daylight in the past. Now they think that a night assault, using infra-red searchlights and masses of tanks, will do the job. Of course they have an advantage there, as we're blind at night, though there are problems, I hear, with the infra-red.'

Adam shrugged. 'Can't be helped. Anything about where and how soon, and their strength?'

'Strength we can't say. But the tanks will rendezvous with the armour's despatcher a mile north of the city, at Shorab, at

eleven p.m. local time – that's in just under two hours. Wait.'
He listened again. 'Yes. About opposition. They do not expect
any until they reach the Kabul gate, at the city boundary. That
means they don't know about us or any other guerrillas in the
vicinity.'

'Right. Let's keep going then. There's a gully I know, half a
mile north of the assembly-point. Let's head for it and let them
have it with all we've got.'

Adam shouted to the sergeant who was driving to go faster,
while Zelikov started to sharpen his knife for the third time
that day. 'Zelikov, if you keep that thing in your boot like that,
it'll cut your toes one of these days!'

'*Da, preents.* I don't mind.' Although he was no hero, the
tiny Russian was game.

They were about three miles from their target. In twenty
minutes they had left the trucks and were climbing the rocky
outcrop, which commanded the road along which the Russians
were due to pass. Exactly an hour after they had moved into
position, the clanking of the T-62 main battle tanks could be
heard distinctly. Soon they could pick up the thump of the
seven-hundred-horsepower diesels, and then the crunching of
asphalt as the thirty-seven-ton monsters chewed up the surface
of the road.

3

*Pendergood's Army
approaching the Airport
18 kms from Kandahar*

2140 hours

Helicopter patrols were out, clattering busily around Kandahar International Airport as the Pashtun *lashkar* approached. It had made record time but with the loss of two vehicles bogged down in the sand. These were the only ones whose drivers had disobeyed Pendergood's orders to deflate their tyres slightly to increase traction where the sand was soft. If the Russians were using infra-red spotting, it was ineffective. They had obviously not seen the guerrillas approach.

There was no sign of Russian ground patrols anywhere, the Pashtun scouts reported: but Pendergood and Callil had been reluctant to use the excellent surface of one of Asia's best highways, the metalled road from Pakistan. Surely it would have a Russian checkpoint on it, somewhere?

They were twenty-five miles into the Afghan national territory of Yaghistan, Land of the Turbulent, when a boy, no more than twelve years old, with Pashtun shoulder-length ringlets, hopped onto the running board of Callil's truck.

'If you're going for the airport, why not take the highway? It leads straight to the bridge, and you've got to cross the river anyway. There's no *Rouss* anywhere on it.'

'How do you know, O great man of wisdom?' Callil called out.

'Smell. You can smell them for three or four kilometres. Smoke, *tabak*, dirt – and *sharab*, drink. Anyway, I'm the king of this whole area.'

The smell of Russia. People had reported it for centuries.

'King, eh? And who are your subjects?'

The lad brandished his pan-pipes and gestured into the darkness.

'Goats. We have every kind of goat, and I am their king. Go on, you may use my road. It's the *Kinar-Wayt* Road.'

'The what?' Maryam asked.

'The *Kinar-Wayt*. The Kinar-Wayt Company, of Danwar, Colorado. They built it.'

'Oh . . .' She translated for the others. 'He means the Ken R. White Company, a well-known construction firm, of Denver.'

'Yes. *Kinar-Wayt*. I got it from them. One of their chiefs said I could have it, when they left. Are you afraid? Maybe you only *look* like soldiers?'

He jumped down onto the sand, and disappeared, as if he gave directions to attacking armies every day of the week.

Callil signalled Pendergood and they struck north along the blessedly smooth broad tarmac, and their vehicles rolled across the Arghastan River bridge unchallenged. The *lashkar* stopped.

The airport itself, now only a mile and a half away, was brilliantly lit. Pendergood, Callil and Maryam focused their night-glasses on the control tower, its tall steel pylons bright with lights to warn approaching aircraft. Three groups of guerrillas were busily setting up the M-1937 mortars, Soviet-made ones, bought on the international market, spoils sold by the winners of an earlier war. A useful weapon, weighing only 121 pounds, the M-1937 could hurl a shell packed with over seven pounds of high-explosive for a distance of nearly two miles. It was also extremely accurate.

Hamza Khan was in charge of the battery, and loved it. He had taught Pendergood the necessary commands. In return he claimed the job of fire-master.

'Mortars in place.' Pendergood could almost feel Hamza's grin in the darkness. He had served in the Iranian army as a mercenary during the long Oman counter-insurgency campaign. He had plenty of experience with captured Russian guns, which the Oman rebels had obtained from the USSR via South Yemen.

'How many mortars operational, Hamza?'

'Five assembled, set up and awaiting your orders,' said the Pashtun. His voice betrayed that he was itching for action.

'What's the range, from here to the control tower and radio masts?'

'Rangefinders show tower lights to be 2,371 metres distant. Maximum effective range of mortars is 3,069 metres. Targets well within accurate range.'

Pashtu lends itself well to military terminology, Pendergood reflected. Now, cripple the transmitters in the tower. That should cause confusion among the Russians attacking the city eighteen miles away.

'Those are the targets. There is no sign of enemy troops between us and the airport perimeter. But if they do appear, lay down smoke by mortar in front of them, without further command. Understood, Fire-Master?'

'Understood, Commander.'

'Now, Hamza, load all five mortars with high-explosive for ranging shots.'

Hamza relayed the order. 'Loaded for ranging shots.'

'Following ranging shots and any necessary correction of sights, prepare for high-explosive barrages, rapid fire. Understood?'

'Understood . . . Order relayed . . . Mortars ready.'

'Mortar battery, ranging shots ready . . . FIRE!'

Hamza passed on the command: '*Da khampara khalas krah!*'

Two mortars fired short, a third hurled its round too far, just over the control tower, falling on the far side. Two struck the transmitting masts and the control tower.

'Seriously damaged,' Pendergood murmured. 'Not bad, Hamza! Now re-range: three on the tower, two on the masts, and move!'

Within seconds, as Pendergood and Callil watched through their night-glasses, the masts collapsed in orange flame and the tower itself, made of concrete but not designed to resist high-explosives, was severely damaged. Most of the lights went out: those that were still on in the main building alongside it were blanked out by smoke and debris.

The nine huge arches of the passenger terminal, designed in the style of the magnificent entrances to the ancient Afghan imperial palaces, collapsed. The bright fluorescent Pashtu-language signs, A A A – *Da Ariana Afghan Hawai Shirkat* – Ariana Afghan Air Company, went with them.

Fires were soon burning fiercely in the great 50-metre by 75-metre hangar, built by the American Federal Aviation

Agency for the Royal Afghan Government and designed for the largest intercontinental jets on the Far East route.

'Fire-Master: cease fire! *Aferin, Muhjahidin!* Well done!' The commanders clapped, and the Pashtuns, always delighted at the sight of fireworks of any kind, gave a loud cry of *Allahu-Akbar!*

At the airport, all was confusion. At first, the commanding general thought that an air raid was taking place. He shook plaster out of his hair and ran for the dugout shelter which was all that was available to him, general or not. His adjutant managed to raise the administration building on his small transceiver, but only after several minutes.

'*Gospodin* general! Mortar attack from the east!'

'Mortar? What mortars? Is it more Afghan deserters? Is it the Pashtun force from Pakistan – or the bandit "Eagle" from the north?'

'I do not know, Comrade General.'

'Find out then, you fool! And see what perimeter defence is doing about it. We'll be overrun at any moment at this rate!'

The general was fed up with the war, with Afghanistan, with the airport on this sunbaked plain and its stifling heat. He wanted to retire, to go fishing, to read books in his dacha in the cold Baltic birch forests. He was a Balt, anyway. What was he doing here in Central Asia? The general pulled out his last Havana cigar, a long thin Romeo y Julieta, and bit off the end. Thank God he wasn't in charge of defending this place. Colonel Antonov was commanding the perimeter. Moscow, or even Afghanistan High Command, would make someone pay for letting the attackers get so close. Moscow had warned of two guerrilla bands due in the area soon . . .

Suddenly he remembered. The tank attack on Kandahar. Due in an hour. That was what he was here for. No communications, no attack.

'Mikhailov!' He called for his adjutant.

'*Gospodin* general?'

'Get some communications fixed with Tank Attack Command. They're on the way to Kandahar already, and they're radio-deaf, on the normal network, or we are, or both! We've got to get things together or call off the attack! We're the nerve centre of the *Sistema Svyazi*, the whole troop command and control communications system.'

'At once, General.' The man clicked his heels and went off at the double.

Of course, it wasn't up to him, a communications man, to call anything off, the general realized. He'd probably get court-martialled, or reprimanded, anyway. Great God . . .

The mortars could not do much to the helicopter patrols, the general thought. It had been a surprise attack, and communications were disrupted: but the Mi-24s would surely be able to deal with the guerrillas.

The three huge rotorcraft, radio-deaf through the loss of the airport's transmitting mast, at last spotted the Pashtuns and swooped to the attack, searchlights blazing down.

Pendergood, seeing them wheeling overhead, signalled to his small air defence squad and breathed a prayer of thanks that he had agreed to buy the small Russian bazookas and rockets from the sleazy arms dealer from Cyprus, that day in Istanbul.

All the same, the men had not had any hot firing experience with the weapons: the rockets had cost too much to waste on training.

The Pashtun rocketeers, chosen for their sniping experience, picked up the launcher tubes as if they had been handling them all their lives. They aimed at the aircraft over open sights, pressed the triggers halfway and waited until the red light came on, for 'Seeker locked onto target'.

As the red turned to green, 'fire', they squeezed the triggers all the way.

With a roar the boost charges fired, and the missiles leapt from the tubes, at the speed of Mach 1.5 – one and a half times the velocity of sound.

The helicopters were very low – not more than 800 feet – when the first missiles struck. A British Hawker Hunter fighter-bomber, it was known, had been hit by a SA-7 over Oman at fourteen times that height, and the effect on the Mi-24s was correspondingly great.

Although not destroyed, the helicopters were soon out of action. One had its supposedly blast-proof windscreen blown in; the second exploded as the missile found its exhaust pipe; the main rotor of the third was twisted. It was only with difficulty that the three aircraft managed to land back on their pads within the airport's perimeter.

4

The Eagle's Force
North of Kandahar City

2151 hours

There were three hundred MBTs, big battle tanks, in the main formation sent to attack and occupy Kandahar that night. As they moved forward to their baseline position, awaiting the assault order, Azambai tuned in to their radio traffic.

He listened for a moment or two, and then turned to Adam with a grunt.

'Something's gone wrong with their command and control communications! They are using a makeshift, highly unsuitable, frequency, and they are getting all kinds of orders and messages. It's made them quite annoyed.'

'Why unsuitable?'

'There's static, for one thing. For another, not all of them have radios which can pick it up. They're mostly crystal-calibrated, you see, which means they can't switch to unplanned frequencies.'

'Bit of luck for us. Any reason why it happened?'

'Yes. Someone at Tank Command says, hysterically, that the main control headquarters, communications, has been knocked out. At the airport. Guerrilla action.'

'Great! We have friends at work.'

Bands of heavily armed men were always appearing unexpectedly in Afghanistan. They might just as quickly melt away.

Adam turned and peered over the rocks at the silent tanks below. They were in a long line in the gully, three abreast, risking the choking of their line of approach with breakdowns, as the Russians always seemed to do. Just like that dawn attack at Paghman.

He ordered the guerrillas to disperse in two lines, to try to reach the end of the column, and to be prepared to attack from above at his signal.

Ten minutes later, a runner came up, and whispered: 'Eagle, all the men are in position, right to the end of the column, on both sides, in battle array.'

'Good.' The tanks were still stopped, every turret open. Men were smoking, the red glow of their *papirosas* lighting up faces and outlining their black, padded tank helmets. Sitting targets, almost literally. Some had got out of their vehicles to urinate, some were chatting, probably discussing the breakdown in communications. They were all Russians: there was no sign of the Afghans who were usually sent in ahead, to take the first enemy fire.

The Russian tank commander had not been able to get through to Afghan Infantry Headquarters. The attack was going to be delayed: it was only sixty minutes to zero hour, and still no readiness alert had come through.

With machine-guns, grenades, rocket-launchers, and tank-killing grenade launchers, the guerrillas stood, silently, on the rocks above, like veritable hawks hovering over their prey.

Adam lobbed the first grenade, signalling the attack. It was one of the terrible Russian RKG-3Ms; spinning on its potato-masher handle, it plunged right down into the open turret of the first tank.

The impact-fused half-kilogramme of high-explosive, which could penetrate six inches of armour, exploded with such violence that The Eagle himself, twenty feet away, felt as if he had been struck with a giant hammer. Winded by the shock, he leant against a rock while the men of the rebel formation, hearing the explosion, went into the attack. It sounded like something straight from hell.

Men screamed, automatic fire rattled, shells exploded in all directions. From the blazing tanks came the radio operators, frenziedly trying to beat out the flames on their uniforms and get away before the ammunition exploded. The dismounted tank crews were utterly bewildered. The darkness was lit by the red-orange explosions, while the yellow of the diesel flames and the choking black smoke mingled with the stench of burning rubber and human flesh. The Russians had put up field-flares, but this only helped the Afghans to see their targets better.

The war cry of the Muhjahidin, *Allahu-Akbar!* was, again and again, drowned out by the explosions, the howls, the unearthly scream of metal as, within ten minutes, all three hundred tanks were turned into scrap.

There had been nine hundred men in the tank crews. No more than a hundred escaped the slaughter. Now the guerrillas jumped down among them. In the narrow defile, eager warriors leapt and stabbed, man to man, lunging, swearing, killing. The heat from the burning tanks filled the place, flames flickering, rising and falling, the scene like something from Armageddon.

As the full moon came up, the carnage continued. Ten Russian armoured personnel-carriers, with a hundred and fifty paratroops aboard, attempted a rescue. Their vehicles could not get past the wreckage of the tanks.

Nobody could tell how the battle was going. The Afghans, although keen and motivated, lacked combat experience. The Russian *parashyutniks* were the cream of the Soviet Army. Well trained, well armed, these were regulars: not the bewildered conscripts who made up the majority in the USSR's motor-rifle formations.

It took three hours to deal with them. Neither side took prisoners or showed any mercy: the Afghans determined to rid their country of its oppressors, the Russians aggressive – and afraid of death or court martial if they failed.

In the end, the battle followed the pattern pioneered by the Russians themselves during World War II, when small, determined parties of partisans took on the lumbering German armour and overcame huge formations of the enemy.

By two o'clock in the morning, the Russian survivors had withdrawn, their ammunition exhausted and their entire tank fleet destroyed or abandoned. It was an impressive victory, but not the end of the Soviet assault on the city of Kandahar.

The smell of burning, of cordite and of high-explosive still hung in the night air as The Eagle and his companions mustered at their rallying point. As Adam was receiving the reports of casualties, a battered car came jerking along the road from the direction of the city.

An old man, waving a large flashlight and dressed in a western-style business suit, turban awry, slammed to a halt and jumped out. 'Kara Kush! Eagle, sir, Kara Kush! Where is he?'

Adam stepped forward. 'I'm Kara Kush. What's the matter?'

The ancient ran to him, grabbed his hand and kissed it. 'I'm Neknam, son of Yakub, from Kandahar. Sent by Ashraf, patriot commander there. Lieutenant Tura is my son-in-law. The Red Afghans, traitors, supported by Soviet Airborne, are attacking us from the west, from the Herat highway direction.'

Adam suddenly felt tired out, but this was hardly a time to think of rest. So that was where the Afghan Army was: the Russians must originally have planned a two-pronged thrust, and it had got out of phase, with the interruption of their radio communications. 'Let's get back to the command truck,' he said, 'and see what we can do.'

When they had assembled, Adam was pleased, selfishly as he immediately thought, that none of his close friends had been seriously hurt. Under the butane gas lamp they saw that the newcomer had a bullet-wound in his left arm, which Noor dressed for him. His suit was covered in oil. Adam looked at the others, smeared with soot, blood, dust, grime, sand.

'What's the situation in Kandahar?' Adam asked.

Neknam shrugged. 'We've got what's left of the Russian occupation force surrounded in the Chowni, the garrison area. We've had them trapped there for a week. We can't get in, they can't get out. They've a lot of arms and ammunition there. Ashraf Khan was trying to breach the walls, leading a suicide squad with gelignite, as I left. God willing, they may have succeeded by now.'

'How many of the enemy are there, and what kind of arms have they? Any tanks?' Adam wanted to know.

'I heard our patrol's report,' Neknam told him, 'it was dark and they couldn't see much, but they are mostly infantry in trucks, that's all. The Karmal conscripts, the Afghan Army as they call it, in front. Just issued with guns they hardly know how to fire. No tanks.'

'Any chance of falling on them from the flank, or from behind, Neknam Khan?'

'Eagle, there's every chance! There's a spur from Highway 75, the main road only half a mile from here. Get your people into trucks and we can drive straight there. I'll show you the way.'

The Eagle shouldered his AK-74 carbine. '*Rahla, rahla,* march, march,' he said.

5

Pendergood's Army
Kandahar Airport

SEPTEMBER 16
0100 hours

The Russians at Kandahar Airport had now rallied, and got three gunships into the air. Spraying the Pendergood army with machine-gun fire, hovering close to the ground, they sought their prey by the invisible light of their infra-red searchlights, operated by the co-pilots.

Pendergood called for the captured Dashka: there were no SAM-7 rockets left now. Aiming at the sound of the rotors in the dark, the men of the Yusuf-Zai brought the heavy Russian machine-gun into play. They exhausted three of the fifty-shot cartridge belts to bring down one craft and cripple the other two. The armourers who had installed the Dashka in its Russian tank in the first place had not intended it to be used against aircraft. For a swivel mounting, therefore, the Pashtun gunners had to hold it against the free-spinning wheel of an overturned truck.

As the last helicopter limped away, fresh Soviet infantry appeared, in an endless stream of vehicles, from their huge encampment on the Kabul road. They had arrived in the country only five months before, during the annual spring rotation of forces, and had not seen real action: only punitive raids on unarmed villagers.

They fired white magnesium flares, constantly, to keep the battlefield well lit. 'Afraid of the dark?' Pendergood shouted.

Scouts observing them as they poured from their armoured personnel-carriers, estimated that there were about eight thousand men: four regiments, outnumbering the Pashtuns by about two thousand. When Pendergood heard this, he laughed a great laugh. Pashtun performance, regardless of what war it had been, was quite consistent. The tribesmen had never been beaten, in all their history, by odds of anything less than ten to one. He snatched up his machine-carbine and signalled to his ammunition-carrier to follow him. This was the life. Who'd be a transport king in England when there was this kind of work to do?

The Russians advanced in line abreast, wave after wave of them, their NCOs howling the Russian Army's constant cry, in war or peace, '*Daway, daway* – faster, faster.' The men ran easily, as if charging across the barren steppes of their native land. Their khaki summer field uniforms showed up a dull green in the chemical light of the star-shells, and their assault rifles spat red flames. To Pendergood, the muzzle-flashes looked like fireflies as the first wave kept up a constant fire. The Pashtuns threw themselves flat on the ground, drew their killing knives, and waited. Shouting to keep their fervour up, the Soviet infantrymen were upon them with amazing speed. They had been liberally dosed with vodka half an hour before: forty-five per cent alcohol.

Whether or not he had been in action before, every Pashtun was determined to see blood flow that night. There was hardly one of them who had not lost a close friend or relative in the Russian attacks against the civilian population. The rebels had seen the broken bodies of men and women, old and young, of children, too – from Zabul, Paktia, Nangrahar, Kunar – carried to the few hospitals there were beyond the frontier, journeys of unimaginable misery, only to die, often terribly mutilated, and in the most extreme pain.

Such is the strength of the Pashtun's commitment to the code of retaliation, that the presence of a large contingent of Ishak-Khel Warriors, from the Isaac Clan, in Pendergood's army, was due to a single incident. They volunteered when it was known that their kinsman, Riyaz Khan, and several of his relatives, had been murdered by the *Rouss*.

When the helicopters destroyed his village in Khair Khana valley, Riyaz Khan, blinded by the chemical bombs, shouted to the survivors to leave him where he was. They refused, and two men and two women started to carry him past the ruined mosque when the Russians came back. The aircraft swooped and spattered them with machine-gun fire, riddling Riyaz's cousin, Askar, and putting two bullets into the blind man as well.

The three villagers who were unhurt, carried their friend two hundred miles over the mountains to Pakistan, lifting, pulling, fording rivers; their only stretcher two sacks stitched together.

The journey took thirty-nine days, and the group, begging food from one village to another and living on wild onions, grass and leaves, were attacked and strafed by Russian helicopters three times on the way.

When they reached Pakistan, they heard about the tiny hospital run by dedicated Afghan doctors who had escaped from the communists. It was so well run and excellently equipped that even the International Red Cross delegation described it as their inspiration. But the journey had taken too long. Riyaz Khan died three days after reaching safety, at the Afghan Surgical Hospital.

His three friends eventually reached the refugee camp at Nasirbagh, in Pakistan, twelve miles from Peshawar. They sat there in the dust, listlessly, for days, without food, drinking only a little water, traumatized by shock. All felt a sense of overwhelming failure. Nobody could convince them that they had not let Riyaz Khan down.

But the murderers of Riyaz Khan were about to learn what it meant to hold the life of an Afghan too cheaply.

That night, the long Khyber knives took a hundred lives for every one who had perished in the village of Riyaz Khan. His name, from every throat, were the last words heard on earth by many a soldier of the Fraternal Limited Contingent. As each man of the Ishak-Khel felled a Russian, he shouted 'Riyaz Khan!' – and the night's watchword '*Ala al-hisab!* in part-payment!'

For three hours, as if in a medieval combat, the fourteen thousand men fought hand to hand.

Salahuddin Khan, named after Sultan Saladin and descended from the Sons of Qais, unstrapped his battleaxe from the side of his jeep and spat on it for luck. Its handle was four feet long and it had a tempered steel blade inlaid with silver – made and signed by Salman the Smith six hundred years ago. Salahuddin's family had been wiped out in the destruction, that April, of the town called Hussain Kot.

His ancestors had fought the Ephalites, the White Huns, the Greeks, Persians and Indians. They had dealt with the Mongols, the Arabs, the Tartars and the British. He didn't know all that, but he did not need to.

The terrible weapon glittered in the flare-light as Salahuddin swung it around his head – and threw. Its five-inch spear point, protruding from between the crescent-shaped double blades, caught a Russian – who had just brought down a Muhjahid – in the exact centre of the back of his neck. The Russian turned over, eyes rolling, mouth moving – then lay still, his spinal cord broken.

Salahuddin ran up and jerked the battleaxe away.

'*Shabash, changhalah!* Well done, Sweetheart!' Most Pashtun weapons had their own, special names.

A Russian knelt, turned around and pulled the pin from a grenade, hurling it too soon at the tiny form of Simab Khan, a lad of just thirteen. Simab saw it coming, reckoned – rightly – that the fuse was a four-second one, caught it like a world class sportsman would receive a ball, and hurled it back, throwing himself to the ground at the same time.

When he looked up the Russian was lying in a hollow depression, his head blown off, the neck still spurting blood. Simab Khan was violently sick, and lay there, amid the shouts and the screams, the explosions and cordite fumes, retching, his vision swimming. It was his first kill. He had no weapon: he'd joined the battle to get hold of one. Forcing himself up, he crept forward. There. Now, at last, he had a Kalakov, one of the new AK-74s, and two – no, three – magazines in a satchel. He ran forward, squeezing the trigger. The gun setting was on 'AV', automatic. Within ten seconds half a dozen Russian riflemen were writhing in the sand.

Ten seconds more and Simab fell, dead, riddled with automatic fire. He was so small the bullets had lifted him into the air. He had been the last survivor of the genocidal air attack on the village of Pul-i-Sufian.

Pendergood was jerking his bayonet from the last of a bunch

of Russians, surrounded by a knot of Pashtuns, when a great flash lit up the sky to the east. A new type of flare, he thought, as he paused to wipe the blade clean. Callil came running up, a broad grin suffusing his face. 'All my own work, Pendergood!'

'Where did you get the flares?' Pendergood said wondering at the same time why Callil had lit or fired them.

'Flares? I haven't seen any.'

'What's that light, then?'

'Oh, that.' Callil, elaborately, affected indifference. 'That's only thirty Nikolai amphibious battle-vehicles, BTR-60s, coming to get us, to wipe us out, that's all . . .'

'What do we do?'

'Nothing. Our scouts spotted them, coming down the Arghistan River – you know, the one just south-east of here. I thought I'd do something.'

'Such as?'

'I'd noticed a 10,000 gallon oil tank installed at the water's edge and my engineering training – that you sneered about so much, back in Pakistan – came in handy. I released the lot into the water. A match did the rest.'

'And the rest was?'

'Up to five hundred and forty men, armed to the teeth, enough to swing this battle the wrong way, burnt to a crisp.'

'Poor bastards!'

'Oh, I don't know; I'd call it poetic justice. They are a specialist unit using napalm. They normally operate against civilians, with blazing oil, napalm and toxic chemicals. Those five hundred and forty have probably killed several thousand civilians. They specialize in the destruction of villages which help rebels, near Pakistan. The Pashtuns know them by their unit badge.' He stopped talking. The Russians were coming on again.

6

*The Eagle's force
Herat Road boundary
Kandahar city*

0230 hours

The Eagle's force arrived at the Herat Road boundary of Kandahar to find the Russians, using the Red Afghan Army infantry conscripts as a shield, about to force their way into the city. They had laid down a barrage of high-explosive and phosphorous shells.

Forgetting their exhaustion after the battle against the tanks, the guerrillas pushed through the demoralized Afghan conscripts' left flank, and went straight for the Russians' rear, catching them unawares. In the confusion, many of the Afghan soldiers simply took to their heels.

Azambai led a charge which crippled a whole line of Soviet personnel-carriers, losing a finger in the process. Adam, attacked by three huge Russian infantrymen, went down under the hammer-blows from the butts of their empty rifles, rescued only in the nick of time by Haidar, the Turkestani. In a maniacal manoeuvre he cut the throat of one Russian, bayoneted the second, and shot the last one dead.

Helping Adam to his feet, Haidar was briefly off his guard. A Russian sergeant came for him, Kalashnikov spitting fire. The Turkestani went down, just before a Pashtun tribesman shot the sergeant through the head.

The battle surged away, leaving Adam standing by the motionless form of his friend.

The Eagle knelt beside the man of Sher-Qala, Haidar, the Weapon-Bearer of his Battle-Lord, and saw the blood soaking away into the still warm sand. Haidar's left leg was torn off: ripped away at the hip.

'You'll be all right, *ghazi*, hero, Haidar . . .'

The Turkestani's eyes were wide open, gazing as if into the distance, the pupils tiny in the bright flare-light, his face and neck muscles stretched with the agony of the pain. He tried to speak. The Eagle put a water bottle to his lips.

'My Lord Captain Juma. The Russian helicopter . . .'

'Yes, Haidar. Stay still. We'll get you help.'

Haidar's voice again, whispering, like a sound from far away . . . 'Present and reporting! I come, my Lord, I come. Just reach out your hand . . .'

His eyeballs moved upwards. With a shudder he was gone.

Adam passed his hand across the eyelids, closing them.

The sky was bright with Russian field-lights, flooding the battlefield in a ghostly glare.

The battle was not going well. Although the people of Kandahar had rallied and were flooding from the city to join the fray, they lacked both weapons and ammunition. Sometimes knots of three or four men, and women, shared a single gun. The deadly machine-gun fire of the Russians flailed through the rebels like a hailstorm destroying a wheat field. The Russians, in the Chowni garrison complex, still held out, guarding their abundant arms and ammunition.

Just when The Eagle thought that all was lost, and the guerrillas were wavering, a contingent of horsemen, at the end of a headlong gallop of thirty miles, entered the fray.

At first Adam thought it was a delusion: the thundering hooves, the rumbling of the cry, nearer and nearer: '*Ajala, Ajala! Ajala, Ajala!* Hasten, Hasten!' The roar of the men matched the drumming of the hooves. Then he saw them.

A messenger from Kandahar, riding a motor-cycle at suicidal speed along the Asian highway's impeccable asphalt, had reached their mountain stronghold with the message: 'Come to battle! To Kandahar.'

These men, whose home was the great Paropamisus range north of Herat, the Afghan Caucasus, were feared and respected wherever, in the East, tales of war and romance were told. Like the dervish knights whom Adam had seen setting out from their monastery, their motto was 'Ride and die!' Calling themselves 'The Agwans', they were, in ancient times, the Argovani of the First Crusade.

They wore scale armour, light and strong, and flowing cowelled and sable-lined cloaks. Long rosaries of wooden beads hung around their necks. Their shoulder-length hair was bound with tight turbans, and their great, square-cut beards rippled in the wind.

Their medieval appearance belied their extraordinary discipline and outlook. In addition to their skill with the sword and dedication to horseriding, they could march fifty miles a day with a sixty-six-pound pack. They alternately marched and rested through the twenty-four hours, and were prepared for battle at the end of it.

Their present leader was no stranger to the modern world. Samuri Zilzila 'Earthquake' Khan, knew something of Western Europe and the Soviet Union. He had borne the Russians no ill-will – until they had invaded his own land. Indeed, he still had a high opinion of Slavic chivalry, based on a visit some years before to Leningrad.

Although a warrior, he was interested in literature, and his Intourist guide had taken him to the Petrograd side of the Neva River to see Maxim Gorky's memorial. Zilzila mentioned that he was related to the Tartars who appointed the first Russian Grand Dukes, the Kipchakov, and therefore effectively founded the nation.

Within fifteen minutes, he had been whisked away to the five-storeyed Military School nearby where the guard was turned out for him to inspect. The commandant, a soldier of the old school, invited him to review the 'fighters of Russia, the country which his ancestors had helped to create'. Such courtesies always have a profound effect on military men.

Tonight, Zilzila Khan led his men against the Russians in a wholly professional spirit. If the Soviet Union wanted to rule Afghanistan, they would have to fight for it. He doubted, though, whether Russian soldiers would willingly fight, year after year, in a foreign land where people had done nothing hostile to the USSR.

Zilzila Khan's standard-bearer raised the ancient battle-ensign, whose embroidered motto now came roaring from the throats of his three hundred cavaliers: '*Al janna fi zill-as-saif!* Paradise is in the shadow of the sword.'

Grey-faced, the Russians turned, as their NCOs began to

shout hoarse orders. The riflemen, Kalashnikovs in hand, started to obey; but their eyes stayed too long on the weird figures, the warriors who, they had been told, skinned prisoners alive and called out to death to take their enemies.

The Afghans smelt the terror. '*Tarsnak* – Coward!' they cried.

Suddenly, as if at a signal, the Soviet ranks broke. Men ran, pushing each other away like children on a playground, and cringed as the long swords came down, across throats, through uniform jackets, deep into their vitals.

'*Hala, Hala, Hala!* – Attack, Attack, Attack!' The battle group *Tufan*, the Storm, caught the main body of the Soviet infantrymen as they tried to scramble up a sheer rocky hillside, urged on by the distorted call to the assault which came from Malik Ramazan Khan's loud-hailer, snatched from the hands of a dying Russian sergeant.

The men of the Storm battle group were, for the most part, almost giants, all of them over six feet tall, and broad in proportion. Before the partition of India they used their size to good effect, wandering all over the country and managing their mysterious affairs, intimidating the people of the subcontinent, it was said, simply by looming over them.

'*Hala, Hala, Hala* – Attack, Attack, Attack!' the guerrillas roared. 'Nikolai: it is time to be afraid!'

The Russian helicopters were there too: but, as on that day in Paghman, the choppers were unable to drop their bombs, use their guns even, for to do so would have been to destroy, together with their enemies, their own men, inextricably mixed with the Afghans in the whirling death-dance below.

'*Hala, Hala, Hala!*' The partisans now had the Russians penned in, crushed in their hundreds against the rocks of a gully with no exit, into which they had dashed like lemmings, scrabbling at the rocks, desperate to get away from their tormentors.

As the first gleam of the false dawn appeared from behind the mountains where far-off Kabul lay, the surviving Russians surrendered. The guerrillas tied up the three hundred who were still alive, allowed the *pomashes* to attend to the injured, and set up a camp of their own, to rest and to assess the situation.

It was broad daylight before all the reports were in: Haidar, Roman Zelikov and three Nuristanis, as well as fifty of the Afghan defectors of Lieutenant Tura's group, were dead.

Adam, Noor and the others sat, slumped listlessly on ammunition boxes, numbed by this bitter news. Good friends who had fought side by side, who had survived the glaciers of Kara Dagh, who had laughed and sung with them, now lay, inert bodies covered with sacking, waiting merely for their hole in the ground: food for the earth.

An irrational, savage urge to kill the prisoners, or to make them suffer and to watch it happen, came over Adam. Noor read what was in his eyes. All she said was, 'Don't.' The moment passed. Adam looked at the terrified prisoners. Some were gibbering. They were suffering enough.

Adam lifted the pieces of rough cloth covering the faces of his dead friends, one by one, and looked at them for the last time.

'Kara Kush, they have tasted martyrdom, and they have found it sweet,' said Karima; perhaps, he thought, because she saw the tears running down his cheeks, making furrows in the orange sand-dust which covered them. Then she said, 'I have killed seven men today, *komondon*. And this I know: I have had enough of killing.' She didn't cry, but she was trembling. Noor put an arm around her. 'Karima Jan, we did not ask for this. God knows. We must not let it change us. Now we must forget.'

'Not yet.' Karima stiffened. 'We have to cleanse the land.' Very quietly she said, 'Mr Zoltan, why does the world not help us? Have we done wrong? I wish that you were here to explain it all to me.'

The guerrillas had laid the Russian wounded in rows, waiting for whatever medical aid might be forthcoming from the city. Suddenly Noor saw a very small, neat Russian KGB officer walking freely along the lines of groaning men, himself unwounded and unrestrained.

As he reached each man he stooped, placed his handgun to the nape of the man's neck, and killed him with a single shot. The automatic's nose had a long black extension, a silencer, and made only a dull thud as it was used.

The Russian had a pouch full of Makarov magazines slung at his side. When he had killed eight men, and the gun was empty, he reached for the bag and, with a practised movement, changed magazines. He even put the empty cassettes tidily back in the pouch.

Noor screamed and ran at him, head down, from a dozen yards away. The little man raised his gun as he stepped aside.

'*Stoi!* Stop!' There was murder in his voice.

In a moment, he was on the ground, felled by a karate chop from Adam's hand. The weapon fell into a sand-drift.

Adam picked him up and shook him like a dog worrying a rat.

'I have to shake him anyway,' he explained to Noor. 'The blow has paralysed him.'

To the Russian he said, in Dari, 'Give me your belt.'

He spat on the Soviet star shining from the buckle as he tied the Russian up. For some reason he mumbled to himself in English.

The Russian, recovered now, spoke in English too. 'Capitalist, fascist, lackey! *Angliski*, English, interventionist!'

Adam said, 'If anyone in the entire world were told of what you have done, murdering your own men, they wouldn't believe it. They'd think we'd made it up.'

The Russian screwed up his face in fury. 'You'd have tortured and killed them, anyway!'

'No we wouldn't. It's you people who do that. You cultured people of the new civilization.' He spat.

'Extreme conditions, extreme solutions.' The Russian was calmer now. Polemic suited him. He went on, 'If they got back to the Red Army, they'd be shot, anyway.'

'Shot?'

'Yes, for violating their written undertaking to commit suicide if captured, whether wounded or not.'

Noor looked wildly around, wondering if she was dreaming. The words 'I don't believe that this is happening,' went through her mind, but she rejected them. It was happening all right.

'Are you *quite* mad?' Adam picked the little man up by the hair and put him down again. His hair, he noted, was unusually long, unlike that of the ordinary soldiers, which was close-cropped. Perhaps this was an affectation, or a privilege, of the political police.

'No, *Afganski* bandit, or Englishman, whatever you are: we are not mad.' The Russian was sneering.

'Huh!' Adam couldn't find the right word.

'We feel love, just like you. Love for Russia. Recently, as I heard on the radio, a Russian spaceman in the Salyut vehicle pined for the Motherland, *Rossya*. And we hate, we hate dirty imperialists, like you. Unlike you, we know about higher duty. The duty of the guiding role of the Party of our country, to help the working class of all peoples . . .'

'God help you!' shouted Noor.

The Russian ignored her. 'Kill me now, bandit,' said the Russian, 'since you are too superior to torture me.' He was not a coward.

Adam signalled to two of his warriors. 'Take this prisoner to the city with the others, and don't harm him. Captives are protected by God.'

To Noor he only said, 'God help the human race.'

7

Pendergood's Army
Kandahar Airport

0800 hours

The Pashtuns had now broken through the Russian defences at the airport three times. At dawn, ravenous, they had attacked the food storage area *en masse*, and taken away large quantities of canned goods, before being driven off by concentrated machine-gun fire. They lost fifty men, but, as Pendergood said, 'That's evidently the price of breakfast in this damned war.' The Pashtuns' food trucks had been blown up in the fighting.

Five-man *hala-zumras*, assault groups, kept getting through the Soviet lines, now the sun was up. One struck at the oil-fired electricity generators, another cut the twenty-five mile long high-tension cable bringing power from the small Arghandab turbines, not realizing that they could have destroyed the supply as it ran through their own lines. The diesel supply for the airport's service vehicles went up, creating a fireball which melted the thick soundproof windows at a hundred feet.

The greatest successes were when the Pashtuns tackled the aircraft. There were more than fifty reconnaissance and fighter-bomber planes on the ground. Using hand-grenades or two-kilogramme high-explosive demolition charges, the attack groups wrecked cockpits, destroyed the air-intakes of the jets and blew off landing gear. Callil and Pendergood themselves took part in several of these actions. The airport was so huge that the Russians could either control the perimeter or guard the aircraft, but not both.

By now, talking by radio to Kandahar, the Pashtun commanders knew that the Russian attack on the city itself had been beaten off.

Callil eventually got through to The Eagle, briefly explaining how he'd accompanied the Pashtuns from the Yusufzai country.

'*Kara Kush!* May you never be tired! We're holding them here at the airfield. But we can't finish them off ourselves, and now it's daylight they can have strafing planes here from Shindand airfield within an hour or so. If you have men and materials enough, how about coming over and lending a hand? Nothing's happening at the moment: complete silence.'

'We'll be with you by eight-thirty – in half an hour – but we haven't much in the way of anti-aircraft guns.'

'Never mind, we have some, and every little helps.'

'Right – understood.'

'See you in half an hour.'

Adam turned to Qasim. 'Get every man and every vehicle, ours and the Kandaharis, out to the airport. It's eighteen miles north-east, along the signposted road. We've got to stop the Monsters before the Nikolai army or airforce comes back.'

At the airport, Pendergood called his group commanders together. 'Help is coming. From The Eagle in Kandahar. Prepare to attack the Sea Monsters, those things that just came in. It'll soon be time for the real *saza*, the retribution.'

The great Afghan strategic airbase at Shindand, headquarters of the West and South Air Commands, seventy-five miles south of Herat, was packed with Russian warplanes. The Ninth Air Fleet had been receiving confusing and contradictory reports and orders about Kandahar, via Kabul, since the night before. Now, finally getting through on the Air Force's own radio network to Command Headquarters at Bagram, north of Kabul, the Shindand's commanding general, Kowalski, was ordered to put every suitable plane into the attack.

'Ignore Kandahar City. Destroy bandits besieging the International Airport. Protect the secret craft, surface-skimmers located there.' The first wave were the Mikoyan MiG-23 fighters, the type called 'the Flogger' in the West. Carrying over six thousand pounds of bombs, their Tumanski R29B engines could attain Mach 2.3 at high altitudes – almost two and a half times the speed of sound. Kandahar was three hundred and fifty nautical miles from Shindand. The operational radius of the Flogger was only five hundred miles. And that was without using dust filters, or gunning the engines. The pilots knew that if they switched on the afterburners to gain maximum speed, their fuel consumption would rise so much that they wouldn't make it home. Fuming, they nursed their engines as they made for Kandahar.

'First wave off, fifteen aircraft,' Kowalski reported to Bagram HQ.

'Total organic aviation – essential to break the siege of Kandahar Airport,' Bagram answered. Kowalski reached for his book of Soviet military definitions. 'Organic aviation,' he read, 'means aviation units supporting major army field forces, in direct support of their combat activities.' The general looked at his resources.

There were sixty Mi-23s on the apron, as well as ten Mi-17s. Lacking auxiliary fuel tanks, neither type of craft had the range to reach Kandahar, to carry out bomb and strafe missions and to return to Herat or Shindand. Kowalski ordered them off the operational zone.

That left three waves, each of five aircraft, with the necessary range. The general asked for the situation report.

'Fifteen aircraft, Comrade General. Ten operational, the rest under servicing.'

'I want more than ten! Recheck the five, tell the mechanics to get at least another three into service. This is a war, not a picnic!' Kowsalski had been in the Air Force long enough to know that Russian mechanics could always do better than they said.

The Floggers, fighters being tested in Central Asia for their possible use against NATO's fighters in the West, roared on at fifty thousand feet, each armed with over three thousand kilogrammes of death-dealing ordnance.

As they came down to six thousand feet, over the rectangular American-built town of Lashkar-Gah, eighty nautical miles west of Kandahar, the great wind hit them. The Black Wind, the Wind of a Hundred and Twenty Days, blows for as long as four months during the summer. Starting from the Iranian border near Hamun Lake in Seistan, it roars up to the mountains north and east of Kandahar. Carrying huge quantities of sand as fine as dust, positively ionized and causing madness, this wind is one of the most fearsome natural forces in the world. It blows up to one hundred and ten miles an hour – hurricane force – burying everything in sand, stripping trees, choking people and animals, filling and obliterating vital wells.

The air-intakes of the Russian jets were protected by extra filters, but nothing could keep out the dust of the Black Wind. Just before they reached the airport, six of the Floggers were in deep trouble. The mighty Tumanskis coughed and roared, afterburners were slapped in to clear the thick dust sucked into the engine nacelles. But Flogger afterburners take six seconds to attain maximum combustion. Moments after the wind hit them, the six 'all-weather' MiG-23s were heaps of burning wreckage in the Registan, the Sea of Sand. Flogger pilots carry no parachutes.

The nine surviving aircraft, wobbling from the wind's punishing force, made their first pass across the airport, which their pilots could hardly see. Clusters of anti-personnel bombs, each containing thousands of steel or plastic needles and ball-bearings, burst in the dunes. The sandstorm had hit the Pashtuns two or three minutes before the MiGs arrived, covering them and their vehicles, blotting out the rising sun, piling up banks of sand which acted as protection against the attack. Designed to explode on impact, under these unusual conditions the bombs burrowed deep into the soft dunes before the triggering mechanism worked. The sand baffled their effect, and the main force of the explosions was spent, uselessly, into the air.

When they had heard the whine of the approaching wind, and seen the dust-devils – swirling pillars which rose a hundred feet into the air – the guerrillas had covered their guns as best they could. But, although they could hear the attacking planes, even above the wind, they could not see them, much less stand up in the blast to load their six anti-aircraft guns.

The army of the Muhjahidin lay there, huddled, waiting for the worst of the *shigatupan*, the screaming storm, to pass over.

The Eagle's convoy, with every available man from Kandahar aboard, was three miles from the airport when the wind struck. As the blanket of sand hit them, the men jumped from their trucks and lay to the leeward of the wind, covering their noses, shielding their faces as best they could from the millions of stinging particles. Adam wondered, as he tried to keep his eyes shut against the burrowing grains, whether the engines would ever start again. Three miles meant nearly an hour's march and that might be too late . . .

The planes made three more passes before the red winkers on their fuel dials signalled danger level. The pilots could now see nothing of the ground below. They could not land at Kandahar: its radio beacon was out of action. Reporting to Shindand, they got Kowalski's order to return. Above the howl of the wind, The Eagle's men and the Pendergood-Callil force heard the last screams of the Turmanskis as the MiGs climbed, steeply, out of the dust curtain and back to base. Clogged with dust, their engine speed had dropped by twenty per cent.

The wind raged for two hours more, darkening the sky until one could see only inches ahead. But now it was dropping, bringing less and less sand by the minute.

Within the airport's perimeter, the coughing, retching Russians staggered about, not knowing what to do in a storm such as this. Because the surface was hard-packed, the sand did not pile up into dunes, and the troops could not dig in. The sand scoured them like sandpaper pulled across their bodies. Their weapons were clogged, and many had their uniforms torn ragged, even ripped off, by the Black Wind.

Three miles away, Adam and his men tried to start the motors of their trucks, and found that only half of them would work. Abandoning the useless vehicles and double-loading the others, they reached the caravan which Pendergood and Callil had made their headquarters, in a quarter of an hour.

Pendergood had shovelled the sand out of the caravan and patched the windows through which it had poured. Red-eyed and coughing, he, Callil and Maryam came forward.

They shook hands and embraced.

'Kara Kush! Welcome.'

Adam interrupted him. 'Pendergood: we're in the middle of a battle. Let's get ready to face the next Russian attack, shall we? Or work out how to overcome the resistance at the airport. We could easily be surrounded, if they bring up enough fresh forces, and I doubt if we'd ever fight our way out of that.'

'Let's get right down to it,' said Pendergood.

BOOK 14

The Secret Weapon

The Russian Army is an undisciplined shower – an oafish army who abandon their weapons, loot civilian cars at roadblocks, sell their equipment for hashish, and leave the wretched Afghan Army to do all the dirty work. The Muhjahidin fed me on Soviet Army rations sold on the black market.

Col. Colin Mitchell
in *Sunday Telegraph*

1. Stand to Arms!

North of Kandahar Airport

SEPTEMBER 16, 1000 hours

Divisional General Zagarov, sitting in his air-conditioned caravan trailer thirty miles north-west of Kandahar Airport, looked at his maps again. 'Captain Miskiny, this is quite irregular. I suppose you want a decoration for heroism in the field?'

'No, sir! With the General's permission, Captain Miskiny only desires to call for volunteers to close the gap and pull tight the noose on the bandits infesting the airport, sir!'

Zagarov did not know much about Miskiny: generals, after all, did not waste their time with captains, and especially in active service conditions. He looked steadily at the young man, a scowl masking his indecision. Miskiny was not a Party member, but he was a good officer, keen and efficient. But his idea sounded as reckless as a Siberian's.

'What is your nationality, Miskiny?'

The captain maintained the formality, speaking in the third person, required of a very junior officer replying to a general 'Beg to report, *gospodin* General: Captain Miskiny is from Krasnovodsk, Caspian Sea, Turkmenistan.'

'So you understand these people better than we do, eh – you're their little cousin?'

'The Soviet Fraternal Limited Contingent is in Afghanistan to help the legitimate government of socialist Afghanistan against bandits and foreign interventionists, sir!'

Zagarov nodded. 'Very well, Captain. Let's go into your plan, and if I agree, you can call for volunteers. As I see it, striking southwards along the motorway – here – you can occupy the ruins and dunes – here – and enfilade the flank of the bandits . . .'

In the end, the captain got his permission.

The Afghan guerrillas and their Pashtun allies surrounded the airport. To the north, however, the main body of Russian tanks and the 346th Motor Rifle Division's uncommitted troops stood by, ready to crush the Afghans on the open ground. The guerrillas encircled the airport's defenders, but they were spread thinly, and their main hope of reinforcements or escape lay to their east. This was the area which Captain Miskiny had proposed to seal off.

Adam shrugged as the scouts, one by one, came in with the story. Russian infantry, packed in armoured personnel-carriers, were rushing to seal the escape gap.

There was nothing much he could do. Messages had been sent to all the towns and villages for fifty miles around, asking for volunteers for the great battle which was surely to come soon. Callil and Pendergood could hold the main road from Herat in the west against tanks, since they had enough men, guns and mortars. To the south, partly defended by the river, the Kandahar volunteers, now well armed with captured weapons, could prevent the airport's defenders from breaking out: but that was the most they could do. Northwards, the bulk of the Afghan and Pashtun irregulars were dug into sand bunkers, awaiting the attack. If the eastern gap were sealed by the Russians before any sizeable support came from the villages – it would mean stand, fight and die. What he really needed now, Adam knew, was more men and vehicles.

He sent for the Afghan lieutenant. 'Take as many trucks as you can, Tura, grenades and automatic rifles. See if you can occupy the eastern ruins before the Nikolais get there. Reports say there's about two hundred of them, in APCs. If you can keep that area open, well and good. If not, retreat to our perimeter and we'll let you through. God be with you.'

The Afghan saluted and sprinted away, calling to his men – 'Haraka, haraka! Let's go!'

It was then that Adam saw the convoy approaching. White flags fluttered from the whip-aerials of the Soviet armoured personnel-carriers, nine of them, as they came bounding down the road from the east. This looked like a surrender: there would not be so many men, some two hundred in all, if it were a parley party. On the other hand, it could also be a trick, and a dangerous one.

Adam ordered the guerrillas to wave down the vehicles while he positioned grenade squads and marksmen on both sides of the feeder-road leading to the airport. 'Don't trust them,' he told the fighters. 'Any sign of treachery and you kill.'

The APCs came on, slower now. They were camouflage-painted in desert colours, with the red star, national insignia of the USSR, on their front mudguards. No weapons were in sight, but all the men were wearing steel helmets with the coarse mesh netting and the summer uniforms of the Soviet Army: brown battle-dress top, breeches and black jackboots. They were in full battle-kit, with water-bottles, pouches and leather harnesses.

A young officer, tall and handsome, with helmet and smoked goggles, stood up in the first carrier and held up his hands, palms outwards, as if in surrender. He had the star and wreath insignia of the Soviet Motor Rifle Troops on his collar-patches. The thin red stripe and four stars on his shoulder-straps showed that he was a captain.

Jumping down, he called, in Dari, to the motley crowd of guerrillas standing under a stunted tree at their makeshift roadblock. 'Where is your leader?'

Adam stepped forward. 'I am Kara Kush, in charge here.'

The Soviet officer saluted. 'Captain Kurt Miskiny, 346th Division, with two hundred and fifteen men, lieutenants, ensigns, NCOs and privates, reporting, sir!'

'Reporting? You mean surrendering, don't you?' Adam asked him.

'Reporting for military duty, *komondon*!'

Adam looked at the line of vehicles, with the men sitting silently in them.

'You are deserters, all of you?'

'We are defectors, beg to report, sir!'

'Are you all Russians?'

'I am from Krasnovodsk. Most of the others are Russians, though we have several other Soviet nationalities, *komondon*.'

What a remarkable thing, Adam thought. Most of the Soviet soldiers captured at Kalantut field armoury, The Eagle's first big exploit, had wanted to go home. These, however, were

553

changing sides. There must have been quite a shift in the outlook of the occupation troops to make this happen.

He thought rapidly. 'Captain Miskiny, you are most welcome, since as you will know we are likely to be attacked by tremendous tank forces before long. But you will understand that we have to guard against treachery. Come to my bunker.'

Adam led Miskiny to a culvert. Once inside, he said, 'How do you propose that we can use you and your men most effectively?'

'First,' said the captain, 'please tell your people to allow us to disperse our vehicles and cover them with their camouflage nets. Then I shall explain myself.'

When Adam had given the order, he continued. 'We are a volunteer detachment, three companies. Two lieutenants and I have been planning this for months. Briefly, we found out which men from our regiment wanted to defect: then we informed them that we would organize it when opportunity offered. Their instructions were to volunteer for a special mission when we gave them a code-word. Then we did it!'

Adam slapped him on the back. 'Well done!'

'Now,' said Miskiny, 'perhaps we should maintain the fiction for a little longer.'

'How do you mean?'

'I can radio my general that we're pinned down but holding the ruins, and perhaps find out what his plans are. The general did not tell me anything at the briefing.'

'Great. Let's do some suitable firing and then you report.'

A great barrage went up in the air as the guerrillas 'engaged' Miskiny's men. Then Miskiny radioed his headquarters.

General Zagarov himself came on.

'What's the situation, Miskiny?'

'Pinned down but holding the ruins, Comrade General.'

'Good man! Can you enfilade the enemy?'

'No, sir. But we can hold on here for a time, to link up with your attack or synchronize with it. Our location is map reference BB/765/4588, point K.'

'Good. Now, Miskiny, hear me. We will attack from the north, with massed tanks, along the flat, at 1430 hours. That's three hours away. We are bringing up massed multiple rocket-launchers to decimate the enemy before the tanks move in.

Three green flares mean "rocket attack". Two red flares mean "end rocket attack". On the latter signal, go in and kill the bandits. I don't want them grenading our tanks.'

'Understood, *gospodin* General.'

'Good luck, Miskiny, Commander out.'

Within the military zone of the airport, eight immense Hind helicopters, unknown to the guerrillas, had been made ready for action. Shindand, near Herat, was too far for effective intervention, as the commanding general there was now adamant. Military command, at Bagram, near Kabul, had, in any case, radioed that the fixed-wing craft at Shindand were not to be risked further, so the second wave never got off the ground. After the first panic at Kandahar Airport, Bagram, by threatening court martial, had got the ground support force there to realize that salvation lay in more helicopter strikes, in spite of the Pashtuns' success in shooting the Mi-24s down.

After all, they had the men, the aircraft, the munitions.

Foolishly, as it turned out, Kandahar Airport Helicopter Command, after loading the machine-guns and fixing the air-to-surface missiles, decided to test the engines. Great clouds of sand and dust rose in the afternoon heat, as the down draft whirled the deposit from the recent sandstorm around the landing pads.

Pendergood came running to Adam's bunker.

'Eagle, they're going to attack, long before 1430 – helicopters!'

Adam ran outside. Beyond the barbed wire and sandbag emplacements where the Russian defenders crouched, he could see the shapes of the great birds. They were within rifle range: but there was nothing that a carbine could do to the Mi-24s. Neither could the AA guns: the ground was far too open to set them up in safety.

Then the wind started again. He shielded his eyes and looked to the south. 'Painda-Gul, if the wind really gets up, and keeps blowing for a bit, they'll not be able to take off.'

'Right.' Pendergood screwed up his eyes. 'But I don't think we're due for a strong wind yet awhile. We'll have to think of something else. I'll go and see the Kandaharis.'

The wind was rising slightly, but Adam thought that Pendergood was probably right. Once those helicopters got into the air, they would be able to strafe the guerrillas almost at leisure. Whether there was any liaison with General Zagarov, he didn't know; but even on their own the helicopters were a murderous threat.

Fifteen minutes passed. Engine testing must be complete. Then, as he watched, one after another, the great machines rose into the air, the four-barrelled machine-guns in the undernose turrets, and the thirty-two rockets under the stubby wings, clearly visible. The Russians had got all eight of them off the ground.

There was a limit to the degree of dispersal possible for the several thousand guerrillas tightly encircling the airport's perimeter. Taking advantage of the ground cover – such as it was – many of them were packed behind rocks and dunes. Others had dug in as best they could, behind shrubs and the roots of leafless trees. The vehicles stood unprotected, inviting attack.

The wind, though still rising, had little effect on the three thousand horsepower of the mighty double Isotov turbo-shafts as each craft soared, half careened, and came in for the kill.

Suddenly, all around the perimeter of the airport, men in floppy Kandahari robes stood upright, threw things into the air, tugged and pulled, staggered and fell, then stood up again. They looked like clowns in some ludicrous ballet. For a moment, Adam thought that some of the Afghans had gone mad.

Then he saw what they were doing. Each man had thrown into the air, and guided upwards, a *badbadak*, a huge, crude kite. As the flimsy constructs soared, the men paid out twine from huge balls, and anchored the kites at three or four thousand feet, forming a line, like hawks hovering in the sky, facing the mass of rotor-craft making their first pass over the guerrilla lines.

Then each kite moved, as its owner manoeuvred it towards one of the Mi-24s, which were edging closer. Pendergood and Callil came running up to Adam.

The three commanders watched as the helicopters, swaying and clattering, rode the air straight to the kites. Their pilots knew that even if the strings became entangled with the rotors, all would be well. Helicopters of this giant size had even flown into flocks of the great grey geese which migrated south from Russia, many times, without being harmed.

The two Pashtuns, however, clutched Adam's shoulders in excitement as they waited for the moment of impact.

Three seconds later, all eight of the Hinds, with enough ammunition on board to destroy the rebel force several times over, were either down or crippled, as the deadly bunches of grenades tied to the kites exploded.

Three helicopters crashed in flames, killing the crews outright and wounding a dozen guerrillas when they hit the ground. Two more went out of control, and vanished in the direction of Kandahar city, to plough into the desert two miles to the south. The remaining three, one on fire, one with a crippled main rotor, the last with a huge gash torn into its side, struggled back to land within the airport's military zone.

Adam was stupefied by the success of the secret weapon.

'The Kandaharis had been making these kites for weeks,' Pendergood explained to The Eagle when the excitement was over. 'They'd never tried them out with explosives, but perhaps you'd forgotten that the Afghans are among the most skilled kite-flyers in the world.'

Of course. Adam remembered that there were great kite championships held throughout the land every year. This time, instead of attaching knives to the kites, to cut the strings of their opponents, the Kandaharis had used the powerful Russian RKG grenades, designed to kill a tank on impact.

'Whatever made them think of bringing the kites along to the attack on the airport?' Adam asked.

'Well, they were preparing them for the helicopters which would descend on Kandahar; and they didn't have anything else in the way of weapons, so they thought they might come in handy, when they were called to the airport.'

Adam looked at his watch. It was 12.40 hours.

The tank onslaught was only two hours away.

2 Kandahar Airport

The Eagle held a battle-council with his commanders. General Zagarov's forces, mainly the defenders of Arghandab and other hastily assembled units, comprised three regiments of tanks, totalling some three hundred M-62s of the 40th Army, which had tried to get into Kandahar the previous year and had since been re-equipped after heavy losses. There were now no serviceable helicopter gunships left at the airport at Kandahar, but, on previous occasions, the Russians had shown that they were capable of deploying, from the base near Ghazni, as many as 240 of the great Hinds to attack at a time.

The multiple rocket-launchers, which could deliver four and a half tons of high-explosive shells in thirty seconds, were a real example of overkill. Although they were being used against a relatively small guerrilla army, these weapons were more suitable for a major war. Either the Russians were testing some of their most advanced weapons here in Afghanistan, or else they had found that the Afghan Resistance was so tough that only the most powerful punishment had any real effect.

Finally, there were the Frogfoot ground-support aircraft. These were so new, and so secret, that Western intelligence knew next to nothing about them. They were due to come into service in the USSR in 1983 or 1984, but by 1982 they had actually been used, in squadron strength both at Herat and against Kandahar. This Sukhoi-25 had strafed the guerrillas, raking them with gunfire and dropping thousand-pound bombs containing a myriad of steel needles, the bomb-casings themselves fragmenting to lacerate and kill. It had been reported that there were SU-25s at a secret new airfield within striking distance of Kandahar Airport.

Adam, thanks to the Russian general's message to Miskiny,

had been able to locate the Soviet start-points, where their infantry, tanks and rockets were massing, only three miles north of the guerrilla positions.

His scouts had also found eight immense rocket-launchers, the deadly 'Sobbing Sisters', direct descendants of the fearsome Stalin Organs of World War II, drawn up behind the tanks and infantry. They had a range of just under ten miles, and they could, each firing forty rounds in salvo or ripple, so saturate the rebel positions that virtually nothing would be left.

The rockets were obviously the first target. The Eagle decided to select teams, made up of Russian and Afghan soldiers who had seen or worked with these weapons, to take care of them.

It seemed practically a suicide mission. Each team would have to work its way past the massed Soviet army, past the guards on the launchers, deal with the crews, and destroy the launchers, on their massive Ural-375 trucks, with nothing more than hand-grenades.

When the first two hundred men were lined up and the problem had been explained to them, Adam said, 'We need volunteers to take out the eight 122-millimetre BM-21 launchers. Eight parties with three grenade-throwers and three grenade-carriers to destroy each launcher. Forty-eight men. Volunteers one pace forward.'

Every man stepped forward.

'Captain,' said Adam to the Russian Miskiny, 'select the men and handle it, will you? You'll be under Captain Tarik.'

'Right, *komondon*. Sergeants Yakubov, Abbasov, Zakaria. Close in on me . . .'

That was that.

'Now for the tanks. Three hundred, in close formation means we need at least a thousand men to deal with them, three or four to a tank.

'Anti-aircraft guns, lowered to tank-killing trajectory, and Dashka heavy machine-guns in the centre: aim for tracks and other soft spots. They may have vulnerable ammunition boxes or fuel tanks at the sides. Grenades have a range of twenty-two yards and will penetrate six inches of armour. Always throw yourself flat to escape blast after throwing: they have impact fuses.

'Finally, the infantry. This is hand-to-hand work. There may be no time to reload, so use the folded bayonets on the Kalashnikovs and, if you like, knives. Those who have no weapons must accompany a fighter so that if he falls or kills a Russian, the weapon which is then available can be seized and used.'

The battle groups dispersed to their tasks.

It was now only ninety minutes to the time fixed for the Russian attack. Adam thought of the men creeping towards the rocket-launchers, could see them edging forward, attacking . . . If they did not succeed, the whole partisan force would be wiped out.

In the bunker, where a communications man sat drinking tea and smoking a captured Russian 'Java' cigarette, Adam found a newcomer.

He was a Russian helicopter pilot, Viktor Stepanov, whose craft had crashed in the river to the south of the airport. He was short and stubby, with an intelligent face and a cut over his left eye. When Adam came in and the radio-man stood up, the pilot rose to his feet and saluted.

'Stepanov, Viktor, Captain, prisoner-of-war, reporting, Commander,' he said.

'Why aren't you tied up?' Adam asked.

'I have given my word of honour not to attempt escape.'

'All right, sit down, Captain.'

Stepanov sat, for a time, looking at the hissing butane gas lamp. Then he said, '*Komandir*: may I speak?'

'Yes, speak.'

'I had no idea, until today, that you Afghans were people, too!'

Adam looked at him, thought of the million massacred civilians, and could not find anything to say.

The pilot's face began to twitch, and he passed his hand across his eyes. '*Afganski tovarish*: How long will it be before the blood of the innocent is off our Russian hands?'

He bowed his head, and began to sob.

Adam closed his eyes, and willed victory for the attack-group against the rocket batteries.

'There will be plenty more blood shed before tonight, Captain,' he said.

The rockets were there all right. The guerrillas, crawling on their bellies, passed around an outcrop of rocks in the sandy valley where the huge cross-country trucks were drawn up, with the launchers mounted on top. Each battery was manned by four men, with a guard, bayonet fixed, standing in front of it in his long greatcoat, though the temperature was 105 degrees Fahrenheit.

Captain Tarik, of the former Royal Afghan Army, signalled to his grenade teams to withdraw for a conference. He could see that there was no hope of attacking the rockets across the thirty yards of open ground in front of them without being wiped out as they approached.

He looked at his fifty men. Twenty of them were wearing Afghan or Russian uniforms. A ruse was the only hope. That was the only way. He quoted them the Pashtu proverb 'Presence of danger tests presence of mind', and explained his plan.

Leaving thirty of his force under Miskiny, to provide covering fire, Tarik marched the remainder of them, carrying their satchels of grenades, Kalashnikovs slung casually across their shoulders, straight up to the mobile command post where a Russian colonel was sitting, talking into a microphone.

Motioning to his motley band to stand at ease, Tarik approached the colonel and saluted.

'Captain Ahmed Husain, Afghan Democratic Army, and special scratch unit, reporting, sir!'

The colonel turned his beefy head towards him and said, uncertainly, 'Well, man, report!'

'Captain Husain reports, with the colonel's permission, the special guard force against marauders is present and in order, sir!'

'What's all this about, Captain? Where are your orders?'

'Verbal orders, sir! Passed down from Artillery Command HQ. Special unit to guard the rockets against bandits, reported in the locality. Your single guard on each battery is not considered sufficient, sir!'

'All right, Captain. But why are your men in such a disgusting condition, covered in dust, their uniforms incomplete? They are a disgrace!'

'Just out of the battle-line forward, sir! Beg to report we have been in action with no time to refurbish!'

'Oh, very well. But get yourselves smartened up.'

The gunners were standing by their launchers, and the guards, a few steps behind them, showed no suspicion.

Captain Tarik saluted smartly, performed a perfect about-turn, and ordered his men, two to each rocket, to position themselves.

The colonel had pulled down the canvas flap on his personnel-carrier command post, and was lying back with his eyes closed. He had just checked in to General Zagarov's communications centre to report that all was well. It was half an hour to barrage time, and he would be roused in fifteen minutes.

Tarik observed that one gunner in each battery was an NCO, and the rest, including the guards, were privates. That meant that he, notionally at least, out-ranked them all.

Time for a further bluff.

'Sergeant Zakaria, tell the eight guards that they are relieved. The Special Unit will take over security from now. You men may disperse to the rest area.'

Good. The delighted guards, long overcoats flapping, ran to the shelter of a tent, a hundred yards off, to snatch a smoke.

Tarik looked at his watch. Twenty-seven minutes. After five minutes he gave the signal, and his 'guards' threw themselves to the ground.

First the Muhjahidin riddled the Russian rocket gunners with AK fire at close range. Every man went down, without any chance of unslinging his own rifle. Then, crouching ready to lie flat, the men threw bomb after bomb – the terrible tank-killers – into the cabs of the trucks, under the swivel-mounts of the rocket-carriers, and at their sighting mechanisms.

As the trucks collapsed and the swivels crumpled, with a roar and a scream of tortured metal, the eight batteries each slewed around, and the horrific power of the rockets themselves was unleashed.

Thirty-two thousand pounds of high-explosive crashed and howled. Some of the rockets burst singly, on the ground; some entire batteries went up, together, torn from their wildly careering mounts, swooshed through the air like lopsided, demonic catherine wheels. Three hundred and twenty rockets, utterly wasted.

In the five minutes between the rebels' appearance and the moment they struck, there had been no rest for the Russian colonel. His radio screeched, and General Zagarov's voice came through.

'Rocketry! It is now doubly important that you fulfil your task to perfection, pulverizing the bandits before the tanks and infantry go in. There has been a serious problem. A large column of reinforcements, tanks and infantry from Ghazni has been ambushed by irregulars at Moqur, two hundred and forty kilometres north-east of here, on the Kabul highway. The convoy is destroyed, with the loss of many men and tanks. They were due here by now, as our fall-back reserve.'

Before the colonel could answer, Tarik had ripped open the canvas curtain of the mobile command post. The colonel threw down the microphone and jumped up, his Makarov handgun at the ready.

Tarik shot him dead, and wrecked the radio set with his rifle butt.

As he rushed from the vehicle, the rocket batteries were beginning to go up.

The attack group reached the cover of the rocks before any Russian unit could decide what had happened, let alone make any response.

Hearing the tremendous roar, Adam, sitting in his bunker, briefly wished that he was a nail biter. That might have given him some relief from the grinding in his stomach. Would he ever see the suicide group again?

Half an hour later, Captains Tarik and Miskiny ran up, saluting, with their 'Mission a hundred per cent accomplished, Kara Kush!'

The Eagle clapped them on the back. 'Well done, well done!' He was about to ask details, when a runner came up with a message from Azambai, in charge of intelligence. 'Kara Kush, the Russians have set up a field command post six hundred yards from our frontline position. It's located on top of the airport water-tower and will be hard to dislodge.'

'What's it there for?'

'Artillery observation. They've a radio transmitter. They'll be sure to use it for spotting, to direct howitzer fire, the captain thinks.'

Adam turned to Captain Tarik. 'Does that mean they're bringing up guns?'

'I'd say so, sir. Probably a battery of four one hundred and twenty-two millimetre field howitzers. They have high-explosive, as well as chemical shells.' Tarik looked worried. 'They have a range of nearly ten miles.'

'So they'll send over ranging shots, and have them corrected by the spotters on the water-tower?'

'That's right. We can get a group ready to demolish the tower, but they might get some shells into us first. I could send some men to try to locate the guns as well. But in the meantime . . .'

'In the meantime we take a lot of casualties.'

'The howitzers are deadly.'

The Eagle said, 'Right. Attacks, as soon as possible, on both tower and guns.'

Azambai had brought out his Soviet Army radio, and was spinning the dials. Suddenly he gave a thumbs-up sign. 'Adam, I've got the signals from the water tower spotters. They are arranging code-signals. Their call-sign is *pirazhuk*, "small pie".'

'How's that going to help us?'

'We take over if the tower goes up.'

'Yes, if the howitzers don't start first, then ask for ranging directions.'

Tensely the two men waited. Five minutes, ten, twenty.

Had the attack group reached the tower? Adam was going to send a man to find out, when the Tarik appeared, as if from nowhere, and squatted down beside him. 'Finished.'

'Finished?'

'The tower is down. Hardly a sound. We knifed the guards and put explosive charges on the supporting struts. There's no spotter left.'

Azambai grinned, and turned to his radio.

'Pirazhuk calling Ananas . . .'

He paused, listened, and then grinned. 'Report your artillery capability. Yes. I repeat, four howitzers. Good. Now, battalion, obey only my signals. Division here. We have a special unit reporting from the front line. Yes, airborne. That's why you don't know them, yes, they're right among the bandits. You mustn't fire without my signal, or you'll wipe out our own forward units. Understood? Yes, good. Never mind my rank and location! Do you think I'm an Afghan savage talking to you? Of course not! I've taken over "Small Pie". Stand by for divisional firing orders . . . Small Pie out.'

Azambai turned to the others. 'This should give our people time to sneak up on them. In the meantime I'll get them to use up some ammunition and keep them busy so that they'll make a better target for the storm-party.'

He flicked a switch.

'Small Pie to Ananas. I shall now give you traverse and elevation . . .' His voice droned on, almost hypnotically. 'Prepare to fire ranging shots airport direction, all four howitzers, rapid fire, semi-automatic operation.'

He gave the range and stipulated high-explosive shells.

Then: 'Ananas, countdown: five, four, three, two, FIRE!'

From a distance of three-quarters of a mile The Eagle and his men first saw the flashes, then heard the whirling roar, as if four express trains were passing above them, and then saw the crash like thunder as the forty-eight pound shells exploded, far beyond their position. They threw up great geysers of black dust, as they carved huge craters in the tarmac, well within the airport perimeter.

Adam cheered, while Azambai calmly touched the switch to transmit and reported, 'Good shot, Ananas! Now increase range by thirty metres and raise elevation twelve degrees.'

He turned to the others. 'I'm going to try to get them to blot out some of the administrative buildings.'

Three more salvoes and several of the airport buildings were reduced to twisted girders and a pile of dust.

Adam clapped Azambai on the back. 'Yusuf, you're completely crazy! Using the enemy's artillery to shell his own strong point!'

'If I were not so modest,' said Azambai, 'I'd quote you the Pashtu proverb that's current hereabouts. About right action as an art.'

Then the guns stopped. 'What's up?' Adam asked; 'I suppose they're onto us . . .'

Azambai whipped off his earphones. 'Not on your life!

They're screaming blue murder. Our lads have got to them and the howitzer radioman tells me they've killed at least twenty of the twenty-eight men operating those guns. Now they'll spike them, and I don't suppose they'll bother us any more . . .'

'Let's change the old proverb,' said Adam, 'from "A ruse is worth a tribe" to "A ruse is worth almost anything".'

'Less succinct,' said Azambai; 'but I admit it's more accurate. Like those Russian gunners. They're certainly well trained, excellent shots. I wonder how many of their own people they killed in the airport?'

Even deprived of their rockets and heavy artillery, the Russians were sure to attack again. Soviet military texts, rigidly adhered to at all times, harped on the necessity of attacking and 'dealing crushing blows', using every man and every machine available. They still had their infantry, and their battle-tanks, and they had a schedule to fulfil. Adam knew that, short of an order from Moscow, the Russians would be upon his men within minutes.

It was indeed only minutes after the destruction of their guns that the Soviet tank commander made his move. Two formations of guerrilla advance guards, rolled back by the tremendous pace of the Russian armour, came running from their advanced positions. The T-62s, all three hundred of them, with infantry following, had left their start-points in massed formation, dead on time and at full speed.

3   The Tanks must not get through

1436 hours

The huge, squat, low-profiled tanks came on, grinding and clanking, at thirty miles an hour. Smoke, fragmentation shells and super-high-explosive missiles poured from the long snouts of the 115-millimetre smooth-bore guns.

The shells dug deep into the sand, reaching the hard rock below, exploding and then throwing up millions of murderous rock-chips. Or, when the gun was set for a higher trajectory, the deadly cargoes spread far and wide from the air-bursts. First came the roar, then the explosion, a sound which rang like a demonic bell through the head and screamed in the ears, on and on, until men thought that they must soon go raving mad.

Rising to face the tanks, from shallow holes scooped in the sand, the guerrillas threw their grenades; sometimes at the tracks – sometimes at the fuel tanks, sometimes just below the rounded, flattened turrets, where the rivetting had made the armour-plating marginally weaker than elsewhere.

One grenade, lobbed at the main gun of an attacking tank, went straight into its mouth, rolled down and exploded just as it struck the HE shell which the gunner had slammed into the breech a moment before. The tank went up like a single bomb. Jabir Khan, whose triumph this had been, repeated the performance three times before he was cut down by machine-gun fire. Few heard or understood his cry of 'Howzat?' as he did it. He had played cricket for his university when he was studying in Pakistan.

Hundreds of Muhjahidin, unable to get out of the way in time, were crushed to death under the relentless caterpillar tracks. Some discovered that if they lay flat, exactly between the broad tracks, the machine would run over them and they would be unharmed.

Many were blown to pieces where they stood, when they miscalculated the power of their own grenades: or were torn in half by the bullets from the two heavy machine-guns on each tank, whipping among them in a blazing lash of fire. Those guerrillas who lacked training or combat experience were most often the ones who died.

The Russian crews, too, suffered terribly. The modern tanks of the USSR, like the old Churchills, Tigers and Shermans, were little better than death-traps in a fiercely fought battle. Although most of their Warsaw Pact allies had already given up the T-62s, the Russians, relying upon enormous quantities of expendable crews, still favoured them. The Afghans, using at best, grenades, a few heavy Dashka machine-guns and one or two captured Russian AA guns, clearly demonstrated how obsolete the T-62 had become. Even updated with laser firing, with schnorkel tubes and improved guns, these machines would be sitting ducks for the powerful rocketry or air assault capability of any modern army.

When a tank was hit, flames spurted from the 1,000 litres of diesel fuel, then came the blaze of the thick lubricating oil, then the hell of the exploding shells inside. Glowing red-hot, the tank exploded, torn to shreds, almost as easily, it seemed, as if it had been a tin can.

So fierce were the flames, so rapid their spread, that the crew often could not get the turret or escape hatch open in time to get out. Sometimes, in any case, either or both had been hit and buckled by a shell, a rocket or a bomb. Sometimes, as the guerrillas stopped their firing to fall flat on the ground, they would see orange fire belching, at first from the gun-ports, then from holes punched by continual explosions of some of the two or three hundred shells still stored inside.

Long after a tank's crew were dead, the thick, black oily smoke would rise, slowly, into the sky, finally to be joined by the acrid smell of burning rubber and the stench of roasted flesh.

Usually, when they did get out, the men would soon be picked off by the guerrilla marksmen or killed by the indiscriminate fire of their own side.

Those few who did escape from the wrecked T-62s that day were often shocked and deafened, wounded, burned. Weeping, raving, arms flailing, they staggered about in the choking clouds of smoke and the yellow-red dust churned up by the explosions and the tank-tracks.

Some lay down and sobbed, others screamed, again and again, '*pomash!*' – seeking a medical orderly who was not there. Most of them would die in minutes, in any case, from the most terrible wounds.

A few, but very few, having snatched up grenades or automatic carbines before they jumped from their crippled chariots, fought the Afghans like furies, leaping and whirling in the fountains of sand and showers of sparks, unknowing, uncaring whether this was life or death, whether or not they were in a nightmare or had gone completely mad.

These men, 'beetles' as the Afghans called them, from their black, shiny combat suits and ribbed, cowl-like padded canvas helmets, were roaring from the combined effect of the half-bottle of vodka which they were issued, and the *fenamin*, amphetamine tablets, which each tank carried.

Military doctrine, as taught in every country in the world, held that infantry could not fight tanks. Yet out of the three hundred, one hundred and twenty of the T-62s were totally destroyed or on fire. The rest, sound or damaged, turned tail. Fifteen hundred guerrillas lay dead, a thousand or more were wounded. In Afghanistan, reversing the usual ratio, there were more fighters killed than there were wounded, in almost every action.

The supporting Soviet infantry now came in. Wave after wave of them, fresh and well-armed, hurling grenades and firing the latest assault rifles, were slaughtered by the Muhjahidin. Without the protection of the tanks, they had no hope. In twenty minutes the attack was abandoned.

BOOK 15

Zoo-Bear

During the Russians' invasion of Afghanistan they were first thought to have pulled off a masterful land operation. Soon afterwards first-person reports began to surface, indicating that they had misinterpreted their intelligence data on the Afghans. Over-optimism, a common problem with intelligence gathering, caused the Russians to go on charging into combat situations in which they found themselves more disadvantaged than their analysis had predicted. They are still trying to analyse, or fight, their way out of Afghanistan.

James F. Dunnigan:
How to Make War

The Super-Redeyes

Almas Fort
The heights near
Kandahar Airport

1600 HOURS

Colonel Farran, his unit safely laagered in the sprawling ruins of Almas Fort, two miles west of Kandahar Airport, lay stretched out like a lizard in the heat of the desert afternoon. His orders at the Pentagon briefing had been unequivocal, precise. 'Destroy the surface-skimmers. We have to show the Soviets that they are vulnerable. But on no account, repeat, no account, are you to engage Russian troops.'

Easier said than done, Farran thought. His men had been in concealment here for a day, watching since the dark before dawn, a spectacle of attack and counter-attack, of classic tank assault beaten back by a hoard of Afghan warriors. Fingers itching on triggers, they had seen blood, fire, death and destruction. Even nature, with the raging Black Wind, had shown its fury.

But they had not been able to get near the skimmers, shielded so resolutely by Russian defenders that they had not left their task even to help repulse the Afghans when the airport seemed on the point of being overrun.

Farran stiffened. There was a flurry of sudden activity around the mass of great ships. Preparations were being made for takeoff. If the transports got away, the mission would be a failure, like the disastrous one in the deserts of Iran, trying to rescue the American hostages held by Khomeini's men. Black smoke rose from sixty huge exhaust vents as the final engine testing began.

The mission might be only minutes away from failure. Sixteen hundred hours. Farran cursed. If it hadn't been for those crazy Afghan guerrillas, whom he hadn't even been able to help, the

Ekranoplans would be destroyed by now, and he would be on his way home.

Farran's thoughts drifted back to the landing of the Lockheed C-5 Galaxies of Airlift Command, on the hard-packed sand of Baluchistan, three hundred miles to the south, less than eight hours before. Then the decanting of the ten loaded heavy trucks and their dash across the godforsaken wilderness to this spot, with the skimmers sitting almost within reach. Before that, the flight from Arizona to the Arabian Sea, at more than five hundred miles an hour: the magic carpet from the Special Training Camp. Every man a volunteer, knowing little more than that Uncle Sam wanted them 'to help save freedom'. Men of Afghan or other Central Asian descent, the sons of immigrants.

Zubeir ('pronounce it "Zoo-Bear"') Farran was one of the few regular soldiers among them: but at the camp they had had three months of the toughest training America could offer. The CIA had discovered that the skimmers would be used to extend the Soviet empire by rushing in thousands of troops to support coups like the Afghan one, where a handful of determined communists could seize temporary power – almost anywhere.

Kill the Ekranoplans, don't tangle with the Russians. And afterwards? 'You will be evacuated by appropriate United States transportation from the Arabian Sea coast.'

Kill the Ekranoplans . . .

In the Muhjahid camp, Adam, Pendergood and the other leaders ran from the caravan at the sentry's shout. Shielding their eyes against the setting sun, they saw the thirty great ships, black and menacing, belching smoke, their multiple jets roaring, rise slowly to operational height.

They looked at one another, helplessly. No AA shells left: and the craft were now too far away to be reached by Dashka fire. The greatest fortune in the world, floating away.

Adam shook his head. The gold was on its way to Russia: the Soviets had won. Unless there was a miracle.

At Almas Fort, Colonel Farran raised his arm and jerked it down. Then, as each group, guerrillas and Americans, unknown to each other, watched, the very sky seemed to explode.

The American Super-Redeye missiles, streaking within seconds to a thousand feet, locked onto the skimmers' engine-heat and struck, a millisecond apart. Each fearsome weapon tore into the vitals of its victim, the explosion of the fuel turning the belly of the monster into a volcano.

Some of the stricken machines lumbered out of control, spewing liquid fire; men fell like broken dolls, amid the showers of glittering coins which, themselves counterfeiting sunbursts, obscured the sun.

The Ekranoplans were dead.

Halzun, watching the takeoff in Moscow on the television monitor linked to the geostationary satellite above the scene, clutched his head in his hands as the holocaust unfolded before his eyes. Total annihilation, catastrophe, defeat. For a long moment he sat stockstill, head bowed. Then he sat back in his chair. No billions to compete with the West. But the War faction's power was wiped out as the skimmers had so unaccountably been. Halzun was Chairman, and would soon be declared President, of the USSR. Half a loaf was better than no bread.

Colonel Farran's truck screeched to a halt at the Muhjahid command post, and the Colonel, in full guerrilla kit, jumped down and called out in Dari, 'Who's your commander?'

Adam held out his hand. 'Welcome, *Ghazi*, hero,' he said, 'but who are you, where are you from?'

'Just some guys who couldn't let the old country down,' said Farran. 'Sorry we can't wait. We've got to meet some guys down at the Arabian Sea.'

He leapt back onto the truck and sped off towards where the file of Special Force trucks was already moving south.

The Muhjahidin watched them go.

Before nightfall the *lashkar*, the combined forces of Kara Kush and Pendergood, was heading for the sanctuary of the unconquered clans, No Man's Land, where they would rest and re-equip until the time when the Russian Bear would once more hear the call of The Eagle:

'Come to battle, Nikolai: it is time to be afraid!'

Fontana Paperbacks: Fiction

Fontana is a leading paperback publisher of both non-fiction, popular and academic, and fiction. Below are some recent fiction titles.

- [ ] THE ROSE STONE Teresa Crane £2.95
- [ ] THE DANCING MEN Duncan Kyle £2.50
- [ ] AN EXCESS OF LOVE Cathy Cash Spellman £3.50
- [ ] THE ANVIL CHORUS Shane Stevens £2.95
- [ ] A SONG TWICE OVER Brenda Jagger £3.50
- [ ] SHELL GAME Douglas Terman £2.95
- [ ] FAMILY TRUTHS Syrell Leahy £2.95
- [ ] ROUGH JUSTICE Jerry Oster £2.50
- [ ] ANOTHER DOOR OPENS Lee Mackenzie £2.25
- [ ] THE MONEY STONES Ian St James £2.95
- [ ] THE BAD AND THE BEAUTIFUL Vera Cowie £2.95
- [ ] RAMAGE'S CHALLENGE Dudley Pope £2.95
- [ ] THE ROAD TO UNDERFALL Mike Jefferies £2.95

You can buy Fontana paperbacks at your local bookshop or newsagent. Or you can order them from Fontana Paperbacks, Cash Sales Department, Box 29, Douglas, Isle of Man. Please send a cheque, postal or money order (not currency) worth the purchase price plus 22p per book for postage (maximum postage required is £3.00 for orders within the UK).

NAME (Block letters) _____

ADDRESS _____

_____

_____